HANDLOADER'S DIGEST

ELEVENTH EDITION

Edited by
Ken Warner

DBI BOOKS, INC.

About Our Covers

Considering the fact we're doing the 11th edition of HANDLOADER'S DIGEST, I guess you could say we've been around awhile. And so has RCBS.

On our front cover you'll see a nice selection of RCBS goodies. Look closely. Among the "familiar green" you'll see something new. It's the RCBS "Partner" handloading press.

Capable of handling all standard rifle and pistol cartridges, the Partner was designed for the beginner, or the experienced handloader who doesn't have the room for full-tool setup. In fact, the Partner is so handy that it can be taken to the range. If all of the above isn't enough to whet your appetite, here's some more good news: RCBS is selling the Partner press for *under* $50!

On our back cover you'll find a familiar RCBS offering, the RS-3 reloading press, the heir to the fortunes of the old "Jr." press. Look closely and you'll see something RCBS has never done before. Yup, your eyes aren't playing tricks, that's a 12-gauge shotshell you see. And to the left of the press you'll see the new RCBS, 12-gauge Shotshell Die Set. That set contains everything you need to convert the RS-3 to a "shell shucker." Other gauges? You bet, but you'll have to wait a while. Cover photos by John Hanusin.

HANDLOADER'S DIGEST STAFF

EDITOR-IN-CHIEF
Ken Warner

SENIOR STAFF EDITOR
Harold A. Murtz

ASSOCIATE EDITOR
Robert S.L. Anderson

ASSISTANT TO THE EDITOR
Lilo Anderson

GRAPHICS
James P. Billy

COVER PHOTOGRAPHY
John Hanusin

MANAGING EDITOR
Pam Johnson

PUBLISHER
Sheldon L. Factor

CAUTION: Technical data presented here, particularly technical data on handloading and on firearm adjustment and alteration, inevitably reflects individual experience with particular equipment and components under specific circumstances the reader cannot duplicate exactly. Such data presentations therefore should be used for guidance only and only with caution. DBI Books, Inc. accepts no responsiblity for results obtained using this data.

ISBN 0-87349-009-6   Library of Congress Catalog #62-15069

CONTENTS

WILDCATTERS are curious, whatever way you take the word. Other adjectives such as innovative, adaptive, ingenious, irrespressible, clever and persistent may also apply. Their common motivation is wanting a cartridge that isn't. The fancied ammunition they desire is not always a bigger blaster, although this *is* a common motive. Their imaginations brook no bounds.

A wildcat cartridge, for the purposes of this account, is one that was not designed for commercial or military use, and so is not available factory formed or loaded. Almost every wildcat is created by altering a factory cartridge case. Just one to be discussed here, the 22 JGR, which was intended to become a commercial factory round (though it did not), was experimented with using lathe-turned cases for its development. More will be said about it.

These oddballs require chambering or rechambering a rifle barrel. Gunsmith work is necessary, both for the gun and on loading dies. Generally the shooter and experimenter does all or some of the work himself. An element of this article will be explanations of how alterations and adaptations were done for some the author has worked with.

A wildcatter is created by the desire for something he can't find in his gun store, the catalogs, or books. As it is a usual wish, many wildcats are aimed at getting more velocity, somehow, out of an available case than it provides as it comes off the shelf. While some old cartridges can be loaded up for use in new and stronger guns, this isn't safe if it might get into an old gun. A wildcat should not be usable in any firearm not chambered for it

and designed to handle its pressure.

Bottleneck cases have bodies larger than the bullet diameter of their necks. Usually the sides of the case taper toward the neck and the shoulder has a gentle slope. If the case sides are straightened up and the shoulder made more abrupt, even pushed forward a little, there is room for more powder. By reaming the chamber of a rifle to these "improved" dimensions, a regular cartridge with a slightly reduced load may be fired in it to form the case to the new shape by the force of internal gas pressure. Rimless cases headspace on their shoulder, at some point or other, so cutting a chamber forward increases headspace when fire forming. This could become dangerous. And severe case stretching will rupture too many. The improvement attained this way, though limited, may be substantial and has

Confessions of a WILD- CATTER

by EDWARD M. YARD

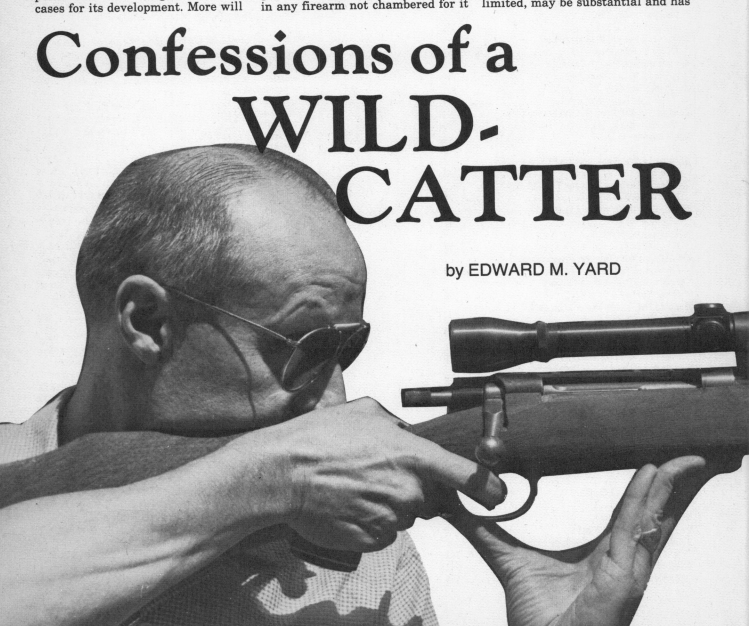

thus attracted many.

A famous and popular example of a fire-formed, increased capacity improved design is the K-Hornet, originated by Lysle Kilbourn. This is one of the easier successful alterations. It was imitated and inspired the Harvey Kay-Chuk, a slightly shortened version to fit a rechambered Smith & Wesson K-22 cylinder. Ballistics for both from the writer's tests will be given.

An equally prevalent practice is to neck down a bottleneck or straight case to a smaller caliber. It is usual to straighten any body taper and to sharpen the shoulder angle as well. The smaller caliber barrel has to be chambered anyhow, so the originator might as well satisfy his whims. This procedure borrows the greater capacity of a larger shell for the smaller and lighter bullets. The 22-250 and

cial loading and the 22-250, the former wildcat, was adopted as a factory cartridge. During its development, the necked-down 250 Savage was also known as the 22 Varminter, a name copyrighted by J. E. Gebby, and as the 220 Wotkyns Original Swift, alluding to Wotkyns' initiative.

Almost every available case has been necked down to 22. A few have been sized to 20 and 17 calibers, with or without improving the case as well. The 17 Remington followed these wildcats to fill a market desire. It is the 222 Remington Magnum adapted to 17 bore. A lesser number of even tinier tubes have been rifled and cased. None compare with the quantity or popularity of the 22s.

Another common cartridge alteration is necking up to a larger bullet diameter. This is accomplished by running a lubricated expanding plug

22-30/30 Ackley Improved is a rimmed cartridge about equivalent to the 220 Swift. The 25-06, once a wildcat custom rifle item, is now factory loaded and production rifles chambered for it. It was long ago called the 25 Niedner.

Improved 30s range from the 30-06 Improved (Ackley) to the 300 Weatherby Magnum, which is about as far as the 300 H&H case can be blown. And it takes a lot more case that will burn heaps of real slow powders to get much ahead of a 30-06 Improved. You will have to shield the chronograph from the muzzle blast to measure it.

These large capacity cases do well when opened up to even 8mm. Then, the regular IMR series of powders can be burned in large charges because of a larger bore volume to expand in to control peak pressure. The larger bullet base area to push on for similar weights produces high velocity and energy. For a while the 35 Whelen and the 375 Whelen were fairly well known. Custom rifles were made by Griffin & Howe of New York. Their improved versions are only slightly better.

Then there is the 333 OKH (for O'-Neil, Keith, Hopkins) a necked up 30-06 and the 334 OKH stretched from 300 H&H, plus other 33s from other cases or these blown out. There are 35s and 375s to parallel them. The 375 H&H Magnum is also blown out and expanded to where it merges with the 458 Winchester being necked down. Then there is "one of the largest wildcat cartridges," quoting Ackley. It is the 475 Ackley Magnum expanded from the 375 H&H. That case is only .463-in. O.D. about an inch from the mouth. Ackley says unnecked Norma Magnum cases are just right. The 378 or 460 Weatherby Magnum case that is .560-in. O.D. at the shoulder could easily be necked up to .475. There certainly are as many ideas in these big bore wildcats as in the small bores, but fewer guns and less ammunition. The small calibers, becoming bench rest and varmint cartridges, see more action.

The simplest sort of wildcat is the improved version of a cartridge. For these a rechambering of the gun is the major expense. Firing regular or slightly reduced loads forms the cases. Subsequent handloading can usually be done with regular dies, except full-length sizing. This can be taken care of by making the roughing reamer to suitably shape the full-length die. When you have a roughing reamer, it is necessarily smaller than the finishing reamer and so can be

The 357 Magnum parent and its wildcat offspring: 22 Sabre, 219 Thor, 25 similar to later 256 Winchester Magnum, 30-caliber intermediate case. Third from left is the 22 Remington Jet that can be improved to the Sabre form.

Opposite: The writer and a Krag single shot rifle now barreled for 22 Sabre.

22-250 Improved are quite successful examples of this approach. A 250-3000 Savage case is necked down for the first, and for the improved version such cases are then fire-formed in a chamber tastefully proportioned with a sharper shoulder.

The 22-250, originated by Wotkyns, inspired the 220 Swift, a Winchester factory hot rod. The factory Swift, however, was a necked-down 6mm Lee Navy case modified to semi-rimmed design to fit standard bolt faces and extractors. Later the 220 Swift dropped in popularity as a commer-

into the neck of the case. The smallest example is possibly the 25 Hornet. It is the 22 Hornet opened up to take 25 bullets and not quite the equal of the 25 WCF or 25 Single Shot. The 222 Remington Magnum has been enlarged to 6mm and is known as the 6x47mm. Its mission is to provide less wind drift than the 22s for bench rest shooting with lower recoil than larger bores.

Many 30-caliber cases have been necked down and expanded, with and without improving them or shortening, into most possible contours. The

The 22 Hornet, two K versions, 22 Midget Magnum, 22 JGR formed from Hornet brass, 22 JGR lathe-turned sample case received from Gower.

sized for the die-making purpose.

Necking down is about as easy, even if the case is to be improved as well. The smaller barrel has to be chambered. The cases have to be necked before the first loading. The writer fitted a chambered 200-222 barrel to a Sako action. Then 222 brass was decapped in a RCBS 200-222 sizing die, recapped, charged and a bullet set in the 200-222 seating die. There was no indication that caliber had changed and a wildcat loaded except that the right dies, the correct charge and a .204-in. bullet had to be used. It was exactly as easy as having reloaded a round of 222 ammo. Even an alert observer might not have noticed the difference.

The chambering reamer is the pass

Micarta laminated plastic bullet-seating guide mentioned in text, shown with 22 Sabre case. It may be used with any loading press. The cavity was formed with appropriate drill.

Final sizing die for 219 Thor cases with mandrel to support neck.

key to the world of wildcatting. Some of the breed are gunsmiths and do the whole job themselves. In a few instances, the wildcat was devised as a house brand to bring in some work. More often, the experimenter sought the aid of a gunsmith, who might have been a shooting friend anyhow. Others learned to make reamers. Some had them custom made by Clymer, Keith Francis, Raton Gunshop, Henriksen Tool Co., or other commercial tool makers. The writer did both—bought some, made some.

Usually the wildcatter is mechanically inclined and does as much of the work himself as he can. This piece will give an idea of how some key things can be done. This will be by suggestions and general procedures.

A full description of making and sharpening reamers can hardly be "part" of an article.

The amateur can make half reamers and fluted ones, IF he has enough equipment and knowledge. They must be heat-treated for hardness before final dimensioning. And they must be sharpened and relieved before they will cut. The reader who tries this must have enough background to carry through.

A half reamer starts by turning, in a lathe, the slightly oversize form of the case on non-deforming oil hardening tool steel, leaving a shank on the base and a pilot beyond the neck. The shank is to drive the finished tool and the pilot is a guide to ride on the lands in the barrel as the chamber is cut.

greater detail. The reader, in the writer's opinion, must still possess previous knowledge and skill. It is possible to learn by trial and error. Barrels may be spoiled as part of the cost of the education.

Having reamers made to your specification (drawing) will save a lot of time for other things that will be needed to get a real wildcat going. Remember to have a roughing reamer, if one is to be used, made to form the full-length resizing die when you are making or finishing your own dies.

One of the writer's projects is an example of this business. The intent was to produce the highest possible velocity from a revolver—not a single shot pistol. So 22 caliber was chosen. This was before the 22 Remington Jet. A

the dies was polished by rotating them on dowels coated with valve grinding compound. This was done in a lathe. A drill press or power arbor will do.

The first die was sized to bring the 357 down to 30 caliber. That was tried out as a wildcat itself. Next it went to 257, also shot and being our own preview of the 256 Winchester Magnum. The final step was to 22 with a short neck and sharp shoulder. The object was maximum powder space for use with short, light bullets from 35 to 45 grains in weight.

All the cases ever formed were made without annealing the necks. Two metal trade procedures were employed. A mandrel was used inside the die to prevent any possibility of the

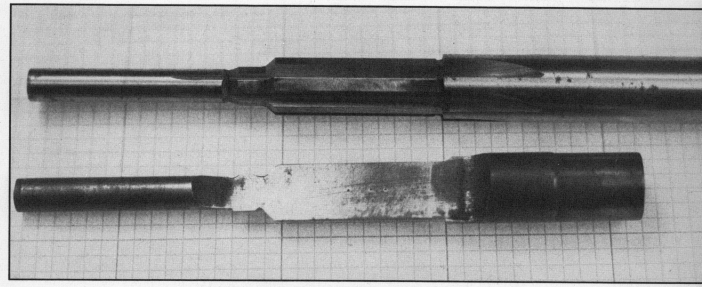

The 219 Thor fluted reamer by Raton (top) and a half reamer for 219 Thor used to chamber experimental revolver.

The whole piece must be heated in a small furnace quickly to a cherry red and quenched with agitation in oil to harden it. If it can't be filed it is hard. Stress-relieve the whole piece by reheating in an oven that is 325 to 375 degrees F for two hours.

Half of the metal is slowly ground away over the length of it that is to cut the chamber. It must not overheat, which would reduce the hardness or warp the tool. The back (round side) must be relieved away from the cutting edge. The edge must be stoned sharp. A fluted reamer is made the same way, but flutes are milled into it before hardening. It must be stoned to relieve and to sharpen the edges.

The *American Rifleman*, December 1951, pages 35 and 36, gives some

357 Magnum case was necked down and the result tagged 219 Thor. The neck was short and the shoulder sharp in true wildcat tradition, so it would have been difficult to blow out the Jet. The 256 Winchester Magnum would have been fine.

It is usual to make dies and to form cases before making any chambering reamers. At least the process is coordinated so that the chamber is for cases that will result from the brass-forming procedure used. One-inch drill rod was threaded 7/8x14 to fit a standard loading press capable of full-length resizing cases. By using fraction and letter size high speed drills, sizing dies were formed. The final body drill point was reground to the desired shoulder angle. The inside of

neck collapsing. And soap, rather than grease or oil or commercial lubricating compound, was used as the drawing lubricant. It does *not* provide the easiest forming effort. But a soap drawing film will not break down. The case can not stick or gall. Dents are not a problem.

A half reamer was made. A 22 Hornet chamber in a revolver cylinder was drilled in steps to remove excess metal. The new chamber was finished with the half reamer. Initial testing was done with just one chamber.

As an indication of how wildcatters work, that revolver cylinder wound up with five different chambers (all 22 caliber) in it for test shooting. Raton Gun Shop made a six-fluted reamer to a final drawing of the 219 Thor, used

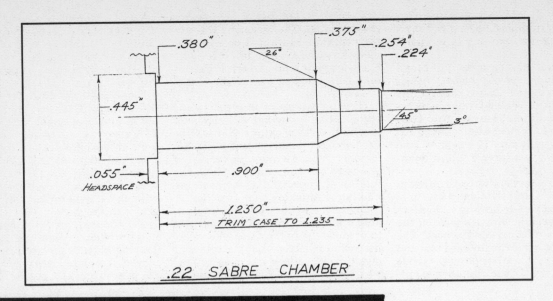

.22 SABRE CHAMBER

TABLE I
How Little 22s Performed

Powder	Charge (Wgt.)	Bullet (Wgt.)	MV (fps)
22 JGR			
Unique	4.0	35 Sisk	2200
Unique	4.0	40 Sierra	2055
H240	6.0	35 Sisk	2360
H240	6.0	40 Sierra	2260
22 Midget Magnum			
2400	8.5	35 Sisk	2550
4227	9.0	40 Speer	2400
22 Hornet			
Factory load		45 HP	2690
2400	10.7	45 Sierra	2705
22 K-Hornet			
2400	12.2	45 Sierra	2900

V.F. Roma created the 22 Midget Magnum by necking down a 32 S&W Long to 22. It has a little more capacity than the Gower case, but less than the Hornet. It easily surpasses the 22 JGR and 22 WRM.

TABLE II
High Velocity Revolver Loads

Powder	Charge (Wgt.)	Bullet (Wgt.)	MV (fps)	Remarks
219 Thor				
AL-7	11.5	35 Sisk	2600	Super Velocity
H240	12.0	40 Sierra	2610	revolver
2400	13.5	40 Sierra	2665	7-in. barrel
22 Hornet				
Factory		45	1950	7-in. barrel
22 Kay-Chuk				
H240	8.0	40 Sierra	1685	S&W K-22
AL-7	7.0	40 Sierra	1820	6-in. barrel

The 219 Thor is a wildcat development of the writer to obtain the highest possible revolver velocity.

for other chambering. Both the half reamer and the Raton fluted reamer are illustrated.

Aside from the satisfaction of creating your own whizzer, which may be all that you will get, the bottom line is performance. The 219 Thor was aimed at getting the highest possible revolver velocity with regular varmint bullets, such as the Sisk 35 and 40-grain. Good results were hoped for with 45-grainers as well.

The top load chronographed at 2665 feet per second with a 40-grain Sierra SP. A second and third were 2610 and 2600 fps. The objective was reached. So far as the writer knows these are the highest revolver velocities achieved to this time. The barrel length was seven inches.

An overlooked wildcat, in the writer's opinion, is the 22 Sabre. E. A. Fisher and C. H. Helbig necked down 357 brass to form an efficient rimmed 22 case they called the Sabre. P. O. Ackley tried but abandoned a similar 17-caliber about the same time. When the 22 Remington Jet appeared, it was blown out by Dan Cotterman et al to a form quite like that of the Sabre. Ackley pulled out his 17 reamers and with 22 pilots formed his 22 Improved Jet. With Cotterman's Super Jet, that makes three very similar cases. As shown in Ackley's book, the writer's chronograph work done for Fisher and Helbig provides much more loading and performance data for the Sabre than the others. Twenty-three loads with five bullet weights and six powders are listed. Accuracy in a variety of rifles with which the writer was then familiar was excellent.

The 22 Sabre is about the ballistic equivalent of the 222 Remington in a shorter, more efficient and rimmed

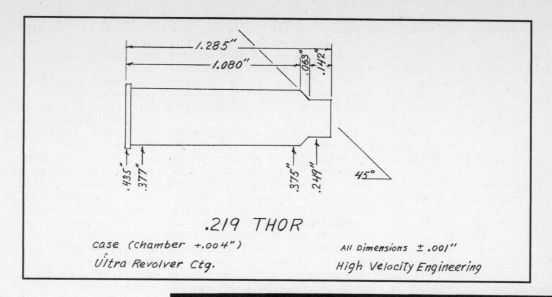

.219 THOR

case (chamber +.004")
Ultra Revolver Ctg.

All Dimensions ± .001"

High Velocity Engineering

case that is ideal for single shot rifle actions such as the Martini Cadet, Winchester High Wall, Ruger No. 3 and Thompson/Center Contender. It would go nicely in Marlin or Winchester lever actions to which it could lend some real varmint zip. Possibly some of the inherent accuracy would be lost in these.

The writer has done more work with this snappy wildcat with a Sabre-chambered barrel on his Krag bolt-action single shot. Chronographing with the Oehler Model 33 and Skyscreens II reaffirmed its excellent performance. In the summer of '84, loads with 45-grain Sierra bullets clocked 3250 fps in temperatures up to 110°F without difficulty. Loads at 3350 fps were also fired without problem. With the right loads, it shoots nicely into an inch at 100 yards. It is the writer's favorite in this class and is sure to receive much more tuning and chronograph attention. There are some dandy wildcats.

Loading wildcat cartridges is usually accomplished with adapted tools. The writer uses an antique Modern Bond tool with assorted mandrels for decapping and priming which are done separately. Sizing dies are made by (or for) the experimenter during fabrication of the case forming set. Bullet seating is done in straight line guides. These can be made for this low volume activity from strong plastic or easily machined metal. This year the writer seated 600 bullets with a die guide made by drilling out micarta laminated electrical insulating material. That die had been used for a couple of years before this past season. Some of these relatively impromptu tools are illustrated.

The 22 JGR is a diminutive car-

TABLE III
22 Sabre

Powder	Charge (Wgt.)	Bullet (Wgt.)	MV (fps)
	22 Sabre		
H240	14.3	45 Sierra	3250
H240	14.5	45 Sierra	3270
H240	14.7	45 Sierra	3300
H110	14.0	45 Sierra	3125
H110	14.5	45 Sierra	3180
4227	16.5	45 Sierra	3160
H240	14.0	40 Sierra	3330
H240	15.3	40 Sierra	3500
H110	14.5	40 Sierra	3300
4227	17.0	40 Sierra	3325

TABLE IV
The Wildcat 30s

Powder	Charge (Wgt.)	Bullet (Wgt.)	MV (fps)	Data Source
		30-06		
4064	54.0	150	3000	Ackley
HiVel 2	45.0	150	3050	Hercules
H205	61.5	150	3100	Hornady
H205	59.5	165 BT	3000	Hornady
		ICL Caribou		
4064	60.0	150	3360	Ackley
4350	62.0	172	3076	Ackley
4350	61.5	180	3030	Ackley
		30-06 Ackley Improved		
4064	55.0	150	3150	Ackley
HiVel 2	55.0	150	3215	Ackley
4350	61.0	180	3053	Ackley
		30 Short Magnum No. 2 (Ackley)		
4895	58.0	150	3100	Ackley
4350	67.0	150	3190	Ackley
4350	67.0	180	3060	Ackley

If more is wanted than the 30-06 or the Ackley Improved provide, it is necessary to go to the 300 Weatherby Magnum, itself an improved 300 H&H Magnum.

tridge that Canadian gunsmith John Gower hoped to develop into a commercial round to surpass the 22 Winchester Rimfire Magnum. He tried to interest ammunition companies but, to our knowledge, no commercial ammunition was ever loaded. Because it received a lot of publicity, the writer tried it out. A couple of Gower lathe-turned sample cases were obtained, but could only be utilized for verification firing.

In true wildcat fashion, JGR cases were formed from much shortened 22 Hornet brass which had the right body diameter. The rims were too big, but that did not matter for performance testing. The internal volume was the same for these as for Gower's turned prototypes which were far from durable. Gower claimed about 2130 fps from a 22-in. barrel for a 40-grain bullet. The writer did a lot of chronographing with a wider variety of loads than Gower or his cohorts used. A velocity of 2260 fps with a 40-grain Sierra bullet was easily attained with a different powder. A few of the many loads tested are tabulated to show that it worked and how. The writer has not even heard of it as a wildcat for a long time.

The 22 WRM did succeed. The public thought the rimfire factory cartridge a better deal than reloading a tiny centerfire. There are several guns available in lever action, bolt and semi-auto with clip and tubular magazines. All the regular cartridge companies make this ammo, with 40-grain bullets FMC or HP.

Anyone doing this experimenting will find the Martini Cadet and Sako short actions convenient. Extractors may be made for the Martini that require a minimum of barrel cut to accommodate them. The Sako is even easier. If the nose of the Sako extractor is partly ground off, the cut in the barrel may be dispensed with. No doubt experience working with other actions will reveal short cuts with them that will simplify fitting many barrels to a single action.

Probably no wildcat has ever been scientifically designed. Since all of them are based on some alteration of existing brass, it is a matter of making do with what is to be had. However, it is a sound approach to do some calculating before selecting the case to be modified. If, after necking and shaping, including any trimming, setting back and fire forming, it has not got the right powder capacity, there is little or no chance that it can perform as intended. The hoped-for velocity, usually what a wildcatter is after, will

be impossible if the final case volume is too small. Efforts to get around this can result in high pressure without coming near to attaining the projected bullet speed. The modern chronograph will make this evident above the sounds of any boasting or wishful thinking.

Choosing too large a case makes for inefficiency. If the desired ballistics require loading way down, uniformity and accuracy may suffer. The powder capacity of a cartridge case should be reasonably well matched to the results it will be expected to produce. Oversize cases are used to obtain a little more velocity at considerable cost. If the velocity is to gain bullet energy, a larger bore is the sound solution.

Predicting the exact performance of any cartridge is difficult. Even an expert like Charles Newton was likely to over-estimate what a production rifle could achieve with factory ammunition. No wonder that wildcatters are prone to be optimistic about their pet variant. Today, there is plenty of tested load data to serve as a guide. The Powley PSI calculator is an excellent guide for approximating pressures of loads in a case of known capacity for IMR powders. The Powley Computer For Handloaders is another slide rule aid that may be used in reverse to find the case capacity for a given velocity goal, and at the same time predict the right IMR powder and its charge.

If it is remembered that all bullet energy is derived from the energy released by the powder charge when it burns, and that similar cartridges are *about* equally efficient, then comparing a wildcat idea to a known cartridge of about the same powder capacity will provide practical guidance.

To make a comparative calculation, Du Pont IMR powders, as they burn in a rifle, can be taken to release about 179 foot pounds of energy per grain weight of charge. For a cartridge in the 222 Remington class, about 27.7% of a full charge energy is transferred to 45-grain bullets, and around 30.1% to 50-grainers. These percentages were figured from loads listed for 4198 in one edition of the *Du Pont Handloaders Guide*. The data varies with the edition date because the powder (or the measurement) changes.

Should a wildcat be expected to burn 25 grains of IMR powder safely, then that amount releases 4475 foot pounds of which 1239.6 could be expected to transfer to a 45-grain bullet. It would have to travel at 3522 fps. This is found by taking the square

root of the number: 1239.6 divided by 45 and multiplied by 450450. Your solarpowered credit card calculator will do the figuring for you. Most of them have a square root key. The number 450450 is a constant that enters all calculations involving bullet velocity and energy to take care of conversions and things that do not change.

This example is valid if there is a powder of which 25 grains can burn in the wildcat at a safe pressure AND at the same efficiency as 4198 in the 222 Remington. There may not be one in the IMR series. Another type of powder may have to be considered. Finally, the proof is in the firing. The load *must* be chronographed. The actual velocity is easily verified. Every wildcatter believes he can estimate "safe" pressure. A real excess becomes obvious.

A wildcat cartridge must be accurate. There is no point to all this exercise if the resulting gun and loads are not at least as good as the nearest factory ammo in a production rifle. Some cartridges do better than others, even if no reasonable cause is apparent. A few targets are shown which indicate one inch or a little less 5-shot groups at 100 yards shot with lightweight rifles running eight to nine pounds with scope mounted, suitable for field varmint hunting. A wildcat must perform this well to endure.

Firearm experimentation and the assembly of ammunition is hazardous. The experience, skill and care of the experimenter and artisan may reduce the danger. Anyone involved in the development, making or use of wildcat guns or ammunition incurs the risk of damage, injury and loss of life. Those who engage in such activity must understand that the hazard exists and be responsible for accepting the risk.

The writer has not experienced a serious accident or sustained injury. Take heed. Be careful, and make sure that what you are about to do is what you intend to do, and that that is prudent. Accidents are not inevitable. Their occurrence must be prevented.

No load information mentioned here is a recommendation. No procedure reported is instruction. The writer's experiences, to the best of his recall, are revealed for reading.

The references, the data, the handbooks, aids, guides, calculators and computers available today, all make wildcat experimenting much nearer to being a science than it was. It remains, though, an art full of surprise or it's no fun. ●

LOOKING DOWN a gun barrel is a hazardous endeavor. Looking from the front end with someone unfriendly behind it is not good for your mental health. Even when you hold the gun, however, looking down the barrel of an unloaded gun can be hazardous. I arrive at this conclusion as the result of many years as a consultant.

People bring burst guns to me to see why they burst. If the problem was not a high pressure chamber burst, but a typical obstruction burst, invariably the shooter had carefully looked down the barrel just before he fired that shot. As a matter of fact, he always looked through the barrel just before he fired every shot, so there

was never any possibility of the barrel having an obstruction in it! But there the barrel is, with a burst obviously caused by an obstruction.

So, somehow a good look down the barrel manages to put something in there which is guaranteed to burst it.

I don't know about you, but I hardly ever look through a gun barrel out in the field unless I suspect I have stuck the muzzle in mud or snow. So when I hear how these folks looked through the barrel just before it burst—obviously from an obstruction—it sounds like wishful thinking. They are wishing they had looked down the bore, because then the gun wouldn't have blown up.

This may seem rather unfriendly, but I reached this conclusion after much experience: if your gun should blow up, it's probably your fault.

Let me tell you some of the reasons for my arrival at that unhappy conclusion.

This young man and his attorney came in to see me. They had a problem. The young man had been shooting a muzzle-loading rifle, when the breech plug came roaring out and hit him in the face. A breech plug in the face doesn't come under the heading of fun and is not guaranteed to improve your looks nor your disposition. There was no doubt the young man had been grievously wounded and

Gun mishaps are most often human error, especially when reloads are involved, so.....

It's Probabaly YOUR FAULT!

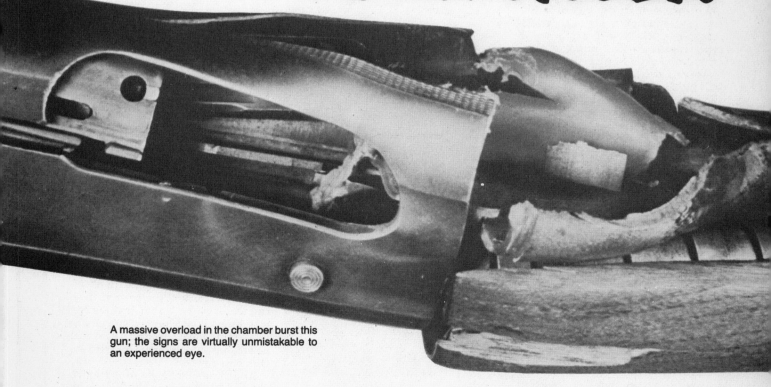

A massive overload in the chamber burst this gun; the signs are virtually unmistakable to an experienced eye.

by COL. JIM CROSSMAN

A veteran of many court cases involving firearms, Jim Crossman has still spent a lot more time in duck blinds than witness chairs.

A rare case of a gun which burst during proof. Note the longitudinal seam in the barrel and the absence of violence in the burst.

Here's another massive overload. It burst this gun in the chamber area, and then took it apart.

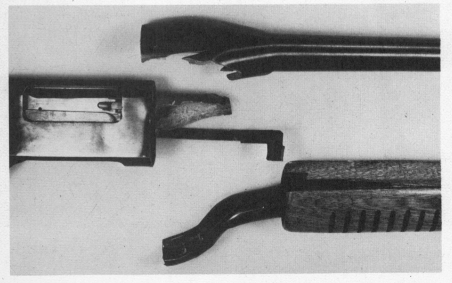

was justifiably annoyed and wanted to sue someone—and so did the attorney, although *he* hadn't been wounded.

They brought the gun and all the accessories, including the can of powder, caps, balls, rod, patches, powder flask—all of it. I found the breech plug a very loose fit, and the back of the barrel slightly bulged. The threads on the breech plug did not show any appreciable damage. The powder in the can was right for the gun. The loads the man had been using were right for the gun and the ball. The balls were the right size, patches the right thickness, and so on. I couldn't find anything wrong, except that the breech plug had obviously come out.

I took photos and showed them to many knowledgeable people. I got a variety of answers—defect in the metal, smokeless powder, overcharge, etc., etc., but none of these answers went with the evidence. The fellow denied any use of smokeless powder and the powder in the can was, indeed, black powder of the proper granulation. I couldn't find anything else that could have caused the problem.

So, finally, I told the people that obviously there was a problem of some sort, but that I didn't know what the cause was and therefore I didn't know who they should sue. I suggested they send the stuff to a chap I know well who is deeply into black powder stuff just to get a second opinion. That they did.

The friend told me later that he had gone through the same things I had. He had found nothing wrong and had arrived at the same conclusion I had—there was a problem, but he didn't know what it was. And so he got ready to pack the stuff for shipment back to the owner.

When he got the shipping box out and was putting things in it, he noticed something unusual—some small black specks in the box. They obviously weren't black powder. Close examination showed that they were particles of ball powder. Ball powder? Where did that come from? He hadn't seen this stuff in his examination before and where did it come from?

He had checked the powder in the can and it was OK, but then he realized he had not checked the powder flask. (And I hadn't either.) And when he did, out came copious quantities of Olin ball powder!

And that solved the problem. Assuming that the man had used the powder from the flask, the fast smokeless powder had given very high pres-

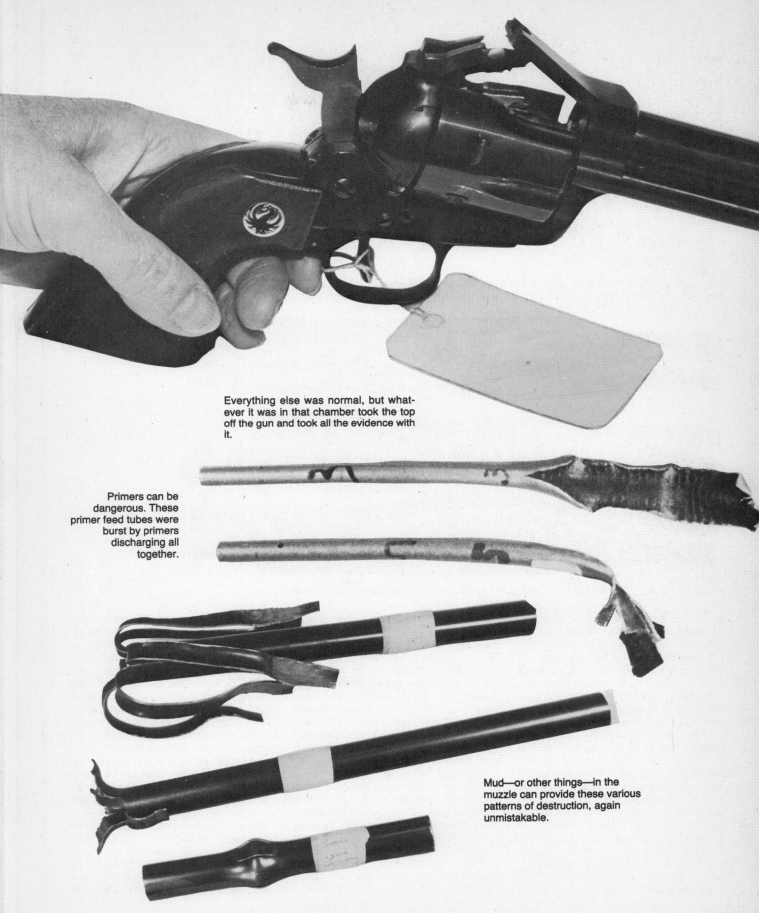

Everything else was normal, but whatever it was in that chamber took the top off the gun and took all the evidence with it.

Primers can be dangerous. These primer feed tubes were burst by primers discharging all together.

Mud—or other things—in the muzzle can provide these various patterns of destruction, again unmistakable.

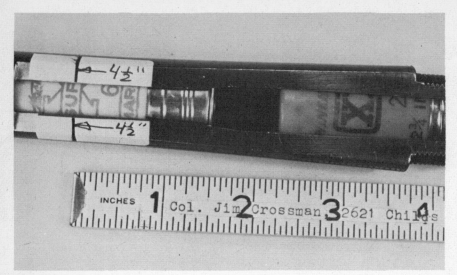

to examine. I glanced at it—then looked again. The burst was not in any of the usual places for a burst. It was well forward of the chamber, but well behind the muzzle, which are the two usual places for shotgun bursts. Further, the burst area didn't have the disruption, distortion and violence typical of most bursts.

When I could get out the microscope and the measuring equipment, the problem was easily found. In making this double barrel shotgun, and "striking" or filing the barrels for contour, its makers had gotten too enthusiastic and had cut the left barrel so that at one place I measured the thickness at about .008". Last year's GUN DIGEST pages ran about .005" in thickness and the cover about. 012".

Calculations showed that the gun could be expected to burst at the thin

This cutaway barrel shows a 20-gauge shell stuck in the barrel, ahead of a 12-gauge shell in the chamber. The 4½-inch measurement is to the base of the 20-gauge shot charge.

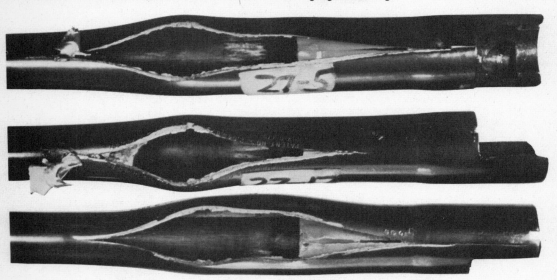

And here is what the classic 12-20 burst barrel looks like—all three times.

sures, causing the rear of the barrel to bulge and letting the breech plug out.

My friend told the young man that it was his fault, that he was responsible for the accident, and it didn't seem to make much sense to sue himself. I thought it pretty dumb of my friend not to have found out about the powder in the flask long before he did.

I have been consulted in cases of several burst shotguns where the shooters swore they were using factory shells, had never reloaded, didn't know anyone who reloaded, and had never used any reloads. But when the shells from the burst guns were examined, they showed clear evidence of having been reloaded several times. In some instances, the primer in the shell was not even made by the people who made the shell, and was of the type sold only for reloading. Even

though you don't reload, when you are shooting with or around other people, it is not difficult to end up with the odd shell which could well be a reload.

It really isn't *always* the shooter's fault. I recall the family who came to see me—a father, mother and son. They had bought a brand new double barrel shotgun for the boy as a Christmas present. Great excitement prevailed when the boy saw what he had been given. He could hardly wait until he could get to the store to buy a box of shells for the gun. And then came the big moment—his first shot with the gun. It was, unfortunately, something less than successful. The left barrel burst on the very first shot. Luckily, the boy's hand was only slightly injured, but a more disappointed kid you never saw.

So they brought the gun over for me

portion at around 2500 psi. While chamber pressure, as normally measured, runs four or five times this, it is measured at the high-pressure point, about an inch forward of the shell base. The burst section on this gun was apparently centered in an area about 7 inches foward. Pressure drops very rapidly as the shot charge moves foward and it would be down to something in the neighborhood of 3000 psi at the center of the burst. In any event, it was high enough to burst this thin barrel and spoil the kid's Christmas. I don't know how that gun managed to pass proof.

So this instance is an exception to the general rule "It's probably your fault!"

Reloading shotshells is not very precise work. It is done not so much with the hope of making better shells as for making cheaper shells. It's much less expensive to reload than to buy factory shells, as the empty hull constitutes a good percentage of the cost. You can reload for two or three bucks a box, or about half the price of factory-loaded shells. And if you shoot a lot of shotguns, shotshell reloading becomes a sort of mechanical thing, without too much thought involved. One merely turns out as many shells in a short time as possible. Once the tool is set up with the right bushings for the powder and shot charge you want, it doesn't take any great amount of concentration or thought to run shells through. Consequently it is easy to do something wrong.

With many reloading tools, if you drop a double charge of powder, you will also drop a double charge of shot, providing the shot tube isn't empty.

the routine, you can get out of step and make a mistake. This is especially true if you aren't paying attention and haven't noticed that you were running out and may have loaded some bad shells before you caught it. The same kind of a problem may arise when you are first starting up after making a major change in the tool.

It's often hard to convince people that they've made a mistake. No one likes to admit he goofed, especially when it resulted in a major injury. I've had a number of people come to talk to me about their busted gun and once in a while I can convince them that they made a mistake, but some people simply don't want the truth. They want to be told that whatever happened is not their fault.

I had a young chap call me some time ago, wanting advice on what

age. These were guns I had blown up in the past, with known charges. And then I took his tool and convincingly showed him how, while difficult, it was possible with his tool to load a shell giving dangerous pressures. After some hours of my convincing demonstrations, he finally packed up all his stuff and away he went.

And he promptly filed lawsuits against the gunmaker and the loading tool maker!

I have been involved in many cases of personal injury due to a gun blowing up, but I have never seen a personal injury from a revolver bursting. Apparently the pieces of the cylinder and top strap, if they come off, usually go up where no one gets hurt.

And there was the case where I was asked to determine why a revolver blew up. The cylinder had opened up

(Left) The hunter claimed a shell blew up in his coat as he was getting his gun out of the car. Actually, his shotgun fired as he was dragging it out muzzle first, and the shot charge hit the shells in his coat. He was very lucky.

(Right) The old British SMLE does not support the case well, and overloads can give you these results in 303 British cases.

You can't help seeing the double charge of shot, as it spills all over the machine and your workbench. You growl and grumble to yourself as you clean up the mess and get on with the reloading. But you can get so involved in cleaning up that you don't notice the double charge of powder lurking down deep in that other shell. The smart thing to do is to take all the shells out of the reloading tool behind the one where you spilled the shot, empty them and start over again.

Many progressive reloading machines have automatic or semi-automatic features designed to keep you moving smoothly from step to step. Once you are set up and rolling in the routine, it is easy to turn out large numbers of good reloads. But when you run out of a component—powder, shots, primers or wads—and break

happened. His pet shotgun had blown up and had badly damaged his left hand. I found out what kind of gun he had been using and I described what his busted gun now looked like and he agreed that it did, indeed, look like this. Then I found out what kind of components he was using and what kind of reloading tool. And I explained to him what kind of a load it took to burst a gun like his and how he could make such a load on his tool.

He was not convinced and was positive that he could not have made such a mistake and insisted on coming to see me. So, some time later, he showed up with his gun in all its glorious pieces and with his reloading tool and all his components. After a bit of conversation, I took him out to the lab and showed him a number of guns like his, with almost identical dam-

at the top chamber, bulging the top strap and badly damaging the two shells in the chambers on each side of the burst. But the three cartridges in the bottom chambers were OK. All five looked like new.

I ran pressures on the three good cartridges remaining. Pressures were perfectly normal, well below the maximum permitted. The spread in pressures was about the same as I got with known factory loads. So it certainly didn't look as if the ammunition was at fault.

Therefore it had to be the gun's fault. To make sure, I sent it off to a metallurgist-shooter I had worked with. After a while he came back with the report that he could find no defect in the material. It was properly heat-treated and looked good. Calculations showed that the gun should hold con-

(Right) This one was not a reloading problem. A 270 Winchester cartridge was forced into a 264 Winchester chamber—which buckled the case. The gun—and shooter—were badly damaged when the cartridge was fired.

(Below) This is the 270 case head after firing in the 264 Winchester Magnum chamber—another violent mismatch.

(Below) Note that the printing on the burst shell is of a different style and in a different location than on the other two shells—some sort of mix-up occurred.

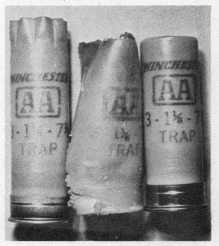

A 300 H&H case converted to a wildcat 338 burst the gun when fired in a 300 H&H rifle.

(Right) The mismatch of the 338 wildcat in a normal 300 H&H chamber created violent pressure as the damaged casehead (right) shows.

siderably higher pressure than I measured and higher than factory maximum.

So what busted the gun?? Obviously it had to be the shell that was in the top cylinder at the time. But that shell casing was gone. I don't know if it had been found and then thrown away or whether it had never been found, but in any event, I didn't have it. And so I don't know what was in the gun when it blew. Based upon past experience, I would say it was very probably a reload. Some pistol cartridges are particularly susceptible to double or triple charging, when using big cases with light loads.

One of the things you have to watch out for is light loads in big cases. No, I'm not talking about the detonation theory some people propound, but I am talking about the possibility of getting a double or triple charge in a case inadvertently. Take that Marlin 444 rifle that came in the other day in pieces. The barrel had burst near the back end, which demolished the forearm, smashed the magazine tube and caused cracks in the receiver, top and bottom. The bolt was not appreciably damaged, nor was the receiver, aside

from the cracks. The locking block showed a heavy imprint of the bolt, but it was otherwise undamaged. The lock and bolt and receiver held together, of course, and the injury to the man came from the burst barrel.

He was a reloader and had been using Unique for some of his reloading. The handbooks show starting loads for the 444 of 11 to 12 grains of Unique, with maximum of 17 to 18, with various cast bullets. But I could load 36 grains of Unique in the case and comfortably seat a bullet. With a bit of effort, compressing the powder, I could load just over 39 grains. Many of the recommended loads compressed the given powder charge, but those were not the relatively fast Unique.

Just taking the 36-grain figure, you can see that it is possible to load a double or triple powder charge and a bullet. All of which is guaranteed to give extremely high pressures! Several 25-grain loads fired in a pressure gun gave an average of about 55,000 CUP, where the SAAMI recommended figure is 47,000. Heavier loads gave markedly increased pressures.

No, I don't know what the man did, but all the indications of extremely

high chamber pressure were there. And by careless reloading, it is possible to get such high chamber pressures. There was no other reasonable explanation for the burst. Therefore, I had to conclude that it was probably his fault!

If at all possible, when using light loads, pick a powder-bullet combination that more than half-fills the case with powder, which should pretty well eliminate the double or triple charge problem. If you can't find such a happy combination, then establish a procedure where you carefully examine each case for the amount of powder before you put a bullet in it.

Many years ago I was doing a lot of high-power competitive rifle shooting. And so I was doing a great deal of reloading, trying to get good, accurate long-range loads, as we had many matches at 600 and 1000 yards. I made up some pretty good loads and my mother, a fine international shot in her own right, got in the habit of bumming some of this fine match stuff from me and often beating me with it.

But one day in a 600-yard match, when she pulled the trigger there was

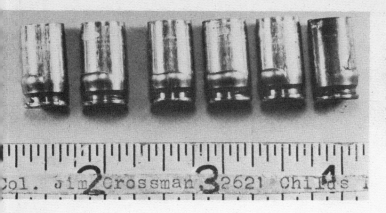

These 9mm pistol cases were fired in a poorly designed gun, one without adequate chamber support for the case—and the resulting case damage is unmistakable.

an unusual report and a cloud of smoke round the breech of the rifle. When we got her untangled from the rifle, her face was marked and burned from powder gas, powder fragments and bits of brass. She was wearing shooting glasses, of course, and her eyes were not hurt.

A look at the fired case showed what looked like a headspace burst, with a circumferential separation of the case ½-inch or so foward of the case head. But how could this be? Her rifle had been put together by a fine riflesmith and had fired hundreds of rounds without trouble.

We finally found that the locking ring on my resizing die had loosened and the die had gotten screwed in too far, so that it was shortening the cases more than necessary. In the process, of course, it was working the brass and hardening it, giving the typical ring you can see on the inside of the case.

So between weakening the case and scrunching it down so that it was considerably too short for the chamber, we ended up with a headspace burst. And it was all my fault! All of which taught me to check and double-check.

And it taught my mother a lesson. She didn't bum reloads from me any more.

And there was another lesson in there—shooting glasses! Don't fire a shot without wearing 'em.

About the same general time there was an experimenter and his wife shooting at the same club. He liked to try things himself, rather than relying on what other people had told him. He did much reloading, mainly attempting to work up various hunting cartridges for the two of them.

Somewhere he heard of a new, easy way of cleaning cases. As I recall, it involved soaking the cases in some mysterious fluid for a few minutes. But he decided that if a few minutes was good, a few hours would be better. Unfortunately, his treatment de-

stroyed the brass structure with the result that his wife had a case fragment in the rifle, filling her face full of brass particles, powder and gas. Unfortunately, she was shooting without glasses. Months later she was still wearing a patch over her eye while the medics were picking tiny bits of brass out of her.

Not that it should be needed, but this emphasized the necessity of shooting glasses. And it also pointed out that in the reloading field, as elsewhere, if you don't know what you are doing, you probably shouldn't do it.

"Instead of putting all the blame on the poor hapless reloader," you say, "how about all these guns bursting from bad metal?"

"So, how about it?" I say. "Show me one!"

I did mention the instance above where the boy's gun burst, not from bad metal, but from too little metal. But bursts due to a defect in the barrel material are extremely rare. Practically all guns made in the U.S. and Europe are "proved" with a high pressure test load, giving pressure well above anything you can reasonably expect to find in the field. If you go into the proof area of a gun maker and ask the fellows when they last burst a gun in proof, they look at each other in puzzlement—and usually can't remember when it last happened. The margin of safety of barrel thickness is so great, in most instances, that any minor defect in the material is not going to weaken the barrel dangerously. So a burst barrel is almost always due to an obstruction or an extreme overload.

As a matter of fact, a burst rifle barrel from high chamber pressure is rather rare. High pressure usually bursts the head of the cartridge case, letting gas loose in the action to damage the wood and perhaps blow off the extractor, but usually without major damage to the metal. Not that this is a good idea, understand, because you can get hurt and may likely lose an

eye if you are shooting without proper glasses. But such a burst is usually less dangerous than a burst shotgun.

The editor of this publication, Ken Warner, told me of an incident reinforcing our discussion topic "It's probably your fault!"

"A fellow club member was mildly boasting of his 30-06 and his marvelous handloads," Warner told me. "He chanced to mention he had never, in 20 years, fired anything in his rifle but handloads from a single batch of 100 cases. My immediate response was to tell him to retire them because he was about to get head separations. We went into the matter at length, but naturally he went ahead because 'after all. . . .' He looked at me very peculiarly the next time we met, for two of the next five rounds he fired had partial separations!"

Since you rely on the brass cartridge case or the metal-and-plastic shotgun hull to keep the gas safely inside the chamber, when that case ruptures it can lead to disaster.

While too much powder can give you high pressures and get you in trouble, too little powder can get you in trouble, too. Such a load can leave the bullet or wad stuck in the barrel. And when the next shot is fired, it can cause trouble. Take the case of the police officer who was chasing a suspect hither and yon in the night, firing some warning shots up in the air in the process. When everything had settled down, the officer noted that all he could hear with his right ear was an obnoxious roaring and ringing. Looking at his revolver, he could see that the barrel was split open about halfway down. Apparently he had fired a "squib" load or one with little powder in it, which had lodged the bullet in the barrel, whereupon the next bullet split the barrel and made a terrible noise alongside the officer's ear. No, he was not a reloader and claimed he was using factory ammunition so you couldn't hang the blame for this around his neck.

But a load which leaves a bullet or wad in the barrel can be dangerous, especially if the load is a "squib" which leaves some unburned powder in the barrel. This can cause a burst barrel on the next shot, in the location of the stuck wad or bullet.

Generally speaking, firearms are mighty safe devices and you can shoot all your life and never have any trouble. Because you are dealing with high pressures, however, if you do some dumb thing, it is possible to get into trouble. Play it safe so it won't be your fault! ●

Don't Pass Up A POTTER

by KENNETH L. WALTERS

Old ain't bad, and neither is cheap.

Representative Potters shown here are the Automatic, Combination, Super Twin and Gem.

THERE IS something about the human spirit which seems to believe that new and expensive is better than old and cheap. When it comes to reloading presses, however, such principles don't always apply. The old and inexpensive Potter presses, for instance, were made way back when a press was really a PRESS, and these fine old tools can not only provide insight to what once was, but also provide outstanding reloading value.

There are three facets of the Potter machines to discuss—namely: exactly how the various models differed; what you need to know in order to buy a good one; and their history.

Most Potters were semi-progressive reloaders, i.e. machines that worked on several shells simultaneously and produced a loaded round with every press cycle. Unlike a true progressive, however, cases must, in most Potters, be manually advanced between the various die stations. Priming and powder charging may be either manual or automatic, depending.

The essential differences between the various Potter reloaders were the number of reloading steps performed per press cycle and the degree of automation involved. The Duplex models did virtually everything for you, except advance the cases. The Super Twin also produced a loaded round per press cycle, but required some additional work in order to prime the cases. The Gem and the Simplex were more like regular single-station reloaders.

Potter Engineering's first commercial press was the Standard Duplex, initially called the Duplex. When other models were introduced, a "first name" was added. This name change occurred in about 1940.

The Standard Duplex was a three-station affair. The first station, which was in the middle, did resizing and depriming. Primers were fed into the mechanism automatically from a primer magazine screwed into the front of the base casting. The primer was actually inserted into the case by using a handle on the left side of the machine. Powder charging was handled on the left; bullet seating and, if necessary, crimping were performed at the station on the right.

Oddly enough, to use the Standard Duplex powder measure, you had to hold the case under it — no shellholder was provided. This was necessary because of the way the machine activated the powder measure. The powder measure was on the upper portion of the reloader far from where the case would have sat had a shell-

holder been provided. Also the base casting would have had to have been considerably enlarged to provide the room for this extra shellholder. Then too, adding this shellholder would have considerably disturbed the proportions of the press and probably required a complete press redesign. Because of this odd arrangement, however, it takes almost no effort to visually confirm that you have the correct charge in the case. All you have to do is tilt the case and look as it goes by.

The Automatic Duplex was virtually identical to the Standard Duplex except that priming was fully automated. To produce the Automatic, an arm was added to the priming mechanism under the base casting, a hole was cut in the base casting and a one-piece primer mechanism activation linkage was provided between the arm and the upper moving portion of the press.

The Combination Duplex was a hybrid of the Standard and Automatic. This unusual reloader could be set up to do priming either manually, as on the Standard Duplex, or automatically, as on the Automatic Duplex. To switch between the two modes of operation, a two-part primer mechanism activation linkage was used which could be readily severed by just pulling one small pin. With the linkage intact, the reloader functioned as a Automatic Duplex. With it severed, the reloader was, essentially, a Standard Duplex.

The factory, incidentally, usually set up the Combination Duplex to operate in the automatic mode and this, of course, is why many current owners cannot tell the difference between a true Automatic and a rare Combination set up for automatic operation. During its production life, a Combination Duplex cost considerably more than the Standard or Automatic. This is undoubtedly why so few were ever sold.

The Super Twin, a four-station machine and Arthur Potter's last design, was essentially a normal Duplex style but one with no primer magazine. Instead, priming was handled manually by placing the case upside down on top of a priming post. The primer was positioned on top of the primer pocket and pressed into place by a punch on the middle, moving portion, of the machine.

It would seem that, functionally at least, the major difference between Potter Standard Duplex, Automatic Duplex, Combination Duplex and Super Twin was how each model han-

dled the priming operation. All four incorporated only two reloading dies.

The Gem was a two-station affair. Built into the machine, on its left, was the primer station complete with a device to hold the case. The remaining main station, on the right, was essentially a normal single-station reloader. The short-lived Simplex was a modified Gem that could be equipped with Potter's automatic powder measure. Thus, the Simplex was actually a three-station reloader.

A true semi-progressive, of course, produces a completely loaded round per press cycle. Because the Gem and Simplex could only hold one reloading die at a time, they aren't semi-progressives.

The first consideration for Potter-buying is price. Excellent tools can cost almost nothing — say $50 — or hundreds — maybe as high as $600 — depending on how much the seller thinks he can get. In my opinion, a machine in excellent condition should cost $150 tops. People who want more almost invariably will settle for this, eventually. After all, there is no collector market here.

Also note that these machines did full-length resizing on pistol rounds but only neck resizing on rifle cases. Obviously if you want to do full-length resizing on rifle cartridges, these aren't the tools for you. Because the Potters were designed before the period of standard die threadings, their dies were unique. Except for, at most, 10 machines made in 1963 and 1964 which incorporated an extra long column and slide, the dies did not use the now standard $7/8$x14 threads. Virtually all Potters used $7/8$x18 threads. Also the dies screwed up into the press, instead of down into the reloader, as is now the norm.

Oddly enough, the last time I checked, new dies were still available from Carbide Die & Manufacturing Co. (P.O. Box 226, Covina, California 91723). Also, given an old die to use as a pattern, there should be any number of places that could make a new one. Thus dies really aren't a problem.

Originally Potter Engineering offered two kinds of factory installed dies. Sets using steel resizers were of their own manufacture. The others, for pistol cartridges, were those made by Carbide Die under their trade name of "Lifetyme."

Potters came with one of two styles of decapping rod. One did cartridge case mouth flaring and the other didn't. If you have a preference, check the die's decapping rod with a micrometer to be sure you get what you

The most popular Potter was the Automatic Duplex, so named because primer insertion was fully automated.

Note how the dies are pressed down over the cases. Most newer machines hold the dies stationary and raise the case or cases on a ram.

A rare Potter Super Twin and the only one ever originally supplied with an early powder measure.

Only one horizontal tool, which Walters owns, was ever made. It worked like bench-mounted tong tools.

want. A new decapping rod, of course, could be made for almost nothing by any good machinist.

Be sure, too, that you get a good primer tube. These things were threaded and screwed into the base of the machine. Be sure that the tube will screw in and that a primer will pass through it readily.

Sometimes the only thing that prevents this is a little dirt in the tube. A simple cleaning should fix that. Q-tips work well. Other times there can be a slight burr across from the hole through which a spring held the primers in place when the tube was being filled. A minor nick there can usually be easily fixed by very carefully using a small file. The spring on the primer tube need not be present as almost any little pin through that hole will do the job.

For machines, old or new, that use a column of stacked primers, the Potter tube was better than most. Because the tube screwed into the machine, if the column ever detonates (I know of no such cases) most of the column would be held in place. That, in turn, offers greater operator protection because the tube isn't likely to be blown out.

Also there is a feel to primer movement and seating in the Potter tools. Assuming that you've cleaned your press up well — RCBS's Crud Cutter does this nicely — and have sorted your brass by manufacturer, you can tell when something's wrong. This isn't really true on all newer equipment and may partially explain Potter's excellent safety record.

Another nice feature on most Potters was a plate (see photograph) that could be moved so that you could see the spent primer fall out of the machine. Using this, you could be absolutely sure that the spent primer was gone before you tried to seat a new one. This, too, minimized primer problems.

Early Potter powder measures were adjustable with two sizes of chambers being offered. It takes almost no time to check the range of possible charges such a drum could throw.

It was, incidentally, a very easy matter to disconnect the powder measure if, for some reason, you didn't want to use it during a particular reloading step. Actually, most reloading steps could be easily disabled if you wanted to use the reloader for just one limited step in the reloading cycle.

Potters used a small flat metal plate that had the required number of shellholders cut into them. Probably because these things were extremely simple, they seem to last forever. If you don't get all the shell plates you need, it is trivial and inexpensive to have them made. Any good machinist could do that quickly.

Like most progressives, the semi-progressive Potters, i.e. the Standard, Automatic, Combination and Super Twin, as well as the Gem and Simplex eject spent primers straight down and out of the mechanism. This means an owner can either cut a hole in his workbench under the machine to let the spent primers fall into some waiting container or periodically remove the machine from the bench in order to clean out the debris. The latter approach wasn't very popular, however, because of the limited room in the base casting. Then, too, on the Duplex models this debris, over time, could damage the various springs that operated the priming mechanism.

Except for the Gem and Simplex where the base casting was too small, another solution to the problem of spent primer debris was possible. Potter offered a sub-base casting upon which the machines could be mounted. Within this casting was a small drawer into which the spent primers would fall. The only odd thing about this casting was the small size of this drawer. Perhaps back then it wasn't expected that a reloader would load all that much ammunition at any one time.

Virtually all the Potter parts, like dies, shellholders, powder chambers, etc., were extremely well made and appear to last forever. Thus it is unlikely that you would ever need to have a part machined unless, of course, you were just adding a new caliber.

AUTHOR'S POTTERS	
Model	**Base Casting Markings**
Horizontal	A.D. POTTER CO. SYRACUSE N.Y.
Automatic Duplex	POTTER DUPLEX A7
Automatic Duplex	POTTER DUPLEX A6
Combination Duplex	POTTER DUPLEX C9
Gem	POTTER 201*
SUPER TWIN	POTTER
* Unimportant pattern number.	

If you need spare parts or help in adjusting an old Potter, you can contact Glen Potter at 40 Lake Shore Drive, Palm Harbor, Florida 33563. Few spare parts still exist but he might have the piece you need.

It might be comforting, too, to note that none of the Potter presses I've purchased over the years was anything less than totally serviceable. Also, I ended up with more than enough spare parts and extra die sets. Partially I think that this was due to the pride and care that was put into the machine's manufacture, i.e. things were made so well they rarely broke. Also I think that many of the people who bought these excellent tools bought every spare part they might ever need and had the wisdom to take care of their equipment.

With any luck at all then, you should be able to buy an excellent Potter that will last you a lifetime for less than you'd have to pay for any of today's equivalent machines. The best place to locate a Potter, incidentally, is via advertisements in *The Shotgun News*.

I have machines using original Lifetyme dies that load 38 Special, 44 Special, and 45 ACP. Eventually I intend to set up the other two to handle 30-06 and 45 Colt. Potters were, of course, offered in all the standard pistol and rifle calibers available up to the mid-'60s.

Initially, in the 1930s, the Potter firm was located at 632 Scoville Avenue in Syracuse, New York. In March of 1941, however, the firm moved to 10 Albany Street, Cazenovia, New York, and, in 1951, they moved again,

The Potter Gem was a two-station press with priming on the left.

Only one Potter lubricator/sizer was ever made. It is quite similar to the corresponding Star Machine Works product.

Perhaps the most unusual Potter was the Combination Duplex. Priming could be either automatic or manual via the handle on the left.

this time to 1387 River Hills Circle, Jacksonville, Florida. In 1958, they moved to their final location, 1410 Santa Anna Drive, Dunedin, Florida. The Potter firm still operates there, but now, with a new owner, it is not in the reloading business.

These physical locations are important because some of the reloaders were marked to indicate the city in which they were made. We know, for instance, that there were presses marked Syracuse. Whether or not the names of the other cities were incorporated into the base casting is unknown, but the educated guess is that they were not. Thus if you should find a press whose base casting has one of these other city names cast into it, you've found a heretofore unknown variation.

Early Potter presses contained a second marking. Located up inside the base casting, which requires turning the press upside down in order to see it, may be a pattern number. These numbers have, essentially, no meaning, but some people confuse them with a serial number. Serial numbers were present on some early machines, but they were located on the top of the main lower casting right behind the shellholders. These serial numbers, starting from 1, indicated how many units of that particular type had been made to date.

Later, the hand-stamped serial number was changed to a letter and number to reflect the type of machine and the year of manufacture. In this third marking, located just behind the right shell position, the prefix A was used to indicate the Automatic model, S denoted the Standard, C indicated the Combination, G was for Gem, ST denoted the Super Twin and, if the Simplex was marked in this manner, it probably carried a two letter prefix starting with S. One Super Twin is known, incidentally, that should but doesn't carry this designation. No machines are now known which carry both a model designation and a serial number.

Originally, the year designation consisted of two digits, like 38 to indicate 1938. The factory used this information on units being returned for repair to determine if the warranty was still valid. Because stamping the units took some effort and a very old reloader could be easily spotted, the year marking was later changed to a single digit, like 5 for 1945. It is true, of course, that a present owner cannot tell if such a marking indicates 1945, 1955 or 1965 but, alas, that is just the way it is.

You can, however, date some Potter

reloaders exactly by using this one digit coupled with noting how some of the parts were constructed. We know, for instance, that Potter used two types of powder measures, discussed later. The all cast iron measures were only produced for the first 15 or so years. Thus, if you have a machine marked AO and it has an an original all-metallic powder measure, you can be pretty sure that it was built in 1940.

Dating can be derived from other parts as well. The Potter firm, for instance, could not get acceptable iron castings made by local suppliers once they moved to Florida. Later machines had bronze arms and aluminium bases once the supply of the original cast iron pieces ran out. Again coupling a one-digit year designation with knowledge of what some of the parts are made out of and knowing when the firm moved to Florida can allow you to determine exactly the date of the manufacture.

Also, once in a great while, exact dating can be found in either correspondence between the original owner and the factory, or an original shipping container complete with a dated postmark. The postmark, obviously, should be from one of the cities listed above.

Press dating can also sometimes be accomplished by noting how the sub-base was made. Originally they were made entirely of cast iron. When supplies ran out and the Florida-based firm could find no local suppliers to make acceptable cast iron parts, first the drawer and later the entire sub-base was made out of an aluminium alloy.

Thus, besides the possible marking to indicate the town in which the press was made, any given machine might have a serial number or a one digit model designation followed by a one or two-digit stamp indicating the year of manufacture. These markings, if present, will be right behind the right-side shellholder. Typical markings on the Potter presses that I own are shown nearby.

Incidentally, while Arthur Potter was employed as an engineer in the automobile industry, he built a horizontal tool. Only one such reloader was ever made and it basically operated like a bench-mounted set of tong tools. Thus, the initial Potter press was a heretofore unknown horizontal. Why this machine was never commercially sold, I don't know. Certainly, later horizontal reloaders, like the Schmidt, weren't all that much better.

It should be noted, incidentally,

The rod which activated the automatic primer seating in the Combination Duplex was made in two parts held together by a pin. If the pin was removed, as shown here, the automatic mechanism was disabled.

POTTER PRODUCTION

Model	Years Manufactured	Total Produced
Horizontal	approximately 1920	1
Standard Duplex	1937 — 1966	600
Automatic Duplex	1940 — 1966	1500
Gem Reloader	1940 — 1953	150
Combination Duplex	1946 — 1966	75
Simplex Reloader	1950 — 1951	30
Super Twin Reloader	1953 — 1966	30

OTHER POTTER PRODUCTION

Type of Equipment	Years Manufactured	Total Production
Electric Furnaces	1937 — 1979	2000 to 3000
Lead Tester	1940 — 1975	200 to 300
Machine Rest	1940 — 1966	40
Sub-base Castings	1940 — 1966	2000
Lubricator/Sizer	1966	1

that the POTTER DUPLEX markings cast into the bases of the Standard, Automatic and Combination Duplex used all capital letters but the size of the letters in the POTTER name are about twice the size of those used to spell out the word DUPLEX. Also you'll notice that, except for the one letter designation behind the right shellholder on some presses, the presses themselves carry no direct indication of exactly what type of press they are. It is true that all three Duplex models had that word in their base casting, but except for the single-digit model designation on some of the later machines, you can only tell the

models apart by noting their exact physical construction.

Also, oddly enough, many owners can not tell a Standard Duplex from a Combination or Automatic since they don't know the meaning of the one letter designation right behind the right shellholder and don't know enough about the physical construction to spot key differences. Thus, I have been sold a rare Combination that had been set up to operate in its automatic mode as if it was, in fact, an Automatic Duplex.

Potter production over the years wasn't large by current standards. Actually it is believed by Glen Potter

This front view of a typical Potter press shows the simple and rugged nature of the basic Potter approach.

On Standard, Automatic and Combination Duplexes, the front of the primer slide could be seen by moving a small plate. This let the operator see the spent primer fall into the sub-base and thus know that the case had been successfully deprimed.

that the total production is pretty close to the figures shown in the chart. You'll notice that the Super Twin has the interesting distinction of being available for a substantial period while having the lowest production ever recorded by a major press manufacturer. Automatic and Combination Duplex reloaders were normally shipped with a sub-base. On the Standard, the buyers had to pay extra for this option.

One last note about differences in the Potter designs. Early production had a cast iron, lidless powder measure with an adjustable cavity. You can spot this easily because the Potter name is actually cast into it. Both a

model for the Duplex reloaders and a bench version complete with a table bracket were available. The later (second) type of powder measure had a plastic hopper with a cast iron base and lid. Eventually, near the end of production, lids were made out of an aluminum alloy. On all these second-style powder measures, replaceable powder cylinders were used. As I indicated earlier, the original powder measure was built for about 10 years, probably ending around 1946.

Although it has been possible to catalog Potter's seven reloaders — six, really, if you consider the horizontal to be a pre-production model — no one now knows how many minor vari-

ations of these basic models were produced. It could well be that numerous uncataloged variations exist.

For the sake of completeness, it is possible to record other Potter production figures, shown nearby. I'm virtually certain that there were actually three different furnaces and two machine rests. These figures, however, are the totals over all models. How many of each individual kind were made is something we'll never know.

Potter Engineering also sold mould blocks, but these were not, I think, of their manufacture. I believe the Potter moulds were actually made by Cramer, i.e. the original owner of the current SAECO line. Also, oddly enough, Potter casting furnaces were sold not only by Potter, but also by Lyman.

Arthur Potter retired in 1972 at the age of 80 and died on July 4th, 1976, at the age of 84. What largely did in the Potter firm, at least in its reloading activities, was the temporary surge in bullet swaging in the mid-'60s that affected the sales of the casting furnaces, and the appearance of numerous inexpensive reloading presses which undermined press sales. Against this double attack, in conjunction with Arthur Potter's advanced age, the firm just couldn't compete. Instead they went on to make non-reloading gear — boat winches, actually — as the mainstay of their business and that business survives to this very day. Arthur Potter's last reloading development effort, incidentally, was a bullet lubricator, but only one prototype was made.

Considered in proper historical context, Arthur Potter was one of the founding fathers of the modern reloading industry. In the 1930s, bench-mounted metallic home reloading presses were just starting to appear, and press designs were far from standardized. Arthur Potter produced the first commercially successful semi-progressive design and a design that was unique.

Arthur Potter's contribution, then, was a high quality product in an era when few such tools existed. None of his contemporaries, except Star Machine Works, survived nearly as long. Also he built quality equipment for as long as he was in commercial production. Times changed but the quality of Potter Engineering's equipment still appeals to reloaders who appreciate fine equipment.

I really don't think you should pass one up. There's something great about using tools in the presence of the ghosts of machinists past. ●

Keeping the VARIABLES in Check

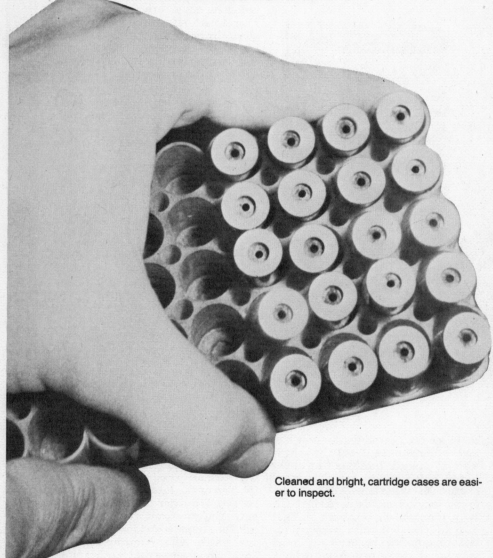

Cleaned and bright, cartridge cases are easier to inspect.

Little things mean a lot.

by SAM FADALA

Handloading is not like baking a cake. One of my handloader friends, in an effort to smooth out the bumps on the reloading road for a newcomer, said that if you can bake a cake, you can reload a safe and accurate round. Possibly, but some of the best bakers grab a handful of this and a scant teaspoonful of that and a pinch of the other and a dash of something else and by the time the mixture does its chemistry, you can have a great cake. Baking is an artistic operation with a touch of science while reloading is a scientific operation with a touch of art.

In part, reloading is a matter of variables. And variables are like gophers. They have to be kept in check or they will dominate the situation.

A friend of mine in Wyoming wanted to know why his 25-06 cases had pierced primers when he used maximum loads. After all, the loads had been lifted directly from the pages of legitimate reloading manuals. The problem lay in the case. "These are GI brass," I told him, "and they are thicker than some other cases."

Being thicker, their volume was less. Less volume and less space for the gas to expand means greater pressure. Greater pressure pops the primer. We switched to W-W brass using exactly the same loads the shooter had been stuffing into that necked-down GI brass and all was immediately well.

Case variations can cause problems because all cases are not created with identical interior dimensions due to variations in brass thickness. You can get general about this, and that's fine. Generally speaking, an RWS cartridge case is thicker than a W-W case. Is that better? Or worse? Neither. It's just different. You may find that in switching from a load worked up in a W-W case to an RWS case, or to Remington brass, that you need to cut back a grain, 2 grains, even 3 depending upon the cartridge, the powder and other factors. The idea is to read which case was used when the data were taken. If you must switch to another brand of case, remember that the results originally obtained will now, most likely, differ.

I have a good load using 58.0 grains of H-4831 with a 140-grain Hornady bullet for one particular 270 Winchester rifle in W-W brass. If I switch to Remington or RWS brass, I cut back to 56.0 grains and the chronograph tells me my velocity is the same. However, cases also vary with the individual cartridge. I used Frontier, Winchester and Remintgon 30-30 brass in a recent chronograph session and differences among these cases were not readily detected by the velocity results. Just be aware of case variables, that's all, and when you have a fine load figured out for a specific cartridge, you may well want to stay with the brass that brought you that load.

Also under the heading of case variables comes that all-important initial step to reloading, checking the fired round for defects. You can't expect good results when cartridge cases vary one from the other, and one way they can vary is through fatigue. It would seem that if you start with a batch of 100 cases, load them all the same, and shoot them all the same number of times, that on one given day each and every case would give up the ghost. It simply isn't so. In spite of superior quality control, some brass cases will indeed have a shorter life

neck (mouth) into the cannelure of a bullet, a thinner neck helps. And the process also gets rid of any thickness here which would pinch the bullet and retard its initial escape into the leade. Such retardation boosts pressures. You might clean the primer pocket, too, since this allows a better view of that important area and aids in correct seating of the primer later on.

When I was a young handloader, I felt pretty smug about the good groups I got with my reloaded fodder. As I look back, I realize the tight groups were products of a good barrel, good bullets, correct bedding and, all in all, a correctly made rifle, plus I

nary factory-dimensioned round, but rather one of my neck-sized-only customs. Luckily, I never lost a head of game because of a sticky chambering situation, and luck was the word for it. You can resize cases at least three ways. The neck-size-only die can be used, in which the neck is squeezed back to normal dimensions, but the body taper is left alone and somewhat as your rifle chamber left it. Or you can use full-length resize dies, but size the case only part-way up the die. Or you can full-length resize.

There may be a slight edge in sizing the neck only, but it's a very slender edge at best, and later on those warped cases may cause accuracy problems, not accuracy enhancement. Forget neck-size only. The gains are generally not worth the hassle of having to force a round home. I began full-length resizing one day as a result of a little demonstration I worked

One factor important to upgraded loads is powder selection. Careful experimentation may lead to a perfect marriage.

span than others. Check for split necks, enlarged primer pockets (the primer slips in too easily), body cracks and so forth before reloading that case. I use a tumbler to clean my cases because I think it makes such inspection easier. Also, I like shiny reloads. It impresses people to hold up a like-new (looking) case, saying, "I reloaded this one myself."

Finally, you will want to chamfer the neck, inside and outside, with — you guessed it — a chamfering tool or deburring gadget. This little tool removes a bit of the metal from the neck area, thinning the neck down at that point. If you need to crimp the case

could see pretty well and I never had any coffee-shakes. But I thought it was my superb handloading technique which had brought the good groups. One thing I never did — I never full-length resized a cartridge case. Why, it only made sense not to. That case was custom-formed to my unique rifle chamber when fired and in no way was I going to squash it back down to that mundane shape the case had when it left the factory.

After a few shots, using full throttle loads, chambering the round got a little sticky. I was happy. After all, the force required to bolt home the round proved that the cartridge was no ordi-

up to satisfy myself that neck-sizing only was bringing a big reward in group size. I had loaded 20 rounds for a particularly accurate bolt-action rifle. Ten of the loads were full-length resized. The other 10 were neck-sized only. You guessed it. No difference at all. The groups were the same from either batch. After running the little "test" again with a couple other rifles, the last neck-sized case left my press. Go ahead and full-length resize. Full-length resizing won't bring a round back to exact factory form, but it will allow that loaded round to chamber easily, if all else is correct, and besides, the full-length resized ammo will most likely work in several rifles, rather than only in the peculiar chamber of your pet.

My pal's expended rifle cases resembled the fingernails of FuManchu — they were getting longer and longer. He not only failed to trim cases at all, but he did not even know there was any such thing as a case trimmer. Plus, his 30-40 Krag leaned to stretch in the first place. Supposing that the long neck of the case extends into the leade or throat of the chamber, and suppose that the bullet becomes effectively pinched between the leade and the case neck? Pressures could go up here. So this tidbit of advice is small in discussion, but big in importance. Cases do tend to grow longer with each firing because brass does stretch.

There are various ways to keep check on case length. The idea is to observe uniformity, keeping your case neck length about the same at all

The author likes to tumble his cartridge cases in order to get them shiny bright. The clean case shows incipient problems, such as minute cracks, much better than a dirty one.

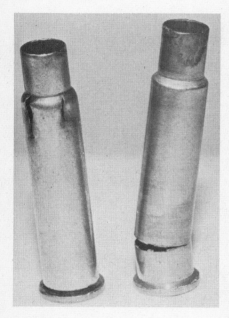

(Left) These kinds of case failure—they happened during fire-forming—are self-evident. However, not all case failures are so dramatic.

times and especially never too long. Yes, minute differences in exit velocity can also be detected if you allow case necks to vary in length, too. I have both trim die and rotary trimmer on my reloading bench. The trim die is very simple to use and it works fine. The cartridge case is inserted all the way into the trim die. Insure that the head of the ram makes firm contact with the base of the trim die when you set it up so that the trim die works properly. If any portion of neck sticks up *above* the top of the trim die, that's excess neck and it should be trimmed off. The trim die is very hard metal, so a file can be used to remove

the extra brass. Then chamfer the neck, after trimming, and the case is correct in length once again.

The rotary trimmer is a bit different. It is a separate tool into which the case is inserted and then a sharp blade is rotated, the blade cutting away excess metal and bringing the case back to normal length. As for the exact measurement of the case, a brand new case can be used to set up the trimmer to begin with. Then all following cases are trimmed back to that dimension. My own trimmer, an RCBS model, uses a series of trim gauges. You simply insert the correct trim gauge, and the trimmer removes just the right amount of extended

This beginning case failure is less evident than it appears in this magnified view. The tiny split will certainly develop into a larger one, so this case is through. Smash the case before throwing it away.

neck to bring the cartridge back to specs length-wise.

Anybody can figure out that if the powder charge varies enough, the exit velocity will also vary, and if the bullets are not leaving the muzzle at pretty close to the same velocity, then they are going to strike a different point on the target. In other words, if your 30-06 shoots one 150-grain bullet at 2700 fps and the next at 3000 fps, you will see some difference in impact at the target. Well, I had all of that figured out, too, in my young days of fancy handloading style. You simply weigh each and every powder charge on a scale. In fact, there is nothing wrong with this method, and I still find it no big inconvenience to weigh charges.

But most of the time, my powder measure does the job these days. As the efficiency of the powder *increases*, variation in the charge means more and more to exit velocity. It only makes sense. I recently read that if you really wanted accuracy from a muzzleloader, you ought to weigh the powder charges, rather than using a powder measure. In fact, blackpowder is not that efficient. My own chronograph cannot tell the difference between 100 grains of FFg in a 50-caliber and 103 grains of the same powder in the same caliber, same ball and patch. You really get a chuckle when told that a charge of 45.5 grains of FFg is *the* accuracy load, meaning that with 45.0, 46.0 or anything *but* 45.5 grains of powder your accuracy is going to depart for the hinterlands. No way.

While it is true that variations in powder charge can foul up accuracy, we tend to get carried away with the idea. Given that a powder measure is *checked* from time to time, and given

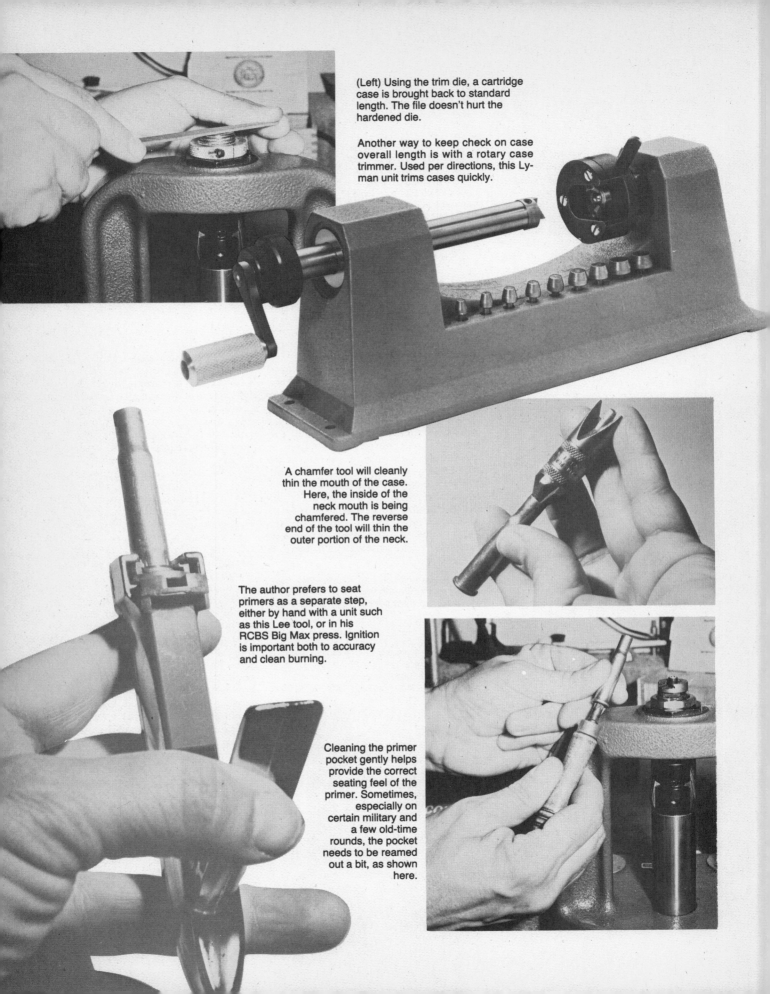

(Left) Using the trim die, a cartridge case is brought back to standard length. The file doesn't hurt the hardened die.

Another way to keep check on case overall length is with a rotary case trimmer. Used per directions, this Lyman unit trims cases quickly.

A chamfer tool will cleanly thin the mouth of the case. Here, the inside of the neck mouth is being chamfered. The reverse end of the tool will thin the outer portion of the neck.

The author prefers to seat primers as a separate step, either by hand with a unit such as this Lee tool, or in his RCBS Big Max press. Ignition is important both to accuracy and clean burning.

Cleaning the primer pocket gently helps provide the correct seating feel of the primer. Sometimes, especially on certain military and a few old-time rounds, the pocket needs to be reamed out a bit, as shown here.

Use many loading manuals. You're more likely to come up with the "best load" for your favorite cartridge if you multiply your choices.

that the reloader uses the measure in a steady fashion, keeping the same *consistent* action on the handle, accuracy will be just fine. (Of course, if the powder measure is not used with consistency, then this little treatise falls apart right away.) In short, other variables are larger in impact than slight variations in powder charge weight.

The missile itself is one of those important variables. In a word, the bullets should be unblemished in terms of damage, especially to the *base* of the projectile. Do this: grab five of your best handloads, with softpoint bullets. Gently tap the points of three of the bullets to flatten them out. Do not beat the bullets violently on a table or counter, but only enough to smash the lead tip. We should maintain seating depth. Now you have two perfect bullets and three smashed-nose bullets. Shoot all five rounds. The group will be normal. Then, when reloading, set aside those five rounds for a little demonstration. Leave two of the new bullets alone, but with a file, cut a little wedge from *the bases* of the other three bullets. Now go shoot for a group. Most likely the three nicked bullets will depart the group at 100 yards, dramatically so at 200 yards and beyond. Bullet bases must not vary.

Ideally, the powder charge should take up all the air space in the cartridge case. This is called 100 percent loading density. If it takes up 80 percent of that space, then you have 80 percent loading density and so forth. I have, to be sure, seen fine accuracy with lower-end densities. But all in all, it is well to adhere to this principle if possible. Therefore, you may experiment with various powders in your pet rifle, using the loads best-advised by the manuals. See if those powders which give closer to 100 percent loading density also render the

best accuracy in your rifle. Recently, I tried a series of 6mm Remington handloads, and the evidence was in favor of H-4350, the powder which gave close to 100 percent loading density. In going to underloads, however, watch out for using slow-burning powder in small charges. Pressure problems have occurred—yet unexplained—with such charges.

Part of the problem, I think, with low loading density is the fact that the primer flash makes contact with the various granules of powder in the case in a somewhat haphazard fashion. That's just my idea. I can no more prove that than I can bicycle from New York to London. But I do know that primer switches have altered accuracy in some of my loads. How the powder is ignited can affect accuracy, and the how in ignition is the primer, of course. I cannot be more specific, except to list many of my own findings, which may or may not help the reader, depending upon his own handloads. I can, however, advise some simple record-keeping. Shooting over a period of time, keep track of group size with a load you have decided on for good accuracy. Then switch primers from time to time and see how the groups match up with your standards. I went from a standard primer to a hot primer in my 257 Weatherby Magnum and accuracy definitely improved. I went the other way with some 30-30 cast bullet loads and accuracy got better. Seat primers carefully, too. I seat primers as a separate function, insuring that the primer is fully inserted into the pocket so that the case will rest flat on its head on a table without wobbling. I also feel the seated primer with a finger to determine that it is fully seated.

Matching the powder with the cartridge case, the primer, the bullet being used in a specific bore size is im-

portant to accuracy. Once again, you can do some safe testing on your own here, using approved powder charges and switching brands until you find the one which is best digested in your cartridge/rifle. Powders vary greatly, especially in rate of state change from a solid to a gas. Read many loading manuals, too, for it could be that the research has been done for you already and your powder selection may be no more troublesome than reading which powder is best for your needs.

One way to begin at the beginning is to match the overall length of the round to fit the magazine of the rifle. Seat the bullet deeply enough into the case mouth so that the loaded cartridge will slide into the magazine. Some believe the bullet should touch the lands of the rifling when the round is chambered. This means a bit more pressure than seating the bullet back so that it must jump into the rifling. Again, it's that initial escape that makes the difference. If a bullet can't get going easily because it is retarded by anything, pressures go up, though they do not rise terribly by seating a bullet so that it just touches the lands.

Some leades or throats are long, or free-bored, which does two things. First, pressures will be a bit lower with freebore. Second, since the bullet does not touch the lands of the rifling, it must follow that accuracy will fall off with freebore. Perhaps I own the exception to the rule—my Dale Storey-built 6.5mm-06 Improved is freebored. It has consistently produced ½-inch groups at 100 yards from the bench, even with me shooting the rifle.

When the variation gremlins run amok over your loading bench, only consistency chases them away. Only when variables are kept in check is the full potential of the reloaded round achieved. Sort those cases. Separate them. Know their differences in volume. Full-length resize your rounds by insuring that the ram is butted up against the base of your resize die. Trim those cases. Keep powder charges consistent from one case to the next. Insure that those bullets are correct in weight, diameter, style and in perfect shape. Try for near 100 percent load density if you can get it with safety. Remember that primers differ. Use the correct one for your round, your load. Use not only the right powder charge, but the right powder for your load. And seat the bullet correctly. And cross your fingers . . .

●

Bigger shot faster? Buffers in steel loads? Gimmicks? Lighter payloads?

WHERE ARE SHOTSHELLS GOING? by DON ZUTZ

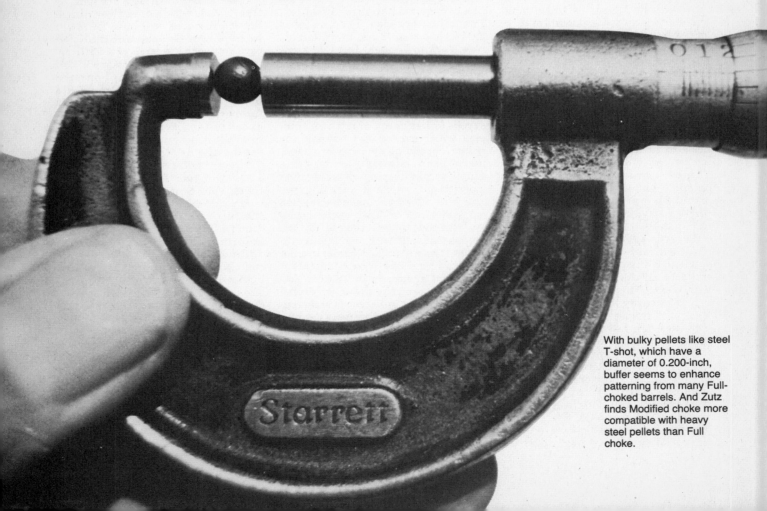

With bulky pellets like steel T-shot, which have a diameter of 0.200-inch, buffer seems to enhance patterning from many Full-choked barrels. And Zutz finds Modified choke more compatible with heavy steel pellets than Full choke.

IT WAS the first warm day last spring when I hunkered down to chronograph some of the newest factory loads for 1986, and if I hadn't known the batteries in Oehler's Model 33 were fresh, I'd have rapped the electronic gizzmo with my knuckles. Velocity figures the likes of which I'd not seen before from the types of ammo I was clocking kept popping up. The first test string, for example, involved 12-gauge, 1½-ounce short magnums from ACTIV Industries, and they averaged 1394 fps. When one is used to seeing them doing 1260 to 1300 fps, a jump of 100 to 150 fps is startling!

And then came Winchester's 3-inch 12-gauge magnums with 1⅞ ounces of copper-plated 6s in what the big red W calls a specialized turkey load. This kind of ammo has never been pushed hard, 1210 fps being a nominal speed for 1⅞-ouncers at the muzzle of a 30-inch barrel. But the first five turkey loads ripped over my skyscreens between 1281 and 1311 fps for an average just below 1300 fps. That's *moving it* for such a long, hefty shot charge!

After the initial test strings, I reached for some known-velocity control loads, and they proved that the chronograph was doing just fine. So the new loads had indeed reached those fancy velocity figures without the help of any elves in the box.

What's going on here? A couple of things, apparently. First, those white-frocked folks who stir things in chemistry labs have come up with still slower-burning propellants which make higher velocities possible with hitherto obese payloads. Upon opening these newest commercial loads, I found a round, glossy black, heavily deterred flake powder new to the shotshell scene. If I had to guess, I'd say that the powders may well have derived from research pointed toward improved steel shot ballistics, but which were found to have lead shot applications, too.

Secondly, although the ultra-slow propellants aren't yet available in cannister lots for reloaders, the trend in shotshell performance is definitely toward higher velocities in hunting loads. Don't be surprised if some BB and buckshot rounds flirt with 1500 fps in the near future.

In fact, hunters who are willing to experiment with hard shot — preferably nickel-plated, with copper-plated pellets acceptable — and lighter payloads can already top 1500 fps in the standard 12-gauge. This is another trend being taken by experimenters,

namely, blending slow-burning powders with less-than-magnum shot charges for optimum muzzle velocity. The barrel should be at least a 30-incher to burn the fuel, and the ample gases will produce a definite rocket effect at the moment of exit, but things can be started briskly. The following reload, for instance, was worked up by Tom Armbrust. who operates Ballistic Reseach in McHenry, IL.

Shell: Winchester 2¾" C/F
Primer: Federal 209
Powder: 38.0/SR-4756
Wad: Remington SP-12
Shot: 1⅛ ounces of hard or plated *lead* shot.
Pressure: 10,100 LUP
Velocity: 1535 fps

For someone who wants to be swift but not *that* swift, here's another to top 1400 fps from a 30-inch barrel:

Shell: Winchester 2¾" C/F
Primer: CCI 109
Powder 31.0/SR-7625
Wad: Remington R-12H
Shot: 1⅛ ounces of hard or plated *lead* shot
Pressure: 10,070 LUP
Velocity: 1440 fps

In some patterning with these loads — which aren't at all "hot," as their chamber pressures are well below the 11,000 LUP maximum for standard 12s — I found the SR-7625-powered recipe to pattern better. With nickel-plated 5s, the patterns were actually quite good from the 30-inch Remington M1100 barrel employed.

Why the sudden coupling of light shot charges with super-duper velocities? It again appears to be a carryover from steel shot experiments. In general, steel shot loads are lighter than lead shot loads, and steel shot must be driven faster than lead if it is to retain adequate energy down range or in the wild blue yonder. This trend has been especially true when it comes to handloading steel shot. The fact is that it's virtually impossible to get more than 1¼ ounces of steel shot into a standard-length 12-gauge hull and still have room for the wad and powder; hence, engineering steel shot loads pivots on getting relatively light payloads to race like crazy.

We can probably make steel duck loads do all we need for clean-killing energy out to 45-50 yards with steel No. 1s. Velocities of 1350 to 1400 fps, which modern steel loads generate, will handle that; and handloaders will find such ballistics within their

reach with steel shot, provided they do some research in the booklets offered by suppliers of steel shot and the related components. The foremost here would be U-Load, Inc. (P.O. Box 443-177, Eden Prairie, MN 55344), Non-Toxic Components, Inc. (P.O. Box 4202, Portland, OR 97208), and Ballistic Products, Inc. (P.O. Box 488, Long Lake, MN 55356).

When it comes to steel shot goose loads, however, reloading becomes a horse of another hue. Geese are the big game of wingshooting. High fliers, heavily boned, and covered with a thick down, geese are dropped cleanly by high-energy pellets only; and, unfortunately, steel shot sizes that do well on ducks aren't adequate on geese as the range increases. Led by experimenter Don Vizecky of Minneapolis, who markets his components and concepts via U-Load, Inc., under the "Supersonic"® label, the trend in steel shot goose loads has swung to specialty reloads with steel buckshot at high speed. The idea, of course, is to drive heavier pellets upstairs so that more energy is retained.

To further the concept of high residual energy, the loads of steel buckshot are being held to relatively light charges of generally no more than 1⅛ ounces and often no more than 1 or 1 1/16 ounces. The reason, of course, is to permit exceedingly high velocities so that each buckball is power-laden for long-range impact. Experiments with these light steel shot charges and ultra-slow-burning powders have produced safe loads reaching 1500 fps and more.

Ballistic Research has done much testing of such high-velocity steel stuff using Supersonic components, and the results in 10-gauge Magnum hulls are attention-getting.

For example, a move is on to allow T-shot, alias T-buckshot (0.20-inch diameter), to be used in states which normally don't permit the buckshot sizes (anything larger than BB) for waterfowling. But T-shot gives the steel shot user about the same energy as he'd get from a lead BB, and therefore, T-shot is deemed more efficient in bringing down geese with steel loads rather than merely crippling and losing them. At Ballistic Research, Tom Armbrust checked out this reload:

Shell: Federal 10-ga. 3½" plastic
Primer: Winchester 209
Powder: 43.0/SR-4756
Wad: Supersonic #1500 plastic wad + 0.200" card

Shot: wad in shotcup
62 pellets T-shot steel
Buffer: 30.0 grains Supersonic graphite
Overshot wad: 1 Supersonic overshot card wad
Pressure: 10,560 LUP
Velocity: 1526 fps

This high-velocity performance from a 10-gauge Magnum reload operating at a nominal maximum pressure figure is due to the combination of a 10's wide bore, which provides gas expansion room, and the relatively light shot charge. In scaling 62 T-shot provided me by Supersonic, I come up with just 503 grains, which is well below the 2-2¼-ounce (875-985-grain) charges we're used to finding in the big 10 with lead shot. Obviously, the buffer helps increase chamber pressures in these steel shot swifties, but it also seems to stabilize the emerging shot strings for enhanced patterns.

The company that supplies Supersonic steel shot components also offers a graphite to mix with the buffer employed for the brand's reloading data and load recommendations. Under setback pressures the graphite will seep out the shotcup's slits.

To help keep chamber pressures down while striving for extremely high velocities with long-range hunting loads of either lead shot or steel shot, experimenters have begun using a dry lube on the outside of the wad. Motor Mica from Ballistic Products, Inc., is specially labeled for the job.

Once known only as a pistol powder, Bullseye now fits into the 12-gauge target load category with 1-ounce shot charge.

This is what a Supersonic reload looks like sliced open. Note the graphited buffer encasing steel buckshot and the use of an overshot wad to keep buffer from trickling out the top.

The people behind Supersonic steel shot supplies believe their buffer helps give the load fluidity at muzzle passage for improved patterning. It appears to be fine beads of expandable polystyrene.

If you think the above reload is fast—you ain't seen nothin' yet! Where pellets larger than T-shot can be legally used on waterfowl, No.4 buck often gets the call. And it can be run another 100 fps faster with this Supersonic combination:

Shell:	Federal 10-ga. 3½" plastic
Primer:	Winchester 209
Powder:	45.5/SR-4756
Wad:	Supersonic #1500 plastic wad + 0.200" card in shotcup
Shot:	28 pellets Supersonic No.4 buckshot
Buffer:	35.0 grains Supersonic graphite

Overshot

Wad:	1 Supersonic overshot card
Pressure:	10,080 LUP
Velocity:	1625 fps!

(Source: Ballistic Research)

In this ultra-fast reload, the stack of 28 No.4 buckshot weighs about 457.5 grains *sans* buffer, which is only 20 grains heavier than a 1-ounce charge (437.5 grains). Add the buffer, and it's still short of being a nominal 1⅛-ounce load (which would be 492 grains) while the above T-shot reload splits the difference between 1⅛ and 1¼ ounces. These are definitely on the lesser side for the Magnum 10, but with the buffer supplying some resistance, they do generate long-range energies for geese.

Although the 12 gauge's bore isn't as efficient as the Magnum 10's, it can also whistle some reloads with T-shot scaling less than an ounce:

Shell:	Federal 3" 12-ga. plastic (plastic base)
Primer:	Winchester 209
Powder:	34.0/SR-4756
Wad:	Supersonic #1200 wad + three 20-ga. 0.100" cards
Shot:	48 pellets Supersonic T-shot
Buffer:	30.0 grains Supersonic graphite
Pressure:	10,960 LUP
Velocity:	1513 fps

(Source: Ballistic Research)

Those 48 pellets of steel T-shot weigh just 389-390 grains, which figures to a trifle over ⅞-ounce. But in my M1100

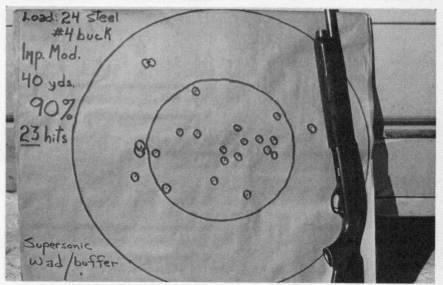

Load: 24 steel #4 buck
Imp. Mod.
40 yds.
90%
23 hits

Supersonic wad/buffer

Through the Improved Modified tube of a WalkerChoke, the Supersonic concept has reliably produced patterns of 90% to 100% with buffered reloads of steel buckshot.

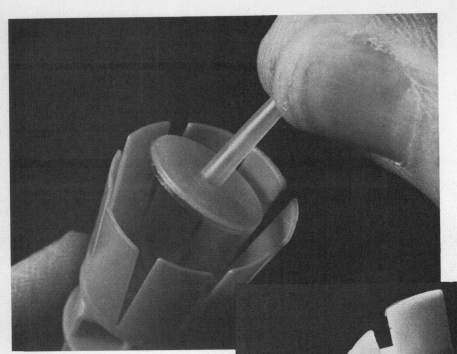

(Below) Testing has shown the Compressor to be mainly effective with buckshot, as shown here, and low-antimony chilled shot, simply dropped around it.

(Above) The plastic shotcup insert known as the Compressor is but a hollow upright post. By giving the pellets some inward relief, the Compressor reduces deformation and improves patterning.

Modified barrel, the round patterns to an average of 93 percent at 40 yards!

Why would experimenters working with steel shot be content with such light charges of shot? It is admittedly the reverse of the lead shot school's "more is better" syndrome. But steel shot doesn't deform, and it normally patterns tightly; consequently, one can start with less steel shot because it retains more in the pattern. In my patterning with steel buckshot in Supersonic fashion, I find five-shot strings averaging 90 percent or better at 40 yards, whereas a lead No. 4 buckshot reload without buffer often falls to 50 percent with 60 percent tops. Some shooting with the standard 12 found more pellets from a buffered 1-ounce load of Supersonic buckshot punching more steel shot through the 30-inch-diameter circle than from a 1½-ounce magnum load of unbuffered lead No. 4 buckshot. The point is simple: It isn't how many pellets you start with, but rather how many find their way into the effective patterning area.

One problem in developing high-performance reloads is making the payload move ahead smoothly and positively so that the combustion area elongates properly for gas expansion. If a payload hangs up ever so slightly with reloads hosting gargantuan powder charges and/or buffered payloads,

chamber pressures can vault sharply and carry interior ballistics beyond safety levels. What also complicates wad slippage is the fire-roughened wall condition of used hulls, something that produces varying degrees of friction despite the self-lubricating characteristic of plastic wads. Indeed, technicians have long told us that one of the main differences between virgin plastics and oft-fired plastics is that the virgin tubes have glassy slick walls which expedite wad movement according to the pressure rise.

To overcome the pressure-causing friction factor in fired hulls, experimenters have begun employing dry lubes on *and in* wads. Ballistic Products, Inc., was the first to offer this concept, marketing mica dust in ½-pound cans along with publishing reloading data for magnum or high-velocity loads employing a brushing of mica dust on the wad's exterior to en-

hance slippage. Of course, mica dust could be brushed on any reload, but BP especially recommends it on their robust magnums which otherwise would offer extreme resistance to powder gases.

At Supersonic the use of dry lubes takes another route. Instead of dusting the wads' exteriors directly, the powdered graphite is mixed with the steel shot buffer and is thus placed inside the shotcup. This method becomes effective when, under firing pressure, the shotcup's slits expand to permit graphite seepage which lubricates case and bore walls as the shotcup moves. One could also dust Supersonic wads directly if desired. But you do see what they mean about skinning the cat! With either Motor Mica or graphite, and either inside the wad or outside, the purpose is the same: to hold down chamber pressures by insuring wad slippage.

The energy that develops so quickly in payloads of high-velocity, high-pressure reloads can be detrimental to patterning if it mashes pellets under setback forces. In general, the lower one-third to one-half of the shot charge feels setback forces adequate to deform pellets, and mutilated shot can either flare from the main mass to weaken patterns or it can slow down quickly to create a long in-flight shot string. At least one experimenter has focused on a method by which some of this energy is soaked up without resorting to buffer to retain pellet form. This is Bernie Ferrie (P.O. Box 769, Trinidad, CO 81082), who operates under the banner of Shootr's Edge.

Inc. Ferrie's idea was to place a hollow plastic tube in the core of the shot charge, thereby giving the interior pellets some relief against mashing by providing a compressible unit to soak up energy. Made by injection moulding, the plastic unit is trade-named the Compressor® and currently is fitted with a base sized for 12-gauge shotcups. This includes the Remington Power Pistons which have rigid buttressing supports inside each shot-cup petal, something the Compressor bases can handle via indentations set at 90 degrees. The 12-gauge Compressor can be fitted to 10-gauge reloads very easily, and ambitious souls can trim the bases to rest in 16- and 20-

gauge wads as well. The accompanying photos should illustrate that the Compressor is merely plopped into an empty shotcup and the pellets are spilled around it.

How does the Compressor work? Like everything else in shotgunning, it can vary from load to load and gun to gun. But in patterning tests I've run using control loads with everything identical except the Compressor, I've found that: (A.) The center density of a lot of reloads could be increased with the Compressor in place; (B.) I could often get reloads to average about 10 percent higher with Compressors, (C.) Compressors were especially good with low-antimony (chilled) shot that is prone to deformation. These attributes appeared as early as my first patterning run with a 32-inch-barreled, Full-choked, Browning A-5 Magnum and the following reload which is 1-grain of powder below Hercules' maximum recommendation:

Shell: Federal 3″ 12-ga. plastic (paper base wad)
Primer: Federal 209
Powder: 38.5/Blue Dot
Wad: Remington RP-12

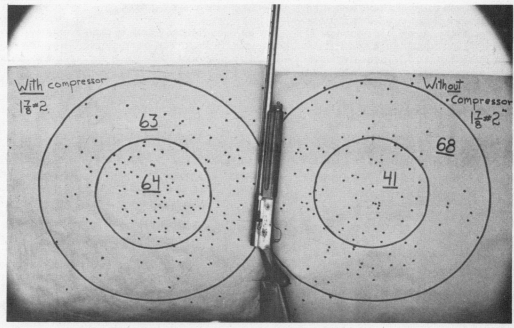

A retrieved Compressor displays the impressions of the interior shot load. When the Compressor looks bad, the pellets were less heavily deformed.

An example of patterning improvement with the Compressor. The left pattern shows how center density tightened for long-range goose hunting when the Compressor was included in a reload which, without the Compressor, turned in average patterns like the one on the right. This amounts to about a 50 percent density increase in the 15-inch diameter core.

Shot: 1⅞ ounces Lawrence brand No. 2 Magnum
Crimp: 6-point fold crimp

In prior tests, this reload gave no better than 67 percent patterns *sans* the Compressor and in *vis-à-vis* shooting the same performance held, meaning it wasn't exactly giving a Full-choke efficiency. When the Compressors were added to the same reload, however, the gun/load tandem averaged 75 percent and showed considerably more center density (as per the accompanying photo). Without the Compressors, the reload would put no more than 37-43 No.2 s into the 15-inch-diameter core at 40 yards; with the Compressors that core count jumped to 61-65 No.2s, which is roughly a 50 percent increase in core density. And as knowledgeable shotgunners know, it is the core density that becomes the effective density beyond 40 yards as the outer pellets split the scene.

Compressors have also shown efficiency with buckshot, especially when fired through a Modified barrel; and they do enhance the density of trap loads for handicap events, especially when chilled shot is employed. According to ATA rules, wad inserts aren't illegal for registered trap events.

Adding anything to the payload is normally deemed to heighten chamber pressures. But the Compressors weigh only 3 grains, which isn't as heavy as a single No. 4 birdshot pellet, and because they absorb energy rather than create significant resistance, they don't appear to cause pressure excursions. Lab tests run with Compressors therefore have indicated that no significant powder reductions are necessary. As printed on material included with each package, Hercules, Hodgdon, and Winchester powders require no reduction, while Du Pont suggested a ½-grain reduction in their propellants.

Although Compressors are now available only as an insert item, the future may very well produce full-sized wads with the compressible post moulded in the shotcup. Moreover, variations of the Compressor concept may turn up in super-patterning buckshot and steel shot applications. The practical use of energy-absorbing posts in shot loads may just be getting started.

As an off-shoot of experiments with the Compressor concept, it appears that steel buckshot may one day catch on with law enforcement agencies, survivalists, and big game hunters for special situations. Unlike big, lead buckshot which often deform on setback and again on impact to reduce pattern density and penetration, it has been found that the larger steel pellets retain their form for deeper penetration. Coupled with a tight-patterning wad concept, steel may also just be getting started. I am told by Bernie Ferrie that steel shot loads including the Compressor show less "dimpling" of the shotcup, meaning there could be a reduction in the chamber pressure as pellets don't wedge so forcefully against the outer walls. But only the future will tell how this all works out.

Not all shotshell experiments are directed toward heavier, faster reloads. A trend in target and "plinker" loads has involved lighter shot charges to reduce the action-reaction principle. In connection with these ultra-light payloads in 12-gauge, some experimenters have gone to the fastest burning powders for efficiency. The primary case in point is Bullseye, which has long been considered just a fast-burning pistol propellant. The fact is that Bullseye isn't an unstable explosive like dynamite, as some spooky handloaders believe. Bullseye is only a bit faster-burning than Red Dot, and with target-velocity reloads it can be used for shot charges of 1-ounce or less in the 12-gauge. For example:

Shell: Winchester 12-ga. AA
Primer: Winchester 209
Wad: Federal 12SO
Powder: 16.5/Bullseye
Shot: 1-ounce
Pressure: 8700 psi
Velocity: nominal 1145 fps
(Source: Hercules *Guide*)

For an even lighter-recoiling practice reload, Bullseye can be employed efficiently with just ⅞-ounce of shot in the 12-gauge hull:

Shell: Winchester 12-ga. AA
Primer: Winchester 209
Powder: 16.5/Bullseye
Wad: Federal 12SO
Shot: ⅞-ounce
Pressure: 7400 psi
Velocity: 1200 fps
(Source: Hercules *Guide*)

On a purely theoretical basis, Bullseye jibes with these light 12-gauge loads because it tends to generate chamber pressures over 7000 LUP or psi, a requirement some technicians believe necessary for enough chamber heat to produce load-to-load uniformity and positive ignition in each round. Going below 7000 pressure units, be they psi or LUP, these technicians argue, shows erratic interior ballistics (at least in some handloading combinations). Skeet and trap shooters who cringe at the thought of launching 1⅛-ounce loads with 18-19 grains of Red Dot or "Hi-Skor" 700-X, or with 19.5 to 20.5 grains of 452AA Ball® or Trap-100, will find a new world of comfort with their first box of 1-ouncers propelled by just 16.5/Bullseye, and Mom, Sis, and Junior will enjoy the ⅞-ounce plinker reloads on hand-trapped clays in Grandpa's gravel pit.

For beginners who start with 20-gauge, an economical, low-recoil handload can be predicated on just a ¾-ounce shot charge. In general, Red Dot is too fast burning for the 20-gauge, but that changes when just a ¾-ounce payload is dropped. Then Red Dot holds safe pressure levels. Here's a load published recently by Hercules:

Shell: Winchester 20-ga. AA
Primer: Winchester 209
Powder: 12.0/Red Dot
Wad: Winchester WAA20 wad + 0.135″ card in cup
Shot: ¾-ounce
Pressure: 10,900 psi
Velocity: nominal 1200 fps

Thus, shotshell reloading is heading toward extremes, from the ultra-fast to the ultra-mild. The emphasis seems to be placed upon improved patterning, not merely increasing the shot charges as was the case a triple decade ago when experiments were predicated upon the more-is-better concept and all we heard about were heavier and heavier shot charges for each gauge. We're apparently smarter now. Hunters have learned that they don't need a ton of lead if they can gain patterning efficiency with lighter, faster charges; trap and Skeet shooters don't want to spend their weekends being hammered by recoil. Moreover, such advances are possible now that we have a wide variety of components, a bit more savvy built up by years of theorizing and experimenting, and receptive labs equipped with pressure guns to lead the way into a scientific assessment of theories and brainstorms. Where will it all take us? Given time, we're headed toward even higher velocities for hunters, tighter patterns for everyone, and less recoil for clay target buffs and beginners. A world of innovations ever since the plastics revolution of the 1960s, shotshell handloading will become even more so in the future. ●

THE RECENT influx of a new batch of used foreign military turnbolts has introduced a new generation of Americans to such esoteric cartridges as the 7.65 Argentine, the 6.5x55mm Mauser, and the 7.92x57 Mauser (better known as the 8mm Mauser). In many ways, the best of these is the 6.5x55. Also known as the "Swedish 6.5 Mauser, Model 94," or simply "The Swede," the 6.5x55 is interchangeable with (not identical to) the Norwegian 6.5mm Krag-Jorgensen, aka "6.5mm Norwegian." The words 6.5 Krag-Jor-gensen often denote a *rifle* as well as a cartridge.

There have been many 6.5mm cartridges imported to the United States; none has achieved overwhelming popularity. The 6.5x54 Mannlicher-Schoenauer was the Greek army cartridge (and rifle) and managed at least to get the attention of Americans when chambered in the beautiful Austrian Mannlicher-Schoenauer sporting carbines and rifles of years gone by. The 6.5x50 Arisaka fits more than a few military castoffs now in American closets. The Italian 6.5x52 Mannlicher-Carcano is not unknown in U.S. hunting circles, and neither is it thought well of. And then there are the obscure 6.5x58 Portuguese Vergueiro and 6.5x53R Mannlicher (used by the Dutch and Romanian military establishments and many, many British shooters in Africa) not to mention the only slightly less murky 6.5x57 Mauser, in both rimmed and rimless persuasion. Of this list of worthies, only the 6.5x54 Mannlicher and the 6.5 Swede have created much stir,

These are the four factory loads tested here.

THE RESURRECTION OF THE

6.5 Swede

It took 90 years and a second wind, but the Swede is here to stay

by CLAY HARVEY

with the Arisaka a distant third.

Commercial 6.5s have fared no better. The 6.5 Remington Magnum—a short, fat, belted misfit—is offered by no riflemaker today, to my knowledge, unless on a special-order basis. It is no loss. The big-bellerin' 264 Magnum will forever reside in the shadow of the 7mm Remington Magnum, as it should. No one will notice. There are too many European sporting 6.5s to discuss here (10 according to Barnes' *Cartridges of the World*, not counting Britain), including the hot 6.5x68 Schuler, which supposedly kicked a 123-grain bullet along at 3450 fps! BSA once made a sizzling, belted 6.5 (dubbed the 26 Rimless Nitro-Express) that was shown as delivering a 110-grain bullet at 3100 fps. Alas, it has gone the way of the 5-cent cup of coffee.

And so, due to these several factors, the Swedish 6.5 emerges victorious among the .26-bores. What factors? Well, attrition for one. The Swede has simply hung on where most others have turned loose all holds and slipped into the void. And availability—there have always been a few Swedish Mausers around for sale, and Parker-Hale, BSA, and one or two others have offered the chambering off and on for decades. Husqvarna did likewise, until some time in the '60s. Such semi-custom outfits as Ultra Light Arms will make you a 6.5x55 if you'll tender a roll of earnest money up front. And now it can be told: U.S. Repeating Arms Company produced around 1000 Model 70 Featherweights so-chambered in the summer of 1986.

Mild recoil, moderate muzzleblast, availability of factory hunting ammunition, a reputation for outstanding accuracy . . . all these attributes counted too. All of it combined kept the Swede alive for more than 90 years.

Notice we haven't discussed ballistics. Smith and Smith's *The Book of Rifles* showed the original military ammo, a 156-grain round-nosed projectile, as achieving 2400 fps from only 41,000 psi. Although Smith and Smith doesn't say, I'll assume that such lofty numbers were taken in a 29.1-inch barrel, despite the fact that

the first military arms produced were Model 94 *carbines*, with 17.7-inch tubes. In such abbreviated ordnance, muzzle speeds ran more like 2150 fps with the heavy blunt-prowed bullet. Later, the Swedish military switched to a lighter pointed bullet, as had many other armies of note in their respective cartridges. The new load was quoted as a 139-grain bullet at 2625 fps. That's pretty potent, especially from a small cartridge. Remember that the 30-06 of that era provided only 2700 fps for its 150-grain bullet, and the ought-six boasts a much larger case capacity, and is loaded to higher chamber pressures.

When the Swedish army made the transition from the antiquated turn-bolt to a modern selfloader—the Ljungman AG42—a shift to a more potent battle cartridge was not warranted. The 6.5x55 was retained, and proved itself equal to any task required of a World War II infantryman, although the round was fired on few battlefields indeed.

For those of you who have recently purchased a fine old Swedish Mauser (as I did some months ago), fret not about the strength, quality, or accuracy of your acquisition. And there must be quite a number of you—on the RCBS "Top 30" list of reloading die sales, the 6.5x55 placed 29th in 1985. I've been keeping tabs on that list since 1976; and this is the first time the 6.5 has appeared on it.

Further evidence of its growing popularity: When Lee Precision introduced its new Lee Hand Press in the summer of 1986, the 10 *standard* rifle calibers included the 6.5 Swede! Ignored for such treatment are such numbers as the 6mm Remington, 25-06, and 300 Winchester Magnum

though Lee makes the outfit for all of these, too. Moral: Someone out there likes the 6.5x55.

Early military-issue ammunition was loaded with Ballistite, a highly erosive, double-base (high nitroglycerine content) powder. Primers were mercuric and hence extremely corrosive. Avoid using this stuff. Further, according to Smith and Smith, large quantities of Danish-made surplus 6.5x55 ammo was once dumped on the U.S. market-place at tempting prices. Some of this ammunition was erroneously identified as being of Swedish manufacture. The Danish bullet jackets are of soft-rolled copper, which causes severe bore fouling. When military steel-jacketed bullets—or gilding-metal component bullets—are fired through a barrel that has not been properly cleaned after use with the Danish ammo, there is a very real danger of blowing up the rifle. Beware. I suggest that military-surplus ammo be avoided altogether, as a precaution.

At present, the Norma sheet shows the following loads: a 77-grain semi-pointed softpoint at 2725 fps and 1271 foot pounds of muzzle energy; a 139-grain semi-pointed boattail softpoint at a listed 2526 fps for 1967 foot pounds; a 139-grain Protected Power Cavity (hollowpoint) at 2854 fps and a whopping 2512 foot pounds; a 140-grain Nosler Partition softpoint at the same speed, yielding 2532 foot pounds (!); and the original 156-grain round-nose (this one's a softpoint) at a quoted 2645 fps and 2423 foot pounds. Wow! Some ballistics! Barrel length isn't specified in the Norma brochure, but let's see how *my* lots of ammo did in my test guns.

One batch of the Dual-Core Plastic

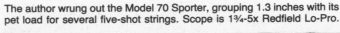

The author wrung out the Model 70 Sporter, grouping 1.3 inches with its
pet load for several five-shot strings. Scope is 1¾-5x Redfield Lo-Pro.

Point, which isn't listed now, but may be later, managed 2742 fps in my Model 70 Winchester Sporter. Bullet weight was 139 grains. That's pretty fast for a 22-inch barrel and exceeds one of the listed speeds for 139-grain ammo, but falls more than 100 fps shy of the other. One test lot of the 139-grain softpoint boattails managed 2580 fps in my M70 Featherweight, beating factory-quoted speed by 54 fps; a second lot hit a zippy 2659 from my M70 Sporter. The 139-grain Protected Cavity clocked 2590 from my Featherweight, 2805 fps from my 22 inch-barreled Ultra-Light Arms M20,

(Above) For loading at the range, Harvey used the Lee dies shown here. At home with the RCBS Big Max, RCBS dies worked fine.

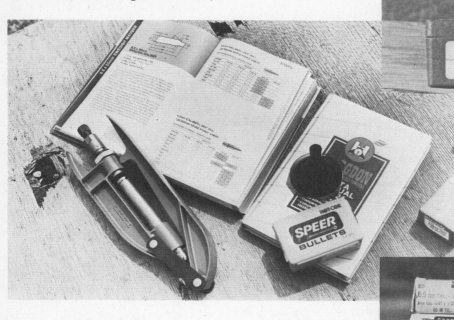

(Left) Plenty of loading data is available for the 6.5x55, and with new small presses, loading at the shooting bench saves development time.

These are the best four propellants for use in 6.5x55, in the author's experience.

(Above) Here's the sampling of component bullets tested by the author in his 6.5s, beginning at 100-grain weight, going up to 160 grains.

Harvey's Model 96 Swedish Mauser was built in 1906 by Carl Gustafs Stads Gevarsfaktori. The rifle is very accurate, grouping five shots into less than 2 inches with regularity, using issue open sights. It shoots high, of course.

The Parker-Hale Model 81 is readily obtainable in 6.5x55, offers a British view of American styling.

Harvey also shot a Model 70 Featherweight in 6.5x55. Less than 1000 of these have been produced for sale in the U.S. That's a 4x B&L scope.

Shooter Bob O'Connor tries out the little Ultra Light Arms Model 20. The rifle shown here is the only ULA ever built in 6.5x55; scope is a Leupold 4x.

and 2831 when fired in my 29-inch Model 96 Swede. Thus, even in a super-long tube, my test lots wouldn't quite achieve advance notices.

The 156-grain round-nose hit 2387 from my M70 Featherweight, and 2392 when checked in its Sporter sibling. Good, but not 2645! The long-spout M96 upped the ante, getting 2584 for 2312 foot pounds. Still short of factory claims, but potent indeed for such a small cartridge.

I have tested none of the 77-grain softpoints nor the 140 Nosler-bulleted factory loads, although I have some of the latter item on the way. The 77-grain load may no longer be imported, except by individual Norma distributors in some cases. (Norma distributors are the only probable sources for Norma bullets, by the way, although few such components were brought over in 1986. The situation will likely improve in 1987, good news for fans of Norma bullets.) Norma brass is imported by several distributors, as well as Norma's American branch, Federal Cartridge Co.

A recent (20 minutes ago, as I type this) phone conversation with Federal's Mike Bussard elicited some interesting information. First, Norma has not been able to keep up with the tremendous increase in demand for 6.5x55 ammunition. (The amount sold in 1985 was from three to four times the number peddled in 1984, and 1986 sales doubled those of 1985!) Second, sales of component bullets in .264-inch diameter have picked up for all the bulletmakers. Mike figures there are several reasons for this, not the least of which is the legion of inexpensive military-surplus rifles. In the 1950s, Mike told me, while there was a similar stream of 6.5x55s coming into the country, most shooters rebarreled their rifles for such cartridges as the 308 Winchester. Not so today. Although hunters are still "customizing" their Swedes—with new stocks, abbreviated barrels, scopes—they are retaining the original caliber.

It's a good thing that Norma ammo is easily available, and will be even more so in the future. The 6.5x55 is not readily formed from any other case. Since it is slightly larger in head and rim diameter than such cartridges as the 30-06 and 7x57 Mauser, reshaping such to use in a Swede is not a good idea. The cases generally bulge quite a bit in the head/web area upon firing. While this may not actually be dangerous (then again, it *could* be), it is unslightly, unseemly, and not recommended. Use cases headstamped "6.5x55mm." Period.

Let's consider for the moment that you are looking for a new hunting rifle, and a military gun is not on your agenda. Just why, you ask, should you essay such an esoteric choice as 6.5mm Swede when you could have a 6mm Remington, or a 257 Roberts or a 7mm-08, or even a 270? Aren't all of them better, more *common* than the 6.5x55? More common? Certainly. Better? More versatile? Maybe. Maybe not.

The 6mm clan are better vermin cartridges, assuredly, providing flatter trajectory with varmint-weight bullets, less recoil, and at least equal accuracy. But bullets no heavier than 105 grains are available from a major bullet company, and so for the heaviest game the Sixes should be avoided. For big game, the 6.5 is superior to 6mms under come-what-may conditions.

The 257 Roberts is ballistically similar to the 6.5x55. Both are capable of punching 100-grain bullets out their respective muzzles in the 2900-3000 foot-second neighborhood when loaded to standard pressures. Thus, for light-boned whitetails, the two are on par. Except for one detail: 100-grain 25-caliber bullets are considered to be suitable for deer-sized critters; not so 100-grain 6.5 projectiles. Deer bullets begin at 120 grains in .264 diameter, and *end* there for the 257 Roberts, as far as common component bullets are concerned, which is all we'll consider here.

The 6.5 offers bullet weights up to 140 grains for deer, and will kick them along about as fast as a Roberts can boost 120-grain slugs when both are loaded to industry-standard pressures. In fact, 6.5x55 factory loads (in some lots) will move 139-grain bullets 200 fps faster than even the quickest lots of Plus-P 257, 117-grain iterations. The Roberts vs the Swede? It's no contest ballistically.

The 270 Winchester is as good a big-game load as the 6.5 will ever be. It shoots flatter, is available in more rifles of nearly all action types, comes in a much broader array of factory ammo, is at least equal in hunting-rifle accuracy, offers reloaders bullets just as heavy as those for the Swede, and hits with more energy. It also makes more noise, is tougher on barrels, costs more to shoot, and—more importantly—it belts you more soundly at the back end. How much more soundly? Well, using data derived from a typical 270 load, i.e. a 130-grain bullet propelled by 55 grains of powder to 3000 fps at the muzzle, and fired in an 8-pound rifle,

The most accurate loads in two Winchesters and the Model 96 Swede were built around this powder and these two Nosler bullets. Oddly, the 125-grain Nosler refused to group in the ULA when tried with this powder.

A top accuracy choice in the Model 70 Featherweight, and the best load in the ULA, utilized 42.8 grains of IMR 4350 and the 160 Hornady. Groups ran just over an inch with both rifles.

The Lee Hand Press is made for any cartridge, but the box is pre-printed for the 10 Lee best-sellers. One of the 10 is the 6.5x55. (Dean A. Grennell photo)

the 270 carries 18.2 foot-pounds of recoil. Push a 139-grain bullet to 2700 fps with 42 grains of propellant in an 8-pound 6.5x55 and you get a 13-pound shove at the buttplate. The 270 plugs you 40 percent harder! Important? Perhaps, to those young, or slightly-built, or arthritis-plagued, or distaff hunters. To us healthy, muscular, he-men, naw . . .

Further—and realizing that the 270 bore offers the benefits of a 160-grain Nosler Partition bullet—there is likely nothing in .277-inch persuasion that will penetrate with the 160 Hornady round-nose. Nothing. Only two component bullets offer sectional density superior to the 6.5mm 160-grain: the 220-grain 308 and the 500-grain 458. And they don't shade it by much: the 6.5 shows .328, the 220-grain, 30 gets .331, and .341 is shown for the 458. Even the heralded 175-grain 7mm Nosler carries an SD of only .310 and its reputation for digging deep into bone and flesh is virtually without peer.

The 7mm-08 (or 7x57 for that matter) offers slightly superior ballistics to the 6.5x55, at the cost of a minor (2.1 foot-pound) increase in back thrust. The 7-08 is equal to the 6.5 in accuracy, and shades it in new rifle availability. But then there are no 7mm-08 surplus rifles. (Although there are some military 7x57s.) The 7-08 offers only one bullet weight in factory-rolled form; the 6.5 can be found in two weights and three styles, as we've seen. (The 7x57 is even broader in scope.) The 7mm boasts a vast selection of component-bullet weights and configurations, although the 6.5 suffers not in this regard. In short, when trying to decide between a 7mm-08 (or 7x57) and 6.5x55, the toss of a coin might be the best approach.

Aside from their exemplary military and target-range records, 6.5-diameter bores have garnered accolades in the field. Famed entrepreneur Charles Sheldon hunted for years with a Jeffery-built Mannlicher chambered to 6.5x53R, a cartridge ballistically identical to 6.5x54 and close kin to the Swede. With it he slew more than 500 head of big game, including at least 70 Alaskan brown bears and grizzlies. Early Arctic explorers relied on the British 256 Gibbs Magnum, which utilized load data that was virtually interchangeable with that of the 6.5x55. W.D.M. Bell used a little 256 on elephant, taking brain shots of course. Today, I am told, about half of Sweden's annual moose kill (75,000 animals) is handled by the 6.5x55. In case you haven't noticed, moose are *big* critters. Former African professional hunter Finn Aagaard, now residing comfortably and productively in Texas, feels that his 6.5x55 is about the ultimate whitetail load. He may be right.

I could go on. And on. But no need. As has been proven time and again, the 6.5 Swede is all you need providing you can shoot and know how to choose a proper bullet.

Speaking of which, let's see what you *can* buy. From Hornady, the following: 100-, 129-, 140-grain spire points, and the good old 160 round-nose softpoint. For match shooters there is a new 140-grain hollowpoint boattail. Nosler lists these: a 120-grain Solid Base; 125- and 140-grain Partition spitzers. Speer carries both 120- and 140-grain softpoint spitzers, and is working on a match bullet similar to Hornady's. Sierra sells two

This time, this test, Harvey was able to do a large portion of his handloading at the range with the Lee Hand Press.

Not one of these Ultra Light rifles is a 6.5x55 because it's in North Carolina, but Harvey thinks there will be more ULA 6.5s.

varmint slugs, both hollowpoints, at 85 and 100 grains in weight; a 120-grain softpoint; a 140-grain softpoint boattail; and a 140-grain Matchking hollowpoint boattail. Not counting bullets from such smaller makers as Barnes and imported bullets from Norma, that is a total of 15 component bullets available right now. Something for everyone.

Despite its compact case, the 6.5x55 has an abundance of capacity for its bore size. Even with such slow-burning and bulky propellants as Du Pont IMR 4831, there is room aplenty. None of my loads is compressed, which means no foot-long drop tube and tedious one-kernel-at-a-time case-filling techniques. (Hallelujah!) Perhaps if I used IMR 4831 in conjunction with the lengthy 160-grain Hornady, or switched to the even slower Hodgdon H-4831, I might encounter mild compression. I can conjure no reason for doing so, being fully satisfied with the accuracy and velocity provided so easily by the Du Pont propellant.

After experimenting with five 6.5x55s to date, I have settled on four powders: IMR 4064, IMR 4350, IMR

4831 (all Du Pont numbers, of course), and Hodgdon's H-380. Although I have spent little effort working toward a varmint load for use in my various 6.5s, I found it no trick to manage about 2900 fps with acceptable accuracy using IMR 4064 and H-380. For 2700-plus at the muzzle, I pair H-380 with Nosler's fine 120-grain Solid Base. Switching to IMR 4831, I can reach nearly 2800 fps with the same bullet in my Model 70 Sporter, and with superb grouping ability. The 125 Nosler Partition exceeds 2800 fps by a goodly margin when boosted by 47.0 grains of IMR 4831, and shoots under 2 inches for average *five*-shot groups in my open-sighted Model 96 Mauser. It's even more precise in my Featherweight, albeit much slower. Top load in my Ultra Light M20 consists of 42.8 grains of IMR 4350 under the 160 Hornady round-nose; groups average 1.2 inches and the Oehler says 2438 fps.

Such fast-to-medium propellants as IMR 3031 work acceptably in the 6.5 x55 so far as accuracy is concerned, but muzzle speeds simply aren't up to par. Best to stick with the medium-to-slow powders.

Choose whichever primers you like; magnum caps are not a requisite with a case this size in most instances. I make it a rule of thumb to pair magnum primers with such slower ball powders as H-380 and H-414, and feel this aids in avoiding any ignition difficulties. With stick propellants, even IMR 4831, I use what's on the shelf.

No special techniques are necessary when working with the Swede. Some handloaders dislike long necks, complaining of the nuisance factor in removing lube from the inside of those necks. Not me. I don't lube the inside of case necks, and when I did, I used a dry lube such as graphite. Nowadays I simply remove the residue from inside the necks with a stiff-bristle brush; then necks slide over an expander with little difficulty.

If you insist on forming 6.5x55 brass from another cartridge case (*not* recommended), be sure to scrutinize the swelling of the case web. If a crack appears, dump that case.

Well, that covers it. I suspect that if you'll give the old 6.5x55 a thorough and impartial trial, you will be quite pleased. Maybe so elated you'll do a backflip. Like I would. If I could. ●

6.5 × 55mm LOAD DATA—HANDLOAD AND FACTORY

Bullet	Wgt.	Powder Type	Primer	Case	Instrum. Vel. (fps)	Energy (fp)	ES	Remarks
100 Winchester SP	44.0	IMR 4064	WIN LR	Norma	2882	1844	83	Good velocity in M70 Sporter
100 Hornady SP	45.3	H380	WIN LR	Norma	2889	1837	66	Accurate in Parker-Hale M81
120 Nosler SB	43.0	H380	FED 215	Norma	2622	1832	27	Sub-max; accurate in M70 Sporter
120 Nosler SB	44.2	H380	FED 215	Norma	2711	1958	37	MAX in M70 Sporter
120 Speer SP	44.2	H380	WIN LR	Norma	2695	1935	22	MAX in M81; consistent velocity
120 Nosler SB	46.0	IMR 4831	CCI 250	Norma	2630	1843	46	Mild in M70 Sporter
120 Nosler SB	47.0	IMR 4831	CCI 250	Norma	2722	1974	41	Accurate in M70 Sporter; most accurate in M81
120 Nosler SB	49.0	IMR 4831	CCI 250	Norma	2793	2078	97	Most accurate in M70 Sporter.
120 Speer SP	48.0	IMR 4831	CCI 250	Norma	2692	1931	78	Accurate in M70 Sporter; MAX
125 Nosler Part	47.0	IMR 4831	CCI 200	Norma	2652	1952	47	Very accurate in M70 Featherweight
125 Nosler Part	47.0	IMR 4831	CCI 200	Norma	2875	2294	41	Most accurate in M96 Military Rifle
129 Hornady SP	43.5	H380	WIN LR	Norma	2673	1903	75	MAX in Parker-Hale M81
140 Speer SP	40.0	IMR 4064	WIN LR	Norma	2534	1996	69	MAX in M70 Sporter
140 Sierra SPBT	42.8	H380	WIN LR	Norma	2557	2032	41	Accurate in M81
160 Hornady RN	33.0	IMR 4064	CCI 200	Herters	1953	1355	41	Extremely accurate in M70 Featherweight
160 Hornady RN	42.8	IMR 4350	CCI 200	Norma	2438	2111	50	Most accurate in ULA M20
160 Hornady RN	42.8	IMR 4350	WIN LR	Norma	2424	2087	69	Very accurate in M70 Sporter
139 Norma PP		Factory Load			2742	2320	51	Fair accuracy in M70 Sporter
139 Norma SPBT		Factory Load			2580	2054	27	Very accurate in M70 Featherweight
139 Norma SPBT		Factory Load			2659	2182	10	Second most accurate in M70 Sporter
139 Norma PPC		Factory Load			2590	2070	25	Most accurate in M70 Featherweight
139 Norma PPC		Factory Load			2805	2428	42	Accurate and fast in ULA M20
139 Norma PPC		Factory Load			2831	2473	52	Very high velocity in M96
156 Norma RN		Factory Load			2387	1973	57	Very accurate in M70 Featherweight
156 Norma RN		Factory Load			2392	1982	39	Very accurate in M70 Sporter
156 Norma RN		Factory Load			2584	2312	38	Very fast in M96

Both Model 70 Winchesters had 22-inch barrels, as did the Ultra-Light Model 20; the Parker-Hale M81 had a 24-inch barrel; the Model 96 Swedish Mauser had a 29-inch barrel. All loads chronographed using an Oehler Model 33 chronotach with Skyscreens III system; speeds instrumental at 12.5 feet.

Abbreviations: **SP**—Soft Point   **SPBT**—Soft Point Boattail   **SB**—Solid Base   **RN**—Round Nose   **Part**—Partition
PP—Plastic Point   **PPC**—Protected Power Cavity   **ES**—Extreme Spread

Yard system universal receiver on cradle. Opened-up view shows barrel ready to enter adaptor threads. Cartridge is pulled partly out of chamber. It will be fully chambered and jam tightly against the breechblock when barrel is screwed into the adaptor. The top board and bolts will grip the receiver.

Hitherto, firing chamber pressures were measured in pounds per square inch or atmospheres, whether LUP or CUP. Now, in a different sense, we have . . .

PRESSURES BY THE YARD

by EDWARD M. YARD

Cartridge in front of universal receiver shows protruding primer cup. This is how the Yard system works. The primer cup is forced out of the primer pocket by the chamber pressure. It enters a piston hole. The piston compresses a standard copper crusher made for measuring gun pressure. (The wood ring is there only to position the cartridge case for this photo.) Note the threads to the left of wood block that mate with barrel threads to adapt many different barrels to a single universal receiver.

THERE IS now an easy way to measure breech pressure in your gun. It does not require drilling a hole in the barrel, but it does measure the gas pressure in the chamber. Right now there is a practical design of a simple mechanical breech device that crushes a standard lead or copper crusher and reads pressure from a regular Tarage table. The writer, who invented this, has built and is using a universal breech embodying this system with several different gun barrels. Adaptors make it possible to insert and remove many others.

In the future, this can be as easy as hooking your gun barrel to the device, or your gun with device attached, to chronograph screens, a chronograph, a computer or TV. You may get digital, graphic, or both, pressure indications, plus muzzle velocity, action time, barrel travel time and more, all simultaneously.

The system using crushers is fine as it now stands. It corresponds with the usual industry procedure. Doing it this way allows comparison to a vast store of industry and laboratory information gathered over most of a century. The crusher method is universal, simple and has minimum calibration problems. This method of measuring breech pressure is the point of entry into a realm handloaders and wildcatters have hoped to find for years.

Just down the road is a gun with a window in the side like that in the Crosman Model 84. The Crosman reads the gas pressure in the reservoir for that shot. Our forecast is that it will be possible to read the chamber pressure of each shot fired in a port lo-cated at a convenient point on the gun. The extent to which a gun could be instrumented and computerized is really no longer limited. Whatever we imagine can be made real.

The purpose here is to reveal how the pressure measuring part of all this works. Without input, all the chips and computers of Apple and IBM won't read out a thing. First we must have some mechanical action that corresponds to pressure. That is what the new gizmo does. It functions like other currently accepted and used devices that measure pressure mechanically—it allows the high pressure gases in a gun chamber to force a piston against a standard copper or lead rod compressing it somewhat. How much the solid cylinder is compressed depends upon the force that acts on it. That force is the prod-

Sliding the breechblock, in the very foreground, into the slot in the receiver, will position the copper crusher under the anvil. The crusher is the longer cylinder in the vertical slot. The piston head is the lower and brighter cylinder. The anvil is the taller of the three cap screws.

Barrel end view of Yard system universal receiver. The spot at the center of concentric circles is the firing pin hole, surrounded by the piston, the bushing and the adaptor ring. Screw heads at right are attached to breechblock.

uct of gas pressure and piston area. The piston area is fixed and the crusher cylinders are all the same in any test set. Therefore, the amount the cylinder is compressed for each shot is due entirely to the amount of the gas pressure. The number value of the pressure measured is found from a table known as a Tarage Table, made up by the crusher manufacturer from a calibrating procedure and supplied with each lot of crushers.

Until this invention, that gas pressure has been brought in contact with the piston by drilling a hole through the side of the gun barrel into the chamber and placing a piston in that hole. A gas check is placed in the hole between the end of the piston and the gases to prevent leakage of gas and damage to the piston stem. This works very well and the arrangement has been used for a long time. When it is desired to make the measurements in a standard firearm, a clamping device is used to hold the parts to the barrel over a hole into the chamber. This clamp assembly is called a yoke.

The obvious disadvantage of this procedure is that the hole in the barrel renders it unsatisfactory for any other use. It becomes a special purpose part, a test barrel. It is not *the* barrel that is used in the real shooting done with any gun. It may be very much like some production barrel(s), but must differ a little or a lot from all of the barrels it simulates. Test results of shots fired in it must differ from values that would have been found in another barrel of the same caliber and chambering, especially if from another manufacturer, with all the differences that occur. It is accepted that the pressure reading variation can be substantial.

So it would be extremely valuable to be able to measure ammunition pressure in the very same barrel in which it will be shot in the field in normal use. This has not been possible before. An observation by the writer has now revealed that there is no need to drill a hole in the barrel. In fact, there is no reason to alter the barrel in any way. That means that it is possible to measure chamber pressure in almost any gun barrel without modification or change. *(Please note the author does not mean that at this time, pressures can be measured in your gun, but that in his test outfit, he could measure them with your barrel: Editor)*

This observation was that there is a hole into the chamber of every centerfire gun through the base of the cartridge which admits the primer flash to ignite the charge. Every time the

STEP BY STEP

To use the universal receiver version of this device constructed by the writer, the barrel is removed from the gun. This must be done carefully by a competent person to avoid marking or damaging it or the gun. Unless the prospective tester has adequate gunsmithing skills, he should seek competent professional assistance. We will limit our comments here to those barrels attached with a screw thread.

In these cases the barrel in which tests are to be made is unscrewed from its gun action. A suitable adapter is screwed into the universal receiver. This will have an outside thread that fits the receiver and an inside thread that fits the barrel. The barrel should turn easily as the cartridge head is to be seated firmly against the breech face. A commercial pressure test facility would need an assortment of adaptors as there are many different barrel threads in use.

The action is made ready by placing the piston containing a firing pin and cross bar in the breechblock. The head of the piston should seat against the block. The cross bar may be secured with a strip of adhesive plastic tape. The breechblock is positioned in the frame. It is held in place by socket head screws. The hammer is cocked and retained by a well engaged sear. A positive safety is positioned.

(Because after the action is cocked, which is necessary to place the crusher, a premature discharge could be disastrous, the writer uses a ¼-inch solid steel bar passing completely through the hammer and blocked by the action frame on both ends as the safety. With this stout pin in place, the hammer cannot fall if the sear is released or broken. The safety must be placed before proceeding with loading.)

The hammer now completely clears the head of the piston. The receiver is set on the bench to put the piston head up and horizontal. The head is accessible through the rear of the receiver. A lead or copper crusher is placed on it with tweezers. The head is recessed about .015-inch just larger than crusher diameter to facilitate centering. With a crusher placed, screw down the anvil until the crusher is very firmly clamped. Adjustments are made to the yoke bar.

The action is ready. When positioned in the firing cradle it may be loaded. The user should confirm that the safety bar is in place before proceeding. The device is loaded by placing a cartridge in the barrel chamber and screwing these into the adaptor. The barrel should turn freely so that the cartridge head contacting the breechblock can be felt. Turn to a very firm contact.

The loaded test gun needs to be secured in the firing cradle. The writer limits movement of this rig by placing one 20-pound sandbag on top of it and another one behind it, leaning against the back. To fire the unit, which should be behind a baffle, the safety bar is pulled out, then the gun is fired by prying the pivoted sear upward to disengage it, while the operator's hand stays behind the baffle.

After firing, the anvil is unscrewed slightly and the crusher picked out of the action with tweezers. The length of the crusher is measured with a micrometer. The remaining length of the crusher is found in the Tarage table and opposite that value a pressure in pounds per square inch is listed. That is the breech pressure for that shot

Edward M. Yard

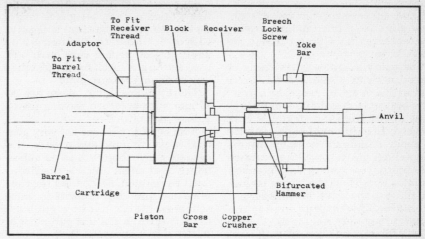

Yard's universal receiver is designed for strength and versatility. The lock, a renewable bushing to compensate for erosion, and the firing pin in the center of the piston are NOT shown to simplify the drawing. The device is fired when the two-pronged hammer (bifurcated) strikes the cross bar. This drives the firing pin into the primer. The primer cup enters the piston hole, forcing the piston against a standard copper crusher.

Yard Universal Receiver

7.62 Nato M80 Ball WRA 66

Crusher Length	CUP psi
.424	48,700
.420	50,100
.415	51,900
.410	53,600
.423	49,000
Average 50,660 psi	

30-06 IMR 4064 54.0 CCI 250, Speer 150

Crusher Length	CUP psi
.423	49,000
.426	48,000
.424	48,700
.420	50,100
.410	53,600
Average 49,880 psi	

gun is fired the full chamber gas pressure pushes the primer cup against the breech of the gun. The higher the chamber pressure is, the harder the primer thrusts against the breech, flattening the primer and impressing the markings of the breech face in the metal of the primer cup.

For many years this flattening of the primer cup has been widely used, and with some confidence, as a pressure indicator, despite frequent warnings about the inaccuracy of this method. Regardless of expert advice to avoid judging pressure by observing primer flattening, the practice has persisted among experienced handloaders. They, the writer included, clung to the fact that chamber gas pressure did what was done to the primers they were looking at.

In a flash, while considering such

pressure guns. This way, the barrel needs no alteration at all. It may remain unmodified in any way.

This idea allows a simple straight line motion of chamber gas forcing a moveable piston against a regular copper cylinder restrained by an anvil. In fact, primer cups have been used as the gas check for the piston in conventional pressure guns.

There was one thing: how to fire the primer with pressure-sensing piston against its entire face?

A lot of ideas that are not very good tend to pop to mind and must be discarded. Such thoughts as somehow using heat or an electric discharge must be rejected. Aside from the complication and bulk of parts for such schemes, that is not how guns are fired. Discharge of a test gun must be initiated as it always is, by the blow of

complished.

A slot through the piston head at right angles to its long axis intersects the hole in which the firing pin lies. A small bar placed through the slot, sized to just slide freely, can contact the end of a firing pin sized to move freely. The pin and bar are sized so the pin will protrude about .060-inch from the front of the piston when the bar is forced foward by a two-pronged striker. This is a perfectly normal gun discharge.

The writer has a lathe and a drill press and limited machinist ability, but with each step having to be worked out to use available materials and skills, he built a pressure gun. It is a strong, safe, reliable device that clearly demonstrates practicality. It provides good pressure measurements easily. The techniques, skills and pro-

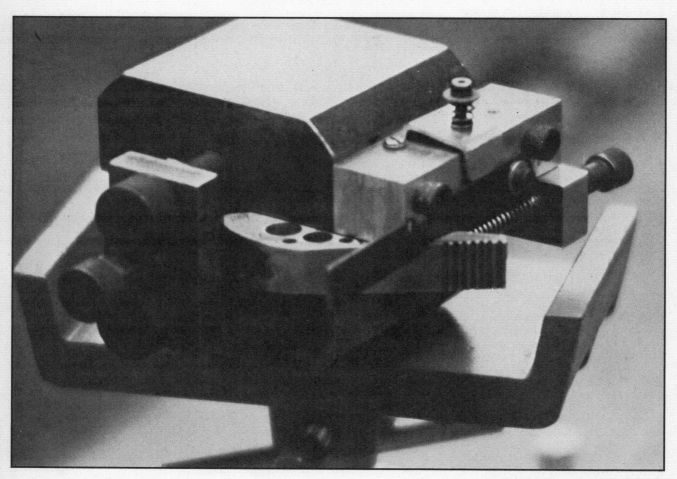

matters, it became obvious that a piston could be placed against the primer, and a regular copper crusher held in place by an anvil against the piston head. Let the primer blow right out of the cartridge case to act as the gas check on the piston stem. And there it was—the same action as in regular

a firing pin that indents the primer cup. The force of the blow can be made standard.

This dictates that the pin must be in the middle of the piston, and it can be put there. Some schematic diagrams and the following description will show how, then, striking it is ac-

Lock side of receiver of Yard pressure measuring system. The anvil assembly is at left.

cedures are the same as those used for standard pressure guns. The crushers are the same.

A massive steel frame with a heavy, screw-locked sliding breechblock was on hand and was used as a universal receiver with little adaptive alteration, but a lock had to be designed and installed. The two-pronged striker was cut from a solid block of tool steel. The anvil was fashioned from a socket head screw. Turning, drilling, slotting and fitting the piston to the breechblock was slow work. The breech-locking screws and piece of bar stock form a yoke.

The action was threaded to take 1.5-inch diameter threaded rings. These adaptors at 24 tpi, could then be drilled and tapped to match a variety of barrels.

At the first moment of truth—firing a 30-06—the system worked. The cross bar, easily replaced, lasted one shot. The piston, not so readily substituted, lasted for three. Beefing up the bar was simple enough and required a piston detail change. The doubly needed stronger, more rigid piston was made much faster than the original. Drawing on the experience, an even more rugged one for a backup was made almost in a jiffy. The struck bar still needs replacement from time to time, which is no problem and that can be corrected if desired.

There is considerable technique to be acquired in using pressure testing equipment. Some came quickly from long experience with muzzleloader pressure guns and blackpowder and Pydrodex. A common desirable practice is to keep the crusher cylinder centered. Other references do not

fore each shot. Industrial test laboratories have enclosed, steel baffled ranges and safety interlocks. Testing outdoors requires the routine safety check of the apparatus and the range before firing every round. The slow shooting pace makes it much more likely someone may stray into or near the line of fire between shots. Good mechanical safeties and proper procedures must be used to prevent accidental discharge.

From the early results with this primer-actuated pressure measuring device and system, two sets of readings are presented in a table and summarized. These were chosen to be widely recognized and understood as well as typical of the performance with standard high-power cartridges. Five shots of 308 Winchester ammunition, specifically WRA '66 MIL 7.62

Yard method pressure device ready to fire, safety rod removed. The universal receiver is clamped in the cradle. A baffle, ordinarily between the firer and the breech, has been removed for photography. The wood stick in the foreground pries the sear upward to discharge the cartridge. The center screw at the very left of photo is the anvil that supports the copper crusher.

mention this and illustrations may be seen showing the crusher off center. The piston and anvil of this device were soon altered to make centering almost automatic.

Firing a pressure gun is more a mechanical act than target shooting. It is easy to forget to check the range be-

Nato M-80 Ball, were fired, averaging 50,660 CUP pounds per square inch. And five rounds of a 30-06 handload with 54.0 grains of Du Pont IMR 4064, a 150-grain Speer Spitzer bullet and CCI Magnum primer were tested giving a mean of 49,880 CUP pounds per square inch. Olin Mathieson .225-

inch × .500-inch Copper Crusher Cylinders and Tarage Table 275 were used. The figures are straight from the table. No factors are applied.

These results were from very ordinary rifle barrels, each chambered for one of the cartridges. They were screwed into a suitable adapter ring threaded into the pressure breech action. It would be impossible to tell that they have ever been used in a test of chamber pressure.

By the time these tests were run, operating procedures were routine, just as much so as those of chronographing. It is easy to arrange to chronograph each round as it is pressure tested. The velocity information greatly enhances the pressure result. If the purpose of the work is load development and evaluation, both are necessary. Previously, when pressure could not be measured, it was estimated. It should be routine to combine the tests. When both peak pressure and the muzzle velocity of a load are known, it is possible to calculate the pressure versus bullet travel curve using the Le Duc equation and its derivatives. This allows accurate estimation of the velocity to be expected from different barrel lengths and the muzzle pressure.

The writer has programmed a Radio Shack (Tandy) computer to make these calculations and to print out a spread sheet. By taking a down range velocity measurement, or several, external ballistic data can be computer generated, printing a tabulation of these automatically. Oehler Sky-screen IIIs have a big enough sensitive area to make the down-range velocity measurements practical at a modest cost. With a little imagination, a computer and the necessary *ad hoc* programs, plus a few well-aimed shots with your custom designed ammunition, very meaningful and desirable data is readily available. The interposition of a computer and a printer takes all of the drudgery out of this work. The ultimate of feeding all of the readings directly into the computer for on-the-spot processing is now possible. This will almost never be needed by amateur ballisticians or by handloaders, though it is fascinating to contemplate.

More realistically, the easily garnered values, averaged and selected, may be fed to the computer for quickly printed spread sheets for the most promising loads under consideration. Load development can henceforth be more scientific, accurate, efficient and successful. The availablility of the correct pressure of the load is vitally important. That value contributes a small part to these calculations and has nothing to do with the computer capability. But how fruitless to have meticulous tabulations for impractically over-pressure loads!

Equally frustrating to any serious load developer, wildcatter, or long-range target shooter would be to work out a combination, or several, satisfactory for a purpose, but not know if there was really any safe leeway. Could the mix become critical later and have to be reduced and the effort re-started ? Or would it be tolerant and permit variation? And quite important, just what do the variations themselves do? Well, now we can know.

The elements of the Yard pressure measuring system may be built into a gun. If they are incorporated in a bolt, this special bolt may be substituted in the gun for the regular one. Pressure measurements can then be taken with the same barrel ordinarily used.

Thompson/Center Arms, the Rochester, New Hampshire, maker of the renowned Contender single shot pistols, plans to adapt the system for their guns. It will soon be available for both the Contender and the T/C 80 rifle. Thompson/Center shooters who have multiple barrels will be able to make pressure tests by the Yard system with just one special action for Contenders, a second to test the TCR 80. As barrels are added to the battery, they are eligible for pressure testing, and would also qualify for any of the rest of the program of tests to which we have been alluding.

By the time you read this, Thompson/Center should have completed prototype tests. All inquiries about this development should be addressed to their plant: Thompson/Center Arms, P.O. Box 5002 Farmington Road, Rochester, NH 03867.

The Yard pressure measuring system has few inherent limitations. It is easily adapted to single shot actions, bolt actions, and universal receivers. It is a system you can put to use yourself, measuring, if you will, your own pressures by the yard. ●

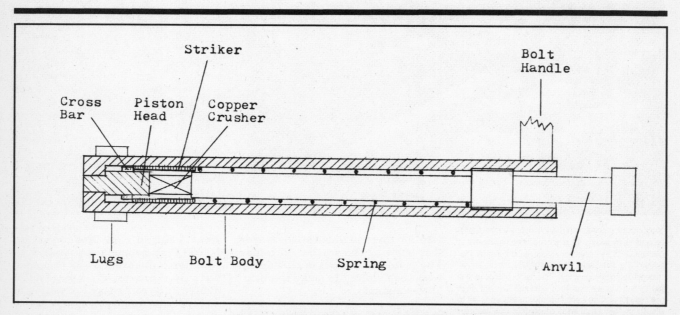

The Yard pressure system may be incorporated in the bolt of bolt-action guns. Shown schematically is one arrangement for a Mauser-type rifle bolt. It adapts easily to single shots.

Cases, primers, powder, shot, wads and glue are needed, but that's all one needs to make shot loads.

SHOT LOADS *For* Big Bore HANDGUNS

You can get up to 200 grains of shot in these loads.

by R.H. VANDENBURG, JR.

HAVE YOU ever wished for a shot cartridge in 41 Magnum? How about a shot cartridge for the 45 ACP that will feed through a magazine, cycle the action, not lead the barrel and produce suitable patterns?

These obviously experimental examples have eminently practical sides. No one who has tried to knock off a rattlesnake or pot a grouse for supper with a big-bore handgun ever wished for more power. More likely, a round ball load that shot to point of aim or a shot cartridge that worked was what was really wanted.

But where does one get such creations? There are no commercially available shot cartridges for the 41 Magnum. What shot cartridges are available for other chambers are generally expensive or have a poor reputation for performance. None of them begin to function in an autoloader. The answer is, of course, to handload. So let's take a closer look at a few shot cartridges for big-bore handguns:

Shot loads have been available, in one form or another since the early days of fixed ammunition. Many blackpowder cartridges that served double duty in rifles and handguns such as the 38-40 and 44-40 were offered in shot form. As time progressed

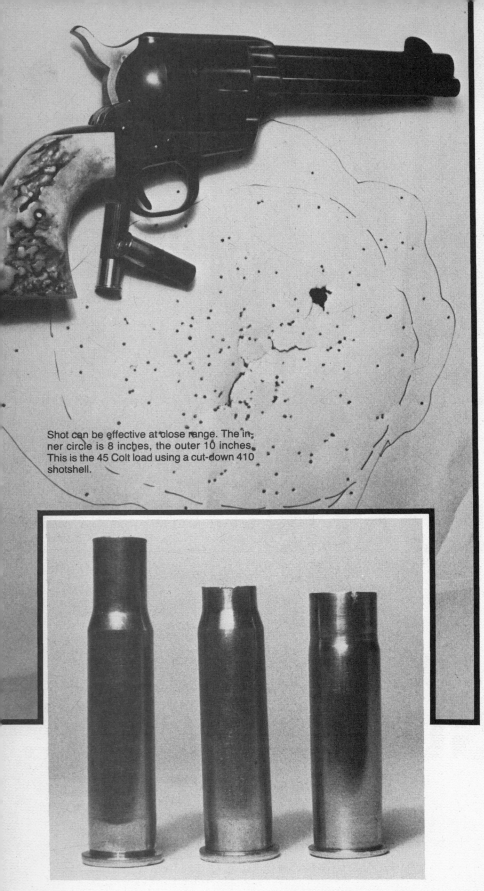

Shot can be effective at close range. The inner circle is 8 inches, the outer 10 inches. This is the 45 Colt load using a cut-down 410 shotshell.

A typical sequence would be (from left) the original rifle case, that case cut to length, and then that case fire-formed.

the list of shot cartridges was expanded to include virtually all of the larger handgun calibers and some of the smaller. Indeed, shot cartridges for 22 rimfires are still being manufactured.

Most of these early shot cartridges were simply standard length cases charged with powder and an over-powder wad, then filled with shot and crimped with an overshot wad. Later efforts included the addition of bullet-shaped containers of wood or paper which had the effect of increasing shot weight and, no doubt, improving feeding, especially from rifle magazines. In general, none of these cartridges held much shot.

However, times change, and there are few handgun shotshell cartridges commercially available today. There are two primary reasons for this—one practical; one legal; both dealing with the barrel rifling. That spiral twist is mandatory for accurate control of a single projectile in flight, but it has just the opposite effect on shot loads. The centrifugal force created causes an almost immediate dispersion of individual shot, creating a doughnut-shaped pattern with shot everywhere except where they are wanted—at point of aim.

There is an obvious solution to this problem, of course: the smoothbored barrel. Unfortunately this approach has been deemed illegal. According to interpretations of the National and Federal Firearms Acts of the 1930s and of the current Gun Control Act of 1968, a smooth-bored pistol or revolver becomes, in effect, a sawed-off shotgun due to its now smooth bore and its barrel and overall length. Federal law mandates that to be legal a shotgun must have a barrel of at least 18 inches and an overall length of at least 26½ inches.

Before this unfortunate turn of legal events, a fair amount of experimental work took place in developing workable shot loads for handguns. One Bud Dalrymple of South Dakota, for example, received a good deal of publicity back in the '30s for his work with smoothbored revolvers. Working predominantly with single-action Colts, he would shorten, rebore and insert a choke (method unknown) in what were discarded rifle barrels and refit them to the revolver frames.

In the '50s, Jim Harvey of Lakeville Arms, using Smith & Wesson double-action revolvers, brought the art to its highest level. Harvey, generally working with 44- and 45-caliber guns, would bore the cylinder chambers straight through. Using suitable rifle cartridges, he would create cylinder length cases blown out to the new chamber dimensions. The barrel would be opened up at the forcing cone, smoothbored its full length and given a slight choke at the muzzle. These guns worked remarkably well, giving the ballistic equivalent of the ½-ounce 2½-inch 410 shotgun shell.

However, as we've noted, the authorities intervened, declaring such weapons to be subject both to registration and a stiff transfer tax, and the market dried up. Still, the idea persisted. Many efforts were made to overcome the rifling requirement, and today much of the ground gained by men like Dalrymple and Harvey has been recovered. The key term in describing the earlier advances was, of course, smoothbore. Today it is *encapsulation*.

The concept of encapsulation is not new but the materials, largely petroleum-based plastics, are of fairly recent vintage. These capsules, which supplant the earlier and largely ineffective wood and paper efforts, offer the shooter increased shot capacity over the standard case alone, can be purchased in loaded ammunition or as full or empty capsules for reloading and, most important of all, protect the shot from the full effects of the rifled bore.

Several variations of these capsules are, or have recently been, available. REMCO capsules are available in 38-, 44- and 45-caliber. In 45, two sizes are produced, one for the 45 Colt and a smaller one for the 45 ACP. These capsules are clear, come filled with No. 9 shot, and are skirted at one end. The skirted end is inserted into the case first with the skirt assisting in keeping the powder in position. The capsule is then crimped in place.

This approach has proved satisfactory most of the time. The capsules are reasonably sturdy so a fairly high failure rate—that is, failure of the capsule to open when leaving the barrel—has been reported. My own experiences support this, with a single keyholing projectile finding its way to or near the target as much as 20 percent of the time. Another difficulty is getting sufficient crimp on the capsule to hold it in place when adjacent full-power bulleted loads are being fired. The result of crimp failure is a cartridge suddenly too long to allow turning of the cylinder. The likelihood of this is greater in 44 Magnums than in 38 Specials. The capsule designed for the 45 ACP is, by the way, too long and the wrong shape to feed from a magazine.

Speer offers empty capsules for reloading in 38 and 44 calibers. They

are packaged 50 to a box and the reloading procedures are the same as for the REMCO capsules except, of course, the capsules must be filled with shot. The capsule material is colored—the ones I have are yellow—and of a somewhat different material from the REMCO offerings. They are also constructed differently, having a ribbed front surface and appear to be more brittle. My experiences, and those of others that have appeared in print, favor the Speer product. Crimping does not present a problem nor have there been any failures of the capsule to break up. The Speer capsules, on the other hand, don't hold as much shot as do the comparable REMCO products nor are they offered in as many calibers.

Thompson/Center Arms, makers of the famed Contender single shot pistols, also provide filled shot capsules for reloading, but these are replacement articles for their Hot Shot line. They also are available only in 38 and 44 calibers and were designed to be used in Contender 357 Magnum and 44 Magnum Hot Shot barrels which include a removable, recessed choke. The loaded Hot Shot rounds are too long to be used in conventional revolvers.

While a book could easily be written about the T/C pistol and its impact on handgun shooting and hunting, suffice it to say, that within the context covered here, the T/C Hotshot barrels and cartridges offer the shooter the epitome of handgun shotshell performance. The capsules themselves hold more shot than either the REMCO or Speer loads. The internal choke, which is removed when standard ammo is fired, is also rifled but the rifling is straight, parallel to the bore. The effect of this rifling and choking is to arrest the spin imparted by the spiral rifling and shred the capsule, insuring a consistent, usable pattern. The Hot Shot barrels have a ventilated rib to improve the sighting plane and some impressive shooting has been done in the game field and on the Skeet range with these guns.

An interesting aside, Thompson/Center at one time offered a 45-410 barrel which was chambered deeply enough to accept a 3-inch 410 shotgun shell as well as the standard 45 Colt cartridge. It had, as an accessory, a smooth choke which extended from

(Author's Note: As a result of a recent BATF ruling, T/C has reintroduced the 45-410 barrel. It is offered as a plain bull barrel or with a rib such as with the 357 and 44 Hot Shot barrels. Choke is of the newer internal style.)

the muzzle. Subsequent consultations with authorities led T/C to drop it. Other barrels with standard chambers were offered with the extended choke as well. At that time the normal Contender barrel length was 8½ inches. After the development of the 30 Herrett, which was offered in a special 10-inch bull barrel, T/C decided to make this new barrel its standard. In doing so it laid the groundwork for the current recessed choke barrels described earlier. While the aforementioned Hot Shot shotshells are offered only in 357 and 44, 45 Colt barrels are also available with the recessed choke. When the choke is removed, on any of these barrels, the effective length of the barrel once again becomes 8½ inches.

For those who would use shot capsules on limited occasions and in calibers for which they are available, Speer offers loaded shotshells in 357 Magnum and 44 Magnum. Thompson/Center sells Hot Shot cartridges for their Contender in the same calibers. The 22 Long Rifle and 22 WMR shot cartridges are also available.

For those who want only a few, but for a caliber other than 22, 357 or 44, there are a number of custom loaders who would no doubt be happy to supply a small quantity for the right price. For those who want a larger quantity, or at a more attractive price, or would simply prefer to load their own, another option is open. You can, using available components, produce shotshells for any centerfire caliber you wish while retaining the advantages of encapsulation. In addition, these loads will hold more shot than any of the commercial offerings with the exception of the T/C Hot Shot cartridges.

Let's begin by examining the components needed to produce shot cartridges.

Case: The case used for shotshells in a revolver must be rimmed, longer than the cylinder and as close in body diameter to the chamber as can be found. All will be brass except that one option in making 45 Colt loads allows the use of a standard 410 shotshell. For the autoloading 45 ACP, a rimless case is required. Specific recommendations for each caliber will be covered later in the text and identified in Table I.

Primer: Large pistol primers will be used in all brass cases. The standard 410 shotshell primer will be required in the 45 Colt load using that shotshell.

Powder: Powder selection will usually be a fast-to-medium burning pistol powder; since low velocity and low

Helpful tools for depriming, cutting and seating wads, and tamping shot.

From left: The 22 WMR factory load, Speer 44 Magnum factory load, reloadable Speer shot capsule, REMCO shot capsule, and a 44 Magnum handload, assembled using a cut-down rifle case.

White epoxy permits indelible ink marking for immediate identification besides creating a good seal at the case mouth.

power produces better patterns, the choice is seldom critical.

Shot: Size and hardness can vary or be tailored for a specific need but unplated No. 9 was used throughout these tests and is recommended for general use.

Paper Wads: Overpowder wads are required in fire forming and in the regular 41 Magnum loading. Overshot wads will be used in all loads except fire forming.

While most any thin cardboard is suitable, empty bullet boxes or backs of note pads make good wads, as do primer box sleeves or the inserts from new or laundered shirts. The simplest method for cutting the overpowder wad is to sacrifice one of the rifle cases to be fire-formed. Cut it off about an inch from the rim, discarding the neck portion. Trim and chamfer sharply. By placing a piece of soft wood under the material and tapping the case through it with a hammer, wads can be cut rapidly à la cookie cutter.

Overshot wads must be slightly smaller. For convenience, these wads can be reduced slightly in size with scissors or be cut using a case of a slightly smaller caliber. The fact that they will be epoxied gives some latitude in precise fit not otherwise afforded.

Plastic Wads: These wads are the key to the successful development of handgun shotshells. Regular 410 shotshell wads, cut to length, they serve as overpowder wad, shot cushion, shot protector and, with overshot wads, form a container which "encapsulates" the shot charge. By preventing the shot from contacting the rifling, patterns are improved and leading significantly reduced.

Epoxy: In order to have both shot and regular cartridges in the gun at the same time, the shot cartridge must be able to withstand the recoil generated by firing regular ammo. This is accomplished by solidly epoxying two overshot wads into place. No other type of glue tested was able to withstand the recoil.

While it is recognized that in most instances gas checks could be substituted for the overshot wads and epoxy, I felt that the crimping requirements would unnecessarily complicate matters and probably shorten case life.

Special Tools: In addition to the normal reloading equipment—dies, press, case trimmer and so on—there are several other items necessary to make the project as simple as possible. These include: a hacksaw for cutting cases; a hammer and block of soft wood for cutting wads; a small nail for extracting wads from cases after cutting; a small vise; a depriming tool; a small rod, about 3 inches in length and ⅜-inch in diameter. One end should be concave to a depth of approximately ⅛-inch—used for inserting wads, tamping shot, etc.

We will not cover calibers smaller than 41 Magnum. While shot loads exist in 38/357 in several forms, most will agree that below 41-caliber, the quantity of shot which can be held within a revolver cylinder chamber doesn't warrant the effort to be described.

Once a case of proper length and diameter has been found, the first critical dimension becomes the rim diameter. If cases can be inserted in the chambers and be turned without binding on each other or the cylinder ratchet, no modification will be necessary. If some reducing is required, the preferred way would be to use a lathe, but simply holding the case in the hand against a moving abrasive such as a wheel or sander will accomplish the same result. The case must be continually turned while in contact with the abrasive. In the absence of these tools, a simple file can be used. A micrometer set to the desired diameter to serve as a go-no-go gauge will greatly assist in ensuring the turned rims are reasonably round, but careful work can be done without one.

Next the case must be cut to proper length. The method used most often is to remove the cylinder from the gun if a single action, or simply swing it open if a double action. Insert a case in one chamber and mark a line on the case where it protrudes through the cylinder. Cut the case off at this line and trim to just under cylinder length. Generally it is best not to chamfer the case at this point. Wait until after fire forming. While there are a number of ways to cut the case to the proper length, depending on the tools available, one way is to insert a bullet of the appropriate caliber in the case mouth being careful not to go deeper than the scribe line, then put the case mouth in a vise. The bullet will keep the case from collapsing. Then simply hacksaw away.

Now the case can be inserted in the gun with the cylinder in place. Rim thickness must be checked next. In some instances the thickness of the rim will be greater than the distance from the rear of the cylinder to the recoil shield. In such cases the cylinder cannot be rotated and a reduction in rim thickness is required. While it is understood that the proper way to reduce rim thickness is to remove metal from the forward edge so as not to obliterate the headstamp or reduce the depth of the primer pocket, this is difficult to do without a lathe. It is also an unnecessary concern in that pistol primers are used in the loads described. Being somewhat shorter than rifle primers, there should be little chance of one not being seated flush or below the case head even after a substantial reduction in rim thickness. This reduction is affected in the same manner as the diameter, with wheel, sander or file, removing a small amount of metal, checking for fit and repeating if necessary. (*This seems to be one instance where reducing rim thickness from the back is the way to do it. Editor.*)

Once the cases have been prepared in this manner, fire forming is the next step. In general this involves priming each case, dumping some powder in—and 4.5 to 5 grains of Bullseye or something comparable is as good as any—inserting an over-powder wad and filling with shot. Care must be taken to insure that the overpowder wad is seated on the powder. Instead of the traditional overshot wad at this point, for fire forming we simply need something to hold the shot in place. Grease or Crisco is often used, as is soap. Wax is preferable though: It offers good shot retention, mild lubrication, is free of moisture and easy to use.

The newly loaded rounds are then chambered and fired, one at a time. The firing expands the brass to chamber dimensions, creating a container of maximum size for subsequent reloading. After fire forming, a final trimming may be desired, followed by a slight chamfering. The trimming may be omitted, but the case mouths should be cleaned up as neatly as possible.

One note of caution: Since bottleneck cases will not accept the plastic wads until after fire forming, the unprotected shot will contact the rifling when fired and severe barrel leading can be expected. Two alternatives are suggested. If only a few cases are to be made, simply fire several jacketed bullets after each fire forming shot and follow the session with a good cleaning. If large quantities are to be made, insert a plastic sleeve in each case before filling with shot. These sleeves can be cut from garbage bags or drop cloths or something similar. While not serving all the purposes of the plastic wad to be used later, the sleeve will save the user much "bench time" after the shooting is done.

Having come this far, things get simpler. The cases are ready to be deprimed and reloaded. Depriming, depending on reloading die style, may best be done separately. If the depriming stem also contains an expander it cannot be used, as the operations would expand the case mouth, destroying the chamber fit fire forming just created. Even if neck expansion were performed separately, depriming would be accompanied by body sizing and sometimes this is not desired. Generally, depriming is best accomplished by using a nail turned to fit or one of the hardened steel tools made for decapping crimped military brass.

The concept of sizing needs to be understood. Generally speaking the rifle cases used to make shot cartridges are undersized in comparison to the handgun cartridge body dimensions. At the same time, fire forming creates a tight fit at the chamber neck and a mildly bottlenecked case. As most of us realize, bottlenecked cartridges usually give less than satisfactory performance in revolvers. When the gun is fired, pressure, from the gases created by the burning powder, forces the case surfaces out and back. The rearward movement, until arrested by contact with the recoil shield, allows the case shoulder to be blown forward. When the pressure subsides, the case's new shape, with the shoulder repositioned, prevents it from returning to its original position, thereby sometimes locking up the gun.

The problem is not consistent, however, or insurmountable. In calibers where the case/chamber fit is close, such as with the 45 Colt, no problems may be encountered at all; where the fit is poorest, as with the 41 Magnum, depending on case used, the most difficulty can be expected.

Much can be done to minimize the difficulties. First we are dealing with low pressure levels so the problem doesn't reach the magnitude of bulleted ammo. So don't load-em-up; less powder usually produces better patterns anyway. Second, by not body sizing, the problem reduces itself with each firing of a particular case. Third, by making certain the chambers are free of oil or other lubricants, adhesion is improved, reducing case setback. If severe case setback does occur, neck sizing the case, setting the shoulder back only enough to insure rechambering, and refiring often overcomes the problem. It is not unusual to have setback at fire forming but not in subsequent firings.

If difficulty in rechambering fired cases persists, body sizing followed by neck sizing may be required. If case setback still causes cylinder backup, some rim thinning may be required. Proceed slowly. By paying close atten-

The 45 ACP shot cartridge will feed through the magazine and cycle the action, if made according to this prescription.

Sometimes rims must be reduced in diameter, thickness. Hand tools will do it if no lathe is at hand.

tion, it may be that a particular case or two or a particular chamber is the culprit. By discarding the oddball case or loading the traditional five rather than six chambers, the problem of additional rim thinning may be avoided. Generally, the tighter the case body to chamber fit before firing, the less the setback afterwards. Hence the admonition against unnecessary body sizing.

Reloading cases in final form is next. Deprime as described. Neck size and reprime using standard pistol primers. Clean the inside case necks with a dry brush or, if necessary, steel wool. Insert powder and wad (after cutting to proper length) and fill with shot. By filling slowly and tamping

down often, the amount of shot each case will hold can be maximized. Fill to within approximately $3/32$-inch of the mouth. Apply epoxy glue to the edges of an overshot wad. Insert in case, forcing the wad down on the shot with firm pressure. Apply more epoxy, this time to the inside of the case mouth and to the top surface of the inserted wad. Insert a second wad, again with firm pressure. Apply a final coating of epoxy filling the case to the mouth. The loads are now complete. They should be set aside to dry, mouth up, for 24 to 48 hours before using.

The actual trim length of the shot wads will be based on brass length, amount and powder used, and wad

thickness. The lengths given in the detailed cartridge descriptions and the table are based on the combinations used in the actual loads described.

Now to review each cartridge individually:

41 Magnum

This caliber may be the most frustrating, and yet rewarding, to load for. The 41 body diameter lends itself to the use of three rifle cartridges for shot cases. None are ideal although the 303 Savage is the most satisfactory. The 41 Magnum chamber dimension in front of the head measures .4368-inch. The 303 Savage dimension at this point is .4390-inch; the 32 Winchester is .4199-inch and the 30-30 Winchester .4195-inch. Given that the chamber dimensions are minimum and the case dimensions are maximum, through careful case selection 303 Savage brass can be found that represents a very close fit. If 303 Savage brass is found to be oversize, it can be sized down in a standard 41 Magnum sizing die but the case must be driven into the die flush with the rim. This can easily be done by reversing the die in the press so that the mouth is up. Then place a well-lubed case in the die and with a flat plate over the head, tap the case in the die with a hammer until the rim comes in contact with the die bottom. Reverse the die and drive the case out with a dowel. Regardless of the case chosen, the rims must be reduced in diameter to approximately .488-inch.

After cutting and trimming the cases to cylinder length, they must be primed, a powder charge dropped and an overpowder wad inserted. Due to the narrow neck diameter even the paper wad is tedious to insert. Care must be taken to press the wad down evenly on top of the powder. To protect the bore from leading a plastic sleeve of some sort is desired. One solution, when other material is unavailable, is cutting across the wad, remove the head from a 410 shot cup and then, cutting lengthwise, remove one of the three "fingers." The remaining piece can be shortened by about $3/8$-inch and inserted in the case before filling with shot.

After fire forming, the same material can be used. Then remove the head and, cutting lengthwise, make a single slit between two of the fingers, creating a single plastic rectangle which can be inserted into the case. In this instance, roll the plastic and insert about ¼-inch. Then insert the tamper rod into the case until it touches the paper wad. Now complete inserting the plastic. This technique will insure that the plastic is forced to the outside, contacting the case walls. A slight overlapping will occur at the case mouth. The same technique may be helpful in inserting other material.

Practical performance varied with the case used. My 303 Savage cases fire formed well with no neck splits or unreasonable setback. The 30-30 and 32 Special cases sometimes split when fire formed and almost always demonstrated setback, effectively tying up the gun. The smaller cases also tended to take on a pear shape after firing due to the dimensional differences in case and chamber. This presented no real problems and successive firings tended to reduce setback. Rim thickness trimming was necessary in some instances with the smaller cases.

Due to the large dimensional differences beween chamber and case when using the 30-30 or 32 Special, fired cylinder-length cases tend to have a neck or shoulder that is not concentric with the case body. While neck sizing minimizes this, cases often had to be rotated a bit before insertion into a given chamber. No such problems occurred with 303 Savage brass.

When body sizing is required, the regular 41 Magnum sizer is used. Neck sizing is accomplished using the 41 Magnum seating die with the crimping shoulder performing the sizing. Neck sizing should always be done in such a manner as to set the shoulder back only as much as needed for rechambering. Any more simply reduces shot capacity.

The powder charge which proved most successful was 5.7 grains of Unique. Patterns were 10 inches or smaller at 10 feet and held together fairly well. Considering the 41 shotshell holds less shot than most of the other cartridges loaded for and has a narrower bore, performance was quite good.

44 Special

Loading shotshells for this caliber was fairly simple and everything said here was also true for the 44 Magnum.

Krag 30-40 brass was used. Rim diameter had to be reduced from the Krag's .545-inch to approximately .515-inch. The Krag rim thickness of .064-inch was also excessive. The normal 44 Special rim specs call for a maximum .060-inch. The plastic wad trimmed to 1⅛ inches fit well. The powder charge finally settled on was 5.5 grains of Unique, but as the revolver loaded for was a custom built Ruger rather than a factory Colt, Smith or Charter, more experimenta-

tion may be called for.

Body sizing when desired can easily be accomplished using the 44 Special/ 44 Magnum full-length sizing die with the decapper removed. Neck sizing is best accomplished with a 41 Magnum sizing die. Screw the die into the press, insert the case in the shellholder and slowly resize the mouth a little at a time, setting the shoulder back just enough to allow easy insertion of the resized brass in the chambers. If a 41 Magnum die is not available, use the 44 seating die letting the crimping shoulder serve as the sizer. This method will not reduce the neck as much as the 41 sizer die and could prove unsatisfactory. If so, a flat washer, or any steel plate with a hole drilled and polished to the proper diameter could be used.

Patterns were adequate, averaging about 10 inches at 10 feet. As distances increased, pattern size grew and density decreased at a faster rate than with other cartridges. A reasonable expectation, as case volume is less in the 44 Special to begin with.

44 Magnum

As indicated, loading details are similar to the 44 Special. The powder selection turned out to be 6.0 grains of Unique, and the wad was cut ⅛-inch longer to an overall length of 1¼ inches.

Revolver headspace was less in the 44 Magnum (a Ruger Super Blackhawk) than in the Special, and there was less evidence of blowback. The 30-40 Krag cases required a reduction in rim diameter and thickness as with the 44 Special.

Generally speaking, the key factors in the performance of shotshells in handguns is quantity of shot and length of barrel. The greater case capacity and larger barrel of the magnum showed itself. Ten-foot groups of 8-inch diameter were the norm and usable patterns held together to distances approaching 30 feet.

45 Colt

This cartridge is unique in that there are two very practical approaches to shotshell construction. One utilizes 444 Marlin cases in the same manner as the other calibers discussed. The second utilizes 410 plastic shotshells.

In the former, the 444 Marlin presents an almost perfect fit. The rim diameter is within 45 Colt chamber specs; no reduction should be necessary. Rim thickness, though, may require some modification. While the factory specs on the two cartridges vary only by .003-inch, short of very

careful case selection, some reduction is likely. Powder selection is again recommended at 6.0 grains of Unique, and wad length should be about 1⅛ inches.

Resizing the body is done using the standard 45 sizer without a neck expander. Neck sizing is best accomplished with a 44 full-length sizing die. In the absence of such, the 45 seating die can be substituted using the crimp shoulder for reduction. As with other calibers, should this approach prove unsatisfactory, a washer or other steel plate with a hole of appropriate size can be utilized.

Performance was good although some case setback was experienced at first. Groups at 10 feet average 10 inches. Usable patterns were maintained past 20 feet. This level of performance could have been improved with a longer barrel. The gun used in development was a 4¾-inch Colt Single Action Army.

The other approach, using a 410 shell, may be the best of all the examples discussed. Fired 410 shells are simply deprimed and cut to cylinder length. Cutting should be done neatly with a sharp knife or tube cutter as case trimmers do not perform satisfactorily on the plastic case material. Unless the reloader has shotshell reloading equipment, priming the 410 case can be perplexing. However, using the special tool discussed earlier in conjunction with a small vise, it becomes easy. Simply insert the tool, concave end first, into the shell, start a primer and carefully align the three components in a vise. By slowly tightening the vise, the primer can be seated flush within the pocket. The concave end of the rod prevents contact between it and the primer cap, eliminating any unnecessary flattening of the latter.

Due to the dimensional correctness of the shell after shortening to cylinder length as well as the flexibility of the material, no neck sizing or setback problems were experienced. Ejection of the cases after firing can sometimes be stiff, though. In fact, in such instances a short dowel of suitable length is recommended for ejection to eliminate possible damage to the ejector rod or the case. Unlike most of the brass shells discussed, full-length resizing of the plastic shell is advised.

Six grains of Unique again proved to be a very good charge in front of the R-P 97-4 shotshell primer. The shortened wad length was 1⅛ inches. Patterns were very good, averaging 8 inches at 10 feet and holding together well beyond 20 feet. Again, with a longer barrel, performance would have been even better. To one with access to 410 cases, this approach to 45 Colt shotshells is close to ideal.

45 ACP

This shotshell is both the most difficult to make and the most satisfying in that it not only provides the desired result on target, but it feeds through a magazine and cycles the action of an autoloader. One especially nice factor, if great quantities of shotshell cartridges for this caliber are wanted, is that RCBS makes 45 ACP shotshell dies which will greatly facilitate production. However, without these dies shells can still be made with a little effort.

Credit should be given here to C. E. Harris, who, while a member of NRA technical staff, developed these first truly workable autoloading shotshells. In fact, RCBS made the first dies to his order.

Regardless of the approach taken, the result is a bottleneck cartridge that headspaces on a shoulder formed by necking-down cut-off rifle brass. No fire forming is required.

The case to be used must conform to certain limitations regarding diameter and extractor groove dimensions. Fortunately the 243, 308, 358 family of cases serve admirably. The 30-06 can be used but in any event, commercial cases are preferable to military as the latter are often thicker which could cause extractor wear or damage. Excess neck thickness of the military cases can also result in damage to the wads during insertion.

The cases must first be cut to a length of approximately 1.250 inches and trimmed to 1.180. Body sizing is done with the 45 ACP sizer. Decapping after firing must be done in a manner so as to not expand the neck areas of the case. Neck sizing, initially and later on, can easily be done with a 41 Magnum sizing die but care must be exercised to insure that the shoulder is not set back so far as to allow the case head to be positioned below the barrel extension when chambered. Improper positioning could cause hang or misfires due to the then lighter than normal firing pin below. Each case must be checked individually as it is being formed. Both body and neck sizing are recommended after each firing.

Powder choice in this load varied, with pressure sensitivity being of greater concern in an autoloader than a revolver. In order to insure proper cycling of the slide, pressure had to be kept higher than when pattern efficiency was the sole criteria. Nevertheless, Unique performed well as did W-W 231—about 6.0 grains of either. Wads must be shortened to ¾-inch or so, depending on powder charge.

Because the case mouth will be crimped in this example to facilitate feeding, an option to the epoxied paper overshot wads is presented. A 38-caliber gas check seated skirt down may be used. In this instance the case should be slightly over-filled with shot before seating the gas check to insure solid seating. The gas check may be seated below the case mouth as the paper wad would be or in such a manner as to allow the mouth to crimp in the skirt. Without the RCBS dies, the handloader may find the paper overshot wads simpler.

Paper wads, if used, are seated and epoxied as described earlier, but crimping should be done before applying the final topping of epoxy.

Crimping can be most readily done with the RCBS dies if used but also by simply using a 38 sizing die. Crimping is slight and must be done carefully if standard dies are used. If case neck thickness makes crimping difficult, an intermediate crimp with a larger die such as a 30-30 sizer can be applied. An alternative crimping method is to obtain a short piece of pipe of proper diameter and bevel the inside of one end at approximately 60 degrees. Simply place the beveled end over the case mouth and tap with a hammer. Practice will determine the amount of force to use.

While production methods employed in 45 ACP shotshell manufacture are much more critical—body and neck sizing, crimping—than those required for revolver loads, the results are very satisfying. Testing revealed 8- to 10-inch patterns at 10 feet, holding together well past the 20-foot mark. More importantly, properly prepared rounds feed through magazines, cycle the slide and eject spent shells without a hitch.

In summary, then, functional and effective shot loads for revolvers and the 45 ACP autoloader can be produced with relative ease. They, along with low and midrange lead loads and high performance jacketed rounds provide a range of versatility and pleasure unknown to the nonhandloader. ●

TABLE I

CALIBER:	41 Magnum	44 Special	44 Magnum	45-410	45-444	45 ACP
Shotshells (1)						
Case	303 Sav.	30-40	30-40	410 Ga.	444 Marlin	243 Winchester
Cut Length	1¾	1²¹/₃₂	1²⁵/₃₂	1²³/₃₂	1²³/₃₂	1¼
Trim Length	1²³/₃₂	1¹⁹/₃₂	1²²/₃₂	1²¹/₃₂	1²¹/₃₂	1³/₁₆
Rim Dia.	.490	.514	.514	N/A	N/A	N/A
Wad Length	1⅛	1⅛	1¼	1⅛	1⅛	1¹¹/₁₆
Primer	CCI 300	CCI 300	CCI 300	R-P 97-4	CCI 300	CCI 300
Powder	5.7 Unique	5.5 Unique	6.0 Unique	6.0 Unique	6.0 Unique	6.0 Unique
Shot (2)	200 gr.	170 gr.	200 gr.	185 gr.	185 gr.	90 gr.
Body Sizer	41 FL	44 FL	44 FL	45 FL	45 FL	45 FL
Neck Sizer	41 Crimp	41 FL	41 FL	N/A	44 FL	41 FL
Crimp Die	N/A	N/A	N/A	N/A	N/A	38 FL (3)

(1) All dimensions in inches
(2) Shot weights are approximate.
(3) May use intermediate step such as 30-30 FL die.

8mm Mauser:

Mauser Mod. 88, Cal. 7,9 mm.

Mauser Mod. 1907 Cal. 7,9 mm „S"

by KONRAD F. SCHREIER, JR.

DADDY OF THEM ALL

EVERY military rifle and most every high-power sporting rifle in use today fires jacketed bullets from rimless centerfire bottle-necked cartridges loaded with smokeless powder. This design and layout is now just about a century old and the first to get it all together for wide use was the 8mm Mauser.

Metallic cartridges were invented before our Civil War and were used in it. They were all rimfires ranging from the 22 Smith & Wesson revolver up to Spencers over 50 caliber. At the end of that war, the first practical centerfire cartridges were introduced.

From then until the late 1880s, the standard military rifle cartridges were all big bored and straight-cased — rimmed cases holding black powder. However, as early as the 1860s chemists had been trying to improve gun powder to replace black powder. They wanted less smoke and more power. Black powder made dense, often blinding, clouds of smoke.

By 1870 or so the first smokeless nitrocellulose-base powders were being successfully tested. Then, as so often happens, one thing led to another. Without the dense clouds of smoke riflemen could see to aim better, and both military and civilian shooters began seeking rifles with improved effective range.

This started the development of modern smokeless powder rifle ammunition. While military inventions such as improved artillery ammunition were deep, dark secrets, improvements for smokeless powder rifles were not. They were widely known, written about and discussed openly.

The credit for beginning the development of the modern rifle cartridge goes to Major Eduard Rubin, a Swiss Army ordnance officer. About 1871 he was assigned to the famous Thun Government Ammunition factory where he began working on ways of improving rifle ammunition.

Top: The 8mm Type 1888 cartridge (above) the 8mm Type S (below) as these Mauser cartridges were shown in the Alpha catalog of 1911. **Below:** German Army infantry about 1900, before the *stahlhelm* and also the Gew. 98.

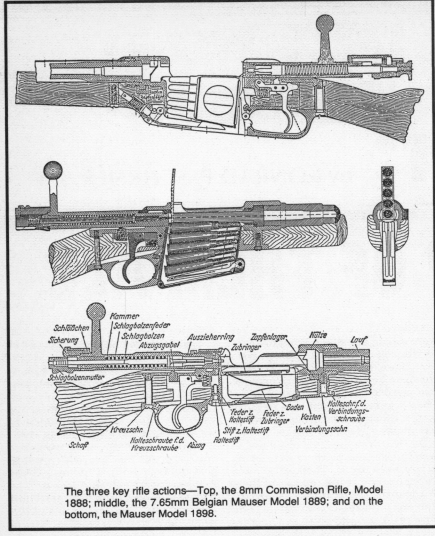

Schlößchen   Kammer   Schlagbolzenfeder
Sicherung   Schlagbolzen   Auszieherring   Zapfenlager   Hülse   Lauf
Abzugsgabel   Zubringer
Schlagbolzenmutter
Kreuzschr.   Feder z.   Feder z.   Boden   Halteschr.f.d.
Haltestift   Zubringer   Kasten   Verbindungs-
schraube
Schaft   Halteschraube f.d.   Stift z.Haltestift   Verbindungsschr.
Kreuzschraube   Abzug   Haltestift

The three key rifle actions—Top, the 8mm Commission Rifle, Model 1888; middle, the 7.65mm Belgian Mauser Model 1889; and on the bottom, the Mauser Model 1898.

By about 1880 Major Rubin had developed a number of radical new ideas: He found that reducing the caliber of a rifle and firing smaller, lighter bullets made the rifle shoot with a flatter trajectory which improved its long range accuracy. He also discovered these higher velocities increased friction so the bullet lead alloy melted and deposited in the rifle's bore; he overcame this by putting jackets of alloys with higher melting points on them. This gave him the jacketed bullet.

In order to fire jacketed bullets at high velocities, Rubin needed cartridge cases which would hold enough powder to do it, and he achieved this by adapting the familiar bottle-necked case design. Then he eliminated the old cartridge rim, replaced it with an extraction groove, and — this is important — used the case shoulder for headspacing. He had the foresight to observe that his new rimless, bottle-necked cartridges would feed better from magazines than the old rimmed style.

Major Rubin had developed the rimless, bottle-necked cartridge by the mid-1880s. Curiously, he had not come yet to smokeless powder. Then something happened which accelerated the whole development.

In 1886, the French Army adopted the first successful smokeless powder military rifle cartridge — the 8mm Lebel. The Lebel was used into World War II, but it was not truly a modern cartridge design. The case was developed from the old French black pow-

German Army in field-gray in early 1915, armed with the 8mm Type S Mauser Model 1898 rifle.

der 11mm military cartridge, remodeled slightly smaller to hold the desired charge of the new smokeless powder and tapered to hold the 8mm bullet. It had a rim, and at first fired a roundnose jacketed bullet based on Major Rubin's designs.

The French Lebel set off an arms race. Within the next five years or so, every major country in the world adopted new small bore smokeless powder military rifles and ammunition!

The first were the Germans, ever watchful of French military developments. In 1888, they adopted a new rifle to fire the revolutionary new 8mm Mauser cartridge designed in 1887. It was the first ever adopted to have a rimless, bottle-necked case, a jacketed bullet, and smokeless powder. It was the first ever adopted using Major Rubin's ideas, and very possibly — records are not complete — was put together with his cooperation.

The Model '88 rifle's design used features from the latest experimental Mauser, Mannlicher and other new experimental bolt action military rifle designs. As for the new case, its very useful diameter was chosen to accommodate the desired charge of smokeless powder; by chance as much as anything else, the 8mm case has proven ideal ever since. It worked out so well that few general-purpose cartridges stray very far from it, and it is still in wide use.

The length of the loaded cartridge was about 3¼ inches. The long, cylindrical, roundnose bullet weighed 226 grains. The whole combination of case, powder charge and bullet had been worked out to give a muzzle velocity of 2,100 fps (feet per second).

The basic .470-in. diameter case of the 8mm Mauser cartridge is easily modified to change its capacity by changing its bottleneck and length. Further, relatively moderate changes of the basic case cover a useful range of powder capacities. It is the direct ancestor of today's 7.62mm NATO rifle cartridge which has the same diameter, as does the 30-06, and the 7mm Mauser, and another ten or more widely used military rifle cartridges. Along with these go another 20 or more sporting rifle cartridges. The original 8mm Mauser case is the basis for more cartridges than any other ever designed — not bad for the first modern military cartridge case design ever.

Another first for the 8mm Mauser cartridge was the way it was loaded into the bolt action Model '88 rifle: The rimless cartridges could be stacked one atop another without the problem of rim-over-rim jams, so a five-round expendable clip holding five of them was invented. The clip itself became part of the rifle's magazine when it was loaded, falling out of the action as the last round was stripped from it. This worked well, and was the basis for the system used in the M1 Garand rifle 40 years later. Its one big disadvantage was that the rifle's magazine could not be loaded with loose cartridges, and it was very difficult to load additional cartridges into a partly empty magazine.

Then, in 1889, as the German army armed with the 1888 commission rifle, Mauser, a huge private military arms manufacturer, introduced its own smokeless powder, small bore military rifle, the 7.65mm Belgian Mauser. Its case was a variation of the 8mm Model '88 cartridge. With this rifle came another first — a new loading system using a five-round charger. The charger held the cartridges by the extractor grooves in their heads so all five could be quickly pushed into the magazine; then the charger was discarded. In this system, loose cartridges could easily be loaded into a partly-loaded or empty rifle. This new charger-loaded magazine was a great advance over the German Model 1888 rifle system, and the charger was the type which is still used for most military rifle ammunition to this day. The magazine still stacked the cartridges in a straight column.

Next, in 1892, Mauser introduced the 7mm Mauser cartridge, another 8mm variation. In 1893, they introduced the Spanish military rifle in 7mm which incorporated another major magazine improvement: The charger-loaded staggered-column box magazine. This design streamlined the stock by eliminating the protruding single column magazine, and there are very few magazine-loading rifles today which don't employ the staggered-column magazine.

In the mid-1890s, the German armed forces began evaluating the advantages of Mauser's improved bolt

Adapted to Mauser, Sauer-Mauser and Schilling-Mauser Model 1888 and Haenel-Mannlicher Model 1888 military and sporting rifles

8 M/M (7.9 M/M) Mannlicher—

	Wt. case	Per 1000
Smokeless powder, soft point bullet (236-grain)...73 lbs.....		$95.00
Smokeless powder, metal cased bullet (227-grain)..75 lbs.....		95.00

20 in a cardboard box; 1,000 in a case.

8 M/M Special (7.9 M/M)—170-grain bullet.

	Wt. case	Per 1000
Smokeless powder, soft point bullet.............65 lbs.....		$95.00

20 in a cardboard box; 1,000 in a case.

8 mm. (7.9 mm.) Mannlicher

Adapted to Mauser, Sauer-Mauser and Schilling-Mauser Model 1888 and Haenel-Mannlicher Model 1888, Mannlicher-Schoenauer Model 1908 military and sporting rifles.

	lb Case	Fact. List THOUSAND
Smokeless, soft point bullet (200-grain)	76	$95.00

Twenty in a cardboard box; 1000 in a case.

8 mm. Mauser (7.9 mm.)—170-Grain Bullet

	lb Case	Fact. List THOUSAND
Smokeless, soft point bullet	70	$95.00

Twenty in a cardboard box; 1000 in a case.

These are typical of 8mm Mauser listings in American illustrated cartridge catalogs of the 1920s and 1930s. Very concerned about mix-ups, ammunition companies basically loaded all their ammunition so the Model 1888 rifle could handle it. The problem must still exist since even today's loads are such that the Model 1888 rifle can handle them. Reloaders handbooks are equally cautious. They are all very correct, because it is dangerous to fire any 8mm Type S ammunition in a Model 1888 rifle.

German Infantry in action in World War I in the fall of 1914 armed with 8mm Model 1888 rifles, presumably set up for S Type ammo.

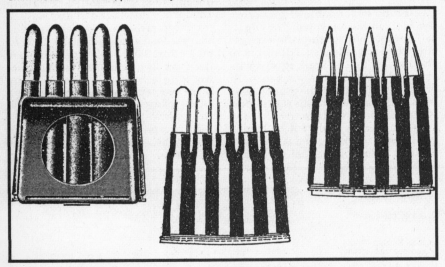

Left: The 8mm Mauser cartridge clip for the 1888 rifle; middle: the charger for the Model 1889 and Model 1898 loaded with Type 1888 cartridges; at right is the same charger with 8mm Type S cartridges.

action military rifles. They found the Mauser superior, simpler and less costly than the Model '88, so they adopted the Model 1898. As adopted the '98 Mauser fired the same ammunition as the Model '88.

By the turn of the century, the old round nose, cylindrical Model '88 bullet was fast becoming obsolete. People had not stopped experimenting with ways to improve rifle ballistics, and by 1900 it had been proven that a lighter, pointed bullet could be fired at a higher velocity with improved

range and accuracy. Mauser and their cartridge supplier DWM — Deutsche Waffen und Munitionsfabriken — were leaders in this development with their pointed "spitzer" (from the German *spitz,* or pointed) bullets. In 1898, and in deep military secrecy, the French had adopted the pointed, streamlined solid bronze Balle D bullet for their 8mm Lebel cartridge. The new jacketed pointed Mauser bullets were easier to make and much less costly than the Balle D. By 1902 or so, the Mauser spitzer bullets, although

still in the experimental stage, were well known.

Mauser offered spitzer bullet ammunition in 1903. The German army began testing it and in 1904 adopted a new 8mm Type S cartridge for the Model '98 Mauser rifle. "S" was for *Spitzer*. In the next five years or so every other major country in the world also changed bullets and many of them paid royalties to Mauser and DWM for both the bullet design and charger loading system which went with it.

The new Type S cartridge fired a 154-grain bullet at about 2,800 fps. Overall, it was a massive improvement in range, accuracy and effectiveness compared to the old Type '88 load, but there were interchangeability problems.

When they adopted the new S bullet, the German military changed bullet diameters and caused problems and confusion which still persist today. The Type S was .323-in.; the old Type '88 was .317-in. in diameter. The groove diameter for the Type S bullet was .323-in., while it was .318-in. for the Type '88!! This meant that Model '88 rifles have never been able to fire Type S ammunition safely.

The reasons for this annoying change in the 8mm Mauser bullet diameter have long eluded arms students. Research by arms and ammunition authorities William H. Woodin, Robert W. Faris, Peter T. Vogel and Erik Windisch has recently uncovered them.

The German reasoning revolves around the basic profile difference between the two bullets. The critical bore-bearing area of the Type S bullet is only about a quarter that of the older cylindrical bullet, and the Germans were concerned that the shorter bearing area would make the Type S less stable in the bore than they needed. The new bullet was also harder than the older one to give it better penetration. Further, there were problems with bore wear in the Model '88 barrel which had very shallow rifling.

To ensure their new Type S bullet would perform, they enlarged its diameter to .323-in., and cut rifling to a .323-in. groove. This change in dimension, if unsafely confusing, had advantages:

The new Type S bullet took the rifling and stabilized very well, and the deeper rifling wore better. Gas sealing with the new bullet was better. In the Type '88 bullet, the seal was made by the base of the bullet enlarging into the grooves; the Type S bullet already fit them. As a result of the better bore seal, Type S rifle bores had much better life than the old Model '88s.

A few Model '88 rifles were re-bored to fire the new Type S ammunition; this proved unsafe because the Type S cartridge developed appreciably higher chamber pressure than the Type '88. Model '98 Mauser rifles made after 1904 were bored for the Type S ammunition, and most of the older ones were reworked to fire it. Unit armorers were issued kits to do the job as a part of their routine rifle maintenance.

The 8mm Mauser rifle and Type S ammunition became standard in the German armed forces in 1904. Then, when World War I grew to much larger proportions than anybody had planned for, old Model '88 rifles and Type '88 ammunition were used in large quantities. The Mauser '98s could fire the old Type '88 ammunition, and the pointed bullet of the Type S ammunition was enough identification to keep it from being used in Model '88 rifles. The use of the '88 ammo in World War I, and the destruction of many of the '88 rifles the Germans surrendered at the end of the World War I pretty well took the Model '88 rifle out of circulation.

The 8mm Mauser '98 rifle and Type S ammunition were still the standard of the German armed forces when they surrendered at the end of World War II. After World War II, the rifle and cartridge were used by many other countries, and they will still be found in limited military service.

And 80 years after the 1904 bore change, the names of 8mm Mauser rifles and cartridges are yet confused. Both types are still encountered: the Model 1888 rifle and its Type '88 ammunition with cylindrical, round-nosed bullets, and the Model 1898 Mauser rifle and its pointed bullet Type S ammunition.

The Model 1888 rifles and Type '88 ammunition are now antique collectors' items, and firing them is not recommended. Type '88 ammunition has not been commercially loaded for half a century, and it has never been safe to fire Type S ammunition in an '88 rifle.

On the other hand, the 8mm Mauser Model 1898 rifle and Type S ammunition are still common. The cartridge is now known by many names including 8mm Mauser, 7.92mm Mauser, 8x57 Mauser, 7.92x57 Mauser and others, and any of these are safe to shoot as long as they are marked as suitable for rifles — fur Gewehr. Mauser am-

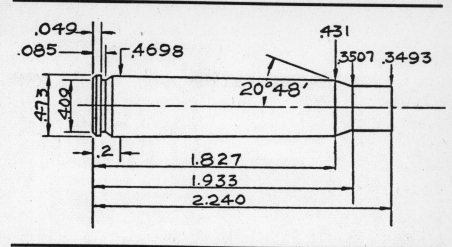

The 8mm Mauser basic case dimensions from the 5th edition of Frank C. Barnes' *Cartridges of the World.*

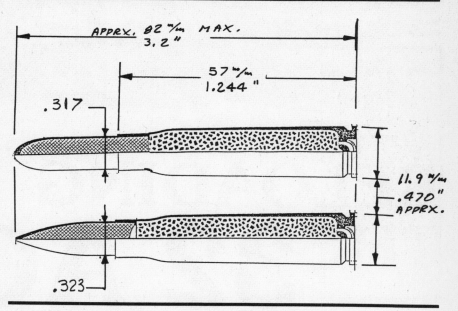

Basic major dimensions of the 8mm Mauser Type 1888 and Type S cartridges; the Type S the lower.

munition made and marked for use in machine guns — *fur MG* — is too hot to be fired safely in rifles.

Confusion aside, the 8mm Mauser cartridge became the basis for a century of arms and ammunition development. The Type '88 was the first centerfire, small bore, rimless, bottle-necked smokeless military cartridge adopted; today's 7.62mm NATO rifles and ammunition — used throughout the world — are direct descendents. Will that same convenient container last another 100 years? ●

Acknowledgement: Prime sources for this article are U.S. Army official and semi-official publications, *American Rifleman* and its predecessors, and the writings of Ludwig Olson and W. H. B. Smith. The work of William H. Woodin, Robert W. Faris, Peter T. Vogel and Erik Windisch published for the first time was their invaluable contribution to the story.

Powders and bullets used in test, fully charted, produced definite best choices.

RELOADING THE 32 ACP

by R.H. VANDENBURG, JR.

You go for accuracy, not punch, and it's fun.

NOT TOO long ago, I was shooting with a couple of friends when one, an inveterate gun trader, began commenting on his latest acquisitions. It wasn't until he said Walther PP that I really began to pay attention. Sensing my interest, he allowed the piece was "new in box" and that he had gotten a great deal. We both agreed he should

bring it along the next time we got together.

Sure enough, the next time we met, he presented me with a small black box. Inside was a target, an instruction manual, a cleaning rod, two magazines and a shiny new Walther PP pistol. It wasn't until then that I realized the caliber was 32 ACP rather

than the 380 I had hoped for. Anyway, after some soul-searching and the obligatory haggling, the Walther was mine. In the following months came factory ammo, components, much shooting and a few surprises.

Historically speaking, not a great deal need be said about the 32 ACP cartridge. It is a semi-rimmed, small capacity autoloading cartridge. Designed by John Browning and introduced in 1899, it has enjoyed wide popularity in Europe where it is called the 7.65mm Browning. At the same time, in the U.S., it was mildly popular up until the end of World War II, then sales fell dramatically. Used almost exclusively in pocket autos of blowback design, its relatively low pressure limits of about 15,000 psi coupled with a FMJ 71-grain bullet hardly inspired praise as a defensive, target or hunting choice.

Indeed, from World War II until recently there were few guns made in or imported into the U.S. for this caliber. Looking through offerings of 10 years ago, I uncovered about four models. The *1985 Gun Digest* lists 11 different models. There are probably more. Perhaps of even greater importance are the hordes of used Walther PPs imported into the U.S. in recent years as French and other law enforcement agencies replaced their sidearms. The result has been an interest in the small caliber. In fact where in pre-

vious years, the 32 ACP was nowhere to be found, the current RCBS reloading die popularity list shows the 32 in the top 20.

So with the increased interest in the caliber, and in handloading for it, we must take a fresh look. Perhaps the greatest thing to happen to the 32 lately has been the introduction of Winchester's Silvertip ammo. The hollowpoint 60-grain bullet leaves the muzzle at a reported 970 fps producing 125 foot pounds of muzzle energy. Federal, Remington and Winchester 71-grain MC ammo produce 905 fps and 129 fps respectively. Norma offers a 77-grain MC at 900 fps and 162 fpe, but I was unable to locate any for this test. In spite of the above figures, the Silvertip is infinitely superior to the others in stopping power with a Power Index Rating of 42 compared to the 71-grain rating of 32. That is not awe inspiring, but a definite improvement.

The gun, on the other hand, is a beauty with a surprisingly good fixed sight arrangement for so small a

piece. Barrel length is 3¾ inches. There are two safety systems: first, a hammer safety which is positioned between the hammer and frame and is only moved out of the way when the trigger is pulled back; second is a hammer drop/firing pin safety which, when activated while the hammer is cocked, interposes itself between the hammer and firing pin and drops the hammer. Release the device and the gun is ready for double-action firing again. Overall the safety systems are excellent.

With the hammer block safety system automatically in place, the PP can be carried with a round in the chamber and the firing pin safety off with relative security. To a lefthander like me, that's important.

On the negative side, an ambidextrous hammer drop feature would be nice, but the only real drawback on mine is a grooved trigger. This is OK for follow-up single-action shots, but it makes that all important first shot unpleasant. Not all model PPs have been so encumbered and mine won't be for long.

The target that accompanied my gun was a standard factory target with a slightly-to-the-right-of-center group measuring almost exactly 2 inches center to center, fired at 15 meters. This group was to become the standard by which I judged my efforts. I don't know if the target was fired by hand or from a machine rest or what brand of ammo was used, but it proved difficult to beat.

During the course of testing, Remington factory 71-grain MC ammo was used as were Winchester's 60-grain Silvertip hollowpoints. Federal and WRA headstamped brass were tried but all reported results used either Remington or Winchester. Four different bullets were handloaded: the discontinued Remington 71-grain, Sierra 71-grain, Hornady 71-grain, all metal cased and a 77-grain cast bullet from Lyman mould 311252. A Hornady SWC 90-grain bullet was also tested but, not designed for the 32 ACP, it did not perform well and is not included in the test results. Six powders considered suitable were tried: Bullseye, Red Dot, Unique, HP38, W231 and 700X. All tests were conducted at 15 meters.

My first efforts with the Walther were with factory ammo. The Remington ammo averaged 3.2 inches while the Winchester Silvertips did better at 2.375 inches.

Most of my efforts were devoted to handloads. I tried my components in a variety of combinations and varying powder charge weights. Some worked,

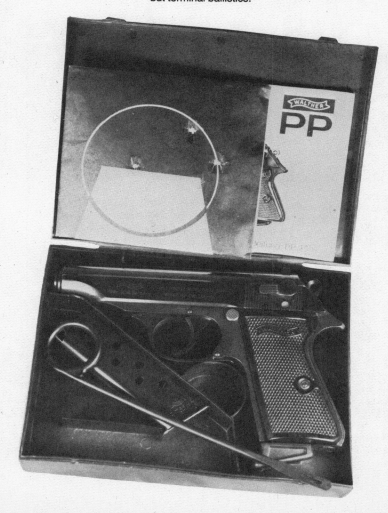

Author's Walther PP, in box, as purchased. In it the 32 ACP cartridge delivers everything but terminal ballistics.

some didn't. Promising loads were chronographed.

Many of the bugaboos often associated with small caliber reloading didn't show up. There were not bulged cases from firing ammo in a gun with an enlarged chamber or one lacking support in the feed ramp area. All the brass had adequate flash holes. The dies, from RCBS, performed perfectly. While there were no cannelures on the jacketed bullets, the cast bullets could be crimped with ease.

On the other hand, the brass did take a beating. In particular, the small rims became nicked and peened from repeated firings, making insertion into a shellholder difficult. A small file usually corrected the problem if it became severe. The brass could also be discarded, of course.

Factory cases varied considerably in weight, at least percentagewise. Caution should be exercised in changing case makes. Cases of different makes should not be mixed. Un-primed cases averaged in weight as follows:

R-P	36.3 grs.
W-W	42.0 grs.
Federal	44.0 grs.
WRA	44.9 grs.

Case lengths varied only slightly. Remington cases averaged .673-inch while W-W brass measured .670-inch. Remington factory ammo measured about .331-inch at the pressure ring ahead of the case web before firing. W-W Silvertips measured .333-inch.

Chart I

Group Size By Case/Bullet Combination

Case	Remington	Sierra	Hornady	Cast	Total
R-P	1.98	2.89	3.5	3.44	3.2
W-W	2.58	1.96	2.38	3.60	2.65

* Accuracy based on 5-shot groups at 15 meters

Cases tried in test: W-W, WRA, RP and Federal. Tests revealed that the PP likes some better than others.

Ammo with bullets used. Remington, Sierra, Hornady and cast bullet handloads; factory Silvertip. A careful test program found a number of useful loads.

Sample ammo with recovered bullets. Left to Right: Remington Sierra, Hornady, cast, Winchester Silvertip. Note that only the Silvertip showed any expansion.

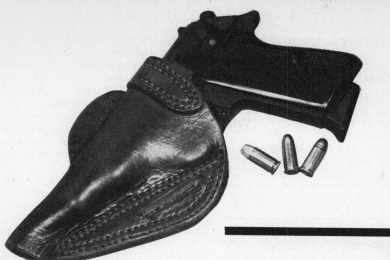

It's hard to beat the factory-loaded Winchester Silvertip in 32 ACP. The difference is, of course, in the bullet.

Writer's packing rig handles factory Silvertip, and both jacketed and cast handloads. The key is that the PP shoots the right loads very well.

Both brands measured, on average, .338-inch after firing. Even when primer or other pressure signs didn't appear severe, case ejection would become violent as loads approached their maximum. I always chose to back off a tenth of a grain or so when this happened.

It wasn't until I began to collect the data that I realized what I was really looking for. In most handloading efforts success is measured by the ability to improve on factory velocity and accuracy or at least improving on one while maintaining or approximating factory efforts on the other. An eye is always kept on both. That's not necessarily so with the 32 ACP. So long as velocity and the attendant pressure are high enough to insure cycling of the action and low enough to insure safety and minimize gun wear, velocity, per se, is largely irrelevant. At the velocities attainable, neither metal cased nor cast bullets are going to expand. And while increased velocity means increased energy, the round noses of the available bullets effectively negates much of the energy transfer. The situation is different with the Silvertip bullet, of course, but it is not available for reloading. At any rate, my goal became accuracy.

I began to chart the data first to insure the proper component mix and second to prevent a combination that looked good initially from swaying my findings and perhaps failing me later.

Chart I reflects the 15-yard accuracy average of multiple five-shot groups by bullet/case combinations. Winchester cases seem to be preferred overall and the Winchester case/

Reloading Data

Bullet	Powder	Charge (grain)	Case	Velocity	Accuracy*	Remarks
Remington 71 gr. MC	Bullseye	2.4	R-P	927	Fair	
		2.4	W-W	939	Poor	Max.
	Red Dot	2.0	R-P	775	Poor	Minimum Unreliable
		2.1	W-W	792	Poor	
		2.3	R-P	840	Very Good	
		2.3	W-W	852	Poor	
	Unique	2.4	R-P	803	Poor	Minimum Unreliable
		2.5	R-P	820	Very Good	Unreliable
		2.5	W-W	834	VeryGood	Unreliable
Sierra 71-gr. MC	Bullseye	2.3	W-W	875	Fair	
		2.4	R-P	905	Good	Near Max.
		2.4	W-W	916	Fair	Max. Heavy Recoil
	HP 38	2.4	W-W	825	Fair	
		2.5	W-W	841	Very Good	
	W231	2.4	W-W	849	Good	
		2.5	W-W	885	Very Good	Most Accurate Load
	700X	1.9	W-W	747	Very Good	Minimum
		1.9	R-P	740	Poor	
		2.0	R-P	820	Poor	
		2.0	W-W	832	Good	
		2.1	R-P	845	Poor	Approaching Max.
	Unique	2.5	W-W	855	Good	
		2.6	W-W	890	Average	Heavy Recoil
Hornady 71-gr. MC	Bullseye	2.3	R-P	868	Poor	Minimum
		2.4	R-P	928	Very Good	Best group this bullet
	HP38	2.4	R-P	829	Fair	
		2.5	R-P	848	Fair	
	W231	2.4	R-P	838	Poor	
		2.5	R-P	864	Poor	
		2.6	W-W	895	Very Good	Violent Ejection
	700X	1.9	R-P	786	Poor	Unreliable
		2.0	R-P	810	Good	
	Unique	2.5	R-P	823	Poor	Unreliable
		2.6	R-P	859	Poor	
		2.6	W-W	884	Average	Heavy ejection
Cast Lyman 311252	Bullseye	1.9	R-P	842	Poor	Erratic
		1.9	W-W	858	Poor	Erratic
		2.0	R-P	860	Fair	
		2.0	W-W	871	Fair	
	Red Dot	2.0	R-P	893	Poor	
		2.0	W-W	910	Poor	
	Unique	2.4	R-P	815	Poor	
		2.5	W-W	840	Poor	
	HP38	2.4	R-P	880	Very Good	Best cast load
		2.4	W-W	891	Good	
	W231	2.3	W-W	826	Good	
		2.3	R-P	820	Average	
	700X	2.0	W-W	900	Average	Approaching Max.
		2.0	R-P	885	Fair	

* Accuracy based on 5 shot groups at 15 meters:
Very Good—less than 1.75″; Good—1.75″ to 2.00″; Average—2.00″ to 2.50″; Fair—2.50″ to 3.00″; Poor—greater than 3.00″.

Chart II
Group Size By Bullet/Powder Combination

Case	Bullseye	Red Dot	Unique	HP38	W231	700X	Total
R-P	J 2.83	J 1.75	J 2.96	J 3.00	J 4.25	J 3.50	
	C 4.00	C 5.12	C 5.12	C 1.00	C 2.75	C 2.58	3.2
W-W	J 2.96	J 3.25	J 2.12	J 2.50	J 1.66	J 1.75	
	C 4.50	C 6.00	C 3.62	C 3.00	C 2.12	C 2.62	2.65
Total	J 2.88	J 2.80	J 2.48	J 2.75	J 2.71	J 2.80	
	C 4.25	C 5.56	C 4.38	C 2.00	C 2.44	C 2.63	—
Grand Total	3.19	4.03	2.90	2.50	2.62	2.71	—

J = Jacketed; C = Cast

Chart III
Group Size by Bullet/Powder Combination

Bullet	Bullseye	Red Dot	Unique	HP38	W231	700X	Total
Remington	3.16	2.5	1.19	—	—	—	2.28
Hornady	3.31	3.50	3.50	3.00	3.42	3.25	3.32
Sierra	2.42	—	2.25	2.50	1.88	1.75	2.29
Cast	4.25	5.56	4.38	2.00	2.44	2.63	3.52
Total	2.88	2.50	2.48	2.75	2.71	2.80	—
	C 4.25	5.56	4.38	2.00	2.44	2.63	—
	T 3.19	4.03	2.90	2.50	2.62	2.71	—

J = Jacketed; C = Cast

Chart IV
Group Size by W-W Case, Sierra Bullet/Powder Combination

Bullet	Bullseye	Red Dot	Unique	HP38	W231	700X
W-W/Sierra	2.69	—	2.25	2.50	1.63	1.75

Sierra bullet combination performed best of all. The Remington case/Remington bullet combination also performed well, but, as noted, the Remington bullet is no longer available.

Chart II reflects the results of the various powders used by case brand. Average group sizes are given for jacketed bullets (J) and cast bullets (C). Totals are provided, by powder type, for jacketed bullets (C). Totals are provided, by powder type, for jacketed bullets, cast bullets and overall. Results are less obvious than in Chart I. Bullseye, Red Dot and Unique had overall averages behind the results of HP38, W231 and 700X. This was due more to their poor showing with cast bullets than their jacketed bullet performance, although both Red Dot and Unique provide somewhat misleading jacketed results. A closer look, as Chart III will indicate, shows Red Dot's best performance coming with the discontinued Remington bullet. And Unique, despite its occasional superb performance, was the most errat-

ic powder of the lot. While there was never a gun related failure during the entire series, i.e. a failure to feed, there were a few failures to eject. Over 50 percent of these were encountered when using Unique.

For the three remaining powders results are close with W231 providing the best jacketed bullet performance, and when paired with W-W cases, it provided some astounding results. HP38 had an even better overall showing due to its cast bullet performance.

In Chart III powders are paired with the various bullets used in the tests. Again, Sierra bullets got the nod, due to the discontinuance of the Remington with which the Sierra was virtually tied for overall performance. Remember it beat out the Remington offering in Chart I by a slight margin. Picking a powder is still unclear, however.

It wasn't until I prepared this chart that I realized Red Dot had received less testing than the other powders.

However, if it followed the path of Bullseye and Unique, the other bullets would only have served to enlarge its jacketed bullet average. Any anyway, it couldn't touch the results of W231 and 700X with the Sierra bullet.

Still having no clear-cut powder selection, I decided to compare the Winchester case/Sierra bullet combination with the various powders. See Chart IV. And there it is.

So my component selection was complete: WW cases, W231 powder and Sierra bullets. It was also comforting to note that the very smallest groups—1 inch—fired in the entire series were also fired with this combination. One or two other combinations matched it but couldn't match the consistency or multiple group average of this combination. It should also be noted that some of the measurements were very close. A different combination might be a winner in another gun.

Then, the recap. For jacketed bullet use, a combination of WW cases, W231 powder, Sierra bullets and CCI 500 primers. For cast bullet shooting I would consider HP38 remembering that this powder achieved its excellent reuslts only in Remington cases. W231 was next overall with cast bullets and performed even better than HP38 when used with WW cases. While it would be a simple matter to maintain two powders, two bullets and two cases, it would be even simpler to reduce the stock to one case, one powder and one or two bullets. Not enough to worry about would be lost in the effort.

So where does all this take us? We've still got a pocket auto in 32 ACP. True, but the load development has demonstrated that the gun can be very accurate. It is not a target arm or a hunting gun but certainly suitable for small game at close range especially with the Winchester Silvertip bullets. I managed to take several grouse during the past season with this combination. More to the point, it is accurate enough to be fun to shoot. Reloading costs are minimal.

While no one I know would recommend the 32 as a defensive choice, I'm not about to stand in front of one when it goes off. If you have something bigger and can shoot it, so much the better. If the 32 is all you have, then reload and practice, reload and practice until you can hit what you aim at, every time. If you feel the need to prepare for more serious matters, stuff your 32 with Silvertips—and remember what you learned in practice. It is really a matter of substituting skill for stopping power. ●

Loading for the GONE BUT NOT FORGOTTEN

by SAM FADALA

AMERICAN SHOOTERS faithfully cling to a group of cartridges long ago superceded by modern rounds. These gone-but-not-forgotten numbers are seldom factory-chambered in today's guns. Some are still factory-loaded. Others are not. The baker's dozen gone-but-not-forgotten discussed here are still around for at least three reasons: they still work well for certain tasks; they may work best of all in some shooting situations; and there are still good rifles around chambered for these cartridges.

Guns have the good trait of lasting a very long time when well-treated. Therefore you can pick up a fine old piece past retirement age, but not

ready to hang on the wall. It could be, however, chambered for one of those cartridges either obsolete or standing by the boneyard waiting for admission. Sure, factory ammo is often still available for guns not built for years and years, but handloading makes a lot of sense with many old-timers.

A few tips for reloaders of gone-but-not-forgotten rounds are in order before approaching the loading bench. First, be sure of your round. Some of those oldies bore headstamps that could be confusing. I have two cartridges in hand right now which fit this category. Both say 25-20 on the headstamp, but one is much longer than the other. An old catalog will show the longer round as the 25-20 Central

Some very fine old rifles are still in use because reloaders can make ammo for gone-but-not-forgotten calibers.

Fire or 25-20 Single Shot. Sometimes the shorter 25-20 goes under the title of 25-20 Marlin. In one catalog, from the Ideal Manufacturing Company of New Haven, the longer 25-20 round shows "Adapted to Single Shot Rifles" under it, while the shorter 25-20 reads "Adapted to Repeating Rifles."

Second, be sure that the old cases, if indeed they are vintage, are in good order, not green with the fatigue of time and use showing on them, and also not of the balloon-head type, which was an older cartridge design with less metal in the head area. Third, be sure that the firearm is in safe working order. And fourth, forget loading "full throttle." Such loads are not necessary, and the older firearm deserves deference—don't strain it. As I say, these loads will get the job done, be that task tin can rolling for enjoyment or putting game in the pot.

The 218 Bee

Its near twin, the 22 Hornet, has survived into modern times, but as this is written, the 218 Bee is chambered in no modern rifle. (*Ahem. Kimber has lately cataloged both 218 Bee and 25-20 in single-shot bolt-action Model 82 rifles. KW*) Winchester has loads with a 46-grain hollowpoint bullet at an advertised 2760 fps MV. The 218 Bee was a bit ahead of its smaller and more successful 22 Hornet cousin, especially with a 55-grain bullet. In my own 22 Hornet handloads, velocities in the 2500 to 2600 fps range using a 55-grain bullet were the rule, while 55-grain bullets in the 218 Bee gained as high as 2800 fps.

Originally, the 218 Bee appeared in the Model 65 Winchester, a lever action. Some 65s produced fine accuracy, with three-shot groups going in the 1-inch range at 100 yards from the bench. However, the 218 was considered less accurate than the Hornet by many shooters. Winchester chambered it in their Model 43 bolt-action rifle anyway and this 1938-style necked-down 25-20 performed quite well in these.

Load (Cast Bullet)

A cast bullet load makes sense in the 218 Bee, for accuracy is good and shooting economy high with these homecast projectiles. This load gives 22 Long Rifle velocity with 22 WRF punch, super for small game and sufficient for varmints at close range.

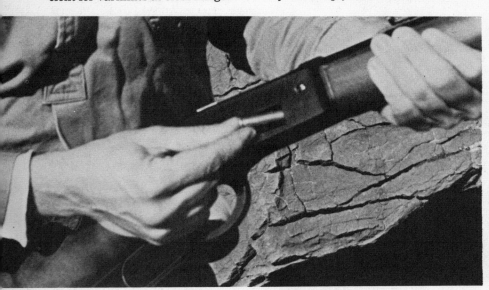

There is a special joy in shooting old-timers, whether they are risen from the world of obsolesence or are more than 100 years old but have never been completely abandoned.

Bullet: 45-grain/Alloy No. 2/
Lyman No. 225415
Powder: 3.0 grains of Red Dot
MV: 1300 fps

Load (Jacketed Bullet)

Every major bulletmaker offers projectiles suited to the 218 Bee. The load shown here is for the 55-grain jacketed bullet, and it delivers good accuracy and varmint hunting authority out to 200 yards or a shade more. Don't load pointed bullets in tubular magazines.

Bullet: 55-grain jacketed
Powder: 14.0 grains of H-4198
MV: 2700 fps

The 219 Zipper

The 219 Zipper was a good idea at the time—the Zipper had plenty of poop to pop a woodchuck at 300 yards. But it went the way of the dodo and other such birds and by 1961 no rifle in America was chambered for this hotshot 22. In 1962 Winchester gave up on the ammo and Remington did likewise soon after. Based originally on a 25-35 Winchester necked down to 22 caliber, the Zipper was available in 1937 in Winchester's Model 64, a Model 94 dolled up a bit, the Zipper 64 having a 26-inch barrel and a neat bolt-mounted peep sight, the 98A.

The Zipper was a 300-yard cartridge chambered in a 200-yard rifle. And later chambering in the excellent Marlin 336 did not alter the fact by much, though this rifle would wear a scope centered over the bore. Accuracy was simply not there in either rifle.

Of course, when the rimmed Zipper was fitted in a single shot or a good bolt-action rifle, it proved the fact that accuracy depends mostly on good bullets out of good barrels and the little cartridge's bullets chewed the X-ring out. Ballistics listed by Winchester in 1939 show a 46-grain bullet at 3420 fps and a 56-grain bullet at 3100. Later, the last listed ballistics would give a 56-gr. bullet 3110 fps MV.

As with so many cartridges, the Zipper's passing was greeted with die-hard reloading, and to this day Zipper fans with old 64s, 336s and custom rifles shoot Zipper ammo. Naturally, bullets are not problem. All of the major missile makers turn out 22-caliber bullets that fit this round, and cases can be formed from 25-35 Winchester brass, even 30-30 Winchester brass, using caseforming dies and cutoff dies. The 222 Remington, that little man resembling a miniature 30-06, made more sense than the Zipper, all right, but this gone-but-not-forgotten oldie hangs on in the shadows and is even brought out into the sunshine from time to time in custom rifles and pretty hot handloads. Our handloads are utilitarian in nature, however.

Load (Cast Bullet)

Loaded this way, the 219 Zipper will drop small game with head shots, and it will put any wild turkey in the woods out of action with one shot. Accuracy is good, hunting-wise, in the Model 64, in which the load was tested, and 50-yard groups of 1½ inches for three shots were common.

Bullet: 54-grain/Alloy No. 2/
Lyman No. 225462
Powder: 21.0 grains of IMR-4198
MV: 1800 fps

Load (Jacketed Bullet)

Don't load pointed bullets in tubular magazines.

Bullet: 55-grain jacketed
Powder: 26.0 grains of IMR-3031
MV: 3100 fps

The 22 Savage Hi-Power

You and I may not thrill and clap hands in delight at the thought of a 70-grain .228-inch bullet zapping forth from the muzzle at a scintillating 2800 fps; however, plenty of shooters around 1912 did, because the Savage 22 Hi-Power was on the scene in the excellent Model 99 lever-action rifle. The famous Charles Newton had developed the round, which was based, once again, on a 25-35 necked down. In a 1939 advertisement, the 22 Savage Hi-Power was said to be, "Accurate at long range. The ideal cartridge for use on small and medium game, from woodchucks to wolves."

Some thought it just right for deer, too, but it did not prove to be all that superior on game larger than the bigger varmints, at least not with the 70-grain bullets available at the time. Naturally, the round was carried onto the Dark Continent where reports of the 22 Savage Hi-Power's proficiency on big game, even lions, germinated, bloomed and were well-seeded back in the U.S.A. Europe liked the round. It was called the 5.6x52R over there, and it was chambered up in some very nice rifles, bolt actions and even doub-leguns.

Although Canada's C.I.L. offered 22 Savage ammo for a very long time, even that source has dried up. Today, no ammo company churns out 22 Savage Hi-Power fodder on our shores, but look overseas, 22 Savage fans, and you will see RWS factory-loading a 71-grain bullet, an SP, just for you. Also, RWS offers its excellent brass in 22 Savage Hi-Power, and the company also has a reloader's softpoint bullet in 71-grain weight, .228-inch, and the same in full metal jacket. So the 22 Savage fan can buy ammo (from Old Western Scrounger, 12924 Highway A-12, Montague, CA 96064.) And Hornady makes a fine 70-grain .227-inch bullet for 22 Hi-Power fans. The round is gone, but hardly forgotten.

Load (Cast Bullet)
Bullet: 78-grain/Alloy No. 2/
    Lyman No. 22835
Powder: 9.0 grains of 2400 rifle
    powder
MV: 1600 fps

Load (Jacketed Bullet)
Bullet: Hornady, .227-inch, 70-
    grain softpoint
Powder: 26.5 grains of IMR-3031
MV: 3000 fps

The 25-20 WCF

Joyfully we plinked and plunked with the 25-20. Recoil was nil and accuracy plenty for modest-range work on informal targets and small game. I had a Marlin Model 27, and she'd shuck shells faster than a popcorn machine through an action smoother than porcelain. My *amigo* had the Remington pump, Model 25. One day when I left my hat at home and got too much sun, I traded the Marlin for a rifle which had more pizazz and a lot less class. The 25-20 was no more than a 32-20 necked down to accept 25-caliber bullets. It was good for small game, though certainly not necessary in most instances, and it would put a tom turkey on your meat post faster than a rattler's strike. On javelina, it was fine if the hunter got close and placed his shot. And, of course, it was touted for deer, but never was the little charmer meant to crop much venison.

J.R. Mattern, in his 1926 classic *Handloading Ammunition* (available through Wolfe Publishing Company) said, "This highly interesting little cartridge can be loaded to give velocities of 2200 fps for woodchuck, jackrabbit and waterfowl [remember, this

was in the 1920s] shooting, and from that down to velocity of only about 600 fps for indoor work or killing trapped game." (p. 280)

The 25-20 showed up in the 1890s and it fitted the Model 92 Winchester's short action just right. It was also chambered in the Model 65, another lever-action Winchester, as well as the Marlin and Remington named above, a Savage 219 single shot, a Savage bolt action and other rifles.

You can't call the 25-20 obsolete, but it qualifies as a goner. Winchester and Remington load the round today with an 86-grain bullet at 1460 fps MV, and data I have from a 1932 source shows the 25-20 with an 86-grain bullet at 1380 fps MV, an 86-grain bullet at 1730 fps MV and a 60-grain bullet at 2200. Since factory loads are available, cases are no problem, and Hornady makes a .257-inch flat-point bullet in 60 grains weight for the 25-20. With a cast bullet the 25-20 is still a turkey-taker. With the jacketed bullet it will put down game up to javelina size.

Watch out for very old brass cases, such as this loaded round. To reload this old one might be unwise. Its primer tells us it was loaded many decades back.

Load (Cast Bullet)
Bullet: 88-grains/Alloy No. 2/
    Lyman No. 257312
Powder: 5.0 grains of Unique rifle
MV: 1500 fps

Load (Jacketed Bullet)
Don't load pointed bullets in tubular magazines.

Bullet: Hornady, .257-inch, 60-
    grain
Powder: 12.0 grains of IMR-4227
MV: 2100 fps

The 25-35 Winchester

No rifles have been chambered for this old-timer for a few decades, but

the 25-35 did make history. It was introduced in 1895 in the Model 1894 Winchester. Its 117-grain bullet had pretty good sectional density and hunters willing to hunt and get close put plenty of venison on the table with 25-35s. In fact, what's said to be the largest grizzly ever to roam the vast reaches of Utah was dropped with a 25-35 in the hands of trapper Frank Clark. The bear was called Old Ephraim, and he was said to be almost 10 feet tall with a weight of about 1100 pounds. And the skull resides in Smithsonian. So reads a plaque in honor of bear and man, this monument resting near Logan, Utah to this day.

Mild report and recoil made the 25-35 easy to hit with, but it did not make the hit—A-bomb proportion—of the 30-30 and so it grew dimmer and dimmer and its light almost went out. However, it is loaded today with a 117-grain bullet at a listed 2230 fps MV. In 1932 the same bullet was rated at 2115 fps MV. Hornady makes a 117-grain round-nose softpoint bullet for the 25-35, too. Of course, cases are available from Winchester. My own experience with the 25-35 comes through a rifle, Model 94, 26-inch barrel and a carbine that looks as if it were used to hoe gardens in Montana from whence it came. The 25-35 is accurate in the 94, plenty so for hunting.

Load (Cast Bullet)
Bullet: 110-grains/Alloy No. 2/
    Lyman No. 257231
Powder: 8.0 grains of IMR-4227
    rifle powder
MV: 1200 fps

Load (Jacketed Bullet)
Don't load pointed bullets in tubular magazines.

Bullet: Hornady 117-grain RN
Powder: 26.0 grains of H-4895
MV: 2125 fps

The 303 Savage

This round has had no play for a very long time, and it's certainly a goner in terms of factory-chambered rifles. The 303 Savage came out in 1895, a development of Savage, and it was chambered in the fine Savage 1899 rifle. Although the rotary magazine allowed for pointed projectiles, Savage ammo was loaded with blunt-nosed missiles only. Later on, the fine 300 Savage round, which was ballistically a mini-30-06 and still is, finished off the 303 for good.

But the round is still loaded today by Winchester, and with a 190-grain bullet. It was that 190-grain bullet which made the reputation of the 303 Savage. Many considered it much better than the 30-30. In fact, it's a near twin to the 30-30, and I handload my own 30-30 with those round nose 190-grain bullets at 303 Savage velocities. Some experts claimed the 303 was always a shooter of .308-inch bullets and that Savage's claim to .311-inch bullets was unfounded. This is false. I have pulled old-time 303 Savage ammo and indeed the bullets did mike out at .311-inch, not .308-inch. Today, however, the 190-grain Silvertip used in the 303 Savage is .308-inch diameter.

Load (Cast Bullet)
Bullet: 169-grain/Alloy No. 2/ Lyman No. 311291
Powder: 37.0 grains of W748
MV: 2350 fps

Load (Jacketed Bullet)
Bullet: Any 150-grain .308-inch modern bullet
Powder: 36.0 grains of IMR-4320
MV: 2444 fps

The 32-20 WCF

"It used to be the most popular cartridge in existence," said Mattern on

This little 25-20 round is small even when compared with the modest-sized 25-85 Winchester round. It's still loaded, but not chambered in any modern rifle.

My own Model 1899 303 Savage, with a personal handload, manages over 2500 fps MV using a pointed 150-grain bullet. I feel it's up to deer-sized game at 200 yards and even beyond with that handload. Factory data shows the bullet at 1940 fps MV today. The figure was generally quoted as a flat 2000 fps MV in the past. The 303 is a good cast bullet shooter. And with handloads or factory fodder it will drop big game at modest ranges. William T. Hornady, the naturalist, used the 303 Savage for his museum collections, including the grizzly bear.

page 296 of his aforementioned text on handloading. While that may be debatable, I would personally say that I've known no better wild turkey round than the 32-20, its bullet doing the job neatly, but without undue loss of meat. In fact, I've used the 32-20 on small game with success. Head shots preferred, of course, but if the chest is the target, not to worry. The bullet from a factory load will not devastate the edibles. My 32-20 usage has been within a 30- to 60-yard radius, I'd guess, and the round does shine there, up close, for it's not exactly a Swift in

trajectory.

The 32-20 showed up in 1882, chambered in the Model 73 Winchester and also in a host of other rifles, as well as handguns, for this was a round with two *personas,* slipping into rifle or handgun chamber, with mild handgun loads being OK for either, but of course rifle loads could be too hot for some handguns. A deer round? Winchester said so for a time. And without a doubt, the 32-20 tipped over a venison steak or two in its time. Its time? Although the 32-20 was chambered in the Model 53 lever-action Winchester (Model 92 action actually), the neat Model 25 Remington pumpgun, that fine Model 27 Marlin pump, as well as the bolt-action Savage 23C, it's been a long time since a rifle was chambered in this caliber. However, quite recently Thompson/Center saw reason to offer a Contender barrel in 32-20. I got one as soon as possible.

Winchester and Remington still load the 32-20, 100-grain jacketed softpoint bullet or lead, about 1210 fps MV. These are good loads for most 32-20 work and they come highly recommended. The handloader must be careful of obtaining a correct 32-20 bullet in jacketed style, and he must also watch out for using loads intended for rifle in the handgun. All in all, I like cast bullet loads in the 32-20, though I did have some good 100-grain Remington softpoint 32-20 bullets which I used in a Model 23C Savage in superb condition, the load being 14.0 grains of IMR-4227 powder for about 1900 fps MV.

Load (Cast Bullet for rifle only)
Bullet: 115-grain/Alloy No. 2/Lyman No. 3118
Powder: 9.5 grains of IMR-4227
MV: 1400 fps (rifle only)

32-40 Winchester

This blackpowder 1884 round gained much prominence as a high-accuracy cartridge. It used a 165-grain bullet with 40 grains of Fg blackpowder, hence its 32-40 name, 32 for caliber, 40 for powder charge. No rifle has been made for this one in about a half-century, except for the Winchester John Wayne Commemorative, a Model 94, complete with collector 32-40 ammo as well as rifle. Today, no ammo is being offered by the factory. And yet this favorite round of Harry Pope continues to stir seemingly dead coals which, now and then, give off heat of interest. In the 1930s, a 32-40 Semi-smokeless load gave the 165-grain bullet a MV of 1450 fps. At the same time, a smokeless powder load pushed the same bullet at 2065 fps—here is 30-30 power, or almost so.

Today, the only 32-40 shooting going on is in the rifles of yesteryear which have survived time's rusty breath. Finding jacketed bullets of .320-inch diameter is no easy trick and besides, some of the older rifles should not be used with hotter smokeless powder/jacketed bullet feedings. Should a 32-40 fan have a rifle in good condition, gunsmith-checked, and made for smokeless powder shooting, 27.0 grains of IMR-3031 will give the 165-grain bullet about 1925 fps MV. But the following cast bullet load is probably today's shooter's best bet.

Load (Cast Bullet)
Bullet: 184 grains/Alloy No. 2/ Lyman No. 321297
Powder: 8.0 grains of Unique
MV: 1225 fps

The 348 Winchester

This round was offered in one rifle and one only its entire life, that rifle being the Model 71 Winchester lever action, a firearm which was supposed to post-date the Model 70, but which in fact appeared in 1936 ahead of the 70. The 71 was an updated 1886 Winchester. The 348 was an updated 33 Winchester round. Born in '36, the rifle was scrapped in 1958. Nonetheless, the round and rifle both receive plenty of respect among hardy woods hunters to this day. Rugged as an iron girder, the reliable 71 could take hard use and go on functioning in workman-like fashion, and many elk hunters swore that nothing put a big bull down faster and more permanently than the 348 round at timberland distances. Browning has this year re-created the Model 71 and in 348, in fact.

Today, Winchester loads a 200-grain Silvertip bullet for the 348 round. It leaves the muzzle at about 2520 fps. Two good bullets I have handloaded in the 348 include the Hornady 200-grain and the 250-grain Barnes. Winchester offers unprimed brass for the reloader as well as the good factory load. Forget cast bullets here. The 348 was made to do a job, that job being the knockout of big game at modest ranges. Francis Sell spoke highly of the cartridge and its hunting accuracy out of the Model 71, as did many other well-known hunter/writers of its day, and using the loads below, the 348 in its Model 71 rifle will take on anything this continent has to offer if the ranges are not too great.

The 25-35 cartridge, right, compared with the 30-06, is still factory-loaded, but no modern rifle is chambered for it. The 25-35 was a very early smokeless sporting round.

The 22 Hi-Power is still loaded (by RWS of Germany), but very hard to locate. It can be loaded today with a Hornady 70-grain soft-point. The 30-06 is at right.

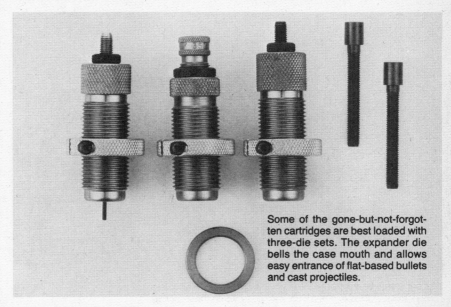

Some of the gone-but-not-forgotten cartridges are best loaded with three-die sets. The expander die bells the case mouth and allows easy entrance of flat-based bullets and cast projectiles.

Load (Jacketed Bullets)
Bullet: Hornady 200-grain SP
Powder: 63.0 grains of IMR-4350
MV: 2564 fps

Bullet: Barnes 250-grain SP
Powder: 49.0 grains of IMR-4064
MV: 2150 fps

The 38-40 Winchester

Old-time literature is replete with 38-40 talk. One hunter explained that if you simply had to have plenty of punch, why go ahead and buy a 30-30, but as for him, his 38-40 was plenty. In 1874 this round was born. In the Model 73 Winchester, it was well-received. The 38-40 also saw chambering in a great number of other rifles, such as the Remington 14½ slide action, Winchester Model 92, Marlin '94 and others, and in handguns. The round has, on the one hand, been gone for 50 years—that is, no rifles have been chambered in 38-40 for about that long. And yet it lives on all the same. Winchester loads a 180-grain bullet at 1160 fps MV today. But that .401-inch bullet is not to be found on the handloader's shelf. Also, there are many very old rifles in 38-40. The shooter simply must have his rifle checked out before loading for it.

Load (Cast Bullet)
  Bullet: 170-grain/Alloy No. 2/
    Lyman No. 40188 (sized to
    .400-inch)
  Powder: 10.0 grains of Unique
    MV: 1500 fps

Load (Cast Bullet)
  Bullet: 269 grains/Alloy No. 2/
    Lyman No. 375296
  Powder: 7.0 grains of 700X
    MV: 1000 fps

Load (Cast Bullet)
  Bullet: 220-grain/Alloy No. 2/
    Lyman No. 429434
  Powder: 9.0 grains of Unique
    MV: 1250 fps

The 38-55 Winchester

This one made a name for itself in the Model 94 rifle introduced in 1894. The round itself was extant in some form as early as 1884, however. It was so good that it was essentially copied in modern times by Winchester. The 375 Winchester is much like the old 38-55, though the two are not interchangeable. Winchester still loads a 255-grain bullet at 1320 fps MV for 38-55 fans, though no rifles have been chambered for this one since knickers were in vogue (except for the Winchester M94 "Chief Crazy Horse" Commemorative). This factory load is a good one for the older rifles. Remember that the 38-55 was chambered

The 44-40 Winchester

Zombies are mythical creatures which are supposed to be both alive and dead at the same time. That, more or less, describes the interesting 44-40. Not that long ago, chamberings in 44-40 were more rare than downpours on the Sahara. However, the 44-40 has made a comeback, especially in a host of replica rifles, as well as revolvers. The 44-40 showed up in 1873 and was listed in the Winchester '73 for a long while. It was also offered in many a handgun, thereby giving a shooter one ammo interchangeable in long or short arm.

In the Remington 14½, the 44-40 made a good close-range showing as a deer rifle caliber. In the Winchester

The 405 Winchester

Moribund is probably the best word for this old-timer. But though the round is gone, it is not forgotten. The 405 was, perhaps, the most powerful of the rimmed numbers to chamber up in fast-action lever rifles of its day. Born in 1904 for the 1895 Winchester rifle, the round was obsolete by 1936 and it's not loaded today. But it was a good one for up-close big game hunting. Teddy Roosevelt used it in Africa and liked it. And surely the 405 was ample for anything on this continent. Just in case the reader has an 1895 Winchester in good shape and in 405-caliber, here are a couple of loads.

Load (Cast Bullet)
  Bullet: 290-grain/Alloy No. 2/
    Lyman No. 412263
  Powder: 40.0 grains of IMR-3031
    MV: 1500 fps

Load (Jacketed Bullet)
  Bullet: .412-inch size—if they can
    be located
  Powder: 55 grains of IMR-4895
    MV: 2200 fps

Epilogue

Do we need these oldies but goodies any longer? No. I suppose not. In each case, there's a modern round to do the work of the gone-but-not-forgotten cartridge. For example, I praised the 32-20 as a great turkey-taker. I think it is. But a down-loaded 30-30 will perform just like a 32-20 any day. The 348 Winchester was a dazzler in the timber but the 358 Norma just has to be better yet. The 25-20 is a joy to shoot, and it will do considerable work from small game up to javelina-sized huntables, but other rounds have taken its place.

And yet, it's the "not-forgotten" aspect of these rounds which keeps them alive after their time. It is also the good, shootable, well-designed and long-lived rifles chambered in these long-ago cartridges which insist that we not abandon them totally. Therefore, the factories continue to offer many of these old-timers, and reloaders handcraft fodder to broaden the application of the old rounds, or to make ammo when the companies finally do cease manufacture. Therefore we have among us a host of cartridges born oftentimes in the last century, but bound to be around in the next. ●

While it is true that bullets for the gone-but-not-forgotten are not always easy to locate, it is a very rare case when these bullets cannot be homecast from a mould. Many good moulds, both custom made and commercial, are available today.

into blackpowder rifles, meaning it was around prior to nickel steel.

Yes, one can find jacketed bullets for the 38-55, but the showing here is for a cast bullet only. There are simply too many tired rifles around to risk hot loads. However, if a reader does own a smokeless powder 38-55, he may find valuable loading data in the older manuals. Then a jacketed bullet can be pushed away at fairly decent velocities for a close-range punch that will put any buck in the freezer with one well-placed shot.

Model 92, it was equally successful as a cartridge for medium-sized game, as it was in Marlin's '94 rifle. In fact, the 44-40 was a pretty good round for the handloader when he had a topnotch rifle of high quality and a supply of .427-inch jacketed bullets. He could push these along at a bit over 2000 fps MV. Today, Winchester and Remington offer loads with a 200-grain bullet at about 1190 fps MV. The handloader may not find .427-inch jacketed bullets for his 44-40 rifle, but he can use the following cast bullet and load.

The mechanical powder measure is very useful, but dippers have always done the job in . . .

Lee's Loads

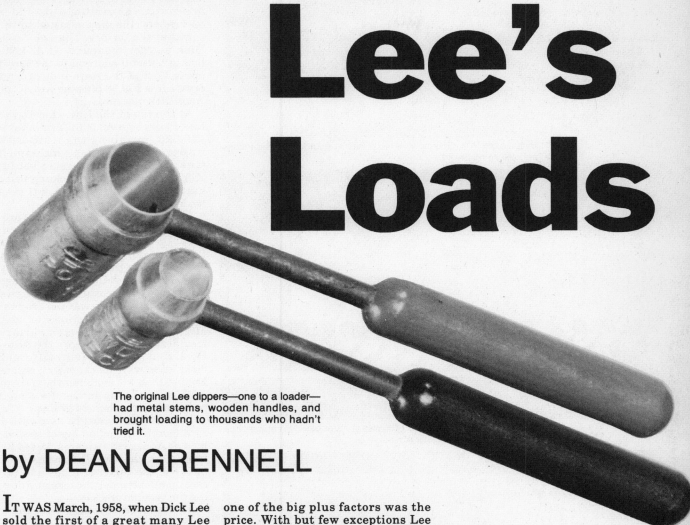

The original Lee dippers—one to a loader—had metal stems, wooden handles, and brought loading to thousands who hadn't tried it.

by DEAN GRENNELL

IT WAS March, 1958, when Dick Lee sold the first of a great many Lee Loader kits. In the beginning, Lee Loaders were for use with shotshells, in 12-gauge, and he sold about 1500 kits in the first year of operation. By that time, they'd added the 20-gauge and 16-gauge, and continued another 12 months, racking up sales of comfortably more than twice that of the first year and so it went.

As time went on, Lee added a number of new products and continues to do so. There were Lee Loaders for bottleneck rifle cartridges, followed by kits for handgun calibers. Public response to the handgun kits was beyond all expectation, with several of the handgun kits outselling the rifle numbers.

Quite apart from the fact that the Lee kits were simple to use, accompanied by clear instructions and capable of producing excellent ammunition,

one of the big plus factors was the price. With but few exceptions Lee Loaders carried a retail price of $9.95, raised to $9.98 in 1971. The current catalog quotes a price of $16.98 for any of the 60 or so different kits for rifle and handgun calibers. Lee Loaders for shotshells are no longer listed, but there's the Load-All Junior, at the same $16.98 price, capable of doing anything the kit could, better and more easily. It is offered only in 12-gauge but the Lee Load-All, at $42.98, can be had in a choice of 12-, 16- or 20-gauge.

If you prefer to work a lever, rather than tapping with a mallet, Lee has a variety of presses that accept conventional 7/8-14 loading dies and the so-called universal shellholders. If you already have your dies and shellholder, the 2001 challenger press retails at just $39.98 or, if that's too steep, there's the new Lee hand press

for only $29.98 with complete kits available that include dies, powder measure, shellholder, load data, powder funnel, ram prime tool, instructions and a tube of case lubricant. The kits start at $44.98 for the two-die rifle sets in the hand press; $59.98 with the 2001 Challenger; $54.98 for three-die carbide pistol kits with the hand press and $69.98 for the same with the Challenger. If you get the set with the carbide dies, the case lube is not supplied, not being required for use with carbide dies.

That is by no means all. There is the unique three-station Lee turret press, in a choice of three configurations and price levels. At $65.98, the basic turret press comes with one turret and the double-headed primer arm that reverses to change between

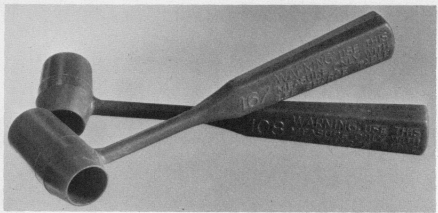

By the early '70s, dippers were red plastic, graduated in cubic inches, and still doing the job.

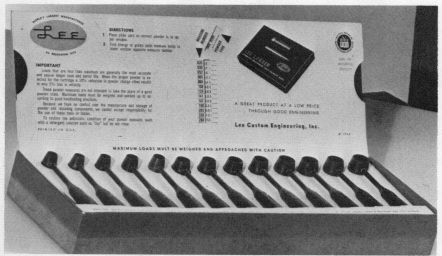

A Lee measure kit, circa late '60s, was still graduated in cubic inches, offered 13 dippers in black plastic.

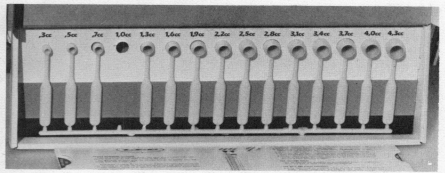

Today's Lee kit has 15 yellow plastic dippers, graduated in cubic centimeters.

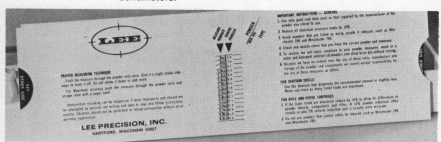

This slide table will provide a very wide range indeed of loads, powder by powder, all dipped.

small and large primers. The handle reverses for right- or left-hand use. The Auto-Index accessory, ordered with the press, brings the price to $79.98 or it's $30 by itself and will fit any Lee turret press. As before, kits are available with the Auto-Index feature and the dies adjusted in the turret at the factory. The Lee Auto-Disk powder measure, at $24.98, makes a useful addition to the turret press. Cost of the Auto-Index turret press kit is $99.98 plus the cost of the Auto-Disk measure.

At the top of the line, there's the Lee Progressive 1000 and that's $204.98, including the Auto-Disk measure. All of the items included, if purchased separately, would list for $229.92, making the package price quite attractive. An optional case feeder is $25.

All of this equipment, from the prototype 12-gauge Lee Loader of March, 1958, up through and including the Lee progressive 1000, have at least one important trait in common: they operate fixed, volume-type powder measures. The measures come in two basic formats. There was the original dipper, still in production and use, after having gone through various modifications. Then there's the Auto-Disk that employs four different disks, each with six chambers, with a Double-Disk kit enabling the user to stack one disk atop another for charge weights greater than 24 grains.

The Auto-Disk must be used with a case mouth expanding die of specialized design, made and marketed by Lee. In use, the Auto-Disk is installed in one of the turret stations and the case mouth actuates the measure during the regular press cycle.

As noted, the dippers have been modified from time to time. Originally, they carried numbers such as 12 or 10M. Then the designations were changed to decimal fractions of one cubic inch. Currently, they are designated according to the volume in cubic centimeters (cc).

When you buy a Lee Loader kit or set of dies for use with the Lee turret press, you get one dipper and the accompanying load data sheet is set up for use with that particular size of dipper.

Let's look at an example, to see how the system works. The Lee Loader kit for the 300 Winchester Magnum comes with a 4.3cc powder measure and the load data card covers seven ranges of bullet weights, from 130-140 grains up to 210-220 grains. For the 130-140-grain weight, they list but one powder: Hodgdon H4895, noting that the 4.3cc measure dispenses

59.0 grains of it for an approximate velocity of 2800 fps.

Moving on to the 140-150-grain weight, they list H4895 again, still at 59.0 grains, with 2750 fps and also list Hodgdon H414 at 65.1 grains for 2970 fps.

Next up the line is the 150-160-grain class, with five different powders from which to select: H4895 (2700 fps), Du Pont IMR-3031 (56.4 grains, 3000 fps), *(Writer Grennell prepared this article before Du Pont sold its IMR powder line to IMR Powder Co., RD #5, Box 247A, Plattsburgh, NY 12910.—KW)* Du Pont IMR-4895 (59.0 grains, 3000 fps), IMR-4320 (60.1 grains, 3000 fps) and H380 (62.2 grains, 2900 fps). I find it interesting that switching from Hodgdon 4895 to the Du Pont variety boosted the approximate velocity by 300 fps.

The 160-165-grain weight class lists three powders: H380 for 2900 fps, IMR-4320 for 3000 fps and IMR-4895 for 2700 fps.

The 170-180-grain bullets are handled by one powder: IMR-4064 at 57.7 grains for 2800 fps.

The 200-210-grain class gets 65.1 grains of Hodgdon H450 for 2500 fps or 62.2 grains of Hodgdon H205 for 2600 fps. H205, as you know, is discontinued and H450 may be a little hard to find at present.

At the bottom lines, the 210-220-grain bullets can be loaded with H205 for 2550 fps, IMR-4350 at 58.5 grains for 2500 or IMR-4831 at 58.5 grains for 2550 fps.

The listing closes out with a few warnings: "Do not use bullets heavier than listed for each type of powder as they will cause dangerous pressures. Be sure your measure is 4.3cc. Push the measure through the powder only once. Give it a light shake to level it off. Do not add more or shake down."

The data listings and warnings are identical on the sheet that accompanies a set of loading dies in 300 Winchester Magnum. The warning against using heavier bullets with a given charge of powder is entirely valid and should be observed scrupulously. There is, perhaps, a tendency on the part of some to scan the listings and wonder what might happen if 59.0 grains of IMR-4895 were to be loaded behind a 130-grain bullet in place of the prescribed 59.0 grains of H4895. If it drives the 150-grain bullet 300 fps faster, might it not be helpful with the 130-grainer? Both of the 4895 powders are pleasantly even-tempered within sensible limits. That is, IMR-4895 is not apt to encounter a light-charge detonation if the weight

of the bullet is decreased by 20 grains. I would not advocate anyone else trying such an experiment, but I might do so myself, if time were available.

How do the dipped charges stack up for accuracy? I can answer that from first-hand experience. Up to the mid-'60s, I lived in Wisconsin, not too far from the Lee facilities in Hartford. Then, as now, I pounded out copy for the firearms press, and I first met Dick Lee early in 1960, as closely as I recall the date. It was the beginning of a long and mutually rewarding friendship, one that's still going on.

Like most of you, I've never been overly well supplied with places to shoot and Lee had an informal rifle range set up in a pasture he called the Back 40. I spent many a blissful Sunday afternoon burning powder in that bucolic facility. Lee also had a chronograph; a rare and prized instrument in the early '60s, and I recall taking one of the very early Model 600 Remingtons in 350 Remington Magnum up to Lee's Back 40 for establishment of tentative load data. By the time the sun sank in the west, we'd gotten the 180-grain Speer JSP bullet out of the short barrel at up to 3400 fps. I didn't quote that particular load in my review of the new carbine and cartridge and was most grateful when the next edition of the Speer Manual came out with a much lower maximum velocity.

On another occasion, probably an earlier one, we were doing 30-06 out of a nice old Springfield for which I'd squandered a whole $25 in a mad moment. With the master himself dipping the charges of IMR-3031, I managed a five-shot group with the 130-grain Speer JHP bullet that spanned a thin trifle under ⅝-inch between centers at 100 yards.

From that day down to the present, I've never had any qualms over fancied sacrifice of accuracy from dipping charges instead of weighing them.

You must understand, however, that we are speaking of charges some-

what below maximum charge weights. If you are going to load to the highest sanctioned charge weights you can find, in the first place, you shouldn't and, in the second place, you'd best use a good powder scale, with great care and with your fingers crossed.

Barring the occasional rare exception, nearly all rifles, nearly all handguns, turn in their best groups with loads that are somewhat below the firewall maximum levels. This is the area in which the volume-based Lee loads operate. The approach is made necessary by the hard fact that any given powder will vary somewhat from lot to lot; some more than others. They will vary both in density and in burning charcteristics. The dose dispensed by a Lee measure has to be modest enough to assure a margin of safety with any powder, out of any maker's lot. To the best of my knowledge, they fill that requirement in fine shape.

If you hanker to explore all the safe possibilities, after thoughtful consultation of reliable sources of load data, $6.98 buys one of the Lee powder measure kits, with 15 different dippers and a cardboard slide rule giving thousands of different charges you can throw with this or that dipper, this or that powder. If it pleases your fancy to make up test loads at the shooting site and if your facility lacks a wind-sheltered spot for use of a powder scale, the Lee powder measure kit can be used quite effectively in anything short of gale-force winds and to excellent effect.

The 1986 Lee catalog, on page 6, has a small box, revealing that, on page 632 of the Guinness Book of Records—edition number not specified—"Rick Taylor is listed as holding the record for the smallest group in target shooting at 1000 yards. He used a Lee Loader to accomplish this amazing feat."

Based upon my own experience, I do not find that in the least incredible. ●

Auto-Disk measure comes with 4 disks, each having 6 cavities, but merely automatic gauging powder charges by volume in the grand Lee tradition.

by DON ZUTZ

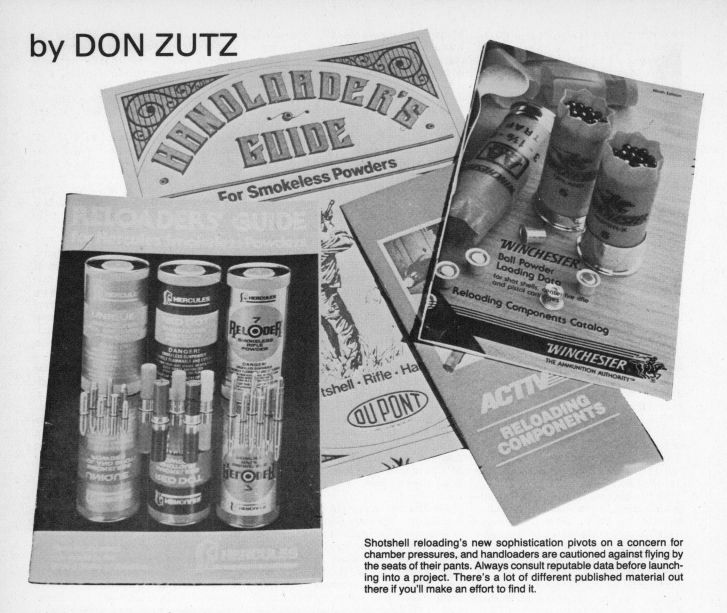

Shotshell reloading's new sophistication pivots on a concern for chamber pressures, and handloaders are cautioned against flying by the seats of their pants. Always consult reputable data before launching into a project. There's a lot of different published material out there if you'll make an effort to find it.

SHOTSHELL SOPHISTICATION *IS UP TO YOU*

THERE WAS a time when advanced riflemen could legitimately scoff at the sheer simplicity of shotshell reloading. When I picked up my first batch of shot, powder, wads, and primers back in the early 1950s, the gunsmith who dispensed them locally was a NRA tournament rifle shooter, and he waved off shotshell handloading as mere child's play.

"Sure is easy, isn't it?" he snickered as I gathered up the packages, "Punch in a new primer, pour in a measure of powder, ram in the wads, drop shot, and close it up. Frontier farmers did it with nothing more than a rusty nail to poke out the old primers and a wooden dowel to push in wads."

And he was right, of course. Until we got into the second half of the 20th century, shotshell reloading was basically a crude affair. Compared to the way accuracy conscious riflemen went through all sorts of steps in their quest for accuracy and uniformity—case segregating, careful priming, case trimming, neck turning, deburring, flash hole regulating, scaling precise powder charges, and straight-

A concern for proper chamber pressures is the most important aspect of sophisticated shotshell handloading. Failure to operate within the industry's established pressure parameters can cause a burst like the one which nearly bisected this sturdy pumpgun.

Wider steel shot drop tubes and plastic shot bottle mouths will also enhance the flow of bulky lead shot.

Steel shot conversion kits, like this MEC package, not only help in the handloading of steel shot, but have other advantages.

line bullet seating—shotshell reloading practices were blatantly gross and devil-may-care.

The reason was undoubtedly that few people expected much from the smoothbore. Riflemen knew all about accuracy and its importance to long-range target or field work, while the shotgun was accepted as a purely short-range proposition, scattering shot hither and yon. Under the prevailing conditions, the performance was generally more hither than yon. Typical hunters lived with it, and few took a hard look at what the shotshell might become when developed with a view to scientific sophistication. Those who handloaded shotshells did it to save money or because they couldn't obtain desired factory loads in their outlying areas.

Shotshell reloading didn't come out of the Stone Age until the plastic revolution erupted in the 1960s. Then, and almost overnight, it went from primitive handiwork to an increasingly complex science which, in this writer's opinion, has actually bypassed metallic reloading in its sophistication. From the early 1960s to the present, it has been no longer a matter of only pushing in fresh primers, pouring in powder, ramming wads, and dribbling shot. That brand of simplicity was gone. As the shotshell's efficiency was being improved, and as we began to see its expanded potentials, we also began to observe that each of the new components and concepts had its own individual pressure-building characteristic. And it is that element—the pressure factor—which carries shotshell reloading to new levels of sophistication.

Handloaders can now make shotshells do wondrous things—throw Full-choke patterns from a Skeet gun or Skeet patterns from a Full choke; hold nearly 100 percent shot strings from the ol' duck gun; whistle steel shot to 1600 fps; manipulate distribution within the 30-inch patterning circle; utilize shotcup inserts, buffering agents and different hardnesses of lead shot; and engineer certain pressure levels by juggling components. But these advances may only be accomplished at a price: the handloader must obtain a foundation of theory and data by becoming well-read in the field of shotshell performance and component characteristics. Without such information and a basic understanding of how a shotshell works, the use of modern, high performance components can be counterproductive and potentially dangerous.

For the person who will read and think, shotshell reloading concepts and techniques now laid before the public can be employed to turn the once indifferent "squaw gun" into a most effective sporting arm. Even without the screw-in choke systems, the smoothbore now has greater capabilities because of what one can wring from it via handloading. During the past year, I have made an extra-full-choked 12-gauge spray Cylinder bore patterns, a Modified-choked 3-inch 12 do 100 percent with steel buckshot, and a Skeet gun run Modified-choke averages with 1½-ounce short magnums.

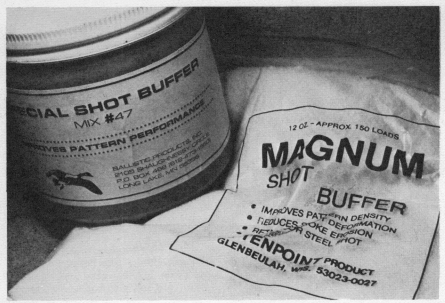

Buffers not only help encase pellets for retained spherical form, but they also enhance the load's fluidity through the choke constriction for better patterns. Buffers differ from supplier to supplier, so follow only the published data from the manufacturer of the buffer you're using.

The secret to all this isn't just cobbling together random assortments of plastic stuff. The key is applying the basics. For the basics are still . . . well . . . basic. That immediately means a concern for chamber pressures. Ignoring pressure limitations can do everything from generating excess recoil to stressing a gun, affecting patterns, and causing bursts. Thus, while the new shotshell sophistication does deliver fancy results, they must be predicated on the same old pressure parameters of yesteryear. By SAAMI standards, the 12-gauge reaches the industry-established maximum at 11,000 LUP, as does the 16-gauge. Because it takes more pressure to drive a given weight through smaller bores than it does through larger ones, smaller gauges have slightly higher allowable average working pressures. The 20-gauge, in either standard- or magnum-length hulls, has a peak of 11,500 LUP. The 28-gauge rises to 12,000 LUP, while the pee-wee .410-bore can be taken to 13,000 LUP. When the piezo-electric transducer, reading in pounds per square inch (psi) is used to check chamber pressures, those maxima can be about 500 units higher and still be considered safe.

All this palaver about safe and sane chamber pressures, along with various published warnings that, "Component switching can cause dangerous pressures," has caused more than a few reloaders to become locked into one particular recipe; they fear that any change will dynamite their pet bird gun. If they're using 18 grains of Red Dot with WAA12 wads and CCI 209 primers, any thought of using other components will leave them quivering and quaking. And the thought of using buffer material or steel shot makes them shudder. Each modern component and assembly *does* have its own pressure characteristic,

Winchester "Grex" is a high-denisty buffer that improves patterns, and it is now available as a handloading component. Use it only according to data printed on the bottle.

When buffers are compressed under the setback pressures of firing, they exert a lateral force and can produce a friction factor that builds chamber pressures rapidly and dangerously if used without a plastic shotcup or shot wrapper. The buffer can "cake" as shown here to cling in the porous interior surface of a shotshell and retard ejecta movement long enough for dangerously high pressures to develop. Always load buffer with a plastic shotcup or wrapper.

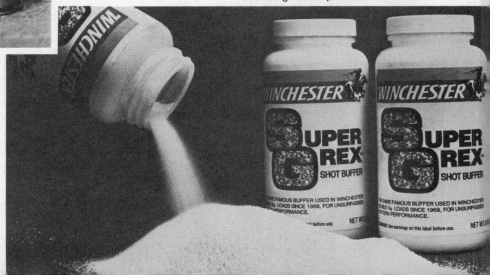

but they can be utilized and combined for excellent results *without* blowing up any guns. Nor are such specialized reloads only for atomic physicists or chaps with PhDs in chemistry. The theory and practice of such reloading is open to anyone who can read intelligently and appreciate the importance of pressure levels.

For example, many handloaders cringe at the thought of switching or substituting a component in a given reload, because there are so many published warnings against that practice. However, switching is safe if the handloader will bother to peruse the vast amounts of literature supplied by component makers. There is so much load data around these days that one can often stumble upon numerous variations of any one reload. Let's say that a trap shooter is turning out the following load which is printed in Du Pont's *Handloader's Guide for Smokeless Powders*:

Shell: Winchester Double-A
Primer: CCI 209
Powder: 18.0/Hi-Skor 700-X
Wad: Pacific Versalite
Shot: 1⅛ ounces
Pressure: 8200 LUP
Velocity: 1145 fps

Now let's say that our reloader runs out of CCI 209 primers and that his nearby dealer has nothing on hand but the known-to-be stronger Federal 209 primers. What to do? Reloaders who are poorly read might shy away, worried that the F209 will be overboard on pressure. But will the fellow's expensive Italian trap gun be blown up by such a primer substitution? Heck, no! Take a look at these figures also printed in the same Du Pont Guide:

Shell: Winchester Double-A
Primer: Federal 209
Powder: 18.0/Hi-Skor 700-X
Wad: Pacific Versalite
Shot: 1⅛ ounces
Pressure: 10,300 LUP
Velocity: 1190 fps

Thus, although the Federal 209 primer did produce an increased chamber pressure over the CCI 209s, it wasn't a dangerous jump. The average pressure of 10,300 LUP by Federal 209 primers is still within the limits of safe 12-gauge chamber pressures.

And what if the same handloader, now using Federal 209s, suddenly ran out of Pacific wads and could only find Remington RXP-12 wads? Could he make that further substitution without seeing his Italian trap gun light up like Mt. Vesuvius? Here's what the Du Pont lab says:

Shell: Winchester Double-A
Primer: Federal 209 primer
Powder: 18.0/Hi-Skor 700-X
Wad: Remington RXP-12
Shot: 1⅛ ounces of lead shot
Pressure: 8,500 LUP
Velocity: 1145 fps

In other words, safe again!

The point is that component switching isn't automatically dangerous. It will frequently produce ballistics changes, but many of those changes will still be within the realm of acceptable pressures. To prove this to himself, a reloader need do nothing more than read carefully through the lab-tested data published and distributed by industry sources. There is so much published these days that a little research will often turn up the exact assembly being considered by a handloader, or it'll produce one mighty close. Moreover, by reading a lot of data, one can get an understanding of the pressure-building qualities of each individual component. Initially, then, the new sophistication means having the ability to read analytically relative to chamber pressures and comparative component performances.

Besides the pressure factors in conventional lead shot reloads, two relatively new concepts have appeared which, despite their field potentials, have introduced handloading complexities: steel shot and buffer. Both affect chamber pressures, sometimes significantly, and *neither* can be added haphazardly to a reloading situation the way it is often possible to switch components in a conventional, nonbuffered, lead shot reload and still retain safe pressures.

The big difference between steel shot and lead shot is that steel shot tends to generate higher chamber pressures because it doesn't deform. Under high pressures—even excessively high pressures—lead shot will generally compress and move from the chamber into the bore to provide increased space for the ever-expanding powder gases. This swaging action of lead shot has undoubtedly saved many reckless handloaders who somehow got too much powder aboard.

Steel shot, on the other hand, remains round and hard regardless of the chamber pressures. It won't swage down for positive bore passage. Hammer a charge of steel pellets on the fanny with a high, sudden gas pressure, and the pellets bind together to form a virtual solid slug that exerts a lateral force against the shotcup petals and hull/chamber walls. In turn, this lateral expansion and binding of steel shot creates added friction, and chamber pressures can mount steeply before the ejecta move forward. Therefore, if an unsophisticated reloader mistakenly thinks he can put steel shot into a conventional lead shot reload using light plastic shotcups and fast-burning powders—forget it! The sharp pressure rise of a fast-burning powder causes the pellets to bind, and the lateral pressure will perforate light shotcups intended for compressible lead shot, thereby impressing themselves into the plastic hull and, eventually, into the bore's surface. In other words, the sophisticated handloader realizes there's a new set of basics for steel shot reloading, and the thinking hunter/handloader will read all he can on the subject before plunging in with both feet.

Essentially, handloading with steel shot pivots on: (A) getting the payload moving smoothly so there is a minimum of wedging, binding, expanding laterally; and (B) using a specially tough shotcup to deter perforations and to supply a self-lubricating quality. Point A requires ultra-slow burning powders. Commercial loading companies apparently employ slower powders than those currently available to handloaders in cannister lots; however, initial steel shot reloading can be brought off successfully with the likes of Hodgdon HS-7, Hercules Blue Dot, and Du Pont SR-4756. Some additional data has been worked up with 2400, which has very slow-burning characteristics in shotguns, but erratic ignition in cold weather plagues this number. Point B is satisfied only by the use of hard, high-density plastic shotcups designated specifically for steel shot.

I have been receiving letters from waterfowlers who suddenly find themselves with boxes of lead shot when new steel-shot-only laws take effect in their areas, and they ask, "Can I replace the lead shot with steel shot to utilize the remaining loads?" The answer is a thundering NO! The chamber pressures and wad toughness of lead shot loads are entirely *wrong* for steel shot. *Never* substitute steel shot for lead shot in either factory loads or reloads!

Using buffer in shot charges is another sophisticated step for reloaders, and it's a step not to be taken lightly.

Using different primers can alter interior ballistics, but it can often be safely done within safe pressure parameters. Again, check the various manuals and learn the pressure-building characteristics of various components.

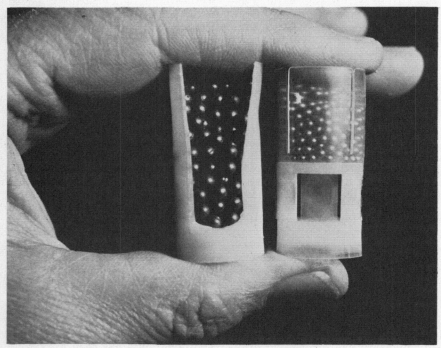

Steel shot requires a tougher wad than lead shot. The steel shot wad is shown here on the left, while a conventional lead shot wad is on the right. Steel shot needs no cushioning.

A trio of different 12-gauge reloads which, despite having different wads and primers, are all quite safe with the same charge of 18.0/Hi-Skor 700-X. Yes, components switching can be done safely if one takes time to check through manuals to verify his data.

The purpose of employing buffer with lead shot is twofold: (1) it keeps pellets in-the-round for their best aerodynamics; and (2) it enhances the fluidity with which coarse shot and buckshot flow through the bore and choke constrictions for improved patterns. When it comes to steel shot, buffers may tend to stabilize the shot charge and influence fluidity only. Buffer isn't needed to keep steel shot from deforming.

Although it is commonly understood that buffers "cushion" pellets against deformation, there is a more accurate explanation. For buffers do not cushion pellets the way pillows cuddle your head. Instead, buffers work best when they surround each pellet, virtually encase it as if it were in a mould, so that when the compressive force of setback strikes, the pellet can't find any open room into which to flow out-of-round. Pellet deformation normally occurs when there is room between pellets for flow and/or when adjacent pellets can mash against each other. Encase each one in buffer, and neither mashing nor flow can occur to any extent.

The concept of fluidity becomes important because coarse shot sizes and buckshot move poorly through bores and choke constrictions. Too, some of the larger pellets can actually take on a spin, or "English," as they ramble up the choke's taper and curve off after exiting the muzzle. Another problem with coarse pellets and buckshot is the jostling and bumping that occurs on emission without buffer. When bedded in buffer, however, the bulky pellets can shift about within their mass and compress as a mass like sand flowing through an hour glass, thus funneling through the choke more fluidly.

But just knowing that buffer improves patterns isn't the height of sophistication. Reloaders must understand that buffers inject a compression factor into interior ballistics, and that means variously higher chamber pressures. Indeed, sifting buffer casually into any old reload can be dangerous! Some years ago, I selected a 1⅛-ounce 12-gauge Magnum reload with a published chamber pressure of 10,000 LUP, indiscriminately added buffer, and sent it off to a lab for pressure testing. Darn thing churned up chamber pressures topping 13,000 LUP, which is well above the 11,000 LUP maximum working average set by the industry. Thus, while some sources offer general rules of thumb for adding buffer—such as, "Reduce the powder charge by 10 percent when buffer is added," or "Use buffer only with loads having published pressures below 9000 LUP—it is far better to ignore all such by-guess-and-by-golly reloading and to rely on scientifically developed data for specific reloads printed in reputable sources.

When buffered reloads first received publicity, plain kitchen flour got a play in magazines and 100 percent patterns were bragged up. It didn't take long for the lab boys to learn that flour caused chamber pressures to vault dangerously, however. For when flour is made slightly damp, as often happens in waterfowling, it tends to cake; and when it cakes, it becomes a veritable solid slug that compresses tightly against the shotcup and/or case walls and offers resistance to smooth initial payload movement. The best buffers are plastic sawdusts designated specifically for reloading. The newest such product is Winchester's Grex, which was released early in 1986. Each bottle of Grex has load data on the backside label.

Buffered reloads must always be used with full-length shotcups or plastic shot wrappers. If buffer contacts the porous, fire-roughened hull wall, it can compress into the pores under setback pressures and cause a "cling" factor which impedes payload movement according to the intended pressure curve. In experiments with buffered reloads lacking plastic shotcups or wrappers, I have had the forward segment of the case shoot off and leave the muzzle like a slug because the compressed buffer imbedded itself solidly into the wall pores and wouldn't release. One can only guess what chamber pressures were present. Thus, the self-lubricating feature of plastic wads and wrappers, along with a dusting of mica or powdered graphite, are always utilized by sophisticated handloaders to insure improved payload movement with buffered shot charges.

In recent years, a series of shotcup inserts have come along for either tightening or opening patterns. (*Mentioned elsewhere*—Editor). Our concern for chamber pressures, however, argues that all such inserts must be used according to instructions from the various suppliers. For putting more material into the ejecta segment of a reload enhances the potential for higher chamber pressures due simply to more forward resistance. In other words, once more it is read before reloading.

Thus far we have looked mainly at reload building, but a sophisticated handloader also carries that quality into his equipment. To get the ballistics published for a certain assembly, one must drop definite amounts of powder and shot uniformly; and with the automated presses and charge bars of today, that means scaling charges for accuracy. Never trust a shot or powder cavity!

For example, shot bushings of all sizes will invariably drop different charge weights for each pellet size because the amount of air space between pellets varies with shot size. Heavier pellets like BBs, 2s, and 4s tend to offer lighter charges from any given bushing, while smaller shot like 8s, 8½s, and 9s become heavier charges because they pack tighter. In general, many shot bushings seem drilled for pellets in the range of 6s and 7½s. As a sample, I used five different sizes of chilled shot to strike these five-load averages from a given 1⅛-ounce bushing:

No. 9 shot	505.5 grains
No. 7½ shot	504.0 grains
No. 6 shot	493.5 grains
No. 4 shot	485.1 grains
No. 2 shot	472.0 grains

Since there are 492 grains in 1⅛ ounces, we find somewhat more than a $\frac{1}{16}$-ounce differential between the 9s and 2s. If we were reloading 20-gauge Magnums and came up with that error, it could be meaningful. The shot charge would not only be packing fewer pellets, but it would also offer less resistance to the powder gases and would, therefore, have a different ballistic characteristic than a reload with the full 1⅛-ounce shot charge.

Getting the bulkier pellets—say, those bigger than No. 6s—to flow smoothly through a drop tube without bridging is tough. But the hopper-to-hull transition can be effected better by employing the wider steel shot hoppers and drop tubes that have been coming along. A case in point is the MEC Steel Shot Kit, which includes a two-part drop tube assembly with a larger interior diameter and funnel. Moreover, the MEC steel shot hopper has a wider mouth to expedite pellet passage. There's no law against using steel shot equipment for lead shot if it makes the operation more efficient.

When it comes to powder, the problem is found in press vibrations, which cause the powder to pack down. Never test a powder bushing by simply running the charge bar back and forth. It's inaccurate. The final powder charge that drops from a bushing is influenced by the machine's vibrations; therefore, check powder samples by running the machine through entire cycles so that the normal operating vibrations are felt by the powder. Ignore the first powder charge and begin taking samples only after a full actual reloading sequence has been run.

Another point is that cannister lots of the same powder can vary. Nothing is perfect except scientific theory. One lot of a given powder can be lighter and fluffier than the next lot, meaning one given bushing will not drop the same weight from each lot. Given the correct charge weight, the same chemical energies will be present, of course. I have had some lots of flake-type Skeet and trap powders show up 1 grain lighter or heavier than the preceding lot, and the handloader must make adjustments to his powder bushing for the correct charge weight. These variations in shot sizes and powder lots are one reason why adjustable charge bars are catching on.

The key to the new sophistication in shotshell reloading, then, is an awareness of pressure parameters and component variations. Given a scientific concern for those aspects, we can manipulate reloads for tight patterns, tight*er* patterns, wildly scattered spreader loads, light-kicking practice or clay target rounds, or high-speed stuff. We can substitute components if, by the same token, we bother to study both published data and each component's individual pressure-building characteristic. We can add inserts or buffer, and we can reload steel shot safely. But if we're going to balance all these combinations so that we come up with effective velocities while still retaining safe chamber pressure averages, we must do some homework. We are not savvy handloaders just because we can yank the handle of any press ever built or because we once got a B+ in high school shop. Handloading involves the release of chemical energy in the form of ever-expanding gases, and you don't learn about that on a drill press or a lathe.

Put all these variables and load possibilities into one lump, however, and it comes up more detailed and with more performance potential than even the most advanced metallic reloaders ever bumped into. In a word—sophisticated. ●

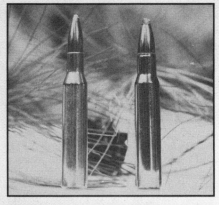

Gun to gun the 30-06 turns in very much the same ballistics, but not the 270, Matunas says.

The only place the 270 stands taller than the 30-06, says Ed Matunas, is in photos like this, as he points out . . .

The Real Differences Between the 270 and 30-06

TABLE I
Best 270 and 30-06 Factory Ammunition Ballistics (22-inch barrel)

Caliber	Wgt. grs.	Bullets Brand & Type	3 yds	100 yds.	200 yds.	300 yds.	400 yds.	3 yds	100 yds.	200 yds.	300 yds.	400 yds.	Comments
270 Win.	100	adv. (1) ballistics	3430	3021	2649	2305	1988	2612	2027	1557	1179	877	
270 Win.	100	Rem. softpoint	3149	2773	2431	2115	1824	2202	1708	1313	993	739	lowest lot—3113 fps
270 Win.	100	Win. softpoint	3043	2650	2324	2022	1744	2057	1560	1200	908	676	lowest lot—3032 fps
270 Win.	130	adv. (1) ballistics	3060	2776	2510	2259	2022	2702	2225	1818	1472	1180	
270 Win.	130	PMC softpoint	2624	2380	2152	1937	1734	1988	1636	1337	1083	868	only lot tested
270 Win.	130	Win. Power Point	2860	2594	2346	2110	1889	2361	1943	1589	1285	1030	lowest lot—2785 fps
270 Win.	130	Rem. Pt. Core Lokt	2718	2465	2229	2006	1796	2133	1754	1435	1162	931	lowest lot—2618 fps
270 Win.	150	adv. (1) ballistics	2850	2585	2336	2100	1879	2705	2226	1817	1468	1175	for pointed bullet
270 Win.	150	Win. Power Point	2800	2540	2295	2063	1846	2612	2149	1755	1418	1135	
270 Win.	150	Rem. Core Lokt	2762	2427	2116	1828	1568	2542	1963	1492	1113	819	RN bullet ballistics
270 Win.	150	Fed. partition	2809	2548	2302	2070	1852	2629	2163	1765	1428	1143	lowest lot—2769 fps
270 Win.	150	PMC softpoint	2624	2380	2151	1934	1730	2294	1887	1541	1246	977	only lot tested
30-06 Spring.	125	adv. (1) ballistics	3140	2780	2447	2138	1853	2736	2145	1662	1269	953	
30-06 Spring.	125	Win. softpoint	3125	2767	2436	2128	1844	2711	2126	1647	1257	944	lowest lot—3075 fps
30-06 Spring.	125	Rem. softpoint	3100	2745	2416	2111	1829	2668	2092	1621	1237	929	lowest lot—3069 fps
30-06 Spring.	150	adv. (1) ballistics	2910	2617	2342	2083	1843	2820	2281	1827	1445	1131	
30-06 Spring.	150	Win. Power Point	2841	2555	2286	2034	1799	2689	2175	1741	1378	1079	only lot tested
30-06 Spring.	150	Rem. Pt. Core Lokt	2870	2581	2310	2054	1818	2744	2219	1778	1406	1101	lowest lot—2848 fps
30-06 Spring.	165	adv. (1) ballistics	2800	2534	2283	2047	1825	2872	2352	1909	1534	1220	
30-06 Spring.	165	Rem. Pt. Core Lokt	2762	2500	2252	2019	1800	2796	2290	1859	1494	1187	
30-06 Spring.	180	adv. (1) ballistics	2700	2469	2250	2042	1846	2913	2436	2023	1666	1362	for pointed bullet
30-06 Spring.	✱80	PMC softpoint	2638	2412	2198	1944	1756	2782	2326	1931	1511	1235	only lot tested
30-06 Spring.	180	Rem. Pt. Core Lokt	2668	2440	2223	2018	1824	2846	2380	1976	1628	1330	lowest lot—2635 fps
30-06 Spring.	180	Fed. partition	2660	2432	2217	2012	1817	2829	2365	1965	1618	1322	extr. uniform ballistics
30-06 Spring.	180	Win. Silvertip	2640	2414	2200	1997	1805	2786	2330	1935	1594	1302	lowest lot—2600 fps
30-06 Spring.	220	adv. (1) ballistics	2410	2130	1870	1632	1422	2837	2216	1708	1301	988	
30-06 Spring.	220	Win. Silvertip	2369	2094	1838	1604	1398	2742	2143	1651	1257	955	extr. uniform lot to lot
30-06 Spring.	220	Rem. Core Lokt	2347	2074	1821	1589	1385	2692	2102	1620	1234	937	extr. uniform lot to lot

Header note: Velocity in fps at: (3 yds, 100 yds, 200 yds, 300 yds, 400 yds); Energy in fpe at: (3 yds, 100 yds, 200 yds, 300 yds, 400 yds)

(1) advertised ballistics are for 24-inch barrel. All tested ballistics are for the popular and universal 22-inch barrel length

THE MERITS of the 30-06 have been eulogized by many. Ditto for the 270's strong points. Few will deny that the 30-06 is an extremely universal cartridge that has been successful, although admittedly stretched, when used on varmints as tiny as gophers or on mighty Alaskan moose and grizzly. And that the 270 is a superb varmint rifle cannot be denied. Too, the most ardent 270 fan will usually admit that the 270 is at its best on light big game such as deer, antelope and goat, and that large caribou are the upper limits, with respect to size, of potent performance for the 270 Winchester.

Few hunters and even fewer reloaders have missed the point that both the 270 Winchester and the 30-06 Springfield are very well suited to the hunting of North American big game. Most shooters have been inundated with written words on just how similar the two cartridges are. But I'm here to tell you that there are more differences between the two cartridges than there are similarities. I'm also going to state right now that I am a very big fan of both the 270 and the 30-06 cartridges, but not for identical applications. There are many times when one is a very poor choice and the other a very good choice. When I select a pair of rifles for a hunting trip, two out of three times they will be chambered for either the 30-06 or the 270. But I make very clear distinctions for those situations in which I will choose one or the other.

Before going into specifics, there are a few basic assumptions that will be made as the differences of the 270 and the 30-06 are discussed. The first of these is the acceptance that it takes a minimum change of 250 foot pounds of energy (fpe) to show up as a notable change in field performance. There simply is no real difference between a 180-grain bullet that strikes a target with 1600 fpe or one that strikes a target with 1450 fpe, all else being equal. Neither game nor hunter will be able to notice any difference when energies are but 150 foot pounds apart. However, when the differences in energy reach or exceed 250 foot pounds, definite differences in bullet penetration and expansion, as well as game reaction to the shot, begin to be apparent, depending upon circumstances, naturally. When energy differences reach 300 foot pounds, or more, field performance differences can be noted even by inexperienced persons.

Another assumption we'll make is that it takes an absolute minimum of 1000 foot pounds of *striking* energy to humanely kill deer-sized animals on a *consistent* basis under *varying* conditions. Further, that game the size of elk require an absolute minimum of 1500 foot pounds of striking energy to be killed cleanly, while very heavy game (big moose and grizzly) should be dispatched with no less than 2000 foot pounds of striking energy.

Finally, it will be assumed that a trajectory change, to be of a notable or meaningful amount, requires a minimum change of 250 feet per second (fps) in velocity as measured at the muzzle. However, some shooters, based on capability to estimate range and holdover, may require 350 fps muzzle velocity change to be able to detect a trajectory change in the field.

To begin with, it is essential to compare actual ballistics of both cartridges in all their various loadings. There are, indeed, some real surprises when one looks at real life results as opposed to advertised claims for the 270 Winchester. Often the 270 simply does not come close to the advertised performance level. The 30-06 invariably peforms in the hoped-for fashion.

Table I lists the performance of a goodly number of factory loads for both cartridges. The results shown in this table include the highest velocities obtained with specific loadings as well as the advertised velocities. Additionally, the comment column shows some of the lowest velocities obtained for similar ammo of different lots. Table III reflects the average velocity expected based on numerous tests.

The first example of disappointing performance comes with a review of the 270's varmint weight (100-grain bullet) loads. Advertised velocity is 3430 (all advertised specifications are for 24-inch barrels), while the actual velocity obtained was 3149 and 3043 for two different brands (actual results are for the popular 22-inch barrel length). The lowest recorded velocities were quite similar to these highest levels. It would be fair, based on these and many other test results, to say that 3100 fps is the average level of velocity to anticipate from factory 100-grain 270 loadings. The difference of 300 fps is a very substantial velocity loss; one easily recognizable in the field by even novice hunters. Reloading is not the answer, as a velocity of 3200 fps is about all I have ever obtained consistent with good accuracy when using 100-grain bullets. However, the 90-grain Sierra hollow-point can be driven at 3500 fps and at this velocity it will supply the flattest possible trajectory commonly available with the 270 Winchester cartridge.

The greater disappointment with the 270 comes with the 130-grain bullet and factory loads. The advertised nominal muzzle velocity for the 130-grain factory load is 3060 fps. Adjusting this for a 22-inch barrel, it is reasonable to assume a nominal muzzle velocity of 3000 fps. This certainly is not borne out by the results of the testing of a great many factory loadings over recent years. The single highest average velocity I have seen in recent times is 2860 fps, some 140 fps less than anticipated. Indeed, the average velocity of 130-grain factory loads, from a 22-inch barrel, seems to be more on the order of 2725 fps, some 275 fps below the hoped-for nominal velocity. Disappointing? You bet! But disappointing results are often the norm with the 270 when factory 100- and 130-grain loads are used.

Of course, handloading can correct some of the shortcomings of the 130-grain factory loadings and a muzzle velocity of 2900 fps is about average. I have some 22-inch barreled 270s that consistently turn in about 3050 fps and some that will do but 2825 fps. But the average handload is some 175 fps faster than the average factory load. And the average reloaded velocity of 2900 fps is close enough to the expected level to cause no notable change in field performance from the anticipated level.

The 270 does as expected when 150-grain factory loads are used. At least all the tests I have conducted indicate expected performance whether the ammo be Remington, Winchester, Federal or even of handloading vintage. Only the PMC ammo proved to be substandard with respect to velocity (see Table I). Advertised velocity, adjusted for a 22-inch barrel, suggests a muzzle velocity of 2810 fps. Discounting the PMC ammo (2625 fps) the average velocity of all the recently tested factory loads is 2800 fps. That's as advertised! And it's easy to do likewise with reloads. Don't ask me why actual velocities with 150-grain bullets are faster than with the 130-grain bullets. I have some suspicions, but this question is best directed to the ammo loaders.

The 270 has been described by one well-known factory personality as "not the favorite cartridge of the ammunition makers." This expression, I'm sure, was in part stimulated by the difficulty in meeting advertised claims with the 100- and 130-grain bullets.

Velocity testing with 270 rifles does point out another disconcerting prob-

The author with a nice and recent buck. The 270 is, these days, tops for author's deer hunting.

lem—velocity variation from rifle to rifle is notable. In a test using three Remington 700s and five Winchester Model 70s, the velocity average for the same lot of ammo from the fastest barrel to the slowest one showed a loss of 250 fps. The particularly slow rifle was eliminated from our test considerations. However, such rifles do exist and are encountered not infrequently. While 270 barrels that produce higher velocities do exist, they are quite elusive. If one takes the disappointingly low velocity of the average factory 130-grain load (from an average barrel) and adds to it one of the frequently encountered "slow" barrels, a velocity of just over 2600 fps may be realized instead of the hoped-for 3000 fps. That's a whopping 400 fps difference.

The velocity variations encountered with the 270 result in proportional variations in energy. Instead of an anticipated 1500 foot pounds at 300 yards (130-grain bullet) one could, in extreme cases, come up with just under 1100 foot pounds, a notable difference indeed. In fact, we could, by fault of velocity variation, go from a round suitable for elk to one just a tad better than needed for deer. No wonder we hear one hunter highly praise the 270 as an elk cartridge and another say it is a minimum for long-range mule deer work. The truth is, that depending upon the actual ballistics produced by the individual lot of ammo in a specific gun, both statements can be accurate. At best, good 270 performance requires ammo and rifle to be proven capable of the high-

er velocities by use of a chronograph. At worst, the 270 can be very disappointing.

A look at the performance of the 30-06 cartridge brings about a different scenario. Indeed, in almost all rifles the 30-06 performs as expected. The factory varmint loads' advertised ballistics (adjusted for a 22-inch barrel) suggest a muzzle velocity of 3100 fps for the 125-grain bullet. Actual test results show an actual average velocity of 3100 fps—absolute perfection. And it's no trick to duplicate this performance with reloads. Indeed, with the lighter 110-grain bullet, reloads can be driven with good accuracy as fast as 3300 fps.

The usual 150-grain factory 30-06 load turns in 2855 fps against an assumed 22-inch barrel performance of 2870 fps (based on factory claims for a 24-inch barrel). Now, a mere 15 fps difference can be considered as advertised, from any practical viewpoint.

The 165-grain 30-06 load does exactly as expected, turning in 2760 fps. Ditto for the 180-grain loading which turns in 2640 fps average velocity against the expected 2660 fps. And the 220-grain factory loadings of the 30-06 are no exceptions in turning in the anticipated performance. The adjusted advertised velocity for a 22-inch barrel is 2390 fps while the actual average velocity is 2360 fps. No one can quibble over 30 fps, not meaningfully.

The expected and obtained velocities of the 30-06 do not seem to suffer extreme variations when one gun is compared to another. Indeed, in a test of four different Winchester Model 70s and two Remington 700s, the largest extreme variation that could be found was a 63 fps reduction, this

TABLE II
Best 270 and 30-06 Handloads (22-inch barrel ballistics)

Caliber	Wgt. grs.	Bullet Make and style	Powder charge wgt. in grains	Vel. in fps at: 3 yds.	100 yds.	400 yds.	Energy in fpe at: 3 yds.	100 yds.	400 yds.	Comments
270 Win.	90	Sierra HP	55.0 / IMR 4350	3021	2620	1552	1824	1372	481	in slowest bbl—2858 fps
270 Win.	90	Sierra HP	60.0 / IMR 4350	3532	3090	1955	2494	1909	764	in slowest bbl—3301 fps
270 Win.	100	Speer spitzer	59.0 / IMR 4350	3253	2930	2090	2350	1907	970	accuracy varies greatly, rifle to rifle
270 Win.	130	Speer spitzer	55.0 / IMR 4350	3045	2795	2135	2677	2256	1316	in slowest bbl—2831 fps
270 Win.	130	Nosler partition	55.0 / IMR 4350	3033	2785	2120	2656	2239	1298	in slowest bbl—2833 fps
270 Win.	150	Speer spitzer	53.0 / IMR 4350	2813	2615	2080	2636	2278	1441	250 fps slower in one barrel
270 Win.	150	Nosler partition	53.0 / IMR 4350	2802	2600	2075	2616	2252	1434	in slowest bbl—2600 fps
30-06 Spring.	110	Sierra HP	61.0 / IMR 4350	3071	2580	N.M.	2304	1626	N.M.	in slowest bbl—3050 fps
30-06 Spring.	110	Sierra HP	58.0 / IMR 4064	3300	2783	N.M.	2660	1892	N.M.	in slowest bbl—3280 fps
30-06 Spring.	125	Sierra Spitzer	61.0 / IMR 4350	2947	2655	1875	2411	1957	976	very uniform load, rifle to rifle
30-06 Spring.	125	Sierra Spitzer	55.0 / IMR 4064	3120	2830	2035	2703	2224	1150	in slowest bbl—3099 fps
30-06 Spring.	150	Speer Spitzer	60.0 / IMR 4350	3018	2764	2090	3034	2545	1455	in slowest bbl—2955 fps
30-06 Spring.	150	Speer Spitzer	52.0 / IMR 4064	2844	2594	1940	2695	2242	1254	in slowest bbl—2828 fps
30-06 Spring.	165	Speer Spitzer	58.0 / IMR 4350	2825	2600	2050	2925	2477	1540	in slowest bbl—2801 fps
30-06 Spring.	165	Nosler partition	50.0 / IMR 4064	2775	2552	1999	2822	2387	1464	in slowest bbl—2749 fps
30-06 Spring.	180	Nosler partition	57.0 / IMR 4350	2761	2550	2040	3047	2600	1664	in slowest bbl—2719 fps
30-06 Spring.	180	Nosler partition	49.0 / IMR 4064	2690	2490	1950	2893	2479	1520	in slowest bbl—2675 fps
30-06 Spring.	200	Nosler partition	55.0 / IMR 4350	2625	2460	2025	3060	2688	1822	very uniform load, rifle to rifle

N.M. = not measured at this range

with a handload. Factory loads showed a maximum velocity loss, from high to low, of only 50 fps. Thus, the 30-06 ammunition user gets what he pays for and there are no performance surprises. On the other hand, the 270 user must reload to get advertised ballistics with a varmint bullet or with the very popular 130-grain bullet; at that, not every barrel will deliver the desired velocity. The 30-06 user who reloads can actually surpass advertised ballistics. It's possible to get 3000 fps with the 150-grain 30-06 bullet when loading with Du Pont IMR 4350. And 2750 is possible with the 180-grain bullet and the same powder (see Table II).

Of course, having a cartridge that delivers less than hoped-for, or having one that delivers exactly as expected, does not necessarily mean that one cartridge will provide better results in the field. The two need to be compared on an actual delivered ballistics basis.

The 270 varmint factory loads (100-grain bullet at 3100 fps) perform almost identically to the 30-06 varmint factory load (125-grain bullet at 3100 fps), with there being but a 1-inch difference in trajectory over 400 yards when both are sighted 2 inches high at 100 yards. But that does not tell the whole story. Because of less recoil (12.1 foot pounds with a 9-pound rifle) the 270 Winchester is easier to shoot than the 30-06 (14.7 foot pounds recoil). Albeit the difference is not overwhelming, almost all shooters do better when recoil is lessened. And an approximate 20 percent change in recoil is enough to be noticed, But even more in favor of the 270 is the improvement that can be made to varmint load trajectories by handloading

This buck fell to a 180-grain 30-caliber bullet when both the author and the 30-06 were somewhat younger.

(see Table III). A 3-inch difference at 400 yards is not monumental but does give a slight edge to the 270 as a varmint load. Even when one of the 270's "slower" barrels is encountered, it will usually be able to duplicate the 30-06's trajectory and still have less recoil, noticeably so. The 270's accuracy with varmint weight bullets also gives it an edge. I've grown to expect ¾- to 1-inch groups from a well-tuned 270 using the Sierra 90-grain varmint bullet. The 125-grain 30-06 handloads normally have produced 1- to 1¼-inch groups.

All this considered, the 270 will do a better job in the varmint field than the 30-06, though it is true that the difference is not overwhelming. Nonetheless, the serious varminter who also hunts deer-sized game with a single rifle will simply do best with a 270.

When the light bullet big game loads are compared (130-grain 270 versus the 150-grain 30-06 loads) differences are notable at shorter ranges (to 200 yards). However, performance is on a near equal footing at the longest ranges.

With the average muzzle velocity of 2725 fps obtained with the 270, we have a substantially reduced level of performance versus that anticipated. This translates to energies of: 2144 foot pounds at the muzzle, 1795 foot pounds at 100 yards, 1494 foot pounds at 200 yards, 1237 foot pounds at 300 yards and 1015 foot pounds at 400 yards. Based on the earlier mentioned assumptions, the 270 with a 130-grain bullet might well be considered

TABLE III
Selected Trajectory and Recoil Comparisons: 270 and 30-06 (22-inch barrels)

Cartridge	Bullet Wgt. (grs.)	Type	Load Type	Avg. Expected Velocity fps at 3 yards	100 yds.	Trajectory in inches at: 200 yds.	300 yds.	400 yds.	Free Recoil in a 9-lb. rifle (fpe)
270 Winchester	90	HP	Handload	3500	+2.0	+1.7	−3.0	−15.0	12.2
270 Winchester	100	spitzer	Factory	3100	+2.0	+1.0	−5.5	−19.0	12.1
270 Winchester	100	spitzer	Handload	3200	+2.0	+1.4	−4.4	−17.0	12.6
270 Winchester	130	spitzer	Factory	2725	+2.0	⊕	−8.9	−26.0	13.6
270 Winchester	130	spitzer	Handload	2900	+2.0	+0.6	−6.6	−21.0	14.2
270 Winchester	150	spitzer	Factory	2800	+2.0	+0.4	−7.1	−22.0	15.8
270 Winchester	150	spitzer	Handload	2800	+2.0	+0.4	−7.1	−22.0	15.8
30-06 Springfield	110	HP	Handload	3300	+2.0	+1.0	−7.4	N.M.	14.2
30-06 Springfield	125	spitzer	Factory	3100	+2.0	+1.0	−6.3	−18.0	14.7
30-06 Springfield	125	spitzer	Handload	3100	+2.0	+1.0	−6.3	−18.0	14.7
30-06 Springfield	150	spitzer	Factory	2850	+2.0	+0.2	−8.1	−24.0	16.2
30-06 Springfield	150	spitzer	Handload	3000	+2.0	+0.8	−6.0	−20.0	18.9
30-06 Springfield	165	spitzer	Factory	2750	+2.0	⊕	−8.3	−25.0	16.7
30-06 Springfield	165	spitzer	Handload	2800	+2.0	+0.2	−7.7	−23.0	19.0
30-06 Springfield	180	spitzer	Factory	2650	+2.0	−0.4	−9.9	−27.0	17.7
30-06 Springfield	180	spitzer	Handload	2750	+2.0	⊕	−8.5	−25.0	20.5
30-06 Springfield	200	spitzer	Handload	2600	+2.0	⊕	−9.0	−25.0	21.3
30-06 Springfield	220	RN	Factory	2350	+2.0	−2.9	−19.0	−50.0	18.9

a 200-yard elk rifle or a 400-yard deer cartridge, though many would insist that the 130-grain bullet is not suitable for elk.

Compare this with the 30-06's 150-grain bullet average energies of: 2744 foot pounds at the muzzle, 2219 foot pounds at 100 yards, 1778 foot pounds at 200 yards, 1406 foot pounds at 300 yards, and 1101 foot pounds at 400 yards. The 30-06 delivers as much at 200 yards as the 270 does at 100 yards. But by the time the bullets get

tridges (with 130-grain versus 150-grain bullets) leaves nothing from which to choose. Typically, both turn in very fine results and 1-inch groups with good handloads are possible in both calibers. But for those who are recoil shy, the 270 will be the easier cartridge to master, with about 3 foot pounds less recoil, about a 20 percent reduction.

When the 270 decides to turn in a substandard performance with respect to velocity, the 30-06 will then

simply a no difference situation despite the '06's hefty energy advantage at shorter ranges.

But there is another difference that is more than worth considering. The 270 accomplishes all that it does at a peak chamber pressure level of about 52,000 to 54,000 CUPs (copper units of pressure) while the 30-06 gets the job done at a more modest level of perhaps 48,000 to 50,000 CUPs. The 10 percent lower pressure level of the 30-06 will mean longer barrel and fire-

to the 300-yard mark both cartridges are performing on a near equal footing. If one compares 270 handloads to 30-06 handloads, the results are similar. A fast 30-06 load will have a 200-yard energy equal to a fast 270 load and at 400 yards things are about equal. Generally speaking, this means game shot at short ranges will be subjected to about 400 foot pounds more energy (depending upon exact range) when the 30-06 is used instead of a 270.

Accuracy between the two car-

best its long-range performance. At 2600 fps (at the muzzle) 130-grain 270 load turns in a 400-yard energy of only 900 foot pounds. However, that extra 200 foot pounds of 30-06 energy falls short of the amount needed to make a notable difference in the field. Actual trajectories are practically identical for either cartridge.

So, the truth is, it matters not which cartridge is chosen *for deer-sized game*. Both are capable of getting the job done to out about as far as anyone can make a clean kill. This is

arm life, as well as a longer cartridge case reloading life. So, if you are a more than occasional shooter, the 30-06 might make a better selection based on a longer useful life or a cost per round basis. For the one-gun hunter, longer barrel life might be the very best reason to choose a 30-06.

Those who favor the 130-grain bullet for elk-sized game when using the 270 should review the results shown in Tables I and II. The 150-grain 270 bullet will always deliver more energy at the longest ranges. So, when considering the 270 versus the 30-06 for heavy game it makes good sense to compare the 270's 150-grain bullet with the 30-06's 180-grain bullet. And here the differences between the two cartridges are indeed notable.

Typically, the 30-06 will deliver a 300-yard energy in excess of 1600 foot pounds when a 180-grain bullet is used. The 270 delivers about 1400 foot pounds when it's performing at its average level (and if a spitzer bullet is used). Thus, the 30-06 is well above

comparison of a 180-grain bullet (30-caliber) to a 150-grain bullet (27-caliber) suggests. When hunting heavy game, most knowledgeable shooters select their ammo with the desire to put the maximum possible energy on the target. The 270's 300-yard energy peaks at about 1400 foot pounds with the use of 150-grain bullets, whether factory ammo or handloads are used. However, a handloaded 30-06, 180-grain bullet driven at a muzzle velocity of 2750 fps will have a 300-yard

should appreciably shorten the range at which elk or larger game are shot.

To summarize the comparisons of ammo ballistics, the 270 Win. cartridge often does not deliver the promised performance with factory ammo when 100-grain varmint or 130-grain big game loads are used. Only the 150-grain load delivers the hoped-for results. Handloading can help to obtain the desired ballistics unless the particular barrel happens to be one of the many 270 barrels that are simply very "slow." And the 270 must be run at 52,000 to 54,000 CUPs to get the best it has to offer.

The 30-06, on the other hand, almost always delivers the desired results with either factory ammo or reloads. Indeed, it is often possible to improve upon factory advertised ballistics by as much as 100 fps. The actual trajectories delivered by the 30-06 are generally very close to what can be obtained with the 270 (see Table III). Still, with a handloaded 150-grain spitzer, the 30-06 (at 3000 fps) turned in the flattest trajectory of all the big game loads tested in the two cartridges. And the 30-06 gets its effectiveness at a modest 48,000 to 50,000 CUPs. However, recoil is al-

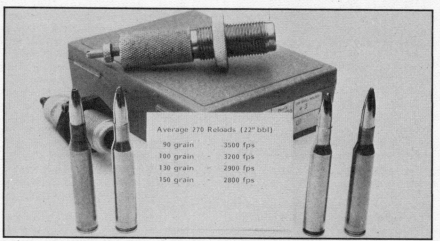

Average 270 Reloads (22" bbl)

90 grain	3500 fps
100 grain	3200 fps
130 grain	2900 fps
150 grain	2800 fps

The 270 performs quite satisfactorily with most reloads, though some specific rifles will prove disappointing.

(Opposite) A pressure gun and chronograph will show the 30-06's superiority over the 270 with respect to any heavy game application or even barrel life. The 270 operates at considerably higher average pressures.

Reloads for the 30-06 can vary immensely. From left to right: 110-grain with IMR 4064, 125-grain with IMR 4350, 150-grain with IMR 4350, 165-grain with IMR 4895, 168-grain with 760, 180-grain with IMR 4350, 190-grain with H380, and 220-grain with IMR 4831. Each is highly accurate at the desired level of performance.

the minimum 1500 foot pounds required for bigger game at this range while the 270 is below this level. Albeit the actual difference is a questionable 200 foot pounds, in that the 1500 foot pound level is accepted by most knowledgeable hunters as a minimum, the difference in performance becomes noteworthy. Indeed, the 30-06's actual field performance on heavy game with 180-grain bullets puts it notably ahead of the 270 with 150-grain bullets.

But there's even more to it than this

energy of almost 1900 foot pounds. That's nearly 500 foot pounds more than possible with the 270, making the 30-06 a magnum performer in comparison.

But for those who like recoil in easy doses, the typical 270 with 150-grain bullets pushes back with just under 16 foot pounds of recoil. The fastest 180-grain 30-06 reloads approach 21 foot pounds of recoil. In that accuracy is closely related to recoil tolerance, some shooters might still prefer the 270 for heavier game. But they then

ways notably heavier for the 30-06 with comparative loads.

But paper or actual ballistics are not the only factors a shooter should use to evaluate a specific cartridge. The actual results obtained when a cartridge is used should be the final area of evaluation.

Reloaders know that both cartridges are relatively easy to reload. But the choice of practical components for the 270 is somewhat limited. Accuracy with the 90-, 100- and 110-grain varmint bullets invariably

The data book listings (and catalogs) may not accurately reflect the performance of any specific 270 as actual velocities are sometimes less than predicted.

peaks with only IMR 4350 or IMR 4064 powders. The 130 as well as the 150-grain bullets seldom do their best unless propelled by charges of IMR 4350, IMR 4831 or Hodgdon 4831. With the sole exception of the 90-grain Sierra hollowpoint, every bullet seems to shoot best at maximum or near maximum pressures. While bullets heavier than 150 grains are available, selection of such bullets invariably leads to reduced down-range energies. Therefore, the 270 effectively handles a bullet range of only 60 grains—90 to 150 grains.

The 30-06 shoots very accurately with almost every powder that will produce factory level ballistics, and that encompasses a great many propellants. I have had fine accuracy with Winchester 760 and Du Pont IMR 3031, IMR 4895, IMR 4320, IMR 4064 and IMR 4350. Too, Hodgdon H380, H4350, H414 and H4895 will all work mighty well. If I were to select a first try powder for 150- to 120-grain bullets it would be IMR 4350. For the 110- or 125-grain varmint bullets my first selection would be IMR 4064.

The 30-06 works well with bullets up to 200 grains. Going heavier will result in a decline in delivered energy. Thus, with 110 to 200 grains being practical, the 30-06 has a bullet selection range of 90 grains, half again as much a spread as the 270.

And while the 270's groups might, as a whole, average ¼-inch or so smaller than the 30-06, either cartridge is fully capable of delivering very close to minute-of-angle accuracy with a well-tuned rifle and carefully worked up handloads. So, for all practical purposes field accuracy with either cartridge will be more than ample for the most demanding shooting.

Most big game struck with a suitable weight bullet from the 270 react as expected, except in the instances when a slow barrel causes a drastic reduction in anticipated velocity. I have killed a great many deer with a 270 and 130-grain bullets. I believe the reaction of each of those animals was nearly identical to the almost like number I have taken with the 30-06 and 150-grain bullets. But I have always felt the need to verify the performance of any 270 taken into the field with a chronograph. I will not use a slow barrel. And I chronograph every lot of 270 ammo used. The urgent need for double-checking is simply not there when I use 30-06 rifles.

I must admit, however, that for a deer-only rifle I prefer the more modest level of recoil of a good 270 over the 30-06. But if I did not own a chronograph, I would forsake the 270 pronto, as I insist on handloads averaging at least 2900 fps when using the 270.

As stated earlier, the 270 does make a better varmint rifle because the reduced recoil and the flat trajectory of a 90-grain HP at 3500 fps makes hitting tiny targets at great distances easier than it would be if a 30-06 were used. However, if factory ammo were to be used I would pass by the 270 in favor of the 30-06—for any purpose.

When game in excess of 300 pounds is to be hunted, the 30-06 will prove a better choice when 180-grain bullets are used, compared to the 150-grain loadings of the 270 rounds. Invariably the 30-06 180-grain bullet creates a larger wound channel and penetrates deeper. Even a small moose will weigh 400 to 500 pounds. And if the only shot presented is a difficult going

The 30-06 can be successfully loaded with any of these or a goodly number of other powders, making it very versatile.

away angle, the 30-06 will prove most capable of anchoring the game where it stands. I would not hesitate to take a broadside heart-lung shot with a 130- or 150-grain 270 load (using a bullet of ample construction) at an elk or moose that weighed as much as 800 pounds. But equally, I would pass up any shot that was not a broadside one when using the 270 on such game. Experience has shown that it's near impossible to consistently drive even a heavily constructed 270 150-grain bullet through heavy bone and muscle and get the necessary penetration required for difficult angle shots on heavy game. Yet, my experience shows that a 180-grain Partition bullet fired from a 30-06 at 2750 fps is easily up to the task. With but one exception, if I know beforehand that the game to be hunted will run in excess of 300 or so pounds, I will invariably select a 30-06.

If the quarry is to be caribou, and knowing that a big one may go over 300 pounds, I will, nonetheless, select a 270 with 130-grain bullets. It's my experience that a wounded caribou most often will just stand there until it is too weak to do anything but fall over. I'm sure there may be exceptions, but until I see the first one, I'll continue to use a 270 for caribou. But for any other animal that tips the scale, or could, at 300 pounds, the 30-06 just seems to be the better round for anchoring game where it stands.

For one lighter animal I also prefer the 30-06. Sheep, of all kinds, seem to

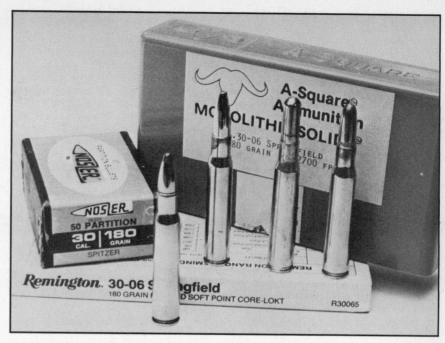

The energy champ of all 30-06 and 270 loads is the 30-06 with 180-grain bullets, especially so when reloads are used.

cling to life with unexplainable grip. Shots that would anchor a similar animal where it stands often will result in a sheep running 100 or more yards. So, because of the 30-06's ability to create a larger wound channel, I favor it for sheep.

In conclusion, with factory loads only, I prefer the 30-06's as-advertised performance over the usual well-below advertised level of the 270 Win. With handloads the 270 is the

better varmint cartridge. And because of its reduced level of recoil, many shooters will find they will do better when using a handloaded 270 on light big game. But when the game gets tough to anchor, a 30-06 is to be preferred.

We are not dealing with the old 30-30 Winchester versus the 32 Winchester Special argument when comparing the 270 with the 30-06. The 30-30 and 32 Special both shot identical weight bullets of identical construction at identical velocities with identical pressures. The lab evidence, and the field evidence, clearly show that there are notable differences in the 270 versus the 30-06. If the ammo factories always loaded the 130-grain 270 bullet to advertised claims some of the differences between the two cartridges would disappear when light big game was condsidered. But the 30-06 would always continue to be the champ on heavier game, and it would do so with a longer barrel and case life, though it would always recoil a notable amount more.

It is important to note that while the nearby tables of ballistics were based on only a dozen or so current test rifles, the listed ballistics compare favorably with a great many 270 and 30-06 rifles and test barrels that I have used during the past 35 years of ballistics work and hunting. The numbers cited are by no means isolated ones, but rather very much representative of what occurs on a day-in day-out basis. ●

The 270 is best loaded with one of three powders, IMR 4350, IMR 4064, or H4831, depending upon bullet weight required.

FOR THOSE OF us who have a certain fondness for sporting arms, there simply is nothing to match the crisp lines of a fine custom rifle. Several writers over the years, in particular, the late Jack O'Connor, extolled the merits of classic stock design. My own preference leans to the classic style; however, I also acknowledge the merits of the Monte Carlo stock for a scope mounted rifle.

Stock design was only one major consideration when, in the '70s, I got the late Lenard Brownell to build a classic stock on a Siamese Mauser action—drop at the comb was to be ⅝-inch; drop at the heel 1½ inches. The rifle was to be chambered for the 25 Krag Improved cartridge, which was another major consideration.

Caliber selection was based on my desire to have a 25-caliber cartridge chambered in a bolt-action rifle. The cartridge needed to be flat-shooting. Thus, it was either the 25-06 in a rimless case, or the 25 Krag Improved for a rimmed case.

One could ask, "Why the Siamese Mauser?" Simply the facts that several Siamese actions were on hand and the Krag rimmed case fits perfectly to the Siamese bolt-face. Ballistics performance of the Krag Improved cartridge was not an open book, while the 25-06 is standardized.

In the fall of 1978, I took delivery of the rifle. It had a premium grade Douglas barrel, with 1-12 twist. The 12-inch twist was decided to be a good compromise in case I might want to shoot some 87-grain bullets at Pennsylvania woodchucks.

My interest in the wildcat 25 Krag cartridge goes back almost 30 years when, as a young fellow in high school, I was engulfed in a newly acquired edition of Philip B. Sharpe's book, *Complete Guide to Handloading*. It was fascinating to learn what some of those early small-arms ballistic pioneers, such as Dr. F.W. Mann and Charles Newton, did to achieve higher velocity and "flat-shooting" cartridges.

As recorded in the December, 1941, issue of *The American Rifleman,* such noted riflemen as H.A. Donaldson, N.H. Roberts and Colonel Townsend Whelen all had A.O. Niedner assemble rifles chambered for the 25 Krag. Charles Newton also at one time had more than a passing interest in the cartridge. Newton tried unsuccessfully to sell Savage Arms on the idea of using a shortened, refined 25 Krag for the Model 99 rifle. Savage opted for a cartridge based on the 30-06 rather than one on the 30-40 Krag. The 250 Savage was too limited in powder capacity to allow a 100-grain bullet to be driven to 3000 fps which had been the desired goal. The lighter 87-grain bullet did reach this level of velocity; thus was born the 250-3000 Savage cartridge.

There has not recently been a great deal written about the 25 Krag Improved. In fact, my search found only two recent articles—one by James Clyde Gates, "25 Krag Improved," which appeared in the 67th issue of *Rifle;* the other was by Hal Stephen, "The 25 Krag Improved," published in the 1963 *Gun Digest*.

There is a point that needs to be considered in any discussion of the 25 Krag. Over the years since 1907, this wildcat, now almost 80 years old, has had several different sets of dimensions given to it. Newton had a short version. A.O. Niedner made a 25 Krag using the standard length 30-40 Krag case (2.30 inches). F.C. Ness indicated

the
25 KRAG IMPROVED
in a bolt action

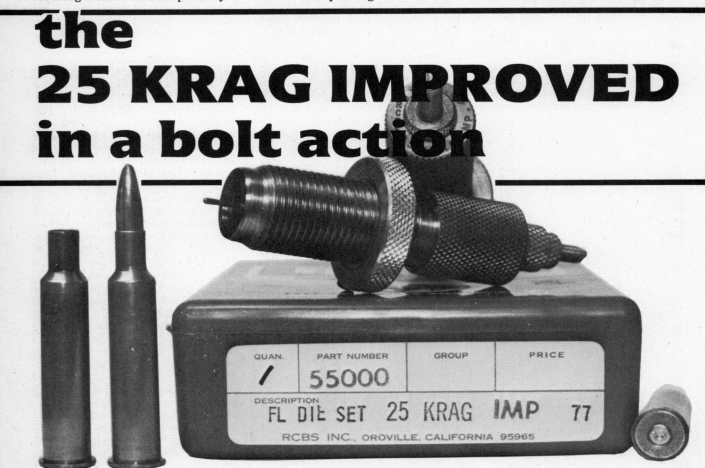

in his book, *Practical Dope on Big Bores,* that there also was the 25 Krag HP (High Power), developed by an unknown designer early on. P.O. Ackley had two different designs for 25 Krag wildcats. The lesser known of the two is the 25 Short Krag; the more prominent is the 25 Krag Improved and the subject of this article.

This version is based on the full length 30-40 case necked down to 25-caliber and blown out by fire forming to obtain a cartridge with minimum body taper and 40-degree shoulder. This Ackley cartridge design was conceived through ballistic experimentation and proved to be most efficient for "over-bored" cartridges and slow-burning powders that were developed in the early 1940s. Ackley concluded that the minimum body taper and sharp shoulder of all his "Improved" designed cartridges reduced case stretching and barrel throat erosion. And, of course, this conclusion would also apply to the 25 Krag Improved.

The late Lenard Brownell built my 25 Krag on a Siamese Mauser action. There were several custom metal alterations that Lenard made to the Siamese action. They were as follows:

- install Brownell hollow bolt handle and three-panel checker the knob;
- drill and tap for Brownell scope bases and install rings;
- fit Canjar trigger and tang safety;
- fill safety notch in the bolt sleeve;
- alter and hone extractor to fit Krag case rim and allow for ease of chambering cartridge;
- slim, contour and polish trigger guard and receiver.

The scope mounted in the Brownell rings was a 4x Leupold. I had an extra set of Brownell rings in which a Weaver K10 had been installed. The Leupold 4x was pulled and the K10 mounted for the load development work, which will be described later. (Kimber of Oregon now makes the Brownell scope rings and bases for most standard rifles. Special custom bases for those that Kimber does not make can be ordered from Billingsley and Brownell, Dayton, WY.)

Before one can start shooting a 25 Krag, it is necessary to convert 30-40 brass. Probably the simplest way is to use RCBS forming and file-trim dies along with a full-length sizing die. I would recommend the use of the form-ing dies to make the 25 Krag Improved; however, that was not the way that cases were formed for use in the test rifle. I was in too much of a hurry. I had not taken the time to order in advance a set of the forming dies, and when the rifle was received, there was a set of RCBS full-length sizing and seating dies included with the rifle. So I jerry-rigged it.

Starting with new Winchester Super-X 30-40 cases, they were successively run through .284-, .270- and .264-inch dies to reduce the neck diameter. Following the case neck reduction, the cases were then full-length sized in the 25 Krag Improved die. Measurements were made to be sure that the inside neck diameter would be of the proper size to accept 25-caliber bullets. Comparison was made with some 257 Roberts new factory brass and the newly formed 25 Krag cases, and there did not appear to be any excessive brass which could cause increased chamber pressures.

Just to be on the safe side, I took five cases and fireformed with 9 grains of Bullseye powder. I put a piece of fiber filler as a spacer over the powder, filled the case to the shoulder

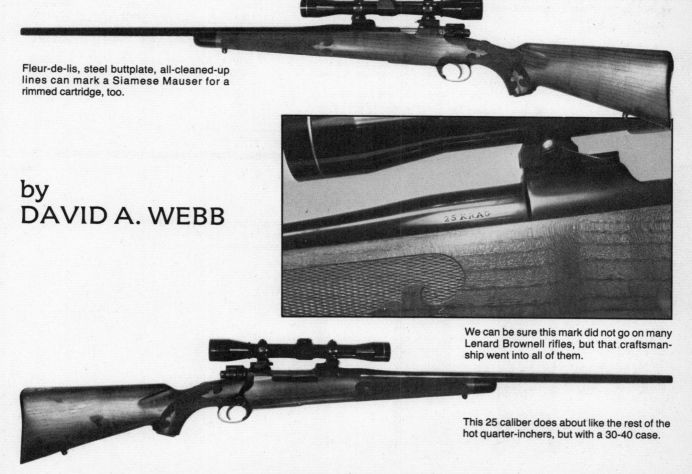

Fleur-de-lis, steel buttplate, all-cleaned-up lines can mark a Siamese Mauser for a rimmed cartridge, too.

by
DAVID A. WEBB

We can be sure this mark did not go on many Lenard Brownell rifles, but that craftsmanship went into all of them.

This 25 caliber does about like the rest of the hot quarter-inchers, but with a 30-40 case.

All these were stable at permissible velocities in author's Brownell Siamese Mauser 25 Krag.

Nothing's perfect, especially the twist rate in his 25 Krag rifle. It won't stabilize these.

Heavy 25-Caliber Bullets	Weight (grs.)	Ballistics Coefficient	Diameter (inches)
Hornady, spire point	100	.336	.2569
Nosler, Partition	100	.409	.2569
Speer, spitzer boattail	100	.393	.2571
Sierra, spitzer flatbase	117	.404	.2569
Sierra, hollowpoint boattail	120	.370	.2566*
Speer, spitzer	120	.410	.2572
Speer, spitzer boattail	120	.435	.2571
Nosler, spitzer solid base	120	.471	.2567*
Nosler, Partition	120	.454	.2568*
Barnes, semi-spitzer	125	.386	.2567*

*Bullet would not stabilize in test rifle (twist 1-in-12).

In this case, the writer got lucky with the first bullet—Speer's 120-grain spitzer—and load he tried and never could improve on it.

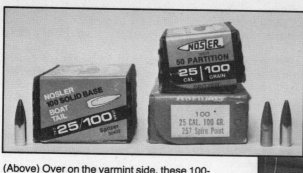

(Above) Over on the varmint side, these 100-grainers zip right along; the 87-grain bullets may get tried, but not yet.

(Below) Not only does Webb have a Brownell rifle with Brownell mounts, but he has two sets of rings and shoots sometimes with a 4x scope, sometimes with a 10x.

with corn meal and topped it with another wad of fiber filler. After fire forming, trimming and deburring the cases, the inside neck diameter was measured to be sure that sufficient neck expansion had occurred to release bullets and not cause any potential pressure problems. All systems were in a "go" condition and the loading and shooting of the 25 Krag Improved rifle commenced. Out of the 40 Winchester cases formed in the above manner, I buckled just one neck in the press.

There is a reasonably good selection of 25-caliber bullets. Because the twist was 1-in-12, I knew that it might be difficult to stabilize the heavier bullets, i.e. the Barnes 125-grain semi-spitzer softpoint. But then I was curious about the matter so it was decided to test and attempt to develop loads for the heavier bullets first. I list the heavier bullets initially tested here and give ballistic coefficients and measured diameters.

The selection of powders was based on previously published information from the articles by J.C. Gates and Hal Stephens; also P.O. Ackley's fine reference book which gives loads for the 257 Roberts Improved were compared as the case volume for the Improved Roberts is similar to the 25 Krag Improved.

Loads for the 25 Krag are given in the table. The optimum performance of the cartridge was best achieved when slow burning powders were used. Load development must be approached with a degree of caution. Several other handloaders have cited,

and my own experience also has shown, that load development with calibers having a bore diameter less than 308 has a tendency to be sensitive. Small incremental increases in the powder charge or a change in the bullet (type, diameter, etc.) can often cause a rapid increase in chamber pressure. Powder charges should be increased in ½-grain increments and when changing to a different bullet make with the same weight, reduce the charge by 10 percent and start from there again.

The loads given with this article were developed in the test rifle, a Siamese Mauser bolt action. Load data for the 25 Krag Improved in a bolt action has not been previously published. Therefore load development in your rifle using data presented in this article must be carefully used.

Now let's take a look at some of the results. My original intent was to utilize a bolt-action Siamese Mauser and develop loads primarily with the heavier bullets for long-range open plains shooting.

There are times when most everything goes according to plan. The very first load that was tried gave excellent performance, grouping in less than 1 inch at 100 yards. The load was the 120-grain Speer spitzer plain base bullet in front of 48.0 grains IMR-4831 Du Pont powder with Winchester cases and Winchester large rifle primer. The Oehler Model 33 chronograph with Skyscreens measured that first firing at 2990 fps. My initial thought was that there was not much room for improvement and "why test more loads?" But as with most handloaders, curiosity prevailed.

The majority of the loads tested were for heavy 25-caliber bullets. A few loads were tried with Winchester's slow-burning ball powder, WW-785; no extensive testing was done due to the limited availability of this propellant. Primary focus was on four slow burning tubular powders: Accurate Arm's MR-3100, Hodgdon's H-4831 and Du Pont's IMR-4831, plus their new IMR-7828.

Several loads were tried with the ball powder H-870. A few preliminary case-full loads showed no advantage. Although accuracy was excellent, there just is not enough room in the 25 Krag Improved case for this slow burner.

The conclusion reached from the load testing was that the best overall load was the first one tested—120-grain Speer with 48.0 grains of IMR-4831. Several loads as shown in the table were close seconds. The 117-grain Sierra (flatbase) and 120-grain Speer (boattail) gave fine accuracy with IMR-4831 and MR-3100 respectively. The 120-grain Nosler, Partition and Solid Base, Sierra HP and 125-grain Barnes SP, although fine bullets, just would not stabilize in my rifle. Undoubtedly both the rifling twist of 1-in-12 inches and the bullet diameters had something to do with the lack of accuracy of these bullets in the test rifle.

As the reader can observe by perusing the data given in the table, there were certain loads that gave fine accuracy. With respect to the heavier bullets—115 grains and up—diameter of the bullet was a factor in determining whether or not the bullet was stabilized by the 1-in-12 rate of twist. With the 100-grain bullets—Hornady, Nosler, Sierra and Speer—the diameter of less than 0.2570-inch was not a significant accuracy factor.

At this point, I believe a brief explanation should be given as to why it took so long from the time that Lenard Brownell completed the 25 Krag rifle in 1979 until now when this article is being written detailing the results of the handloaded development for the rifle. I guess I really do not have any important reason for the delay. When the rifle was first received, it was determined rather quickly that the load using the 120 Speer/IMR-4831/48.0 grains gave MOA accuracy. I thus knew the rifle would shoot, and it was then used the next several years to hunt whitetails in the western part of my home state of Pennsylvania. When the possibility of an antelope hunt in Wyoming developed, it was decided to revive the old project that had never been completed of "determining the ballistics performance of the 25 Krag Improved cartridge in a bolt rifle." I wanted to know what was the best possible handload that could be used for open range shooting. So I shot enough to find out. ●

Table 1
Loads for 25 Krag Improved

Bullet	Charge (grs.)	Powder	Case	Primer	Cart. Leng. (in.)	Cart. Head* Expansion (in.)	Velocity (fps)	Accuracy**
100-gr. Hornady	45.0	IMR-4350	Super Speed	Win	3.04	0.4576	2997	C
	46.0	IMR-4350				0.4583	3049	B+
	47.0	IMR-4350				0.4584	3127	B
	46.0	WW-760				0.4583	3073	B
	49.0	IMR-4831				0.4579	3172	A
100-gr. Nosler Partition	46.0	IMR-4350	Super-X	Win	3.02	0.4581	3143	B
	49.0	IMR-4831				0.4582	3192	C
100-gr. Nosler (Solid Base)	46.0	IMR-4350	Super-X	Win		0.4583	3145	B
	49.0	IMR-4831				0.4581	3195	B
100-gr. Speer Spitzer (boattail)	46.0	IMR-4350	Super-X	Win		0.4582	3095	C
	49.0	IMR-4831				0.4583	3167	A
117-gr. Sierra Spitzer (plain base)	51.0	H-4831	Super-X	Win	2.98	0.4586	3032	B
	48.0	IMR-4831				0.4580	3047	B+
	48.0	H-4350				0.4584	3001	B
	48.0	MR-3100				0.4584	3019	B
	51.0	IMR-7828				0.4584	2981	C
120-gr. Speer Spitzer (plain base)	48.5	H-4831	Super-X	Win	2.95	0.4579	2818	A
	49.0	H-4831				0.4582	2867	C
	50.0	H-4831				0.4586	2998	A
	47.0	IMR-4831				0.4581	2947	B
	48.0	IMR-4831				0.4580	2990	A
	49.0	IMR-4831				0.4587	3109	B
	50.0	IMR-7828				0.4583	2944	B
	51.0	IMR-7828				0.4584	3013	C
	52.0	IMR-7828				0.4587	3073	B
120-gr. Speer Spitzer (boattail)	49.0	H-4831	Super-X	Win	2.99	0.4583	2895	C
	50.0	H-4831				0.4584	2967	C
	48.0	IMR-4831				0.4583	3053	B
	48.5	IMR-4831				0.4585	3061	C
	50.0	IMR-7828				0.4585	2962	B
	47.0	MR-3100				0.4583	2911	B
	48.0	MR-3100				0.4585	3078	A
	48.0	WW-785				0.4580	2830	C
	47.0	H-4350	Super Speed			0.4581	2945	C
	48.0	H-4350				0.4585	3046	C
	54.0	H-870				0.4578	2664	B
	56.0	H-870				0.4580	2709	B
	57.0	H-870				0.4582	2855	A

*Measurements taken at base of case on "pressure ring."
**A—less than one MOA; B—between one and two MOA; C—between two and three MOA.

A Handloading Mystery

by H.V. STENT

A SPECIAL NOTE

This collation of comments and commentaries circles around and around our hobby. Writer Bert Stent quandarized from out in the boonies in the first place; then, with Stent's permission, just about everybody in the handloading business was asked to comment on what he had written. Since this panel involved several of the people who actually prepared the loading manuals Stent cites, a certain acerbity was expected though not much arrived, all things considered.

The idea was to clear up the mystery for Bert Stent and for you. I'm not so sure that happened.

All were written several years ago, but in the interim there have been a lot more old manuals consulted.

Ken Warner

The old ones and the new ones hardly ever agree. Why not?

IF I NAMED the cartridge now, you might read no further and miss an intriguing conundrum relevant to all handloaders. Let's just call it cartridge X.

X has long suffered from a poor press, mostly because its bullets are comparatively slow. Therefore I was electrified to find in Lyman's *Reloading Handbook No. 45* a suggested handload for X giving a velocity of 2900 feet per second (fps) to a light-weight bullet. That would jump X into the high speed class, right there with, in velocity, the 270, 30-06, and 7mm Remington Magnum.

Nothing would do but that I try out this load for X at once. Bullets were bought, cases, primers, and dies were on hand; but the powder involved, Hercules' RelodeR 11, was nowhere obtainable. Its manufacture had been discontinued.

But there are other handloading manuals besides Lyman's, and leafing through an old *Speer's No. 7,* what did I find but a still faster load, 2959 fps, with good old Du Pont 3031, which was not scarce at all.

Lovely. Just to be on the safe side, I checked it out with Speer's latest, No. 9, to find there that the highest recommended load with that powder and bullet in cartridge X was only 2584 fps. The maximum load of 3031 had been dropped from 40 grains to 33 grains.

My dreams deflated, I wrote Speer asking why. Back came a form letter saying that they check all their recommended loads for each new edition of their handbook, and there are bound to be changes. No explanation of why such a big drop for this particular load. I looked up a 3031 load for a different weight bullet in the same cartridge; it, too, was down, from 34 grains to 28.5.

Had 3031 developed higher pressures between the publication of Manual No. 7, in 1966, and No. 9 in 1974? We hear of different lots of powder varying. But if pressures were up, velocities for the same amounts of pow-

This familiar silhouette is about as old as the idea of loading manuals.

der would surely be higher too. They weren't; as far as I could see, there was no appreciable difference.

This posed a problem, for obviously if 33 grains was maximum, as Manual No. 9 had it, then the 40-grain load recommended in No. 7 would be a dangerous overload, enough perhaps to blow rifle and me into bite-sized bits. Who yearns to be scattered over the landscape?

Better check with Lyman's. Yes, its 33.5 grains of 3031 giving 2603 fps for a 110-grain bullet pretty well matched Speer's 33-grain and 2584 fps for a 100-grain slug. Glance at their recipes for another weight bullet—150-grain: Speer had a top of 28.5 grains for 2153 fps; Lyman showed 29.5 grains giving 2274. Close as a courting couple.

A bit of a start to open a Hornady Handbook, then current, and find the top load with 110-grain bullet was 10 percent higher than Lyman's limit— 36.6 grains as opposed to 33.5. Start swelled to shock waves when I compared loads for the 150-grain bullet: Lyman and Speer were cozy with 29.5 grains and 28.5 grains for 2274 and 2153 fps respectively, but Hornady jumped to 33.8 grains, upping velocity to 2400. What's more, Speer in 1966 agreed with Hornady in 1973; Speer's No. 7 gave the 150-grain bullet a max of 34 grains of 3031 for 2407 fps.

All bloody bewildering here on the backside of British Columbia.

To settle this disagreement about amounts of powder, go to the guys who made it, of course. Du Pont's *Handloaders' Guide,* bearing no date but obviously post-1973 since it includes data for 4759 powder, out of production until that year, was called in.

It ignores 100- and 110-grain bullets in X. But for the 150-grain— brace yourself—it gives 35.5 grains which produces 2370 fps. More powder than even Hornady or Speer's No. 7, but with lower velocity than they got, and also lower chamber pressure. Lyman gave 39,400 Copper Units of Pressure for their 29.5-grain, so Du Pont's 35.5-grain should make their CUP runneth over, but they give its pressure as only 37,700.

Six grains more powder—an increase of over 20 percent—yet *less* pressure, and only 96 fps more velocity? What gives here?

Just to muddify the mixture more, back around 1950 BC (Before CUPs) the *American Rifleman* ran a test on a load of 35 grains of 3031 with 150-grain bullet and got a pressure of 49,400 whatchamacallums.

It all makes what Sherlock Holmes might have called a very pretty little problem. And if you've deduced by his methods that X is the too-often condemned (in the papers) 30-30, don't think the same thing can't happen to your more modern cartridges. The bell may toll for them, too.

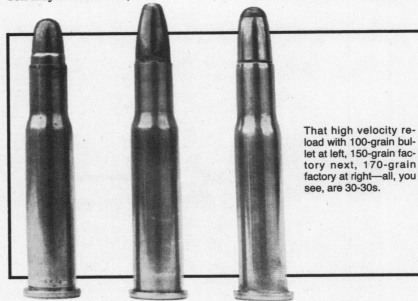

That high velocity reload with 100-grain bullet at left, 150-grain factory next, 170-grain factory at right—all, you see, are 30-30s.

For example, the 7mm Remington Magnum. With H450 powder, max loads given in Speer's No. 9 were 59.5 grains for 160-grain bullet (2850 fps) and 58 grains for 175-grain slugs (2781 fps). Lyman offered 67 grains for the 160-grain bullet (3016 fps) and 65.5 grains for the 175 (2939 fps). Speer warns that their top loads must be "used with caution"; Lyman indicates that a 7-grain difference with H450 can mean up to 15,000 CUPs difference in pressure. Or enough to worry anybody.

Going back now to my little 30-30.

What would its pressures soar to if I loaded it up into the 2800-3000 fps speed zone? Its pressure limit is supposed to be 40,000 whatevers.

Still, Speer listed that load of 40 grains of 3031 the 100-grain bullet for years; some handloaders must have tried it; and none has blown past me. And if Du Pont, whose maximum for 170-grain bullets is 32 grains of 3031, finds it safe to go up to 35.5 when bullet weight is cut to 150 grains, their corresponding load for the light 100-grain bullet would be somewhere around 44 grains. Surely, then, 40 would be safe, even if only in British Columbia.

To test a maximum load it's always wise to start well below it and work up. I loaded new 30-30 cases with 36, 37, 38, 39, and 40 grains of 3031 behind 100-grain Speer plinkers, and shot one of each, in that order, through two Winchester 94s and one Marlin 336.

Rear-locked lever actions will warn, the theory goes, of excessive loads by sticky extraction well before their safety limit is reached. I've had it more than once, but all these loads, including the 40-grain, extracted slick as grease after firing. Empties looked OK, and primers were not extruded, flattened, or cratered. Chronographed in a 26-inch-barreled single shot, the 40-grain load gave 3143 fps. When shot through a 20-inch-barreled carbine, that speed would, I figure, come down to almost exactly the 2959 fps that Speer prophesied.

So here's a load that can transform the old slow-poke thutty-thutty into a high speed, flat-shooting varmint buster. Or at least it would if the rifle's basic grouping ability was up to the job.

But with this one, as with max loads in all calibers, the big question is: how safe is it for frequent use? When different guidebooks, even different editions of the same guidebook, disagree so much, what are we to believe?

Are the discrepancies caused by variations in powder lots? Can there be wide spreads between readings of different pressure guns? How reliable are pressure measurements calculated from minute alterations in bits of copper or lead?

Can we trust the pressure limits we've set for various rifle actions and cartridges? Consider the Model 99

Different prescriptions for the use of this splendid 3031 in 30-30 have been printed over the years—all seem to work.

Savage; it started out with 30-30 type pressure limits of 40,000 foot pounds; now it's chambered for the 243 and 308, where pressures run up to 52,000 CUPs (?) and has been issued for the still hotter 284 Winchester. If pressure limits for the 99 were long set too low, could those for some other rifles be set too high?

Unthinkable? No more so than a velocity of over 3000 fps for a 30-30. Remington's "Accelerator" reaches 3400 fps, but that's both different and a *lot* lighter.

There *is* a mystery.

The Experts Speak:

ED MATUNAS: "There is no mystery, simply a gross lack of knowledge . . . only current data should be used . . . this just points up the problems of using old data . . . "

SIERRA: "The whole purpose of the piece is murky and the subject trivial . . . an adversarial tone . . . unfair . . . what constitutes a safe load will vary, a function of numerous factors not least of which is the humans involved . . . ballistics is not always an exact science . . . "

HORNADY: " . . . as reloading manufacturers gained technological sophistication, we learned information developed in our rifles could be significantly different from what could be safe in others . . . our latest manuals developed data using a standard CUP pressure gun to establish upper limits . . . we then published data developed with standard factory firearms . . . in some instances, loads did not appear to be maximum in our guns, but reading pressure signs in some firearms is very difficult . . . none of us want to furnish 'inferior' data . . . but we still get letters from reloaders who try their first loads at maximum . . . "

HODGDON: "About the 30-30: Yes, data can be confusing! There can be a big difference between data worked up in a rifle and that worked up in a pressure gun. Some data sources keep loads purposely on the low side. We do this. Some data sources want to keep 30-30 loads super safe, below 35,000, and some crowd it to 45,000 or more . . . pressure measurement is not an exact science . . . dozens of variables enter."

OMARK: " . . . find the article confused—a fog-bank of uninformed opinion . . . implies error or incompetence . . . 10 years ago, the user of reloading equipment, components and data was considered to be somewhat responsible for his own actions . . . the courts have changed to a stricter view . . . and as accurate pressure testing equipment became available, the loading data was revised . . . the difference between *maximum, safe pressure in the test gun* and *Industry Standards* resulted in many changes . . . these changes and normal variations create the confusion pointed out by Stent . . . there are a *lot* of answers to Stent's questions in the manuals, but not in the data tables . . . early 99s actually cracked actions with factory 30-30 loads . . . it took redesign and modern metallurgy to make the 99 safe for modern calibers . . . "

LYMAN: " . . . it is futile (not to say invalid) to compare data from the '50s and '60s with recent data. Components do change . . . so may conditions . . . one of the very basic tenets is to use the *current* edition of a given data source . . . "

A POWDER MANUFACTURER: " . . . how can data be the same when everything that goes into its development is different? . . . Stent is not comparing apples to apples . . . to extrapolate reloading data is not a prudent practice . . . when one has a basic understanding of the subject, one can appreciate that the differences in data will continue to exist."

A Second Special Note

I don't think writer Stent implied any incompetence anywhere in his text. Adversarial? Only in a Socratic sense. Unfair? Hardly. Murky? Not on purpose. Error? Well, errors there are, but Stent didn't say so. Ignorant? Of course—when it comes to these aspects of the loading manual business. That was the point. So are almost all of us. Less so now, of course.
Ken Warner

Me And Life With

ONE OF THE few observations that can be made about loading presses and their design, without fear of much contradiction, is that not everyone agrees on what's good and not so good. What follows is a collection of one guy's opinions on the topic. I've been using loading presses for 30-some years and have worked with a greater variety than most. I've encountered features I liked very much and others that I didn't like at all. The discussion will be confined to those presses that are incapable of producing a loaded round with each stroke of the operating handle: turret presses will be included, but not the all-out progressive designs, which will be discussed elsewhere in this issue.

If a press carpets the floor with spent primers, I tend to regard that as an unforgiveable design flaw. Some presses have primer-catcher receptacles that are held in place by rubber bands or such. It has been my experience that such devices capture some of the primers but not necessarily all of them. The ideal solution to the control of spent primers, I think, was the one introduced in the old Model A-2 RCBS press and still used on the Heavyweight CHampion by C-H. The ram is hollow, angled back slightly, so that the primers drop down through the ram and on out through a small vent bored in the rear side of the ram. Put a can or similar receptacle beneath that and you'll catch every single spent primer. The Model A-4 RCBS press has the hollow ram of its remote forebear but they've provided a small plastic cup that snaps over a flange on the bottom of the ram. That is supposed to catch the primers and usually does so, provided you remember to remove and empty it at regular intervals. If you happen to knock it loose, you have dead primers all over the place.

The RCBS A-2 and C-H Heavyweight CHampion share another feature I admire warmly and seldom if ever encounter in other presses. At the completion of the cycle, the ram is at the bottom of its stroke and the operating handle is well to the rear. The front member of the O-frame is positioned so that it's convenient to remove the processed case with your right hand as the left hand is putting a fresh case into the shellholder. This arrangement of things makes for maximum efficiency and speed of operation.

If the press is to be used for high-stress operations, such as bullet swaging, the C-H Heavyweight CHampion gets my vote. Its ram appears to be heat-treated and quite tough in the

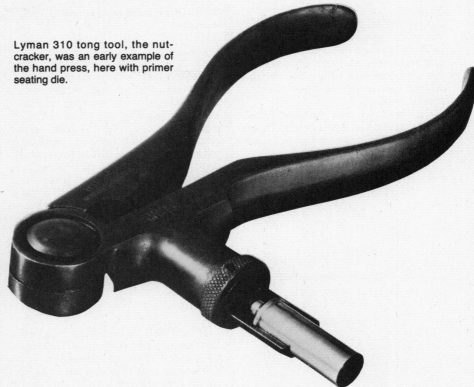

Lyman 310 tong tool, the nutcracker, was an early example of the hand press, here with primer seating die.

THE NON-

area that secures the shellholder. If you subject some of the other presses to comparable levels of strain, the milled lips will distort and you'll not be able to insert a shellholder in the usual manner until you pry them back to normal configuration with a screwdriver and a sheepish expression on your face.

Another feature I appreciate warmly is what we usually term the compound toggle linkage, as found on

quite a few of the contemporary presses. The leverage increases progressively over the arc of the operating stroke, approaching infinity at the very end of it. The principle is a little difficult to explain, but it becomes clearly apparent if you operate the handle and watch the interaction of the linkage at the end of the stroke.

There are times, such as in loading small handgun cartridges, when you do not need an extravagant amount of leverage and the generous arc covered by the operating handle seems excessive. At such times, a shorter handle would be a welcome convenience. In fact, I went to a bit of bother to make up a custom stubby handle for use on my old Hollywood turret press in such situations.

Leave it to designer/maker Richard Lee to follow such a concept to its logical conclusion. When the Lee Precision Model 2000 press appeared, the radius of its operating handle was easily wrench-adjustable to any desired length. If you needed more leverage, increase the handle radius: just that simple.

of 2-inch plank, perhaps 12 inches square or so. The mounting holes are counter sunk on the underside to leave the bolt heads flush with the lower surface, so the assembly can be attached to the working surface by means of C-clamps. Toward the rear edge of the upper surface of the plank, I fasten an old die box or similar container, by means of a sheet metal screw in each of the four corners. That provides fairly secure storage for all the pesky—but vital—little hunks of hardware. To the present, this seems to have worked out quite well, and I commend it to your consideration for that reason.

A-4 had never used an A-2, so as to know the joy of a really efficient arrangement of parts.

In cold actuality, if you have two functional hands in the first place, the procedures of reloading tend to make you more or less ambidextrous. I am right-handed, as noted, but my left hand does an awful lot of the needed work and, were I forced to reload with my left hand in my pocket, I'd cut my output by an estimated 70 percent.

Any loading press design that hampers access to the area around the shellholder by either or both hands is not a good design, in my humble opinion.

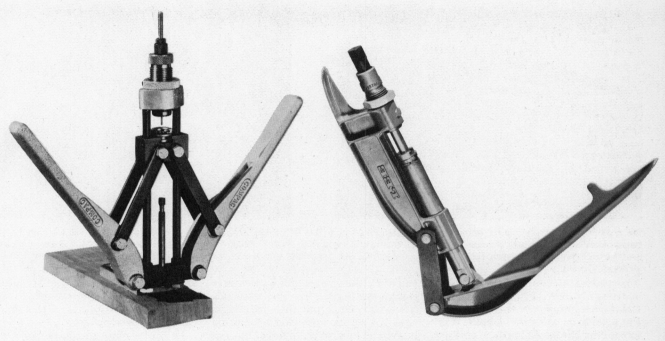

Huntington Compac press is an improved version of the old Decker press. A W design, it works with standard dies.

Lee Hand Press, shown partly open, is the latest arrival in the non-bench tool class.

PROGRESSIVES

Most loading presses come out of the box with an assortment of small hardware items consisting of collars, punches, springs and such-like to permit seating primers of either diameter, perhaps other items, as well. Keeping track of such vital gizmory offers something of a challenge.

I've contrived a solution of sorts and it works fairly well, for me. I offer it for your consideration. My usual approach is to mount the press to a piece

The RCBS A-4 press, I'm told, was designed by a southpaw and offers the option of switching the handle position for the convenience of either persuasion. Being a natural northpaw, I've tried the handle in both positions, finding myself less than gruntled with either of them. The operating handle, at the top of its stroke, blocks access to the area around the shellholder on one side or the other. It was obvious to me that the designer of the

In making these observations, I'm well aware that my own case is unusual. I have several presses and most reloaders have one, perhaps two at the outside. Thus, I have and cherish a C-H Junior CHampion but, if it were my only press, I would mutter darkly about it. Compact and light in weight, it has the compound toggle linkage and is, in many respects, a delight to use. Expelled primers, however, have to be caught by hand for dis-

 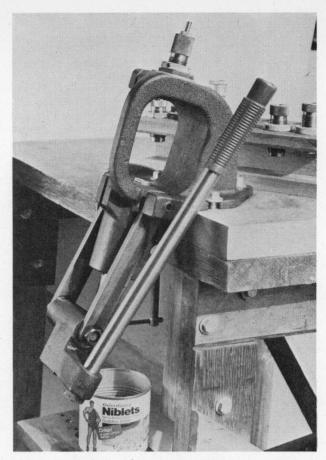

Since early 1959, my good friend and staunch companion has been this RCBS Model A-2 (at left). I like it because it's well adapted for two-handed feeding and removal of cases. Spent primers drop into the big can on a shelf below the press and I empty them out, every year or so. The C-H Heavyweight CHampion (at right) has hollow ram to put spent primers into a container, and it's heat-treated and tough enough for bullet swaging.

posal and it's a vexing, time-consuming chore. I leave the Junior CHamp mounted near the other press I happen to be using and employ it for expanding the case mouth or perhaps for seating the bullet.

Primer seating is another operation that is not always handled as well as it should be. As a general observation, I don't much care for any design in which primers are seated at the end of the handle upstroke. They require application of moderate to considerable horizontal force on the handle. I often work on surfaces that are not rock-solid in the horizontal plane and using such presses requires grabbing the press in your free hand to keep from overturning the bench. I prefer to seat the primers at the end of the handle downstroke, thus bypassing the problem.

I like the Lee Auto Prime II system and customarily reserve two presses with Auto Primes installed and ready to go; one each for the small and large primer diameters. Picking up primers and putting them inside the collar of a priming punch is a fumblesome chore at best and the Auto Prime relieves

you of it, likewise avoiding the risk of contaminating the primers with oily fingertips. Once put into the magazine, the primers are fed to the priming punch by gravity: a force that has not faltered in many millennia.

I have long harbored a personal dislike for those little pivoting primer arms that have to be held in place to seat primers on the downstroke of the ram. The ram goes up to size and deprime the case, back down to seat the primer, back up again to allow the priming arm to pivot outward and—particularly with bottleneck cases—the case mouth re-encounters the expanding plug and frictional resistance. More often than not, the ram will lurch upward, knocking out the new primer. I think this is an eminently nettlesome arrangement.

My opinions are a lot mellower when it comes to turret presses and the old eight-station Hollywood press gets a great deal of use. As with the Junior CHampion, it is not designed to catch spent primers and new primers are seated at the end of the handle upstroke. My solution to that consists of a little plastic can, originally con-

taining a roll of 35mm film. I trimmed a little off the top and attached it beneath the shellholder with tape to catch the spent primers.

Of course, that prevents use of the regular primer seating post, but I don't mind. I remove the priming post and replace it with ½-inch, ⁵⁄₁₆-18 bolt to keep debris out of the hole. The primer catcher is of translucent plastic—from Fuji colorprint film—so I can see when it's time to empty it. Primers are seated as a separate operation on one of the presses equipped with the Lee Auto Prime II units.

Having anywhere from three to eight turret stations available at the flick of a wrist is an appreciated luxury. For example, when I'm loading the 44 Magnum case, I start by running it up into an RCBS carbide resizing die that also punches out the primer. Next comes a Hornady carbide sizing die that's slightly smaller in diameter than the one from RCBS and I have that adjusted so it only sizes about the top ½-inch of the case neck another thousandth or two.

Next comes one of the Lyman M-type mouth expanding dies. The lower

RCBS A-4 (left) features ambidextrous handle, primer catching cup and lots of leverage. It also blocks access at the top of the stroke. Hornady Model 00-7 (right) has primer catcher, an ingenious priming arm, compound toggle linkage, and plenty of handle.

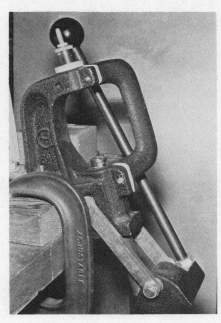

The C-H Junior CHampion is a handy little press, light in weight, with lots of leverage. I often use this one for seating bullets, rarely for resizing, as it has no provision to catch spent primers.

portion of the punch is about .002-inch smaller in diameter than the bullet and, as the case mouth goes over that, it comes to an expanding area that's about .002-inch larger than bullet diameter. When suitably adjusted, the Lyman M die expands the top .010-inch or so of the case mouth just enough to permit hand insertion of the bullet base, but there is not an extravagant flare or funnel effect to weaken the brass.

Having run the cases through those three dies, I prime them and add the powder charge by means of other facilities. While it's possible to install a rotary powder measure in the Hollywood turret, I do not trust myself not to forget to actuate the darned thing. To my mind, there's no satisfactory substitute for having all the charged cases reposing in a loading block, so as to be able to visually inspect the level of powder in each case before starting the bullet into the case mouth by hand as a preliminary to final seating and crimping. Handled thus, I damn-well *know* there is one charge of powder behind each bullet: no more and no less.

The hand-started bullet returns to

the press for seating to the desired depth. My bullet seating die, for the record, is an old one made by C-H for the 44 Russian cartridge but there's no need for you to be that exotic. The final operation is performed by a taper-crimp die originally made by RCBS for use in reloading the 44 Auto Mag cartridge.

By following the outlined approaches, I've never had a bullet migrate forward in the case from recoil. The bullet is held in the case neck so securely that it takes a lot of hard whacks with the inertia-puller to get it back out, should you wish to do so. I do not like to use the hard roll-crimp that's usually recommended, for several reasons. For one, it work-hardens the case neck and, for another, it may scrape and distort the base of the bullet, particularly with cast bullets.

If you do not have a good, firm grip of the case neck on the bullet base, even the most savage roll-crimp is not enough to hold the bullet motionless against the hammering effect of recoil. If the case neck has a good grip on the bullet base, you do not need the roll-crimp; just that simple.

Press designs come to be characterized by letters of the alphabet. Thus, we've had the C-press—once quite popular, now seldom seen—and the closed version of that, called the O-press and still in wide use. Huntington Die Specialties' revised version of the Decker hand press could hardly be called anything but a W-press and Lee Precision's new hand press could be termed an L-press. The old Lyman #310 tong tool is more or less a V-press and the original Lee Loader, powered by a billet of wood—perhaps a mallet aforethought—could, arguably at least, be called an I-press. While it's admittedly intriguing to speculate upon a firm called American Reloading Products, marketing something called the American X-press, the fine details of its working principle seem a bit hazy. That still leaves several letters unassigned, although the H-press is well rooted in the art. The late Charles Heckman, whose obituary appeared in the first edition of this book, called his firm C-H Tool & Die Corp., and made both C-presses and H-presses; good ones, too.

Most turret presses are modifications of the C-press design, although some have a tie-bar that can be installed for high-stress operations, such as bullet swaging, thus converting them into O-presses, temporarily, at least.

The tong-type press must be nearly as old as the fixed metallic cartridge and I can't say who first came up with the idea. I have a tong tool, in 44-40 WCF, made by Winchester, and it may antedate the Lyman tong tool. I have an Ideal tong tool, in 32-20 WCF, that includes a single-cavity bullet mould at the front end. It's nickel-plated and still was reasonably functional, the last time I used it, which was not recently.

I do not like surprises when I'm shooting and that is the reason for my insistence upon a thoughtful visual check of the powder level in each case before seating the bullet. I do not begrudge the time that takes. Recently, I had to terminate some test-firing with a 44 Magnum revolver until I could get it home and make up a suitable rod to drive a lodged bullet out of the bore. That was not one of my loads. Rather, it was a *factory load!* These days, I lead a fairly vegetative existence—living in peas and hominy, as it were—but I was right grateful I didn't trigger that particular round in a chips-down confrontation.

All that notwithstanding, I'll use any reasonable approach to get the work done as quickly as possible, barring any concession to reliability. In bench presses, my taste runs strongly

The beloved old 8-station Hollywood turret press, with priming post installed. (Is your bench always this messy, Mr. Grennell? No it's often considerably messier . . .)

toward presses that offer free access to both left and right hands when the ram is at the end of the downstroke, examples being the cherished old RCBS Model A-2 that I've been pumping contentedly since some unrecorded date in 1959, the C-H Heavyweight CHamp or the big old Hollywood.

It is, however, in the nature of my job description that I have to work with all sorts of presses, one time or the other. For those of us who must cope with a press accessible only to the left hand, I'd like to re-offer details on what I call the "three-finger shift." I wrote it up originally for *Gun Digest* in '64 or so, but I think the details might bear repeating.

At the conclusion of the press cycle, pick up an unprocessed case, mouth-up, between the left thumb and left forefinger, moving it toward the shellholder. Grasp the processed case in the shellholder between the left forefinger and left center finger—the one occasionally employed in communicating with fellow motorists. Withdraw the processed case and substitute the new one in its place. With just a bit of practice, the replacement of cases can be made almost as fast as when using both hands; possibly even just a tiny squintch faster. Give it a try and, if you find it useful, pass the word along.

The mentioned piece in the long-ago *Gun Digest* essayed to apply the studies of the late Frank Gilbreth to work simplification at the loading bench. Gilbreth was the father of time-motion study; a role played by Clifford Webb in the film, *Cheaper By The Dozen.* Reloading involves a lot of simple, repetitive motions and anything that can be done to streamline

Recently acquired and just a delight to use is this Redding MatchGrade powder measure. The micrometer is precise and free of backlash. There's a locking screw on the far side to prevent movement of the mike, once adjusted to taste. It lives on Hollywood.

Admittedly inelegant but undubitably functional, here is my primer-catcher for the Hollywood press, a 35mm film can held on with drafting tape. This precludes use of the priming post, so primers are seated in the old Wells press.

the flow of the work is very much to the long-term good. It is a situation in which you're both labor force and management. If you can figure out a way to do it a little quicker, no one is apt to accuse you of trying to drive down the piecework rate. For your collection of minor trivia, I'll note that the unit used in time-motion study for each segment of an operation is the *therblig,* which is Gilbreth, spelled backwards, with minor concessions to make it pronounceable.

I am not morally opposed to using systems in which primers are fed from a tube or magazine and I work with such rigs, every now and again. One should be keenly aware that, any time you have two or more primers jostling against each other, there is some actuarial risk of a chain detonation and such a thing can be distressingly messy as well as painful. Many years ago, I became a fanatical believer in wearing shooting glasses when shooting. Some while later, as the gear became available, I added earmuffs to the must-have category (too late, as it turned out). Along the way, having shooting glasses in place when I really needed them saved my eyesight on at least four or five memorable occasions. I also wear them when casting bullets and that represented one of the times.

It is profoundly educational to look at your mug in a mirror and be able to see the outline of a pair of shooting glasses amid the scars, scabs and pockmarks. It is an experience you do not soon forget. And you are most bodaciously glad to be able to view the spectacle.

What I'm leading up to saying is that I've long since amended working practice to include wearing eye protection when engaged in any aspect of reloading. I have not as yet gone so far as to reload while wearing earmuffs but, if you prefer to do so, I promise not to laugh at you for so doing.

A great many loading presses have abode their destin'd hour and went their way. Some were stunningly great and, for some of the others, minimum discussion constitutes maximum charity. In my considered opinion, the worst loading press I've enountered to date was contoured to resemble one of the meaner species of snakes and named accordingly. Its maker has long since gotten out of the business of making loading presses, suggesting that others shared my feelings about it.

Over a number of years, a lot of loading presses came out of Minnesota, often applauded by florid catalog copy and names such as Model Perfect and Krupp-American. Basically, they were C-presses, ruggedly built and heir to all the assets and liabilities of that design concept. Most if not all of them utilized an arrangement whereby the shellholder was removed from the end of the ram and screwed into the position usually occupied by the loading die. A priming post was screwed into the end of the ram and that was your method for seating the primer.

In my lengthening career at the loading bench, I have encountered one example of that particular genre.

I got it about 1961 or so and still have it. This one is branded R. F. Wells/ Howard Lake, Minn., and it's identified as the Professional Model C.

I would say its handle has been worked up and down about as often as any other press I've ever had and/or still have. The curious thing is, I don't recall that I've ever loaded a complete round of ammunition on that press, but I've seated a thundering goshawful lot of primers with it. I have both sizes of priming punches and have lovingly accumulated 14 different shellholders for use with it. The threads on the holders are cut all willy-nilly, requiring some number of homemade shims to lock them in position with entry slot to the fore. I made the shims from obsolescent calling cards, cutting a ⅞-inch hole in the card and trimming to suit. The chart above the shellholder rack specifies anywhere from zero to six shims for use with any given holder. With so soul-balmy a widgit available, you may understand why I don't worry if I lose track of the pivoting primer arm that came with this or that press to be tested and evaluated.

The Purdey/Bonanza presses, out of Faribault, Minnesota, were an entirely discrete operation from what we might term the Model Perfect breed. They include some examples of really gifted engineering and continue to be available from Forster Products.

I would be the first to concede that, in the ranks of reloaders, I am a maverick's maverick. My activities, needs and shaped tastes are anything but typical. One time or another, I've had a chance to use a lot of presses and have continued to use those that impressed me favorably. Some, such as the old A-2, are edging toward their 10th hashmark, i.e. 30 years of service.

I do not know of a really bad design of loading press in today's marketplace. Some are better than others and hardly any—with the exception of the C-H Heavyweight CHampion— are quite as good as I wish they were. Fred Huntington, designer of the A-2, claims it could not be built in today's labor market for a price that any sane soul would be inclined to pay. The big C-H rig is by no means cheap, but you could purchase three of them and have enough change back from the price-tag on a Colt Python to tip a waitress right handsomely.

How much is it worth to own a press you can use for the better part of 30 years and feel happy as a kid on Christmas morning every time you work the handle on it?

Persecution rests . . .

I don't prime with the A-2, and in fact long ago lost its priming arm. I do deprime a lot, though, and I have an improvement.

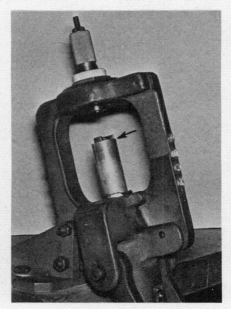

The short section of aluminum tubing (arrow) is slipping over the ram to cover the slot in the front of it . This positively prevents escaping primers and, should I wish to try it, enables decapping of cases with live primers, with little risk.

Checking Out

PROGRESSIVE

LOADERS

More than ever, you pays your money and you takes your choice . . .

John Neese assisted the author in setting up the many presses tested. Here he is with the C-H Auto Champ. Note easy visibility of all operations with C-H.

by CLAY HARVEY

ARTICLES on progressive loaders are encountered infrequently in the shooting press. Why? First, progressives are generally more expensive than single-stage units, although the price gap is today nowhere near the yawning abyss it once was. Secondly, progressives are viewed by many as tools for very advanced hobbyist practitioners, those reloaders who are less concerned with ammunition accuracy than the "rest" of us and handgunners who shoot a lot, probably in competition, and thus are interested primarily in huge quantities of ammo, such as police departments.

Some truth lies in all that. Generally, a progressive tool *is* more difficult to assemble, requires greater attention to details when producing ammo, demands more time and mechanical ability to change from one caliber to another, needs much more maintenance, and indeed usually hits you harder in the wallet than similarly sophisticated single-stage or turret presses. Consequently, they are most often purchased by experienced handloaders. However, a degree in mechanical engineering is not a requisite, nor do you have to be an executive with General Motors to afford one. On the other side, despite what you may hear, a progressive loader will not perk coffee as you load, at least at this stage of development.

The assertion that the progressive press owner is a dimwit who cares more about ammo quantity than quality is specious. *Of course* quantity is important to a progressive owner; it's why he bought the tool. The implication that such a gent manufactures slipshod ammo is where the truth wanders off. Handgun ammunition loaded on a progressive is fully as good as the best of fodder fabricated on a single stage or turret. Besides, the user of a progressive is cognizant of the fact that weighing charges and hand-seating primers in no way affects handgun ammo precision *at the target.* You are in doubt? I suppose, then, that you figure Remington and Winchester and Federal have elves hand-filling their 38 Special and 45 ACP target ammunition, perhaps in a hollow tree somewhere.

Naturally, since competitive handgunners and police officers probably burn up more cartridges than the rest of us, they are the ones most likely to need a progressive. I have difficulty perceiving the slight in this, but have known detractors of progressives to imply that prospective purchasers of such tools who are *not* one of the above might be suspect, and should be relieved of their Serious Shooter cards. (Serious Shooters, by the lights of these elitists, worship at the altar of accuracy for its own sake, above all else, including practicality. A pox on them.) (The elitists.)

Now, some of you may be wondering at this point exactly what a progressive press is. I'm not surprised. If you read up on these new-fangled gadgets (only 50-odd years old), you'll get even more confused. Definitions vary, terms vary. For instance, you will run across such terms as pseudo-progressive, semi-progressive, straightline, circular, universal, fully-automated, hand-indexed, and more. Before discussing such idiomatic terminology, let's find a working definition for the word "progressive."

One gentleman proffered this one in the shooting press: "A hand-operated progressive reloader is a press that works on six or more cartridge cases simultaneously."

Why six? I dunno.

The same gent, later in his career: "A progressive is a press that works at relatively high speed and with considerable uniformity on several shells simultaneously and does not require the operator to handle the shells individually between the various reloading stations."

Not too bad, but why "relatively high speed?" Speed has nothing to do with *defining* a progressive. Why not include automatic case feed in the definition, or bullet feed, or primer feed?

Here's another, and now we're getting close: "A machine that performs a function on several cartridges at once and produces a loaded round with each press cycle."

If we settle on this one, then such hand-indexed units as the Dillon 550, RCBS 4X4, and the basic Star *are* true progressives.

Dave Pickens offers the following: "To be a *true* progressive, a tool should produce a loaded cartridge after each complete cycle, with the operator having nothing to do but work the handle."

He means aside from putting powder, bullets, primers, and brass in their appropriate containers, of course. He has a point. And if you agree with him, then the only true progressive I know of is the R.D.P.

Such manufacturers as Lee and C-H would like progressives to be defined as tools with auto-indexing capability as well as automatic case feed, priming, and powder metering. Which is understandable; their machines offer these features and most of their competition do not.

I'm about to jump into the fray, to wit: "A progressive reloader, using a single case-securing mechanism, provides one fully loaded cartridge with every complete up-and-down cycle of the operating handle, regardless of the number of supplementary operations required during said cycling, and regardless of who or what performs these maneuvers."

Have I covered all the bases? Mentioning simultaneous work being done on multiple cases would be redundant; how else could a loaded round be fabricated? No need to mention high speed or uniformity, since such are dependent on operator skill, even with self-charging loaders. Yep. That covers it. I'll stand by my definition, which eliminates the old three-station H-styles, by the way.

Now we can discuss and dismiss such vague terms as *pseudo-* and *semi*-progressive, both of which refer to units bereft of self-indexing. Outdated, unneeded. A *fully-automated* press is one that is totally self-operated, usually electrically, and requires attention only at hopper-filling time. A *universal* press offers caliber conversion capability. A *straightline* articulates with all the cartridge cases lined up in a row, like cans in a brewery. A *circular,* by far the most popular and versatile, has a rotary shell plate; the cartridges go round like a carousel. Circulars, with one or two exceptions, are easy to change from caliber to caliber, usually by changing the tool head. Perhaps I should have said "relatively easy," since cartridge switching even with the most advanced progressive is more complicated than simply replacing the dies in a single stage or turret.

Having arrived at a point wherein we are working with a clearly defined set of parameters, and now that we've examined the argot, let's slip into the past and see where the progressive suffered its genesis.

In 1930 or thereabout, much cerebration was going on in San Diego. Several shooters, not content with the simple hand tools available heretofore, were casting about for better (read *faster*) ways to produce prodigious quantities of handgun ammo. Fathered by all this cranial activity were such presses as the Star (still with us today), the Buchanan (later bought out by PESCO), the Shockey (which offered several die positions, but only a single shellholder), the Hill (a *very* rare straightline), the Potter (which some say was not quite a true progressive), and the fully automated Dircks (which led to the Tri-Standard). Thus we leap from around 1930 to the early '70s when C-H brought

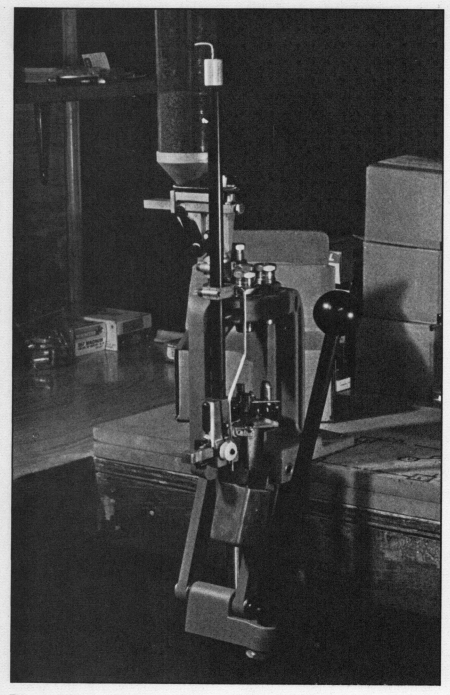

This is the Dillon RL-550. Note John Neese's homemade primer level measure, a long rod bent at the top.

out the Auto-Champ, the only straightline that came and stayed rather than came and went.

Such Star-related presses as Phelps (which was first, I'm told, to offer rifle cartridge capability), Berdon, CPM, and Hollywood made a ripple here and there, and were said to be well built. Now dead. Ransom designed a machine, sold by C'Arco, but I'm unsure of its current status. Ponsness-Warren, of shotshell fame, made a type of progressive metallic loader. And then there was the defunct Jet. Alas, except possibly for the C'Arco "Grand Master," these too are gone, so far as I know.

Currently available progressives are the C-H Auto Champ, Dillon's 550 and new Square Deal, Hornady's Pro-Jector, Dick Lee's 1000, the RCBS 4X4, and R.D.P.'s "The Tool." As mentioned earlier, Star is still in business but saw fit to contribute neither a

press to test nor pertinent information.

Without fanfare, here are the contenders for your buck.

Star

I wanted to get Star out of the way first, since I have so little to relate on the subject. Early Star machines were "simple" progressives, available in one caliber only. Both straightline and circulars were offered, though only the circular survives. In addition to reloading tools, Star manufactures sprinklers for California's citrus and avocado farmers.

Star's universal press is used primarily for handgun calibers, although a rifle version is sold. Since the press is not as stout of construction as some, I have read that Star recommends that 30-06-size cases be sized on a single-stage unit, which kind of negates a progressive's advantages. The Star is not self-indexing in standard form, although various options are said to be available, including an auto-advance device.

Although I have neither examined nor yet used one, Star loaders are said to be reliable and well made. Their reputation is excellent. However, one tester wrote that he considered the Lee 1000 to be a close second to the Star, and this gentleman had not yet tried the Dillon Square Deal or the R.D.P. Star's well-earned and long-lived first place slot can no longer be taken for granted.

C-H Auto Champ

C-H got into the progressive business in 1970, and offers the only popular straightline design on the current market. There's a good reason; it's a hell of a press. It works, is extremely well made and designed, and you don't have to hock your Rolex to scare up the purchase price.

When C-H was contemplating going into the progressive business, they studied a batch of elderly units with a critical eye. The one that impressed them most was Joe Dircks' Tri-Standard in-line. A direct clone would have been both too expensive and too formidable to mass produce, so C-H settled for a less expensive but similar design. After 17 years and various permutations (Mark I through the current Mark V-a, in natural progression), the C-H Auto Champ is a successful progressive indeed.

The Mark V-a is a four-station press featuring auto case, primer, and powder feeding/charging. It is also self-indexing, naturally. Station one (not counting the case feed as a station) sizes and decaps the brass. Station two primes, expands, bells, and decants propellant. Station three can both seat the bullet *and* crimp it with such roll-crimped revolver cartridges as the 38 Special, or simply seat the bullet. Station four is used to taper crimp ammo to be used in auto pistols, such as the 45 ACP. Finished rounds are ejected automatically down a chute.

The factory provides you with one powder bushing (the measure is not adjustable as most are) and one bullet seating stem. Although caliber changing is possible, it is very complicated and best left alone if you aren't blessed with considerable mechanical aptitude. The powder measure has a shut-off gate; it can be emptied without removal from the tool, a nice feature. As with most progressives, handgun-caliber dies feature carbide inserts in the sizing units, relieving you of a case lubing job.

As is requisite with a straightline (indeed, with circulars, though not quite on the same scale), the Auto Champ must be kept meticulously clean for proper functioning. This is no easy chore, but a minor nuisance. Removal of a case from one of the stations is nearly impossible, but since all of the little buggers are right out in front, unobscured, I don't feel that's much of a problem unless you are afraid you've failed to seat a primer. Stopping in mid-stroke can double-charge; the manual repeatedly warns of this possibility. So don't stop your stroke. Last of the negatives: the powder will dump even if no case is at that station.

Good points: the press is sturdy and extremely well made. It should be long-lived. It is provided with a primer supply measure, which every press should be. Its in-line case flow offers superb visibility of the various operations. And there's a clear, well-written, complete and concise operating manual.

If all you want to do is load a lot of, say, 38 Special ammo very fast and efficiently, do not intend to experiment with various loads and bullets, and don't want to spend more than a thousand bucks for a heavy-duty progressive, the C-H merits a very long look.

Dillon RL-550

Might as well face it; Dillon's the name in moderately priced progressives. Despite the fact that Mike Dillon has ruffled a feather or two in the industry—for doing things like leaving out the middleman and selling his presses direct to the shooting public—his reloaders are state of the art. In

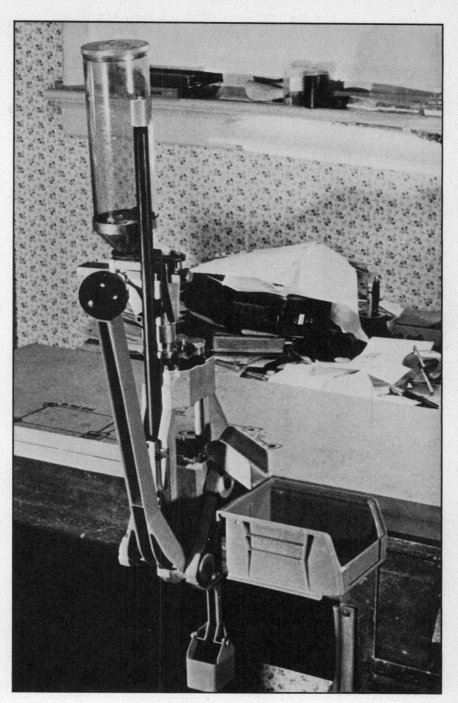

This is the Dillon Square Deal— the new design for everyone to try to beat, which might be tough at $135.

fact, except for one other firm—which makes a much more expensive press—no one equals Mike's progressive attitude toward progressives. No one.

In the mid-'70s Mike offered a conversion unit to switch the ubiquitous Star to 223 Remington capability. He peddled it under the sobriquet "Super Star." It gained a following. And then came the RL-300 progressive. The 300 evolved into the RL-450, which set the

industry on its ear. Dillon became not *a* name to reckon with, but *the* name to reckon with. It still is.

The current hot item from Scottsdale, Arizona, we'll get to in a moment, but for now we'll peer closely at Mike's 550. It is a non-indexing tool that boasts automatic primer feed and powder charging, though you have to pump the cases and bullets yourself. Of course it's a circular, and offers easily interchangeable tool heads for

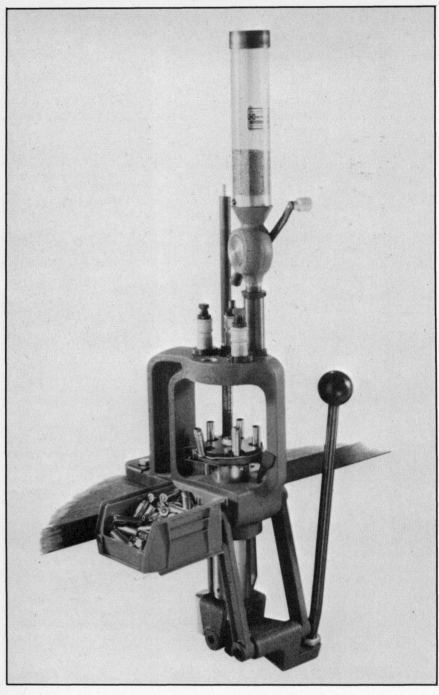

Hornady's Pro-Jector has a "Brass-Kicker" (in operation here) and is a sound and solid design.

adjustable powder measure, a chute to accept loaded rounds, is easy to set up, is of very good quality, and wears an indexing star to make shell plate rotation easier.

To some, the 550's prime advantage over other progressives is its safety tube for the primer column. The single most condemned feature of progressives is the columnar primer feed. Due to various causes—friction, a cocked primer, trying to prime a case with a primer already present, trying to prime a case when none is present at the priming station—there have been a few instances where a primer detonation caused the whole primer column to explode, injuring the operator. Some loaders are so concerned about this rare phenomenon that they avoid progressives altogether, and don't use auto-priming devices on their single-stage or turret presses.

Dillon made it all better. First, he improved his priming mechanism. Second, he provided users with a stiff tube of steel to cover the primer tube. One tester, who admits to a mistrust of priming tubes, loaded 500 rounds on his Dillon without mishap. Undaunted, he shot into the protective cover and priming tube (full) with a rifle. He succeeded in initiating simultaneous detonation of the primer stack, but the steel cover *held together*. He still isn't happy with auto-priming devices.

The only negative I can come up with on the Dillon is that it does not come with a primer-column measuring rod. My local progressive expert, John Neese, who helped with the set-up of most of the presses under discussion, made a simple rod on his own.

At $234.95 direct (less dies), the Dillon offers a terrific return on your investment. Dollar for dollar, only the tool we are about to cover can approach it on an initial-cost basis.

Dillon Square Deal

If this press isn't the number one seller among progressives within a year, I'll turn in my crystal ball. For an incredible $135, Mike Dillon will sell you a progressive that is self-indexing, auto-priming, and offers the Dillon auto-dispensing powder measure. All you do is feed it cases and bullets, and work the handle. Further, the tool comes virtually set up in the caliber of your choice. Simply fill the powder hopper and set your charge (after attaching it to the press, of course, and the press to a sturdy bench), attach the spent-primer receptacle, fill the primer magazine, and make ammo.

a quick caliber shift. The design is four-station, and the powder-charging die won't dump a load unless a case is waiting below because the case itself trips the mechanism. If you need to switch head sizes, a shell plate and three locator pins are required and not too expensive.

Dillon offers his own dies. The sizing, crimping, and seating dies are funneled for easy entry of cases, something not all die makers consider. The

seating die carries a bleed hole for excessive cast bullet lubricant. Nice touch.

Dillon will update your RL-450, incidentally, for a modest fee, making it virtually into a 550. The cost is a bit under a C-note.

The RL-550 has much to recommend it, and little to go wrong. I know many users in my area, and hardly ever hear of a problem that wasn't the user's fault. The press has an easily

Not only is the Square Deal a square deal, but it's really square. The body is angular, the ram square, the primer catching cup, the bullet collection box—nearly every part is box-like. The circular shell plate is inletted into the top of the ram, supported all around its circumference. The ram, being square, won't torque or twist in operation.

There are no conventional dies but inserts (like automobile cylinder sleeves) that function like dies and are held captive in the head by a holddown plate; they are *not* screwed in. Aside from that, they perform and are adjusted like standard reloading dies.

The press has virtually no metal-to-metal contact at any of its working points. Instead there are compressed Delrin bushings, self-lubricating, at all points of friction. The slickness that results is amazing. Since close-tolerance machining (or casting) is not necessary, the cost of the machine is held quite low. Dillon claims that the Delrin bushings will not wear out, period. If they do, he'll replace them.

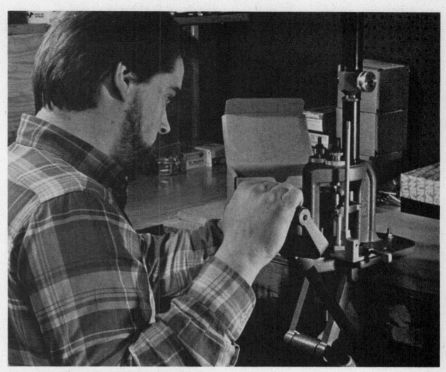

As shown, the RCBS 4x4 requires nearly all operations to be done by the operator, but then, on the other hand, provides plenty of control at each step.

All the Allen wrenches needed to adjust or disassemble the Square Deal are included with the press. A great idea. Dillon's typically concise and well-illustrated manual is a pleasure to read as well as being informative, just like the one pertaining to the 550.

Hornady Pro-Jector

Hornady's newest progressive is an updated version of their Pro-7, which was a five-station, auto-priming, auto-indexing "O" tool that would handle magnum-size rifle cartridges. The Pro-Jector boasts these features and then some, such as the shell-ejecting "Brass Kicker." A set of Durachrome dies comes with the unit, plus a loaded-round receptacle, priming tube with a Dillon-type cover that leaves a short portion of the priming tube poking out of the top (not so good), and a powder measure adapter. The Hornady, by the way, is one of only two tools that doesn't come with a powder measure, presumably to keep costs down. In theory, leaving it up to the user what type of propellant dispensing device to choose is a Good Thing, but here it translates to additional cash outlay. Considering that the Pro-Jector carries a $335 tab, it's tough for me to swallow that premise, especially since the Dillons and Lee 1000 sell for *much* less than the Hornady and include a measure. But no

The Lee 1000 is a relatively inexpensive press that does nearly everything automatically. John Neese checks primer depth here.

Free.

Is the press foolproof? Nothing is. But it's pretty close. Example: the shell plate can be rotated forward or *backward* if need be without fouling anything up. Another? A primer is not dispensed unless the ram is shoved forward and there is a case in the priming station. No case, no primer. As with the RL-550, cartridges are ejected down a chute, automatically. As with the 550—no case in place means no propellant is dumped. If you forget to do something, like replenish your primer supply, you can set things right easily. It's a very forgiving press.

Again as on the 550, there is a steel cover for the priming tube. On the Square Deal, a threaded cap locks it in place and covers the upper end of the tube, something not present on the older 450, but built into the 550. Alas, still no primer-level indicator.

one asked me.

Steve Hornady tells me that he expected purchasers of his tool to be experienced loaders, but notes that newcomers to handloading are attracted to the Pro-Jector. Others have surmised that certain styles of progressives might become the C-presses of the future, and here's some corroborative evidence.

The Pro-Jector's frame is cast aluminum. The cylindrical ram contains a drive shaft that is attached to the shell plate at its upper end and the index wheel at its lower. The toggle, directly beneath the index wheel, contains two spring-loaded pawls that actuate the shell plate through the index wheel. Priming is done at the top of the handle stroke, indexing near the bottom.

There is an error in the loading manual, which, by the way, is not the clearest of tomes. According to the book, the " . . . carriage completes its vertical travel (upward), moves (the shell plate) into the five stations and *performs all the loading operations except priming.*" The strong implication here is that everything is automatic; not so. Case feed, bullet feeding, and powder dropping must all be performed individually by the user.

Set-up of the Pro-Jector is not the easiest of tasks, and demands above average mechanical ability.

It's tough for mechanical engineers to grasp that not everyone is gifted. Tools that are even moderately difficult to set up should be done at the factory. Ignoring this—or developing the attitude that if the user isn't smarter than the press, he shouldn't buy it—will cost any manufacturer many sales. One reason that progressives have been relatively slow to

Sue Pickens illustrates her two-handled technique with the R.D.P. Auto case feed funnel is just in front of her face; the bullet collator is at upper right.

catch on is their set-up complexity, and the difficulty of caliber change in some units.

Manufacturer's attitudes are more of a problem than you might think. One outfit's spokesmen opine that the operator "has to be smarter than the tool." Another claims in a press release: "We do not care to have this unit in the hands of reloaders who feel that they are much smarter than the machine." Neither of these firms is Hornady. The bottom line is that a tool should be designed for the lowest common denominator if it is to be widely successful. Or, if such is not feasible, then the unit should be provided to the end user in fully-functional readiness.

Once set up, the Pro-Jector works. It's a burly tool, beautifully made and finished, and smoothly functional.

Extra shell plates are available for nearly any cartridge, including the 32 ACP. The price is not exorbitant. And for 30 bucks, Hornady will update your Pro-7, turning it into a Pro-Jector. Good deal!

Lee 1000

Dick Lee bills his new Progressive 1000 as "The World's Fastest handloading Press." I'm not sure of the validity of that claim but after my press was worked on a bit, to smooth feeding, it turned out ammo pretty quick.

One problem. In some of Lee's literature, there is the following: "This press is so trouble free you can actually process one case at a time without spilling powder or *causing a jam . . .*" Wrong. If you don't remove the primers by hand after each indexing of the shell carrier, the press'll jam tighter than Zorro's hatband. And if you're not careful when clearing the jam, but work the handle a bit, you can get a double charge. Be careful.

I had heard of a few problems with the Lee, which is not unusual. Claude Davis of Chigger Ridge Reloading Supplies in Reidsville, NC, has a Lee set up in his shop, and that's not unusual either. He's loaded hundreds of rounds on the machine with no problems that he himself didn't initiate. He was, to put it mildly, a fan of the 1000 when I talked to him. He uses the tool for demonstration, so it is subjected often to the ministrations of inexperienced operators. No problem.

Lee's 1000 offers auto case, primer and powder feeding and is self-indexing. Carbide dies are included, as well as Lee's nifty Auto-Disk powder measure. Changing shell plates and the shell plate carrier (to effect a caliber change) is simple and inexpensive.

Lee doesn't use a typical priming

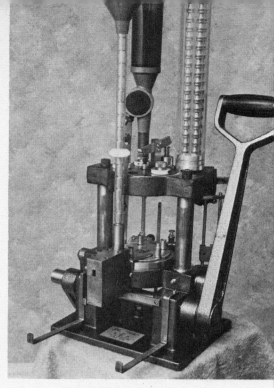

This is it, the big one, the R.D.P. The money is steep, perhaps, but the value is high.

tube, but a circular tray with cover like the ones used in his Auto Prime hand tool. Primers are gravity fed down a trough to the proper station; an agitator pin is provided for recalcitrant caps.

Although not a heavily-built machine, the Lee is warrantied for 2 years. Unconditionally. Quality of fit and finish is generally acceptable. If the Dillon Square Deal weren't available, the Lee would look quite attractive at its price of just over $200. Still, Lee has an excellent reputation and backs his products, and this is the least expensive progressive having an automatic case feed, so it's worth consideration.

RCBS 4X4

Although RCBS once offered a tool capable of loading a batch of ammunition handily and quickly—the Green Machine—the 4X4 is their first progressive. Unlike most other such tools, the 4X4 does nothing automatically. The operator must feed the brass, rotate the shell plate, manually move primers from the primer tube to the priming cup with the priming lever (whew), drop the powder, stick a bullet atop a case, and remove the loaded round. Oh; the spent primers are captured as they exit by a "de-priming bottle" that lives at the end of a bent tube below the press. Since the RCBS unit has no automatic functions, it can be used readily as a single-stage press, which is a good selling point.

Quality of assembly and finish is the same as with all RCBS products I've used: super. The 4X4's price is $303.50, and does not include dies, measure, or *shell plate*. (The plate runs $26.50.) High!

An unusual aspect of the 4X4 is its counter-clockwise shell rotation. And while the operation is velvety and precise, some device aside from the plate itself (or one of the cases) would be handy to facilitate cycling. I vote for a star similar to Dillon's.

Although some reloaders complain of the many manual operations needed to work the 4X4, this is more a mild inconvenience than a serious problem. Still, for the same money (and less) you can buy machines that perform all or most of these tasks for you.

The RCBS tool does not offer a primer tube cover as is used on the Dillon, Pro-Jector, and C-H presses. It's an oversight that should be remedied, especially since the tube is located at the right front corner of the frame, near the operator's face.

A long threaded powder measure adapter is provided, to be attached to the press then receive the measure itself. Inside the adapter is a drop tube that is lifted by a case as it enters the adapter, centering the tube over the case mouth. Three drop tubes are provided: small bore rifle, large bore rifle, and handgun.

The 4X4 is not the most innovative progressive, nor the least expensive, nor yet the fastest. But it offers RCBS quality, simplicity of use and set-up, and the benefits of a single-stage press when one is desired. And it's backed by one of the most respected firms in the business.

R.D.P. "The Tool"

Let us not mince words: The R.D.P. progressive is the best there is, and you can say I said it. Nothing else anywhere near its price range ($1265 pistol, $1315 rifle) is as heavily built, reliable, tough. Hell, it weighs over 100 pounds!

The basic unit provides automatic priming, bullet feed, and a self-indexing five-station shell plate. For extra money ($250) you can buy a case feeder. For more extra money ($180) you can get a vacuum priming system that keeps the priming punch and cup clear of crud, not to mention sucking a primer down onto the punch. If feeding the bullet tubes—five of them, holding about 185 45-caliber bullets, or 155 357s, or over 200 9mms, depending on the slugs, and which must be rotated into position by hand—be-

comes too much of a chore, for $695 you can buy a bullet collator that will feed them automatically, base down. Remember that none of these is necessary, only nice to have; the basic unit is complete.

The Tool comes set up—in a huge drum—in the handgun or rifle caliber of your choice. If you'll let them know beforehand, they will prep the machine for your exact load, including bullet configuration. Should you decide to add accessories, it's easy. (Even for me, and I barely know a wrench from a gherkin.)

There are R.D.P. presses in existence that have loaded well over a million rounds with no problems that can be laid on the tool, and with scant discernible wear. How can it be so? Because all gears and parts are made of tool steel—except where brass will offer less friction—and precision castings. The construction quality is astounding, and uncompromising.

The primer tube has a protective housing, plus it's at the left rear of the press, away from the user. There is a failsafe built into the priming mechanism, to preclude, as much as possible, a detonation. The primer shuttle carries a detent into which a spring-loaded ball on the main slide fits. If there is a cocked primer, the slide continues to function, but slips past the shuttle detent, so there's no priming.

The powder measure is activated by a link connected to the lower platen. If no case is present at the powder station, propellant will be dumped anyway, but there's not much reason for a case not to be present. The measure is an RCBS Uniflow.

Of course there is an automatic ejection system that dumps loaded rounds into any kind of box that you have around. At the front of the tool there are fixtures to hold that receptacle in place.

Caliber changeover requires about 15 minutes once you're familiar with the job. Converting to another caliber can cost as much as $158, but possibly much less, depending on several factors. Switching from the 45 ACP to the 308 Winchester would not require a different shell plate, for example.

A final option bears mention. For 50 bucks you can buy an extra tool handle, and it makes all the difference in the world. Why? Isn't the press smooth enough with just one handle? You bet. So smooth, and so fast, and so trouble-free that you will be churning out ammo at the rate of around 1000 rounds an hour. Know what'll happen if you use one handle? Your working arm will fall off, or burn so badly from lactic acid buildup

you'll wish it would. With two handles, both arms work—in unison. Much easier. Spring for the extra handle.

If you can afford the tariff, The Tool is The Only Tool. Any other press is . . . simply another press. Don't take my word. See one for yourself. Then if you don't buy it, it'll be because either you can't afford it or you don't really feel you need its awesome capability.

Negatives? Well, I suppose in theory the fact that powder can be dumped without a case at station is a negative. But I can't see it as much of a problem with this tool. And the R.D.P. doesn't offer a primer column metering device. That's it.

To make up for the foregoing oversights, R.D.P. makes an auto-lubricating full-length rifle-cartridge resizing die. Yes, that's what I said—the die lubes the brass all by itself. (Assuming you keep it filled with lube, of course.) How's that for innovation! Single-stage pre-sizing of rifle cases is a thing of the past with The Tool. Neat?

Conclusion

That covers the tools, now let's close by examining the premise. Is a progressive right for you?

If you shoot a lot of ammo and don't do much experimenting with various charges and bullets, I'd say yes if you choose your tool carefully. If you don't load 300 rounds a year, or most of your ammo is used in benchrest matches, then a progressive is probably not for you. If you shoot competitive rifle or handgun events (other than benchrest), and aren't tied in to one of the OPEC nations, then you need to look hard at a progressive if you haven't already. If primer feed tubes scare you to death, avoid progressives, not to mention similar devices designed for single-stage and turret presses.

A fellow once recommended against progressives because of the necessity of purchasing scads of components at one time. Brilliant. If you shoot a lot, you'll be buying lots of components to begin with; how else would you shoot a bunch? Progressives and large quantities of bullets, primers, and propellant go together—how could it be otherwise?

Finally, if you are simply *uncomfortable* with a progressive reloader, don't *buy* one. Just don't knock them! Folks who fear chain saws avoid them like the plague, using an ax instead. But they cut down few trees. If you want to see chips fly, use a modern tool. There's a moral there somewhere. ●

The Polywad Spred-R wad is basically a plastic toadstool, with a long solid stem and a circular top.

OPENING PATTERNS

by DON ZUTZ

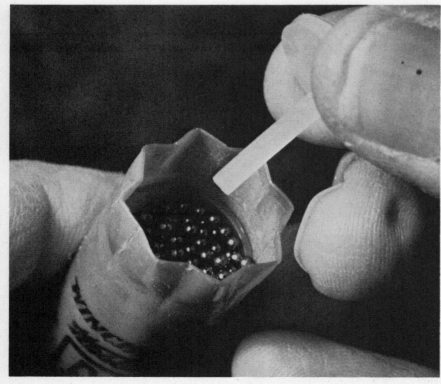

The Spred-R wad is simply poked, post down, into the shot charge just before the closure is made—like a thumbtack.

IT IS IRONIC that my favorite upland double is choked to within an inch of its life and provides patterns woefully unbecoming to close-range gunning. A Merkel over/under, it has barrels marked Modified and Full chokes, but actual testing with most upland loads proves that it performs more like a gun choked Full and Extra-Full. At 21-yard Skeet range, which duplicates a lot of quail, woodcock, and ruffed grouse work, both tubes slam their entire shot charges into just 15 or 17 inches; and as most hunters know, that spells either misses or mincemeated birds, neither good for morale.

Despite its tight-patterning, however, the straight-gripped Merkel fits me beautifully and, at 6¾ pounds, responds spiritedly. For whatever reasons, I score better with it on flushing game than with any other double I've ever owned or tried. It is a natural pointer for me, and with it I can wring out the best that my personal hand-to-eye coordination has to offer. So much for getting gushy over a gun—except to tell you why I have let it force me to experiment with a number of different scatter-type reloads.

My goal hasn't been only to find rounds that would deliver consistent 30-inch patterns at 20-25 yards for fast-action, close-range wingshooting. I needed a load that would make the Merkel's lower tube spray Cylinder bore shot clouds because more than a few woodcock are taken right off the muzzle. In the past, this has meant added fiddle-dee-dee at the reloading bench as cardboard wads had to be fashioned and then placed in the load to divide the shot charge into even layers. It was something I could have done without.

That's why I sat up and paid attention when Jay Menefee of Macon, Georgia came along with his new concept in scatter-type inserts known as the Spred-R. It is something entirely different in this business of making choked barrels throw more open patterns. For whereas other cardboard and plastic divider wads and scatter inserts were made to be bedded in the shot charge—such as the B-card dividers and cardboard and plastic X-shaped dividers—Menefee's Spred-R is made to fit the very top of the shot charge *almost* like the old-style overshot wad. The main difference is that the Spred-R has a lengthy 0.656-inch shaft extending downward from its center to penetrate the upper layers of shot, and it looks like a flat-topped plastic toadstool. I make the top disk to be 0.718-inch in diameter and about 0.062-inch thick. Menefee tells me that thicker disks have been tried, but they contribute nothing except extra weight and bulk.

The method for loading Spred-R inserts is ultra-simple: Merely take the reload through all the stations on a press and, after the shot charge has been dropped, press the Spred-R home, post first. The disk will lie atop the shot charge like an overshot wafer of yesteryear, and the crimp will be

McHenry, IL 60050), the powder charges of published reloads should be dropped by up to 1 grain if they are listed with chamber pressures below 10,000 LUP and the powder reduction should be carried to 1½ grains if they show a published chamber pressure of 10,000 LUP or more. It does not seem to be the Spred-R's weight which causes higher pressures, but rather the fact that the crimp must open more fully to permit the plastic disk's escape. This opening takes a mite more time, and that means powder gases will increase more than normally would happen if the Spred-Rs weren't in place. In any case, a wee bit of sacrificed velocity doesn't upset results over the short ranges involved.

How does the Spred-R insert influence pellet distribution? For many years, I have argued that the mere presence of an overshot card wad *doesn't* automatically spell blown,

donut, or more open patterns. I have fired too many patterns with reloads and factory loads having roll crimps and overshot wads to believe that; for many such wafer-topped rounds have given me excellent Full-choke densities even with a relatively heavy overshot card in place. My own contention has always been that wad pressure from behind instigated pattern scattering, either by ramming into the shot charge at muzzle exit and pushing center pellets toward the outside of the mass, or by sandwiching the pellets betwixt the overshot card and the following cushioning wads. Without that rear end pressure, however, the chances for uniform and consistent scattering is remote; the final patterns are a matter of chance relative to the action of the trailing wads.

What Jay Menefee has apparently done with his plastic toadstool is to insure some control of the overshot disk

IS EASIER THAN EVER

folded over it.

Although the Spred-R is relatively light, some load adjustments must be made for chamber pressures and crimping space. According to testing done by Tom Browne of Hodgdon Powder Co. and Tom Armbrust of Ballistic Research (1108 W. May Ave.,

This is the average pattern fired by the Merkel's lower barrel at 20 yards with a 1-ounce charge of 9s and no Spred-R.

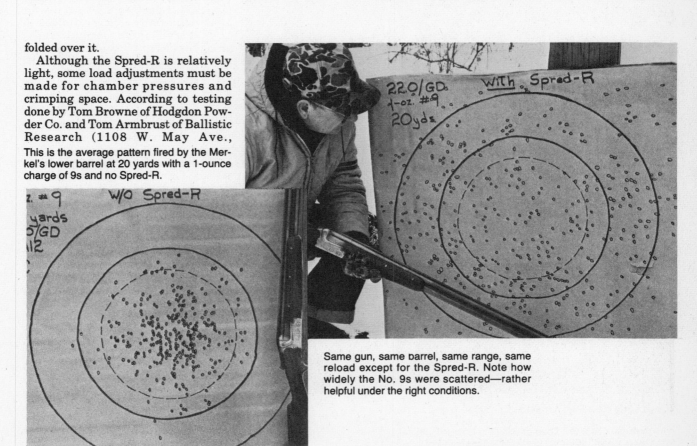

Same gun, same barrel, same range, same reload except for the Spred-R. Note how widely the No. 9s were scattered—rather helpful under the right conditions.

The wide patterns thrown by Spred-R-equipped reloads and 1-ounce of 9s helped make the writer's tight-shooting Merkel quite effective on close range woodcock.

This splayed AA case shows how the Spred-R wad sits inside a 1-ounce shot charge to leave the center a void and to effect the old overshot wad condition. Theoretically, the long post assists by stabilizing the Spred-R insert via pressure from the pellets.

so that the trailing wads can influence pellet distribution on every shot. This is done by the shaft which penetrates the shot charge and is held in place by the pinching pressure of pellets as they squeeze together during their trip through the bore and the choke constriction. Thus, the disk is held in place squarely before the exiting pellets; and, combined with the following force of the gas-urged trailing wads, can cause central pellets to move quickly toward the fringe. This tandem of a stabilized front disk and a ramming rear end blow produces a sandwiching effect on each shot for greater consistency in producing semi-blown patterns. In the old shotshells with cardboard overshot wafers floating in place, the light overshot cap could be easily blown away by the shot charge for little or no effect on the patterns. With the Spred-R anchored in the shot charge, however, the disk can't be brushed aside, and the pellets must climb over it and toward the side rather than proceeding straight ahead.

It does not seem as though the plastic shaft generates a post-wad effect, meaning that pellets push into it during bore travel and then spring away after leaving the muzzle. If this action is present, it doesn't seem significant. The post is deemed a bit skinny for the spring-away concept. Indeed, if the central shaft contributes anything besides stability to the disk's position, it may be a weakening of the shot charge's core prior to firing so that the trailing mass below the shaft has a void into which it can push and force leading pellets in an outward direction. In any case, the darn thing works, and some woodcock in my freezer regret that very much.

Due to an active duck and goose season, I got behind on my woodcock and grouse hunting last fall, but on a sunny bright day when the waterfowl weren't moving, I put Spred-Rs to the test in a small, picturesque covert that flowed from a hillside cedar stand into a flat comprised of pasture and corn stubble. Nearly 40 years of visiting this cover taught me to expect some birds along the very fringe where slashings grew. The first one came up just as my eyes caught the first glimpse of splashings, and it was almost stymied by overhanging willows to its side. But break through it did, and when it was silhouetted against the faint blue sky, the Merkel reached for it. The pattern enveloped the bird nicely and it lay where it had fallen. Perhaps 100 paces further the same scene was replayed. Neither bird was more than 17 yards from the gun's muzzle; neither was missed; neither was mincemeated.

The reload I used for that initial outing with Spred-Rs was one contained in company literature for a chamber pressure below 10,000 LUP, and it read like this:

Shell: Winchester AA
Primer: Winchester 209
Powder: 22.0/Green Dot
Wad: Winchester WAA12
Shot: 1 ounce of Lawrence 9s
Velocity: approx. 1300 fps

When I later used that same reload for patterning, I found that my Merkel was up to its old tight-shooting tricks: *without* the Spred-R insert, said reload slammed itself mainly into the 15-inch-diameter core of the patterning circle (see accompanying photo). There are about 585 pellets in a 1-ounce helping of No. 9s, and of that total only 35-38 ever showed up in the area between the 15- and 20-inch rings. Moreover, in five test patterns there were never more than 4-6 perforations in the annular ring comprising the area between the 20-inch inner circle and the 30-inch-diameter circumference.

When I switched to the same reload with the Spred-R insert aboard, however, the picture changed significantly. The accompanying photo illustrates the average result when 22.0/Green Dot/1x9 was fired over the same range. The pellets scattered across the entire yard-square sheet, putting 190-198 into the annular ring. The 15-inch core received only 90-95 pellets, on average, while the area between the 15- and 20-inch inner rings picked up 81-86. More No. 9s liberally dotted the space immediately outside the 30-inch circle. Thus, as anyone can perceive, the presence of the Spred-R insert did *indeed* alter the Merkel's patterning characteristic! The item is no fraud.

During further shooting, though, I found that the Spred-R didn't cause every recipe to fan out in similar style. One of my pet grouse reloads uses 1⅛ ounces of No. 7 shot, and I assembled it in this manner for the trial:

Shell: Winchester AA
Primer: Winchester 209
Powder: 17.5/Red Dot
Wad: Windjammer
Shot: 1⅛ ounces No. 7

This is deemed a safe assembly, as Hercules lists 18.5/Red Dot at 9900 psi and 1200 fps; hence, my reduction

to 17.5/Red Dot meets the caveat for using Spred-R inserts. But at the patterning board, this particular reload merely spread itself around evenly inside the 20-inch-diameter core, sending no more than 8-10 pellets into the annular ring.

Some reloads respond like crazy to the Spred-R's presence, but it is possible that others may perform differently. Reloaders will want to check their individual gun/load combo's delivery on patterning sheets. In general, the results I get from my particular load of 1⅛x7 gives me something closer to Modified choke percentages at 40 yards than it does Improved Cylinder. That's not all bad, of course, because it finally gets the Merkel's Modified barrel to shooting an honest Modified cluster, whereas it had mainly been doing a de facto Full choke. It is possible that, in some situations, the higher per-pellet energy of larger shot sizes can overcome the Spred-R wad and remain a tighter pattern than shown by the test loads of No. 9 woodcock persuasion.

Developer Jay Menefee has had Tom Armbrust at Ballistic Research run off a few pressure tests with heavier hunting reloads for use with the Spred-R insert, and they are as follows:

Shell: Winchester AA
Primer: Winchester 209
Powder: 25.0/Hi-Skor 800-X
Wad: Winchester WAA12R(red)
Shot: 1⅜ ounces
Pressure: 9740 LUP
Velocity: 1247 fps

Shell: Winchester AA
Primer: Winchester 209
Powder: 32.0/540 Ball®
Wad: Winchester WAA12
Shot: 1¼ ounces
Pressure: 10,320 LUP
Velocity: 1237 fps

The Spred-R can be used in 10-gauge reloads for those days when birds aren't holding ultra-high and rifle-like shot strings aren't needed. One test by Jay Menefee saw an AyA Matador II respond reasonably well for an expanded hitting area for gunning inside 40 yards. The particular reload was:

Shell: Remington 3½"
Primer: Remington 57*
Powder: 43.0/SR-4756
Wad: Ballistic Products Pattern Driver
Shot: 2 ounces
Pressure: approx. 9800 LUP
Velocity: approx. 1230 fps

Using Lawrence copper-plated No. 4s bedded in 20 grains of Ballistic Products buffer, this reload sent 255 pellets into the 20-inch core at 20 yards, leaving only 4 in the annular ring. With the buffer left out and a Spred-R insert atop the copper-plated 4s, however, the 20-inch core count fell to 185 while the annular ring picked up 55. While that's not exactly a riot gun pattern, it does show a more rapid opening of the shot mass for wider, easier-to-hit-with patterns between 20 and 40 yards.

Speaking of riot guns—shooting Spred-R top wads through a Cylinder bore can create the "donut" pattern effect, meaning the core is almost devoid of pellets while the annular ring and adjacent areas receive heavier perforations. To remedy this core weakness when the Spred-R is used with open-choked guns, Menefee has devised a method for keeping more pellets in the center: he punches little holes in the disk, a method which theoretically lets pellets escape straight ahead to hit within the core of the cluster rather than being influenced outwardly. Spred-Rs so modified are not available; the holes are made by a leather punch. My samples had holes about ⅛-inch in diameter. I do not have a Cylinder bore per se, but I removed the screw-out choke tube of a M1100 barrel and tested it. Darned if the modified Spred-R didn't seem to work, although not always with extreme uniformity. However, there can't be too many hunters who want patterns larger than Cylinder bore, anyway.

The Spred-R has been applied to steel shot reloads to open the patterns for close-range shooting. If there is one problem with steel shot, it is a penchant for extremely tight patterning from Modified and Full chokes. The following steel shot Spred-R reload was lab tested by Tom Armbrust at Ballistic Research, and he put it to practical use on four jump-shot mallards. It is intended to shift steel shot from its normal heavy core density to better overall distribution within the 30-inch circle with steel 4s and 2s. My own M1100 Full choke ran 55 percent with it, but I have not employed it on game.

Shell: Federal 12-ga. 2¾" plastic field (paper base wad)
Primer: Winchester 209
Powder: 29.5/Blue Dot
Wad: Supersonic #1200 steel shot wad
Shot: 1⅛ ounces No. 2 or 4
Pressure: 9960 LUP
Velocity: 1221 fps

Apparently enough pellets squirt through these holes to fill up the hole in a doughnut pattern when Spred-Rs are used in open-choked guns.

A variation of the Spred-R on the right shows holes punched through the overshot disc so that some pellets can seep through and strengthen the center of patterns in open-choked guns. Without these holes, patterns take on a doughnut configuration in open chokes.

That's not very swift for steel shot, but it is adequate for the short ranges over which the open-patterning round can be legitimately applied.

One problem confronted in reloading with the Spred-R is insufficient space for a good crimp if the original wad is used. Merely cutting the powder charges by 1-1½ grains isn't going to free up enough space to compensate for the Spred-R. A solution is going to the next larger shotcup wad within the same basic wad line. For example,

with 1⅛-ounce loads use the Winchester WAA12F114 instead of the WAA12. In the Federal line, select the 12S4 rather than the 12S3. And, of course, the various sizes of Remington Power Pistons also lend themselves to such manipulations. Staying within a family of wads tends to reduce the chances for pressure excursions.

After the world had forgotten the overshot disk, then, the Spred-R concept brings it back in a sophisticated

form for the practical purpose of scattering pellets as widely as an hunter would want from a tightly choked shotgun. At this time they are available in 12-gauge only, but smaller-diameter units could become a reality if there is a public demand. Meanwhile, the 12-gauge item is already quite versatile in both 10 and 12 bores. Further information and distribution materials can be had from the company known as Polywad (P.O. Box 7916, Macon, GA 31209). ●

WEATHERBY LOADS FOR NEW IMR 7828

Test work on IMR 7828 completed just prior to DuPont's sale of its smokeless powder business to IMR Powder Co. is now made available by the new source—that is, all the IMR-series powders are made in the same facility as before.

As the slowest of the series, IMR 7828 is an excellent choice for Weatherby calibers. It will be available in 1-pound, 8-pound and 2-pound containers. We reprint here IMR Powder Co.'s recommendations.

Reloading Data For DuPont IMR 7828 In Weatherby Calibers

Caliber	Primer	Bullet	Cartridge Overall Length (Inch)	DuPont Powder	Powder Charge (Grains)	Velocity (fps)	Chamber Pressure (CUP)
240 Weatherby Magnum	Fed. 210	Hornady 70-gr. Spire Point	3.063	IMR 7828	56.0C	3505	47500
		Hornady 87-gr. Spire Point	3.063	IMR 7828	54.5C	3360	50700
		Nosler 100-gr. Spitzer	3.063	IMR 7828	53.5C	3240	52000
257 Weatherby Magnum	Fed. 215	Hornady 87-gr. Spire Point	3.250	IMR 7828	76.0	3825	54000
		Hornady 100-gr. Spire Point	3.160	IMR 7828	74.0	3680	54400
		Nosler 100-gr. Spitzer	3.160	IMR 7828	73.0	3655	53100
		Hornady 117-gr. Boat Tail Spire Pt.	3.225	IMR 7828	70.0	3390	54200
		Nosler 120-gr. Spitzer	3.250	IMR 7828	69.5	3375	53700
270 Weatherby Magnum	Fed. 215	Hornady 100-gr. Spire Point	3.250	IMR 7828	78.5C	3645	48200
		Nosler 130-gr. Spitzer	3.250	IMR 7828	76.0	3500	53000
		Hornady 140-gr. Boat Tail Spire Pt.	3.350	IMR 7828	74.0	3355	52800
		Nosler 150-gr. Spitzer	3.250	IMR 7828	73.5C	3280	54100
7mm Weatherby Magnum	Fed. 215	Hornady 139-gr. Flat Spire Point	3.068	IMR 7828	76.0C	3335	51500
		Nosler 140-gr. Spitzer	3.250	IMR 7828	76.5C	3390	53300
		Hornady 154-gr. Spire Point	3.337	IMR 7828	74.5	3250	53400
		Nosler 160-gr. Spitzer	3.337	IMR 7828	73.5	3210	53500
		Hornady 175-gr. Spire Point	3.355	IMR 7828	72.5	3045	54100
		Nosler 175-gr. Semi-Spitzer	3.350	IMR 7828	71.5	3040	54500
300 Weatherby Magnum	Fed. 215	Nosler 150-gr. Spitzer	3.563	IMR 7828	89.0C	3425	49900
		Hornady 180-gr. Spire Point	3.554	IMR 7828	86.0C	3225	53000
		Nosler 180-gr. Spitzer	3.563	IMR 7828	86.0C	3240	52500
		Nosler 200-gr. Spitzer	3.563	IMR 7828	83.0C	3065	50600
		Hornady 220-gr. Round Nose	3.563	IMR 7828	81.0	2940	52400
340 Weatherby Magnum	Fed. 215	Nosler 210-gr. Spitzer	3.608	IMR 7828	90.5C	3070	51600
		Hornady 225-gr. Spire Point	3.645	IMR 7828	89.0C	2965	51000
		Nosler 250-gr. Spitzer	3.658	IMR 7828	87.5C	2885	53800
		Hornady 250-gr. Round Nose	3.658	IMR 7828	87.5C	2860	53100
378 Weatherby Magnum	Fed. 215	Speer 285-gr. Grand Slam	3.625	IMR 7828	117.0C	3060	51600
		Hornady 300-gr. Round Nose	3.644	IMR 7828	118.0C	3055	53700
460 Weatherby Magnum	Fed. 215	Hornady 500-gr. Round Nose	3.720	IMR 7828	117.0C	2360	41900

Notes:
Brass = Weatherby Factory Shells; C = Compressed Load; Barrel Length = 26-inch; All Nosler bullets used were Partition type; Recommend using only primer shown for each load.

TOUGHEN UP YOUR CAST BULLETS

by J.R. (DICK) SCHROEDER

"In SPITE of an auspicious beginning, the day had progressively dwindled to miserable. Now here he was, red-faced, knuckles skinned, cussing at the culprit—the lead deposit in the bore of his handgun that was ever so slowly giving way to an energetically applied brass brush."

Sound familiar? Well, tighten up your cinch and ride on. There is a way out of that box canyon.

The following mix/method, carefully adhered to, will substantially harden your cast bullets. You can reduce, and in many cases completely eliminate, the leading caused by soft, plain-based bullets, even in magnum loads. It won't cure problems in a rough or pitted barrel, but it will help even them to a degree.

The only equipment you will need, in addition to your usual casting set-up, is a coffee can and some heavy cloth. Blue jean material works well.

The Mix

Pure lead, 25 percent and wheel weights, 75 percent. To this add 1½ percent tin by weight.

The Method

Melt down the lead, then add the wheel weights, removing the small steel clips as they float to the top. When this mix is hot enough to quickly char the end of a tightly rolled tube of newspaper, you are ready to proceed. You did open the window and start the fan?

Using a commercial flux, or a glob of beeswax or bullet lubricant, flux the metal while stirring thoroughly. Get rough with it, not enough to cause a splash, but try to get some air down into the mix. Now skim off the impurities that floated to the top. Be careful not to remove any metal when skimming, just get the impurities off.

Looks clean and bright doesn't it? Uh-huh. Flux and stir again—then skim the impurities that floated to the

Frequent fluxing and stirring and more fluxing and stirring is important—you have to cast good ones to be worth the trouble.

top of that apparently clean mix.

Now add the tin. As an example, here's how I do it. My melting pot holds 8 pounds of metal. To this I simply drop in a quarter of a 1-pound bar of 50-50 solder. Solder being half-tin, half-lead, that amounts to ⅛-pound, or 1½ percent of 8 pounds, of tin. The

extra ⅛-pound of lead about equals the weight of the metal clips that were removed.

Now flux and stir again, skimming if necessary, although the amount of impurities should be negligible by this time.

You are now ready to start casting

bullets. As usual, a few will probably have to be discarded until the mould heats up. When you start getting good castings, tap a couple out on a piece of soft cloth to air cool. These will be used later in a comparison test.

The coffee can, mentioned earlier, should be about a quarter-full of water and standing close by. The cloth is fastened like a loose drumhead across the top of the can, leaving a shallow pocket. Secure it with a rubber band or whatever, then take a sharp knife and cut a slit in the bottom of the

a ruckus not soon forgotten.

The bullets must be hot enough to produce a sharp sizzle when they hit the water. However, as you cast, observe each bullet before you tap it from the mould, and at the first sign of a frosted appearance, quit casting—the mould and bullet are too hot. Lay the mould aside to cool down a bit. Placing it on a concrete floor works well.

No, you don't sit back and light up a smoke while waiting. Use this time to flux and stir the metal again. Doing

too much.

When the casting session is completed, use your thumbnail to compare the hardness between the air-cooled, and the water-cooled bullets. The water-cooled bullets should be markedly harder.

Use a good lubricant, such as an Alox/beeswax formula when sizing. Be sure that you size these hard bullets down to groove diameter. *An oversize hard bullet will increase pressures.* And don't expect hollowpoints to expand with this mix — they are

Tap hot bullets directly from mould into splash-proofed can of water, and do it some distance from all that hot lead.

pocket maybe 1½ inches long. Tap all of the bullets, from now on, directly from the mould through the slit in the cloth and into the water.

Don't neglect to use the cloth. It prevents any water from splashing out. One small drop of water landing in your pot of molten metal will cause

this every time the bullets get too hot accomplishes two things: One — the mix must be fluxed and stirred frequently anyway; and two — the bullets must be as hot as possible. The amount of time it takes to flux and stir allows the mould to cool down just the right amount without cooling off

just too hard to open up reliably.

So load up a batch and try them out. Then, when you are back home after the shooting session, sit back and light up that smoke (the one you passed up while fluxing and stirring), instead of scrubbing out a leaded barrel that didn't shoot well.   ●

Buckshot loads can be easily assembled with an inexpensive loader. Cast muzzleloader balls are reasonably good buckshot substitutes.

HANDLOADING THE
410 FOR DEFENSE

The little fellow is bigger than you think.

by C. RODNEY JAMES

At left, a 410 Federal hollowpoint slug expanded to .602-inch when fired into wet packed snow. At center, the Federal slug unfired. The flat point slug is a Remington.

THE 410 shotgun is generally written off by firearms experts and others as a "mouse gun" fit for small game, taken at very close range, and nothing else. Now I am not about to recommend that a person rush out to buy a 410 as a defense weapon, but for those who own one or are considering buying one for hunting, here are a few facts I feel are worth passing along.

A shotgun at close range is the most lethal small arm there is. There are records of such dangerous big game as lion and tiger having been killed, in close range encounters, by charges of light bird shot! At 10 feet or less, a charge of any size shot acts as a nearly solid mass—churning through tissue, delivering its total energy in a devastating "rat hole" wound. At longer ranges lethality is greatly reduced—a safety factor which gives the shotgun an advantage as a self-defense arm over the handgun or rifle.

Authorities can never seem to agree on an exact definition of "shocking," "stopping," or "devastating" power, nor can they agree on the best way of measuring it. I will not confound the issue with further definitions, but will reiterate one point most agree upon—that the effect of simultaneous hits by multiple projectiles can have as great or greater effect than a single hit by one, even if it is larger and moving at a higher velocity.

While law enforcement personnel rely on the 12-gauge riot gun with 18 to 20-inch barrel and self-defense expert Massad Ayoob gives this his blessing, Ayoob raises an important point in reference to using high-powered long arms for indoor defense shooting—the blast is deafening and stunning. It can disorient the shooter for critical seconds when all his faculties *must* be functioning.[1] For this reason Ayoob favors the less powerful and more difficult to master handgun over the shotgun as the best defense weapon.

I disagree. I prefer the 410.

In addition to the noise of a powerful weapon, recoil and rate of fire must be considered, as I found out the time I attempted to fast-fire a 12-gauge autoloader. The first shot, at a stationary target, was on center. The remaining four passed over it as the muzzle jumped violently upright. The gun was so out of control that had I fired a sixth shot, I would probably have been thrown on my back, and this was with trap loads.

Theorists of defense shooting seem to fall into two groups—those who feel, when it comes to caliber, that bigger is better and those who believe that a hit with a 22 is better than a miss with a magnum, particularly one that is recoiling all over the place. It is a fact—a heavy gun, even in the hands of an expert, is going to have a slower rate of accurate fire than a less

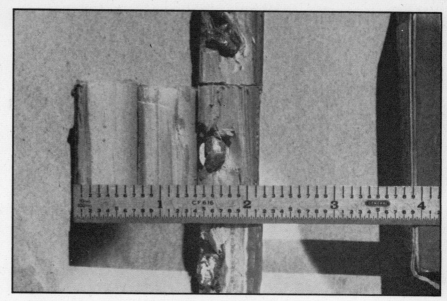

Buckshot fired 20 yards passed through two pieces of hard pine barn siding and into a third. Deepest penetration (top) is 00 buckshot from a 12-gauge. Center is 00 buckshot from a 410. Bottom is a .310-inch diameter lead ball from a 410.

A sectioned handloaded 410 buckshot load—recoil is mild and 00 buckshot remains in a tight pattern to 20 yards.

powerful weapon of the same general size, weight and action. Defense shooting is a situation wherein seconds, even fractions of seconds, can make critical/fatal differences. I tend to position myself with the second group, particularly when someone other than a well muscled adult male with extensive combat shooting experience and practice is shooting. It occurred to me, though, there might be a way to have rapid fire, multiple projectiles and adequate lethality at a reasonable noise level.

In testing the 410 as a defense weapon, my first surprise was to find that six pieces of 00 buckshot—*two thirds* of the 12-gauge riot load— will fit in a 3-inch 410 shell. A Cylinder barrel is the most accurate for buck and slug loads and will group six pellets in 12 inches at 20 yards. This is about the maximum range for such a weapon. Surprise number two: recoil is *mild*—a slight jump—no more than

any other maximum 410 load. The report in 26- or 28-inch barrels is little louder than a 38 handgun. In a pump or autoloader, the delivery of five shots is virtually as rapid as with a 22 rimfire autoloader. I was amazed to find velocity and power equal to the 12-gauge. Penetration in pine boards at 20 yards was virtually the same.

Intrigued by this performance with buckshot, I decided to see what slugs would do. Two five-shot groups were fired from the same Model 42 Winchester with a Cylinder barrel, using a sand bag rest, at 35 yards. The largest group measured 5 inches, the smallest 3.2 inches. They could be kept on center by holding 3 inches low at that distance. The use of a rear sight might well have tightened these groups, but for close-range defense is not necessary. The 95-grain slug at a muzzle velocity of 1470 and muzzle energy of 460, though woefully inadequate for deer, is a rough equivalent

of a light-weight, high-velocity 38 handgun load. The soft slugs upset well, expanding more than half their original diameter in soft targets.

Since buckshot loads are not commercially available, the handloads I made up were based on data from the NRA "Handloader's Guide," which recommended a charge of 16 grains of 2400 for a ¾-oz. charge of shot. An inexpensive MRC loader was used to assemble shells which proved to be of good quality.

Commercially made buckshot is now sold only in 25-pound bags—enough for 541 six-pellet loads—far more than I wanted. I made several by extracting buckshot from odd-lot 12-gauge paper shells that had seen better days. As an experiment, I bought a bag of 100 muzzleloader balls with a diameter of .310-inch. They did not fill the shell and required an additional wad cut from the base of a plastic shot holder. My theory was that pro-

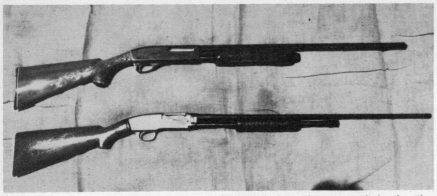

Model 870 Remington (top) is a far better house gun choice than the longer, obsolete Model 42 Winchester, but these loads work well in both author's guns.

Slugs from author's 410s will group in less than 5 inches at 35 yards when fired through a cylinder barrel, aimed with standard shotgun bead.

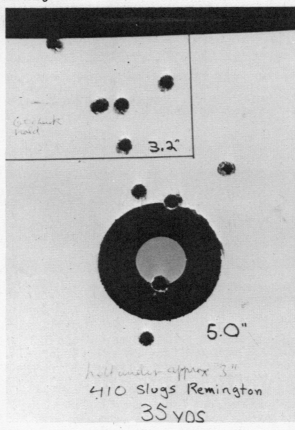

3.2"

5.0"

410 Slugs Remington
35 YDS

This 00 buck from a 410 Cylinder barrel at 20 yards stayed within a foot circle, penetrated well.

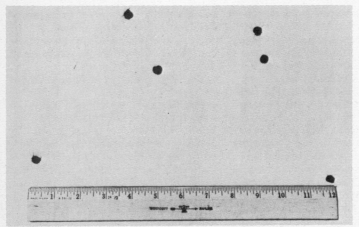

viding an extra cushion for the soft, pure lead shot would result in less deformation. It didn't work; but although the lead shot deformed more than the commercial hardened shot, patterns were not adversely affected. In the future I would use cast balls of .33-inch—the same as 00 buckshot. The Lyman reloading handbooks recommend casting buckshot of #2 alloy.

Any ammunition used for defense should be made with the greatest care and precision. Only new or once-fired shells should be used and the finished product should be checked to see that it will function flawlessly in the gun intended to use it. Crimps should be tight. If the ammunition is to be used in an autoloader, heat sealing the crimp in the center with a soldering pencil might be a good idea.

I agree with most experts that no single barrel, double, or bolt-action shotgun can cycle fast enough for defense shooting, although according to a reliable source such cut-down 410s are a new favorite with street gangs. This leaves, as legal options, the Remington 1100 autoloader and 870 slide action and the Mossberg 500 as the only practical guns of recent manufacture. The pump guns have the advantage of handling both 2½- and 3-inch shells, allowing the use of commercially made 2½-inch slug loads. Slugs for the 1100 would have to be handloaded in 3-inch shells. A Cylinder or slug barrel generally gives the best results with buckshot and slugs, though for stack-loaded buckshot this may not hold true.

Mossberg now offers the 500 in a "security" model featuring a six- to eight-shot magazine and 18- to 20-inch barrel. As of this writing the Italian firm of Luigi Franchi is developing a line of special-purpose automatic shotguns (SPAS) for military and police operations. Franchi's guns utilize space-age plastics and bullpup assault weapon designs. One prototype is the SPAS 410 with a 10- to 12-round box magazine and a capacity for both automatic and semi-automatic fire. The SPAS 410 will fire the 3-inch shell for which is being developed a special load containing five metal shot in a discarding sabot.[2] With this kind of firepower the 410 would indeed be a weapon to be reckoned with, but my own guns aren't out of the home defense running. ●

Notes:
1. Massad F. Ayoob, *In The Gravest Extreme.* p. 100
2. Roger Frost, "Luigi Franchi's Special Purpose Shotguns." *International Defense Review,* April 1986. p. 463

THE 22-caliber wildcat cartridges of today are the products of many years of experimenting, as are most of our commercial cartridges, many of which were themselves once wildcats. The father of many cartridges, Charles Newton, who got ahead of his time due to the powders of that era, based many designs on the shortened 30-06 case, but one of his early cartridges was the 22 Newton based on the 7x57 Mauser case, a favorite for experiment early in the century.

In this original design, Newton used .228-inch bullets. I doubt Newton ever achieved the velocities we do today. With powders such as 4350, we certainly can take his old design, load

seems rather slow, we must consider the retained velocity of such a long bullet and its ability to maintain a greater percentage of its velocity (and energy) over long range.

The 226 Barnes Q.T. I was privileged to shoot for a while was very accurate considering that it was a light sporter. With a barrel only 24 inches long, and weight of only 8½ pounds, it produced an average of 1.1-inch groups for three five-shot groups at 100 yards. The barrel was made and chambered by P.O. Ackley. The action was a Mauser.

Kill reports are always interesting, especially if bullets are recovered. In the case of the 226 Q.T. none were re-

ing, one where the case is formed in a 22-250 die which squeezes in the walls of the case a bit, thus making it a bit longer. It is really a 22-250 case shape, except it is .16-inch longer. It saves the cost of buying loading dies, since 22-250 dies can be used by backing them up .16-inch.

There is a 22-6mm made the same way using the 22-250 dies, shaping this case, too, like the 22-250, but in this case the length is .335-inch longer than the 22-250, necessitating backing the dies up that much for loading.

The 257 Roberts and the 6mm case being the offsprings of the 7x57 case, any of the three can be used for form-

Long-Bulleted 22s

They're peculiar, but they reach way out there.

by HAROLD HARTON

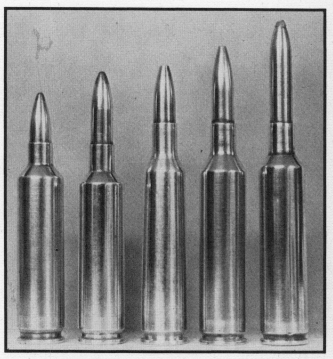

Left to right: 22-243 Ackley, 22-243 Durham, 22-6mm (formed in 22-250 dies), 224 Clark, 226 Barnes Q.T.

it with 40 grains of 4350 and a 70-grain bullet and achieve 3250 fps (feet per second). In this same case using 38 grains of 4350 and a 90-grain bullet we can get 3100 fps and 920 fpe (foot pounds of energy). This is a cartridge designed in 1912.

Such preliminary work led to the design of one of the most interesting, if not the most popular, wildcats of our day, namely the 226 Barnes Q.T. Based on the same 7x57 case but with straight walls and a 40-degree shoulder, this cartridge shoots a 125-grain bullet at 2700 fps. This 22 bullet is 1.420 inches long and requires a 1-in-5¼-inch twist. Although the velocity

covered. Complete penetration on both elk and mule deer were the case. One kill was a grown cow elk facing toward the hunter. The bullet entered the chest and exit was out the left ham. For a total of five elk and seven mule deer killed, none were lost and none required a second shot. This is a fine record for any caliber.

Today we have several such wildcats in 22-caliber worth considering. They are based on the 243 and 6mm Remington cases. The 22-243 Ackley and the 22-243 Durham are very similar with interchangeable loading data and equal ballistics. There is another version of the 22-243 worth consider-

ing the wildcats using this case length. One such wildcat that enjoys much popularity these days, in the windy West especially, is the 224 Clark. This case is very similar to the 226 Q.T. but using lighter bullets such as 70 to 85 grains. These require a twist of one turn in 8 or 9 inches of barrel to stabilize.

With the new Sierra 69-grain bullet and the Hornady 68-grain bullet, a whole new world of long-range shooting experience awaits those enterprising souls that don't mind forming cases, fire-forming, trimming and loading. To many of us, that is just a pleasant part of being a gun nut. ●

SORTING OUT ACCURACY

Take one step at a time and you can learn some things.

by H.W. SAKSCHEK

It SEEMS I'm *continually* sorting out accuracy and searching for smaller groups. I sometimes wonder if all this fuss about small groups is really worth the trouble, but it must be because I spend endless hours in search of them, like so many other handloaders.

Every time I acquire a rifle—new, used, or other built from scratch—I'm faced with the task of squeezing out every last bit of accuracy. The long procedure has become almost robotic. The glass bedding, the fine tuning tricks, and finding the most accurate

load that particular rifle will shoot better than all others has been repeated for hundreds of rifles.

On my latest rifle, a Remington Model 700 Varmint in 222 Remington, I spent some time to find which factors are important, and to what degree they improve accuracy. I sorted out accuracy improvement from glass bedding, from tune-up tricks, and from load work-up, compared to the total improvement that ultimately resulted in smaller groups.

The 222 Remington cartridge has lived and continues to live an accu-

Author with Remington Model 700 heavy barrel varmint rifle in 222 Remington. Tasco 24x target scope was used because an accurate high-power scope, and a mirage tube is necessary for ultra-small groups.

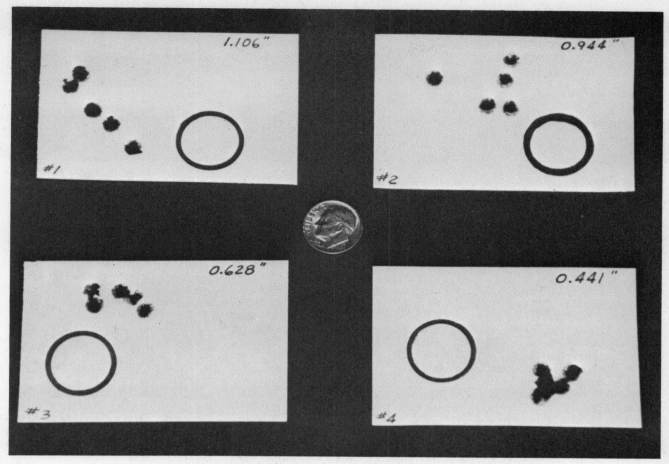

Typical groups from different stages of testing. Target #1 was fired with pet load and the factory-new rifle. Target #2 was fired after the glue bedding operation. Target #3 was shot after crowning and lapping; and #4 came after load work-up.

rate life. Since the day of introduction, it has been noted for fly-speck groups. There are any number of good varmint cartridges around, and this is not to detract from any of the others, but I always loved the cute little 222, and I chose this one for varmints and sunny day plinking.

To start this project, the Model 700 was first topped with a Tasco 24x target scope. This is my personal choice as "best for the money" in a reliable scope for target and varmint application. The 222 was to be my crow and fox eater. A good high-power scope is necessary.

For the first trip to the range, I took some of my pet handloads for the 222. These consisted of 23.5 grains of Winchester 748 powder, with Nosler 52-grain HPBT match bullets, and Federal M205 match primers. This load has performed well or reasonably well in every 222 I have owned, so it was a good starting point. I never use, nor do I intend using, factory ammo for long-range varmint hunting. I always make sure I'm the one that controls the components of the cartridge, the

main reason for handloading in the first place.

I installed a Harris Bipod on the forearm and used a Teflon-taped sandbag under the rear of the stock. Supporting the rifle the same for each shot is necessary for accuracy testing. I began shooting my pet handloads and the factory new rifle. Those first groups averaged 1.187 inches center to center. I fired four groups of five shots each, and did so for all accuracy testing reported here. The largest of the groups was 1.198 inches, smallest was 1.085 inches. This wasn't bad for out-of-the-box, but could it do better? The data was noted.

The first thing on the agenda for improved accuracy was bedding. Because there is always a chance that a bedding job could be less than perfect, I decided to glue-bed this rifle. Glue bedding is very similar to conventional bedding, with one exception, the action is actually glued into the wood for keeps. It can be removed—one way, they say, is by placing the rifle in a freezer for a couple of days, and then rapping it sharply; another is by heat-

ing the barrel in the area of the bedding—but all my glue-bedded rifles are still glued.

The idea is that approximately 5 inches of the back of the barrel, and the front inch or so of the action, is supported by the bedding material. From the bedding forward and back, the metal floats in the stock. Because the stock is permanently joined to the barreled action, it is not necessary to hold the action in place with any screws. These screws, some theorists believe, are the major reason conventional bedding sometimes gives less than desired performance because the tension of the screws, and their clamping action on the stock, must be kept constant to insure continued accuracy. No screws, no tension, no problems, or so the glue theory goes.

There are some minor differences in preparing for glue bedding instead of conventional bedding. First, provision must be made for future removal of the trigger assembly. Therefore, the trigger area is opened up to allow the trigger assembly to be dropped from the bottom of the stock. Clearance

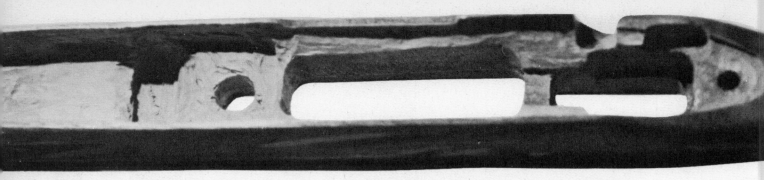

Before glue bedding, the stock is opened up so that none of the action parts contact the wood. The trigger area is enlarged to allow the trigger to be dropped out the bottom. Recoil lug area is opened to surround lug with bedding.

holes are drilled through the side of the stock to allow driving out trigger retaining pins in the case of the Model 700.

Next, the stock is opened up considerably larger than is normally required. This is best accomplished by tracing the outline of the barreled action, about $\frac{1}{16}$-inch larger, onto the stock using a scribe. All the wood is removed from under the barreled action, up to the scribed lines. The area around the recoil lug is opened very wide to hold a lot of bedding material, because it is important not to allow the recoil lug to contact any part of the stock. The lug should be totally surrounded by the bedding. The trigger assembly must not contact any part of the stock or the trigger guard—the action, its sides and its tang must all vibrate without contacting the stock.

At first this may seem like a lot of wood removal, but it's fast if you use a Dremel tool. You don't have to be very fussy, because no one is ever going to see under the action after it's glued. You should be a little careful along the top sides of the forearm, but that's all.

Next comes the routine of masking off the sides of the stock and the top of the forearm along the barrel channel with tape. Then, the bottom of the barrel and the action are cleaned to remove any oil or grease so the bedding can grip. Check to see that everything clears by spacing the front of the barrel and the back of the action tang off the stock with a piece of heavy tag board (or two matchbook covers). There should be no contact between the wood and the action, except at these spacers.

Apply release agent to the front action screw and into its threaded hole. Take care not to get release agent on the action bottom around the hole because the bedding must grip in this area. Insert the front action screw into the stock and hold it there with tape. Seal bare wood that will not be covered by bedding with varnish; don't forget the side holes. The varnish seals out moisture and oil that could absorb into the wood which could later cause warpage.

If all looks well, prepare the bedding material. Any of the conventional bedding materials will work because they are actually adhesives if you just don't use any release agent. I prefer to use a product called Micro-Bed. Micro-Bed is a little thicker than most, so it doesn't run as much, and has a nice brown color after mixing. I've used it on many rifles in the past and have always had excellent results.

Now, take a deep breath and apply bedding material to the bottom of the action and into the stock. Put in plenty; it's easy to wipe off. With spacers in place, slowly bring the barreled action down into the stock, allowing trapped air to escape and extra bedding to ooze out. Turn the front action screw into the receiver just a little; it's only there to provide the fore-and-aft location of the action.

While the extra bedding is oozing out, make sure the action is seated straight up in the stock with plenty of space evenly around it. Use toothpicks to keep spaces even on all sides. You can wipe away some of the excess bedding, but I prefer to wait about 3 hours until the bedding starts to set up. I then remove the tape, peeling the excess bedding with it. I let everything dry overnight.

Next morning, I remove the front action screw, and clear away any bedding that has run into the magazine area. I install the magazine and floorplate, and loosely install the front action screw. I use a drywall insert and a reshaped sheet metal screw to hold the floorplate in place at the rear. The factory screw is not used.

With the glue-bedded rifle and more pet loads, I returned to the range. Much to my surprise, the average of the next four 5-shot groups was only slightly below 1 inch, 0.937-inch average. Largest group was 0.955-inch and smallest group was 0.915-inch. This improvement, only ¼-inch,

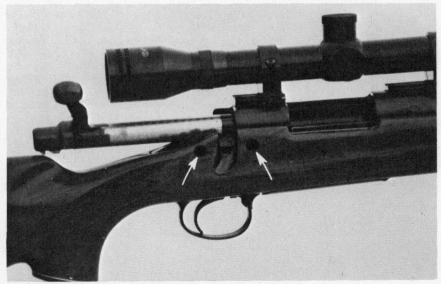

These holes drilled into the sides of the stock line up with the trigger assembly pins. To remove the trigger, pins are driven out, and trigger is dropped out the bottom of the stock.

was somewhat disappointing. I have bedded many rifles in the past and almost all showed much more than ¼-inch improvement after the bedding.

Slightly sub-1-inch groups don't excite me, but there was certainly no reason yet to use the rifle as a tent stake. I proceeded with my next accuracy trick.

I crowned the muzzle of the heavy barrel 222 with a muzzle-crowning tool. This little tool is equipped with a pilot to fit the bore and a very precise cutter designed to insure perfect perpendicularity of the face of the muzzle to the bore. Then a second cutter bevels the inside edge of the bore, recessing it slightly, but squarely.

I carefully slid the bolt, less its innards, into the action, pushing it hard forward as far as it would go. I then slowly rotated it to the fully closed position, and pulled it to the rear, trapping the grinding compound between the back of the locking lugs and the lug recess faces. While applying steady rearward pull, I lifted the bolt handle just short of the camming point, and then closed the bolt fully again. I could feel the grit cut, as the lifting and lowering of the bolt handle motion was repeated a couple of trillion times—10 minutes worth.

Care was taken not to open the bolt too far. If it gets to the point where it starts to move rearward, the oper-

stock, but I had little choice since the two were married. I then reassembled and installed the bolt.

The third trip to the range provided some very interesting results. The average of the next four 5-shot groups went to 0.650-inch The largest group measured 0.705-inch, and smallest measured 0.610-inch, for another improvement of ¼-inch-plus. This was more improvement than the bedding step had accomplished, especially percentage-wise.

Although I'm sure the bedding operation was necessary to improving accuracy, it did not have as much gain in improving accuracy as the muzzle crowning and bolt lug lapping oper-

Glue bedding: the rear of the barrel and front of action are glued while everything else floats. Toothpicks are spacers while the bedding dries and tape protects the stock exterior.

This little precision job takes only 3 minutes, but insures that a bullet will not be upset by escaping gases at the moment it leaves the barrel, as is the case if the muzzle is slightly off square. I can't really say I noticed any "out-of-square" while crowning, but I had the added confidence of knowing that the muzzle was not going to be a "lack of accuracy" factor.

Another trick which is helpful in improving accuracy is to lap the locking lugs in the action. This is usually performed prior to installing a barrel and insures fully mated surfaces between the back of the locking lugs and the corresponding surfaces inside the receiver. I had to do the lapping operation post-glued.

I dismantled the bolt and applied a very small amount of fine grinding compound to the back of each of the two locking lugs. Care was taken to cover only the back face of the lugs. No other area of the bolt or action should be submitted to the cutting effects of valve grinding compound for obvious reasons.

ation would grind away at the edges of the locking lugs rather than their faces. A thumb, precisely placed, can keep the action from accidentally opening, and constant rearward pull keeps the lapping at the back of the lugs.

After the trillion (10 minutes) up-and-downs, I carefully slid the bolt back out of the action and wiped it clean. The back of one locking lug was polished bright, but the other had only a small bright spot near the bolt body. It was apparent that both lugs were not seated evenly. I cleaned off the locking lugs and wiped out the action. I applied more grinding compound and repeated the operation. By the end of the second trillion (10 minutes more) up-and-downs, both lugs were equally bright. I cleaned up the action and bolt again.

I switched to a very fine jeweler's rouge, and repeated these steps a third time to produce a mirror bright finish on the back of both lugs. I then cleaned both the action and the bolt thoroughly. Cleaning was not easy with the action glued into place in the

ation. This was not only a surprise to me, but it made me realize that sometimes it's the little things that have the biggest effect on improving accuracy, or keeping you from it.

Not satisfied enough to stop looking, I continued. The next step was to vary loads, examining various primer-powder-bullet combinations. We're all familiar with this time-consuming procedure. There are no shortcuts. I sometimes think there must be a scientifically acceptable procedure, but have never found any method other than good old trial-and-error.

It's possible to eliminate some variables like bullets, because of end use, but changes such as bullet seating depth must be tried in increments of every hundredth or so. Once a good seating depth is found, it necessitates looking back at other loads and com-

Case preparation tools included (left to right) Buck Stix Flash Tool for removing burrs around flash hole, primer pocket reamer, neck turning tool and benchrest dies to insure straight bullet seating.

binations that were rejected earlier. After testing hundreds of rounds, you'll feel like a tail-chasing dog.

If you think that working up a load is easy, consider that there are about eight kinds of primers, 16 kinds of powder, 18 different bullets (unless eliminated by application), six to eight usable bullet seating depths, and about six kinds of brass manufacturers. If you wanted to try every possible combination, firing four groups of five shots each, you would have to shoot over 2 million rounds. If you fired 1000 rounds per day, it would take you 5 years to finish testing, and you'd have shot-out 400 barrels. I'm sure your wife would have left also.

No one has ever tried all the possibilities, and I'm not going to be the first. By testing, I found 24.5 grains of BLC2 and a 50-grain Sierra Blitz, with Federal brass and M205 match primers, shot better in this rifle than my earlier pet load. I used the Blitz bullets not only for accuracy, but because they had proven, in past use, devastating for eating those crows and foxes. Bullet seating depth was an ever-so-slight touching of the rifling, for an overall length of 2.200-inches. My resulting four 5-shot groups averaged 0.450-inch, largest group measuring 0.490-inch and smallest measuring 0.435-inch. This was another improvement of $^2/_{10}$-inch, and groups finally started looking

like small clusters, rather than spreads.

I had come a long way since that first group of $1^3/_{16}$ inches, but I had one last rabbit in the hat. I purchased 100 Federal nickel-plated match cases, and fired each of them once with my latest load. I then neck-sized, trimmed to length, and outside neck-turned the cases. I only removed enough material to clean up all the way around the necks, because I still had a standard factory chamber, not a tight benchrest chamber.

Next, I cut the primer pockets to uniform depth with a tool designed for this purpose. I then used a Buck Stix Flash Tool to clean up the flashholes, and remove any burrs that may have been left from the factory manufacturing process. *(Author, by the way, owns Buck Stix, which sells a variety of hunter products.)*

Last, I weighed each and every case, marking its weight on the side with a marker, and grouped them accordingly. I found 29 cases that were not only identical in weight, but also identical in outside dimension. This supposedly insures that the select few were identical in wall thickness and volume, the whole reason for hours of squinting at the scale.

For the final accuracy test, I was very meticulous in the loading procedure. The neck sizing die was set to touch the shoulder lightly, making sure that the case was centered when the neck reached its final reduction. This insures chamber centering. Primers were carefully measured, using a caliper, and I selected 29 that were exactly the same height, measured top to anvil base. Bullets were weighed, selecting those with identical weights and absolutely no imperfections, especially around the base. Powder was thrown using a Bonanza Benchrest powder measure, and bullets were lastly seated using a set of Bonanza Benchrest dies, lapped to fit a fired case.

I returned to the range, with 29 of the most perfectly loaded cartridges I could muster. The first four shots were fired to foul the barrel which had been very meticulously cleaned with Sweets and Gold Medallion before leaving home. These first four shots were fired over a chronograph and velocity averaged 3072 feet per second (fps)—3077, 3072, 3071 and 3068, to be exact.

I was actually hyper as I settled to squeeze off the final 20 shots. The first five shots were a small one-holer. The next five looked about the same through the 24x scope. I was hyper again. The third five-shot group looked a tad bigger, and the last group of five looked better than the first two groups.

The calipers came out quickly, and I measured the last four groups in the same fashion as I measured all of the previous groups. I measured outside to outside of darkened edge around the hole—0.595, 0.590, 0.615, and 0.550-inch. I then subtracted the bullet diameter to find my center to center measurement. The four groups thus measured: 0.371, 0.366, 0.391,

Description Modification	Group Size (inches) Average	Approximate (percent) Improvement
1—None, Factory New	1.187	—
2—"Glue Bedding"	0.937	21.0
3—Crowning & Lapping	0.650	24.2
4—Load Work-Up	0.450	16.8
5—Special Case Prep	0.363	7.4
Total Improvement	−0.824"	69.4

and 0.326-inch, for an average of 0.363-inch or another improvement of 8/100+-inch.

Before you whip out to the range to start your testing, let me tell you about shooting sub-half-minute groups. Don't waste your time trying to use your trusty 3x-9x variable hunting scope. You can't shoot at what you can't see. Even with the 24x Tasco Target scope, I can aim reliably at a circle no smaller than ½-inch; it has crosswires that subtend about ⅜-inch. If I continue to see if this rifle will out-do what it has done, I will use a 36x or 40x benchrest scope (probably Leupold; it's come to be the standard for benchrest).

The 20 shots fired for the last test took me over 40 minutes to shoot, doping the wind, waiting for mirage to settle, and carefully gripping the rifle the same for each shot. All these factors can cloud the true accuracy potential of the rifle if not taken into consideration. Every benchrest technique for consistent shooting was used during my accuracy testing. You can do it if prepared, but not unprepared.

With testing finished, I reviewed my notes on the now-sub-⅜-minute factory rifle. In fact, I charted the data.

I was very surprised during the data review. The glass bedding, even when glued, did not give a remarkable improvement, but a necessary one I'm sure. Had I used the BLC2 load first, bedding improvement may have been more significant. All factors interact. The case preparation steps, for example, accounted for only a 7 percent improvement to accuracy, not a big improvement, but measurable. I expect the 7 percent would not have been measurable, had it not been for the fact that the rifle was perfectly bedded. Which was actually more important? This is the chicken and the egg of the reloading game—still tail-chasing.

I guess I would conclude that if you are surprised when an improvement to accuracy is not as great as you expected, it still enters into the picture. It may be the improvement that lets the others show up.

I can say, however, you shouldn't give up the search for that one-hole group until you are absolutely satisfied you have tried all the possibilities, and even then you may get a surprise. I did. Remember I said that I went to the range for the last time with 29 cartridges? The last five were the same as the other 24, with the exception that I substituted 52-grain Nosler match bullets for the 50-grain Blitz bullets.

I had only 24 Blitz bullets, so I thought I would check to see how the Nosler bullets shot at the seating depth used for the Blitz bullets. I don't even know exactly what that seating depth measures on the Nosler bullets—I just used the dies as set for Blitz, and brought along the extra five rounds. I figured that as long as I had the super-prepared, weight-matched cases, I might as well shoot them all.

I shouldn't have, because these last five went into one ragged hole, measuring 0.421-inch, edge to edge. Center to center for this last look-see group equals an amazing 0.197-inch. That's less than $\frac{2}{10}$-inch from a factory barrel for five shots. Was this just a five-shot fluke?

Fluke or not, you can bet that I'll spend a lot more time sorting out accuracy. Who knows, it could well turn out that I found me a better pet load! ●

(Editor's Note: At press-time, author Sakschek had acquired a 223 because this 222 shot too well to use on prairie dogs and crows. The last number he mentioned was "14," whatever that means. KW)

That last "look-see" group measured less than 2/10 inches, center to center. This load was unexpected and it shows a reloader is never finished.

The muzzle crowning tool has a precision pilot and cutter. The operation is easily accomplished by hand and takes less than five minutes to produce a perfectly square crown.

Bryan Murphy of Murphy's Gun Shop in Tucson sells a lot of 22-caliber merchandise, including 40-shot Mini-14 magazines.

Are 22s
All You Need?

**Maybe so, when push comes to shove.
The small bores can stretch to cover
a lot of ground.**

by BILL R. DAVIDSON

YOU CAN LIVE and hunt in most of the United States with a few rifles, nothing larger than 22-caliber. For a time, while I was between jobs and some of my family was around but not employed full-time, we got by using just 22s. We did it primarily for economy, but there were some other good arguments.

When the financial crunch came down, we religiously cleaned and lightly oiled or sprayed our high-power rifles and stored them safely. Handguns and shotguns were kept out and in use for whatever emergency might come up. We kept two short-barreled shotguns and a 223-caliber rifle loaded for coyotes, the occasional bobcat and so on.

The main rifle in our 22-caliber bunch was a Model 77 Ruger 22-250 varminter with 24-inch medium-heavy barrel. It is very accurate even though it has been used a good deal since it was acquired new about 10 years ago. With a 4x Lyman scope, it will usually put three shots into something between ½-inch and 1 inch at 100 yards. When it fails, the failure is usually the shooter's. Although the rifle has been hauled around and used in a wide variety of climates and terrain, it has never changed point of impact to any appreciable degree; even

cinch-girthed, simon-pure big-bore believers, these four puny calibers kept us partway fed and wholly free of mastodons, saber-toothed tigers and biphibians for a respectable period in the Colorado plateau country.

The 22-250 was not the most-used caliber, but it was the cornerstone of the idea. With 70-grain bullets—and perhaps with 63-grain ones—it downs deer-sized animals—whitetails, mule deer, antelope. Few, even among its main fans, will endorse it for elk, but it will do the job when used by a careful, conscientious and skilled shot. It is certain punishment on predators. And 22 bullets are still cheap enough to allow their use on predators.

The 22-250 is a remarkably flexible cartridge in reloading. As most gun buffs know, it was a wildcat caliber until about 20 years ago, and may be the most widely-used caliber in this country in the space between the smaller 222 Remington and the traditional 30-06. It has become what the 220 Swift might have been—the staple large 22 centerfire.

Three bullets were used in the 22-250—Sierra's 55-grain softpoint spitzer, Sierra's 52-grain hollowpoint and Speer's 70-grain softpoint. There was some experimenting with others, but the three listed here were the best

for meat in a special season. The 55-grain softpoint was not as explosive as the 52-grain HP on larger predators, but it damaged pelts less—and today's coyote pelt is well worth preserving.

Some predator hunters, using their big-game rifles, shoot coyotes with the same strong-jacketed, large-caliber bullets they use on elk, deer and so on. On predators, these do not open up at all; the hunters prefer to drill a fairly small 7mm or 30-caliber or perhaps even bigger hole completely through a coyote, which they feel will be collected in better condition than if shot with a light, frangible bullet that damages the pelt.

There is a good deal of confusion about predator hunting. The standard scoped flat-trajectory bolt-action rifle is the best instrument for long shots in open country. But in thick brush at short range—the ranges at which coyotes and bobcats are shot when called in—the scoped bolt gun is at a serious disadvantage. There, someone with an iron-sighted carbine—lever-action or semi-automatic—is better equipped. The traditional "wisdom" on such hunting is sometimes just error. The best running shot this writer has made on an animal was with a Marlin 30-30 carbine at a zigzagging coyote in creosote brush at about 200 yards—right after two expert varmint callers had repeatedly missed the animal with their scoped bolt guns.

That gets to the AR-15 223-caliber semi-auto rifle. It is kept mainly for fast jackrabbits (using softpoint, not hollowpoint rounds, as a rule), for anti-coyote medicine and for protection. The purposes here did not require a scope, and the gun was iron-sight-zeroed at 200 yards. In fast-swinging brushy conditions, a scope would have been a hindrance.

The virtue to the AR-15 was that of any good semi-automatic rifle—fast followup capability. The 223 is perhaps a bit more cartridge than is required, but in colder climates the jackrabbit is no sluggard and a very tough animal for his size. In southern Colorado, the jacks are particularly spooky and tough—perhaps from a mix of incessant coyote predation and the demands of the climate.

Riflemen using scopes frequently can't adapt to the fast-swinging requirements of such shooting. With the 223 (we also used a Ruger Mini-14 at times), we shot jacks for dog food and used the cottontails for people-feeding.

Experiments with the AR-15 showed ours shot best with loads a grain or so under maximum, and that

Gary Higgins Jr. takes a firm stand hunting jackrabbits with the Mini-14 in the desert north of Tucson.

when changing elevations between 7,500 or 8,000 feet and sea level, it has required only minimal adjustments for elevation. That's it; the Model 77 shoots better now than when it was new.

The other do-it-all calibers are the 223 Remington, the 22 WMR and the 22 Long Rifle. To the consternation of

performers. Since we were not playing numbers games on chronographs, but sticking to serious surviving in a lean time, we did not try the lighter range of 22 bullets on which the Swift's reputation (or notoriety) was founded.

The 70-grain did well on the one deer collected, a mule deer doe shot

Big 22 centerfires appeal widely. Here, Tucson shooter Ray Somogye zeroes in his Model 700 Remington 22-250, a top choice.

Author's daughter Liz with her 22, a Remington Nylon 66 that is still in the family, has produced a lot of meals.

4198 powder in particular was efficient and accurate. We tested a variety of loads in two ARs and the Mini-14 over a period of a year or so. (A list of loads for the two centerfire 22 calibers accompanies this article). All three 223 rifles shot well and were adequate for the purpose; we kept the more reliable of the ARs plus the Mini-14. The better AR-15 was the one which behaved best with 4198 reloads. The Mini-14 is a good back-up for it. But with a wide range of reloads and factory loads, all three did especially well. All three were sensitive to relatively minor changes in hold and sling tension—so no one use a sling in shooting.

The 22 WRM should be sublabeled "The Farmer's Friend," based on our experience with it. No other caliber is as widely adaptable for general farm use. The factory loadings in hollowpoint and full-jacketed bullets both have their uses. Ours was used on jackrabbits, cottontails, turkeys,

coyotes; my older son—a good shot—and I would not have been afraid to use it on a deer up to 125 yards, granted a good stalk and tight holding. The Mossberg Chuckster we have is superbly accurate, shooting as well up to 100 yards as much more expensive rifles. It is kept in a rack by the front door with the gun unloaded but two or three magazines beside it, filled and ready to lock in.

The Chuckster is kept zeroed at 100 yards with iron sights. This may surprise some people who conceive of any 22 rimfire rifle, even a magnum, as a 50- or 75-yard rifle. But that's ballistics-tables ritual thinking; actually, the 22 Magnum is as accurate as it can be held up to 150 yards. One of our children has a Savage 22 Magnum/20-gauge over/under gun which is the ultimate short-term survival weapon; its 22 Magnum barrel is almost as accurate as the Mossberg's longer tube. Our experience with the 22 Magnum made us happy Winchester kept the cartridge alive in the 1960s when it was subjected to heavy criticism and some other major ammunition companies discontinued it.

The only difficulty experienced with our Chuckster was with magazines. Of the original three, two required replacement—something Mossberg cheerfully handled. Now two magazines are kept partially-loaded with three hollowpoint cartridges each; one is empty, and one is loaded with a shotshell on top and two full-jacketed bullet rounds under it. The empty magazine is rotated about monthly to give each magazine's spring relief from heavy pressure.

Finally, the 22 Long Rifle rimfire caliber guns: A bolt-action Remington

513S sporter and a Ruger 10/22 semi-automatic. The Remington is an excellent training and small-game hunting rifle for children and grandchildren, and the Ruger is good on moving small game and a satisfactory defense rifle for people who are not too expert with heavier-caliber guns. It is short, light and handy—and adequately accurate for moving-game shooting.

The 513 Remington is our oldest gun. Like the Mossberg, it's kept unloaded but with a couple of magazines loaded nearby. One is loaded with hollowpoint bullet cartridges, the other with standard-velocity round-nose bullet loads.

The Remington is fitted with a Redfield sporter-type receiver sight, but the Ruger 10-22 is as-was when it left the factory—folding-leaf rear sight, blade front sight. Both are zeroed at 75 yards, following the traditional zeroing with 22 Long Rifle rimfires, so that the bullet is on zero at 25 and drops back to zero at 75 yards—more or less.

No one will reasonably claim the 22s—centerfire and rimfire—are omnipotent. They are, however, adequate to satisfactory for most hunting and shooting that Westerners will do. They and their components are light, portable and economical, at least compared to other calibers. Aside from brown-Kodiak-grizzly bears and elk and moose, one or the other will do whatever you need to do in the field with a rifle. ●

Personal 22 Centerfire Loads

Bullet (Grains)	Powder/Grains	Remarks
22-250		
52-53 HP	4895/35.5	
	760/38.6	
	4064/36.2	
	4320/36.5	preferred load
55 SP	760/39.0	
	4320/36.0	preferred load
	4064/36.0	
	4895/35.5	
70 SP	4831/40.0	
	4350/39.0	preferred load
223		
52 HP	4198/22.0	preferred load
	748/27.5	
	4895/26.5	preferred load
55 SP	748/27.0	
	4895/26.0	preferred load
60 HP	4895/25.0	
	748/27.0	
70 SP	748/23.5	
	4895/24.0	

HP—hollowpoint; SP—softpoint.

SHOT

by DON ZUTZ

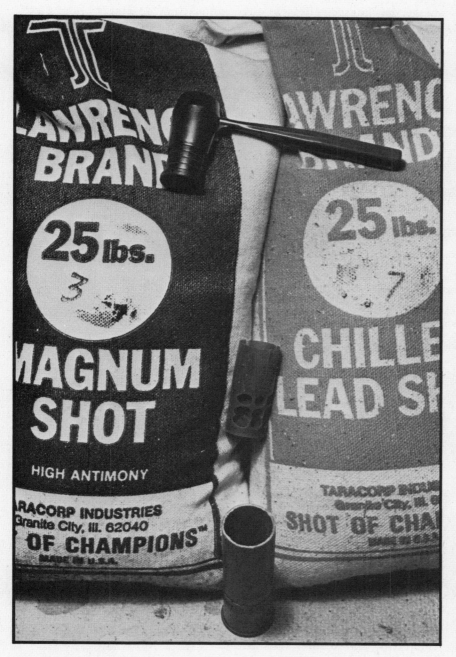

It's everything it used to be and more.

IN THE complete lexicon of shotgunning, there are pellet sizes and designations with which most current hunters and handloaders aren't familiar. Some of the old labels buried in books, such as "swan shot," undoubtedly belong to the ages. But there is other nomenclature which, either forgotten, recently devised, or resurrected, pinpoints pellets that have a definite bearing on scattergunning's present and future. Collectively massed under the generic title of "Shot," their numbers and nuances are not without purpose. Thus, a background in the methods and meaning behind these multiple shot-making madnesses should help wingshots and reloaders understand where we are in pellet development and application, how we got here, and where we're going . . .

Initially, pellets were not standardized. Shotmakers had their own numbering systems. A No. 6 from one maker could be larger or smaller than a No. 6 from another source. In the late 19th century, there were still several major US suppliers who set their own sizes and weights: Tatham & Bros. of New York, the St. Louis Shot Tower of Missouri, Raymond Lead Co. of Chicago, T.N. Sparks of Philadelphia, the Sleby Co. of San Francisco, Merchant's Co. of Baltimore, the Dubuque Co. of Iowa, and the Le Roy Co. of New York were the apparent leaders. Surviving documents and references relative to those Yankee shot-droppers differed broadly on sizes and standards. Number 4 birdshot from Tatham & Brothers, for example, was published to count 132 pellets per ounce, whereas the St. Louis Shot Tower advertised No. 4s at 159 per ounce while the Le Roy Co. listed 121. The same mess was present in letter-designated pellets. Tatham called pellets with a 0.230-inch diameter FF, but Raymond Lead called its 0.230-inchers 000 shot.

And that was only the American scene, of course. When one considers that the British and Europeans also had various shot-designating systems, he can appreciate the megamess. Ordering No. 6s could bring anything from 4s or 5s to 7s or 7½s, depending upon the source of supply. Just recently I opened some new, plastic-cased, Belgian-made 24-gauge loads stamped "6" and found they measured 0.100-inch, which is the basic American No. 7. On an international plane, then, the lack of uniformity still exists.

At the tag end of the 19th century and during the early 20th century,

America gradually settled on a pellet size and numbering system akin to that of the Tatham standards, and the system has been adopted by SAAMI. The Tatham figures ran like this:

Pellet Designation	Diameter (inches)	No. Per Ounce
FF	0.230	24
F	0.220	27
TT	0.210	31
T	0.200	36
BBB	0.190	42
BB	0.180	50
B	0.170	59
1	0.160	71
2	0.150	86
3	0.140	106
4	0.130	132
5	0.120	168

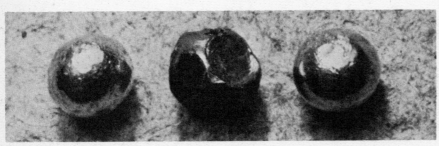

Pellet deformation has been the bane of shotgunning, and various methods—the use of greater amounts of antimony and/or plating with copper or nickel—have been devised to help retain pellet form under setback pressures. The deformed BB in the center shows how the forces of pellet-against-pellet in the chamber and during bore travel can affect relatively soft shot.

The larger pellet sizes have been becoming more popular in steel shot loads for their greater downrange energy retention for goose hunting. Sizes like T- and F-shot provide steel pellets with energies similar to those of lead BBs, with F-shot hitting even harder at 50 yards than high-velocity lead BBs.

T-Buck 0.20"   #4 Buck 0.24"   #00 Buck 0.34"

6	0.110	218
7	0.100	291
8	0.090	399
9	0.080	568
10	0.070	848
11	0.060	1,346
12	0.050	2,326

If a sharp reader compares today's SAAMI chilled shot table with the above Tatham listings, he'll see a pair of discrepancies. One is the absence of half sizes; they were added later, as our narrative will point out. The other is that current SAAMI tables show a few more chilled shot per ounce for each number, which can be explained by the use of an antimonial alloy in modern shotmaking; for hardeners

are lighter than lead itself, and with chilled shot having a 2½ percent to 3 percent mixture of arsenic and antimony, it simply takes more pellets of any given size to scale a full ounce (437.5 grains).

Exactly why the Tatham system was accepted by the industry cannot be documented. But the system makes sense for a reason beyond arbitrary establishment. It isn't only linear in nature, but there is also a handy mathematical basis for the number-designated pellets: by subtracting the pellet's number from 17, one will find the diameter of that specific shot. For instance, subtract No. 6 from 17 and the remainder will be 11—which, with an appropriately placed decimal point before it, is the nominal diameter of No. 6 birdshot, namely, 0.110-inch. Thus, there was a system behind the system.

Not all pellet sizes gained popularity, of course. With the exception of BBs, the letter-designated sizes have largely been ignored since the early 1900s. One reason why BBBs, Ts and Fs have been unpopular is because various states have outlawed anything larger than BBs for waterfowl. Another reason is that hunters operating under the more-is-better syndrome have opted for buckshot. Where buckshot is legal on geese, hunters pick No. 4 buckshot.

Recently, though, the 20-caliber pellet known as T has been making a comeback, albeit not in lead. To pro-

vide waterfowl hunters with more per-pellet energy on geese, states that formerly restricted loads to BBs have legalized T-shot in *steel*. This gives a goose hunter about the performance he would get from a lead BB, and, in this writer's experience, provides a positive penetration on Canadas out to at least 50 yards. As provided by U-Load, Inc. (P.O. Box 443-117, Eden Prairie, MN 55344) under the Supersonic tradename, steel T-shot dropped a trio of geese for me last October at guesstimated distances of 35-45 yards, and all were anchored where they hit. Their impact on the major first wing bone was shattering. Thus, T-shot—which is now being called T-buck, which may be a mistake in the original nomenclature—may have a brilliant future as a steel projectile.

When it comes to lead Ts and Fs, they are being offered by Ballistic Products, Inc. (P.O. Box 488, Long Lake, MN 55356) in 5-pound bags with a higher antimonial content for improved patterning.

At one time, No. 7 shot was widely used in the uplands and by trap and live pigeon competitors. The 12-gauge loading of 3¼-1¼-7 is still a very effective recipe which patterns beautifully. And when Charles Askins the elder wrote *The American Shotgun* back in 1910, he selected 1 ounce of 7s for his pet duck load in the 16-gauge. My own first venture into shotshell reloading back in the 1950s was prompted by my curiosity to see how an ounce of No. 7s would work on ruffed grouse and ringnecks in my 20-gauge, and I can't say I was disappointed. At roughly 300 pellets per ounce, No. 7s give more energy than 7½s and greater density than 6s. I was pleasantly surprised to find my

A 2mm pellet, nominally a 9½ by American standards, is widely used for international Skeet under the rules of the International Shooting Union.

above-mentioned 24-gauge shells hosting basic 7s, and they have acquitted themselves perfectly on grouse and woodcock.

Number 7s aren't exactly out of it. I have a couple 25-pound bags on my loading room floor. Lawrence brand shot (Taracorp Industries, 16th & Cleveland Blvd., Granite City, IL 62040) is still being dropped to said specification each year, but the run is small and one must generally write the company to obtain information about its availability and distribution. Hopefully, No. 7s will also make a comeback one day in high-antimonial form, as they rate huzzahs on grouse and wild-flushing quail like the desert species.

What took No. 7s out of the picture? Number 7½s. I have been unable to document the first manufacture of 7½s, but they were around in the early part of this century. The popularity of 7½s traces mainly to the period between the World Wars, thanks to the writings of hunters who we can gath-

ered momentum, the market for 7s fell off while the demand for 7½s expanded. At 350 per ounce as opposed to 300 for No. 7s, the No. 7½ load was expected to put more shock-inducing hits on each bird, and the public bought it. After WWII, therefore, No. 7s weren't brought back as a regular factory loading.

In the 1970s, another half-sized pellet entered the scene, the No. 8½. This was purely a target load play. Theoretically, 8½s filled out patterns for 16-yard trapshooting. But it was actually introduced by the industry in hopes that both Skeet and trap shooters would accept 8½s so that Skeet 9s could be dropped and the list of loadings simplified. As it turned out, 8½s only increased the number of loads, because Skeet shooters kept insisting on 9s. In general, 8½s are best in 1-ounce trap loads or Modified-choked trap guns for added density with 1⅛-ounce ammo.

No. 3s never really got off the ground, although the late Elmer

sometimes used in International Skeet loads and are still obtainable from Taracorp. To be precise, ISU rules specify 2mm shot for Skeet, and that figures out to about 9½ shot on our SAAMI scale. I have opened Winchester International Skeet rounds to find pellets averaging 9½ (about 0.085-inch).

While No. 11 shot is forgotten, No. 12s still find use in 22 Long Rifle shot loads and some 9mm garden gun ammo. Number 12s may also have been loaded for trick shooters of the old wild west shows to break balloons as they rode by on bucking broncos. However, another smaller pellet, known as dust shot, has also been used for such showmanship. Dust shot, according to current American specs, has a diameter of 0.040-inch and tallies 4,565 per ounce.

No documentation explains the use of the letters "T" and "F" in the Tatham system, but it isn't too difficult to think of them in terms of "turkey" and "fowl" pellets, as turkeys were taken by body shots at that time, as were waterfowl raked at long range. The coarser pellets beyond Tatham's FF were generally derived from a British carrying-on known as swan shot. These were not actually round pellets. Hunters hacked cube-like projectiles from lead sheets to take His Majesty's swans with ancient blackpowder guns, a nominal count being anywhere from 200 to 250 cubes per pound of lead plate. Today the swans of England are protected, but the idea lives on. For American settlers applied the same practice on whitetails, and the name simply changed from swan shot to buckshot. Essentially, the letter-graded pellets of the Tatham and the current SAAMI systems were not regarded as a part of this category, meaning that

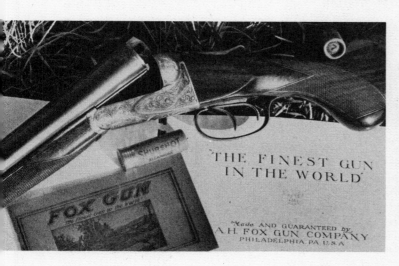

During the so-called Golden Years of American scattergunning, the No. 7 shot was important for upland hunting, trapshooting, and box pigeon events. It has since been replaced by No. 7½s in popularity, but it is still a good upland pellet.

er under the heading of the "fine-shot school." These people argued that penetration wasn't the only factor in a shotshell's terminal effect, but that shocking power due to multiple hits was even more important. Their argument stated that the impact of a pattern on a bird's nervous system was equivalent to the square of the number of pellet hits; hence, the more shot one got on a bird, the better were his chances supposed to be of killing it cleanly. Thus, five to six hits on a ringneck with 7½s were said to be more positive than two to three heavier 4s or 6s.

Not everyone agreed with the fine-shot school's theory (including this writer, who tends to disagree), but the idea was new and flashy. As it gath-

Keith swore by them for geese and long-range mallards. I spent the past autumn taking mallards with reloads using Lawrence brand Magnum-grade 3s, and the results were most excellent. They split the difference between the density of 4s and the energy of 2s to produce clean kills on green-heads. Moreover, a No. 3 steel pellet is available from Non-Toxic Components, and it may have better application in the uplands than on waterfowl for heavy-bodied birds like pheasants and prairie grouse. I have never been totally satisfied with steel 4s.

The finer sizes of lead shot served special purposes, too. Number 10s were once regarded as snipe shot. Not too many sportsmen demand special loads for snipe these days, but 10s are

At .10-inch, the No. 7 bagged in the U.S. provides about 300 pellets to the ounce.

Number 3 shot almost evaporated in the last 50 years, but it is now coming back in the form of steel shot and high-antimony Magnum-grade bagged shot for reloading.

Ts and Fs are not true buckshot. They should rightly be termed T-shot and F-shot if historical factors prevail.

As the US ammunition industry standardized buckshot, the final list reads like this:

Buckshot Designation	Diameter (inches)	No. Per Pound
#4	.240	338
#3	.250	299
#2	.270	232
#1	.300	173
#0	.320	143
#00	.330	130
#000	.360	100

(*As listed in *1986 Winchester Ammunition Guide*.)

Unlike birdshot which is formed by dropping molten lead, buckshot is made by moulding or rolling. Some companies have also made use of swaging equipment. Until recent years, buckshot was made extremely soft, perhaps because hunters wanted pellet expansion on target. However, soft buckshot is subject to extensive deformation on firing setback and during bore travel; and that deformation, along with anything *but* a fluid flow characteristic, caused terrible patterning. Hunters who shoot soft, naked buckshot at high geese are ignorant of shotgun performance. And that brings us to the subject of pellet quality . . .

While birdshot and buckshot sizes were becoming standardized in each

nation, and while the various sizes were finding their particular niches with hunters and shooters, parallel advances were being made in pellet quality. This advance was actually more important than standardizing sizes and numbers, as a poor quality pellet doesn't perform well in patterning or penetrating regardless of its number or letter. Yet, even in today's supposedly sophisticated world, hunters pay more attention to shot numbers than to shot quality. To most chaps, a No. 4 is simply a No. 4, and they'll buy the cheapest shot they can find. But among metallurgists and shotgun experimenters, there's a lot more to it.

Lead has always been considered the best metal for shotgun pellets. It is cheap, easily formed, and possessed of a very high density to overcome air

Magnum No. 3s measure .14-inch and deliver 112 or so pellets to the ounce.

resistance. However, the malleability of lead is an Achillean heel. For the ramming force of expanding powder gases (setback) and the pressures of bore passage combine to deform lead pellets, and deformation means they'll lose velocity quickly and/or flare from the main cluster as air resistance acts upon their flattened, irregular shapes. The results of pellet deformation are weak, patchy patterns and long in-flight shot strings.

Much in the history of shotshell development pertains to overcoming lead shot deformation. This doesn't mean research and improvements have dragged. The answers were known in the 1800s. Ballisticians knew all about the woes of pellet deformation before the modern percussion gun became established. Some British waterfowlers bedded their pellets in ground bone dust to encase them against raw pellet-to-pellet mashing, and German shotmakers

blended antimony, which is a hardener, with lead to make a harder pellet which became known as "chilled shot."

Essentially, the name chilled shot is a misnomer. It is not hardened by any cooling process, but is toughened only by the inclusion of antimony. (Arsenic is also employed in the making of lead shot, but it merely helps provide surface tension to draw the falling lead droplet into spherical form.)

Chilled shot is not the beginning and the end of improved shotmaking, although many casual hunters and handloaders aren't aware of that. In fact, chilled shot is considered relatively soft by modern standards. Today's shotgunner has three levels of shot hardness available: The softest is known as drop shot and has either no antimonial content or, at the most, a meager ½-percent antimony content. Chilled shot is an intermediate quality which, according to data supplied by Taracorp for Lawrence brand shot, has a 1 percent antimonial content in BBs, 2s, 4s, 5s, and 6s, while the target sizes of 7½s, 8s, 8½s, and 9s receive a 2 percent dash of hardener. The highest quality black shot is known as Magnum grade, and it will probably vary in antimony content slightly depending on which outfit makes it. The Lawrence Brand Magnum shot finds BBs and 2s having 2 percent antimony, 4s and 5s bearing 3 percent antimony, 6s and 9s with 4 percent, and trapshooting 7½s and 8s with a whopping 6 percent antimony.

Buckshot has generally been made of 100 percent pure lead. However, in recent years, Dave Fackler of Ballistic Products has persuaded the industry to make buckshot with at least a 3 percent antimonial content for improved patterning.

With low-antimony drop shot, it is difficult to get patterns beyond 50 percent at 40 yards regardless of the gun's choke. There is simply too much pellet deformation. With chilled shot, patterning can also be dicey, with 57 percent to 63 percent being about tops for many Full-choked guns that should be doing 70 percent or better. Those *el cheapo producto* factory loads one buys at bargain prices normally have a low grade of chilled shot, and serious patterning with such inexpensive loads uncovers terrible performances. Said factory loads look nice on the outside, but inside they have soft, deformation-prone shot. One reason why such loads are cheap is because antimony is an expensive metal, and by not using antimony the price of ammo can be lowered. Unfortunately, so will effectiveness decline. Hunters who use anything but the hardest pellets are being penny-wise and pound-foolish.

Another step to improved patterning was plated shot. John M. Olin is given credit for pioneering copper-plated (Lubaloy) shot in the US in the 1930s. However, Sidney Pitt of England took out a patent for plating lead shot in 1878, so the idea was already 50 years old before Olin picked it up. Initially, Pitt plated with tin or zinc to reduce the potential for game contamination with lead. Too, in those days of leaky card/filler wad columns and fast-burning powders, it was hoped that plating would eliminate "balling," which is the fusing of black shot into clumps.

The project soon turned primarily toward improved patterning, which is

harder shot. Typical hunters can be snug with a buck. And few weekend shotgunners actually understood the potential performance difference between the various hardnesses of pellets. Why pay $7 for a box of ammo marked "hard shot" when another box at $5 looked just as good and had round pellets, too? As late as the 1960s and early 1970s, Winchester was having a tough time selling their bagged Lubaloy shot because hunters didn't want to pay the necessary price.

The tragic thing is that now, just as we've convinced the public that hard shot and plated pellets are the way to go—and that the factories are giving us both commercial loads and reloading components that pattern beautifully—we can't use them. The trend is toward steel shot.

Nothing lately has had a more revolutionary impact on shotgunning

plicate. A No. 2 steel pellet does about the work of a No. 4 lead pellet; a steel BB performs close to a lead No. 2; and a steel T-shot does the job of a lead BB. The added size is required so that the steel pellet has more weight to overcome air resistance. Winchester's *1986 Ammunition Guide* illustrates this comparison:

A Winchester load of No. 4 lead shot exiting at 1330 fps has a retained energy of 4.4 foot-pounds at 40 yards, and 2.7 foot-pounds at 60 yards. A Winchester steel shot load of No. 2s launched at 1365 fps has a per-pellet retained energy of 4.4 foot-pounds at 40 yards, and 2.6 foot-pounds at 60 yards, meaning roughly similar performance. However, steel No. 4s leaving at 1365 fps strike with only 2.5 foot-pounds at 40 strides and 1.4 foot-pounds at 60 yards, a definite difference from lead 4s and steel 2s. To enhance hitting power with steel for longer-range goose hunting, the trend is slowly sidling toward steel T-shot and buckshot, as its greater momentum carries positive penetrating energy farther than the steel birdshot sizes. In fact, I understand that a wad experimenter has the FBI interested in whopping steel buckshot loads because steel buckshot of considerable size penetrates deeper than the traditional lead #00 buck which, upon impact, mushes out to expend its energy quicker. And wouldn't that be a revolution in shot selection if the FBI went to steel buck?

Thus, the subject of shotgun pellets isn't old and it certainly isn't bland or simple. Not all pellets are pure lead as many shotgunners think, and steel and lead sizes aren't equivalents. Sometimes we split hairs over sizes and alloys, and indifferent hunters view this as comical. But most often, an in-depth look at pellet sizes, purposes, alloys, and field and patterning results is meaningful. Entire industries have grown up around these dinky spheres, from the old Newcastle Chilled Shot Co. of England to the modern makers of steel shot, and the end isn't in sight. Perhaps one day there'll be a lead substitute that'll appeal to hunters more than steel shot currently does. Maybe one day we'll have a biodegradable material. In any case, the next time you're out to buy a bag of shot for reloading, you might give it more thought than they did when great grandpa was restuffing brass hulls for his battered Parker. Pellets aren't just pellets anymore. And to the fussy few, they never were.

High-antimony F-shot has been brought into long-range shotgunning by Ballistic Products, Inc. for those who dote on high energies per-pellet for optimum goose hunting distances with the big 10-gauge Magnum.

where it remains. Today, plating is copper or nickel, the latter being harder and more expensive. Olympic trapshooters use nickel-plated shot almost exclusively, and hunters who have used such trap loads on grouse in the coverts swear by it.

Plating alone doesn't render a pellet perfect. The nucleus must be high-antimony lead. Plating soft shot permits deformation as extensive as that of soft unplated shot. In many respects, high-antimony Magnum black shot is preferred to copper-plated shot with soft-lead interiors.

Ammo suppliers are now beginning to make copper-plated buckshot, and Ballistic Products, Inc., has sent me some trial copper-plated #4 buck for reloading. It's another step.

The big problem in pellet quality improvement wasn't the technological side. Ballisticians and metallurgists knew about that more than a century ago. The difficulty was getting the public to pay a little more for

than steel shot. Its exterior ballistics are different than those of lead shot, something which the public is having a tough time understanding. Because steel shot doesn't deform, it A.) patterns very tightly, and B.) has a relatively short in-flight shot string. These two factors are enough to make many typical hunters miss, as they demand greater pattern-placement precision than unpracticed weekend warriors can manage. And it goes a step further: steel loads may require slightly less forward allowance close in, since they are fast out the barrel and, initially, retain velocity reasonably well for 25-30 yards. But then, alas, steel loads tend to slow down quicker than lead pellets of the same diameter beyond 40-45 yards when air resistance works against them more efficiently than against the denser lead spheres.

The current rule of thumb in selecting steel shot is to pick two sizes larger than the lead pellet you wish to du-

A Fresh Look at 17-Calibers

by H. WALT LAM

MANY shooters bypass 17-caliber cartridges in their search for a good varmint gun. The reasons are varied, based mostly on the assumption that the 25-grain bullet does not perform well under windy conditions, and that it lacks sufficient punch to be effective against woodchucks at long ranges. This reasoning is not necessarily correct, and the actual performance of the 17 deserves a fresh evaluation.

A typical 22-caliber 50-grain bullet at a muzzle velocity of 3800 fps still has 2850 fps at 200 yards and 2430 fps at 300 yards. A 25-grain 17-caliber at the same muzzle velocity is still moving at 2400 fps at 250 yards and 2240 fps at 300 yards. Thus, the difference in velocity at 300 yards between a 17 and a 22 is about 190 fps — not a difference a woodchuck would know about.

Wind drift, as indicated in Hornady's manual, shows that in 250 yards, a 22-caliber 50-grain bullet with a coefficient of 220 traveling at 3800 fps will drift 7 inches, while the 25-grain 17 with a coefficient of 190 will drift between 7-8 inches. With these performance characteristics in mind, there is little on paper to find fault with the 17.

Being interested in small caliber rifles, I acquired my first several years ago. A Martini Cadet action was the base for the 17 Ackley Bee. I field-tested the rifle extensively to see its capabilities firsthand. Mounted with an 8x Unertl scope, the rifle performs very well.

Zeroed 1 inch high at 100 yards, several groups were shot on days with little or no wind. I was pleasantly surprised with ⅝-inch groups using 11.5 grains of 4198. Shooting in a good crosswind, the results were not alarming: 1- to 1¼-inch groups, only slightly off center. The results convinced me to try the cartridge on a few hunting trips.

The first day out a breeze was blowing, and on the first shot, a crow exploded at a range of approximately 200 yards. Two more crows fell victim to the 25-grain bullet and a woodchuck dropped at 150 yards. Several weeks later, in a stiff breeze, two chucks were taken at 200+ yards and one at 100+ yards. This convinced me that all the negative comments I had heard did not apply to the Ackley.

My experiences with the Ackley Bee led me to purchase what is now my favorite varmint rifle, a Remington 700 BDL in 17 Remington. Rem-

Between two 22-caliber bullets, the 17 is dwarfed.

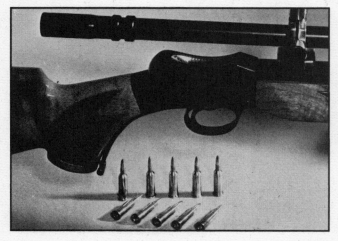

Author's 17 Ackley Bee on a BSA Martini action, built by P.O. Ackley, works well in the field.

The Remington BDL is an excellent rifle and in 17 Remington killed off a lot of wildcats.

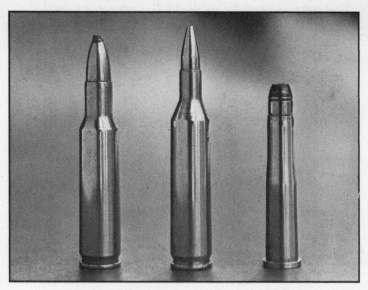

Between the 222 (left) and the 22 Hornet (right) the 17 Remington stands taller and shoots lots faster.

A 6x Bushnell scope works out about right for the 700 Remington 17-caliber.

The author with one of the many prairie dogs that fell victim to the 17 Remington.

ington introduced this cartridge in 1971, and a lot of the wildcat 17s fell by the wayside. Today, Remington still produces rifles and cartridges in this caliber. Only Sako, among all the rest, also produces a 17-caliber rifle.

Remington ammo is listed at approximately 4000 fps, and these velocities can be obtained. However, I have had better results by loading down to 3600-3800 fps.

I mounted a 6x Bushnell scope on my 700 and zeroed 1 inch high at 100 yards using factory ammo. Groups measured ½- to ¾-inch. Reloads consistently produced slightly smaller groups. After firing 50 rounds, the smallest group measured just under ½-inch, and the largest just over ¾-inch. Averaged out, they came in a little closer than factory ammo. Using 30-grain bullets, groups opened to over 1½ inches. Some 18-grain bullets were tried and the first two shots showed promise. Unfortunately, the next three completed the group with a measurement of 2¾ inches, so it was back to the 25-grain bullet.

In the field, 19.5 grains of 4198 and the 25-grain bullet killed two chucks at 150 yards. A close look at the chucks showed the entrance hole but no exit — another plus for the 17. Both shots were in the chest.

On a recent bird hunting trip to South Dakota, I packed the 700. Regrettably, I took only two boxes of cartridges. I wasn't sure about the weather for varmint hunting in October. As it turned out, the temperature was in the 70s and prairie dogs were plentiful. Our host took our party on a tour of his ranch and pointed out a section full of prairie dogs. We shot and killed 38 within a few minutes time; the Remington proved itself. Since that trip, many crows and chucks have fallen victim to my 17.

It is not difficult to obtain permission to hunt on small farms in my area. The 17's noise level is relatively low and does not frighten livestock and families as much as larger calibers do. Also, the thin jacketed bullet literally explodes on contact. No ricochets go screaming off across the landscape.

Pelt hunters will find the 17 does a lot less damage to fur-bearing animals. Turkey hunters will find a lot less damage to the meat with a well-placed shot.

If you are in the market for an excellent mid-range varmint or hunting rifle, check the 17s. You may be surprised, as I was, with the results. You may even be able to use the 30-grain bullets that my rifles do not seem to digest well. ●

HOW HAL HARTLEY SAW IT:

1. PENETRATING

Wᴴᴱɴ I WAS 7 years old (1916) my Dad would, under his strict supervision, let me shoot his Stevens Favorite 22 rifle. Since then I have shot many American-made guns, and a goodly number of foreign guns, and I have learned a few things. I have learned that unless you are prepared to do battle, you should not kick a man's dog, nor make derogatory remarks about his guns.

When hunters, riflemen, target shooters and plinkers get together, it is a pretty safe bet that someone will say that he has a gun that will out-shoot, shoot further, shoot harder and is more accurate than any other gun in the crowd. On one Saturday, people began to gather in my gunshop, visiting and talking. This sure plays havoc with a work schedule, but there is nothing else to do but to join in. Of course the talk dealt with guns and shooting.

One of the fellows, we will call him "Bud," said he had the hardest shooting 30-06 he had ever seen. I had been reloading some 220 Swift cartridges and held one up and said, "I *think* this cartridge, shooting a 55-grain bullet, will penetrate more steel than your 30-06 180-grain soft nose bullet."

Bud's jaw dropped, and he became glassy-eyed and began talking in an unknown tongue. He soon regained his sanity and bet his rifle against mine.

I had a 16x⅜-inch plate of hot-rolled steel that I had been planning to use in bullet penetration tests. So, we went out to the 100-yard range and set up the plate. Years earlier, I had made a few tests and felt sure the 220 would penetrate the plate at 200 yards.

Bud elected to shoot first. His bullet penetrated the plate, and Bud gave me an "I told you so" look. I then fired the 220, and the fellow on the spotting scope said, "It penetrated."

Bud seemed a bit uncertain after that announcement.

Then we set up at 200 yards and Bud shot first. The spotter said, "He hit the plate, but I don't think there is a hole in it."

I said I thought the report sounded a bit weak and that we should give Bud another shot. He agreed that the recoil was noticeably weak. We shot again, and again the spotter said, "A hit, but no hole."

We sent a runner to check the target, and to put pasters over the holes made at 100 yards and to paster Bud's bullet splashes.

Then it was my time to try the 220. After I fired the spotter said, "A hit, and I think a hole." We all went to the target and held a postmortem over the results of the tests. Of course, I didn't claim Bud's rifle.

After that test I carried out more extensive tests, using different cartridges, different calibers and loads. These tests proved some reports and theories, and disproved some others. Once, I tried the 219 Donaldson Wasp, the 219 Improved Zipper, the 225 Winchester, the 22-250 Remington, the 220 Swift, the 6mm Remington, the 25-06 and the 30-06. All the 22 calibers were loaded with the Sierra 55-grain Spitzer bullets. The 6mm shot Sierra 60-grain hollowpoints. The 25-06 was loaded with the 100-grain spitzers. The 30-06 shot the 180-grain spitzer. The AP load was the LC-53 cartridge.

The load for the 219 Don-Wasp was 28 grains of 3031, 55-grain Sierra. The load for the 219 Improved Zipper was 32 grains of 4064, 55-grain Sierra. The load for the 220 Swift was 38½ grains of 4064, 55-grain Sierra. The load for the 6mm Remington was 48 grains of 4831, 75-grain Sierra. The load for the 25-06 was 53 grains of 4831, 100-grain Sierra spitzer. The load for the 30-06 was 48 grains 4064, 180-grain Sierra spitzer.

One day I was doing some of these

Labelled bullet holes tell their own story. Hartley loved the way the small-bore speedsters performed on steel.

by HAL HARTLEY

STEEL 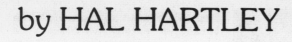 PLATES

tests when a good friend drove up. He watched what was going on and asked if he could check his Remington 17 caliber. I told him I would be happy to see how it would perform. He told me some astonishing stories about the accuracy and flat trajectory over 500 yards. I try to keep from forming opinions of something controversial until I have the opportunity to try it out, so this was a good chance.

The plate was set at 100 yards for the first shot. The bullet failed to penetrate. We then set the plate at 50 yards. Still no penetration. We set the plate at 25 yards and the bullet did penetrate. When I say penetrate, I mean that the bullet went *through* the plate. Friend was a bit chagrined at the performance, but we agreed that it was remarkable that a tiny 25-grain bullet would go through ⅜-inch steel.

Now for the details of the bullets versus steel. I started all the cartridges at 100 yards on ¼-inch hot-rolled steel plate and all of them penetrated, even when moved from 100 to 200 and to 300 yards.

Then I set up the ⅜-inch plate at 100 yards and started with the 219. It penetrated. Then the 225 Winchester penetrated, as did the 22-250. The mighty 220 Swift might have been

shooting through butter. The 6mm Remington failed to penetrate with either the Sierra 60-grain or 75-grain. This was a bit of a shock to me because the cartridge is a favorite of mine. The 25-06 penetrated, as did the 30-06.

Then on to 200 yards. Here the 219 penetrated less than half the thickness of the plate. The 225 Winchester made a large bulge on the back of the plate, but did not penetrate. The 220 Swift penetrated. The 22-250 penetrated. The 25-06 failed, as did the 30-06.

We went to 300 yards, where the 22-250 and the 220 Swift failed. The Swift blew a large bulge on the back, larger than the 22-250.

The next test was the 30-06 with armor piercing bullets. I had never tried this and didn't know what to expect, so I started at 100 yards. The bullet jacket was left in the plate, but the steel core went through. At 200 yards, it was the same story. The jacket stuck in the plate, with the steel core going on. The same story at 300 yards.

Then I put up a piece of ½-inch plate at 300 yards and got the same results as with the ⅜-inch plate. I then shot at a piece of truck spring steel ½-inch thick, placed at 40 yards. The 220 Swift made a crater ¼-inch

deep. A 30-06 180-grain softnose bullet made a faint lead smear—no penetration at all. The 25-06 made a ³/₁₆-inch crater. The armor piercing bullet went through, but from the looks of the entrance hole it had a bit of trouble getting "traction." The hole shows a bit of twisting of the steel, with a hint of keyholing. The steel core must have broken for there were two ragged holes in the backstop. If there is a moral to this story it would be: if you think someone is going to shoot at you, get on the opposite side of a hill, because ⅜-inch steel plate doesn't offer much protection.

From the state of these experiments I noticed that around the entrance hole there was more of a crater built up than was shown around the exit hole.

I had planned to fill a plastic milk jug with water and try the 220 Swift for penetration, but I stopped by a place where a fellow was doing some painting, and I saw some empty paint buckets, the 1 gallon size. I got one and brought it home. Some paint in the bucket was still fluid and when I filled the bucket with water it turned the water white. I set the bucket on a block of wood and set a 36-inch square of cardboard behind it. Then, from 40 yards, I shot the bucket with the

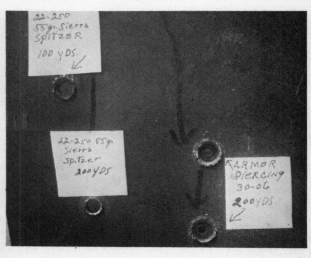

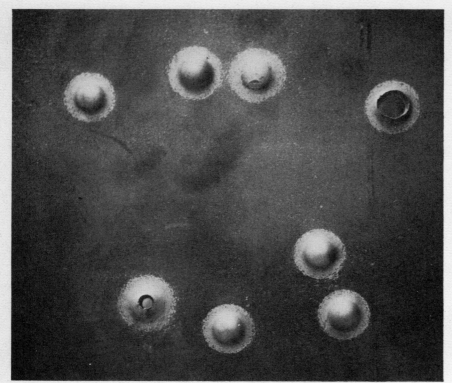

Swift. Talk about an explosion!!! The bucket lid went at least 20 feet. The white water was spread over a 60-foot circle. The bucket was split in two halves. It had a split at the weld down one side and opposite that it had split straight down the other side from top to bottom, as if it had been a second welded seam. The bottom had been blown out and was 20 feet off to one side. Water was dropping from the trees. On examining the backstop cardboard I found two ragged holes about 3 inches apart. The backstop was leaning against a rick of firewood and there were signs where the bullet particles had ricocheted. The halves of the bucket were bulged and twisted. It showed a terrific force had been released.

When I tried the 25-06 at 100 yards,

The backside of Hartley's plate at long range shows how hard many try and how few succeed.

2. ABOUT THOSE

WHEN THE evening meal is finished a lot of men around here get kicked out of the house until bedtime, and some of them come to my shop, where the talk turns to guns and shooting, though politics and the state of the Nation has been getting considerable of our attention, too. On one particular night, our champ varmint hunter was telling of missing a crow.

Seems that when he started to load his rifle he dropped the cartridge and when he picked it up he noticed that the lead tip had been somewhat flattened. He chambered the cartridge and rested the rifle on a sand bag on the car door. It was a perfect set-up: The crow was about 150 yards; a superbly accurate rifle; the scope a 15x Unertl Ultra Varmint; a solid rest; no wind; a good sight picture. He touched the Canjar set trigger, and got a clean miss.

He was positive the miss was caused by that flattened bullet tip. All varmint shooters have had these unaccountable misses and most of us won't admit human error is to blame. This particular miss brought on a long discussion of the importance of using only perfect bullets. They agreed that caliber 224 bullets should never vary in weight more than ½ grain, must be perfectly round and with *no battered points*. Case closed, and quick!

Back when the 22 Hornet was king of the varmint cartridges I had made a few tests, using bullets on which I had filed the tips to various shapes. The results had been enlightening, so I now ventured to say that the bullet tip could be pretty badly mis-shaped without greatly affecting the accuracy. Jaws dropped and eyes went glassy, but soon the group regained its strength and quickly had me backed

into a corner. When they quieted down some I filed three bullets (to the shape of #1 shown here although not quite so drastic) and bet I could fire them into a 2″ group at 100 yards.

I told them that the condition of the base had more effect on the flight of the bullet than the point did and here came more derisive hoots. So I filed three bullets to the approximate shape of #2 and bet that they would spread at least 12″. We loaded three of each of these #1 and #2 bullets and agreed to meet the next evening to try them on targets.

The evening was clear, with no wind, as we prepared for the tests. I was shooting a single shot rifle chambered for the Winchester 225 cartridge and as I placed the cartridge with the filed tip in the chamber I turned the filed edge to 12 o'clock. Shots 1 and 2 were ½″ apart. Shot 3 dropped 1⅜″.

I was shooting from sandbags placed on the car hood. After I had fired, I placed the rifle in the car and leisurely walked to the target. I had placed two baffles of pine boards behind the steel plate in order to catch the slug that would be punched from the plate, and to see what the condition of the bullet might be. As I was separating the baffles, I found the slug had gone through both baffles and was just hanging on to the target holder plank. I reached for the slug and pulled it free, then I realized that the slug was just short of being *RED HOT!!* I tried to turn it loose, but it wouldn't let go. Finally, I slung it loose. My fingers had a nice blister and charred meat on each. It had been fully 5 minutes since I had fired that shot, but the slug was too hot to handle. Engineers say that pressure will create heat. I would like to know what that peak pressure was when the bullet hit the steel, and to know what the temperature was.

Some years ago, when the Winchester 458 had just appeared on the mar-

ket, a fellow brought one by the shop. We were slightly in awe of it and were making predictions of what it would do. The owner asked if I would like to shoot it. I hesitantly agreed. I had a piece of ⅜-inch spring steel I was planning to test some 220 Swift loads on. I stuck the steel in a bank about 20 feet away, braced myself, took aim and fired. After the blood started flowing normally through my shoulder and arm, we went to the spring to examine it. The front of the spring showed a very shallow crater. The back showed a slight bulge with two hairline cracks in the shape of a cross. I reset the spring, loaded the Swift, and aimed and fired. The bullet easily penetrated the spring. The owner of the 458 said, "Something don't add up right." I think that said it all.

From these tests I learned that jacketed bullets of 224-caliber, traveling at better than 3500 fps (feet per second) penetrated more steel than bullets of 243 caliber and larger traveling at around 3300 fps did. What

benefit did I derive from this? It could help me prove a point if I should be involved in an argument about a certain cartridge, and the penetration of steel. A friend of mine was in college and the professor of the class flatly stated that a 224-caliber bullet would not penetrate a ⅜-inch steel plate. He said there was no way a soft metal would penetrate a harder metal. The professor granted permission for my friend to bring his 219 Improved Zipper to the class and to prove, or to disprove his statement. They went to a target range and set up a target at 100 yards. He fired three times, and each bullet penetrated. Friend said all the rest of the school year that professor was a bit "cold" to him.

More tests, involving more cartridges and more sizes of bullets could be conducted in order to learn just where the dividing line between speed, bullet weights and bullet diameter peaks, of course. As I see it, the 220 Swift is king of the standard factory cartridges in this regard. ●

BATTERED BULLETS

Then I turned the rifle over to one of the doubters and had him to fire the three loads with the filed bases. He had a shot at 12 o'clock, one at 3 o'clock and one at 5, and a spread of 20″.

This really got the ball to rolling, and back at the shop we filed bullets to shapes as shown in #1, #2 and #3. We fired a series of targets, using both 50- and 55-grain bullets, with results following a fairly set pattern. Shape #3 gave wider spreads than the other two.

I had never made any similar tests on 30-caliber bullets, but thought this would be a good time to do it. I decided to file the bullets to more different shapes and to use both 125 and 180-gr. pointed. I thought that the greater sectional density of the 180-gr. would cause it to carry truer than the 125-gr. but the tests didn't bear this out. In fact the 125-gr. averaged slightly better groups. The targets were 3′x3′,

cut from white wrapping paper, with the aiming point in the center. A few of the more drastically filed bullets missed the paper, but those that hit showed not the slightest indication of tipping, or keyholing. I had expected those which were filed on the base and tip to tumble, but none in either 224 or 308 did.

In shooting several targets with bullets #1, #2 and #6 I found that by placing the filed area in the chamber in the same position for each series of three shots the bullets would usually land strung out, rather than scattered. Shape #4 couldn't be tamed; it always scattered. I marked loads with the base-filed bullets when I seated them, so I could tell how to place them in the chamber.

In shooting the 30 caliber, in both weights, of #4 and #5 bullets I would see a big orange bloom in the scope.

Evidently the filed area deflected the flame and gas as the bullet cleared the muzzle. I can't recall having ever seen this happen in any other instance.

These tests were carried out over a period of weeks, as time and weather permitted. The targets selected for this article are not the best, nor the worst, but are the average. I will be the first to say that any one could make a similar test and would come up with different results, depending on the amount and the angle of filing, but I'm sure he'd have an interesting time as he checked the targets.

I feel sure that the greatest factor in the great shooting done by modern bench rest and varmint shooters is the near perfect bullets that have been developed over the past 30 years. So, if you should happen to bruise that tiny lead tip don't throw it away. It will travel true, if the base isn't battered. ●

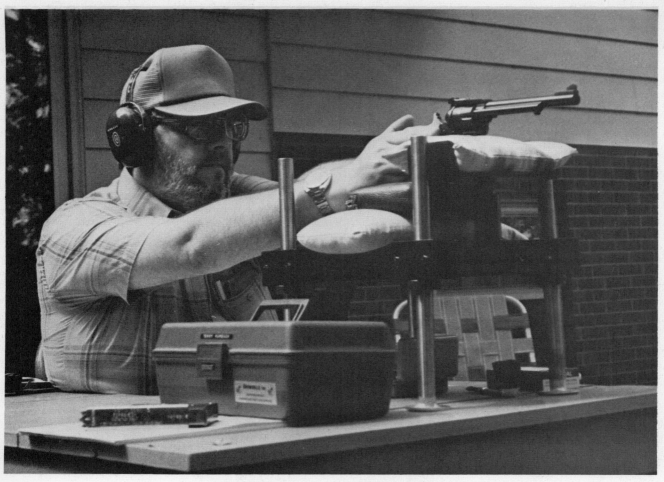

The author tested three Ruger SSM 32 Magnums off sandbag rest to find the consecutively numbered guns quite alike.

CONSECUTIVE NUMBERS

May Mean Something

This three-gun test
describes very nearly
matching performances.

by TERRY MURBACH

REVOLVERS are as individualistic as people. Your Smith & Wesson M19 may look like mine, my Python looks just like yours, but inside those barrels and cylinders, they are as different as night and day. Each revolver has different tastes in factory ammunition. And handloaded ammunition must be assembled with care because your mild load may be hot as hell in my gun. That same load, mild in yours, hot in mine, may even be giving several hundred feet per second more velocity in your gun than mine.

These differences are caused by minute built-in tolerances in chamber sizes and smoothness, in several dimensions of the barrel, the barrel/cylinder gap, forcing cone size, shape, and smoothness, plus a myriad of other things including how hard your revolver's hammer hits a primer in comparison to my revolver's hammer. These slight differences in guns are caused by tooling wear, changes in tooling, different machine operators, slight differences in the metal being cut, and many other things that must keep gun manufacturers up nights pulling out their hair.

The opportunity to test three Ruger SSM 32 Magnum revolvers with consecutive serial numbers promised a new experience. Instead of comparing guns made years apart these three might have been made the same day. Would these revolvers show the vast differences in performance that are much in evidence among other guns? The guns, numbers 8842, 8843, 8844, were like three peas in a pod to look at them.

The polish and blueing were as good as I've ever seen on a Ruger product. The grip frames fit the main frames nicely and the anodizing on the grip frames matched the guns blueing. They are timed alike. The cylinder bolt on 8842 has slightly marked the cylinders, but that's of no real consequence in my opinion.

Another problem with 8842 concerned the mainspring. It was a major effort to cock the hammer and afterwards the hammer hit the transfer bar like a brick dropped on your kitchen floor. Cocking the gun with the stocks removed revealed the mainspring was compressed to its absolute limit when the hammer came to full cock. After I thoroughly dismantled my workshop trying to find two spare Blackhawk mainsprings I've owned for 15 years, I cut two coils off 8842's spring with a cutoff wheel in the Dremel tool. The now shorter mainspring provided a markedly easier cocking pressure, less hammer slap on the transfer bar and a lighter trigger pull.

The second Ruger, 8843, had a very smooth action and an entirely usable trigger pull right out of the box. The third, 8844, was virtually identical to 8843 in feel. I couldn't actually tell which one was which without looking at the serial numbers. Shooting was to reveal 8844 had one endearing trait not shared by the other two: it shot factory 32 Magnum 85JHP ammo into virtually the same point-of-impact as it shot 32 Long handloaded ammunition using Alberts 100-grain HBWC bullets. Why one gun out of three put most everything into the same POI is an intriguing mystery that begs for a logical answer. Your guess is as good as mine 'cause I haven't the foggiest idea.

All test firing was at 25 yards using a variety of factory 32 ammunition. Several 32 handloads were tested also. I used 8842 to develop 32 Magnum handloads using Hornady's 85-grain JHP and 2400 powder. The best shooting load developed was then tested in the other two guns.

This particular load in 32 Magnum brass used 11.5 grains of 2400, CCI 500 primers, and the 85-grain JHP bullet. Velocities were markedly above factory ammo, over 300 fps more, which is astounding. In none of the three test guns did this handload show any case pressure ring expansion greater than that measured on factory ammunition. All three guns ejected the fired brass from the handloaded cartridges without a hint of stickiness. Until the chambers got dirty, ejection consisted of pointing the barrel up, rotating the cylinder, and letting the cases drop out, courtesy of gravity. The CCI 500 primers did show a slight bit more flattening than did the Federal primers, but I believe it is because they are a bit softer. Besides the fact this load shoots fast and accurately, it also burns 2400 so

The three Rugers were externally very like. One had a very strong mainspring, compared to the other two.

Author's Note

After this article was all finished, I had an opportunity to test one cast bullet load in 8842. The bullets were SAECO #325.32 SWCs weighing 99.4 grains lubed. These were loaded in 32 Magnum cases over 8.0 grains of 2400, sparked by CCI 500 primers. Velocities averaged 1190 fps with an Sd of 24. The first five shot into .625-inch. The second five measured 1.375 inches.

This group was the first five rounds out of the 8844's brand new barrel using the 32 Long handload discussed. It measures .43-inch and seemed to epitomize the SSM's eager-to-please nature.

The top gun, a Ruger Super Single Six, was purchased by the author in early 1965, if memory serves. The SSM was bought late winter of 1985. Author finds them complementary.

cleanly you won't believe your eyes. If you look close, you may find a flake or two of yellowed unburnt powder, but in comparison to popular loads using 2400 in the 357 or 44 Magnum, the 32 Magnum burns 2400 totally and completely. That's amazing.

During load development with 8842, group averages suddenly started increasing while retesting what appeared to be the best shooting 32 Magnum loads. After much searching, head scratching, and theorizing I measured a full length-sized 32 Magnum case. I was dumbfounded when the dial caliper read 1.085-inches, a full 10 thousandths of an inch over factory specifications. A check on other cases showed some as short as 1.075-inches. After three loadings all had grown, a few as much as .015-inch. I ran the whole batch through the Forster trimmer and accuracy averages returned to the previous levels.

Many handloaders tend to ignore case lengths in straight walled pistol cases. That is a mistake, particularly in revolver cases that must be crimped firmly and evenly. It is equally strange to note though that these differences in case length, which must affect crimp pressure, made themselves known by opening up groups. There was no corresonding change in velocities or velocity standard deviations, nor were there pressure indications. This further reinforces my feelings that the 32 Magnum cartridge in the Rugers shows remarkably uniform ballistic properties plus

Don Wilks, the author's testing associate, was so impressed with his SSM that he bought a Single Six.

THE RESULTS

SSM8842	Velocity	S.d.	Group Average	Groups Fired
Federal 32 Long 98 gr. RN	728 FPS	9	2.68-in.	5
Federal 32 Long 98 gr. WC	770 FPS	8	1.70-in.	5
32 Long Handload[1]	905 FPS	7	1.57-in.	15
Federal 32 Magnum 85 gr. JHP	1098 FPS	13	1.68-in.	10
32 Magnum Handload[2]	1479 FPS	22	1.50-in.	10

SSM8843				
Federal 32 Long 98 gr. RN	715 FPS	18	2.21-in.	5
Federal 32 Long 98 gr. WC	765 FPS	12	1.83 in.	5
32 Long Handload[1]	899 FPS	9	1.54-in.	16
Federal 32 Magnum 85 gr. JHP	1071 FPS	18	2.21-in.	5
32 Magnum Handload[2]	1443 FPS	15	2.29-in.	5

SSM8844				
Federal 32 Long 98 gr. RN	729 FPS	5	2.59-in.	5
Federal 32 Long 98 gr. WC	782 FPS	7	1.93-in.	4
32 Long Handload[1]	902 FPS	8	1.59-in.	15
Federal .32 Magnum 85 gr. JHP	1049 FPS	14	1.83-in.	5
32 Magnum Handload[2]	1442 FPS	22	1.47-in.	5

[1] Sako Brass
Alberts 100 gr. HBWC bullets
2.4 gr. HP38 powder
CCI 500 primers lot A17JD
L.O.A. .930"

[2] Federal Brass
Hornady 85 gr. JHP bullets
11.5 gr. 2400 powder
CCI 500 primers lot A17JD
L.O.A. 1.325"

a very high level of ballistic efficiency. In effect, ladies and gentlemen, this is one hell of a slick little cartridge that launches bullets fast, straight, and true. All three revolvers shot well with 32 Long ammunition. These neat little cartridges are superior small game loads particularly with the wadcutter bullets. They go in bigger than 22 hollowpoints come out and deck small game—like rabbits and squirrels—without messing up the good eating parts. Also, assuming you already own 32 Long brass, if you shop around and buy your bullets and primers at a decent price, you can load 32 Long cartridges at less cost than buying 22 LRHP ammunition.

The Ruger Single-Six 22 revolvers always were a class act, and I believe Ruger's market for the SSM 32 Magnum is assured for eternity if only one out of two Single-Six owners buy an SSM. The two guns do complement each other so much. My associate Don Wilks, Technical Advisor to Woodland Associates ballistics test lab, who has owned one to six of every handgun under the sun, wouldn't give a Single-Six so much a a passing glance. After test shooting 8843, which is his, for a month or so he ran, not walked, down to a local emporium and bought a Single Six. Mine is 20 years old this year and I'm glad he finally saw the light.

The original idea was to see if three ostensibly identical guns would be as alike as their lineage would indicate. After 4 months of testing, I remain amazed at how alike they are. There were no wild swings in accuracy, no big changes in pressure indications from one gun to another, velocities were amazingly alike. They were indeed like three peas in a pod. ●

Neither the author nor the publisher assume any responsibility for your use of the above noted handloads. It is *your* responsibility to develop loads for your guns.

All velocities listed were chronographed on an Oehler Model 33 and are instrumental at 11.5 feet. All groups fired at 25 yards.

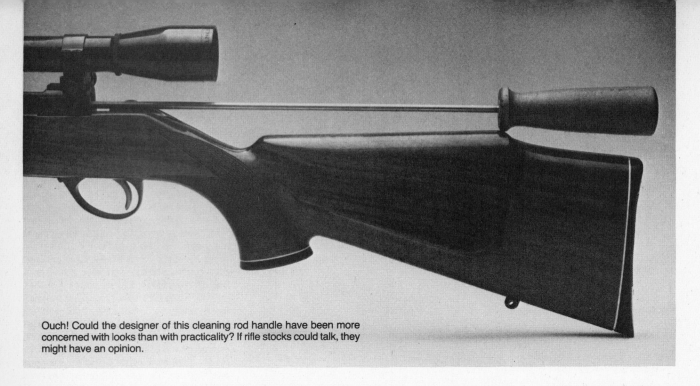

Ouch! Could the designer of this cleaning rod handle have been more concerned with looks than with practicality? If rifle stocks could talk, they might have an opinion.

SHOOTING PAINS

Real problems don't always
have solutions. Here are some.

by JOHN CAMPBELL

WE'VE ALL felt them, those unmitigated pangs in the backside that come too often in the shooting game. Some of these irritations make us wonder why solutions haven't been engineered already. Others leave us puzzled at whether The Doctor has ever been in. A few have all the earmarks of being psychosomatic.

From my experience, little quirks in shooting equipment create the most persistent shooting pains. If you've been around guns and shooting very long, I'll bet you've run into at least a few of them. Here's a sufferer's sampling in no particular order:

CLEANING ROD THREADS that never seem to match the brush you're using. Whether it's due to misdirected proprietary interests or blatant orneriness, the two giants of the gun cleaning equipment industry refuse to standardize on certain brush/tip/bob thread sizes, particularly for 22 caliber brushes. Buy a brush from one maker and try to use it with the

cleaning rod of another and you're in for trouble. It will either refuse to thread in at all because of its oversized thread or, screw in very sloppily and strip out on the first backstroke, because its threads are undersize. I know of no outfit that's gone broke because things like loading press shellholders are standardized. What's the big deal with cleaning equipment?

CASE TRIMMER PILOTS AND COLLETS are other things that ought to be standardized. Whenever I realize that I need another pilot, or collet, it seems I rediscover that my local gunshops carry another brand—which invariably won't work.

OVERSIZED CLEANING ROD HANDLES that would look more appropriate on beer taps than on tools for scrubbing out rifle bores. Voluptuous and nicely finished handles have their place, I suppose, but I'd rather not contend with them while trying to clean a high-combed or even moderately straight-combed rifle. The

darned things can beat the hell out of a good stock, and bending the rod so the handle can clear the comb puts unnecessary wear on a rifle's throat. It all makes you wonder if the guys who design these things ever use them.

UNDERSIZE 22-CALIBER BRUSHES that aren't worth a hoot in any 224 centerfire rifle. It seems that the Big Two have also decided that a 22-caliber brush should be the proper diameter for cleaning 22 rimfire rifles—in other words, rifles with .223-inch groove diameters. If used in anything from a 222 Remington to a 220 Swift, these brushes are pretty much ineffectual because they don't contact the bore surface firmly enough. Granted, there are doubtlessly far more 22 rimfire rifles floating around than 224 centerfires, but why not make a brush only .0015-inch larger in diameter to work in both?

A BORE BRUSH ORGANIZER of some sort would also work wonders for my mental tranquillity. There's virtually nothing on the market designed to organize, store and keep rifle and shotgun bore brushes clean. Whatever it might be would keep 22-caliber brushes separate from 243-caliber brushes, etc., would be dustproof so crud wouldn't build up on them, and contain a nonflammable solvent that would soak brushes clean between uses. Here's hoping.

UNMARKED BORE BRUSHES are something else that could use a little consideration. I don't know about you, but I've spent more than a little time trying to eyeball a pair of brushes to decide which one was the 27-caliber and which was the 28-caliber. I invariably choose the wrong one, too. If there can't be a bore brush organizer available, why not stamp the caliber on each brush shank? I, for one, would be willing to pay the extra 10 cents per brush in production costs.

SCOPE RINGS WITH BLIND-HOLE, BOTTOM-ACCESS tightening feature. I'm all for sleek design, but this brainstorm is a benchmark in unnecessary grief. A rational man could easily understand *The Shining* after trying to keep the reticle square and even out ring gap with this system. Gunsmith supply houses offer special round-head Allen wrenches in an effort to ease the problem—and, I suspect, to contain the nation's suicide rate among gun cranks. Meanwhile, I'll take the good old traditional through-hole, top-screw-access rings every time.

SHORT-TUBE COMPACT SCOPES that won't work with some mounting systems. Frankly, I'm a fan of compact scopes, but I can't understand why some manufacturers fail to tell potential buyers that the short tubes of these scopes often demand narrow ring spacing. Try to mate a compact scope with a two-piece mounting system on a standard length bolt action and you'll see what I mean. If the scope has an objective bell (usually those of 4x or more magnification), it simply won't work. The solution is either a one-piece base, which moves the rear ring forward of the action bridge, extension rings, or a full-size scope with a longer tube length. The final answer is to hope that scope builders will give us more information on what will—and won't—work—in advance for a real change.

FULL-SIZED 3x SCOPES are slowly passing into oblivion. That hurts because they're perfect for woods rifles or big-bore dangerous game rifles like the 375 H&H. Weaver's 3x died with the company. Leupold recently dropped its M8-3x for some unexplicable reason, and Lyman seems to be out of hunting scopes altogether. That still leaves us with 2.5x models from Redfield, Bushnell and a few others, but I'm not reassured. Just to be on the safe side, I buy every odd Weaver, Lyman or Leupold 3x I come across.

BAND RAMP FRONT SIGHTS are virtually extinct, and I don't understand why. Redfield, Burris and Lyman have all stopped making them. For about $50 you can still buy a band ramp front sight from Jaeger or London Guns, but it's a real pain to pay that kind of money for something the big makers offered for only a quarter of the price just a few years ago. Now that these sights have regained their deserved classy image among shooters, I hope someone sees fit to make them available again at a reasonable price.

BALL-TYPE SHOTGUN CLEANING MOPS are another useful item that have almost bitten the dust in favor of longer brush-like mops. For my money, the ball mops are far better. You can soak a large patch with solvent, push it through a shotgun bore with a round mop, and have only the wet patch contact the inside of the barrel. With a long mop, the patch falls short of completely covering it, the mop gets filthy and keeps putting fouling back into the bore you're trying to clean. So far, I've gotten along fairly well by cutting long mops in half with snips, but it's still a pain.

LONG RIFLE-TYPE BORE BRUSHES in 375 and 458 calibers are as rare as sympathy from the IRS. About the only thing that comes close for the big H&H round is a 444 brush. The bristles are too long, though, so

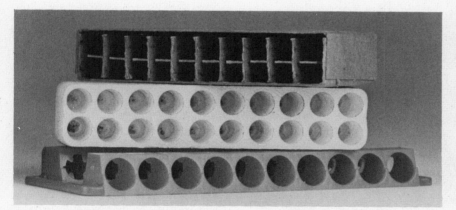

On top of the heap for reloader-friendly cartridge boxes is the good old-fashioned pasteboard design. Rounds slide in and out like butter. You can write on it with a pencil and it's biodegradable.

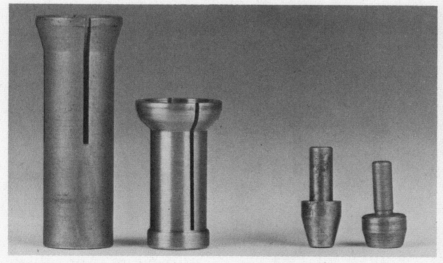

Why not standardize case trimmer collets and pilots just like shellholders? What manufacturers lose in proprietary advantage would probably be more than offset by increased and hassle-free sales.

they over-flex and break down quickly. The same brush is too small for the 458 and so are the various 45-caliber pistol brushes. As a consequence, my rifles in these calibers often don't get cleaned as well as I'd like.

ALL-BLACK BULLSEYES are another thing that leave a lot to be desired. Your scope reticle disappears against them, which does little to tighten your groups. For the good of us all, target makers should follow the lead of one well-known company and print white center targets. And with iron sights, this design allows a perfectly normal six-o'clock hold.

ONE-PIECE PLASTIC WADS for 16-gauge shotguns are something else you don't stumble over every day. Remington produces those that are available, but they're designed to accommodate 1-ounce and 1⅛-ounce loads—nothing much heavier or lighter. Since I'm a fan of the fading 16 bore, I'd like to see a little adrenalin pumped into the gauge by making

it more versatile. That requires new wads. Wouldn't it be great to load ⅞-ounce of shot in a light target load that would kick less than a 20-gauge yet pattern even better? How about stuffing the 16 with a 1⅜ or even 1½ ounces of shot to virtually duplicate the 12 gauge in a handier gun? For aficionados of the 16, it would be pure heaven. For now—another pain.

FOAM AND PLASTIC CARTRIDGE CARRIERS are definitely on my poignant pains list. Shooters who aren't reloaders probably have little objection to them, but those of us who have to reuse such containers time after time know how frustrating or useless they can be. My hands-down favorite among factory ammo boxes are those that have plain pasteboard dividers inside a sliding pasteboard sleeve. Brass is easy to get in and out, you can write your load on them easily with a pencil, and you can erase it just as easily. They're also made of "renewable resource" materi-

als and are biodegradable. And scarcer and scarcer.

PLASTIC GUNSTOCK FINISHES: Scratch them, and covering the scuff becomes a real task. Dent them, and steaming the ding back out is no fun either. Remove the whole finish? No commercial stripper except sandpaper I know of is worth trying. I'd rather trade off their weatherproof qualities for a finish that's a little more "user friendly." Varnish/linseed oil would be nice.

PLASTIC SHOTSHELL WAD FOULING is something we all have to live with, but there's no commercial firearms solvent that really dissolves it. Shotgun cognoscente have been quietly resorting to carburetor cleaner for some years now, but the danger of spilling the stuff on your stock finish is always a major terror. The alternative is to use good old Hoppes, a bronze brush, and a lot of elbow grease. Stainless steel brushes are a third option, but I can't bring myself to use them on high grade shotguns. So, as the TV anchormen tend to say, the situation remains unchanged and painful.

GUN SCREW SLOT SIZES offer unnecessary infinite variety. Not only do foreign guns have a galaxy of slot sizes, but domestic firearms have their own wild ones. I've even found different slot sizes between the two guard screws of one American-made bolt-action rifle. A set of "gunsmith screwdrivers" helps, but doesn't solve the problem. To really clear things up, America's gunmakers should simply standardize on a certain number of slot widths and depths—all geared to common hardware specifications. Think of the buggered screws it would prevent.

ASSAULT RIFLES THAT PELT YOU WITH BRASS at the range are another thing that should be prevented. Anyone using a benchrest to the immediate right of some of these paramilitary peculiarities had better be prepared for 308 cases clunking them in the head or 223 hulls banging into their rifle and equipment. The culprit, aside from the bozo firing the weapon, is the ejection system of many of these arms. Whoever designed them was apparently concerned with getting expended cartridge cases out of the gun and nothing more. If I ever have a choice of assault weapons to shoot next to, it will certainly be one of those foreign jobs that respectfully kicks its brass forward, out toward the muzzle.

WRITERS THAT GO ON AND ON about firearms esoterica can also be a pain. So I'm quitting right here. ●

Where are they now? The highly sensible ball-type shotgun mops, left, seem to be following banded ramp front sights, center, and 375-caliber Nosler Partition bullets along the road to oblivion.

One down and something to go. Scopes 3x magnification like this old Weaver, foreground, are as extinct as the dodo despite their great usefulness on brush guns or big-bore rifles like the 375 H&H. And, sooner or later, someone will invent a solvent that removes plastic wad fouling as well as carburetor cleaner does—and is safer to use around a shotgun.

Ammunition, Ballistics and Components

Remington has introduced a high velocity 3-inch Magnum 12-gauge slug. Velocity and energy levels are impressive.

by EDWARD A. MATUNAS

FOR THOSE who think a full-time gun writer's life is all grins, I can, based on this past year, tell you otherwise. A favorite rifle wore out and I had to purchase three new ones before I felt it properly replaced. A planned hunt for my favorite game—caribou—failed to materialize because the herd did not show up on the normal migration route. Too, several hard deer hunts left everyone with unfired rifles. Sure, there was a nice eight-point, very heavy buck and a few lesser deer. And some fine quail shooting. Ducks and geese did not cooperate as normal, though there was still plenty of shooting, and as the federal people can tell you, woodcock populations were definitely down, at least in the Northeast. But there also were 2 days when a great many deer were passed up in hopes of a shot at what will, next season, prove to be a state record buck.

And there were opportunities to stress that a 6x hunting scope is not nearly as practical as a 4x for general big game. Indeed, I've also become less enamored with variables during the year. One could say that I've developed a very biased approach to hunting scopes during the last 12 months. I spent quite a few dollars converting almost all of my big game rifles to 4x scopes.

But I've learned more this past year than in a good number of similar time frames. Or perhaps I just relearned a few forgotten lessons: Like—long eye relief and big fields of view are more important than magnification and zoom features. And that a 4x scope is perfect for any big game animal at any range—long or short. And that components can vary greatly from lot to lot. Ditto for factory ammunition.

Steel shot is with waterfowlers forever. I've come to accept that, I guess.

Proof that Remington's new slugs get the job done is this 8-point buck. Also shown are a happy author and a Remington 870 with a Hastings rifled barrel.

Remington's new Premier target ammo in a cutaway view.

Remington's new Power Piston wad has a unique figure eight support section.

Most states are demanding full conversion to steel for waterfowl prior to the 1991 federal deadline. Here at home, we make the conversion in 1988. So I've spent a great deal of time learning what I can about steel. The advice to shoot two sizes larger in steel than would be selected for lead shot seems about perfect. Thus, I've been using steel 2s to replace lead 4s and steel Bs to replace lead 2s (BBs in factory loads.) And it's super obvious, from this season's waterfowling, that a bit higher velocity is often better than a bit higher pellet count when steel is being used.

I also find current ammunition pricing most interesting, even exciting. For the first time since 1953, when I entered the industry, there has been no general price increase. Rather there has been a *substantial* general price decrease.

Remington's new distribution policy of fewer distributors and more sales direct to qualifying dealers may be at the core of the price down-turn. With such a hard ball approach to marketing, Remington may have found it easy to realize one of the major problems of the shooting industry was a lack of entry-level pricing on quality firearms. So they decided on a $200 Model 870 and similar efforts. Then they backed it all up with a pronounced decrease in the price of all ammunition. This caused, I believe, a we-gotta-match-it attitude at Winchester, who also announced drastic price reductions, except on a few pro-

prietary loads such as 218 Bee and 351 Winchester Self Loading. And while no word has reached me at the time of this writing, I expect Federal will do likewise. One industry joke has it that PMC is complaining of the competition in the sporting ammo market.

The shooter who stocks up on all of his favorite ammunition, at the new 1987 prices, will be doing a smart thing. I'm willing to bet that ammo will *never* be this inexpensive again. There are some loads selling for $5— even more—less per box this year than last.

But it's all not that easy. Preliminary investigation has shown that some dealers are reluctant to decrease the price on ammunition inventory put into stock at 1986 pricing. Too, other dealers seem to feel the general public will never know about the price decrease. Thus, a few unscrupulous types may prevent some shooters from having easy access to lower priced ammo. Too bad, because lower ammo and firearms prices are just what this aching industry needs to start forward recovery.

Now, let's get into the interesting new items for this year.

Remington

In recent years, Remington has marketed 12-gauge target ammo only in blue cases with a Peters headstamp. However, around mid-1986, Remington reintroduced a 12-gauge target load with a Remington head-

stamp. This new case has internal volume that makes the data for it quite similar to the data for the Peters Target Load. Actually, when using Hi-Skor 700-X, for example, powder charges for the new Premier Target Load are about ½-grain less for similar velocity levels.

Hard shot, a new Power Piston wad (with legs that resemble a figure eight) and a new primer with a covered flash hole are all incorporated into the new shell. The Premier Target Load is available in light (2¾ dram equiv.) and heavy (3 dram equiv.) target load specifications. Too, these new components are available to reloaders with designations of TGT12 Power Piston (figure eight) wad and Premier 209 primer.

The tubes used on these hulls have extra tough bodies. My reloading of 250 empty cases, over and over and over, has indicated a better than expected reloadability. If succeeding lots provide such reloading longevity, this case may become the most popular with handloaders.

Also new from Remington are some very special shotshells called Multi-Range DuPlex. These shells use two different shot sizes loaded into each case. Available shot combinations are BB x 4 and 2 x 6. Total shot charge weights are 1½ ounces for the 2¾-inch shell and 1⅞ ounces for the 3-inch shell. The 2¾-inch loading employs ⅜-ounce of the larger shot with 1⅛ ounces of the smaller shot. The 3-inch length uses ½-ounce of the larger shot with 1⅜ ounces of the smaller shot.

In order to prevent blown patterns, the larger shot is loaded on top of the smaller. Remington suggests that greater energy deposits will be made on the quarry. When underestimating the range on passing waterfowl, if the shooter is using a BB x 4 loading, the few BB pellets might well prove very effective in bringing the bird to bag.

The best news, to me at least, is that the new MultiRange DuPlex loads are to be made available in steel shot. These loadings, with two different size pellets, may prove to be just what's needed to get highly effective killing patterns from steel.

The 2¾-inch steel MultiRange DuPlex loads will utilize ¾-ounce of the smaller size shot in conjunction with ⅜-ounce of the heavier pellets, for a total of 1⅛ ounces. Muzzle velocity is quoted as 1275 feet per second (fps). The 3-inch loadings will use ⅞-ounce of the small shot and ⅜-ounce of the large shot, for a total of 1¼ ounces at 1375 fps. Shot combinations for both shell lengths will be BB x 2, BB x 4,

Green Remington target loads have been absent for some time. The Premier loads are top shelf and the fired cases will prove popular with reloaders.

and 2 x 6. Not being easily pleased, I believe I would prefer a load of B x 2. But lacking that, I'm going to give the steel BB x 2 loads a real work-out.

For those interested in such things, the lead 3-inch BB x 4 is proving to be a very, very effective duck load that fits nicely into the occasional need for bagging a goose; just enough so that it is becoming my favorite waterfowl ammo selection.

Another new steel shot load from Remington includes a 1¼-ounce 2¾-inch 12-gauge load with 1275 fps velocity. Available shot sizes include 1, 2, and 4. Also new are the 20-gauge 1-ounce steel loads with 2, 4, or 6 size shot.

Slug shooters also have two new Remington 12-gauge loads. The 2¾-inch High Velocity load uses a 1-ounce slug at 1680 fps, an increase of 120 fps over existing Remington slug loads. That's enough extra velocity to bring muzzle energies up to 308 Winchester levels.

The 3-inch Magnum 1-ounce slug loading has an impressive muzzle velocity of 1760 fps. That's sizzling fast enough to duplicate the muzzle energies of a 30-06 round. Naturally, slugs lose velocity quickly, but these new loads should make 100- to 125-yard shots practical, at least with a sight-equipped slug barrel.

Remington is also making available 7mm BR (Bench Rest) Remington unprimed cases. The case, as serious shooters would hope, comes with a small rifle primer pocket. With a 30-degree shoulder and an overall length of 1.520 inches, this case will elimi-

The new Remington Special Purpose Multirange DuPlex shotshell will appeal to waterfowlers and turkey hunters, loaded in a drab olive green case with blackened head.

A first for factory loads are the new Remington DuPlex shotshells which are loaded with two different sizes of shot. These are available with lead or steel pellets.

The fully formed 7mmBR case will also make it easier to form 6mm or 22-caliber BR cases.

The Remington 7mmBR case, in a loaded configuration, will prove a real boon to those who have had to form brass.

New handgun rounds from Remington: a 140-grain jacketed 357 Magnum hollow-point, and a 225-grain 45 Colt lead semi-wadcutter.

New Remington ammo includes a 300-grain jacketed hollowpoint 45-70 Govt. loading.

A 257 Roberts 100-grain high velocity load from Remington has +P velocity without +P pressure. Also new is the 338 Winchester Magnum cartridge in 225- and 250-grain loadings.

nate the tedious chore of forming cases from the earlier straight-walled Remington Bench Rest case. Too, those wishing to form 6mm or 22-caliber BR cases will find the task goes easier when starting with the 7mm BR case as opposed to starting with a straight-walled case. This all ties in nicely with the availability of the Remington XP-100 silhouette pistol in 7mm BR Rem.

New in the handgun cartridge lineup is the semi-jacketed hollowpoint 140-grain 357 Magnum load. This bullet weight gets the very best out of the 357, combining flat trajectory, good energy levels and moderate recoil. It makes a good selection for the individual who wants to use a single bullet weight for varmints, light big game and even self-defense. Indeed, the new load provides a flatter trajectory and higher energy levels than

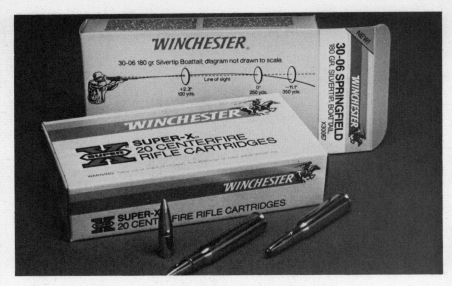

Winchester's new 180-grain boattail Silvertip bullet in the 30-06 cartridge adds some down-range ballistic improvement for a premium price. The box shows how.

12-Gauge Remington Slug Ballistics

Shell	Range in Yards					
	3	25	50	75	100	
2¾" H.V.	1680	1467	1286	1144	1045	Velocity
	2741	2091	1606	1272	1061	Energy
3" Mag.	1760	1538	1345	1189	1075	Velocity
	3009	2297	1756	1372	1123	Energy

Remington Ballistics

Caliber	Bullet (grains)	Velocity at yards:			Energy at yards:		
		0	50	100	0	50	100
357 Mag.	140	1360	1195	1076	575	444	360
45 Colt	225	960	890	832	460	395	346

Remington 45-70 Govt. 300-Grain Ballistics[1]

	Range in yards				
	0	50	100	150	200
Velocity	1810	1647	1497	1362	1244
Energy	2182	1806	1492	1235	1031
Trajectory	−1.5"	+2.0"	+1.7"	−2.0"	−11.4"

[1]Based on barrel length of 24"

Remington 257 Roberts 100-Grain Core Lokt H.V.

	Range in yards						
	0	50	100	150	200	250	300
Velocity	2980	2818	2661	2510	2363	2222	2085
Energy	1972	1762	1572	1398	1240	1096	965
Trajectory	−1.5"	+1.0"	+2.0"	+1.7"	0.0"	−3.3"	−8.3"

New Winchester Loads

Caliber	Velocity at yards:					Energy at yards:				
	0	100	200	300	400	0	100	200	300	400
7x57, 145-gr.	2690	2442	2206	1985	1777	2334	1920	1568	1268	1017
30-06, 180-gr. BT	2700	2503	2314	2133	1960	2913	2504	2140	1819	1536

the 125-grain 357 Mag. loads and does it while generating less recoil than traditional 158-grain loads. Bullet expansion during brief tests was superb.

Another new handgun load is one that will appeal to a great many fans of the 45 Colt. It uses a 225-grain plain lead bullet with a Keith-style shape that is easy on the bore, easy on recoil and plenty accurate. It has sufficient punch for medium size varmints or personal protection too. Ballistics for both loads are shown nearby.

Remington has now joined the ranks of ammo manufacturers who offer a 300-grain 45-70 load. Remington's bullet is a semi-jacketed hollowpoint with a muzzle velocity of 1810 fps. This 300-grain bullet makes it practical for use at ranges of 150 yards if you sight in to be 2 inches high at 50 yards. The bullet design should also ensure expansion to 150 yards. Also note that unlike other manufacturers, Remington is retaining, for now at least, its traditional 405-grain load in the same caliber.

Rifle shooters who favor the 257 Roberts cartridge will want to be sure to try Remington's new higher velocity load in this caliber. It utilizes the excellent 100-grain Remington Pointed Soft Point Core Lokt bullet. This load will add 50 yards to the practical range of the 257 Roberts compared to standard loadings in this cartridge.

Unlike other 257 higher velocity loads, the Remington round, through careful propellant selection, obtains near 3000 fps velocity without Plus P (+P) level pressures. A good bullet at high velocity and modest pressures is

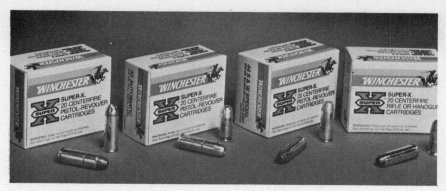

A number of Winchester's heavy handgun cartridges are now available in 20-round boxes, a bit easier on the wallet.

Super Steel non-toxic waterfowl loads in shot sizes T and BBB are now available in 10-round boxes from Winchester.

about all anyone can ask. It's enough to give me reason to contemplate another rifle chambered for the Roberts round, now that it's an effective 300-yard deer cartridge.

That the 338 Winchester Magnum has become the favorite heavy game cartridge in North America is undeniable. And indeed, there is good reason for this popularity. Sure, the 375 H&H bests the 338's muzzle energy by about 400 foot pounds, but depending upon the loads being compared, the difference is only about 200 foot pounds in favor of the 375 H&H at 100 yards. At 200 yards there is no difference, while at 300 yards the 338 has about a 200-foot-pound advantage over the 375 H&H. And as the range gets longer, the 338 looks even a bit better.

But none of this is enough to favor one cartridge over the other. Both are very accurate cartridges. However, the 338 offers a few other advantages that include a short action (on most rifles, anyway), a somewhat flatter trajectory, as well as notably less recoil. All of which makes the 338 a heck of a lot more shootable and thus the better choice.

While the 200-, 210- and 225-grain loads available from Winchester and Federal have proven to be good ones, Remington has introduced two 338

Winchester Magnum loadings. The first is a 225-grain bullet, a very slightly modified Hornady projectile. The second is a 250-grain bullet, a premium grade Speer Grand Slam, and it's the bullet weight I favor in this cartridge. This Speer bullet is accurate and expands beautifully while maintaining most of its original weight.

The 338 Winchester Magnum and the 300 Winchester Magnum are the two wisest choices when stepping up from the 30-06. The choice between the two becomes even more interesting now that Remington is loading the 338 round. If recoil is not a factor in your decision, the 338 will never disappoint you, especially if you select the new Remington 700 Classic which, by the way, will be available only this year chambered for this 33-caliber North American heavy game favorite.

Winchester

Well, if you own a 348 Winchester Model 71, Winchester is planning to run a lot of 348 ammo during mid-1987. This will satisfy owners of the old 71 as well as owners of the new Browning Model 71.

A new 145-grain 7mm Mauser load has been added to the line. It has a Power Point style bullet. The heavier

175-grain bullet continues in the 7x57 line. Also new is a 180-grain Silvertip for the 30-06 with a boattail base. However, I'm hard pressed to see the justification for a $4.70 per box premium for the boattail over a flat base Silvertip. It's just not the kind of thing for which most folks will spend an extra 5 bucks. The ballistics of these two new rifle loads are shown nearby.

Look for some 41 Magnum, 44 Magnum, 45 Auto and 45 Colt ammo to be available in 20-round boxes. It's about a break-even on per round cost, and it makes it easier for a modest ammo user to purchase his needs without going deeply into his wallet.

Winchester is really doing something for the shooter with making it easier to purchase steel shot loads. Steel shot selection is not the same as lead shot selection. Bigger shot sizes and lighter shot charge weights have to be dealt with.

To make consumer selection easier, each box of steel shot loads manufactured by Winchester, starting a while back, bears one of three labels. One

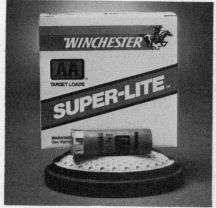

A Winchester 1⅛-ounce target load at a reduced velocity, for reduced recoil, is now available and is called Super-Lite.

label pictures an alighting duck and carries the word "Decoy." Another shows a duck flying overhead and has the word "Pass." And the third shows a goose and the word "Goose."

I don't agree with every suggestion made by Winchester, but I do agree that this system is a jillion times better than letting the novice steel shot load purchaser go unassisted during his transition from lead to steel.

Winchester is adding a new 1⅜-ounce steel shot load to its 12-gauge 3-inch Magnum ammo. This load will have a muzzle velocity of 1265 fps and is to be available in BB, 1, 2, 3 and 4 size shot. Based on the "two sizes up" rule for shot selection when choosing steel, Bs are the proper replacement for lead 2s, yet no one is offering them.

A new 12-gauge 1-ounce loading with steel 2 and 4 shot is also available. Looks like the ammo companies know the states are going to be making us use steel for all bird hunting before long. Why else a 1-ounce loading, except for upland use?

Also new in steel shot loads are a 10-gauge 3½-inch Magnum loaded with T and BBB shot. Ditto shot sizes in 12-gauge 3-inch Magnum steel loads. I don't know that these low pellet count, super big sizes are going to do anything but create a new generation of sky busters. But I'm willing to give them a try where legal (which ain't in my home state of Connecticut).

Overall, Winchester has spent money on the expansion of its very wide range of Copper Plated Steel Magnum, Steel Magnum and Steel Game loads. Even steel shot size 3 is now available in all 12- and 20-gauge Winchester loadings, save one.

A lot of folks have missed noting that the newly returned Xpert brand field shotshells are employing Double A style wads, i.e. one-piece plastic

coil (obtained by reducing velocity slightly).

Owners of rimfire rifles chambered for the Winchester 22 WRF cartridge should be out stocking up on this ammo as Winchester's limited run (late 1986) of these cartridges may never again be repeated. And if you own a 22 Magnum and have been wishing for a lighter loading, the 22 WRF works just fine in most 22 MRFs, but not semi-autos. It's like using a Short in a Long Rifle chamber.

Like everyone else, Winchester is now offering rimfire ammunition in blister packs. But I doubt if it will become very popular once the shooter realizes he has to pay a premium for these cute, point of purchase packages. And once again, the Ball Powder Propellent Loading Data booklet has been revised by Winchester. If you use Ball Powder, a copy of the 1987 update is a must.

Federal

Federal has added six new steel shot loads to its line of non-toxic waterfowl ammo. These include a 10-gauge 3½-inch Magnum with F or T shot, a new 12-gauge 2¾-inch Mag-

num with No. 3 shot, and a new 12-gauge 2¾-inch with steel BB shot.

I believe, despite the success of some to the contrary, that BB shot is as big as practically needed when hunting waterfowl with steel shot. Yet I'm sure Federal is equally convinced that there is a market for the T and F sizes or it wouldn't bother to load these. I think there simply are too few pellets in loads with such large shot sizes as BBB, T and F pellets. Indeed, the steel F 3-inch Magnum 12-gauge load has but 48 pellets. Compare these to the 1¼-ounce load of lead BBs with 62 pellets or a 1½-ounce load of lead BBs with 75 pellets. And both lead BB loads have proven to pattern too sparsely for consistent long-range use on geese (see 1987 GUN DIGEST). But shooters and time will make the final decision on monster pellets such as BBB, T and F.

The sixth new Federal steel shot load is a 20-gauge 3-inch Magnum with $^{15}/_{16}$-ounce of No. 2 shot. That's 117 pellets and this load may prove effective if ranges are not long. Federal is now marketing a total of 28 different steel shot loads.

Slugs are taking on a new meaning with heavier loadings, rifled bores and such. We are at the beginning, I think, of real progress in the search for accuracy and game-stomping ability with slugs. Federal's newest 12-gauge slug is a 3-inch loading using a 1¼-ounce slug with a muzzle velocity of 1560 fps; a bit less in the usual 20- and 22-inch barreled slug guns. This adds up to a bit more than 2000 fpe at 50 yards compared to the 1175 fpe at the same range with a 2¾-inch 1-ounce standard velocity slug. That's a heap more energy and, yes, you guessed it—a heap more recoil.

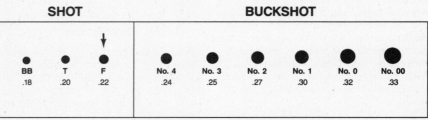

Winchester made a one-time run of the long obsolete 22WRF cartridge. If you own a rifle so chambered, now is the time to stock up.

wads which incorporate a shot cup. Xpert shells are available in 12-gauge 1¼ ounces (1220 fps), 1⅛ ounces (1255 fps), and 1 ounce (1290 fps). Also available are a 16-gauge load of 1⅛ ounces (1185 fps) and two 20-gauge loads—1-ounce (1165 fps) and ⅞-ounce (1210 fps).

New in the shotshell line is a 12-gauge 1⅛-ounce AA Target load called the Super-Lite. Shot sizes available are 7½, 8, 8½ and 9. This load's claim to fame is its reduced re-

SHOT			BUCKSHOT					
BB	T	F	No. 4	No. 3	No. 2	No. 1	No. 0	No. 00
.18	.20	.22	.24	.25	.27	.30	.32	.33

(Diameter in inches, actual size.)

Federal has added F-size shot to its line of 12-gauge steel pellet ammunition.

A jacketed 50-grain hollowpoint in the 22 WRM? You bet, if you find some of Federal's newest. Sixteen percent more energy at 100 yards should get most 22 magnum users to give the new ammo a try.

The new 12-gauge 3-inch Magnum slugs from Federal feature a small hollowpoint.

Federal 12-Gauge 3-inch Magnum 1¼-ounce Slug
(30-inch Barrel Ballistics)

	Muzzle	50 yards
Velocity	1560	1285
Energy	2953	2010
Drop	—	2.0"

Buckshot sizes 000 and No. 1 have been added to the 12-gauge 3-inch Magnum Premium ammo line. Like all Premium ammo, high antimony content, copper-plated pellets and a granulated polyethylene buffer are standard. Pellet counts are 10 for the 000 size and 24 for the No. 1 buck size.

The addition of a 250-grain Nosler Partition bullet in 338 Winchester Magnum caliber will gladden the hearts of many of those who recognize the 338 for what it is—one of the finest North American heavy big game cartridges. All the accuracy associated with Federal Premium ammunition and all the deep penetration capabilities of Nosler Partition bullets will make this loading a winner for moose, elk and grizzly.

Two other new Premium loadings that use the excellent Nosler Partition bullet are a 140-grain 7mm Remington Magnum and a 120-grain 257 Roberts +P, both of which are worthwhile additions. Finally, there is a round-nose 30-06 load for the Hi-Power line and a 117-grain boattail softpoint 25-06 load for the Premium line. Ballistics for all the new Federal rifle loads are shown nearby.

A Nylon-clad lead hollowpoint 124-

I guess a few folks still prefer round-nose bullets, despite their lower efficiency, for Federal has introduced a 180-grain round-nose 30-06 loading.

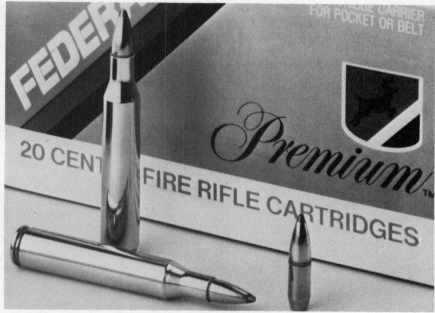

New for 25-06 fans is a Federal Premium load with a 117-grain boat-tail Sierra bullet.

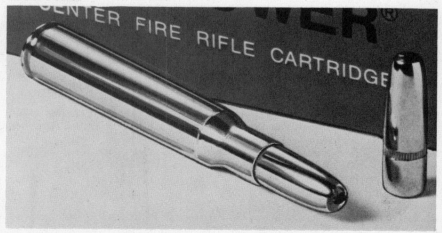

The popular 338 Magnum cartridge is now available from Federal with a factory loaded 250-grain Nosler Partition bullet—in the Premium line, naturally.

Federal's new 9mm Nyclad hollowpoint ammo is devastating, as attested to by these photos of bullet performance in a clay block.

Ballistics for New Federal Rifle Loads

Caliber	Type	Bullet Wgt. (grains)	Bullet Style	Velocity in fps at yards: Muzzle	100	200	300	Energy in ft. lbs. at yards: Muzzle	100	200	300
338 Win. Mag.	Premium	250	Nosler-Partition	2660	2400	2150	1910	3925	3185	2555	2025
30-06 Spring.	Hi-Power	180	Round-Nose	2700	2350	2020	1730	2915	2200	1630	1190
7mm Rem. Mag.	Premium	140	Nosler Partition	3150	2920	2700	2500	3085	2650	2270	1940
25-06 Rem.	Premium	117	Sierra Boattail	2990	2770	2570	2370	2320	2000	1715	1465
257 Roberts (+P)	Premium	120	Nosler Partition	2780	2560	2360	2160	2060	1750	1480	1240

grain bullet is now being loaded for the 9mm Luger in Federal's Nyclad ammunition line. With a muzzle velocity of 1120 fps this bullet has 345 fpe at the muzzle and 290 fpe at 50 yards. Energy transfer to the target is superb with this very reliable, positive expanding bullet. High PIR values are guaranteed. Recovered bullets consistently show 60-caliber expanded diameters.

A heavier 22 Magnum rimfire cartridge is also being loaded. It's a 50-grain hollowpoint which, according to Federal, possesses 16 percent more energy at 100 yards than the 40-grain hollowpoint. Muzzle velocity is 1650 fps with an energy of 300 fpe. At 100 yards, retained velocity is 1280 fps and retained energy is 180 foot pounds.

Dan Arms

During the past year some 20-gauge Dan Arms ammo has been brought into the United States. While there has not yet been a wide variety of loads available in the 20, spokesman Don Brinton indicates that more variations are on the way.

I did get to use Dan Arms' 20-gauge 2¾-inch, ⅞-ounce Super Dove load. It worked just fine on New England partridge. Too, some 1⅛-ounce, 2¾-inch

Magnum loads also proved more than satisfactory.

New from Dan Arms this year are two steel shot loads, both in 12-gauge. At 1 ounce with No. 5 shot and ⅞-ounce of No. 4 shot, these loads have a very light shot charge by U.S. standards, albeit they do have very high muzzle velocities. I am told that 1⅛- and 1¼-ounce 12-gauge steel loads will be available at a later date. Such loads would prove more popular, I am sure.

The new Dan Arms 12-gauge slug load uses a 1⅛-ounce slug with which I have been averaging about 5-inch groups at 50 yards. This is a bit better than one U.S. brand slug, but not as good as two other U.S. brands. As with all Dan Arms ammo, prices are rock bottom.

For a free, rather complete loading data booklet for 12-gauge Dan Arms cases write to: Don Brinton, Dan Arms, 2900 Hamilton Blvd., Allentown, PA 18103. He probably would appreciate a self-addressed, stamped envelope. Loads for the 2¾-inch 12-gauge Dan Arms case are shown for 1 ounce to 1⅝ ounces of shot.

Hercules

Hercules has finally decided that the market void left by their discon-

tinued RelodeR 11 powder needed filling. The new powder is called Hercules RelodeR 12 and is said to be suitable for a wide range of medium capacity cases. Data for a dozen different cartridges, ranging from the 222 Remington to the 45-70 Govt., are being supplied by Hercules. The nearby table reflects some of this data.

Cartridges in the 308 family seem well served by RelodeR 12, as do those in the 7x57 Mauser family. But data are also given for the 7mm Remington Magnum, the 300 Winchester Magnum, and the 303 British.

In their 1987 data booklet, Hercules is listing data both in LUP (lead units of pressure), CUP (copper units of pressure) as well as in actual PSI (pounds per square inch) as obtained by piezoelectric testing. The reloader should keep in mind that LUP, CUP and PSI are different test media which result in different numbers. Nor is there a direct relationship between CUP and PSI. Thus, 50,000 CUP cannot be generally assumed to mean 62,000 PSI as the relationship changes with the specific cartridge being tested. But do remember that the listed variations caused by these different methods of testing, do not reflect any change in pressure. Rather, they simply reflect a change in the pressure recording system used. A table nearby will help clarify all of this.

Hercules' new data listings also show extensive coverage for such components as the new Remington Premier Target 12-gauge shell as well as Remington's TGT12 wad and 209 Premier primer. Twelve and 20-gauge Fiocchi shells are listed as is the 20-gauge Activ shell. Coverage in some other areas has been expanded.

IMR

This is a press release:

"The Du Pont Company has sold the assets of its Smokeless Powder business to the IMR POWDER COMPANY, an affiliate of EXPRO Chemical Products Company of Valleyfield, Quebec. EXPRO has been the manufacturer of all Du Pont powders since 1978.

"The sale included the 'Hi Skor' trademark, equipment, and technical know-how relating to the business.

"The acquisition affords an excellent fit with the strong manufacturing base at EXPRO. The newly formed U.S. affiliate known as the 'IMR Powder Company' will be responsible for the sales and marketing of all the powders previously handled by Du Pont.

"The packaging and testing of the powders for the handloading market will be done at a new facility to be located in Plattsburgh, N.Y. To assure an orderly transition of the business, Du Pont will continue to package and test powders at their Potomac River Works Plant under a service agreement until the new site is completed.

"The acquisition should not result in any change from the point of view of customers. First and foremost, there will not be any change in the product offering. All the powders have been made at the same plant for more than eight years.

"Secondly, there are no plans to make any major changes in the packaging and distribution of the product line.

"The personnel formerly connected with the Smokeless Powder business at Du Pont will be associated with the IMR Powder Comapny. This will provide the continuity to assure a smooth transition.

"In summary, the principal objective of the IMR Powder Company will be to continue to provide quality products coupled with effective and responsive customer service."

That's all we know at press time. The IMR Powder Co. U.S. address is 122 Lakeside Dr., Glassboro, NJ 08028.

Omark Industries

The increasing popularity of the aluminum-cased Blazer ammunition is due, in part, to the relatively low cost of this non-reloadable cartridge. So, once again, CCI has added quite a few new loads to this line. The new loads are: 38 Special with 125-grain JSP and 158-grain L-SWC; 357 Magnum with 125-grain JSP; 44 Magnum with 200-grain JHP and 240-grain L-SWC, and 45 Auto with both 185- and 200-grain TMJ bullets.

New in the CCI Lawman centerfire ammo line is a 38 Special 158-grain L-SWC-HP bullet.

The 45 Auto is now available in a shot loading. No exposed plastic case on this load—making it different from the 38/357 and 44 Magnum shotshell loadings.

In the component line, new 45-caliber TMJ bullets, in both 185 and 200 grains, are available. These are Totally Metal Jacketed bullets made by plating the jacket to the core.

Both the 209 and 209M shotshell primers have been modified, via an anvil change, to give a larger firing pin sensitive strike area, hence, better reliability.

I often state the benefits of premium quality component bullets. And Speer Grand Slams are, indeed, premium grade projectiles, offering a unique blending of accuracy and highly controlled expansion. These are available, as some of you may know, in .277-inch (130 and 150 grains), .284-inch (60 and 175 grains), .308-inch (165 and 180 grains), .338-inch (250 grains) and .375-inch (285 grains). These bullets are so good that, after extensive testing, Remington decided to use the .338-inch 250-grain version in their newly introduced 338 Winchester Magnum loading of this weight.

But, often a premium bullet is not required for specific purposes. A shooter who takes only broadside, or front end, into-the-chest shots has no need for the deep penetration capability of a premium bullet. Assuming he is using a bullet and cartridge well matched to the quarry's size for such hunting shots, the Speer Spitzer flat base bullets are, in my opinion, near perfect. For most big game-hunting these bullets in 27-, 28- or 30-caliber have been favorites of mine for a very long time. I, and countless others, have bowled over a great deal of game with this style bullet, without a single problem. No, I wouldn't expect to penetrate 3 feet or more with such a bullet, but it's not often such penetration is required. For those times when 18 to 24 inches of penetration is ade-

Dan Arms shotshells are now available in 20-gauge and even a few 16-gauge loads. Good shells at down-to-earth prices.

Dan Arms slug loads use 1⅛-oz. projectile. Accuracy is fair; 12-gauge only at this time.

The long-awaited Hercules replacement for RelodeR 11 has arrived. Called ReloadeR 12 (naturally) it has a wide range of applications.

CUP (Copper Units of Pressure) versus PSI

The following shows some of the relationships that exist between the CUP (crusher method) and PSI (piezoelectric method) values determined by actual testing. Keep in mind that the pressure remains the same for a given line. The variation is due to the differences in the testing method. But do notice that, depending upon the cartridge, CUP to PSI relationships vary.

Cartridge	Max. CUP	Max. PSI
22-250 Remington	53,000	62,000
222 Remington	46,000	50,000
223 Remington	52,000	55,000
6mm Remington	52,000	65,000
243 Winchester	52,000	60,000
25-06 Remington	53,000	63,000
270 Winchester	52,000	65,000
7mm-08 Remington	52,000	57,500
7 x 57 Mauser	46,000	51,000
7mm Remington Magnum	52,000	61,000
280 Remington	50,000	62,000
30 Carbine	40,000	40,000
30-06 Springfield	50,000	60,000
30-30 Winchester	38,000	42,000
300 Savage	46,000	47,000
300 Winchester Magnum	54,000	64,000
308 Winchester	52,000	60,000
35 Remington	35,000	33,500
45-70 Govt.	28,000	28,000
458 Winchester Magnum	53,000	57,500

Hercules ReLoder 12 Data For Popular Applications

Caliber	Bullet Wt. (grains)	Charge Wt. (grains)	Velocity (fps)	Pressure
223 Rem.	50 Hornady #2245	27.0	3335	52,300 PSI
22-250 Rem.	50 Hornady #2240	36.5	3650	58,100 PSI
	50 Hornady #2260	36.0	3550	59,100 PSI
	60 Hornady #2270	35.5	3415	59,400 PSI
243 Win.	75 Speer #1205	34.0	3125	57,500 PSI
	80 Speer #1211	34.0	3060	57,500 PSI
6mm Rem.	75 Speer #1205	39.0	3340	62,200 PSI
	80 Speer #1211	38.0	3205	62,300 PSI
25-06	75 Sierra #1600	48.0	3580	59,900 PSI
	87 Speer #1241	44.5	3290	59,500 PSI
257 Roberts	75 Sierra #1600	39.0	3160	42,800 CUP
	87 Speer #1241	36.5	2930	43,300 CUP
257 Robt. +P	75 Sierra #1600	41.9	3365	48,000 CUP
	87 Speer #1241	39.5	3165	48,000 CUP
6.5x55 Swede	129 Hornady #2620	40.0	2665	44,200 CUP
	160 Hornady #2640	38.5	2405	44,000 CUP
270 Win.	100 Speer #1453	52.5	3355	61,800 PSI
	130 Speer #1459	47.5	2865	62,000 PSI
	140 Sierra #18545	46.5	2790	59,800 PSI
7mm-08 Rem.	120 Hornady #2810	44.5	3000	50,600 CUP
	139 Hornady #2820	42.5	2790	50,100 CUP
	145 Speer #1629	39.8	2635	50,500 CUP
7x57 Maus.	120 Hornady #2810	43.0	2895	48,900 PSI
	139 Hornady #2820	40.5	2660	48,800 PSI
	145 Speer #1629	37.0	2520	48,800 PSI
280 Rem.	120 Hornady #2810	50.5	3080	62,900 PSI
	145 Speer #1629	47.0	2740	62,900 PSI
7mm Rem. Mag.	120 Hornady #2810	58.5	3195	59,000 PSI
	139 Hornady #2820	57.0	3035	59,000 PSI
	145 Speer #1629	48.0	2765	58,900 PSI
30-06 Spring.	125 Sierra #2120	51.0	3055	57,500 PSI
	150 Hornady #3031	48.0	2760	57,500 PSI
	165 Speer #2035	44.5	2555	56,900 PSI
	180 Speer #2053	41.5	2365	56,800 PSI
30-30 Win.	125 Sierra #2020	37.0	2555	39,900 PSI
	150 Sierra #2000	33.5	2320	40,400 PSI
	170 Hornady #3060	32.0	2160	40,100 PSI
300 Win. Mag.	150 Hornady #3031	59.0	3105	61,200 PSI
308 Win.	110 Sierra #2110	50.5	3200	57,400 PSI
	125 Sierra #2120	49.0	3040	57,500 PSI
	150 Sierra #2130	45.0	2755	57,100 PSI
	165 Sierra #2145	44.0	2650	57,200 PSI
	168 Sierra #2200	43.0	2605	57,200 PSI

Some of Sierra's new bullets include this trio intended for use in single shot pistols.

try in a custom-made 6mm PPC with a 10-inch barrel.

Another new bullet is a 90-grain hollowpoint in .312-inch diameter with Sierra's Power Jacket construction. This design will insure reliable expansion for handgunners fond of the 32 H&R Magnum. Or for that matter, it just might work in a 32 S&W Long with near maximum charges, if the ranges are kept short.

There is a new 130-grain 7mm (.284-inch diameter) spitzer flat base bullet and also a 30-caliber 135-grain bullet, both labeled "single shot pistol." Contender owners should enjoy these.

Nosler

A few new Nosler bullets have been added to the Ballistic Tip line. These

quate, these standard grade bullets are perfect; and this covers a great many hunting situations.

I have had exceptional results with Speer Spitzers of 130 and 150 grains in the 270 Winchester, of 150 and 180 grains in the 308 Winchester and 30-06 Springfield, and with the 145-grain in 7mm-08 and 280 Remington. Perfect mushrooming, adequate penetration and superb accuracy are all anyone can ask, and penetration has averaged about 20 inches. That's enough, or more than enough, for antelope, deer, caribou, sheep or goat. Even most elk can be cleanly taken with such bullets as, despite some comments to the contrary, few 800-pound elk are encountered; indeed, one of 500 pounds is quite good.

Sierra

Sierra seemingly always has some new products. No matter how complete the line appears, new products are introduced annually. This year most of the half-dozen new items are for the handgunners. But there are also a few items for the rifle shooters—the first of which is a 7mm (.284-inch diameter) 150-grain spitzer boattail bullet. The samples received grouped well when used in a 7mm-08 Remington Model Seven carbine.

New also is a .375-inch 200-grain, flat-nosed bullet with the cannelure correctly located for use in the 375 Winchester cartridge. Packed 50 to a box, these bullets feature multiple knife cuts in the front end of the jacket—Sierra's Power Jacket construction. These projectiles will give very

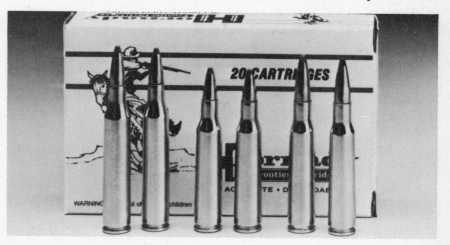

Hornady has introduced a half-dozen new loadings for its centerfire loaded ammunition line—two each in 257 Roberts, 25-06 and 7x57mm.

positive expansion at the modest velocity levels of the 375 Winchester. A brief 100-yard expansion test showed very uniform bullet mushrooming with an average retained weight of 120 grains. This is the first bullet for the Big Bore Winchester that I feel approaches perfection. Accuracy was as good as I get most times from a 94 carbine—about 3¼ inches on the average.

The fist new handgun bullet is an 80-grain 6mm (.243-inch diameter) spitzer clearly labeled "single shot pistol." Of flat base construction, these bullets are, according to a Sierra spokesman, capable of high accuracy as well as good expansion on game, when driven at handgun velocities. I'm not sure specifically what levels of velocity Sierra has in mind for these bullets, but I'm anxious to give them a

Hornady suggests a maximum velocity of 3400 fps for its new 70-grain 6mm Super Explosive bullet. This bullet is a good choice for rifles with short barrels, i.e., the Remington Seven.

are a .257-inch 100-grain spitzer and a .264-inch 120-grain spitzer. If you like bullets that will not suffer from battered noses in the magazine as a result of recoil, and which supply the sharpest possible profile, Ballistic Tip bullets are ideal.

Also new from Nosler are a 9mm (.355-inch) 115-grain hollowpoint, a .410-inch 210-grain JHP and a 45 Colt 250-grain JHP. As always, accuracy is superb with each Nosler bullet. And the handgun bullets appear to offer very reliable expansion.

Hornady

The Hornady loaded ammunition line has been expanded to include two new loads for each of the 257 Roberts, 25-06 Remington and 7x57 Mauser. In both the 257 Roberts and the 25-06 Remington a new 100-grain varmint bullet has been added, at 2900 and 3150 fps muzzle velocity respectively.

Too, both the 257 Roberts and 25-06 Remington are now offered with a 117-grain boattail softpoint at 2700 and 2950 fps. The 7mm Mauser loads include a 139-grain boattail softpoint bullet and a 154-grain flat base softpoint projectile.

Other news from Hornady tells of a new 6mm, 70-grain Super Explosive hollowpoint bullet. This should have applications in single shot handguns as well as in many of those ultra short barrel, lightweight rifles so popular today. Hornady suggests a maximum muzzle velocity of 3400 fps for this new bullet and is claiming positive expansion on varmints as small as prairie dogs. So far, my tests show the bullet to be a good one when Hornady's advice is followed with respect to maximum velocity.

A new 44-caliber 180-grain jacketed hollowpoint from the Nebraskan bullet makers should fill the bill for 44 Magnum owners who want less recoil. If you own a rifle chambered for the 7.62x39, a new Hornady 123-grain .311-inch diameter bullet will give you the capability of reloading for this popular military cartridge.

I've begun some testing on Hornady's loaded ammunition in 30-06, 270 and 22-250.

Finally, there are two new 45-caliber lead bullets, both designed for positive feeding in the various 45 Automatic pistols. The first is a modified Keith-style bullet in 200 grains and the second is a 230-grain round-nose bullet. Each has a 5 percent antimony content.

Accurate Brand Powders

The new 1-pound pack is proving to be a market-wise decision and, indeed, it is attractive. But the big news from Accurate this year is the price on their 3100 speed propellant. When purchased in an 8-pound container the suggested retail price of Accurate 3100 is less than $5 per pound. While 3100 is only one of the propellants offered by Accurate, folks will be looking for ways to burn it because of its new low pricing.

Accurate 3100 can be used in cartridges ranging in size from as small as the 22-250 to some of the big magnums. It is an extruded powder of relatively slow speed and is ideally used in cartridges such as the 243 Winchester, 7mm Mauser, 300 H&H and 300 Winchester Magnum when medium-heavy to heavy-weight bullets are being loaded.

Accurate has also taken on the distribution of Samson (IMI-Israel) components. Brass will be available in a number of handgun cartridges including 380 Auto, 9mm Luger, 38 Special, 357 Magnum, 44 Magnum, and 45 ACP. Rifle caliber brass available will be 223 Remington, 243 Winchester, 30M1 Carbine, 7.62x39, 30-30 Winchester, 308 Winchester and 30-06 Springfield.

A-Square Ammunition

In recent years a lot of small, cus-tom bullet makers and ammunition loaders have made efforts to gain small shares of the shooter's dollars. Some of these have lasted only a short while before fading into oblivion. Others persist.

A-Square offers custom-built rifles of rather large proportions. But they also offer quite a few hard-to-get cartridges, both as brass only and as loaded rounds. Included are such calibers as 375 Weatherby Magnum, 416 Hoffman, 416 Rigby, 404 Jeffrey, 450 Nitro Express (3¼-inch), 450 Nitro Express #2, 470 Rigby, 505 Gibbs and 577 Nitro Express, to mention just some.

Custom loaded ammo, using new brass, is available in about three dozen calibers. Several special bullets are used in the loading of this ammo. One type is the Monolithic Solid. This bullet is of homogeneous bronze construction (no separate core and jacket) and should prove up to the task of very deep penetration without expansion or distortion. I have had the opportunity to use some of the Monolithic Solids on the range. Accuracy was good and the velocities and pressures were normal. Tested ammo was of 30-06 caliber with a 180-grain bullet weight. Other available bullet types include the Dead Tough Soft Point and Lion Load Soft Point.

The Monolithic Solids are available as small as 7mm diameter (175 grains) and as large as .510-inch diameter (700 gains), with about a dozen other in between sizes available. The Dead Tough Soft Points come in .375-inch, .416-inch, .423-inch, .458-inch and .510-inch diameters. The Lion Load Soft Points are available in the same diameters.

For those with an interest, the Dead Tough Soft Point features a thick jacket and hard core for maximum penetration with expansion through heavy muscle and bone. The Lion

---

LOAD CORRECTION

In CARTRIDGES OF THE WORLD No. 5, we printed then-new-data-for Accurate Arms smokeless powder. Two of the loads furnished us were in error for typographic reasons.

Therefore:

The proper load of Accurate Arms No. 9 powder for the 223 in 14-inch T/C Contender pistol should have read 12.0 grains, *not* 22.0 grains are reported. Accurate Arms no longer lists this load.

The proper load of MP-5744 in the 6.5 TCU, again in a Contender, with 120 grain bullet is 19.0 grains, not 29 grains as reported.

Ken Warner

Hornady's new 44-caliber 180-grain jacketed hollowpoint offers plenty of punch with lower recoil.

If you own a 7.62x39 you will want to give Hornady's new 123-grain bullet (.311-inch diameter) a thorough trial.

Two new lead bullets from Hornady are a 200-grain Keith-type for the 45 ACP and a 230-grain round-nose for the 45 Colt.

A-Square offers quite a few variations in loaded ammo and bullets. Shown are 180-grain monolithic solids, loaded in the 30-06 case.

(Right) Accurate 3100 powder is a slow burner that will appeal to large case-heavy bullet enthusiasts. If you purchase it in 8-pound cans it can be had very inexpensively—about $5 per pound.

Load Soft Point has a thin jacket and soft core for rapid expansion with penetration limits in the range of 1½ to 2 feet.

For more details on the A-Square line, contact Arthur B. Alphin, A-Square, Route 4, Simmons Rd., Madison, IN 47250. Mention us when you write.

Non-Toxic Components Inc.

NTC, fully aware that abundant data is the best possible salesman, has continued to expand its reloading recipes for steel shot. From a very humble beginning, NTC data has been expanded to include almost 70 loads. Selections include 10-gauge 3½-inch Magnum info for Federal, Winchester and Remington cases, 12-gauge 3-inch Magnum info for a half-dozen cases, as well as the expected 2¾-inch 12-gauge recipes. Shot charge weights from ⅞-ounce to 1½ ounces are covered.

To coin a phrase, if you are going to load steel shot, then you are going to need NTC. Drop Jack Rench a note at P.O. Box 4202, Portland, OR 97208 and get a copy of NTC's catalog.

Hodgdon

Hodgdon began supplying reloaders with propellants many years ago by repackaging surplus military powders. As time went on, due to the lack of availability and other factors, Hodgdon brand propellants eventually became newly manufactured powder to the exclusion of surplus ones. Now the folks at Hodgdon have "discovered" a source of surplus powders for their H335 and Ball C2.

The nice part of all this is that these surplus propellants are getting to the reloader at about $8 per pound. I should emphasize that these powders are "new" as opposed to salvaged or pulled down powder which is obtained by breaking apart loaded ammunition. Containers of the surplus grade powders (which weigh 1, 5 and 8 pounds) are identified by a special bright yellow sticker. Supplies are not infinite and I expect that one day this specially priced surplus material will be exhausted. If you like to use H335 or BLC2, it's time to buy a year's supply of powder. And if you shoot a 222, 223 or 224 Weatherby Magnum, H335 may just be the most accurate propellant you can burn.

When using Hodgdon data or any other, be sure to keep in mind that 8x57 Mauser data are for ammunition and rifles that accept .323-inch diameter bullets safely. Some European sporters and military Mausers, manufactured prior to 1905, have .318-inch bores. The use of .323-inch bullets in these rifles is, of course, extremely dangerous.

Thompson Center

Successful muzzle-loading hunters are well aware of T/C Maxi-Ball bullets. These effective and superbly accurate projectiles are available in 32-, 36-, 45-, 50- and 54-caliber. But, like all similar muzzle-loading bullets, they will not normally expand in game unless they hit heavy bone. A clean hole, almost cookie cutter-like, in and out is the usual performance of these otherwise superb bullets.

Indeed, the two deer we downed during the past season with 50-caliber T/C Renegades and T/C Maxi-Balls, ran 26 and 250 yards respectively, due solely to lack of bullet expansion. Good hits were made on both deer. The first was shot in the chest, penetrating the heart, lung and finally the paunch. Yet, this thoroughly devastated animal managed a very fast 26 yards. The second took a hit, at an angle, which resulted in penetration from left front shoulder on out through the right rear. A second shot entered within a few inches of the first but at a broadside angle. The distance run by the deer was 200 yards between the first and second shot, and another 50 yards thereafter. Oh, for a rapidly expanding bullet!

Well, Thompson Center has come up with a semi-hollowpoint version of its bullets. Called the Maxi-Hunter, these bullets may well prove to be just what's needed to create a large, permanent wound channel. Such a wound would obviously help do in critters quicker, or at least reduce the length of any death run. I'm going to give them a try this spring on black bear and later this fall on whitetail. I will report in our next issue on any performance change compared to the Maxi-Ball bullets.

Miscellaneous

New custom bullet manufacturers are springing up like snowmobile manufacturers did during the heyday of snowmobiling. I sincerely hope their same fate does not await the new bullet manufacturers. One of the newcomers, Allred, is offering a unique heavy-duty line of 22-caliber bullets for, perhaps, those who believe a 223 is adequate for an 80-pound antelope if the right bullet is used. Hollowpoint or lead tip bullets of 50 to 90 grains are available; so are dual core and triple jacketed bullets. A few double jacketed .308-inch bullets are also available. For a cata-

log and price list write to Terry Allred, Allred Bullets Co., 932 Evergreen Drive, Logan, UT 84321 or call 801-752-6983.

If you reload the 41 Magnum and are looking for a wide variety of custom made bullets, Harrison Bullet Works might be of interest to you. The catalog bullet weights are 170, 200, 210, 225, 240, 250, 255, 265 and 275 grains. There are plenty of options too, such as hollow point, Keith-style, round nose, flat base, cup base, etc., etc. The address is 6437 E. Hobart St., Mesa, AZ 85205.

Conclusion

That's about it for this year. Yes, there were other new items; some, however, were not worthy of discussion. A few others appeared interesting but we decided to wait and see if they will be with us for at least a year or two before devoting too much time to them. And bet we missed a few good items due to circumstances beyond control. We try to get everything worthwhile included in these pages, but sometimes the manufacturer fails to call our attention to an item, or we fail to uncover it on our own.

If you're a collector, you might want to save this issue for its low ammunition prices. It's unlikely that we will ever again see the major manufacturers so reduce prices. Thus, this year's are the lowest in a long time and will, I'll bet, never again be repeated. ●

These chucks were dumped with Hodgdon's new bargain-priced H335. Ball C2 is also now available at "surplus" pricing.

AVERAGE CENTERFIRE RIFLE CARTRIDGE BALLISTICS AND PRICES

Caliber	Bullet Wgt. Grs.	— VELOCITY (fps) —					— ENERGY (ft. lbs.) —					— TRAJ. (in.) —				Approx. Price per box
		Muzzle	100 yds.	200 yds.	300 yds.	400 yds.	Muzzle	100 yds.	200 yds.	300 yds.	400 yds.	100 yds.	200 yds.	300 yds.	400 yds.	
17 Rem.	25	4040	3284	2644	2086	1606	906	599	388	242	143	+2.0	+ 1.7	− 3.7	−17.4	$12.00
22 Hornet	45	2690	2042	1502	1128	948	723	417	225	127	90	+1.0	− 5.3	−27.6	—	21.10*
218 Bee	46	2760	2102	1550	1155	961	778	451	245	136	94	+1.0	− 5.2	−26.3	—	35.30*
222 Rem.	50	3140	2602	2123	1700	1350	1094	752	500	321	202	+2.0	− 0.4	−10.6	−33.1	9.00
222 Rem.	55	3020	2562	2147	1773	1451	1114	801	563	384	257	+2.0	− 0.4	−10.5	−31.8	9.00
222 Rem. Mag.	55	3240	2748	2305	1906	1556	1282	922	649	444	296	+2.0	+ 0.2	− 8.2	−26.3	10.20
223 Rem.	40	3650	3010	2450	1950	1530	1185	805	535	340	205	+2.0	+ 1.0	− 5.9	−22.0	13.34
223 Rem.	55	3240	2747	2305	1906	1556	1282	922	649	444	296	+2.0	+ 0.2	− 8.2	−26.3	9.85
224 Wea. Mag.[2]	55	3650	3192	2780	2403	2056	1627	1244	943	705	516	+2.0	+ 2.0	− 2.4	−12.2	26.00
22-250 Rem.	40	4000	3320	2720	2200	1740	1420	980	660	430	265	+2.0	+ 1.8	− 3.2	−15.5	12.92
22-250 Rem.	55	3680	3137	2656	2222	1832	1654	1201	861	603	410	+2.0	+ 1.3	− 4.3	−17.1	10.20
220 Swift	50	4110	3610	3135	2680	NA	1875	1450	1090	800	NA	+2.0	+ 2.8	+	− 6.9	16.10
22 Savage Hi-Power	71	2790	2295	1885	1560	NA	1225	830	560	383	NA	+2.0	− 0.8	−12.6	—	21.69
243 Win.	80	3350	2955	2593	2259	1951	1993	1551	1194	906	676	+2.0	+ 0.9	− 5.4	−18.6	12.30
243 Win.	85	3320	3070	2830	2600	2380	2080	1770	1510	1280	1070	+2.0	+ 1.2	− 4.5	−14.2	16.67+
243 Win.	100	2960	2697	2449	2215	1993	1945	1615	1332	1089	882	+2.0	+ 0.2	− 7.5	−22.2	12.30+
6mm Rem.	80	3470	3064	2694	2352	2036	2139	1667	1289	982	736	+2.0	+ 1.1	− 4.5	−16.5	12.30
6mm Rem.	100	3100	2829	2573	2332	2104	2133	1777	1470	1207	983	+2.0	+ 0.6	− 6.1	−19.2	12.30
240 Wea. Mag.[2]	87	3500	3202	2924	2663	2416	2366	1980	1651	1370	1127	+2.0	+ 2.2	− 1.8	−10.6	26.00
240 Wea. Mag.[2]	100	3395	3106	2835	2581	2339	2559	2142	1785	1478	1215	+2.0	+ 1.6	− 3.0	−12.8	26.00
25-20 Win.	86	1460	1194	1030	931	858	407	272	203	165	141	+	− 8.2	−23.5	—	23.95*
25-35 Win.	117	2230	1866	1545	1282	1097	1292	904	620	427	313	+2.0	− 5.3	−27.4	—	15.50
250-3000 Savage	100	2820	2504	2210	1936	1684	1765	1392	1084	832	630	+2.0	− 0.6	−10.4	−29.5	12.45
257 Roberts	100	3000	2633	2295	1982	1697	1998	1539	1169	872	639	+2.0	− 0.4	− 9.4	−27.2	13.75
257 Roberts	117	2650	2291	1961	1663	1404	1824	1363	999	718	512	+2.0	− 1.0	−15.0	—	13.75
25-06 Rem.	87	3440	2995	2591	2222	1884	2286	1733	1297	954	686	+2.0	+ 1.1	− 5.1	−18.4	15.55
25-06 Rem.	90	3440	3043	2680	2340	2034	2364	1850	1435	1098	827	+2.0	+ 1.2	− 4.2	−16.6	15.55
25-06 Rem.	100	3230	2893	2580	2287	2014	2316	1858	1478	1161	901	+2.0	+ 0.8	− 5.7	−18.9	13.35
25-06 Rem.	120	2990	2730	2484	2252	2032	2382	1985	1644	1351	1100	+2.0	+	− 7.5	−22.0	13.35
257 Wea. Mag.[2]	87	3825	3456	3118	2805	2513	2826	2308	1878	1520	1220	+2.0	+ 2.7	− 0.3	− 7.7	27.00
257 Wea. Mag.[2]	100	3555	3237	2941	2665	2404	2806	2326	1920	1556	1283	+2.0	+ 2.1	− 1.8	−10.5	27.00
257 Wea. Mag.[2]	117	3300	2882	2502	2152	1830	2829	2158	1626	1203	870	+2.0	+ 1.2	− 5.1	−18.9	27.00
6.5x50 Jap.	139	2360	2185	2035	1900	NA	1720	1475	1243	1083	NA	+2.0	− 1.6	−13.4	NA	21.69
6.5x50 Jap.	156	2065	1870	1690	1530	NA	1480	1215	990	810	NA	+2.0	− 4.6	−23.3	NA	21.69
6.5x52 Carcano	156	2430	2210	2000	1800	NA	2045	1690	1385	1125	NA	+2.0	− 2.0	−14.7	NA	21.69
6.5x55 Swedish	140	2855	2665	2500	2350	NA	2530	2210	1930	1677	NA	+2.0	+ 0.6	− 6.7	NA	21.69
6.5x55 Swedish	156	2645	2415	2205	2010	NA	2425	2015	1701	1414	NA	+2.0	− 1.0	−12.1	NA	21.69
6.5 Rem. Mag.	120	3210	2905	2621	2353	2102	2745	2248	1830	1475	1177	+2.0	+ 0.7	− 5.6	−19.3	21.80
264 Win.	140	3030	2782	2548	2326	2114	2854	2406	2018	1682	1389	+2.0	+ 0.4	− 6.6	−18.4	18.10
270 Win.	100	3430	3021	2649	2305	1988	2612	2027	1557	1179	877	+2.0	+ 1.0	− 4.9	−17.5	13.35
270 Win.	130	3060	2776	2510	2259	2022	2702	2225	1818	1472	1180	+2.0	+ 0.4	− 6.8	−20.8	13.35
270 Win.	150	2850	2585	2336	2100	1879	2705	2226	1817	1468	1175	+2.0	− 0.4	− 9.2	−25.8	13.35
270 Wea. Mag.[2]	100	3760	3380	3033	2712	2412	3139	2537	2042	1633	1292	+2.0	+ 2.4	− 0.9	− 8.9	27.00
270 Wea. Mag.[2]	130	3375	3100	2842	2598	2366	3287	2773	2330	1948	1616	+2.0	+ 1.9	− 2.4	−11.6	27.00
270 Wea. Mag.[2]	150	3245	3019	2803	2598	2402	3507	3034	2617	2248	1922	+2.0	+ 1.8	− 3.0	−12.8	27.00
7x30 Waters	120	2700	2300	1930	1600	1330	1940	1405	990	685	470	+2.0	− 2.0	−11.0	−20.0	15.67
7mm-08 Rem.	140	2860	2625	2402	2189	1988	2542	2142	1793	1490	1228	+2.0	− 0.2	− 8.4	−23.9	13.35
7mm Mauser	140	2660	2435	2221	2018	1827	2199	1843	1533	1266	1037	+2.0	− 1.0	−11.1	−29.7	13.60
7mm Mauser	150	2755	2540	2330	2135	NA	2530	2150	1810	1515	NA	+2.0	+	− 8.4	NA	13.60
7mm Mauser	175	2440	2137	1857	1603	1382	2313	1774	1340	998	742	+2.0	− 2.7	−17.6	—	13.60
7x57R	150	2690	2475	2285	2080	NA	2410	2040	1830	1515	NA	+2.0	+	− 8.4	NA	22.75
280 Rem.	140	3000	2758	2528	2309	2102	2797	2363	1986	1657	1373	—	—	—	—	13.35
280 Rem.	150	2970	2699	2444	2203	1975	2937	2426	1989	1616	1299	+2.0	+ 0.2	− 7.5	−22.4	13.35
280 Rem.	165	2820	2510	2220	1950	1701	2913	2308	1805	1393	1060	+2.0	− 0.6	−10.3	−29.3	13.35
7x64 Brenneke	150	2890	2600	2330	2115	NA	2780	2250	1810	1490	NA	+2.0	+ 0.6	− 8.4	NA	22.75
284 Win.	125	3140	2829	2538	2265	2010	2736	2221	1788	1424	1121	+2.0	+ 0.6	− 6.3	−18.7	17.50
284 Win.	150	2860	2595	2344	2108	1886	2724	2243	1830	1480	1185	+2.0	− 0.2	− 8.8	−25.2	17.50
7mm Rem. Mag.	150	3110	2830	2568	2320	2085	3221	2667	2196	1792	1448	+2.0	+ 0.6	− 6.1	−19.3	16.50
7mm Rem. Mag.	160	2950	2730	2520	2320	2120	3090	2650	2250	1910	1600	+2.0	+ 0.4	− 7.1	−21.6	26.92+
7mm Rem. Mag.	175	2860	2645	2440	2244	2057	3178	2718	2313	1956	1644	+2.0	+	− 7.9	−22.7	16.50
7mm Wea. Mag.[2]	139	3400	3138	2892	2659	2437	3567	3039	2580	2181	1832	+2.0	+ 2.1	− 2.1	−11.1	27.00
7mm Wea. Mag.[2]	160	3200	3004	2816	2637	2464	3637	3205	2817	2469	2156	+2.0	+ 1.7	− 3.0	−12.6	27.00
30 Carbine[1]	110	1990	1567	1236	1035	923	967	600	373	262	208	+1.0	−11.5	—	—	21.40*
30 Rem.	170	2120	1822	1555	1328	1153	1696	1253	913	666	502	+2.0	− 5.7	−27.8	—	14.05
30-30 Win.	55	3400	2693	2085	1570	1187	1412	886	521	301	172	+2.0	+	−10.2	−35.0	12.50
30-30 Win.	125	2570	2090	1660	1320	1080	1830	1210	770	480	320	+2.0	− 2.4	−19.4	—	13.25
30-30 Win.	150	2390	1973	1605	1303	1095	1902	1296	858	565	399	+2.0	− 4.2	−25.6	—	10.45
30-30 Win.	170	2200	1895	1619	1381	1191	1827	1355	989	720	535	+2.0	− 4.8	−25.1	—	10.45
300 Savage	150	2630	2311	2015	1743	1500	2303	1779	1352	1012	749	+2.0	− 1.6	−13.9	−36.6	13.50
300 Savage	180	2350	2137	1935	1745	1570	2207	1825	1496	1217	985	+2.0	− 2.6	−19.7	—	13.50
303 Savage	190	1890	1612	1372	1183	1055	1507	1096	794	591	469	+2.0	− 8.8	−38.1	—	17.05
30-40 Krag	180	2430	2213	2207	1813	1632	2360	1957	1610	1314	1064	+2.0	− 2.2	−15.0	−38.5	14.05
307 Win.	150	2760	2321	1924	1575	1289	2538	1795	1233	826	554	+2.0	− 1.4	−15.4	—	14.85
308 Win.	55	3770	3215	2726	2286	1888	1735	1262	907	638	435	+2.0	+ 1.4	− 4.2	−15.8	14.80
308 Win.	150	2820	2533	2263	2009	1774	2648	2137	1705	1344	1048	+2.0	− 0.6	10.0	−28.1	13.35
308 Win.	165	2700	2520	2330	2160	1990	2670	2310	1990	1700	1450	+2.0	+	− 8.4	−24.3	13.35
308 Win.	180	2620	2393	2178	1974	1782	2743	2288	1896	1557	1269	2.0	− 1.2	−11.7	−31.3	13.35
30-06 Spring.	55	4080	3485	2965	2502	2083	2033	1483	1074	764	530	+2.0	+ 1.9	− 2.1	−11.7	14.80
30-06 Spring.	150	2910	2617	2342	2083	1843	2820	2281	1827	1445	1131	+2.0	− 0.2	− 8.5	−24.6	13.35
30-06 Spring.	165	2800	2534	2283	2047	1825	2872	2352	1909	1534	1220	+2.0	− 0.6	− 9.9	−27.5	13.35
30-06 Spring.	180	2700	2469	2250	2042	1846	2913	2436	2023	1666	1362	+2.0	− 0.8	−10.5	−28.6	13.35
30-06 Spring.	220	2410	2130	1870	1632	1422	2837	2216	1708	1301	758	+2.0	− 2.7	−20.5	NA	13.35
7.5x55 Swiss	180	2650	2460	2250	2060	NA	2800	2380	2020	1690	NA	+2.0	− 0.2	− 9.2	NA	22.75
7.62x54R Russ.	180	2575	2360	2165	1975	NA	2650	2270	1875	1560	NA	+2.0	− 0.6	−10.4	NA	22.98
308 Norma Mag.	180	3020	2780	2580	2385	NA	3645	3095	2670	2270	NA	+2.0	+ 1.4	− 5.9	NA	27.45
300 H&H Mag.	180	2880	2640	2412	2196	1990	3315	2785	2325	1927	1583	+2.0	− 0.2	− 8.3	−23.7	17.50
300 Win. Mag.	150	3290	2951	2636	2342	2068	3605	2900	2314	1827	1424	+2.0	+ 0.9	− 5.3	−17.8	17.50
300 Win. Mag.	180	2960	2745	2540	2344	2157	3501	3011	2578	2196	1859	+2.0	+	− 7.3	−20.9	17.50
300 Win. Mag.	200	2830	2680	2530	2380	2240	3560	3180	2830	2520	2230	+2.0	+ 0.6	− 6.2	−19.1	23.42+
300 Win. Mag.	220	2680	2448	2228	2020	1823	3508	2927	2424	1993	1623	+2.0	− 1.0	−11.0	−29.5	17.50
300 Wea. Mag.[2]	110	3900	3441	3028	2652	2305	3714	2891	2239	1717	1297	+2.0	+ 2.6	− 0.6	− 9.2	27.00
300 Wea. Mag.[2]	150	3600	3297	3015	2751	2502	4316	3621	3028	2520	1709	+2.0	+ 2.3	− 1.2	− 9.2	27.00
300 Wea. Mag.[2]	180	3300	3077	2865	2663	2470	4352	3784	3280	2834	2438	+2.0	− 2.6	− 3.0	−12.4	27.00
300 Wea. Mag.[2]	220	2905	2498	2126	1787	1490	4122	3047	2207	1560	1085	+2.0	− 0.1	− 9.9	−22.3	27.00
7.7x58 Jap.	130	2950	2635	2340	2065	NA	2513	2005	1581	1230	NA	+2.0	+ 0.2	− 7.9	NA	22.98
7.7x58 Jap.	180	2495	2290	2100	1920	NA	2485	2100	1765	1475	NA	+2.0	+ 1.2	−12.2	NA	22.98
7.65x53 Argen.	150	2660	2390	2120	1870	NA	2355	1895	1573	1224	NA	+2.0	− 0.2	− 9.1	NA	21.69
303 British	180	2460	2124	1817	1542	1311	2418	1803	1319	950	687	+2.0	− 2.8	−21.3	—	13.75
8mm Rem. Mag.	185	3080	2761	2464	2186	1927	3896	3131	2494	1963	1525	+2.0	+ 0.4	− 7.0	−21.7	20.70
8mm Rem. Mag.	220	2830	2581	2346	2123	1913	3912	3254	2688	2201	1787	+2.0	− 0.4	− 9.1	−25.5	20.70
8mm Mauser	170	2360	1969	1622	1333	1123	2102	1463	993	651	476	+2.0	− 4.1	−24.9	—	13.75

Caliber	Bullet Wgt. Grs.	Muzzle	100 yds.	200 yds.	300 yds.	400 yds.	Muzzle	100 yds.	200 yds.	300 yds.	400 yds.	100 yds.	200 yds.	300 yds.	400 yds.	Approx. Price per box
			— VELOCITY (fps) —					— ENERGY (ft. lbs.) —					— TRAJ. (in.) —			
8x57 JS Mauser	165	2855	2525	2225	1955	NA	2985	2335	1733	1338	NA	+2.0	+	-8.0	NA	21.69
8x57 JS Mauser	196	2525	2195	1895	1625	NA	2780	2100	1560	1150	NA	+2.0	-2.0	-15.7	NA	21.69
32-20 Win.	100	1210	1021	913	834	769	325	231	185	154	131	+	-32.3	—	—	17.05
32 Win. Spl.	170	2250	1921	1626	1372	1175	1911	1393	998	710	521	+2.0	-4.7	-24.7	—	11.15
338 Win. Mag.	200	2960	2658	2375	2110	1862	3890	3137	2505	1977	1539	+2.0	+	-8.2	-24.3	20.95
338 Win. Mag.	225	2780	2572	2374	2184	2003	3862	3306	2816	2384	2005	+2.0	-1.4	-11.1	-27.8	20.95
338 Win. Mag.	250	2660	2456	2261	2075	1898	3927	3348	2837	2389	1999	+2.0	-0.8	-10.5	-28.2	20.95
340 Wea. Mag.[2]	200	3260	3011	2775	2552	2339	4719	4025	3420	2892	2429	+2.0	+1.6	-3.3	-13.5	44.00
340 Wea. Mag.[2]	210	3250	2991	2746	2515	2295	4924	4170	3516	2948	2455	+2.0	+1.7	-3.3	-13.8	29.00
340 Wea. Mag.[2]	250	3000	2806	2621	2443	2272	4995	4371	3812	3311	2864	+2.0	+1.0	-5.0	-16.8	29.00
351 Win. S.L.	180	1850	1556	1310	1128	1012	1368	968	686	508	409	+	-13.6	—	—	38.70*
35 Rem.	150	2300	1874	1506	1218	1039	1762	1169	755	494	359	+2.0	-5.1	-27.8	—	12.30
35 Rem.	200	2080	1698	1376	1140	1001	1921	1280	841	577	445	+2.0	-5.3	-32.1	—	12.30
356 Win.	200	2460	2114	1797	1517	1284	2688	1985	1434	1022	732	+2.0	-3.0	-18.9	—	20.95
358 Win.	200	2490	2171	1876	1610	1379	2753	2093	1563	1151	844	+2.0	-2.6	-17.5	—	20.95
357 Magnum	180	1550	1160	980	860	770	960	535	383	295	235	+	-23.4	—	—	24.75*
350 Rem. Mag.	200	2710	2410	2130	1870	1631	3261	2579	2014	1553	1181	+2.0	-1.2	-12.1	-32.9	22.00
9.3x57 Mauser	286	2065	1820	1580	1400	NA	2715	2100	1622	1274	NA	+2.0	-2.8	-25.9	—	27.62
9.3x62 Mauser	286	2360	2090	1830	1580	NA	3545	2770	2177	1622	NA	+2.0	-2.0	-23.2	—	27.62
375 Win.	200	2200	1841	1526	1268	1089	2150	1506	1034	714	527	+2.0	-5.2	-27.4	—	18.05
375 Win.	250	1900	1647	1424	1239	1103	2005	1506	1126	852	676	+2.0	-7.9	-34.8	—	18.05
375 H&H Mag.	270	2690	2420	2166	1928	1707	4337	3510	2812	2228	1747	+2.0	-1.0	-11.5	-31.4	21.80
375 H&H Mag.	300	2530	2171	1843	1551	1307	4263	3139	2262	1602	1138	+2.0	-2.6	-17.1	—	21.80
378 Wea. Mag.[2]	270	3180	2976	2781	2594	2415	6062	5308	4635	4034	3495	+2.0	+1.6	-3.4	-13.2	46.00
378 Wea. Mag.[2]	300	2925	2576	2252	1952	1680	5698	4419	3379	2538	1881	+2.0	+	-8.7	-26.9	46.00
38-40 Win.	180	1160	999	901	827	764	538	399	324	273	233	+	-23.4	—	—	28.85*
38-55 Win.	255	1320	1190	1091	1018	963	987	802	674	587	525	+	-18.1	—	—	16.75
44-40 Win.	200	1190	1006	900	822	756	629	449	360	300	254	+	-33.3	—	—	26.90*
44 Rem. Mag.	240	1760	1380	1114	970	878	1650	1015	661	501	411	+	-17.6	—	—	10.20
444 Marlin	240	2350	1815	1377	1087	941	2942	1755	1010	630	472	+2.0	-5.8	-32.7	—	14.85
444 Marlin	265	2120	1733	1405	1160	1012	2644	1768	1162	791	603	+2.0	-6.8	-33.4	—	15.05
45-70 Gov.	300	1880	1650	1425	1235	1105	2355	1815	1355	1015	810	+	-12.8	—	—	15.95
45-70 Gov.	405	1330	1168	1055	977	918	1590	1227	1001	858	758	+	-24.6	—	—	15.95
458 Win. Mag.	500	2040	1823	1623	1442	1237	4620	3689	2924	1839	1469	+2.0	-5.6	-26.4	—	42.45
458 Win. Mag.	510	2040	1770	1527	1319	1157	4712	3547	2540	1970	1239	+2.0	-6.4	-27.3	—	46.00
460 Wea. Mag.[2]	500	2700	2404	2128	1869	1635	8092	6416	5026	3878	2969	+2.0	-0.6	-10.7	-31.3	50.00

From 24″ barrel except as noted (1 = 20″ bbl.; 2 = 26″ bbl.). Energies and velocities based on most commonly used bullet profile. Variations can and will occur with different bullet profiles and/or different lots of ammunition as well as individual barrels. Trajectory based on scope reticle 1.5″ above center of bore line. + indicates bullet strikes point of aim.

NOTES: * = 50 cartridges to a box pricing (all others 20 cartridges to a box pricing)
NA = Information not available from the manufacturer.
— = Trajectory falls more than 40 inches below line of sight.
+ = Premium priced ammunition.

Please note that the actual ballistics obtained in your gun can vary considerably from the advertised ballistics. Also, ballistics can vary from lot to lot, even within the same brand. All prices were correct at the time this table was prepared. All prices are subject to change without notice.

CENTERFIRE HANDGUN CARTRIDGES—BALLISTICS AND PRICES

Caliber	Gr.	Bullet Style	Velocity (fps) Muzzle	50 yds.	Energy (ft. lbs.) Muzzle	50 yds.	Barrel Length in inches	Approx. price/box
22 Rem. Jet	40	JSP	2100	1790	390	285	8⅜	$29.30
221 Rem. Fireball	50	JSP	2650	2380	780	630	10½	10.40*
25 Auto	45	LE	815	729	66	53	2	14.10
25 Auto	50	FMC	760	707	64	56	2	13.00
30 Luger	93	FMC	1220	1110	305	253	4½	23.70
30 Carbine	110	JHP, FMC	1740	1552	740	588	10	14.05
32 S&W	85, 88	LRN	680	645	90	81	3	12.55
32 S&W Long	98	LRN, LWC	705	670	115	98	4	13.25
32 H&R Mag.	85	JHP	1100	1020	230	195	4½	20.92
32 H&R Mag.	95	LSWC	1030	940	225	190	4½	17.25
32 Short Colt	80	LRN	745	665	100	79	4	12.50
32 Long Colt	82	LRN	755	715	100	93	4	13.10
32 Auto	60	STHP	970	895	125	107	4	16.45
32 Auto	71	FMC	905	855	129	115	4	14.90
380 Auto	85, 88	JHP	1000	921	189	160	3¾	15.25
380 Auto	95	FMC	955	865	190	160	3¾	15.25
38 Auto	130	FMC	1040	980	310	275	4½	16.65
38 Super Auto +P	115	JHP	1300	1147	431	336	5	18.75
38 Super Auto +P	125	STHP	1240	1130	427	354	5	18.75
38 Super Auto +P	130	FMC	1215	1099	426	348	5	16.15
9mm Luger	115	JHP	1160	1060	345	285	4	18.50
9mm Luger	115	STHP	1225	1095	383	306	4	20.50
9mm Luger	123, 124	FMC	1110	1030	339	292	4	18.50
38 S&W	146	LRN	685	650	150	135	4	14.00
38 Short Colt	125	LRN	730	685	150	130	4	13.75
38 Special	148	LWC	710	634	166	132	4V	14.65
38 Special	110	STHP	945	894	218	195	4V	19.35
38 Special	158	LRN, LSWC	753	721	200	182	4V	15.10
38 Special	95	JHP	1175	1044	291	230	4V	17.80
38 Special +P	110	JHP	995	926	242	210	4V	17.80
38 Special +P	125	JSP, JHP	945	898	248	224	4V	17.80
38 Special +P	158	LSWC, LHP	890	855	278	257	4V	15.25
357 Magnum	110	JHP	1295	1094	410	292	4V	19.55
357 Magnum	125	JHP, JSP	1450	1240	583	427	4V	19.55
357 Magnum	145	STHP	1290	1155	535	428	4V	21.50
357 Magnum	158	JSP, LSWC, JHP	1235	1104	535	428	4V	19.55
357 Magnum	180	JHP	1090	980	475	385	4V	24.75
357 MAXIMUM	158	JHP	1825	1588	1168	885	10½	9.40*
357 MAXIMUM	180	JHP	1555	1328	966	705	10½	9.40*
10mm Auto	165	JHP	1400	NA	719	NA	NA	12.65*
10mm Auto	200	FMC	1200	NA	635	NA	NA	12.65*
41 Rem. Mag.	175	STHP	1250	1120	607	488	4V	28.35
41 Rem. Mag.	210	LSWC	965	898	434	376	4V	22.00
41 Rem. Mag.	210	JHP, JSP	1300	1162	788	630	4V	25.75
44 Special	200	LSWC HP, STHP	900	830	360	305	6½	19.70
44 Special	246	LRN	755	725	310	285	6½	19.70
44 Rem. Mag.	180	JHP	1610	1365	1036	745	4V	10.50*
44 Rem. Mag.	210	STHP	1250	1106	729	570	4V	11.45
44 Rem. Mag.	220	FMC	1390	1260	945	775	6½V	34.44
44 Rem. Mag.	240	LSWC	1000	947	533	477	6½V	21.35
44 Rem. Mag.	240	LSWC/GC	1350	1186	971	749	4V	25.00
44 Rem. Mag.	240	JHP, JSP	1180	1081	741	623	4V	10.20*
45 Auto	185	JWC	770	707	244	205	5	21.45
45 Auto	185	JHP	940	890	363	325	5	21.45
45 Auto	230	FMC	810	776	335	308	5	20.35
45 Auto Rim.	230	LRN	810	770	335	305	5½	21.65
45 Win. Mag.	230	FMC	1400	1232	1001	775	5	24.75
45 Colt	225	JHP, LHP	900	860	405	369	5½	20.00
45 Colt	250, 255	LRN	860	820	420	380	5½	20.00

Notes: Blanks are available in 32 S&W, 38 S&W and 38 Special. V after barrel length indicates test barrel was vented and produced results approximating a revolver with its cylinder to barrel gap.
Abbreviations: JSP (jacketed soft point); LE (lead expanding); FMC (full metal case); JHP (jacketed hollow point); LRN (lead round nose); LWC (lead wadcutter); LSWC (lead semi-wadcutter); STHP (silvertip hollow point); LHP (lead hollow point); LSWCHP (lead semi-wadcutter hollow point); LSWC/GC (lead semi-wadcutter with gas check); JWC (jacketed wadcutter)
*20 rounds per box; all others 50 rounds per box

RIMFIRE AMMUNITION—BALLISTICS AND PRICES

Cartridge Type	Bullet Wt. Grs.	Bullet Type	Velocity (fps) 22½" Barrel Muzzle	Velocity (fps) 22½" Barrel 50 Yds.	Velocity (fps) 22½" Barrel 100 Yds.	Energy (ft. lbs.) 22½" Barrel Muzzle	Energy (ft. lbs.) 22½" Barrel 50 Yds.	Energy (ft. lbs.) 22½" Barrel 100 Yds.	Velocity (fps) 6" Barrel Muzzle	Velocity (fps) 6" Barrel 50 Yds.	Energy (ft. lbs.) 6" Barrel Muzzle	Energy (ft. lbs.) 6" Barrel 50 Yds.	Approx. Price Per Box 50 Rds.	Approx. Price Per Box 100 Rds.
22 CB Short (CCI & Win.)	29	solid	727	667	610	34	29	24	706	—	32	—	**$NA**	**$10.38(1)**
22 CB Long (CCI only)	29	solid	727	667	610	34	29	24	706	—	32	—	**NA**	**5.18**
22 Short Match (CCI only)	29	solid	830	752	695	44	36	31	786	—	39	—	**NA**	**5.18**
22 Short Std. Vel. (Rem. only)	29	solid	1045	—	810	70	—	42	865	—	48	—	**1.80**	**NA**
22 Short H. Vel. (Fed., Rem., Win.)	29	solid	1095	—	903	77	—	53	—	—	—	—	**1.80**	**NA**
22 Short H. Vel. (CCI only)	29	solid	1132	1004	920	83	65	55	1065	—	73	—	**NA**	**4.56**
22 Short H. Vel. HP (Rem. only)	27	HP	1120	—	904	75	—	49	—	—	—	—	**1.91**	**NA**
22 Short H. Vel. HP (CCI only)	27	HP	1164	1013	920	81	62	51	1077	—	69	—	**NA**	**4.86**
22 Long Std. Vel. (CCI only)	29	solid	1180	1038	946	90	69	58	1031	—	68	—	**NA**	**4.86**
22 Long H. Vel. (Fed., Rem.)	29	solid	1240	—	962	99	—	60	—	—	—	—	**1.91**	**NA**
22 LR Pistol Match (Win. only)	40	solid	—	—	—	—	—	—	1060	950	100	80	**5.10**	**NA**
22 LR Match (Rifle) (CCI only)	40	solid	1138	1047	975	116	97	84	1027	925	93	76	**4.28**	**8.56**
22 LR Std. Vel.	40	solid	1138	1046	975	115	97	84	1027	925	93	76	**1.72**	**3.44**
22 LR H. Vel.	40	solid	1255	1110	1017	140	109	92	1060	—	100	—	**1.72**	**3.44**
22 LR H. Vel. HP	36-38	HP	1280	1126	1010	131	101	82	1089	—	95	—	**1.99**	**3.98**
22 LR-Hyper Vel. (Fed., Rem., Win.,(2))	33-34	HP	1500	1240	1075	165	110	85	—	—	—	—	**1.99**	**NA**
22 LR-Hyper Vel.	36	solid	1410	1187	1056	159	113	89	—	—	—	—	**1.75**	**NA**
22 Stinger (CCI only)	32	HP	1640	1277	1132	191	115	91	1395	1060	138	80	**3.52**	**NA**
22 Win. Mag. Rimfire	40	FMC or HP	1910	1490	1326	324	197	156	1428	—	181	—	**6.07**	**NA**
22 LR Shot (CCI, Fed., Win.)	—	#11 or #12 shot	1047	—	—	—	—	—	950	—	—	—	**4.58**	**NA**
22 Win. Mag. Rimfire Shot (CCI only)	—	#11 shot	1126	—	—	—	—	—	1000	—	—	—	**4.24**	**NA**
22 Win. Mag. Rimfire	50	JHP	1650	—	1280	300	—	180	—	—	—	—	**Unk**	**NA**

Please Note: The actual ballisctics obtained from your gun can vary considerably from the advertised ballistics. Also, ballistics can vary from lot to lot even within the same brand. All prices were correct at the time this chart was prepared. All prices are subject to change without notice.

(1) per 250 rounds. (2) also packaged 250 rounds per box.

SHOTSHELL LOADS AND PRICES

Winchester-Western, Remington-Peters, Federal

Dram Equivalent	Shot Ozs.	Load Style	Shot Sizes	Brands	Average Price Per Box	Nominal Velocity (fps)
10 Gauge 3½" Magnum						
4½	2¼	Premium(1)	BB, 2, 4, 6	Fed., Win.	$24.90	1205
4¼	2	H.V.	BB, 2, 4, 5, 6	Fed.	23.00	1210
Max.	1¾	Slug, rifled	Slug	Fed.	7.13	1280
Max.	54 pellets	Buck, Premium(1)	00.4 (Buck)	Fed., Win.	6.75	1100
Max.	1¾	Steel shot	BB, 2	Win.	21.05	1260
4¼	1⅝	Steel shot	BB, 2	Fed.	21.00	1285
12 Gauge 3" Magnum						
4	1⅞	DuPlex Premium	BBx4-2x6	Rem.	7.65	1210
4	1⅞	Premium(1)	BB, 2, 4, 6	Fed., Rem., Win.	16.60	1210
4	1⅝	Premium(1)	2, 4, 5, 6	Fed., Rem., Win.	15.40	1280
4	1⅞	H.V.	BB, 2, 4	Fed., Rem.	14.60	1210
4	1⅝	H.V.	2, 4, 6	Fed., Rem.	13.50	1280
4	Variable	Buck, Premium(1)	000,00,1,4	Fed., Rem., Win.	4.00	1210 to 1225
3½	1¼	DuPlex Premium	BBx2-BBx4-2x6	Rem.	6.20	1375
3½	1⅜	Steel shot	BB, 1, 2, 4	Fed.	14.50	1245
3½	1¼	Steel Shot	F, T, BBB, BB, 1, 2, 4	Rem., Win.	13.50	1375
4	2	Premium(1)	BB, 2, 4, 6	Fed.	16.60	1175
Max	1	Slug, rifled	Slug	Rem.	4.05	1760
12 Gauge 2¾" Hunting & Target						
3¾	1½	DuPlex Premium	BBx4-2x6	Rem.	6.60	1260
3¾	1½	Premium(1), Mag.	BB, 2, 4, 5, 6	Fed., Rem., Win.	14.50	1260
3¾	1½	H.V., Mag.	BB, 2, 4, 5, 6	Fed., Rem.	12.20	—
3¾	1¼	H.V., Premium(1)	2, 4, 6, 7½	Fed., Rem.	10.80	1330
3¾	1¼	H.V., Promo.	BB, 2, 4, 5, 6 7½, 8, 9	Fed., Rem., Win.	9.90	1330
3¼	1¼	Std. Vel., Premium(1)	7½, 8	Fed., Rem.	9.45	1220
3¼	1⅛	Std. Vel., Premium(1)	7½, 8	Fed., Rem.	9.15	1255
3¼	1¼	Std. Vel.	6, 7½, 8, 9	Fed., Rem., Win.	8.35	1220
3¼	1⅛	Std. Vel.	4, 5, 6, 7½, 8, 9	Fed., Rem., Win.	7.60	1255
3¼	1	Std. Vel., Promo	6, 7½, 8	Fed., Rem., Win.	5.80	1290
Max.	1¼	Slug, rifled, Mag.	Slug	Fed.	5.12	1490
Max.	1	Slug, rifled	Slug	Fed., Rem., Win.	3.25	1560
Max.	1	Slug, rifled, hi-vel.	Slug	Rem.	3.90	1680
4	Variable	Buck, Mag., Premium(1)	00, 1, 4 (Buck)	Fed., Rem., Win.	3.55	1075 to 1290
3¾	Variable	Buck, Premium(1)	000, 00, 0, 1, 4 (Buck)	Fed., Rem., Win.	2.80	1250 to 1325
3¾	1⅜	H.V.	2, 4, 6	Fed.	14.42	1295
3¼	1¼	Pigeon	6, 7½, 8	Fed., Win.	8.35	1220
3	1⅛	Trap & Skeet	7½, 8, 9	Fed., Rem., Win.	8.20	1200
2¾	1⅛	Trap & Skeet	7½, 8, 8½, 9	Fed., Rem., Win.	8.20	1145
2¾	1	Trap & Skeet	7½, 8, 8½	Fed., Rem., Win.	8.20	1180
3¾	1¼	Steel shot	BB, 1, 2, 4, 6	Fed., Win.	13.50	1275
3¾	1⅛	Steel shot	1, 2, 4, 6	Fed., Rem., Win.	12.40	1365
3¾	1⅛	DuPlex Premium	BBx2-BBx4, 2x6	Rem.	5.70	1365
16 Gauge 2¾"						
3¼	1¼	H.V., Mag., Premium(1)	2, 4, 6	Fed., Win.	15.17	1260
3¼	1⅛	H.V., Promo.	4, 5, 6, 7½, 9	Fed., Rem., Win.	9.50	1295
2¾	1⅛	Std. Vel.	4, 6, 7½, 8, 9	Fed., Rem., Win.	7.60	1185
2½	1	Std. Vel., Promo.	6, 7½, 8	Fed., Win.	5.80	1165
Max.	⅘	Slug, rifled	Slug	Fed., Rem., Win.	3.25	1570
Max.	12 pellets	Buck	1 (Buck)	Fed., Rem., Win.	2.80	1225
20 Gauge 3" Magnum						
3	1¼	Premium(1)	2, 4, 6	Fed., Rem., Win.	12.85	1185
3	1¼	H.V.	2, 4, 6, 7½	Fed., Rem.	11.25	1185
Max.	18 pellets	Buck	2 (Buck)	Fed.	4.52	1200
Max.	1	Steel Shot	2, 4, 6	Fed., Rem., Win.	11.85	1330
20 Gauge 2¾" Hunting & Target						
2¾	1⅛	Premium(1), Mag.	4, 6, 7½	Fed., Rem., Win.	11.40	1175
2¾	1⅛	H.V., Mag.	4, 6, 7½	Fed., Rem.	10.00	1175
2¾	1	H.V., Premium(1)	4, 6	Fed., Rem.	9.40	1220
2¾	1	H.V., Promo.	4, 5, 6, 7½, 8, 9	Fed., Rem., Win.	8.30	1220
2½	1	Std. Vel., Premium(1)	7½, 8	Fed., Rem.	8.30	1165
2½	1	Std. Vel.	4, 5, 6, 7½, 8, 9	Fed., Rem., Win.	7.15	1165
2½	⅞	Promo.	6, 7½, 8	Fed., Win., Rem.	5.80	1210
Max.	¾	Slug, rifled	Slug	Fed., Rem., Win.	3.00	1570
Max.	20 pellets	Buck	3 (Buck)	Fed., Rem., Win.	2.80	1200
2½	⅞	Skeet	8, 9	Fed., Rem., Win.	7.65	1200
2¾	¾	Steel shot	4, 6	Fed., Win.	11.20	1425
28 Gauge 2¾" Hunting & Target						
2¼	¾	H.V.	6, 7½	Fed., Rem., Win.	8.75	1295
2	¾	Skeet	9	Fed., Rem., Win.	9.05	1200
410 Bore Hunting & Target						
Max.	11/16	3" H.V.	4, 5, 6, 7½, 8	Fed., Rem., Win.	8.14	1135
Max.	½	2½" H.V.	4, 6, 7½	Fed., Rem., Win.	6.90	1135
Max.	½	2½" Target	9	Fed., Rem., Win.	7.45	1200
Max.	⅕	Slug, rifled	Slug	Fed., Rem., Win.	2.85	1815

(1)Premium shells usually incorporate high antimony extra hard shot and a granulated polyethelene buffer to increase pattern density at long ranges. In general, prices are per 25-round box. Rifled slugs and buckshot prices are per 5-round pack. Premium buckshot prices per 10-round pack. Not every brand is available in every shot size. Price of Skeet and trap loads may vary widely.

The Handloader's Catalog

Here's the latest edition of the "handloader's wishbook," the catalog section of this 11th edition HANDLOADER'S DIGEST. We've done our best to show you, the reader, what's new and different in the tools with which to ply your hobby or trade. Some of the things are new, some are not, but all are interesting and useful to the modern handloader who wants to turn out the best available reloads he can make.

Like nearly everything else these days, the costs of these tools have risen a bit in keeping with economic conditions. The prices shown in these pages are approximate, suggested retail. If you shop around before buying, you're likely to save some money and the effort will be worthwhile.

If you've got more questions than our catalog has answers for, then be sure to check our trade directory in the back of the book for the manufacturer's addresses you may need. A call or note to them will bring quick results.

Handloading can be a safe, enjoyable and cost-efficient part of the shooting sports, but only if the human element does his part. Be safe, conscientious and consistent in all of your reloading and shooting. Good luck, and enjoy our catalog.

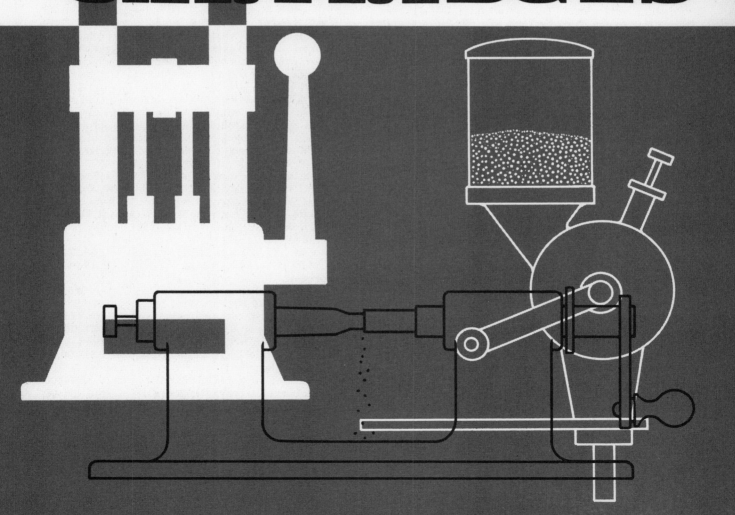

11th EDITION — PART 1

TOOLS AND ACCESSORIES FOR
METALLIC
CARTRIDGES

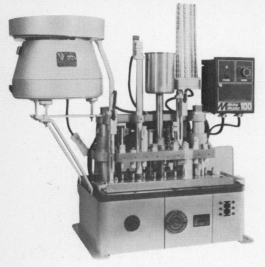

Ammo Load Mark IV

Ammo Load Auto Primer Tube Filler

Ammo Load Machine Stand

Notes on Presses . . .

Presses, like other pieces of machinery, are designed to work within certain limits. The largest and strongest presses will handle any job, from neck sizing the 22 Hornet up to swaging 375 caliber bullets. Before buying a press the novice should keep in mind that, as his knowledge of handloading increases, so will his desire to reload additional cartridges. He should try to anticipate his future requirements—it will save him money in the end.

The handgun shooter, loading for himself only, cannot go wrong buying a simple Hornady, Lyman, Lee or RCBS press. All handle handgun ammunition with ease, of course, as well as rifle cartridges. The Lyman #310 tool, the old reliable, also handles both types of ammunition. These are sturdy but not fast tools. After a few months though, suppose our handgunner decides to handload ammo for several friends. In that case his original choice of a press may not be adequate for larger volume handloading.

Or, let's assume instead that he moves on to bullet swaging. Can his original press handle bullet-swaging pressures?

All these things should be carefully thought out before buying any handloading press. It will save time, breakage and money. In any case, it is better to buy just a little stronger press than your present needs call for.

On the other hand, the shooter who travels, who moves and lives, perhaps, in a confined space or the man who does not do much shooting would be wise to purchase a small, light tool— say the Lee (rifle or shotgun), the Lyman 310 or the Pak-Tool Hand Loader, one of the finest small portable tools. Using this tool a man can sit in his car, canoe or on a log in the woods and reload cartridges with accuracy and dependability.

AMMO LOAD Mark III and Mark IV

Designed for high volume pistol ammo reloaders, these units will reload from 3,600 to 5,000 rounds per hour. Both are powered by a foot-switch-activated ½-hp. motor (110-Volt Mark III/220 Volt Mark IV). The Mark III comes standard with an automatic case feeder, primer magazine (manual), 32-oz. powder flask with removable filter screen, 38-45 capacity bullet feeder and a slide assembly for automatic case positioning.

The Mark IV comes with all those features found on the Mark III plus: a carbide final sizing die, variable speed, DC motor with control box, three shut-off switches for low feed auto shut-off at case feed, primer feed and bullet feed stations, a light panel for low-feed signaling and a special powder flash shut-off assembly.

Available in four standard calibers (38 Spec., 357 Mag., 45 ACP, 9mm), four special order calibers (38 S&W, 380 Auto, 44 Mag., 44 S&W) or eight custom calibers (25 Auto, 30 Carbine, 32 Auto, 32 S&W Long and Short, 38 Auto, 41 Mag., 45 Long Colt). Weight 315 lbs. (Mark III)/323 lbs. (Mark IV). From Ammo Load, Inc.

Price: Mark III **$8,329.00**
Price: Mark IV **$9,445.00**
Optional Features
Price: Automatic Primer Tube Filler **$654.00**
Price: Ammo Load Machine Stand **$939.00**
Price: Case Vibratory Inspection Table (110-Volt) **$1,593.00**
Price: Case Vibratory Inspection Table (220-Volt) **$1,750.00**
Optional Equipment
Price: Powder Flask Shut Off (Mark III) **$60.00**
Price: Carbide Final Sizing Die (Mark III) **$60.00**
Price: Eight Station Bullet Turret (Mark III and IV)**$239.00**
Optional Calibers
Price: Special Order **$462.00**
Price: Custom Order . . . . **Varies**
Motor Options
Price: Variable Speed Motor (Mark III) **$514.00**
Price: 220-Volt 50 Cycle AC (Mark III and IV) . . . **$750.00**

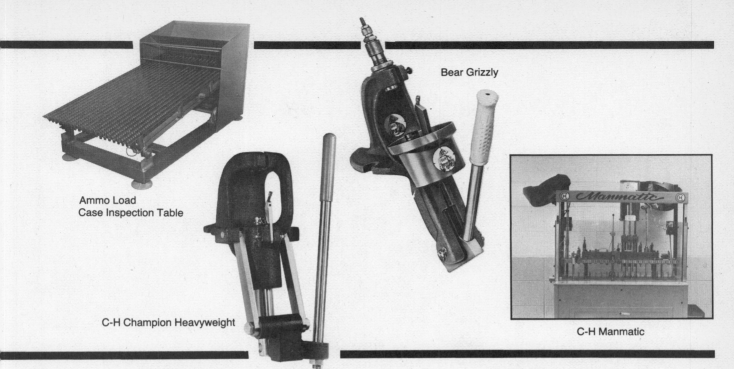

Ammo Load
Case Inspection Table

C-H Champion Heavyweight

Bear Grizzly

Manmatic

C-H Manmatic

BEAR Sportsman's Special

Metallic rifle or pistol reloaders will have everything they need to get started with Bear's Sportsman's reloading kit. The package includes Bear's Grizzly Bear press and primer arm, set of precision dies (reloader's choice), Micro-Measure powder measure, shellholder head, Magna Damp powder scale (510-grain capacity), a chamfer and deburring tool, case lube, *Speer Reloading Manual* and primer catcher. From Bear Company **$98.00**

BEAR Hunter's Special

A kit that includes everything the reloader needs to start reloading rifle or pistol ammunition. The kit includes the Black Bear "C" press and primer arm, set of dies (reloader's choice), Magna Damp powder scale (510-grain capacity), case-hardened shellholder head, chamfer and deburring tool, case lube, *Speer Reloading Manual*, and powder funnel. From Bear Company **$78.00**

BEAR Brown Bear III

This heavy-duty H-type reloading press features a three-station loading sequence, an integral automatic priming system and adjustable primer seating depth. For reloading both rifle and handgun ammo. From Bear Company.

Price: Press. **$150.00**
Price: Press with choice of dies and shellholders . . **$165.00**

BEAR Black Bear

The most economical press Bear has to offer to the reloader. A C-type press made of heavy annealed cast iron. Accepts standard 7x14 dies and interchangeable shellholder heads. A fully automatic primer feed system is optional. From Bear Company.

Price: Press with primer arm **$38.00**
Price: Primer catcher tray. **$4.00**

BEAR Grizzly Bear

This economical and rugged C-type press is made of heavy-duty cast iron. It will perform the most delicate or the toughest of reloading operations. The convenient wide opening "C" allows easy access to the cartridge. Can be adjusted to either up or down operation. A fully automatic primer feed system is optional. From Bear Company.

Price: Press with ram and primer arm **$40.00**
Price: Press with shellholder head, primer arm, one set of dies **$52.00**
Price: Primer catcher tray. **$4.00**
Price: Universal C Press ram for removable shellholder head **$7.00**
Price: Removable shellholder head **$2.50**

C-H Manmatic

This fully automatic press can reload up to 3,000 rounds per hour. Chain driven by a ¾-hp., 110-volt motor, the Manmatic moves cases through its 20 reloading/checking stations. Seven automatic station probes and sensors monitor the cases for problems. If a problem is sensed, a case-actuated microswitch automatically stops the press and an LED light indicates where the problem occurred. Unit is enclosed by Lexan shatterproof shielding. Weight is 525 lbs. From C-H Tool and Die Corp. **$13,700.00**

C-H "Champion" Heavy-Weight

A very heavy-duty O-type press with a ram 1.185″ in diameter. Press is drilled to allow spent primers and debris to fall through. Takes universal shellholders and is threaded ⅞-14 for standard dies. Well suited for case forming and bullet swaging operations. Solid steel handle. Toggle is designed so that it "breaks" slightly over top dead center for extreme leverage. From C-H Tool and Die Corp.

Price, including universal primer arm and shellholder head **$199.00**
Price complete with one set of standard dies **$217.00**

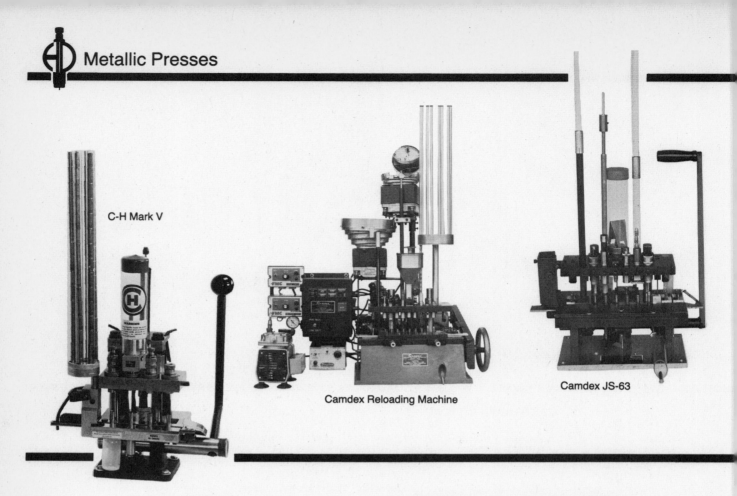

C-H Mark V

Camdex Reloading Machine

Camdex JS-63

C-H 444 H Press

This press offers four-station versatility—2, 3, or 4-piece die sets can be used. Or, a powder measure can be used with 2- or 3-piece die sets. Improved casting design offers increased strength and there is room for the longest magnum cases. Press comes complete with four rams, four shellholders, small or large primer area, and primer catcher. From C-H Tool and Die Corp. **$158.00**
As above, with one standard caliber die set **$174.00**
Extra primer arm **$2.40**

C-H 444-X Pistol Champ Press

This three station, semi-progressive reloading tool is highly suitable for loading large quantities of pistol ammunition. Tungsten carbide sizing die with decapper, Speed Seater seating die, button operated powder measure that dispenses powder and expands and bells the case mouth, fixed powder charge bar (available for different charges). Three strokes of the operating handle produces a finished round. Up to 200 rounds per hour can be loaded. Available in 38 Special/357 Mag., 30 Carbine, 9mm Luger, 44 Mag., 45 ACP, 45 Colt. Press complete with accessories. From C-H Tool and Die Corp. **$269.50**
444-X Conversion Kits:
38/357, 44 Mag., 45 ACP, Colt, carbide **$64.00**
As above, steel **$49.60**
9mm Luger, carbide **$68.40**
As above, steel **$49.60**
30 Carbine, carbide **$81.40**
As above, steel **$49.60**

C-H Mark V Auto Champion Press

A heavy duty H-type progressive loading machine that gives one completed round with each pull of the handle. Powder is dropped through a special "Flow-Through" belling and expanding die. Tungsten carbide sizing die. Fixed powder bars. Automatic case advancing makes double charging impossible. Seating stems are available for any type bullet.
Operating stations are in a straight line at the front of the machine. The three stations are clearly visible with no blind spots. Available only in 38 Special/357 Mag., 9mm Luger, 44 Mag., 45 ACP. Bullet seating stems are available for semi-wadcutter, wadcutter or round-nose. Many improved features. From C-H Tool and Die Corp.
Press, complete (includes 1 primer tube, 2 case tubes) **$699.00**
Extra case tubes (holding 15 cases each), 2 for **$3.60**
Extra powder bushings (specify type and weight) . . . **$2.40**
Bullet seating stems **$1.80**

CAMDEX JS-63 Loader

Choice of either hand or motorized operation. Tube case feeder, takes standard ⅞-14 sizing dies. Spring loaded primer slide is adjustable for pick-up location and seating location. Powder station uses standard Pacific powder bushings. Crimp station uses standard ⅞-14 die. This 8-station press comes completely assembled and ready to go. From Camdex, Inc.
Hand operated with tooling for one caliber, about **$1,950.00**
Automatic (motorized), complete, about **$3,450.00**
Caliber conversion kits **$695.00**

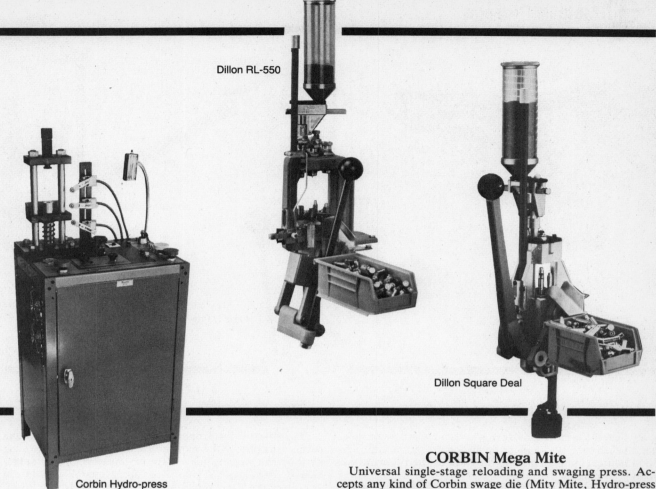

Dillon RL-550

Corbin Hydro-press

Dillon Square Deal

CAMDEX Reloading Machine

This electrically operated loading machine can produce 4400 completed rounds per hour. It is a cam operated index loader that comes with a T-C resizing die, a "Fail Safe" primer control system including a primer pocket probe. Controls monitor and shuts down machine automatically if any of five functions are not satisfied. Machine comes ready to operate with conversion kits available to load any centerfire pistol caliber and several rifle calibers. From Camdex, Inc. Price of machine in one caliber, about..................**$8,000.00**
Automated and Continuous Loader...........**$9,100.00**
Auto primer filler...........................**$675.00**
Conversions.............................**$2,650.00**

CORBIN CHP-1 Mark IV Hydro-press

This hydraulic press reloads any caliber up to 20mm. Ram stroke is adjustable from zero to 6 inches, which makes the press convenient for extruding up to ⅜-inch lead wire with Corbin's extrusion dies. Automatic sensors and safeties assure safe loads. Key switches prevent unauthorized use. Works in either semi- or full-automatic modes. Can also be used for jacket making, bullet swaging. From Corbin Manufacturing and Supply & Co., Inc. Price..................**$4,950.00**

CORBIN Mega Mite

Universal single-stage reloading and swaging press. Accepts any kind of Corbin swage die (Mity Mite, Hydro-press or reloading press) and standard reloading dies. Machined steel construction; all moving interfaces run on bearings. From Corbin Manufacturing and Supply Co........**$650.00**

DILLON RL-550 Progressive Press

A fully progressive O-type metallic cartridge press, it comes with automatic powder measure, and automatic primer feed. The removable tool head holds the die set in proper adjustment. Tool head is threaded for standard ⅞-14 dies. All reloading steps are performed with one stroke of the operating handle. Comes complete to load one caliber, less dies, and with lifetime warranty. From Dillon Precision Products, Inc..............................**$234.95**
Price: Dillon pistol die sets (38/357, 9mm, 44 Mag., 45 ACP)..**$39.95**

DILLON Square Deal Pistol Press

This entry-level progressive press loads only pistol calibers and comes in 38, 357, 9mm, 44 or 45 ACP, with preadjusted drop-in insert dies, automatic primer feed, automatic powder measure, spent primer catcher, and completed round collection box. The only adjustments needed are for powder charge and bullet seating depth. Loading involves only feeding empty cases and bullets at the proper stations. Press comes complete with dies in one of the above calibers. From Dillon Precision Products, Inc.................................**$135.00**
Price: Caliber conversion kit (dies, shellholder, primer punches, primer feed parts)..................**$42.00**

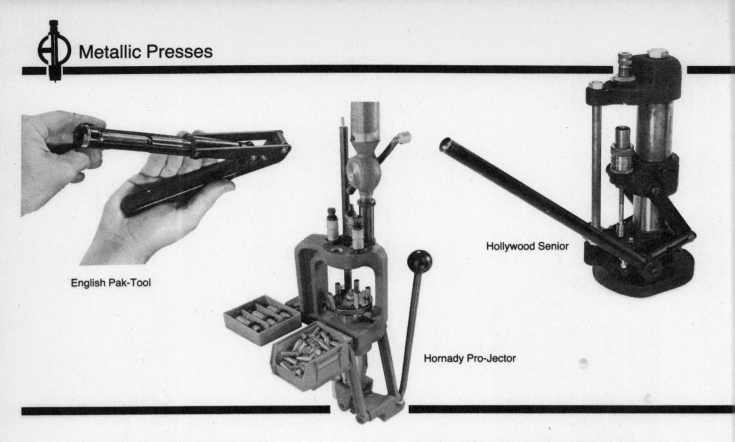

English Pak-Tool

Hollywood Senior

Hornady Pro-Jector

W.H. ENGLISH Pak-Tool

Designed for the handloader who lacks room or facilities for a bench tool, it's ideal for the benchrest shooter, the varmint hunter, the man back in the bush or the rifleman who likes to load at the shooting range.

The leverage of the Pak-Tool makes full length sizing of such cartridges as the 357 and 44 Magnums possible. For rifle cartridges, the Pak-Tool neck sizes only. The Pak-Tool is 100% straight line in all operations. From Roberts Products.
Price complete for one standard rifle caliber **$54.50**
　　Handgun calibers **$59.50**

FORSTER/BONANZA B-2 Co-Ax Press

This press has adjustable jaws which are set against the cartridge case extractor groove with zero tolerance, thereby maintaining perfect concentricity. The jaws will work on most boxer-primed rifle and pistol cases having a rim thickness of .050″ to .070″. All other specs are the same as the B-1 press. From Forster Products......................... **$192.00**
　　Price Blue Ribbon Conversion Unit for the B-1 press **$30.00**

HOLLYWOOD "Senior" Turret Tool

Same superb quality and features as the regular "Senior" except has 8-station turret head. Holes in turret are tapped 1½″ and ⅞″, 4 of each. Height 15″, weight 47 lbs. stripped. Comes complete with one ½″ die shellholder bushing, turret indexing handle, one ⅝″ tiedown rod for swaging, and one adaptor bushing for adapting 1½″ dies down to ⅞″-14. From Hollywood Loading Tools....................... **$550.00**

HOLLYWOOD "Senior" Reloading Tool

A massive (43 lbs. stripped) tool with leverage and bearing surfaces ample for the most efficient operation in reloading cartridges or swaging bullets. The castings are 30,000 PSI tensile strength gray cast iron. Precision ground 2½″ pillar, in one-piece construction with base. Operating handle of ¾″ steel 15″ long gives tremendous leverage and ease of operation with a downward stroke for case sizing or bullet swaging. ⅝″ steel tie-down rod furnished for added strength when swaging bullets.

Heavy steel toggle and camming arms held by ½″ steel pins in reamed holes. Extra holes are drilled for greater leverage in bullet swaging.

The 1½″ steel die bushing takes standard ⅞″-14 dies; when bushing is removed it allows the tool to accept Hollywood shotshell dies. From Hollywood Loading Tools. **$520.00**

HORNADY Pro-Jector Progressive Reloader

Designed for the high-volume reloader, the Pro-Jector can produce hundreds of reloads per hour in both rifle and pistol calibers. The Pro-Jector is the only progressive press on the market with the capacity to reload a wide variety of pistol and rifle cartridges—with automatic indexing of the shell plate. Hornady's Power-Pac linkage reduces operator effort and the angled frame increases visibility in the working area. Accepts standard dies. The price includes features such as the Positive Priming System, Brass Kicker cartridge ejector, as well as a standard set of dies, cartridge catcher, primer catcher, shell plate for one caliber, powder measure adapter, large and small primer tubes and a new Automatic Primer Shut-off. The Pro-Jector also features a five-station die platform for roll or taper crimp dies. From Hornady................. **$335.00**
　　Price: Extra Shell Plates........................ **$25.00**

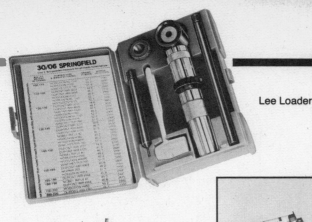

Lee Loader

Lee Hand Press Kit

Huntington Compac

Hornady 00-7

HORNADY 00-7 Reloading Press

Follows the 0-7 design in providing an O-type frame which is angled 30° to one side, but uses special handle-to-ram linkage for extra power in case resizing and bullet swaging. The "Power-Pac" linkage greatly multiples the force applied to the ram through the lever designed to be at a maximum during the final ½-inch of lever stroke. Also includes Hornady's PPS priming system for fully automatic priming. From Hornady...**$124.50**
00-7 auto primer feed...........................**$14.95**
00-7 with Series I die package (includes PPS, primer catcher, shellholder, and one set of dies)................**$163.55**
00-7 with Series II die package (includes PPS primer catcher, shellholder, one set Series II dies).............**$189.15**

HUNTINGTON Compac Press

Designed for those handloaders lacking space for a bench-mounted tool, the Compac is also ideal for loading at the range. Performs all reloading operations. Tool has sufficient leverage to full length resize all pistol and rifle cases, decap military brass, and even perform some light case forming operations. Accepts ⅞-14 dies and standard removable shell holders. Tool weighs about 37 oz. The unique symmetrical design maintains perfect alignment. The Compac Press is made of high tensile steel and aluminum alloys used for aircraft parts. From Huntington. Price, less dies............**$54.95**

LEE Progressive 1000 Press

This variation of the Lee Turret Press combines other Lee options into a complete package. Press includes carbide dies, an automatic index system, four-tube case feeder, Auto Prime II, Deluxe Auto-Disk powder measure and a case sensor. Add a bullet and pull the lever; all other operations are automatic. One loaded round with each pull of the lever. Loaded rounds eject into a chute to a container. Quick die change. Easy to set up. From Lee Precision, Inc...........**$204.98**

LEE Hand Press and Hand Press Kit

A full-size hand-held reloading press that uses standard dies and is large enough to handle 375 H&H Magnum cases. Compound linkage makes even case-forming easy. Weighs 1¾ pounds. Also comes in kit form which includes the Hand Press, 2 rifle or 3 pistol dies, shellholder, die box, powder dipper, powder funnel, load data, Ram Prime tool, complete instructions and case lube (with rifle dies only). Available in most popular calibers. From Lee Precision, Inc.
Price: Hand Press only.........................**$29.98**
Price: Two-die rifle kit.........................**$44.98**
Price: Three-die pistol kit.......................**$54.98**

LEE Loader Hand Loading Tool

The simplest, most economical tool available, it consists of a few dies to be used with a mallet or soft hammer for resizing, bullet seating and priming. Powder charges are measured with a charge cup. All parts of the Lee Loader are fully guaranteed and will be replaced free of charge if they break or prove defective in normal usage. Available for most popular rifle and pistol cartridges. From Lee Precision, Inc...........**$16.98**

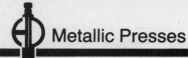

Lee 2001 Challenger

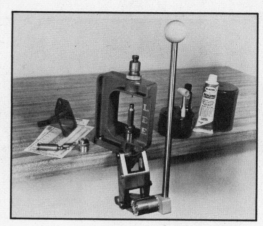

Lee Turret Press Kit

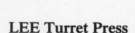

Lee Turret

LEE Turret Press

"O" frame strength with a quick replaceable turret. Entire turret with dies can be replaced in 10 seconds—rotate the turret 30° to lift out. To change primer size, lift out the primer arm and rotate 180°. Accepts all standard ⅞-14 dies and universal shellholders. Built-in primer catcher. Compound leverage and accessory mounting holes.

Press can be easily changed for left-hand use. Handle is adjustable for the most convenient angle at the end of the stroke.

The optional Auto-Index automatically rotates the die turret to the next station. Safety override prevents overstressing should the turret be prevented from turning. The optional Auto-Disk powder measure automatically dispenses an exact charge and is actuated by the cartridge case.

A Lee Turret Press kit is now available and includes the Auto-Index and factory adjusted dies. Kits can be made up for most popular calibers. From Lee Precision, Inc.

Press only......................................**$65.98**
Hardwood box.................................**$34.98**
Extra turret **$10.98**
Press with Auto-Index **$79.98**
Auto-Disk powder measure **$24.98**
Turret Press kit...............................**$99.98**

LEE 2001 Challenger Press

This heavy-duty O-type press has a large opening with 30° offset. Stress limiting design shortens lever travel and makes it impossible to spring the frame from alignment. Compound leverage makes sizing the largest case easy. The lever is adjustable to start and end for most convenience, and for right- or left-handed operators. Frame is cast from ASTM380 alloy. Polyester red finish, large hard maple lever knob. Spent primers eject into the covered built-in catcher. Accepts all standard dies and shellholders. From Lee Precision, Inc. Press only...**$39.98**

Two kits are available—a 2-die rifle kit and 3-die pistol kit. Each kit includes press, set of dies (most popular calibers), powder measure, shellholder, powder funnel, Ram Prime tool, case lube (not included with carbide dies) load data.
Price: 2-Die Rifle Kit **$59.98**
Price: 3-Die Pistol Kit..........................**$69.98**
Price: Hard maple storage box **$34.98**

LYMAN Special-T Turret Press

Combines fast "turret-loading" with the strength and simplicity of the popular "C" press. Frame and 6-station turret are high-silicon iron castings. Verti-Lock Turret secured to frame by heavy-duty ¾" steel stud provides positive stop, audible click indexing.

Turret locks rigidly for swaging; powerful leverage (25 to 1); up- or down-stroke operation. Alignment ramp positions shellholder at top of stroke. From Lyman Products. Price, with ram, priming arm, catcher **$109.95**
All-American dies (specify caliber): Standard: ...**$29.95;**
Deluxe:......................................**$54.50**
Optional equipment: Spart-T auto. primer feed ...**$15.50**
Lyman 55 powder measure **$67.95**

Lyman Expert Reloading Kit

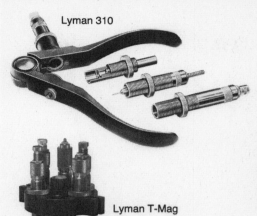

Lyman 310

Lyman T-Mag

Lyman Orange Crusher

Lyman AccuLine

LYMAN Orange Crusher

An O-type press with a large 4½″ opening that accommodates even the largest cartridges. The heavy-duty casting has three mounting holes and is painted in Lyman orange color. The handle design mounts for left- or right-hand use and focuses power between the power links for smooth, easy leverage. Compound linkage design allows case forming and bullet swaging. Primer catcher locks securely to the press, yet is easily removed when emptying spent primers. From Lyman Products. Press with primer catcher, primer arm **$89.95**

Orange Crusher Set includes press, primer catcher, primer arm, shellholder, AA-Standard or Multi-Deluxe die set **$139.95**

LYMAN Expert Reloading Kit

All the tools needed for reloading contained in one kit. The Expert Kit includes: Special T-turret press; Universal priming arm; primer tray; auto primer feed; detachable shellholder; primer catcher; universal trimmer; M-500 reloading scale; #55 powder measure; deburring tool; case lube kit; powder funnel, AA standard rifle or multi-standard pistol die set; quick release turret system; hex wrench; extra decapping pins; ⅞″ x 14 adapter (mounts #55 measure in press turret); complete setup instructions; and *Lyman's Reloading Guide*. Available in 9mm Luger, 38/357 Mag., 44 Mag., 45 ACP, 30-06 Springfield.

Price: Expert kit (dies included) **$329.95**
Price: "No Cal" Expert kit (less dies and shellholder) **$299.95**

LYMAN T-Mag Press

This press allows the reloader to mount six different reloading dies and two primer feeds that can be left in place, ready for reloading at all times. Uses standard ⅞-14 dies, and has a ¾″ steel stud and extra heavy support post holding the turret. Base has three holes for greater leverage and solid mounting. Uses O-Mag primer feed and primer catcher. Press set comes with one standard AA pistol or rifle die set and shellholder. From Lyman Products. Press only, with primer arm, primer catcher **$129.95**

Complete press set **$169.95**

LYMAN AccuLine Reloading Press

This lightweight single-station press is designed for bench-mounted operation but can be adapted to hand-held use by switching the operating handle end-for-end. A low-cost portable tool for smaller-quantity rifle or pistol reloaders. Accommodates all Lyman die and shellholders. The AccuLine press can be purchased separately or packaged in two different reloading sets—standard rifle or carbide pistol die sets. From Lyman Products.

Price: Press only **$29.95**
Price: Press and standard rifle dies **$49.95**
Price: Press and carbide pistol dies **$69.95**

LYMAN No. 310 Tool

Reloads pistol or rifle cartridges. A low-cost portable tool for smaller-quantity reloaders and those who want a compact and handy reloading outfit. An adjustable extractor hook and the Adapter Die let many rimmed or rimless cases be processed in the same handles. From Lyman Products.

Price: Set of 310 tool dies **$31.95**
Price: 310 tool handles (large or small) **$29.95**
Price: 310 tool pouch **$9.95**

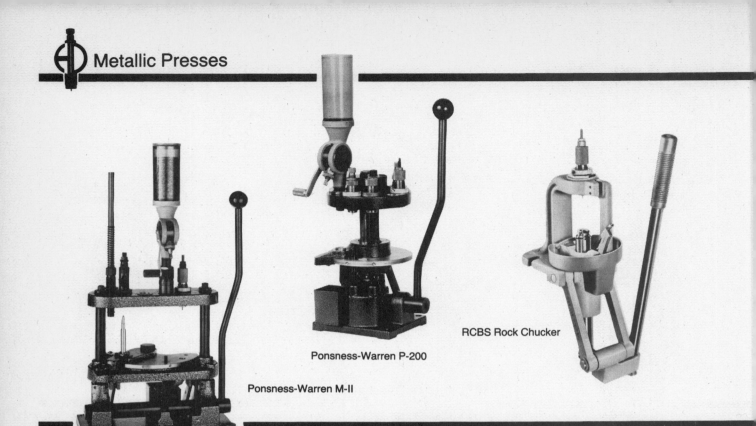

Ponsness-Warren P-200

RCBS Rock Chucker

Ponsness-Warren M-II

MRC Unitized Loader

A simple economical kit with everything needed to reload most popular rifle and handgun cartridges. Includes a Unitized Priming Tool made of strong flex nylon with integral shellholder, a primer pocket cleaner, a few dies to be used with a mallet or soft hammer for full-length resizing and bullet seating, and a Flaring Crimper for loading cast bullets. From Mequon Reloading Corporation................**$23.98**

MRC LOADER Improved Hand Loading Tool

A simple, economical tool, it consists of a few dies to be used with a mallet or soft hammer for resizing, bullet seating and priming. Powder charges are measured with a charge cup. All parts of the MRC Loader have a limited warranty and will be replaced free of charge if they break or prove defective in 2 years of normal usage. Available for most popular rifle and pistol cartridges. From Mequon Reloading Corp.....**$19.98**

MRC Target Model Loader

Designed with the bench rest shooter in mind, this simple, economical tool loads target-quality ammunition at less than the cost of a conventional loading press. The loader features neck line reaming, positive straightline bullet seating, micrometer depth bullet seating. Set includes primer pocket cleaner, chamfer tool, case trimmer, MRC priming tool, neck reamer, bullet seater. All that's needed are the components. All parts have limited warranty and unit is available for most popular rifle calibers. From Mequon Reloading Corp. Price, complete.......................................**$64.98**

PONSNESS-WARREN Metallic M-II Press

This H-type press is capable of loading 200 rounds or more of rifle or handgun ammunition per hour. The die head has four 7/8-14 holes to accept standard dies, powder measure, and other accessories. Conversion from one caliber to another is accomplished in less than 5 minutes. Once the case is inserted into the shellholder, it is not removed until it has been resized, reprimed, charged with powder, a bullet seated and crimped. Case is moved to each station on a side-swinging carrier. Press comes with an automatic primer feed. The Metallic M-II comes without dies, powder measure, or shellholder. Optional features include additional die heads, powder measure extension, and the P/W CAL-die bullet seater. From Ponsness-Warren.

Metallic M-II press and primer feed **$199.00**

PONSNESS-WARREN Metal-Matic P-200 Press

This loader is designed to load straight-wall metallic and 223 cases at the rate of about 200-300 per hour. The 10-hole die head is tapped for standard 7/8-14 dies, and is designed to hold two calibers at one time. Once the case is inserted into the shellholder, it is not removed until all loading operations have been completed. A spring-loaded ball check precisely indexes the shellholder arms as it moves under the die head. The P-200 uses twin guide posts for durability, and comes with a removable spent primer box, large and small priming tools. Made of heavy die cast aluminum. The P-200 comes without dies, powder measures, shellholder, or primer feed (optional). From Ponsness-Warren.

Metal-Matic P-200 ....**$99.00**
Primer feed **$29.95**

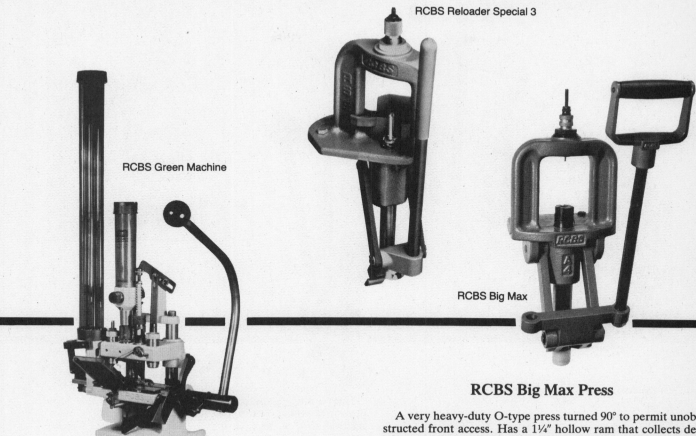

RCBS Reloader Special 3

RCBS Green Machine

RCBS Big Max

RCBS Green Machine

The four station, progressive, hand-operated tool can load 38/357 Mag., 9mm, 45 ACP, 44 Spec./44 Mag. at a rate of 600 rounds per hour. Uses standard crimper and carbide sizer dies, specially designed expander and seater dies. The seater die is the "window" type. Powder is automatically measured from the Little Dandy powder measure. Comes with automatic case feed magazine, primer feed and magazine, dies, powder measure, and dust cover. Machine is pre-adjusted for target loads at the factory. Each pull of the operating handle produces a loaded round. From RCBS.

Price, complete, about........................**$600.00**

RCBS Rock Chucker Press

Using the familiar RCBS Block "O" frame design to reduce springing and allow plenty of room to process cartridges up to the magnums, the Rock Chucker, with down-stroke compound leverage system, eases reloading chores. This 20 lb. press comes with removable "snap-action" shellholder head. From RCBS...................................**$129.00**

Rock Chucker Combo includes rifle or pistol dies (specify caliber) primer arm and primer catcher ....**$157.00** (Rifle); **$160.00** (Pistol)

RCBS Big Max Press

A very heavy-duty O-type press turned 90° to permit unobstructed front access. Has a 1¼″ hollow ram that collects decapped primers. Automatic shellholder fits nearly all cases from 22 Hornet through 458 Win. Mag. (a shellholder adapter is also included for thick or very wide rim cases). As the ram moves up, the shellholder grips, centers and locks the case in place, then releases it at the bottom of the stroke. Solid steel shovel grip mounts left or right and has a rotating walnut handle grip. Flush mounting with no linkage underswing. Frame has standard ⅞-14 thread. Press without dies.......**$233.00**

Special Duty kit includes an extra-long 24″ dual-mounted handle, blank bushing and ram adaptor blank that can be custom machined for additional tooling. From RCBS....**$41.00**

RCBS Reloader Special 3

This press has the capability to reload 12-gauge shotshells in addition to metallic rounds. Rugged "O"-frame design resists springing. Changes to up- or down-stroke in minutes—nothing extra to buy. Standard ⅞-14 dies. Ample leverage to do all reloading and case forming **$89.50**

Reloader Special-3 Combo—includes: RCBS RS-3 Press, primer catcher, removable head type shellholder, universal primer arm and one set of RCBS dies. Available in most popular calibers. From RCBS. Specify caliber ..**$111.00** (Rifle); **$114.00** (Pistol)

Reloading Starter kit—includes: RS-3 press, primer catcher, ram priming unit, Model 5-0-5 reloading scale, *Speer Reloading Manual*, case lube kit, case loading block, powder funnel and primer tray.........................**$162.00**

Shotshell die kit, 12-gauge.....................**$40.00**

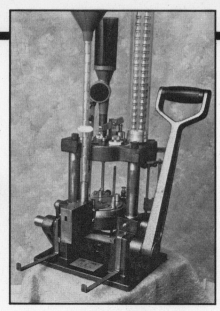

R.D.P. "The Tool"

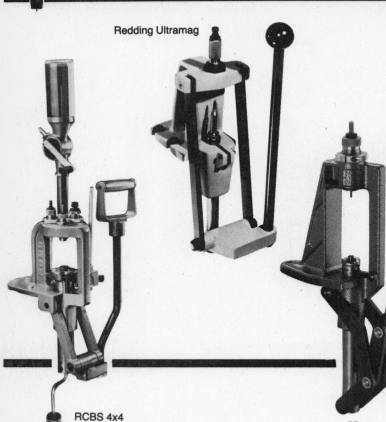

Redding Ultramag

RCBS 4x4

RCBS Partner

RCBS 4 × 4 Progressive Reloading Press

Durable, cast iron "O" frame design. Features four die stations on top and a four-cartridge shell plate on bottom. Comes with large and small primer capability, tube-type automatic primer feed and an adaptor for any ⅞-14 externally threaded powder measure. Mounts securely to the reloading bench. From RCBS.

Price: Press (less shell plate, dies and powder measure) **$303.50**
Price: Shell plate **$26.50**

RCBS Partner Press

This "O" block frame press features compound leverage and has the standard ⅞-14 thread for all RCBS reloading dies and accessories including the primer pocket swager and bullet puller. It also utilizes standard RCBS removable-type shellholders. The partner press is sold without dies and shellholder, in Standard Kit form or as a Deluxe Kit. From RCBS.

Price: Press less dies and shellholder **$45.00**
Price: Standard Kit (Press with primer arm, 505 reloading scale, case lube kit, powder funnel, primer tray, deburring tool, case loading block, *speer reloading manual*, and instructions) **$130.00**
Price: Deluxe Kit (Includes Standard Kit plus dies, shellholder *How-To-Reload* VHS video cassette, box of 100 Speer bullets and certificate for 100 CCI primers.) **$190.00-193.00**

R.D.P. "The Tool" Reloader

Heavy-duty H-type progressive loading machine that produces one loaded round for each pull of the handle. Comes ready to load in the rifle or pistol caliber of choice. Handle converts for right- or lefthand use. Accessories available include: a bullet collator that automatically feeds bullets at the rate of 2,500 per hour and automatically converts to all calibers; a case feeder that feeds all cases just by changing the feed nipple; and vacuum priming system. Lifetime warranty. From R.D.P. Tool Co., Inc.

Price: Reloading machine (Pistol) **$1,265.00**
Price: Reloading machine (Rifle plus lube die and universal powder drop die). **$1,315.00**
Price: Bullet Collator **$695.00**
Price: Case Feeder (small bowl) **$250.00**
Price: Case Feeder (large bowl) **$285.00**
Price: Vacuum Priming System **$180.00**
Price: Shell Plates **$40.00**
Price: Bullet Die and Slide. **$45.00**
Price: Bullet Tube **$40.00**
Price: Expander Plug **$13.50**
Price: Case Feed Nipple. **$15.00**

REDDING Ultramag 700 Press

A new design in reloading presses which has the compound leverage linkage system connected at the top of the frame. This allows the reloader to develop tons of pressure without springing or deflecting the press frame. Frame is of a high grade cast iron. Frame opening is 4¾″, large enough for the 50 x 3¼″ Sharps round. Ram stroke is 4⅛″. Spent primers collect in the hollow ram, emptied via a screw cap. From Redding.

Price: **$192.00**
Price: Press with shellholder, one set of dies. **$225.00**

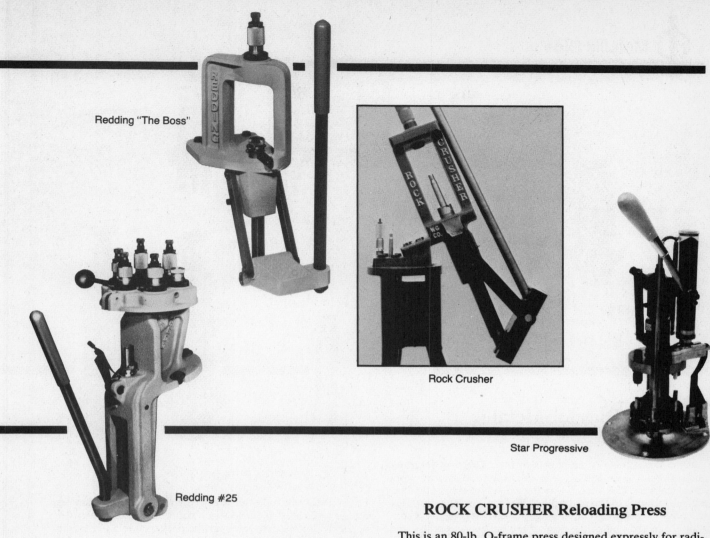

Redding "The Boss"

Rock Crusher

Redding #25

Star Progressive

REDDING "The Boss" Press

This O-type reloading press has a cast iron frame, and a large opening with 36-degree frame offset. The Boss "smart" primer arm automatically moves in and out of position with ram travel and is positioned at the bottom of ram travel for positive feel. Accepts all standard 7/8-14 threaded dies and universal shellholders. Shellholders may be rotated to any position desired. From Redding.

Price: Press only **$84.95**
Price: Kit (includes press, shellholder, choice of Series A dies) **$118.00**

REDDING No. 25 Turret Press

Machined ferrous alloy castings and toggle leverage system combine with a 6-station turret head for increased ease and speed in reloading metallic cases. Extremely rugged frame weighs 24 lbs. Progressive linkage develops 50-to-1 leverage. Ram uses standard shellholders. Turret accepts 7/8-14 dies. From Redding. Complete with 6-hole turret. **$219.95**

Kit form includes press, shellholder, and one No. 10 die set **$253.00**

Extra turrets (6 station) **$54.00**

ROCK CRUSHER Reloading Press

This is an 80-lb. O-frame press designed expressly for radical case forming and reloading ammunition up to 23mm. Has a frame opening of 8½″ x 3¼″. Develops over 20,000 lbs. ram pressure. (Ram stroke is 5¾ inches.) Uses 1½″-12 dies (bushings available to convert to 7/8-14 dies—**$25.95**). Comes with one shellholder (choice of 50 BMG, 20mm Lahti, 20mm Solothurn, 20mm Short Solothurn, or is T-slotted for standard RCBS-type snap-ins.) Press is shown with a 20 mm case in the shellholder, 30-06 case and die on the stand. From Old Western Scrounger.

Price: Press with shellholder **$650.00**
Price: Extra shellholders **$24.95**
Price: Can crusher plates (for flattening aluminum cans) **$14.95**

STAR Universal Progressive Reloader

Handles all popular handgun calibers (38 Spl. and 45 ACP parts in stock), including 30 Carb., 357 and 44 Magnums; 44 Spl., 45 Auto Rim, 45 Colt.

When ordering, specify powder charge and type, primer make, and send sample bullet. If no bullet is available, give complete description or catalog number. From Star Machine Works.

With Lifetyme Carbide Die. **$925.00**
Extra tool head for one caliber with Lifetyme Carbide Die **$345.00**
Additional charge for 30 Carbine, 9mm and 38 Super.

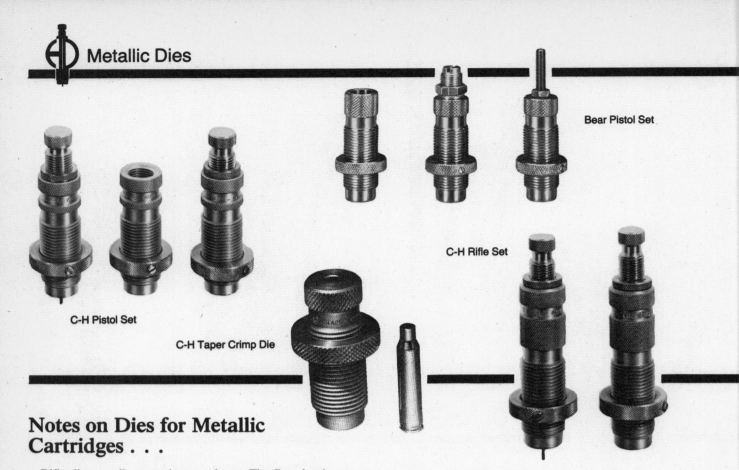

Bear Pistol Set

C-H Rifle Set

C-H Pistol Set

C-H Taper Crimp Die

Notes on Dies for Metallic Cartridges . . .

Rifle dies usually come in sets of two. The first deprimes and resizes. The second die seats the bullet and in some types also crimps the case mouth into the cannelure ring in the bullet. An example of this is the 30-30 Winchester. This cartridge is usually carried in a tubular magazine so that pressure is constantly exerted against the nose of the bullet. As a result, the bullet must be solidly crimped to keep it from pushing back into the case. Recoil can also cause the bullet to be pushed back into the case in some instances.

There are also handgun dies in sets of two that work the same as rifle dies. The seater dies of these sets is invariably a crimping die also. Nowadays, for improved load quality, many handgun die sets consist of 3 or 4 dies. In these the first die simply resizes the case. The second die deprimes and expands (bells) the mouth of the case. The third die seats and crimps the bullet. In the four-die set the third die merely seats the bullet and the fourth die crimps the case mouth into the bullet. For the best and most accurate ammunition, it is always advisable to seat the bullet in one operation, then crimp the bullet in a second operation.

For the man who reloads thousands of cases a year, a sizing die with a carbide insert is the type he needs. This ring of extremely hard tungsten carbide will resize a half-million cases before any wear shows! Ordinary steel dies won't generally, process a third this many. Furthermore, cases don't have to be cleaned when using carbide dies. Dirty cases won't scratch these dies nor will the dies scratch the cases. Instead, the cases come out highly polished.

Some dies are chrome-plated, some are not. If proper case lubrication is used there is little difference between the life of these two types of dies.

BEAR Pistol Die Set

This pistol three-die set is also for rifle cartridges having straight wall cases. It consists of a sizing die, an expander/decapper die and a seater/crimper die packaged in a plastic die box. Available either as a set or each die separately. From Bear Company.

Price: 3-die set	$15.00
Price: Size Die	$6.50
Price: Expander Die	$6.00
Price: Seating Die	$8.00

BEAR Rifle Die Set

For use with bottleneck cartridges. Available as either a two- or three-die set. The two-die set contains a size die and seat die; the three die set includes a neck die. Bear size dies are reamed to precise standards, hardened by a special carbon nitrate process and polished for smooth operation. Available in set form or as individual dies. Packaged in a sturdy plastic die box. From Bear Company.

Price: 2-die set	$15.00
Price: 3-die set	$15.00
Price: Size die	$8.00
Price: Seating die	$8.00
Price: Plastic Die Box	$2.00

BEAR Trim Die

For fast easy trimming of overall case lengths. Doubles as case gauge. Available in 41 calibers—from 219 Zipper to 350 Rem. Mag. From Bear Company $9.50

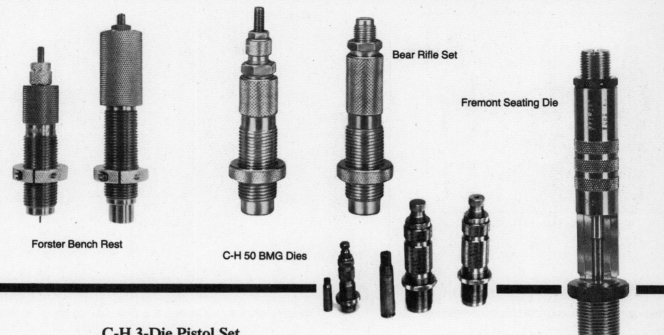

Bear Rifle Set

Fremont Seating Die

Forster Bench Rest

C-H 50 BMG Dies

C-H 3-Die Pistol Set

3-die pistol sets eliminate many of the problems resulting from non-uniform cases or instances of varying wall thickness. These sets are available for all straight walled pistol cases. All C-H dies are made of steel, heat-treated and satin finished. From C-H Tool and Die Corp.....................**$30.00**

C-H 2-Die Rifle Set

Made of chrome-plated steel with a super-hard finish, C-H dies are available for all popular cartridges. They fit all tools having a ⅞-14 thread. From C-H Tool and Die Corp. **$30.00**
3-die rifle set (includes the C-H neck sizing die) . . . **$38.40**

C-H Taper Crimp Die (Rifle)

Available in 308 Win. and 223 Rem., the C-H die allows for a uniform, tapered crimp. Eliminating time-consuming trimming, these dies are especially useful for handloading semi-auto rifle ammo. From C-H Tool and Die Corp......**$17.00**

C-H Taper Crimp Die (Pistol)

Each die is precision honed, hardened and polished to a mirror finish on the inside; the outside has a non-glare satin finish. The taper crimp die allows a uniform tapered crimp, especially useful for autoloaders that headspace off the case mouth. Available in 38/357, 9mm Luger, 45 ACP, 30 Carbine. From C-H Tool and Die Corp.....................**$14.00**

C-H 50 BMG Dies

These chrome-plated steel dies are threaded 1½-12. From C-H Tool and Die Corp. A full-length sizer die and crimp seater die are...................................**$275.00**
Sizer die only...............................**$163.59**

FREMONT Seating die

The Fremont unit is a ⅞-14 straight line bullet seating die that uses a spring-loaded, sliding sleeve to align the neck and shoulder of the case with the bullet. The cut-away into the bullet chamber allows bullet insertion directly into the sliding sleeve. These are universal dies—the 30-cal. die can be used to seat bullets in any of the 30-cal. cases (30-06, 300 Win., 308 Win. and Norma, etc.). These dies do not crimp the case. Short cases require using the Fremont extended shellholder. Calibers available are 224, 6mm, 25, 7mm and 30. From Fremont Tool Works. Price.........................**$24.50**
Extended shellholders, each **$7.50**

FORSTER/BONANZA Co-Ax Bench Rest Dies

Case is supported full length in seating die. Inner sleeve holds case and bullet concentric, while outer sleeve seats bullet. Coaxial design simulates hand-seater efficiency but functions in a press. Seating die is not hardened and does not crimp. Sizing die same as Co-Ax Die. Usable in most presses, these dies are available in most popular calibers. From Forster Products. **$46.50**

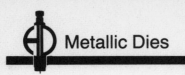

Goodwin Dies

Hart Sizing Die

Hart Seater

Hornady Tapered Expander

GOODWIN Loading & Forming Dies

These loading and forming dies are made in England by James Goodwin and are offered in many unusual calibers. Loading dies (3-die sets) are available threaded ⅞″-14 or 1¼″-12; forming dies are 1-in. unthreaded or with 1¼″-12 threads. The shellholders work with Lyman and RCBS presses. Some dies are special order only. Contact Jack First Distr. (importer) for availability and details.

Price: Loading dies, set of three, ⅞″-14 . . . . **$75.00**
Price: As above, 1¼″-12 . . . . **$108.00**
Price: Forming dies, 1″, unthreaded, each **$22.00**
Price: As above, threaded 1¼″-12, each **$36.00**
Price: Shellholders, each **$10.00**

Goodwin Die Calibers

Rifle		450 N.E. 3¼″
240 Flanged	9.5 Turkish	500-450 3¼″
26 BSA	9.5×56 Mann. Sch.	577-450 Martini Henry
6.5×48 (and Sauer)	9.5×57 Mauser	500-465 N.E.
6.5×68	375 N.E. 2½″	470 N.E. 3¼″
6.5×70	375 Flanged	475 #2 N.E. 3½″
280 Ross	38-56 Win.	476 N.E.
375-303	40-60 Win.	461 #1 Gibbs
318 Westley Richards	40-82 Win.	50-95 Win.
8mm Lebel	400 Purdey	50-110 Win.
8×57 J	450-400 2⅜″, 3, 3¼″	50-140 Win.
8×60R Portuguese	401 Win. S.L.	500 N.E. 3″
8.15×46 R	10.75×68 Mauser	500 Jeffery
32 Win. S.L.	10.75×73 Jeffery (404)	577-500 (and Mag.)
33 Win.	405 Win.	505 Gibbs
333 Jeffery	416 Rigby	577 Snider
35 Win.	10.8 Swiss	577 N.E. 3″
9×56 Mann. Sch.	425 Westley Richards	
360 N.E. 2¼″	11×52R	**Handgun**
360 #2 N.E.	43 Egyptian	7.65 MAS Pistol
9.3×64	11mm (43) Mauser	8mm Lebel Rev.
9.3×72R	45-75 Win.	450 Webley Rev.
369 Purdey	45-90 Win.	455 Webley Auto
9.5×36R	450 #1 Carbine	11.75 Montenegrin Rev.
	450 #2 Musket	

HART Bullet Seater

Designed with the precision handloader/shooter in mind, this straight line bullet seater is adjustable for depth and is available for 222, 222½, 222 Mag., 22-250, 6mm Rem. BR, 25-06, 30-338, 6x47, 6mm Rem., 22 Rem. BR, 308 Win., 7mm Mag., 22 PPC, 6mm PPC. The body, base and head are all made of stainless steel. From Robert Hart and Son . . **$34.95**

HART Sizing Die

Made of hardened steel, this die for the precision loader/shooter, is of the drive-in/drive-out type and is available in 222 Rem., 222 Mag., 6x47, 308, 25-06 and 6mm Rem. The knock-out rod decaps the case at the same time. From Robert Hart and Son. **$46.00**

HORNADY Dies

Guaranteed for life. Heavy-duty solid steel spindles with collet-type hex nuts to insure accurate alignment. Standard ⅞-14 thread with steel lock rings. Adjustable crimper. Cavities are polished after heat-treating. Packed in plastic compartmented box with sizing lube and spare decapping pin. From Hornady.

2-die rifle set . . . . **$31.50** to **$36.00**
3-die pistol set with standard sizing die **$32.50**
3-die set with carbide sizer. **$56.00**
Carbide pistol sizing die only **$38.75**

HORNADY Tapered Expander Spindle Assembly

The tapered expander is used in case-forming operations to expand case necks. Available in 22 cal.-7mm, 22-cal. -30-cal., 22-cal.-6.5mm, 30-cal. -35-cal. From Hornady. **$8.45**

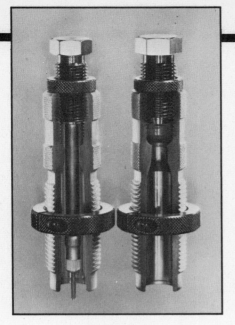

Hornady Dies

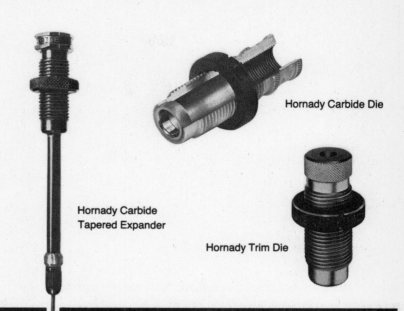

Hornady Carbide Die

Hornady Carbide
Tapered Expander

Hornady Trim Die

HORNADY Metallic Silhouette and Bench Rest Dies

Designed with the competition shooter in mind. Two (rifle) and three (pistol) steel die sets with standard ⅞"-14 threads and blued steel lock rings. Die interior heat-treated and mirror polished. Exterior hard satin chrome-plated. From Hornady...**$36.00**

Two-Die Set	7mm/223 Ingram	357/44 B&D
22 PPC	7 × 47 Helm	30 Herrett
6mm PPC	7mm Rem. BR	357 Herrett
6mm/223	7mm TCU	**Three-Die Set**
6 × 47 Rem.	7mm Merrill	44 Auto Mag.
6.5mm TCU	30 Merrill	45 Win. Mag.

HORNADY Carbide Dies

A must for the serious pistol ammo reloader. Requires little or no case lubrication. Carbide insert is concentric in the die body for alignment of case in die. Doesn't leave belt mark on case as with other TC dies. From Hornady. Three die set **$56.00**

HORNADY Taper Crimp Die

Applies the proper crimp to autoloading pistol cases. Available in 380 Auto, 9mm Luger, 45 ACP and 38/357 TC. From Hornady. **$12.70**

HORNADY Neck Size Dies

Made of steel and finished in a hard satin chrome, Hornady neck sizing dies resize only the neck of cases to be used in bolt-action rifles. Standard ⅞"-14 thread with blued steel lock rings. Interior heat-treated and polished to mirror finish. From Hornady...**$22.00**

HORNADY Carbide Expander Spindle Assemblies

Increases ease of resizing when reloading bottleneck cartridges. The carbide expander "floats" on the spindle assembly, to allow expander to center itself in the neck. Provides chatter-free neck expanding, while eliminating the need for inside-neck lubrication. Also reduces neck stretching. Fits Hornady or RCBS dies. Available from 219 Zipper through 300 Win. Mag. From Hornady. **$18.00**

HORNADY Series IV Die Sets

For dies no longer produced for inventory, Hornady will custom make dies in the calibers below. From Hornady...**$53.00**

RIFLE	6.5 Mann.	340 Wby
	6.5 Carc.	348 Win.
17/222	6.5 Jap	35 Whelen
17/223	6.5×57	350 Rem. Mag.
219 Zipper	6.5×68	358 N. Mag.
22 K Hornet	270 Wby.	378 Wby.
22 RCFM(Jet)	7×30 Waters	9.3×74R
224 Wby.	7×65R	9.3×57
22 Sav. Hi-Power	7×64	9.3×62
5.6×50 Mag.	7×61 S&H	10.3×60
5.6×52R	7.35 Carc.	460 Wby.
5.6×57	303 Sav.	
6mm Int.	300 H&H	
6mm/284	308 N. Mag.	**PISTOL**
25 Rem.	32/40 Win.	32 S&W Short
25/284	8mm/06	38 Super Auto
25/20 Win.	8×60S	38 S&W
256 Win.	8×68S	38/40 Win.
6.5/06	8.15 × 46R	44/40 Win.
6.5 Rem. Mag.	33 Win.	45 Auto Rim RN

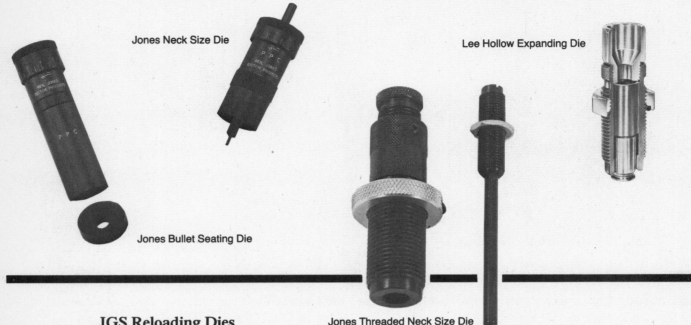

Jones Neck Size Die

Lee Hollow Expanding Die

Jones Bullet Seating Die

Jones Threaded Neck Size Die

JGS Reloading Dies

This maker can supply dies for such large calibers as 50 Russian, 50 BMG, 55 Boyes, 14.5mm Russian, 20mm Lahti, 20mm/M-103, and many other variations. The dies fit the Hollywood or new Rock Crusher presses (1½" dia. with 1-12 threads). A full-length die set includes the sizer and seater dies. From JGS Precision Tool Mfg.

Price: 50 cal. set..............................$295.00
Price: 20mm set................................$395.00

JONES Adjustable Bullet Seating Die

Bullet seating depth is critical to accuracy. With Jones straight line adjustable bullet seating die and bushings, the die can be tailored to specific chamber neck dimensions. Bushings are available in increments of .001". The adjustable cap and stem assembly on the die allows simple and accurate adjustment of bullet seating depth. The seating stem is threaded to provide .050" movement per revolution. Made of steel with black oxided finish. This die is available for all popular calibers including wildcats. From Neil Jones Custom Products $45.00

JONES Threaded Neck Sizing Die

Designed for those reloaders using a conventional reloading press. Standard ⅞" x 14 threaded die but uses interchangeable hardened steel sizing bushings. Bushings are available in increments of .001" so this die with the proper bushing will handle virtually all cartridges having the same head diameter. Expansion mandrels to open up case necks to a larger caliber are also available. From Neil Jones Custom Products.

Price: Die with decap punch (less bushing).......$30.00
Price: Expansion Mandrel $8.00
Price: Bushing $8.00

JONES Adjustable Neck Sizing Die

A neck sizing die fitted with an adjustable cap which is threaded to provide .050" of movement per revolution. The cap is precision scribed in increments allowing adjustments of .00125". Used in conjunction with Jones neck/shoulder bushings, the case neck is sized and the shoulder moved back in very precisely controlled increments. This die is available for most cartridges including wildcats. It also can be used with standard bushings and can be adjusted to size as much or as little of the case neck as desired. Made from steel with black oxide finish. The adjustable decapping punch is suitable for all calibers from 22 on up. A die base is available for use with an arbor press. From Neil Jones Custom Products.

Price: Die (less bushing).......................$37.50
Price: Standard bushing $5.00
Price: Shoulder bushing $7.00

JONES Neck Sizing Die

The unique design of this die requires no special reaming to fit the cartridge case and the polished hardened steel sizing bushings "float" laterally in the die to positively align themselves on the case neck. Sizing bushings are available in .001" increments in all popular calibers. Die body is made of light metal alloy and will not rust. The decapping pin furnished with die suitable for any caliber from 22 up, is fitted in the top of the die for positive alignment, and is retained in the top by means of a spring-loaded ball which can be tension adjusted. A die base for use with an arbor press is also available. From Neil Jones Custom Products.

Price: Die (less bushing).......................$21.00
Price: Die base.................................$7.50
Price: Die Bushing $5.00

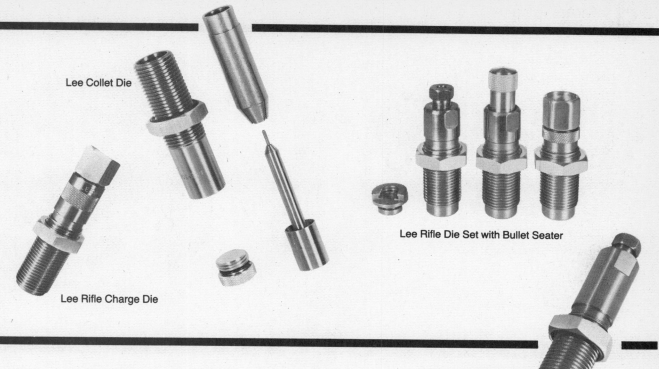

Lee Collet Die

Lee Rifle Charge Die

Lee Rifle Die Set with Bullet Seater

Lee Decapping Die

LEE Hollow Expanding Die

Designed for use with the Lee Auto-Disk powder measure, or separately. On press downstroke, the traveling plug stops to shake all powder into the case. Includes powder funnel adaptor. Calibers 30 M1 Carbine, 32 S&W Long, 32 ACP, 38 Super/38 ACP, 380 Auto, 9mm Luger, 38 Spec., 357 Mag., 41 Mag., 44 Spec., 44 Mag., 45 ACP, 45 Colt. From Lee Precision, Inc. **$10.98**

LEE Rifle Charging Die

Charge through the top of the die. Adaptor accepts Lee powder funnel or the Lee Auto-Disk Powder Measure. Fits all calibers from 22 Hornet through 308 Win. Tapered drop tube allows even large charges through the 22-caliber orfice without bridging. From Lee Precision, Inc. **$10.00**

LEE Decapping Die

One size fits all cases from 22-caliber through 375 H&H Mag. The decapper easily removes crimped-in primers. Cases need not be clean nor lubed when using this die. From Lee Precision, Inc. **$9.98**

LEE Carbide 3-Die Sets

Steel die with carbide insert for straight sided cases. Carbide is so hard and smooth that no case lubricant is needed. Includes Powder Through Expanding Die. Seater die has aluminum bullet adjuster. Calibers 32 ACP, 32 S&W Long, 38 Super & 38 ACP, 380 Auto, 9mm Luger, 38 Special, 357 Mag., 41 Mag., 44 Special, 44 Mag., 45 ACP, 45 Colt, 30 M1 Carbine. From Lee Precision, Inc. Three-die set **$34.98**
30 M1 Carbine **$43.98**
Carbide sizing die only **$20.98**

LEE 2-Die Rifle Set

Lee dies are made to close tolerances and finely polished. The floating bullet seater allows the bullet to be pressed into the case while the point is permitted to float and seek its own center. The decapper is guaranteed unbreakable for two years. Stuck cases are simply pounded out with a drift punch and hammer. Each set comes with a free shellholder, powder measure, charge table, and instructions. Available in most popular calibers. From Lee Precision, Inc. **$22.98**
30 M1 Carbine **$30.98**

LEE Collet Die

This 2-die set sizes only the neck of the case so no expanding is needed. End pressure on the die closes the collet tightly against the case neck while the decapping mandrel limits closing to just under bullet diameter. Since case does not rub against die, there is no need for lubrication and there is no case stretching. Die set also includes dead length bullet seater. The seating plug is free-floating to insure alignment. Available in all popular rifle calibers. Comes with shellholder. From Lee Precision, Inc.
Price: About **$35.00**

LYMAN Small Base Dies

This 2-die set is for loading jacketed bullets when the finished cartridge should be sized to minimum dimensions, especially in auto, pump, and lever actions. Available for 223, 243, 6mm, 25-06, 270, 7mm TCU, 7mm Rem. Mag., 30-06, 300 Win. Mag., 308. From Lyman Products. **$31.95**

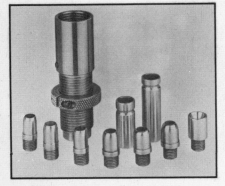

Lyman Multi-Expand/Powder Charge Die

Lyman Bench Rest

Lyman Multi-Deluxe

LYMAN T-C Pistol Die

Tungsten carbide resizing and decapping die for 38 S&W (fits 38 ACP and 38 Super); 38 Spl. (fits 357 Mag.); 41 Mag.; 44 Spl. (fits 44 Mag.); 45 ACP, 45 Colt. From Lyman Products.
Price:.. **$39.95**

LYMAN AA Bench Rest Dies

A precision made and finished 2-die set that has a neck-size-only die and a micrometer-head adjustable seating die for precise seating depth and alignment. The head gives .001″ click adjustments, .025″ per rotation. Seats with or without crimping. Available for 14 varmint and target calibers. From Lyman Products.

Complete set **$59.95**
Micrometer Seating Die only **$38.95**
Neck Sizing Die only **$20.50**

LYMAN Universal Decapping Die

Cases need not be clean nor lubed when using this die. Removes spent primers from all cases 22-cal. through 45-cal. (except 378 and 460 Weatherby). No need for readjustment when switching from one cartridge to another. Comes with a pack of 10 decapping pins. From Lyman Products..... **$9.95**

LYMAN Multi-Deluxe Die Sets

The Multi-Deluxe set has a tungsten-carbide sizing die to eliminate case lubing, a two-step neck expanding plug, and extra seating screws for loading all the popular bullet designs in a given caliber. From Lyman Products. Calibers 32 S&W Long, 380 ACP, 9mm Luger, 38 Spec./357 Mag. & Maximum, 41 Mag., 44 Mag./Spec., 45 ACP, 45 Colt. Set...... **$54.95**
Carbide sizing die only......................... **$39.95**

LYMAN Die Adaptor

This threaded steel adaptor is used to mount smaller diameter 310 and obsolete Tru-Line dies to modern ⅞-14 presses. From Lyman Products. **$3.95**

LYMAN Multi-Expand/Powder Charge Die

Designed as an accessory for the Lyman Pistol AccuMeasure or #55 Powder Measure. Simultaneously expands case mouths and drops a powder charge from attached measure. This standard ⅞-14 die can be used in certain progressive presses, all turret presses and single-station presses. The set includes the die body set and seven tubes—one Universal (non-expanding) powder drop tube and six calibrized expand/powder drop tubes for 32, 9mm, 38/357, 41, 44 and 45 Auto cartridges. From Lyman Products **$19.95**

LYMAN AA Dies

A standard 2-die set for loading jacketed bullets in bottle-necked rifle cases. Available for most calibers. A 3-die set is available for straight-wall cases for loading both cast and jacketed bullets. From Lyman Products.

3-die Multi-Deluxe pistol set (includes Tungsten Carbide sizer, 2-step neck expander and seater)............. **$54.95**
Metric 2-die rifle set **$38.95**
Standard 2-die rifle set **$31.95**
Standard 3-die rifle set, from **$38.95**
Standard 3-die pistol set, from **$32.95**
Two-step "M" neck expanding die for cast rifle bullets.. **$14.00**

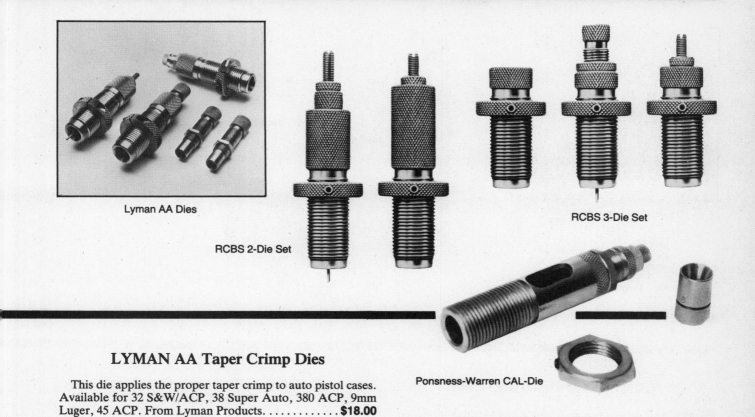

Lyman AA Dies

RCBS 2-Die Set

RCBS 3-Die Set

Ponsness-Warren CAL-Die

LYMAN AA Taper Crimp Dies

This die applies the proper taper crimp to auto pistol cases. Available for 32 S&W/ACP, 38 Super Auto, 380 ACP, 9mm Luger, 45 ACP. From Lyman Products. **$18.00**

PONSNESS-WARREN CAL-die Bullet Seater

Designed for all metallic reloading presses, the CAL-die eliminates pinched fingers and increases reloading speed by 50 percent. Requires only one die body for all bullet diameters from .224″ to .358″. To change calibers, only a different bullet retaining sleeve is required, which slips easily in the die body. The retaining sleeve holds the bullet until the case is pushed into the die and seated. The bullet is simply dropped through the side port of the die body.

The CAL-die comes with a large bullet seating pin for 30-cal. and larger, a small pin for under 30-cal., and a .308″ bullet retaining sleeve. Die body is threaded ⅞-14. Bullet retaining sleeve diameters offered. .224″, .243″, .257″, .264″, .270″, .284″, .308″, .32″, .338″, .358″. From Ponsness-Warren.
CAL-die (with 308 sleeve). **$24.95**
Additional retaining sleeves **$6.95**

RCBS Case Forming Dies

RCBS has long produced dies for forming hard-to-get cases from available brass. Prices vary, depending on the job to be done and the number of dies required. Making 22-250 cases from 30-06 brass, for instance, requires 4 dies, a reamer and an expander. Dies not cataloged will be furnished on special order. From RCBS.

RCBS Competition Dies

Designed with the competition shooter in mind. The sizing die has a hardened ball that is mounted further up on the decapping rod for easier neck expansion. Seater die is fitted with micrometer head with click adjustments in .001″ increments. Die also has a "window" with sliding guide for correct bullet alignment before and during seating. Both dies are made to extremely close tolerances and are finished in black oxide with white numerals. When necessary, an extended shellholder is included for shorter rounds. Each die set comes with a set-screw wrench, hexagonal lock rings, and packed in a fitted hardwood box. Available for: 222, 223, 22-250, 243, 270, 7mm-08, 7mm Rem. Mag., 30-06, 308. From RCBS. . **$85.00**

RCBS 2-, 3-, 4-Die Sets

RCBS dies are manufactured to close tolerances on turret lathes (not on screw machines) and hand polished before and after heat treating. Threaded ⅞-14. Decapping stems in calibers above 264 (6.5mm) are heavy-duty type. Seating dies have a built-in crimper which can be used at the operator's discretion. Special dies are available for semi-automatic rifles which require minimum-dimension cartridges for reliable functioning.

Four types of die sets are available: standard 2-die for bottle-neck rifle and handgun calibers, 3- and 4-die for handgun calibers, and a somewhat different 3-die set for straight-side rifle calibers, such as the old blackpowder numbers. From RCBS. . . . . **$33.60** to **$71.00**
3-die set with RCBS tungsten carbide sizer **$104.00**

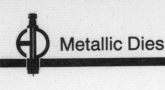

Redding Reloading Dies

Weatherby Universal
Full-Length Resizing Die

Redding Combination Dies

Redding Model #10 Crimp Die

REDDING Model #10 Die Sets

Made from alloy steels, heat-treated and hand polished. All Redding dies are lifetime guaranteed and use no aluminum or plating. Standard ⅞-14 thread. Available in 2- or 3-die rifle sets, 3- or 4-die pistol sets with taper crimp. From Redding.

Series A $34.00
Series B $41.50
Series C $49.00
Series D $56.00

Neck sizing dies are available in most bottleneck calibers. Prices will vary from $22.50 to $37.50 for the neck die only. Sets are from $34.00 with standard seater to $56.00.

Custom-made dies available on special order. Priced from $62.00 and up.

REDDING Form & Trim Dies

The Redding file trim dies are different from others. The internal dimensions are to chamber size and, therefore, do not full length resize the brass unnecessarily. Those accuracy buffs and varmint shooters who neck size their brass only will find this feature a great advantage. For case-forming, these dies perform the perfect intermediate step before final sizing in the proper full-length sizing die. From Redding.

Series A $18.95
Series B $22.95
Series C $27.50
Series D $32.00

REDDING Combination Dies

These special die sets are provided for the shooter who wants the convenience of one die set to load more than one caliber. Available in 38 Spl./357 Mag. and 44 Spl./44 Mag. Other calibers on request. From Redding. $34.00

REDDING Titanium Carbide Pistol Dies

Titanium carbide has the highest hardness of any readily available carbides, yet is not brittle. The smooth micrograins present a slippery, non-galling surface not attainable with other carbides. Available in most popular handgun calibers. From Redding.

Sizing die only $59.95
Complete set $79.95

REDDING Profile Crimp Dies

For handgun cartridges which do not headspace on the case mouth. These dies give a slightly tighter, more uniform roll-type crimp, but require bullets to be seated to the correct depth in a previous operation. In calibers 32 S&W Long, 357 Magnum, 38 Special/357 Magnum, 357 Maximum, 41 Magnum, 44 Magnum, 44 Special/44 Magnum, 45 Colt. From Redding. $19.95

REDDING Taper Crimp Dies

Made to the same high standards as all other Redding dies, then carefully heat-treated and hand polished.

Taper Crimp dies are available in most popular handgun calibers for those who prefer the uniformity of a tapered crimp to the conventional roll crimp. It is especially useful for those autoloaders that headspace off the end of the case. Standard ⅞-14 thread fits most presses. From Redding.

Most calibers $19.95
Specials $27.95

Shell Holders and Rams*

Make	Holder C	Holder H	Ram C	Ram H	Tools Fitted	Notes	Holder C	Holder H	Ram C	Ram H
C-H	X	X	X	X	Most H&C	Held by spring clip, relieved for primer clearance. Floating shell holder action.	$ 4.00	$ 4.00	$10.50	$ 5.25
Hollywood	Special				H'wood only	Order by caliber. Fit H'wood turret and standard presses. Same as C-H.		5.50 6.00		
Lee	X	X	X	X	All	Hardened steel		3.98	3.98	
Lyman	X	X	X	X	See notes	Solid H type (J) fits Lyman AA Turret and Tru-Line; C-type fits Spartan, Spar-T, Pacific, O-Mag, T-Mag, Crusher.	5.25		7.00	
McLean	Special				Most all	Universal cartridge holder.	8.00			
Hornady	X		X		Most C&O types	One-piece holder/ram also available for C tools, $6.25.	5.50			
Quinetics	X	X			Most all	Universal cartridge holder.	12.75			
RCBS	X	X	X	X	Most H&C	Heavy duty style for bullet making, A2 or C press, $4.50. Special ram required for A2, $3.60. Head extension for all rams, $3.00.	5.50	5.50	10.00	10.00
Redding	X		X		Most C types	Snap-in spring action holder. Ram price includes upper and lower links.	6.00		24.00	

*All holders are detachable-head type except as mentioned in notes.

WEATHERBY "Universal" Loading Dies

Bullet is introduced into the sliding bullet guide in the cutaway at the side of the die. This insures alignment of the bullet and cartridge case during the bullet seating operation. Visual observation also simplifies bullet seating to the proper depth. ⅞-14 thread. From Weatherby, Inc.

3-piece set (includes neck sizing sleeve) in 270, 30-06 and all Weatherby Magnum cals. except 224, 378 and 460 . . . **$55.00**

2-piece set, in 270, 30-06 and all Weatherby cals . . . **$50.00**

To neck size, a neck sizing sleeve is inserted into the bullet seating die. Not available for 224, 378 or 460 Weatherby Magnum. **$6.25**

Extra seating inserts, Weatherby calibers **$8.00**

Universal bullet seating die, complete. **$25.00**

WILSON Chamber Type Bullet Seaters

The case is aligned and supported by the chamber section from start to finish of seating, while the bullet is aligned and seated by the close-fitting plunger in the bore section. With this chamber type seater, the case is all the way "home" before any movement of the bullet takes place. From L.E. Wilson Co.

Seaters are available in all popular calibers **$35.00**

WILSON Straight Line Full Length Resizing Dies

These dies place no strain on case rim, and correct headspace is assured at all times.

As regularly furnished, dies are adjusted to produce a resized case correct for rifles of normal headspace. A die for a rifle having less or more than normal headspace can be made ($3.00 extra) if the customer will mail in several fired cases from his rifle. From L.E. Wilson Co.

Price to adjust die to a rifle having less or more than normal headspace. **$7.50**

Available in all popular calibers, including wildcats **$15.75**

WILSON Neck Sizing Die

This neck resizing die uses interchangeable bushings in sizes from .236″ to .343″ in .001″ increments in diameter. This allows a complete choice of the amount of sizing for any case neck in a given caliber regardless of the amount, if any, that has been turned off the neck to true it. The bushing does not float, but is held tightly for maximum concentricity of all parts. Available in most popular calibers. From L.E. Wilson Co. Complete with push-out rod and one bushing. . . . **$43.50**

Extra bushings. **$8.75**

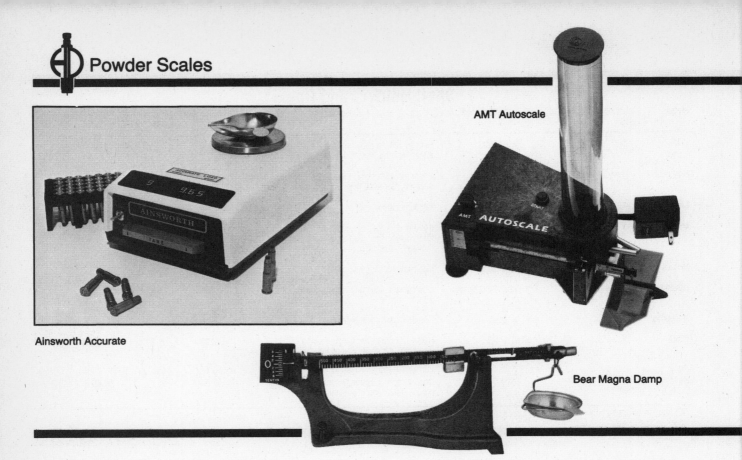

Ainsworth Accurate

AMT Autoscale

Bear Magna Damp

Notes on Powder Scales . . .

Powder scales are probably the single most important tool in the handloader's kit. So many cartridges are today loaded to near-maximum that it is important to know precisely what the powder charge is. A few grains over may cause severe damage to the firearm and to the shooter.

Powder scales vary greatly in both price and quality. Generally, you get what you pay for, but some quite inexpensive models do an adequate job. The critical parts of a scale are the knife edges and the bearing surfaces that these knife edges rest upon. They must be hardened and ground correctly, then polished. Keep them clean and free of rust, but don't use an ordinary oil. A siliconized fluid will work fine, in most cases.

It's always a good idea to keep the scale covered when it's not being used to minimize dirt and dust accumulation. Many manufacturers sell dust covers made especially for their scales.

Powder scales that have graduated beams with sliding adjustments must have these beams properly machined, calibrated and checked, otherwise incorrect readings will result. Notches should be deep enough that the sliding weights will not easily be moved by accident.

Precision weights are available so that any scale can be checked to make certain the marked weights are correct. Once this zero is known, the scales may be used with complete confidence. Most scales have leveling screws since the scales must be level or they won't give the correct reading. Treated with care, today's scales will give many years of service.

AINSWORTH Accurate Load Scale

An electronic scale for precise ammunition reloading, the Accurate load can weigh in either the gram or grain mode. Total capacity is 4,500 grains or 300 grains with sensitivity to ±0.1 or ±0.01. Has large, easy-to-read LED display that gives reading in 3 seconds. Rugged, lightweight and compact, the Accurate load comes with a standard RS-232 interface system to allow computer hook-up or printer attachment. Price includes 1,000-grain-calibration weight, dust cover and powder scoop. From Denver Instrument Co. **$549.00**

AMT Autoscale™

AMT's electronic powder scale uses opto electronics to bring precision and accuracy to the reloading bench. Photons of light sense the position of the balance arm thus eliminating any friction-caused weighing errors. Powder is dispensed through two barrels. The high-speed barrel controls rapid feeding up to 10 grains per second. The final load is controlled by the slow barrel with accuracy better than ±$\frac{1}{20}$-grain. The 9-volt transformer fits any household outlet. Speed control knob adjusts measure to feed any type of powder. From AMT. **$279.00**

BEAR Magna Damp Powder Scale

This rugged compact scale is designed to give fast accurate weighing of powder (or bullets) from $\frac{1}{10}$-grain up to 510 grains, with tenth-grain over and under scale. Magnetic dampening eliminates excessive swing of beam. Precision ground bearings and adjustable leveling screw. From Bear Company. **$20.00**

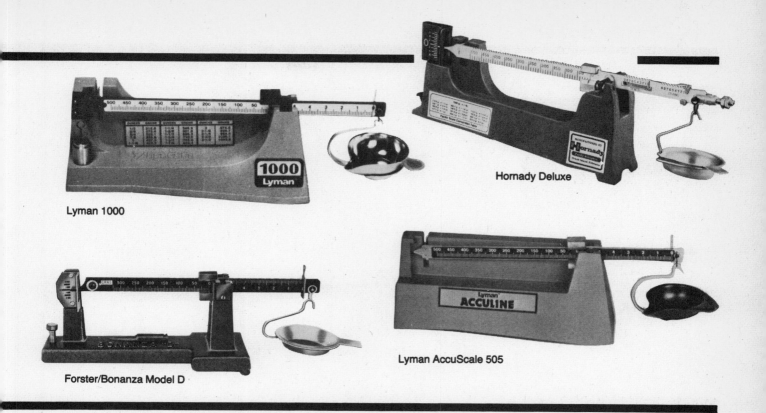

Lyman 1000

Hornady Deluxe

Forster/Bonanza Model D

Lyman AccuScale 505

C-H Powder and Bullet Scale

This scale features a chrome plated brass beam, graduated in 10 grain and $\frac{1}{10}$-grain increments. The pan has a convenient pouring spout and there is a leveling screw on the base. All metal construction. Scale has a maximum capacity of 360 grains. From C-H Tool and Die Corp. **$35.95**

FORSTER/BONANZA "Blue Ribbon" Scale

This scale has 511 grain capacity and three poises for better accuracy. Diamond polished agate "V" bearings. Base is moulded from Cycolac, beam and pan from Lexan. Base has 3-point suspension with wide-stance auxiliary leg. The minimum weight poise is located near the beam pointer so that the eyes need not be shifted during final adjustments. Center poise measurement is 10 grains; right poise 1 grain; left poise $\frac{1}{10}$ grain. Beam is dampened in three seconds. Guaranteed accurate to $\frac{1}{10}$-grain; sensitivity to $\frac{1}{20}$ grain. From Forster Products **$59.90**

FORSTER/BONANZA Model "D"

Easy to read pointer and reference point with definite divisions. New "V" agate bearings at fulcrum reduce friction and wear. The leveling screw is on the far left of the base for easy access. Beam graduations are white on a black background. Die-cast aluminum base with epoxy Bonanza-red finish, 330-grain capacity. Accuracy guaranteed to $\frac{1}{10}$-grain; sensitivity guaranteed to $\frac{1}{20}$-grain. From Forster Products **$44.00**

HORNADY Deluxe Powder Scale

A single beam balance with three counterpoises and built-in oil reservoir for damping if desired. A $\frac{1}{10}$-grain over-under scale is fitted at the pointer end of the beam to simplify sorting bullets, etc. Capacity, 500 grains. Adjustable leg for leveling. Magnetic damping system. From Hornady Mfg.
Price: Model M (grains) **$54.95**
Price: Model G (grains) **$58.25**

LYMAN Model 1000 Scale

A scale for the reloader who wants maximum capacity. Scale has a 1005-grain capacity, magnetic damping, precision-ground knife edge on agate bearings, black on white beam markings, positive pan positioning for consistent accuracy. Comes with a handy ounce-grain conversion table and protective dust cover. Accuracy to within $\frac{1}{10}$-grain. From Lyman Products. **$77.95**

LYMAN Model 500

This scale has a large 505 grain capacity with a white beam marked in black. Magnetically damped for fast readings. Precision ground knife edge agate bearings. Accuracy to within $\frac{1}{10}$ grain. From Lyman Products.
Price: Standard **$55.95**
Price: Metric **$69.95**
Price: Dust Cover **$3.95**

LYMAN Accu Scale 505

For the budget-conscious reloader. Accurate to within $\pm\frac{1}{10}$-grain. Easy to read beam markings, magnetic dampening, plus 505-grain capacity. From Lyman Products. . **$39.95**

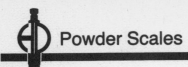
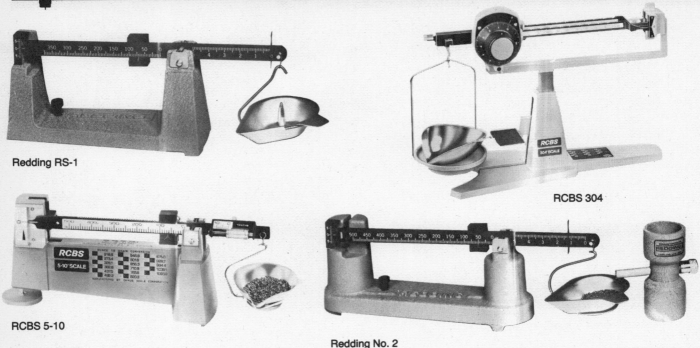

Redding RS-1

RCBS 304

RCBS 5-10

Redding No. 2

RCBS 304 Dial-O-Grain

A laboratory quality scale designed for the serious re-loader. Scale has a 1,110 grain capacity and its features include hardened steel knives and polished agate bearings, magnetic damping, oversized pan, extra-stable die cast base, and powder trickler. As in fine laboratory instruments, the dial is engraved with easy to read increment values from $1/10$ grain to 10 grains. From RCBS. **$227.00**

RCBS 5-10 Powder Scale

This 510-grain capacity scale features both a micrometer poise ($1/10$-grain to 10 grains) and approach to weight system for speed and accuracy. When the attachment weight is added to the beam, the capacity increases to 1,010 grains. Die cast base holds the scale components and converts into a dust proof carrying case. Anti-tip pan and large leveling leg. Magnetically damped and utilizes self-aligning agate bearings. From RCBS. **$79.00**
    With metric reading scale **$91.00**
    Vinyl dust cover **$4.80**

RCBS 5-0-5 Scale

This scale features a three poise system. Calibrations on the left side of the beam are in full 10 grain increments with widely spaced deep beam notches. Two small poises on the right side of the beam adjust from 0.1 to 10 grains. Scale is magnetically damped; self-aligning agate bearings support the hardened steel beam pivots with a guaranteed sensitivity of $1/10$ grain. Maximum capacity is 511 gains and the scale has an improved leveling leg for perfect zero. From RCBS. **$58.00**
    Vinyl dust cover **$4.80**

RCBS 10-10 Scale

This scale features a micrometer poise and approach to weight system for accuracy and speed. An attachment weight, stored in the leveling screw, increases capacity to 1010 grains. Pan is anti-tip design. Sensitivity is $1/10$ grain. Left side of beam is graduated in 10 grain increments, while the right side consists of 1 grain increments. The micrometer poise, which can be locked into place, divides these into 10ths. Approach to weight system alerts user to beam movement before the pointer reaches zero, thus preventing overloading. When not in use, all components can be stored in the die cast base. A hard plastic dust cover is included. An ounce to grain conversion chart for shotgun reloaders is affixed to the scale. From RCBS. **$92.50**

REDDING No. 2 Master Powder Scale

Guaranteed accurate to less than $1/10$-grain, scale has magnetic damping for fast readings. Over/under scale permits checking charge variations without moving counterpoises. Capacity is 505 grains. Blue-black beam with white graduations. Pour spout pan, stable cast base and large convenient leveling screw. Scale has hardened and honed self-aligning beam bearings for lifetime accuracy. From Redding. **$55.00**

REDDING Standard No. RS-1

Gunmetal blue-black beam is clearly graduated, has a total capacity of 380 grains. $1/10$-grain over-under scale allows checking of variations without readjustment of counterpoises.
    Self-aligning bearings hardened and honed to eliminate rubbing and side friction, built-in leveling screw. Guaranteed accurate to less than $1/10$-grain. From Redding. **$44.00**

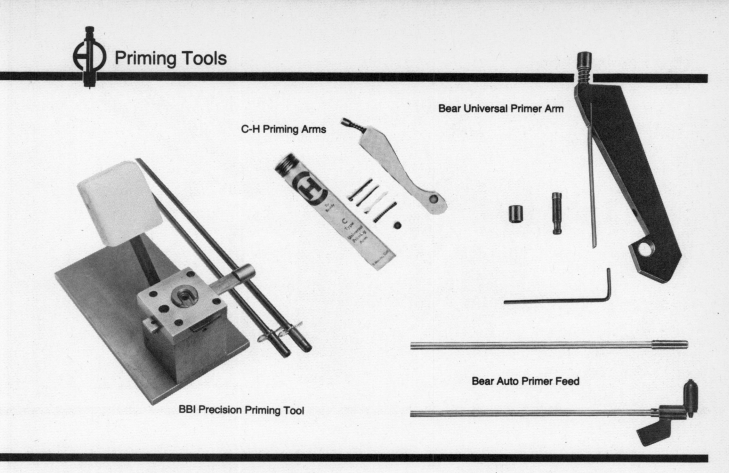

C-H Priming Arms

Bear Universal Primer Arm

Bear Auto Primer Feed

BBI Precision Priming Tool

Notes on Priming and Priming Tools . . .

Often great care is exercised in selecting uniform cases and weighing charges and bullets, but priming is done by many without much thought. Yet uniform seating of primers is essential for best accuracy. Poor alignment with the pocket can result in the pellet of priming compound being cracked as the primer is forced into place. Excessive seating pressure can produce the same result. Variation in seating depth can induce ignition and velocity errors that result in less accuracy.

All these factors can be controlled if one takes the time to do so. Priming as a separate step after resizing allows more attention to the "feel" of the primer going into the pocket. Cases in which primers enter with too much or too little pressure can then be segregated and used for plinking or other not-so-important shooting. The heavy, powerful linkages on many presses prevent one from sensitively feeling the primer enter its pocket. Use of separate priming tools, such as the Lee, RCBS, or Forster/Bonanza, is desirable for that reason.

Many priming arms and punches are said to be adjustable for seating depth. In a sense they are, but the case is supported by the front face of its rim during priming. This means that seating depth will vary as much from case to case as does the rim thickness. In rimmed cases, this dimension will vary as much as .006" to .008", and even more in some rimless and belted cartridges. Unless primer seating depth is controlled by the rear face of the case head, adjustment of the priming punch itself really doesn't accomplish much toward uniformity. A case with a thin rim will usually have a shallowly seated primer, while a thick rim will produce a deeply seated one.

We now have sensitive priming tools that lock the case firmly, allowing uniform primer seating if primer pockets are of equal depth.

BBI Precision Priming Tool

An improved and modified Shoffstall design that uses RCBS shellholders with precision sleeves. Primer size can be changed quickly. Features a Delrin handle, seating-depth adjustment, large and small primer feed tubes and seating punches. Made of machined steel and anodized aluminum. From Beal's Bullets, Inc. **$198.50**

BEAR Auto-Primer Feed

For "C" type presses. Automatically feeds primers into primer arm. Comes with large and small primer tubes. From Bear Company. **$11.00**

BEAR Universal Primer Arm

For fast accurate seating of primers. The flat return spring helps prevent primers from jamming and clogging the action of the Bear Universal Primer Arm. Constructed of durable high grade blue steel and equipped with large and small seating punches and cups. From Bear Company. **$4.00**

C-H Auto Primer Feed

This Automatic Primer Feeder will fit all C-H H-type presses with the priming post at the left-hand station. Will not fit the C-H Magnum "H" press. Easy to install and makes primer feeding a snap. From C-H Tool and Die Corp. For large or small primers **$29.95**
Extra primer stud............................. **$2.65**
Extra primer tube **$3.90**
Extra primer slide **$6.00**

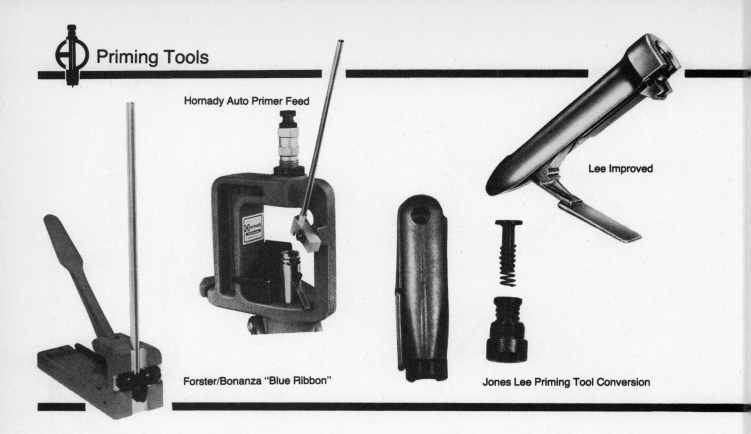

Hornady Auto Primer Feed

Lee Improved

Forster/Bonanza "Blue Ribbon"

Jones Lee Priming Tool Conversion

C-H Universal Primer Arms

Furnished with four seating punches, springs, etc., everything needed to seat all metallic case primers. For most C-type presses. From C-H Tool and Die Corp. **$6.95**
For Model 444 press **$2.40**

FORSTER/BONANZA "Blue Ribbon" Co-Ax Primer Seater

This automatic primer seater has its own built-in primer flipper and loading tray. Primers are seated flat and coaxially with the cartridge case. Primer tube holds 40 primers. Tool's jaws grip the case extractor groove with zero tolerance for precise primer seating. Jaws will work on most Boxer-primed rifle and pistol cases having a rim thickness of .050″ to .072″. They will not work on 45 Auto Rim. For large or small primers. From Forster Products...................... **$45.00**

HOLLYWOOD Priming Arm Special

For use with Hollywood Senior and Senior Turret tools with the universal shellholder and button. Can also be used with the shellholder extension. From Hollywood Loading Tools. **$15.00**

HOLLYWOOD Automatic Primer

This automatic priming accessory fits Hollywood Senior and Senior Turret tools. Allows continuous priming of cases. Requires use of the adapter. From Hollywood Loading Tools.
Price: Automatic Primer...................... **$29.95**
Price: Adapter for above **$14.95**
Price: Automatic Primer and Adapter **$39.95**

HORNADY Automatic Primer Feed

Attaches to Hornady 00-7 or 0-7 press and makes case priming automatic. It comes complete with large and small primer tubes. From Hornady. **$14.95**
Price: Extra Primer Tubes **$6.50**

JONES Lee Priming Tool Conversion

For serious reloaders and accuracy minded shooters, seating primers by feel with a low leverage tool is an improvement over seating primers with a conventional reloading press. This Lee Conversion provides the reloader with a priming tool specially adapted to that operation. The original punch has been replaced with a double punch, with the larger of the two supporting and squaring the entire base of the cartridge in the shellholder assuring the primer will be seated straight. The punch assembly is made of hardened tool steel and is available in two sizes—small rifle and large rifle. A modified shellholder is required and Jones stocks these for common benchrest, varmint and hunting cartridges or can modify one for the reloader. From Neil Jones Custom Products.
Price: Complete for one size cartridge **$30.00**
Price: Large Punch Assembly **$13.50**
Price: Small Punch Assembly.................. **$13.50**
Price: Modified Shellholder **$6.00**
Price: Custom Modification of Shellholder **$2.00**

LEE Progressive 1000 Priming Attachment

The Progressive 1000 Priming Attachment kit is required if the Shell Plate Carrier is being converted to another primer size. The kit contains large and small primer troughs, springs, punches and a tray with cover. From Lee Precision, Inc. **$10.00**

MRC Unitized Tool

Lee Auto Prime II

Lyman AccuLine Ram Prime

Lee Ram Prime

Lee Auto Prime

LEE Auto-Prime

A fast, safe and accurate priming tool that automatically feeds and installs primers as fast as you can place shells in the holder. Thumb pressure allows the reloader to feel primers being seated. Built-in primer flipper turns them right side up. Dump primers in the tray, shake, and replace the cover and it's ready to work. Interchangeable shellholders available for most popular calibers. From Lee Precision, Inc. **$14.98**
Shellholders **$3.98**

LEE Improved Priming Tool

Thumb pressure seats the primer with a "feel." Small enough to be pocketable, yet delivers primer seating qualities sought by precision shooters. Same tool as the Auto-Prime except without the automatic feed. From Lee Precision, Inc.. **$8.98**
Additional shellholders........................ **$3.98**

LEE Auto Prime II

Uses standard shellholders and will fit any brand of loading press with a vertical ram. Primes on the upstroke. Includes primer feeders and punches for large and small primers. Primer tray detaches for filling and serves as a primer flipper. Open feed trough to vent an accidental discharge and a drain to sift primer dust through the die. From Lee Precision, Inc. **$15.98**

LEE Ram Prime

Fits all brands of presses and is supplied with the Lee 2001 Challenger Kit. Primes on the press upstroke for more positive feel. Includes punches for both large and small primers. From Lee Precision, Inc. **$11.98**

LYMAN AccuLine Ram Prime System

An accessory for the the AccuLine press, it mounts in the die station for one-at-a-time primer seating. Can be used on any press threaded for $7/8''$ x 14 reloading dies. Comes with large and small primer punches. From Lyman Products... **$10.95**

LYMAN Auto Primer Feed

For all current Lyman presses. Does away with individual handling of primers. Comes with tubes for large and small primers. From Lyman Products. **$15.50**

MRC Unitized Priming Tool

Made of strong flex nylon, this hand-operated tool is made with an integral shellholder. The low cost makes it practical for each caliber to be loaded. Available for most popular calibers. From Mequon Reloading Corp. **$6.48**

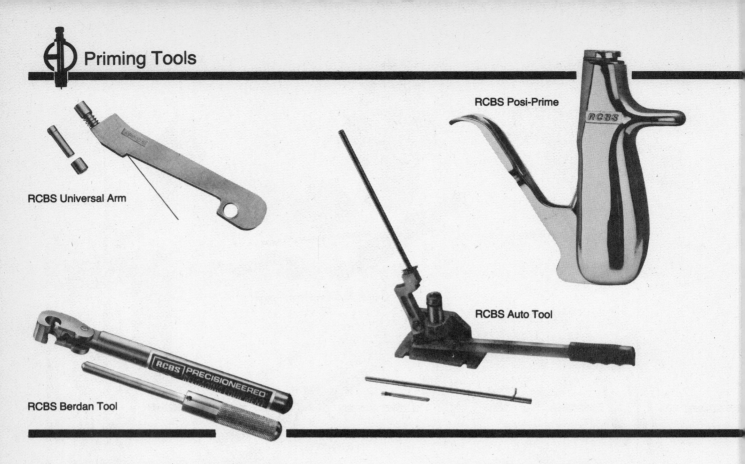

RCBS Universal Arm

RCBS Posi-Prime

RCBS Auto Tool

RCBS Berdan Tool

PONSNESS-WARREN P-200 Primer Feed

Designed for the P/W Metal-Matic straight-wall case loader, this primer feed will fit the ⅞-14 threads of the die head. Handles both large and small primers, and has a shielded tube protector. Fits all existing P-200's. From Ponsness-Warren. **$29.95**

RCBS Posi-Prime Priming Tool

Compact hand-held tool that seats one primer at a time. Primer plugs and sleeves for large and small primers are provided. Accepts all 32 standard RCBS shellholders. From RCBS. **$15.00**

RCBS Standard Priming Tool

This tool is cam operated for sensitive "feel." Tells you when primers are properly seated to the bottom of the pocket. Two primer rod assemblies are furnished to handle all American-made Boxer-type primers. Will accept most popular shellholders. Tool attaches to bench with bolts or a C clamp. From RCBS. Tool, less shellholder **$34.00**

RCBS Universal Primer Arm

Designed for use with RCBS Jr and most "C" type presses. Interchangeable primer plugs and sleeves fit all sizes of primers. From RCBS. **$8.40**
Primer plug and sleeve **$2.50**

RCBS Auto Priming Tool

The single stage leverage system gives user plenty of "feel" when seating primers. Tool permits a visual check of each primer pocket before seating the primer. Primers are fed through the RCBS automatic primer feed. Primer rod assemblies furnished with tool all use large and small rifle and pistol primers. From RCBS. Tool, less shellholder........ **$54.50**

RCBS LACHMILLER Berdan Depriming Tool

Handles a wide range of Berdan primed cases, such as the 8mm Rimless, 6.5mm Mannlicher-Schoenauer, and 11.7mm Rimmed. Offers a dry method of removing about 200 Berdan primers per hour. Comes with instructions. Available from RCBS **$32.50**

RCBS Positive Ram Priming Unit

Standard equipment on the Big Max and Reloader Special-2 presses and can be used on any press with ⅞-14 thread and RCBS-type removable shell holder. Priming is accomplished at the top of the press stroke. Primers can also be seated to a pre-set positive stop. Large and small primer rod assemblies supplied. From RCBS. **$13.70**

RCBS Auto Primer Feed

Feeds primers one at a time into the sleeve of the primer arm. Designed for use with RCBS Jr. press but will work on most C-type presses. Furnished with tubes for both large and small size primers. From RCBS. **$17.50**

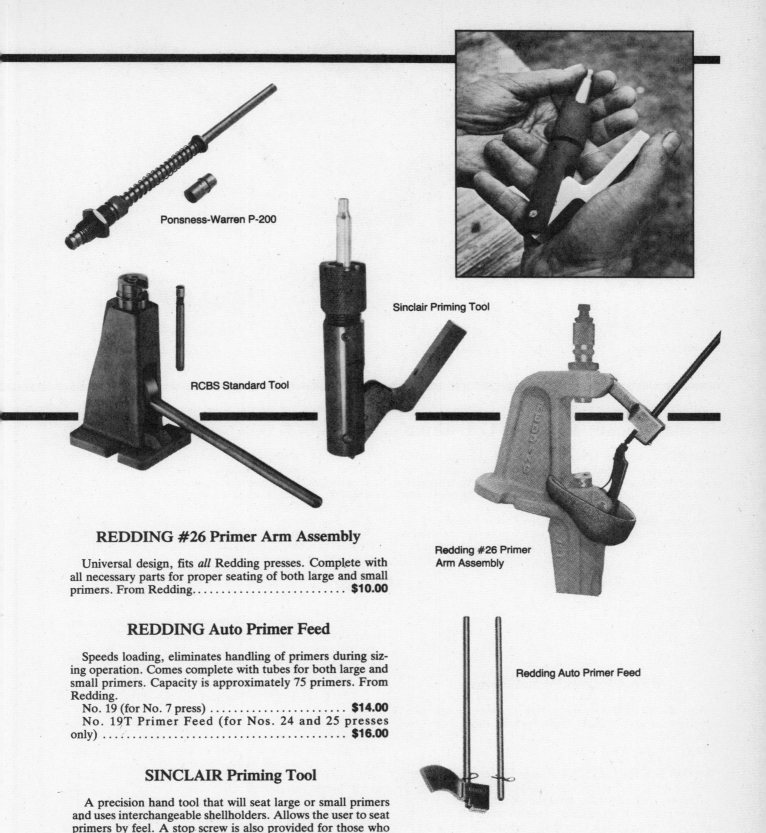

Ponsness-Warren P-200

RCBS Standard Tool

Sinclair Priming Tool

REDDING #26 Primer Arm Assembly

Universal design, fits *all* Redding presses. Complete with all necessary parts for proper seating of both large and small primers. From Redding.......................... **$10.00**

Redding #26 Primer Arm Assembly

REDDING Auto Primer Feed

Speeds loading, eliminates handling of primers during sizing operation. Comes complete with tubes for both large and small primers. Capacity is approximately 75 primers. From Redding.
No. 19 (for No. 7 press) **$14.00**
No. 19T Primer Feed (for Nos. 24 and 25 presses only) **$16.00**

Redding Auto Primer Feed

SINCLAIR Priming Tool

A precision hand tool that will seat large or small primers and uses interchangeable shellholders. Allows the user to seat primers by feel. A stop screw is also provided for those who wish to seat primers to a pre-determined depth. Made of steel, hard coat anodized aluminum all wear points are heat treated. Turning the tool head 90 degrees holds the case to the shellholder before the primer is started into the pocket. From Sinclair Int., Inc.................................... **$72.50**
Shellholders, each. **$2.50**

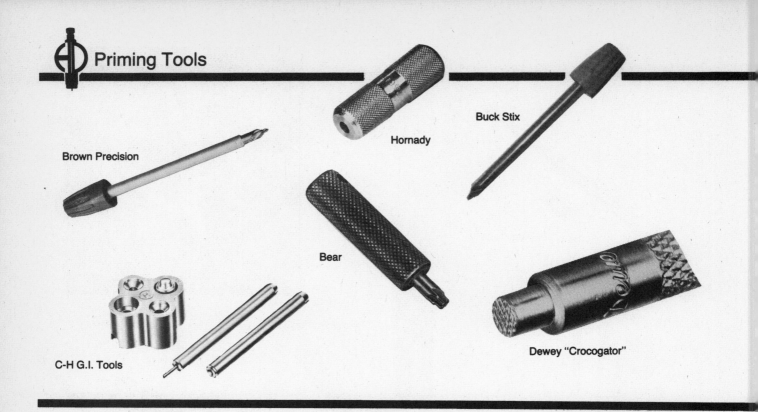

Brown Precision

Hornady

Buck Stix

Bear

C-H G.I. Tools

Dewey "Crocogator"

Primer Pocket Tools for G.I. Brass

All G.I. brass, even newly manufactured, is made with the primers heavily crimped-in. Because ordinary decapping pins may bend or break under the strain of removing such primers, extra sturdy "punch and base" sets are available from several tool makers.

Because these G.I.-brass tools are fast and handy, many shooters use them in preference to other decapping means. Primer pockets, for one thing, are easily inspected, cleaned or gauged.

BEAR Primer Pocket Reamer

A hand-held tool for scraping residue from primer pockets. Available for large or small primer pockets. From Bear Company **$4.75**

BROWN PRECISION Flash Hole Uniformer

A necessary tool for benchrest shooters, it is designed to chamfer the inside flash hole of match cases for round-to-round uniformity. The tool is quick and easy to use. All you need are the tool and fired cases with the spent primer still in place. Simply insert the pointed end through the case neck until it goes into the flash hole, then rotate it until it stops cutting.

Small Flash Hole Uniformer (22-cal. and larger) . **$11.50**
Large Uniformer (7mm and up) **$11.50**

BUCK STIX Flash Hole Tool

This simple, hand-held tool removes the burr around the flash hole and opens up undersize flash holes to make them uniform in size. Has a precision-ground tool steel head that is replaceable. Fits cases from 22 cal. through 460 Weatherby Magnum. From BUCK STIX.

Price: Standard tool. **$10.95**
Price: Replacement cutter **$3.54**
Price: PPC tool. **$10.95**
Price: PPC replacement cutter. **$3.54**

C-H Primer Pocket Reamer

Quickly and easily removes the crimp from military cases. A slight twist on the top edge of the pocket is all that is necessary. Available in either small or large size (specify). From C-H Tool and Die Corp. Price, each. **$4.50**

C-H Primer Pocket Swage Die

Removes the crimp from any military case. Use with any reloading tool and standard shellholder to swage large and small primer pockets. Comes complete for large and small pockets. From C-H Tool and Die Corp.

Shellholder **$4.00**
Extra swage punch. **$4.50**
Shell holder clip . . . . **$.40**

C-H G.I. Decapper/Swager

Does good job of decapping and primer pocket swaging of G.I. cases. Two positions; one for decapping and the other for swaging the crimp from the primer pocket. Large primer size only. From C-H Tool and Die Corp. **$7.00**

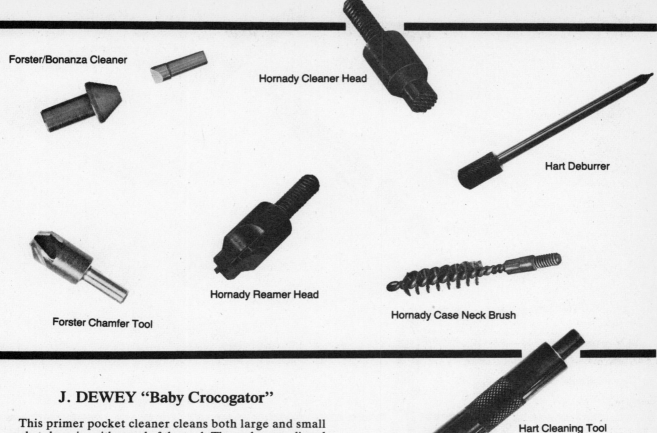

Forster/Bonanza Cleaner

Hornady Cleaner Head

Hart Deburrer

Forster Chamfer Tool

Hornady Reamer Head

Hornady Case Neck Brush

Hart Cleaning Tool

J. DEWEY "Baby Crocogator"

This primer pocket cleaner cleans both large and small pockets by using either end of the tool. The ends are radiused to conform to pocket contours. Small diamond-shaped teeth assure proper cleaning. Made from hardened steel. From J. Dewey Mfg. Co. **$2.95**

FORSTER Chamfering Primer Pocket Tool

Will remove most, if not all, of the crimp in military brass, making it easy to seat new primers. Can be used with either Forster case trimmer. Price includes center. From Forster Products... **$12.90**
Chamfering tool only **$9.90**

FORSTER Primer Pocket Cleaner

A scraper-type tool that mounts on the cutter bar of the Precision Case Trimmer to remove powder residue quickly and easily without removing any metal. Available in .210 or .175 size, with center. From Forster Products. **$7.50**
Extra cleaner **$4.50**

FORSTER Decapping Tool

This replacement decapping assembly fits most popular 3-piece die sets. A spring loaded, tool steel pin allows the decapper to center itself before the full force of the press is in contact with the primer. Simply replace the existing assembly and lock ring with this unit. From Forster Products.
Model A—½-20 thread, Redding dies
Model B—9/16-18 thread, Lyman, C-H, pre-1982 RCBS
Model C—7/16-27 thread, Lifetyme (Star Machine)
Price: **$19.50**
Price: Extra pins....... .... **$1.00**
Price: Adapter **$4.00**

HART Case Flash Hole Deburring Tool

A hand-held deburring tool for removing the burr of metal around the primer flash hole. Comes in two sizes — one standard for all cases and a special smaller version for the PPC cartridge which has a smaller than normal flash hole. From Robt. W. Hart & Sons, Inc. **$10.20**

HART Primer Pocket Cleaner

Suitable for both large and small rifle primer pockets, the Hart Primer Pocket Cleaner will clean out powder residues easily and quickly. From Robt. W. Hart & Sons, Inc. **$6.25**

HORNADY Universal Handle

This tool is made of polished, knurled aluminum and threaded to accept Hornady's case neck brushes, primer pocket cleaners, and primer pocket reamers. Brushes are available in calibers from 17 through 45. From Hornady Mfg.
Handle alone **$2.00**
Handle and primer pocket cleaner brush **$5.00**
Handle and primer pocket reamer tip.............. **$7.00**
Case neck brushes, each........................ **$1.25**
Large Primer Pocket Cleaner Head **$3.50**
Small Primer Pocket Cleaner Head **$3.50**

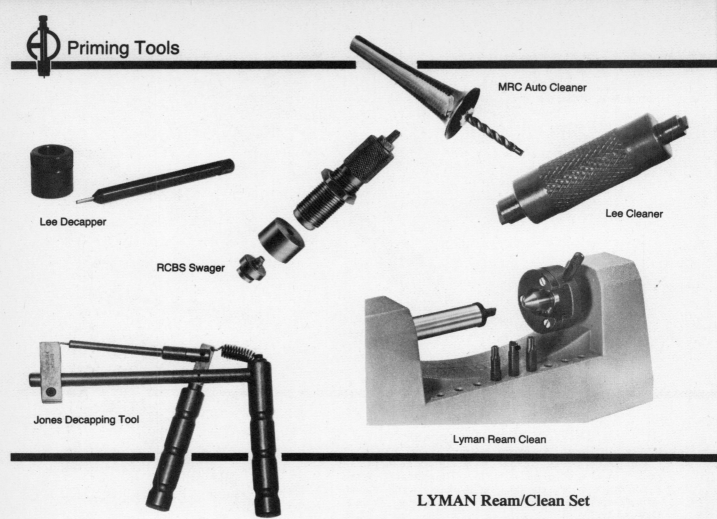

MRC Auto Cleaner

Lee Decapper

RCBS Swager

Lee Cleaner

Jones Decapping Tool

Lyman Ream Clean

JONES Decapping Tool

For reloaders who decap their cases in a separate operation, this tool is said to be faster than using a punch and base set. The shellholder head is reversible to take either .378 or ".473" case heads. The decapping mandrels screw off and standard mandrels for 22-cal., 6mm, 7mm and 30-cal. are available. Mandrels for other calibers available on request. From Jones Custom Products.

Price: Decapping Tool complete for one caliber... **$25.00**
Price: Extra standard decapping mandrels......... **$6.00**
Price: Mandrels for other calibers **$7.00**
Price: Shellholder............................... **$8.00**

LEE Decapper and Base

For removing crimped-in primers from G.I. brass, this tool is guaranteed unbreakable. A simple yet efficient unit that is necessary for working with this type of brass. From Lee Precision, Inc.. **$3.68**

LEE Primer Pocket Cleaner

Hand-held tool for scraping residue from the primer pocket without damaging the pocket or flash hole. Available for either large or small primers. From Lee Precision, Inc........ **$1.48**

LYMAN Ream/Clean Set

Designed for use with Lyman's Universal Trimmer, this set can be used to ream the primer pocket crimp from military brass, and to remove primer residue from all cases. Set contains large and small reamers, large and small primer pocket cleaners, chuck head adaptor for case mouths up to 45 caliber, and a reamer/cleaner shaft adapter. From Lyman Products... **$12.50**

LYMAN Primer Pocket Reamer

Hand-held with a wooden handle that removes crimp burr and carbon deposits from G.I. 45, 38, or 30-cal. cases. Specify large or small primer. From Lyman Products. **$7.95**

LYMAN Primer Pocket Cleaner

Cleans fouling out of the primer pocket bottom with a scraping action. Available in large and small sizes. Wooden handle. From Lyman Products **$7.95**

MRC/Automatic Primer Pocket Cleaner

A fast and easy method of cleaning the primer pocket and flash hole without damaging them. One quick push does the job in the same fashion as a "Yankee" screwdriver. Available for large and small primers (specify). From Mequon Reloading Corp... **$3.98**

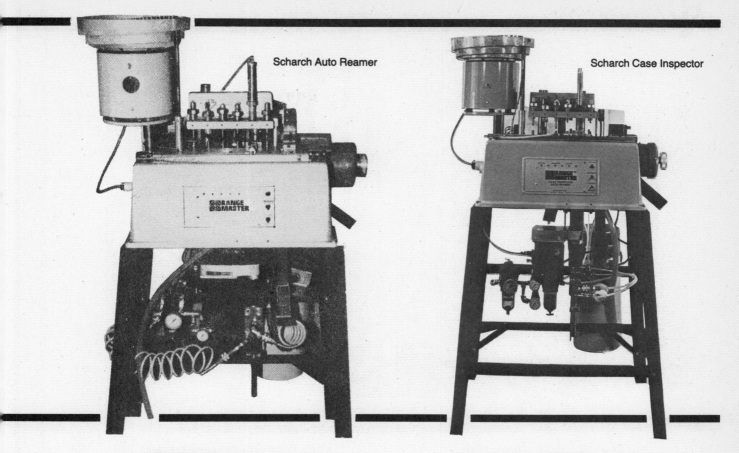

Scharch Auto Reamer

Scharch Case Inspector

MRC Primer Pocket Cleaner

This small, hand-held tool is for scraping residue from the primer pocket without damaging the pocket or flash hole. Available for either large or small primers. From Mequon Reloading Corp. **$1.48**

MRC G.I. Decapper and Base

A two-piece tool used for removing crimped primers from G.I. brass. Carries a 2 year limited warranty. This basic tool will prevent breaking conventional decapping pins. From Mequon Reloading Corp. **$3.98**

RCBS Primer Pocket Swager

Designed for use in presses accepting 7/8-14 dies and removable shellholder heads. Removes the crimp found in G.I. brass; for either large or small primers. From RCBS. **$20.00**
A-2 case stripper washer (extra) **$1.20**

RCBS Primer Pocket Brush

A twist of this tool throughly cleans out the primer pockets. Interchangeable stainless steel brushes, for large and small primer pockets. Attaches easily to accessory handle. From RCBS.
Complete Combo **$10.50**
Brush only, Large or Small **$4.80**

R.D.P. Primer Pocket Reamer

Motor-operated primer reamer that removes military crimps without loosening or distorting the primer pocket. Adjustable for all calibers. Production rate limited only by the operator. From R.D.P. Co., Inc. **$160.00**

SCHARCH MANUFACTURING Range Master™ Case Inspector Auto Reamer

Available for 38/357, 9mm/380 or 45ACP brass, this machine is a high-production case inspector to process military crimp brass. Operating on 110 VAC, the RangeMaster cycles 5100 cases per hour. It allows for two different types of operations: inspecting and reaming military brass or, with the reamer shut down, inspecting commercial brass — functioning exactly as the standard Range Master Case Inspector. The reaming tool gives a perfect ream finish. It full-length resizes the primer pocket and cuts the correct radius at the opening of the pocket. All Berdan and aluminum cases are detected and rejected automatically. In the event of a jam-up or shuttling problem, the machine shuts itself off preventing damage to working parts. 100 percent self-contained, it comes with its own 150 PSI vacuum and auto case feeder. From Scharch Mfg. Inc.
Price: Case Inspector **$5495.00**
Case Inspector Auto Reamer
Price: 38/357 . . . . **$8760.00**
Price: 9 mm/380 . . . . **$9260.00**
Price: 45 ACP **$9260.00**

Sinclair Cleaner

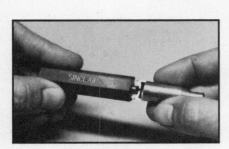
Sinclair Uniformer

Wilson Cleaner

Wilson Reamer

Wilson Punch and Base Set

SINCLAIR Primer Pocket Uniformer

This hand-held Culver-type primer pocket uniformer will cut all primer pockets to a uniform depth and, at the same time, square the primer seating surface with the case head. This allows the primer to be seated to a uniform depth with the anvil resting properly on a flat surface. The tool is fitted with specially ground tool steel cutters for both large and small primer pockets and is fully adjustable for trim length and cutting depth. From Sinclair Int., Inc. **$18.85**
Extra cutters................................. **$5.75**

SINCLAIR Primer Pocket Cleaner

A scraper-type primer pocket cleaner with serrated blades. Cleans both small and large pockets of primer residue. Made of hex stock so it won't roll off the bench. From Sinclair Int., Inc.. **$5.00**

WILSON Punch and Base Sets

The punch, an insert with spherical end, is made of SAE 50100 steel heat-treated to Rc 60-64 for maximum strength. The case-hardened base, recessed at the top to support the case head, is counterbored at the bottom to collect the driven-out primers. Punches and bases available in nearly all popular calibers. From L.E. Wilson Co. **$6.25**
Punch only **$4.35**
Base only....................................... **$1.90**

WILSON Primer Pocket Reamer

Designed for use in the Wilson Case Trimmer, the trimmer acts as a jig for obtaining correct alignment between cartridge case and reamer, and provides firm support during reaming.

By the time the reamer contacts the bottom of the pocket, the outside corner is rounded for easy insertion of the new primer. Since the reamer stops cutting when it hits the bottom of the pocket (no pounding or forcing is used), the flash hole is undamaged and the smooth, neat, properly shaped primer hole insures correct seating of primers. Case trimmer is not included. From L.E. Wilson Co. Reamer and handle only. **$13.50**
Reaming device complete for most rifle calibers .. **$28.80**
Pistol calibers **$30.25**

> **The product prices mentioned in these catalog pages were correct at presstime, but may be higher when you read this.**

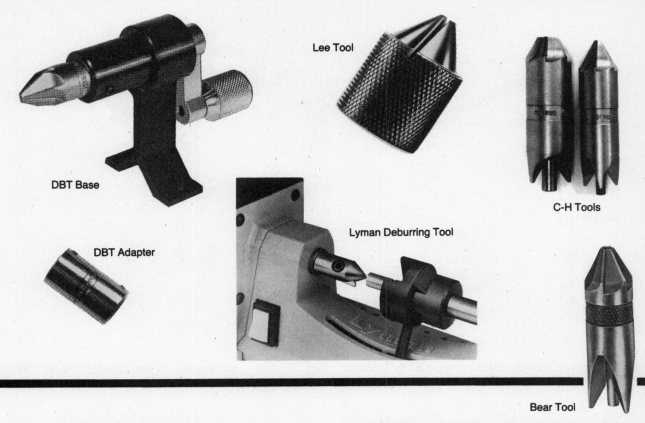

DBT Base

Lee Tool

C-H Tools

DBT Adapter

Lyman Deburring Tool

Bear Tool

Notes on Chamfering Tools . . .

A case after trimming often shows a burred or roughened mouth, both inside and out. Chamfering tools remove these burrs and also cone the inside of the mouth, making for easier bullet seating. Many handloaders chamfer the inside of their untrimmed cases for the latter reason.

The tools mentioned here are all of hardened steel, precision ground to give clean cutting without chattering. They are knurled or relieved for easy gripping and most have a center pin to keep the case aligned during outside deburring. All sporting caliber cases can be processed with these tools. For best results, apply only light pressure; these are not designed to shorten cases materially, but to smooth them.

Some tools have tungsten carbide cutting surfaces for lifetime use, accounting for a higher price. However, it's unlikely that the average reloader will ever wear out any of these tools, no matter how inexpensive.

CHAMFERING Tools

C-H	$8.95
Forster	$9.90
Lee	$2.48
Lyman	$7.95
Hornady	$9.00
RCBS	$11.20
Wilson (17-45 cal.)	$7.00

BEAR Chamfering and Deburring Tool

Eases bullet seating by lightly beveling and smoothing case mouths. An easy-to-use hand-held tool. From Bear Company. **$7.50**

C-H Magnum Deburring Tool

For those who load 45-caliber and larger calibers, this hand-held tool fits all cases from 45 to 60. Shown with a standard-size tool for comparison. From C-H Tool and Die Corp. **$14.95**

LYMAN Deburring Tool

Bevels and removes burrs from both inside and outside of the case mouth. Precision machined and hardened, it fits all cases from 17 to 45 caliber. Knurled for easy gripping. From Lyman Products. **$10.95**

Sinclair Deburring Tool

RCBS Tool

Forster/Bonanza

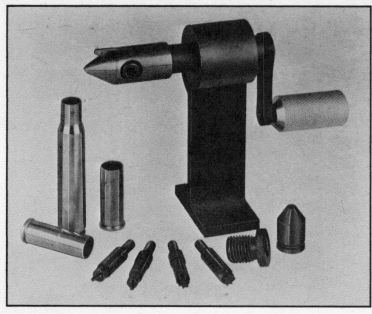

Lyman Case Care Kit

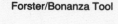

Forster/Bonanza Tool

LYMAN Chamfer/Debur Tool

This tool can be used with all Lyman case trimmers as well as the Pedestal Crank. It adjusts to fit case mouths from 17-45 cal. Simultaneously chamfers and deburs trimmed cases. From Lyman Products **$10.00**

MRC Chamfer Tool

Easy to use hand-held tool used to chamfer the case mouth. Replaceable cutter blades. Comes with one blade. From Mequon Reloading Corp. **$3.48**
Replacement blades, for 3 .... **$1.48**

RCBS Deburring Tool

For beveling and removing burrs from case mouths of new factory cases or newly formed and trimmed cases. To bevel, insert pointed end of tool into case mouth and twist slightly. To remove burrs, place other end of tool over case mouth and twist. Precision machined and hardened. For 17 to 45 calibers. From RCBS. **$11.20**

SINCLAIR Deluxe Deburring Tool

The Sinclair Deburring Tool removes the burr of metal around the primer flash hole inside the case. This allows the primer flash to more uniformly ignite the powder charge. The tool is fitted with a shouldered stop to regulate cutting depth for all calibers. A special version is available for the PPC cartridge which has a smaller-than-normal flash hole. From Sinclair Int., Inc. **$13.00**
PPC version **$12.50**

MRC Chamfer Tool

WILSON Burring Tool

This burring tool is knurled to allow a good grip and has a locator pin that keeps the case in position while the outside is burred. (Other end chamfers the inside of the case mouth.) It services cases from 17 to 45 cal. From L.E. Wilson Co.   **$8.00**

C-H Die Lube

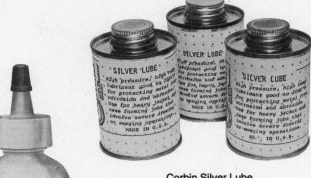

Corbin Silver Lube

Bear Case Lube

Corbin Swage Lube

Notes on Case and Die Lubricants . . .

It is practically impossible to resize fired cases full length without proper lubrication. Some of the smaller handgun calibers may work all right that way, but even there you are courting a stuck case and short die life unless you use carbide dies—these will handle even dirty cases! To do the job properly, the lubricant must have a high film strength under pressure. Ordinary oils and greases do not work well. More than one stuck case has resulted from the use of the family can of oil.

Many commercial sizing lubricants do a fine job. Today, virtually all reloading tool manufacturers offer one under their own trade name at a reasonable price. Probably oldest in use and still one of the best is common anhydrous lanolin, available from many local drugstores. Green soap also works well, as do most soaps, colored or not!

Whatever lube is used, it must be applied sparingly. Any excess is forced to collect between case and die, and it may form unsightly dents in the case. Harmless unless very large, the dents are a sign of sloppy work.

BEAR Case Lube Pad

Bear case lube pad makes lubricating fast and easy and helps eliminate dents caused by excessive lubing. From Bear Company. **$5.00**

BEAR Case Lubricant

Bear's special formula helps reduce wear and tear on dies and eliminates stuck cases. The 2-oz. plastic bottle is unbreakable and has handy spout tip. From Bear Company. . . . **$1.00**

C-H Die Lube

A liquid designed for lubricating dies and full length case sizing. 2-oz. poly bottle. From C-H Tool and Die Corp. **$1.75**

CORBIN Swage Lube

High film-strength under pressure and high diesel ignition point plus rust-inhibiting qualities. Used for forming bullets, drawing jackets and case sizing. Swage Lube forms a film that protects the diamond-lapped surfaces of bullet swage dies and prevents sticking. From Corbin Mfg.
Price: 2-oz. bottle. **$4.98**
Price: Pint bottle **$29.50**

CORBIN Silver Lube

Can withstand up to 2,000 degrees Fahrenheit. Used for the heaviest case forming, jacket drawing and bullet swaging operations. Jobs such as making partitioned bullets with heavy brass or steel tubing on Corbin's Hydro-press require this metal bearing lubricant. Comes in 4-oz. screw-top can. From Corbin Mfg. **$6.50**

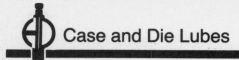

Hornady Case Lube

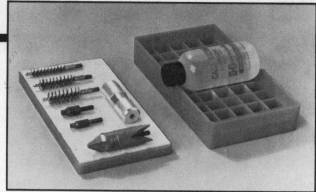

Hornady Case Care Kit

Forster/Bonanza Sport Lube

Imperial Wax and Lube

FORSTER/BONANZA Case Sizing Lube

A high pressure lubricant to adhere to cases when forced into the sizing die. Makes resizing easier and saves equipment. Comes in 2-oz. plastic bottles. From Forster Products. **$1.95**

FORSTER/BONANZA Case Graphiter

Made of impact resistant plastic, this unit has three brushes to lubricate the mouth of any case from 22 to 35 cal. Cover is supplied to keep graphite in and dust and grit out. From Forster Products. **$6.98**

FORSTER Sport Lube

This case lube doesn't gum up cases and won't cause cases to wrinkle in the full-length sizing operation. Sport Lube is a 100 percent animal based product, is clean and easy to use, and washes off with soap and water. Comes in 3-oz. and 16-oz. plastic tubs. From Forster Products.
Price: 3-oz. **$2.20**
Price: 16-oz. **$7.00**

HORNADY Case Sizing Lube

A clean, clear liquid lubricant that stays on the case during the entire sizing operation. From Hornady. 2 oz. plastic bottle. **$2.50**

HORNADY Case Care Kit

Kit concept saves money by including all the items needed to prepare deprimed cases for priming and loading. Kit contains case lube pad, reloading tray, accessory handle, three case neck brushes, large and small primer pocket cleaner, chamfering/deburring tool, case lube. From Hornady **$25.20**

IMPERIAL Dry Neck Lube

A dry, graphite-like powder of special ingredients that doesn't "pack" like graphite. Dipping the case mouth into the tin lubes the neck without danger of contaminating powder charge. From LeClear Industries. Price, less postage, per 1-oz. tin **$1.35**

IMPERIAL Sizing Die Wax

This is an extremely high lubricity wax designed to ease case forming and resizing operations. Only a very light coat of wax is needed and one tin will last for several thousand cases. Resize and reform in one operation. From LeClear Industries.
Price less postage, per 1-oz. tin **$2.50**
Price, per 2-oz. tin **$4.50**

LEE Resizing Lubricant

An industrial deep draw lubricant that eliminates stuck and dented cases. Non-sticky, odorless, non-allergenic white paste that is pleasant to handle — washes off with water. If permitted to dry before use, it completely eliminates dented cases. Has a wax base. A little goes a long way. From Lee Precision, Inc. Per 2-oz. tube. **$1.66**

LYMAN Case Lube Kit

A complete kit for efficient case lubrication. Includes Lyman's improved resizing lubricant, a case lubricating pad, and a handle with three interchangeable brushes covering every caliber for inside neck lubrication. From Lyman Products. **$12.95**
Resizing lube only **$2.50**
Lube pad only **$6.50**

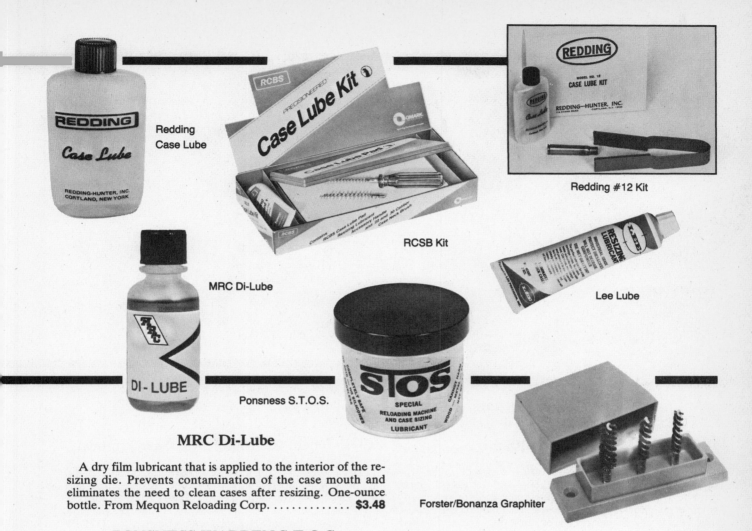

Redding Case Lube

Case Lube Kit

RCSB Kit

Redding #12 Kit

MRC Di-Lube

Lee Lube

DI-LUBE

Ponsness S.T.O.S.

Forster/Bonanza Graphiter

MRC Di-Lube

A dry film lubricant that is applied to the interior of the resizing die. Prevents contamination of the case mouth and eliminates the need to clean cases after resizing. One-ounce bottle. From Mequon Reloading Corp. **$3.48**

PONSNESS-WARREN S.T.O.S.

A grease-type lubricant recommended for reloading equipment, as a case sizing lubricant, and for use on firearms. Has a tackiness to it which creates a self-coating friction-free surface. A clear, completely safe grease. From Ponsness-Warren. 2-oz. jars. **$4.95**

RCBS Case Lube Pad

For lubricating cases or bullet jackets before sizing or forming. A thin coating of lubricant is applied to the pad and cases are then rolled across it to pick up lubricant. From RCBS. **$6.30**

RCBS Resizing Lubricant

Easily applied with the RCBS Case Lube Pad or with the fingers. Comes in 1-oz. tube. From RCBS. **$2.30**

RCBS Case Lube Kit

Contains everything needed for cleaning and lubricating cases inside and out. Includes: RCBS Case Lube Pad, 2-oz. tube of RCBS Resizing Lubricant, and Accessory Handle with interchangeable 22 and 30-cal. case neck brushes. From RCBS. **$12.90**

REDDING No. 12 Case Lube Kit

This case lube pad has non-skid feet on the bottom to prevent the pad from sliding on the bench while lubricating cases. Kit includes 2-oz. plastic bottle of Redding Case Lube. From Redding. **$9.95**

REDDING #21 Case Lube

Compounded to eliminate stuck case and pulled rims. Prolongs life of the dies and makes reforming easier. From Redding. 2 oz. plastic bottle **$2.50**

ROOSTER Case-Forming Lubricants

Three case-forming lubes are available from Rooster Laboratories — CFL-56, CL-WR-14 and CSL-71. CFL-56 and CSL-71 are semi-solid lubes, CL-WR-14 a liquid, and all minimize oil denting and folding and have a brass protectant built into them. Whether resizing or performing radical or moderate case re-forming operations, one of these lubes will fit the reloader's needs. The semi-solids are available in 2.8-oz. tubs; the liquid in 2-oz. or 8-oz. bottles. For further pricing structure contact Rooster Laboratories.
Price: CFL-56, CSL-71 (each) **$5.00**
Price: CL-WR-14 (each) **$3.50**

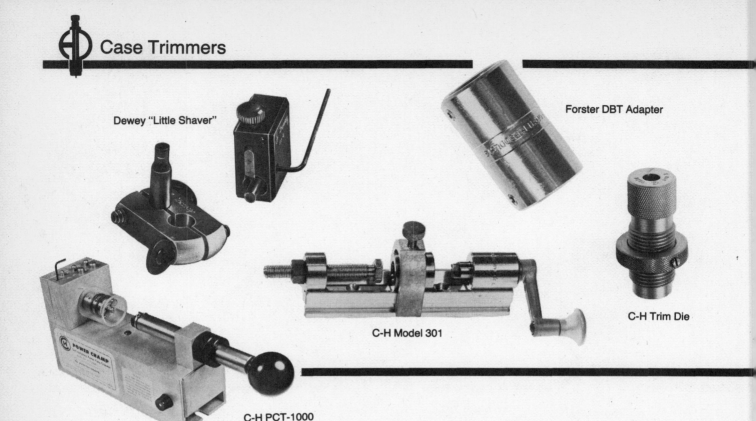

Dewey "Little Shaver"

Forster DBT Adapter

C-H Trim Die

C-H Model 301

C-H PCT-1000

Notes on Case Trimmers . . .

Repeated firings cause brass to flow forward—more pronounced in some calibers than others—and this excess length must be trimmed periodically. Unless such cases are trimmed, chambering effort may be increased, case mouths may wedge into throats and higher pressures result because of lessened neck clearance.

Case trimmers run from hand-held types for minimum in-the-field brass cutting to "file-type" dies, to miniature lathe-style devices.

BEAR Case Trimmer

Sturdy cast iron trimmer uses Bear-type removable shellholder heads. It adjusts to any cartridge length and can be used with a ¼-inch drill for power trimming. From Bear Company.

Price: Case trimmer............................ **$21.00**
Price: Case trimmer pilots..................... **$1.70**

C-H MODEL 301 Case Trimmer

A clamp locks case holder in position, eliminates danger of cutting fingers. Insures uniformity from 22 cal. through 45 cal., either rifle or handgun cases. From C-H Tool and Die Corp. Price includes one case holder............... **$21.95**
Extra case holders **$3.50**

C-H Model PCT-1000 Power Case Trimmer

This motorized tool trims and deburrs the outside of the case neck in one operation. It will accept any case length and has a tough tungsten carbide cutter. Easily adjusted for precise trimming. Comes complete with one shellholder and pilot of your choice. From C-H Tool and Die Corp...... **$179.00**
Extra shellholders, each **$4.00**
Extra pilots, each............................. **$2.50**

C-H Trim Die

For shortening case neck length, these dies are hardened so they will not be affected by filing or a fine tooth hack saw used in the operation. Available for most popular rifle calibers. From C-H Tool and Die Corp..................... **$13.00**

J. DEWEY "Little Shaver"

This is a fully adjustable neck turning tool that will accurately turn cartridges from 17 to 30 caliber with the changing of a properly sized mandrel to fit the case neck. Four fired cases needed when ordering. Case clamp also available for belted magnums. From J. Dewey Mfg. Co. Price, with one mandrel....................................... **$30.00**
Case holding clamp **$7.50**
Extra mandrel **$10.00**

FORSTER DBT Adapter Base

For use with the DBT Adapter, this base offers speed and saves wear and tear on your hands. Installed on your loading bench, the Forster Products DBT Base offers instant availability and ease of operation when chamfering large numbers of cases. (For inside and outside deburring.) From Forster Products... **$16.50**

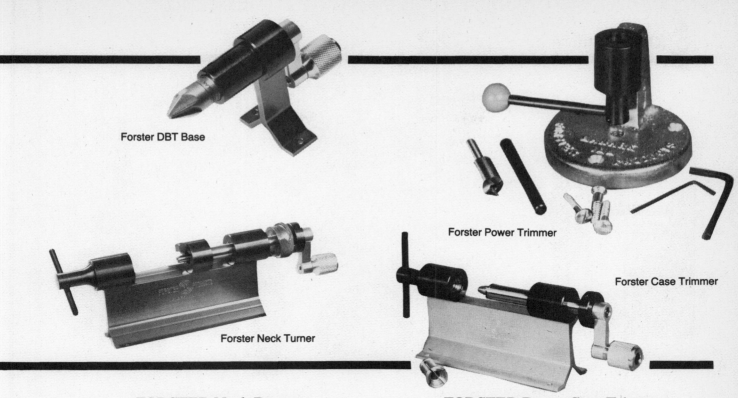

Forster DBT Base

Forster Neck Turner

Forster Power Trimmer

Forster Case Trimmer

FORSTER Neck Reamer

Mounted in the Forster case trimmer, this tool removes excess brass from inside case necks. Available in: 17 (requires 17 cal. cutter shaft), 220, 223, 224, 243, 257, 263, 277, 284, 308, 311, 323, 338, 348, 358, 375, 410, 432, 452, 458, and .239″ plus .4275″. The staggered teeth cut smoothly, and are ground to .002″-.003″ over max. bullet diameter. Give cartridge and caliber. From Forster Products. **$12.00**

FORSTER Outside Neck Turner

The necessary clearance of .002″ to .003″ cannot be maintained between case and chamber neck when repeated firing thickens brass, or when cases are formed from heavier brass. This tool removes the excess metal from the outside of the necks by passing the neck between a hardened pilot and a carbide cutter. The operation is identical in principle to that of lathe-turning on a mandrel. The process produces very uniform neck thickness. Must be used on the frame of the basic Forster case trimmer. Only a new pilot is needed to change caliber. Available in diameters .224″, .243″, .257″, .263″, .277″, .284″, .308″, .311″, .323″, .333″, .338″, .358″, .375″. Price does not include Case Trimmer. From Forster Products **$22.50**
Extra pilots.................................... **$4.50**

FORSTER Precision Case Trimmer

Hardened and ground cutter shaft has four staggered cutting teeth for smooth, chatterless cutting. Collet holds case without any end movement. All cases cut to same length even if head diameter varies. Stop collar features a fine adjustment screw. From Forster Products. **$37.50**
Extra pilots (state cal.) **$1.95**
Extra collets (state cal.) **$6.00**
Extra cutters................................... **$9.00**

FORSTER Power Case Trimmer

Permits use of electric drill press for trimming cases. Accurately lines up by means of a furnished line-up bar. Nonchattering cutter comes with ¼″ shank. Price includes one collet and pilot. From Forster Products **$37.50**

FORSTER DBT Adapter

The DBT adapter allows the reloader to turn the Forster case trimmer into a deburring tool holder. The adapter mounts on the case trimmer cutter shaft and is used with the case trimmer collet housing removed. For inside and outside deburring. From Forster Products.................. **$6.50**

Check Chart of Forster Collets

Forster collets have three steps and each collet will handle the popular cartridge cases shown in the following tabulation:
#1 COLLET—17, 30-06, 6.5mm 243, 264, 270, 308, 338, 358, 401 & 458 Win.; 250 & 300 Sav.; 222, 222 Mag., 244, 35 & 44 Mag. Rem.; 22 Var.; 22-250, 220 Swift, 22 Lovell; 6mm; 243 RCBS, 257 Roberts; 250-3000; 25 Souper; 25-06; 6.5mm Dutch; 6.5x57 Mauser; 6.5mm Jap; 6.5 Mannlicher; 256 Newton; 270 Gibbs; 250, 270, 300 & 375 Weatherby; 7x57 Mauser; 7mm Gradle; 7mm Ackley; 7mm Mashburn; 7x61 S&H, 7x64; 276; 30 & 35 Newton; 300 & 375 Mag.; 303 British; 32 S&W Long; 8x57 & 8x57 JR; 8x60; 35 Whelen; 375-06; 375 Barnes; 38-40; 395-400; 41 Colt; 44 S&W Spec.; 45 ACP; 45 Long Colt; 450 Watts.
#2 COLLET—22 Hornet; 22K-H, 218 Bee & M-Bee; 219 Zipper & Wasp; 22 Sav.; 22/30-30; 6mm/30-30; 25-20; 25-35; 25 Rem.; 30-30; 30 Rem.; 303 Sav.; 32-20; 7.7mm Jap; 9mm Luger; 38 Colt Super; 41 Rem. Mag.; 45 Long Colt.
#3 COLLET—22 Hornet; 22K Hornet; and Krag case; 30 Carbine; 38 Spec.; 357 Magnum; 35 Win.
In addition, Forster has a #3 collet to take 33 Win., 348 Win., 38-50, 45-70, 45-90.

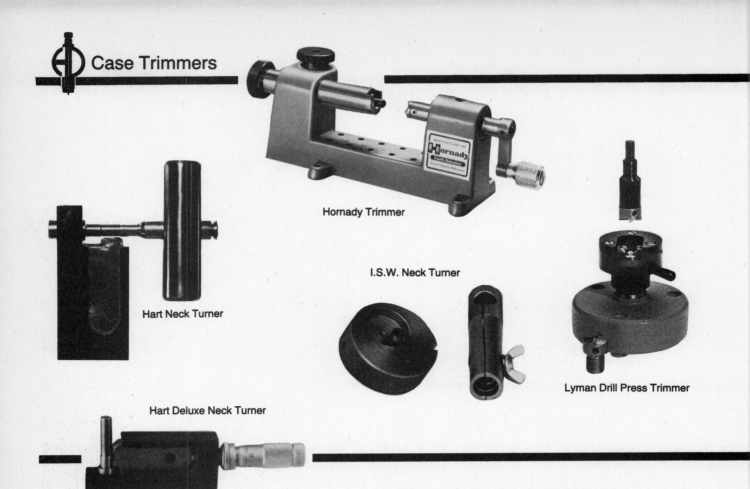

Hornady Trimmer

Hart Neck Turner

I.S.W. Neck Turner

Lyman Drill Press Trimmer

Hart Deluxe Neck Turner

HART Neck Turning Tool

This tool is designed to turn the outside of the case neck to any desired wall thickness and depth. The mandrel has an end stop so that all cases are turned to the same length. Requires a mandrel and expansion plug for each caliber from 22 through 30. Tool will hold a wall thickness of .0003″. Cutter is high speed steel and mandrels are hardened. Additional handles are required for each individual caliber and are available for most calibers to 30-338. From Robert Hart and Son. **$62.00**
Deluxe Model (same as standard but with micrometer dial adjustment) **$98.95**
Extra handles **$6.30**
Extra mandrel and button **$11.75**

HORNADY File Trimmer and Case Former

For trimming and case forming. A fine grade file will not scratch the hardened surfaces. Available in most calibers. Fits ⅞-14 presses. From Hornady. **$18.00**

HORNADY Case Trimmer

Uses regular removable shellholder heads instead of collets, and is adjustable for any length case. Also attaches to a ¼″ drill for use as a power trimmer. From Hornady. Extra shellholder heads ($5.50), extra cutter heads ($6.00) and pilots ($2.40) are quickly installed **$49.95**

I.S.W. Case Neck Turner

This hand-operated case neck turning tool comes with a "universal" hand vise and the turner. The cartridge case is held in the vise and inserted into the cutter and rotated. Comes with a pilot of a single diameter but others are available for standard calibers. From I.S.W. **$45.50**
Extra pilots **$5.50**

LYMAN AccuLine Trimmer

Economically priced, this tool trims all rifle and pistol cases from 22-458 Win. Mag. The centerless ground shaft is adjustable for depth of cut and the cartridge case is positioned using a standard shellholder. Can be bench-mounted, held by C-clamps or in a vise. Available with one cutter or with the Nine-Pilot Multi-Pak. From Lyman Products.
Price: Trimmer less pilot **$29.95**
Price: Trimmer with Multi-Pak **$34.95**

LYMAN Universal Case Trimmer

This simple, yet efficient, trimmer has a chuck head that accepts all metallic rifle or pistol cases, regardless of rim thickness. To change calibers, simply change the inexpensive case head pilot. Cutter has coarse and fine cutting adjustments and rides on an oil impregnated bronze bearing. Cast base can be mounted to bench. From Lyman Products. Complete trimmer less pilot **$54.95**
Multi-Pak Trimmer (Trimmer with nine pilots) . . . **$59.95**
Extra pilots (specify) **$2.95**
Replacement cutter heads (2) **$8.50**

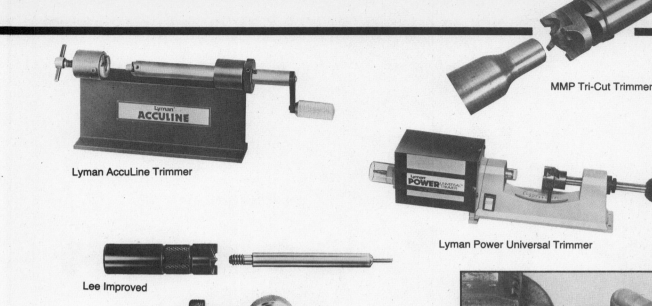

MMP Tri-Cut Trimmer

Lyman AccuLine Trimmer

Lyman Power Universal Trimmer

Lee Improved

Marquart Neck Turner

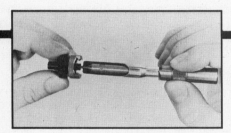

Lee Improved

LYMAN Power Universal Trimmer

Has all the features of the Universal Trimmer except operation is motor driven. This unit is available in 110V or 120V with three-prong grounded cord. Safety covers for operating ends provided. From Lyman Products

Price: 110V **$179.95**
Price: 220V **$180.00**

LYMAN Universal Drill Press Trimmer

The universal chuck head bolts to your drill press. By mounting the cutter head and case head pilot to your drill chuck, you can process large quantities of cases accurately. State caliber. From Lyman Products **$39.95**

LEE Improved Case Trimmer

Trims cases to proper length by hand or by using an electric drill. Price is complete for one caliber. Shank fits ¼-inch drill chucks. Spins cases for trimming, chamfering and polishing. All operations can be done without removing the shell or stopping the tool. Lee Precision, Inc. **$4.28**

Extra pilot and shellholder to change caliber **$4.28**

MRC Case Trimmer

This trimmer is factory adjusted to trim cases to the maximum length. Case mouth is "trued" during trimming, as well as sized. Available for most popular calibers. From Mequon Reloading Corp.

Sizing case holder **$4.98**
Cutter and knockout rod **$3.98**

MMP Tri-Cut Trimmer

Reduces case length, deburrs inside and outside of case mouth simultaneously. Available in two shank lengths — .155" to fit RCBS case trimmer, .186" to fit C&H, Forster, Bonanza, Hornady, Pacific and Redding power trimmers. Available in 224-458 calibers. One year unconditional guarantee. From Muzzleload Magnum Products. **$12.75**

MARQUART PRECISION Case Neck Turning Tool

A very compact and precision device for taking a shaving cut on metallic cartridge case necks. The case holder is held in the jaws of a bench vise; a case is inserted and the jaws tightened. The cutter is then pushed onto the arbor and rotated. The cutter is adjustable in the frame to control the depth of the cut. Tool is accurate to within .0001". From Marquart Precision. Complete tool with one pilot and case holder. **$48.00**

Additional holders. (every case head size, 22 through 378 W.M.) **$8.00**

Additional solid pilots (every caliber, 17 through 30 cal.) **$8.00**

Case Trimmers

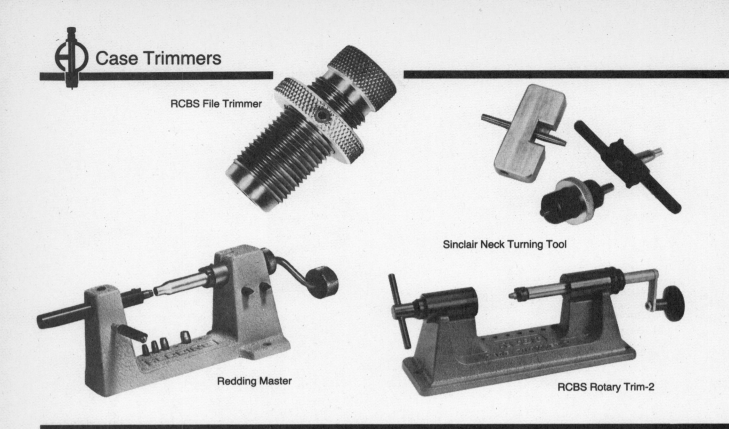

RCBS File Trimmer

Sinclair Neck Turning Tool

Redding Master

RCBS Rotary Trim-2

RCBS Rotary Case Trimmer Power Conversion

Converts the RCBS hand-turned Rotary Case Trimmer into a power driven trimmer. From RCBS.......... **$4.00**

RCBS Outside Neck Turning Accessories

An easy way to remove high spots and case neck out-of-roundness. Head and pilot guide cutter over the outside of the sized cartridge case neck as it is supported by the pilot. Attachable to most ½-inch shaft case trimmers. From RCBS. **NA**
Self-Advancing Attachment advances the cutting tool over the case neck with each turn of the trimmer handle. Adaptable only to RCBS Case Trimmer 2.................. **NA**

RCBS File Type Trimmer

Quickly trims cases to exact length by filing off any portion of the case above the die. Hardened to withstand the roughest use. Standard ⅞″-14 thread. Available in all calibers with over-all case length of 0.875″ or more. Cases measuring shorter than 1.70″ require an extension on shellholder. See catalog for die group references. From RCBS.
   Die group A, B **$18.90**

RCBS Rotary Case Trimmer-2

Working just like a lathe, this unit trims a brass case to the desired length—quickly, easily and accurately. Interchangeable quick-release pilots are available for all popular calibers (17 to 45). From RCBS.......................... **$49.50**
   Collets **$6.50**
   Pilots **$2.60**

RCBS Trim Gauges

Makes adjusting a rotary-type case trimmer to a new caliber easy. RCBS trim gauges are metal collars with an adjustable screw and a locking nut. Basically the reloader adjusts the screw on a trim gauge to the appropriate length and permanently locks it to size with the nut. To trim that case length simply snap the gauge on the trimmer shaft of a case trimmer. Fits most ½-inch diameter rotary shafts. Available in six lengths. From RCBS. **$6.30**

REDDING Master Case Trimmer

This unit features a universal collet that accepts *all* rifle and pistol cases. Frame is solid cast iron with storage holes in the base for extra pilots. Both coarse and fine adjustments are provided for case length. Shipped with two pilots (22 and 30 cals.), universal collet, two neck cleaning brushes (22 through 30), and two primer pocket cleaners (large and small). From Redding.
   Model 1400.................................... **$59.95**
   Model 1500 pilots............................. **$2.50**

SANDIA Power Adaptor

This unit adapts to a ¼-inch or larger hand drill or directly on a ½-inch motor shaft. It is suitable for inside and outside deburring, and for primer pocket reaming on military cases. It will accommodate most deburring tools and Wilson large or small primer pocket reamers. Enables the user to deburr several thousand cases per hour. From Sandia Die and Cartridge Co.
   Power Adaptor **$14.95**
   With polishing attachment **$17.45**

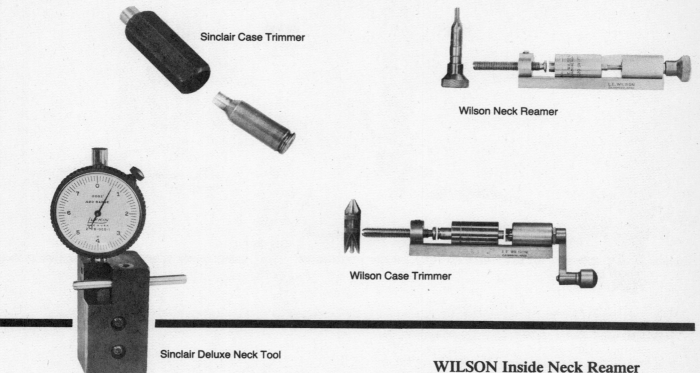

Sinclair Case Trimmer

Wilson Neck Reamer

Wilson Case Trimmer

Sinclair Deluxe Neck Tool

SINCLAIR Standard Neck Turning Tool

To assure that the bullet is sitting squarely in the case, outside neck turning is highly recommended. Sinclair's tool is accurate to .0001″. It uses dual-caliber case mandrels (22/6mm, 25/270, 7mm/30). Single-caliber mandrels available in 17, 6.5, 323, 338 and 358. The tool is supplied with a universal handle which will hold most rimless cases from 222 through the belted magnums. Comes complete with all necessary wrenches, case handle and choice of one mandrel. From Sinclair Int., Inc. **$48.00**

SINCLAIR Deluxe Neck Turning Tool

An improved version of Sinclair's neck turning tool, it can be fitted with a dial indicator and set for the desired neck thickness. Alters neck thickness by as little as .0001″. Tool has a fully adjustable carbide cutting blade and comes with all wrenches and Sinclair's Universal case handle. Accepts any dial indicator with a .375″ mounting shaft. Price, less dial indicator, mandrel. From Sinclair Int., Inc. **$95.00**

SINCLAIR Case Trimmer

Designed for the benchrest shooter, this hand-held case trimmer is fully adjustable for trim length and is made of hex stock so it won't roll off the bench. Presently available only in 22 and 6mm for rifles chambered with tight necks. Can be opened up for standard necks. From Sinclair Int., Inc. **$15.00**

WILSON Inside Neck Reamer

Used with the Wilson case trimmer, and made in popular calibers from 17 to 458. The case trimmer keeps the case correctly aligned while this reamer is run into the neck to remove excess metal, reducing wall thickness. From L.E. Wilson Co.
Price, reamer and handle only. **$15.95**
Complete reaming device (rifle only) **$31.25**
Special size reamer made to order **$20.25**
Complete reaming device with special size reamer **$35.55**

WILSON Universal Case Trimmer

This simple, rugged tool is one of the oldest trimmers on the market, and it does excellent work. Cases are held by the body, not the rim, producing truly square mouths; needs no pilots. Case holders are available in most popular calibers, will accept more than one caliber where body diameter and taper are similar. Regular pistol holders only are hardened. New "Q" pistol holder requires only a tap to grip and release the case. Some "Q" holders service more than one caliber for trimming. Because of slow taper and case expansion, holders for lever action, some bolt and slide action rifle calibers are furnished in two sizes—fired and unfired cases (write to Wilson for details). Fired case size will be furnished unless otherwise specified. This trimmer is used as the basis for other Wilson accessories. Instructions and a table of cartridge case lengths accompany each trimmer. From L.E. Wilson Co. For rifle calibers. **$32.25**
Pistol calibers **$31.25**
Extra shellholder; rifle, **$4.50**; special rifle **$8.00**
Trimmer with "Q"-type pistol holder. **$35.25**
"Q"-type pistol holder only **$7.50**

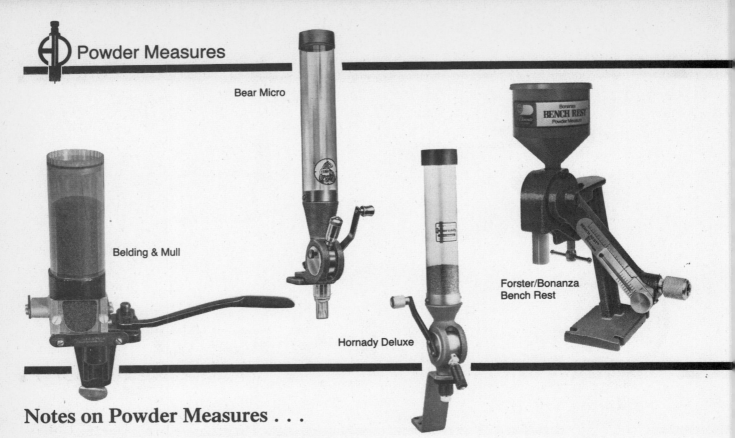

Bear Micro

Belding & Mull

Forster/Bonanza
Bench Rest

Hornady Deluxe

Notes on Powder Measures . . .

The powder measure is a distinct help in speeding up the reloading operation. Throwing loads accurate enough for most hunting purposes, they should not, however, be relied on when loading near-maximum or maximum charges. In any case, the powder measure must always be used in conjunction with an accurate powder scale, using the scale to check the accuracy of the first charge thrown and spot checking subsequent charges as the reloading operation continues. It's a good idea to weigh every tenth charge thrown. An inexpensive set of *gram* weights will check your grain scale for inherent accuracy.

Variations in charges thrown will depend on several factors, among them amount of powder in the hopper, size of powder grains and ability of the operator. Many measures have built-in baffles in the hopper to maintain a more even pressure on the powder going into the charge tube, but even with these it is wise not to let the powder level get too low, causing a decrease in pressure on the powder. In any powder measure there is a slicing action on the powder as it is metered into the charge tube. In cutting the coarser powders the attendant slight jarring of the measure may result in a charge variance of 3 to 4 tenths of a grain. A precise, consistent operator will get less of a variation of powder charges—he will work the handle with the same speed and force, drop the knocker (if measure is so equipped) or gently rap the charge tube to settle the powder down into the metering chamber. As with most reloading operations, consistency is the key word here.

BEAR Micro-Measure

With each turn of the handle the Bear Micro-Measure measures and throws consistent charges. Built-in baffle equalizes pressure of powder entering measuring chamber. Micrometer adjusting screw allows the reloader to record settings for future reference. Comes with two see-through drop tubes. 22-30 caliber and 30-45 caliber. From Bear Company. **$29.00**

BEAR Pistol Powder Measure

Precisely measures powder for pistol cartridge from see-through powder tube. Nozzle accommodates all case sizes. Attaches securely to bench-mounted base plate and is easily detached for powder removal. Equipped with fixed charge rotor. From Bear Company.
Price: Measure with rotor of choice **$12.50**
Price: Extra rotors **$4.00**

BELDING & MULL Visible Powder Measure

The B&M measure feeds powder from the main hopper into a secondary reservoir as needed. Movement of the operating handle then fills the separate charge tube. With this method, powder density in the lower reservoir is near constant; this is believed to aid loading uniformity. From Belding & Mull **$58.75**
With micrometer charge tube **$65.20**
Extra charge tubes, standard **$7.40**
Extra magnum charge tubes **$8.80**
Micrometer charge tubes **$13.90**
Micrometer magnum tubes **$16.25**

C-H Pushbutton Powder Measure

The same measure used on the C-H Pistol Champ press. Can be used with any conventional single station press or turret-type press. Dispenses powder and bells the case mouth as well. Seventeen different bushings available for over 215 powder/load combinations. From C-H Tool and Die Corp. **$37.50**
As above, without Hollow Expander **$28.50**
Extra bushings **$2.40**

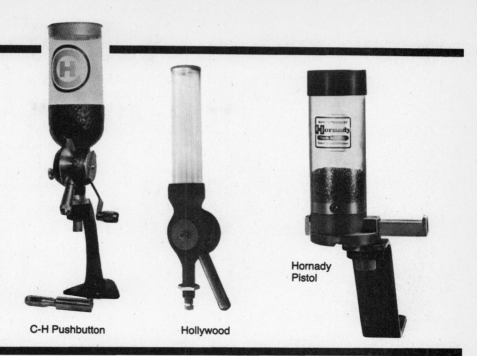

Francis Quick-Measure

C-H Pushbutton

Hollywood

Hornady Pistol

FORSTER/BONANZA Bench Rest Measure

The large plastic hopper may also be used as powder and shot funnel, and the lid is a primer turner. Easily read Vernier on handle can be set by pouring a weighed charge into hopper. Adjustable for charges from 2½ grains of Bullseye to 95 grains of 4350. Minimal powder shearing. Hopper is quickly emptied by removing the charge bar. Two drop-tubes are supplied. From Forster Products.....................**$66.50**
　Long drop tube **$9.00**
　Measure stand.....................................**$16.60**

FRANCIS Quick-Measure

The base, powder chamber and all moving parts of this powder measure are made of solid brass. The special design will normally maintain ± .1-gr. accuracy and will not shear powder. No rotating drum. Once the chamber is set to a "pet load," it can be removed and re-installed with no change to the load. Only requires one hand to operate—place a scale pan or other container under the chamber and lift to dispense the charge. Easily detached from mounting for emptying. From Francis Tool Co............................**$87.50**
　Extra drop tubes **$8.00**

HOLLYWOOD Powder Measure

Adjustable from 2½ grains of Bullseye to 93 grains of 4350. Disc baffle helps assure constant powder pressure on metering chamber. Hard-coated conical bearing surfaces for precise powder cutoff. Threaded 7/8-14 to fit many presses; large lock ring secures measure to tool. Integral thumb screw bracket for bench mounting. One drop tube (22-270 or 7mm-45) supplied. From Hollywood Loading Tools **$100.00**
　Extra drop tubes **$8.00**
　Shotshell drop tube **$9.00**

FORSTER/BONANZA "Bulls-Eye" Pistol Powder Measure

Body of this measure is machined from steel. Rotors are machined from hard brass, drilled for charges of Hercules Bullseye Pistol Powder. Large capacity reservoir; contour of the measure will accept all pistol case sizes. Measure may be mounted to the bench and easily removed for operation with a reloading block. Comes complete with attaching bracket and choice of rotor. Also included is a comprehensive table of equivalents of various brands of powders adapted to most popular pistol cartridges. Each rotor number is listed and cross-referenced for the charge thrown. From Forster Products. Price, less rotor **$18.00**
　Charge rotors in following grain weights: 2.5, 2.7, 3, 3.5, 4, 4.5, 5.3, 5.5, 6.0, 6.5, 7.0, 7.5, 8.4 (for Hercules Bullseye Powder) **$6.00**
　Extra rotor (blank with pilot hole) **$6.00**
　Measure stand.....................................**$16.60**

HORNADY Deluxe Measure

Throws up to 100 gains per charge. All parts are precision finished. Equipped with large capacity powder hopper and micrometer adjusting screw for recording settings. Two plastic drop tubes included (22-30 cal. and 30-45 cal.). Available for either rifle or pistol. From Hornady.............**$69.95**
　Extra drum (rifle or pistol) **$13.50**
　17-cal. drop tube **$2.30**

HORNADY Pistol Powder Measure

This measure is designed primarily for pistol powders. The charge bar has interchangeable bushings that provide a wide range of charges. Price includes measure stand. From Hornady...**$29.95**
　Extra bushings...................................**$2.00**

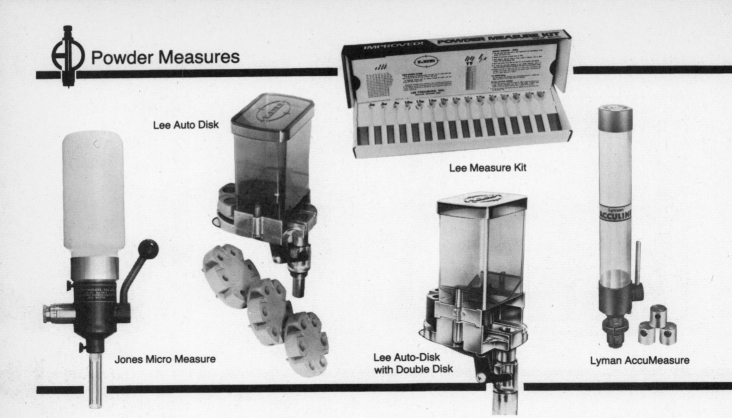

Lee Auto Disk

Lee Measure Kit

Jones Micro Measure

Lee Auto-Disk
with Double Disk

Lyman AccuMeasure

JONES Micro Measure

Measure is made of tool steel that is 100 percent machined. Smooth casting surfaces assure smooth powder flow through the measure. The measure can be changed from one powder to another simply by changing bottles. Bottles have a bottom cutout and plug so powder can be returned to reservoir without removing bottle from adaptor. Two interchangeable measuring drums are available: The standard drum is for most rifle cartridges and has a capacity of 16 to 114 grains with a micro-click value of approximately .3 grain; the small drum meets the needs of the handgunner with a drum capacity of 4 to 65 grains and a click value of approximately .1-grain. Measure can be mounted directly to edge of bench or attached to a powder measure stand. An optional ⅞″ x 14 adaptor also available. Price includes one removeable powder bottle, two 3″ drop tubes (22/6mm and 30-cal.or larger) and complete instructions. From Neil Jones Custom Products.

Price: Large drum measure $180.00
Price: Small drum measure $195.00
Price: Measure with both drums $280.00

LEE Auto-Disk Powder Measure

Designed for the Lee Turret Press, this measure screws into the expanding die mounted in the die turret. While expanding the case, the charge drops through the hollow expanding plug. The case actuates the measure. A built-in powder baffle and charge disks molded of glass-reinforced plastic contribute to uniform charges. Comes with four charge disks with six cavities each. Charges from 2 to 24 grains. Disks are easily interchangeable. See-through powder reservoir. From Lee Precision, Inc. $24.98
Deluxe Auto-Disk Powder Measure (machined metering surfaces, polycarbonate hopper, triple chrome-plated main casting) $34.98

LEE Powder Measure Kit

Contains 15 individual powder dippers and a slide rule chart listing 69 different powders, 1,300 loads. These are the simplest of the measuring devices; not recommended for maximum loads. Over 1,300 loads listed with the kit. From Lee Precision, Inc. $6.98

LEE Double Disk Kit

Conversion unit designed for Lee Auto-Disk and Deluxe Auto-Disk powder measures. Allows two disks to be stacked for fine charge adjustments of .1- to .2-grain. Kit includes four extra disks, two hopper risers and screws. From Lee Precision, Inc. $14.98

LYMAN Pistol AccuMeasure

This measure can be used either free standing, or mounted on all turret and single-stage presses used in conjunction with the Multi-expand/Powder Charge Die. Changeable brass powder rotors handle all ball and flake type pistol powders. From Lyman Products.
Price: With Multi-Pak Starter Set (three rotor bushings) $24.95
Price: Less rotor bushings $19.95
Price: Rotor bushings (each) $4.95

LYMAN No. 55 Measure

Calibrated slides and micrometer screws offer precise adjustments. Threaded drop tubes (large and small) and integral knocker are included. Stem is threaded for Lyman (and other) press mounting convenience. From Lyman Products. $67.95
1-lb. reservoir, extra $9.95
Measure stand $17.00

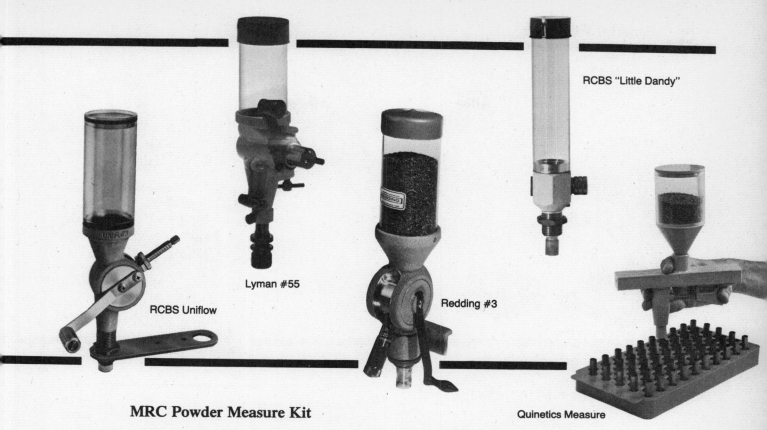

RCBS "Little Dandy"

Lyman #55

RCBS Uniflow

Redding #3

Quinetics Measure

MRC Powder Measure Kit

This kit contains 13 individual powder dippers and a slide rule chart listing 86 different powders. These are the simplest of the measuring devices; not recommended for maximum loads. Over 1115 loads listed with the kit. From Mequon Reloading Corp.......................................**$6.48**

QUINETICS Powder Measure

This adjustable, hand-held powder measure is able to throw charges with a high degree of accuracy. For use with rifle or pistol powders. Special design of the spring-action mechanism eliminates shearing of powder grains. Made of plastic. From Quinetics Corp. Complete........................**$42.95**

RCBS "Little Dandy" Pistol Measure

Designed specifically for pistol shooters and small-caliber rifle shooters, this measure is intended to be hand held but can be used with a powder measure stand. With 26 interchangeable, fixed charge powder rotors available you can load most any popular powder and make up any of 250 or more load combinations. From RCBS.

"Little Dandy" measure **$31.50**
Extra charge rotors, each.......................**$7.00**
"Little Dandy" rotor knob **$2.00**

RCBS Uniflow Measure

Big acrylic hopper. Measuring cylinders are ground and honed, have calibrated screw to record settings. Big cylinder holds to 110 grains of 4350; small one up to 60 grs. 4350. Shank has 7/8-14 thread. Stand plate, 2 drop tubes, and both cylinders included. From RCBS. **$65.00**
Stand (extra) **$17.90**
Drop tube 17-caliber...........................**$5.80**

REDDING #3 BR Match Grade Measure

Designed for benchrest, silhouette and varmint shooters, this measure has an adjustable powder baffle, zero backlash micrometer adjustment and micrometer lock. See-through powder reservoir. From Redding. No. 3 BR with Universal or Pistol metering chamber **$91.00**
No. 3 BRK (with both metering chambers) **$114.50**
No. 3-30 match grade metering chambers (fit only the 3 BR)..**$25.50**

REDDING Powder Measure Kits

Supercharger powder kit contains everything needed for accurate charges. No. 101 Kit includes: No. 1 standard Powder Scale, No. 3 Master Powder Measure, No. 5 Powder Trickler and No. 6 Bench Stand. From Redding............**$135.00**
No. 102 Kit contains: No. 2 Master Powder Scale, No. 3 Master Powder Measure, No. 5 Powder Trickler and No. 6 Bench Stand **$145.00**

REDDING # 3 Master Powder Measure

Has a micrometer-type metering chamber with lock screw right in front for easy setting and reading. The micrometer graduations allow the user to repeat exactly the same setting at a later date. Handles charges up to 100 grains and is supplied with a chart for normal settings. Features a large transparent reservoir and see-thru drop tube (22 to 60 cal.). Critical areas are honed for precise fit to avoid jamming of fine powders. No aluminum parts are used. From Redding.

Model #3 with Universal or pistol chamber **$74.00**
Model #3K includes both metering chambers **$89.95**
Model #3-12 Universal or pistol chamber........**$17.95**

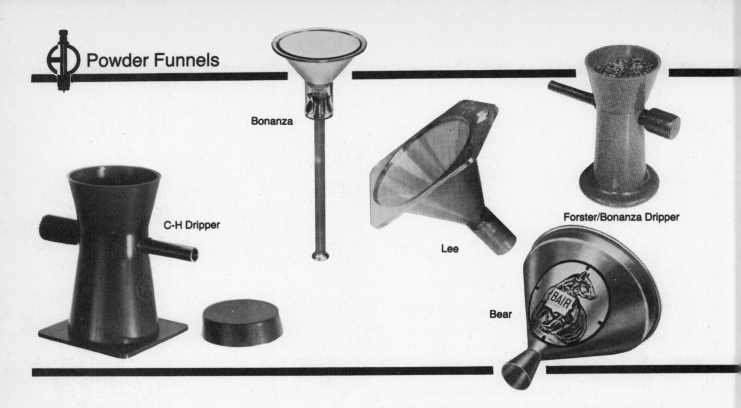

Bonanza

C-H Dripper

Lee

Forster/Bonanza Dripper

Bear

Notes on Powder Funnels . . .

A handy, almost indispensable, accessory for the reloader, the powder funnel provides a means of easy transfer of powder from the scale pan. These universal funnels have tapered shell feed tubes that accommodate all cases from the 22's through 45-70.

BEAR Powder Funnel

This universal powder funnel comes with two inserts — 17-25-caliber and 25-45-caliber. The insert can be removed for a straight-through funnel. From Bear Company **$1.50**

BEAR Powder Dribbler

A fast easy way to balance the scale when weighing precise powder charges. A twist of the knob and powder will dribble into scale pan one kernel at a time. Large adjustable reservoir. The base can be filled with lead shot for added stability. From Bear Company............................. **$3.50**

C-H Powder Measure Stand

Stand can be bolted to the bench or secured with "C" clamps. Will accommodate any measure with 7/8-14 threads. It is made at a convenient height for charging cases. From C-H Tool and Die Corp................................. **$6.95**

C-H Powder Dripper

For use with most scales, a twist of the knob will dispense one kernel at a time to bring charge weights up to specifications. Has an extra large square base to minimize tipping. Base insert furnished allowing ballast to be added for additional stability. From C-H Tool and Die Corp......... **$5.25**

Forster/Bonanza Cycolac plastic **$2.50**
With long drop tube **$8.00**

Forster/Bonanza Powder and shot funnel, large size, Cycolac plastic **$4.00**

C-H Clear, anti-static plastic **$1.50**

Flambeau Anti-static treated to eliminate clinging powder grains. Large flange serves as handle **$1.49**

Fitz Amm-O-Cone—Fluorscent red plastic **$1.50**

Lee Funnel, 22 to 45 cal............................ **$1.98**

Lyman Black opaque plastic......................... **$2.95**

MTM Clear, transparent plastic.................... **$1.88**

Hornady Aluminum; Spill-proof spout 17-cal., 22-270, 28-45 cals. **$3.00**

RCBS Fluorescent green tenite, anti-static treated. Square lips prevent rolling. **$2.60**

RCBS 17 Caliber **$3.00**

Redding Anti-static plastic, 22 thru 50 cal........... **$3.00**

FORSTER Long Drop Tube

Replaces the standard powder drop tube on the Forster/Bonanza Bench Rest Powder Measure. For use with 4831 powder and other slow burning powders where full capacity loads are desired. Convenient for dropping powder charges directly into primed cases in a loading block. From Forster Products.. **$9.00**

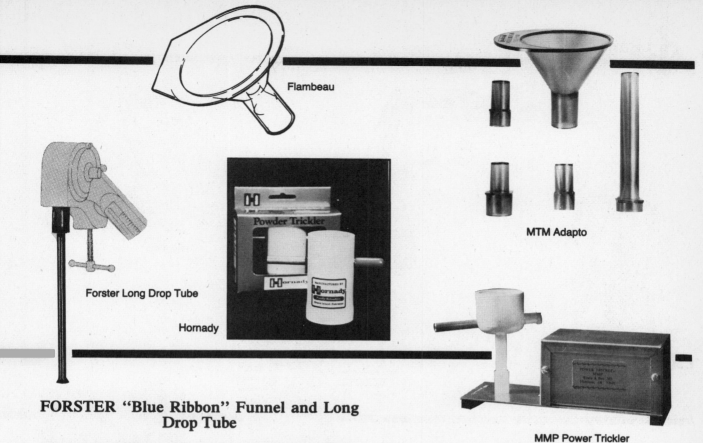

Flambeau

MTM Adapto

Forster Long Drop Tube

Hornady

MMP Power Trickler

FORSTER "Blue Ribbon" Funnel and Long Drop Tube

For use with 4831 powder and other slow burning powders where full capacity loads are desired. From Forster Products.. **$8.00**

FORSTER Large Powder and Shot Funnel

Same funnel as used on the Forster/Bonanza Bench Rest and Bullseye pistol powder measures. Made of tough plastic. From Forster Products........................... **$4.00**

FORSTER "Blue Ribbon" Powder Funnel

Made from cycolac, this powder funnel has been designed with four "ears" to prevent it from rolling off the loading bench. Available for 22-45-cal. and for 17-cal. From Forster Products.. **$2.50**

FORSTER/BONANZA Powder Measure Stand

This cast aluminum-alloy stand is painted in the familiar Bonanza red finish. Can be bolted to the loading bench or a separate block. Will fit either the Bonanza Bench Rest or Bulls-Eye powder measures. From Forster Products. **$16.60**

FORSTER/BONANZA "Big Red" Trickler

Companion tool for the Bonanza powder and bullet scale, this handy item brings underweight charges up to proper reading by adding a few granules of powder at a time. Two piece construction. Ballast may be added for stability. From Forster Products.. **$8.50**

HORNADY Powder Trickler

For use with any powder scale. Hornady's new Powder Trickler is for the serious reloader. Simply fill the large capacity reservoir with powder, rotate the cushioned knob and the powder trickles accurately into the scale pan. From Hornady... **$4.00**

LYMAN Powder Dribbler

Allows exactness with a minimum of effort. Features a large reservoir, ideal height and an over-sized base to reduce the chances of tipping. From Lyman Products.......... **$8.95**

MMP Power Powder Trickler

Operated by a foot switch, the MMP Power Powder Trickler automatically throws a precise charge to "top off" the conventional charge. Features adjustable feed rates and 360-degree feed tube positioning. Powered by a 115-volt AC sealed vibrator motor. Comes with a 5-year warranty. From Muzzleloader Magnum Products.................. **$74.95**

MTM Adapto Powder Funnel

A unique five-in-one funnel with interchangeable adaptor tube to provide an exact fit for all cartridge sizes and to make loading easier. Four different tubes are supplied to fit cartridges ranging from 17 cal. to 45 cal. Eliminates powder build-up around case necks. From MTM. **$3.19**

RCBS Stand

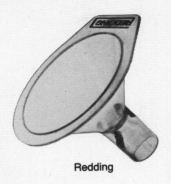

Redding

RCBS

Redding #5

Sinclair

RCBS Powder Trickler

Very useful when weighing charges. Simply set measure to throw an underweight charge, then feed just enough powder to balance the scale with this handy device. From RCBS... **$9.50**

RCBS Powder Measure Stand

Bolted to your loading bench edge or a wooden platform, this stand provides plenty of room for loading block or powder scale. Made of aluminum alloy, in RCBS green, for powder measures with standard ⅞-14 threaded drop-tube. From RCBS... **$17.90**

RCBS Powder Funnel

Plastic funnel with specially designed drop tube to avoid powder spills around case mouths, an anti-static treatment to prevent powder from sticking, and a square lip to keep it from rolling around. Available in one size for 22-45 cal. and one size for 17-cal. From RCBS.

Price: 22-45-cal. **$3.00**
Price: 17-cal. **$4.00**

REDDING No. RS-6 Powder Measure Stand

Provides convenient bench-top mounting for the Redding Master Powder Measure or other measures threaded ⅞-14. This stand is *not* threaded—measure is secured with a lock ring allowing the reservoir to be quickly dumped. From Redding. **$17.95**

REDDING No. 5 Trickler

A companion to the Redding powder measure and scale, this trickler will add the necessary few kernels of powder when loading maximum or highest accuracy ammunition. From Redding.................................... **$13.95**

SINCLAIR Powder Measure Bracket

This powder measure bracket attaches quickly to the corner of a shooting tool box with Allen screws, providing a solid platform to which the on-the-range reloader can attach a measure. Made of anodized aluminum, it will accommodate most measures. From Sinclair Int. Inc. **$12.00**

Case Gauges

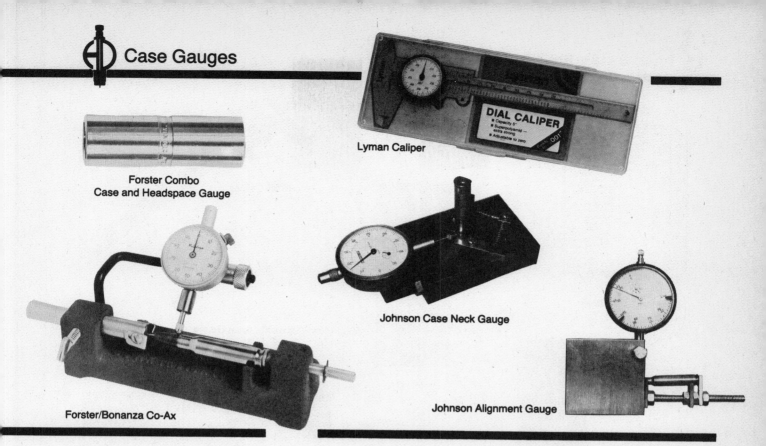

Forster Combo Case and Headspace Gauge

Lyman Caliper

Forster/Bonanza Co-Ax

Johnson Case Neck Gauge

Johnson Alignment Gauge

Notes on Case Gauges . . .

Few beginners realize it, but one of the most important tools a reloader can have is an accurate case length gauge. Made in various designs, some of these are simply measuring devices of the Go-No-Go type. Their purpose is to tell the reloader if the over-all length of a fired case exceeds the allowable maximum. If it does, it must be trimmed, for chambering a too-long case jams it into the rear of the lands, crimping it on the bullet's ogive and leaving no clearance for expansion on firing—therefore boosting the pressure to dangerous levels.

Some combination gauges, such as the Wilson and Forster, also measure head to shoulder length, thus indicate headspace condition and show whether a case has been altered by a sizing die. All in all, these are very useful and important items, and well worth their cost for all reloaders, novice and expert alike.

FORSTER/BONANZA Co-Ax Indicator

Designed to show the degree of concentricity between case and bullet, this device can show misalignment of .0005". The cartridge is held against a recessed adjustable rod by a spring loaded plunger; the case head, held in a "V" block, is rotated by finger pressure. From Forster Products. Price less dial indicator **$39.00**
Dial indicator only **$40.00**

FORSTER Combination Case and Headspace Gauge

Measures head to shoulder length (headspace) as well as over-all length. Available in most popular calibers, including many popular wildcats and belted magnums. From Forster Products. **$15.00**

JOHNSON Case-Neck Gauge

Two spring-loaded stabilizer arms press neck tightly against a hardened steel spindle. As case is rotated, dial indicator shows variation of wall thickness to .001" or less. Price, including the precision dial indicator gauge. Add $4.00 shipping/handling charge. From Plum City Ballistics Range . . . **$64.00**
Without dial indicator **$29.00**

JOHNSON Bullet Alignment Gauge

This gauge accurately measures the alignment (concentricity) of completed cartridges. It is designed to be used with the same dial indicator as used on the Johnson case neck gauge. Price, including precision dial indicator. Add $4.00 shipping/handling charges. From Plum City Ballistics Range . . **$59.00**
Price without dial indicator **$24.00**

LYMAN Dial Caliper

Designed specifically for the reloader, this caliper reads to .001" and opens to 5 inches for measuring loaded rounds. Comes in its own protective case with a comprehensive case length trim guide. From Lyman Products. **$29.95**

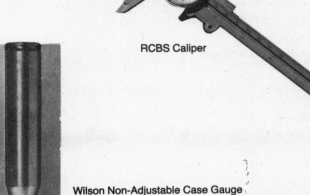

RCBS Caliper

McKillen & Heyer

Wilson Non-Adjustable Case Gauge

Wilson Adjustable Case Gauge

Sinclair Concentricity Fixture

McKILLEN & HEYER Case Length Gauge

A multiple-case gauge, hard chrome-plated, for measuring fired and sized cartridge cases.

Calibers are marked in raised letters for ease of reading. Shows most popular calibers. From McKillen & Heyer, Inc. **$9.00**

RCBS Dial Caliper Case Length Gauge

Easy-to-read dial, 5″ capacity, and measures four ways: outside, inside, depth and step. Handy chart on the back shows maximum and trim lengths for popular calibers. Dial graduations are in .010″ and 1/64″; the Vernier measures in increments of .1mm. Comes in a fitted plastic case with instructions. From RCBS................................. **$28.40**

WILSON Cartridge Case Gauge

An invaluable gauge for checking case cone-to-head and over-all length. Each end has both steps milled at one pass for greater accuracy. They are also useful in setting the case trimmer or—its most important function—in setting up any adjustable resizing die. All popular calibers, including many wildcats. From L.E. Wilson Co..................... **$15.00**

Adjustable Case Gauge for belted calibers. **$20.75**

Case length gauge for cases having no neck and a straight taper. **$8.50**

SINCLAIR Concentricity Fixture

This fixture will accept any dial indicator with a standard .375″ shaft and can be adjusted to read (1) neck runout as a method of checking the operation of a sizing die; (2) bullet runout to check the seating die; (3) case head squareness. Wooden base with anodized aluminum bed, nylon cartridge V-blocks. From Sinclair Int., Inc. **$48.00**

The product prices mentioned in these catalog pages were correct at presstime, but may be higher when you read this.

Bear Puller

Forster Model B

Hornady

C-H Puller

Notes on Bullet Pullers . . .

An efficient means of pulling a quantity of bullets from loaded ammunition can often produce quite a savings in one's shooting. Most often, surplus military ammunition is the target for pulling. Bullets can easily be pulled and replaced with hunting types. This practice is ordinarily safe so long as bullets of equal or less weight than the originals are used. If heavier bullets are desired, then powder charges must be reduced or another powder used.

One may also acquire a windfall of cheap or free ammunition which is of no use in its original loading. Pulling the bullets and salvaging the other components can save money.

Most pullers use a simple screw actuated collet to hold the bullet while the case is drawn off it. This type does not mark bullets and is probably the best choice for general use, even though separate collets are required for each caliber. Semiautomatic types are very fast, but do mark or indent the bullet, making them of little use for reloading. For only occasional use the inertia type is the best choice.

BEAR Bullet Puller

Removes bullets from cases without scratching or damaging them. This collet-design & bullet puller is chrome-plated and has standard ⅞ x 14 threads. Available in all popular calibers. From Bear Company.

Price: Bullet puller and collet **$12.50**
Price: Extra collet **$6.50**

C-H Bullet Puller

C-H puller has positive die-locking action, removes bullet without damage. Heavy-duty handle fully adjustable for ease of operation. Hex locking nut prevents twisting during operation. From C-H Tool and Die Corp. Price includes one collet **$10.50**
Extra collet (most popular calibers available) **$3.25**

FORSTER Bullet Puller

Has standard ⅞-14 threads to fit most reloading tools. Made of steel throughout and designed to tighten the grip on the bullet as pulling pressure is increased. Collets available for 22, 6mm (243-244), 25, 6.5mm, 270, 7mm (280 Rem.), 30, 303, 8mm (32), 358, 357, 45 ACP. From Forster Products **$9.90**
Exta collets 17, 333, 338, 348, 375, 410, 432 (44 Mag.), 458 . . . . **$6.00**

HORNADY Bullet Puller

This bullet puller uses a threaded body in conjunction with a threaded handle assembly. The collet drops in from the top and is available in 13 sizes from 17 caliber to 458. After the collet is installed, a handle is inserted into the puller body. As the handle assembly is screwed in, the collet is pushed down over the bullet and locked into place. From Hornady.

Puller body (no collet) **$10.60**
Collets (specify caliber) **$5.55**

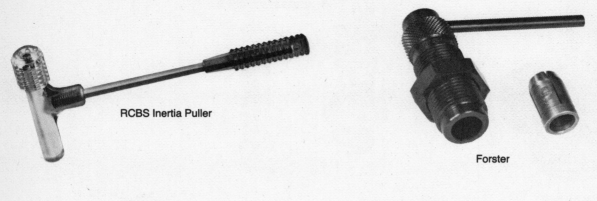

RCBS Inertia Puller

Forster

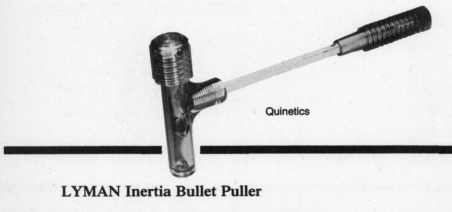

Quinetics

RCBS Bullet Puller

LYMAN Inertia Bullet Puller

Removes bullets from 22 to 45 cal. centerfire cases without damaging case or bullet, even those made of soft lead. This hammer type tool is quick and simple to use and all salvaged components are reusable. From Lyman Products..... **$23.95**

QUINETICS Kinetic® Magnum Bullet Puller

This inertia-type puller features a three-jawed chuck assembly that grips the cartridge quickly and efficiently, allowing speed in operation. User pushes round into the chuck, twist-tightens the cap and raps unit to pull bullet. Handles most cartridges from 22 to 458 Win. Mag., centerfire only. From Quinetics Corp. **$17.25**

RCBS Inertia Bullet Puller

Made of unbreakable plastic with a rugged aluminum handle, this kinetic puller can be used for cartridges from 22 Hornet through 458 Win. Mag. A three-jaw chuck grips the cartridge affording strength and reliability. The hollow head traps components after extraction, leaving case and bullet unmarked. From RCBS. **$24.70**

RCBS Bullet Puller

Usable in all presses with 7/8-14 thread. Working like a draw-in collet chuck on a lathe, the internally machined collets pull any length bullets quickly and easily without damage to them. From RCBS. **$12.30**
Extra collets................................. **$7.20**

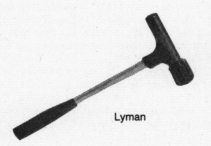

Lyman

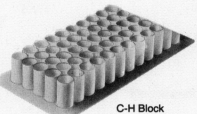

C-H Block

C-H Puller

B-Square Arbor Press

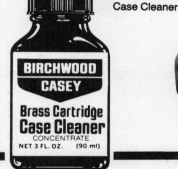

Birchwood Casey
Case Cleaner

Bear Removable Shellholder

Miscellany for Handloaders . . .

Gadgets to lure the reloader are numerous indeed! Just about as many, if not more, have appeared and then disappeared. Some of the accessories available are worthwhile, even—to those ammo makers who load in quantity or who are concerned with ultra-precision cartridges—a real necessity. At the other extreme, of course, are items you can well do without maybe, but you will have to decide that for yourself. In between there are small tools of real utility, products which can be helpful to you or not, as your personal needs—or fancied needs—demand.

Further on, in various other divisions, you'll find additional notes.

B-SQUARE Super Mag Arbor Press

Designed for the bench rest shooter and range reloader. The Super Mag will do all the tasks a conventional arbor press will do plus full length resize, all without bolting or clamping the press down in any way. It resizes all caliber brass. The press head is fully adjustable up or down on threaded posts for secure positioning. The ram, with replaceable brass caps and "spring return," has over a 1-inch stroke. Adjustable for both right and left hand use. Measures 13¾ inches high, weighs 4½ pounds. From B-Square. **$79.95**

BEAR Removable Shellholder Head

Easily changed from one caliber to another. Made of high grade steel, hardened for long life. Fits all basic "C" type presses. From Bear Company. **$2.50**

BEAR Primer Turning Plate

For fast easy primer handling, the Bear turning plate positions primers for insertion into the primer tube. No more misfires caused by handling primers with oily fingers. From Bear Company **$1.50**

BIRCHWOOD CASEY Case Cleaner

A liquid chemical formula for cleaning and restoring the brass to the original natural finish. Does not etch the metal and is easy to use. No harmful fumes or offending odors and will not stain hands or clothing. From Birchwood Casey. 3-oz. bottle. **$2.50**

C-H Stuck Case Puller

This tool kit removes cases stuck in reloading dies. It consists of the drill bit, tip, washer, allen-type screw and wrench. Easy to use and efficient. From C-H Tool and Die Corp. **$5.95**

C-H Loading Block

Holds 60 cartridges for easy reloading. Comes in black, white, red and blue—handy for the reloader who works up cases for different loads, etc. Holes are ¹⁵/₁₆" deep. Not large enough for 45-70 or 348, but holds all sizes up to 375 Holland & Holland. From C-H Tool and Die Corp. **$1.65**

Corbin Cleaner

Dillon FL-2000

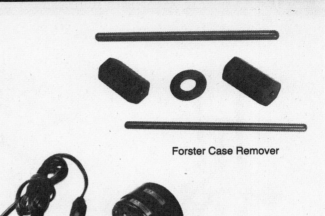

Forster Case Remover

Corbin Vibrator Kit

C-H Case Cluster

An accessory for the Mk I, Mk II, Mk III and Mk IV Auto Champs, as well as for other makes of progressive loading tools, including the Star (assuming that it has a Hulme feeder). This is a spring loaded indexer accommodating six case tubes, and will hold 90 38 Spec. cases, 120 45 ACP, or 138 9mm Luger cases. When one tube is empty, a twist of the unit will index another full tube into position and lock. From C-H Tool and Die Corp.

Complete with two threaded inserts for all calibers. **$39.95**
As above except for the Star machine. **$44.95**

CHEVRON Case Master

The Chevron Case Master is an automatic pistol case feeder that's designed to be used with production ammo loading machines which use a shell case feeding system, such as the Star, Phelps, C&H Model 375, etc. It may also be adapted for filling tubes for use on other machines.

The Chevron Case Master automatically orients and feeds to a constant level, the following pistol cartridges: 38 Spec., 357 Mag., 44 Spec., 44 Mag., 45 ACP, 45 Auto Rim and 45 Colt. To load 9mm, 38 Super and small cases, the company recommends that you purchase their "shell-plate." When ordering this unit specify the caliber(s) needed. No alterations to your loading machine are necessary. From Chevron Case Master. **$199.00**

DILLON Magnum FL-2000 Case Cleaner

A vibratory case cleaner, this unit has a 12½ qt. volume. Cleans 1,300 38/357 cases or 550 30-06 cases per hour. The motor is internally cooled, thermally protected, and turns on ball bearings. Bowl and frame are ¼-in. thick high-impact ABS plastic. From Dillon Precision Products, Inc. . . **$125.00**

CORBIN Vibrator Motor Kit

Complete vibrator motor and mounting kit to make a high efficiency case polisher out of any flat-bottom pail. Motor is mounted to the bottom of the pail, and pail is suspended by a rope. Powerful vibrations churn the contents (regular polishing medium such as walnut shells and rouge). For 115 volt AC operation. From Corbin Mfg. **$29.50**

CORBIN Bore Cleaner

Safe cleaner for fine target barrels, contains no corrosives or harsh abrasives. Removes lead, copper, and powder fouling from pistol, rifle, and shotgun bores. Also removes plastic wad fouling. From Corbin Mfg.

2 oz. bottle **$2.98**
Pint bottle **$18.00**

CORBIN Bullet Polisher Kit

The Corbin Bullet Polisher Kit is an economical method of polishing cases and bullets. Vibratory polishing moves the media rapidly against the cases, rather than rolling the whole mixture and knocking components against each other. It is the preferred method for polishing precision bullets. The kit consists of a mounting bracket, a vibratory motor using an enclosed eccentric weight to induce powerful vibration, a package of Corbin Polishing Medium, instructions and hardware. The motor contains automatic circuit protection and all wiring is finished, ready to use from the box. A line-mounted switch and grounded three-prong plug is standard. The unit is mounted to a container supplied by the handloader (usually, a 3-lb. coffee can is chosen). The container can be suspended from a cord or bail, or an optional steel stand is available from Corbin. For 115-volt, 60 Hz operation. From Corbin Mfg. **$29.50**

Corbin HTO-2 Furnace

Forster Hollow Pointer

Forster Primer Turner

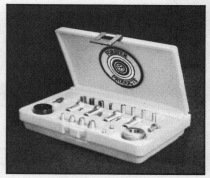

Forster Accessory Case

CORBIN HTO-2 Heat Treatment Furnace

The Corbin HTO-2 is an electronically controlled electric furnace for heat-treating steel and copper, making bonded-core bullets, and general gunsmith and laboratory metalurgical heating jobs. Features extremely fast heat-up time; set-and-forget temperature monitoring and control due to the electronic "brain" of the system; a range of from 0 to 2,000 degrees F. under constant temperature monitoring and control without operator attention; forced-air cooling for the electronics and stainless steel enclosed temperature transducer with fail-safe circuitry. Dual meters read both the absolute temperature compensated for ambient level, and deviation from the selected set-point. Heat loss is measured and stored, then compared to heat gain during alternate cycles, closing in quickly on a control band and holding it regardless of the thermal load or changes in heat radiation. The cavity size is 4.5 x 4.5 x 6 inches. Available in either 200-volt or 115-volt single phase models. Can be operated from ordinary household wiring because of space-age ceramic fiber insulation and low energy required to achieve selected temperatures. From Corbin Mfg. **$850.00**

CORBIN Bore Lap

Compound for lapping rough or badly fouled gun barrels, smoothing minor chatter marks, restoring rusted surfaces. Used on tight cloth patch or lead lap. From Corbin Mfg.
2 oz. jar. **$4.50**

FORSTER/BONANZA Die Box

Box provides a safe, dust-free and dry storage for your dies while not in use. Each box has a moisture absorbent disc to prevent rust and the inside lid provides tips and suggestions to questions or problems regarding reloading. Made of high impact plastic. From Forster Products. **$3.00**

FORSTER Accessory Case

This compartmented plastic case holds Forster's case trimmer collets and pilots, new style outside Neck Turner with pilots, neck reamers, a primer pocket chamfering tool with center, and primer pocket cleaners. Hinged lid with snap latch. From Forster Products. **$5.95**

FORSTER/BONANZA Stuck Case Remover

This five-piece kit will easily remove cartridge cases stuck in either a Bonanza or RCBS sizing die. No drilling or tapping required with this kit. From Forster Products. **$8.00**

FORSTER/BONANZA Primer Turner

The cover of the Bonanza powder measure serves as a primer turning plate. Made of unbreakable pastic, it is helpful in loading automatic primer tubes. May be had separately. From Forster Products. **$3.00**

FORSTER Hollow Pointer

An accessory for the Forster Case Trimmer. Available in either $\frac{1}{16}''$ or $\frac{1}{8}''$ drill size. Complete with guide bushing and drill for any caliber rifle or pistol cartridge. From Forster Products. **$9.00**

FORSTER Polishing Roll

This silicone carbide impregnated cleaning and polishing material won't rust and can be washed and reused. Ideal for cleaning and polishing cartridge cases. Cut it to size for intricate jobs. From Forster Products **$3.96**

Hodgdon Cleaner

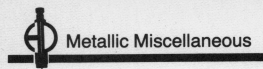

Hanned Precision Nexpander

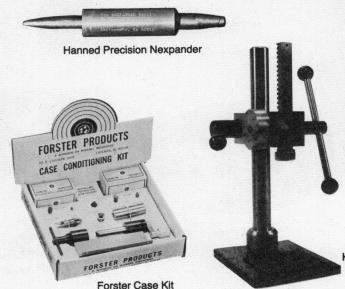

Forster Case Kit

Hart Arbor Press

Hanned Precision K-Spinner

FORSTER Headspace Gauges

These Forster gauges are made to ± .0002″ tolerance to insure accurate testing. Gauges are available in "Go," "No Go", and "Field." Most popular calibers. From Forster Products.

Rimless...$12.00
Rimmed, with pilot............................$12.00

FORSTER Case Trimming and Conditioning Kit

A complete selection of all the Forster tools. Kit includes: Forster Case Trimmer with collet and pilot, deburring tool, DBT Adapter, case length gauge, neck reamer, primer pocket cleaner, primer pocket center, and the outside neck turner. Kit is available in the following calibers: 38 Special, 357 Magnum, 44 Magnum, 219 Donaldson, 222 Rem., 222 Rem. Mag., 223 Rem., 22-250, 243 Win., 30-06, 8x57 Mauser, 257 Roberts, 244 Rem., 7x57 Mauser, 280 Rem., 250 Savage, 270 Win., 300 Savage, 308 Win. From Forster Products. Complete $96.00

HANNED PRECISION K-Spinner

Chuck this manual case-polishing mandrel into the drill lathe or drill press, grab a handful of 0000 steel wool and polish your cases. It polishes cases mirror bright in only 6 seconds. The mandrels come several sizes with one size fitting several calibers. Three rifle sizes are available: SR (17-27 cals.); MR (284-348); and LR (358-458). Pistol sizes available include: Revolver (357, 41, 44, 45), and Auto (380, 45). All orders postpaid. From Hanned Precision.

Price: Each (specify size) $16.50
Price: All six plus mounting block $70.00

HANNED PRECISION Nexpander Tool

A tool to help the reloader get a bullet started into a case. Eliminates lead shaving of cast bullets and mangled case necks caused by jacketed bullets. Two precision-tapered steel rods permit slight case mouth belling when a bullet refuses to seat. Fits calibers 17 through 458 both rifle and pistol. All orders postpaid. From Hanned Precision.................$16.00

HART Arbor Press

This deluxe arbor press combines anodized aluminum and blued steel parts. Height is adjustable from 1″ to 7″ with a 3½″ ram stroke and 2″ stroke per handle revolution. All bronze bushings. Brass ram tip for die protection. Rubber pad on base for die protection. Measures 10½″ high, 5½″ wide and 6″ deep. From Robt. W. Hart & Sons, Inc.

Price:...$94.95
Price: With spring return on ram $109.95

HODGDON Case Cleaner

A mild, acidic solution is diluted with water for soaking or tumbling dirty cases. Cleans brass bright and shiny without etching. Four-ounce bottle cleans hundreds of cases. From Hodgdon Powder Co.............................$2.50

HORNADY Automatic Primer Shutoff

Makes it easy to remove the primer tubes from the Automatic Primer Feed Assembly without spilling a handful of primers. Precisely aligns with the Positive Priming System on Hornady's Pro-Jector progressive press. Standard with the Pro-Jector and is now available as an accessory. From Hornady..$9.50

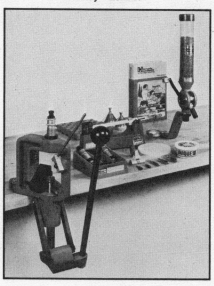
Hornady PacifiKit

Hornady Primer Turner

Hornady Loading Block

Hornady Accessory Pack I

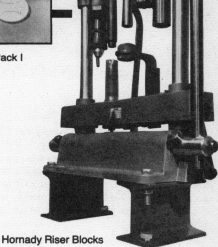
Hornady Riser Blocks

HORNADY PacifiKit

Available in Pro-7 or OO-7 this kit includes all the bench accessories of the Accessory Pack I (deluxe powder measure, magnetic scale, two powder funnels, reloading tray, primer turning plate, case lube, chamfering and deburring tool, three case neck brushes, both large and small primer pocket cleaner with accessory handle, *Hornady Handbook of Cartridge Reloading*) plus either a Pro-7 or OO-7 press. Both PacifiKit presses are equipped with a set of dies, primer catcher, removable shellholder, positive priming system and automatic primer feed. From Hornady.

Price: OO-7 kit with Series I 2-die set **$333.85**
Price: As above with Series II 3-die set **$359.50**
Price: Pro-7 kit Series I 5-die set. **$425.00**
Price: As above with Series II 3-die set **$448.40**

HORNADY Primer Turner

Made of plastic, it permits easy primer handling. After picking up all of the base down primers, merely replace lid and flip over. From Hornady. **$3.95**

HORNADY Handloader's Accessory Pack I

For reloaders who have a press, dies and shellholder but need all the bench accessories for handloading, Hornady offers their Accessory Pack I. It includes a deluxe powder measure, magnetic scale, two non-static powder funnels, a Universal loading tray, a primer turning plate, case lube, a chamfering and deburring tool, three case neck brushes, both a large and small primer pocket cleaner with accessory handle and a copy of the *Hornady Handbook of Cartridge Reloading*. From Hornady. **$172.50**

HORNADY Primer Catcher

Deep-welled and wide-faced to catch all primers and prevent them from bouncing out. Made of durable plastic. From Hornady. **$4.00**

HORNADY 366 Riser Blocks

Mounts your 366 Auto above the counter, and gives you easy access to your finished shells. From Hornady. . . . **$12.00**

HORNADY Loading Block

This universal block accommodates 98% of all popular calibers and will hold 50 cases of any caliber from 25 ACP through 458 Win. Mag. Molded from high-impact red plastic. From Hornady. **$3.50**

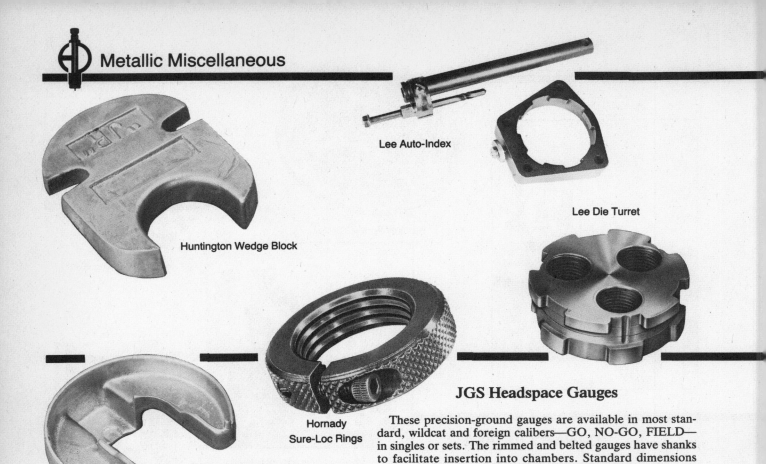

Lee Auto-Index

Lee Die Turret

Huntington Wedge Block

Hornady
Sure-Loc Rings

Huntington Primer Catcher

HORNADY Sure-Loc Die Rings

The Sure-Loc lock ring comes with an allen wrench and has a unique locking screw which pulls the collar tight around the threaded die body. As it tightens, it applies even pressure around the die. This feature prevents seizing but allows the lock ring to be easily loosened. Made of blued steel. From Hornady. Price, each **$1.75**

HORNADY Stuck Case Remover

A new 3-piece tool that consists of a #7 drill, ¼-20 tap and a remover body designed to fit the universal shellholder on any standard press. Easy and fast to use. No wrenches needed. From Hornady. **$9.95**

HUNTINGTON Aluminum Primer Catcher

Designed to fit the RCBS Rock Chucker presses and old Junior presses, the Primer Catcher attaches quickly without screws. From Huntington Die Specialties. **$5.00**

HUNTINGTON Wedge Block

The Wedge Block is designed specifically for the old RCBS Junior press. It elevates the press at an angle that provides a little more ease of operation. From Huntington Die Specialties. **$6.00**

JGS Headspace Gauges

These precision-ground gauges are available in most standard, wildcat and foreign calibers—GO, NO-GO, FIELD—in singles or sets. The rimmed and belted gauges have shanks to facilitate insertion into chambers. Standard dimensions from 22-250 through 30mm. From JGS Precision Tool Mfg.
Price: SAAMI and standard dimensions, rifle, from **$16.50**
Price: Shotgun (to SAAMI specs), from **$16.50**
Price: Custom dimensions, from **$20.10**

LEE Shell Plate Carrier and Case Sensor

To change calibers on Lee Progressive 1000 press, the entire shell plate carrier can be replaced with this unit. Each unit comes complete with shell plate, Auto Prime, case ejector, Auto-Index, and spare parts. From Lee Precision, Inc. **$52.98**

LEE Auto-Index

This conversion unit for the Lee Turret Press automatically rotates the turret to the next station near the bottom of each stroke. The safety override prevents over-stressing should the turret be prevented from turning. Greatly speeds reloading as no time is required to index the turret. Press can be ordered with Auto-Index, or separately. From Lee Precision, Inc. **$30.00**

LEE Case Feeder

Designed for the Lee Progressive 1000. An extra case feeder can be purchased to be mounted on each Shell Plate Carrier, eliminating the need for readjusting when changing calibers. From Lee Precision, Inc.
Price: Large Case Feeder (Handgun)............. **$25.00**
Price: Small Case Feeder (Handgun) **$25.00**
Price: Rifle Case Feeder..................... **$25.00**
Price: Extra Case Feeder Tubes (7-pack) **$6.98**

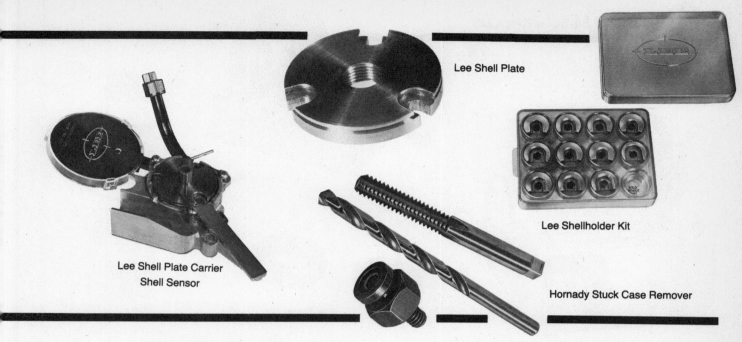

Lee Shell Plate

Lee Shellholder Kit

Lee Shell Plate Carrier
Shell Sensor

Hornady Stuck Case Remover

LEE Shellholder Set

Eleven shellholders that fit over 115 different calibers packed in a durable, see-through plastic box. Includes shellholders #1 through #11 (see chart).

Price: Red Storage Box with 11 holders for Lee Auto Prime $19.98

Price: Green Storage Box with 11 holders for all brands of presses $19.98

Price: Red Storage Box only $2.50

LEE Conversion Kit

The Conversion kit updates and converts the Lee Turret Press to a Progressive 1000 basic press. A Shell Plate Carrier must be ordered with the conversion kit. Factory installation available. From Lee Precision, Inc.

Price: Conversion Kit $25.00
Price: Factory Installation $10.00

LEE Die Box

Lee dies come packed in a round box that permits storage of the turret with the dies installed. Made from a tough, durable plastic. Will also hold dies without the turret. From Lee Precision, Inc. $2.00

LEE Shell Plates

For the Lee Progressive 1000 press and available in all calibers compatible with the Progressive 1000. From Lee Precision, Inc. $20.00

LEE Die Turret

For the Lee Turret Press. Once the dies have been adjusted they never need readjusting. Simply snap the turret and dies into the press. Made of cast and machined aluminum. From Lee Precision, Inc. $10.98

LEE Shell Plate Carrier

Calibers on the Lee Progressive 1000 can be changed easily and quickly by replacing the shell plate carrier unit. Changing the unit rather than just the shell plate extends the life of the press. The Carrier comes complete with Shell Plate, Auto Prime, case ejector, Auto-Index and spare parts. Available in all calibers compatible with The Progressive 1000. From Lee Precision, Inc. $49.98

R1	8mm/06	R5	R7
22 Rem.Jet	8mm Man. Schoe.	257 Wea.	22 Hornet
256 Win. Mag.	35 Rem.	303/25	22K Hornet
38 S&W	35 Whelen	6.5 Rem. Mag.	30 M1 Car.
38 Colt N.P.	358 Win.	264 Win. Mag.	
38 Short Colt	357 Auto Mag.	270 Weatherby	
38 Long Colt	44 Auto Mag.	7 x 61 S&H	
38 Special	45 Auto	7mm Rem. Mag.	R8
357 Mag.		7mm Wea.	33 Win.
41 Long Colt		30/40 Krag.	348 Win.
		300 H&H	40/82 Win.
	R3	300 Wea.	45/70 Gov't.
	22 Savage	300 Win. Mag.	
R2	219 Zipper	308 Norma Mag.	
22 BR	25/35	303 British	
224 Clark	6.5x55 Swed. Mau.	8mm Rem. Mag.	R9
22/250	7.5mm Swiss	338 Win. Mag.	41 Mag.
240 Wea.	30 Herrett	340 Wea.	220 Swift
243 Win.	30/30 Win.	35 Win.	225 Win.
6mm Rem.	32 Win.Spc'l	350 Rem. Mag.	6.5 Jap.
244 Rem.	32/40 Win.	358 Norma Mag.	
6mm Int'l	38/55 Win.	375 H&H	
6mm/284	408 Win.	375 Wea.	
6mm/06		38/40	R11
25/284		44/40	444 Marlin
25/06		458 Win. Mag.	44 S&W Spc'l
250 Savage		455 Webley	44 S&W Rus.
257 Roberts	R4		44 Mag.
6.5mm/06	17 Rem.		45 Colt
6.5mm x 57	221 Fireball		
270 Win.	222 Rem.	R6	
280 Rem.	222 Rem. Mag.	218 Bee	
7 x 57mm Mau.	223 (5.56mm)	25/20 Win.	R12
284 Win.	6x47(6mm/222M)	32 Win. S.L.	220 Rus.
300 Savage	32 Short Colt	32/20 (32 W.C.F.)	PPC
308 Win. (7.62 NATO)	32 Long Colt	30 Luger	7.62mmx39
30/06 Springfield	32 S&W	30 Mauser	
7.7 Jap.	32 S&W Long	9mm Luger	
8 x 57 Mau.	32 Colt N.P.	38 Super Auto	R13
	380 Auto	38 ACP	45 Auto Rim

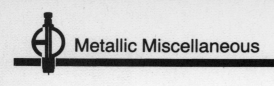

Lortone Pistol Pete

Lortone Model R-40

Lee Rings

Lyman Case Cleaner

LEE Lock Rings

No tools are needed to lock these rings in place, yet they stay put once locked. Easily readjustable. Rubber O-ring on the bottom face. Usable on all brands of dies. From Lee Precision, Inc. Pack of three rings. **$2.50**

LORTONE Precision Case Media

Black walnut shell treated with non-toxic industrial cleaning/polishing agents for long life and easy clean-up. From Lortone.
Price: 24-oz. plastic pouch **$4.50**

LORTONE Brass Machine Case Tumblers Model R-40, R-20

For commercial reloaders, Lortone provides rugged economical high-volume tumblers. Capacity runs from 2,400 38 Special cases to 800 30-06 cases (R-40) or 1200 38 Special cases/400 30-06 cases (R-20). Features heavy gauge welded steel construction; hexagonal steel barrels; neoprene rubber liner and gasket; dual rubber covered drive shafts; heavy-duty bearings and barrel guides. Optional ⅓-hp ball bearing motor available. From Lortone.
Price: Model R-40. . . . . **$325.00**
Price: Optional ⅓ hp motor. **$97.50**
Price: Model R-20. . . . . **$260.00**

LORTONE Pistol Pete Case Tumbler

Cleans and polishes cases quickly and quietly in a solid rubber 10-sided tumbling barrel. Compact steel and aluminum frame fully encloses motor and drive system. Tumbler holds 180 38 Special cases or 75 30-06 cases. A 24-oz. pouch of Gunners Brass Precision case media comes with the unit. From Lortone **$74.50**

LORTONE Brass Machine Case Tumblers, QT-6, QT-12 and QT-66

Large capacity case tumblers for the serious reloader. Feature solid rubber barrels with 10-sided interiors, welded steel frames, fully enclosed drive systems and overload protected ball bearing motors. The QT-6 has the capacity to hold 260 38 Special/90 30-06 cases; QT-12—600 38 Special/200 30-06 cases; QT-66—520 38 Special/180 30-06 cases. The QT-66 features two barrels on a single frame—ideal for cleaning two different batches of cases without mixing. From Lortone.
Price: QT-6. . . . . **$89.50**
Price: QT-12 . . . . **$119.50**
Price: QT-66 . . . . **$129.50**

LYMAN Turbo Cleaner/Degreaser

An industrial strength degreaser, this product removes lubricants from cartridge cases, dies or mould blocks. Packaged in 14-oz. aerosol can. From Lyman Products. **$4.95**

LYMAN Primer Catcher

Made of heavy-duty plastic, this catcher locks securely to the press, yet is easily removable for emptying or cleaning. For Orange Crusher, O-Mag, T-Mag or Special-T and Spar-T presses. From Lyman Products. **$4.50**

LYMAN Ammo Handler Kit

For reloaders who have the press but not the accessories, the Ammo Handler Kit provides the No. 55 powder measure, Model 500 scale, case lube kit, *Metallic Reloading User's Guide, Powder Manufacturer's Loading Data,* powder funnel, deburring tool, primer tray and loading block. From Lyman Products. **$144.95**

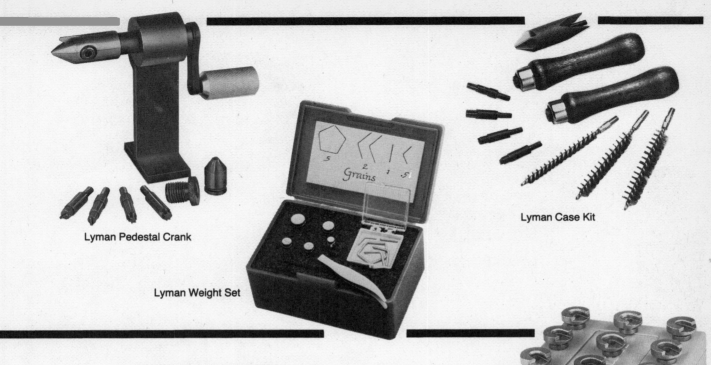

Lyman Pedestal Crank

Lyman Weight Set

Lyman Case Kit

Lyman Shellholder Set

LYMAN Turbo Sifter

A black plastic 14″ sifter that makes it easy to separate cases from the polishing media. Speeds up the processing of cases. From Lyman Products. **$7.95**

LYMAN Case Preparation Kit

Everything needed to prepare cases for loading. Kit contains Lyman's deburring/chamfering tool, large and small primer pocket cleaners, large and small primer pocket reamers, inside-neck cleaning brushes in 25, 38 and 45 calibers, and a pair of wood handles. From Lyman Products **$24.50**

LYMAN The Organizer

A sturdy work station, adjustable for any reloading press, sizer, lubricator or other gear normally mounted to a workbench. Available in kit form, stained and finished or unfinished. From Lyman Products. **$29.95**
The Organizer, stained and finished **$49.95**

LYMAN Pedestal Crank

Hand-operated Pedestal Crank accepts and drives Lyman's primer pocket cleaning brushes, ream/clean accessory set and the chamfer/debur tool. The sturdy base assumes shaft alignment. From Lyman. **$13.50**

LYMAN Die Box

New orange-colored box is made of tough plastic with a hinged, lifetime, snap-lock cover. Holds each die firmly. Impervious to moisture, bore cleaner or oil. From Lyman Products. **$2.00**

LYMAN Reloader's Shellholder Set

This set contains 12 standard shellholders in a handy storage box. Shellholders fit all popular rifle and pistol cartridges and most presses. Includes the following Lyman shellholders: 1, 2, 6, 7, 9, 11, 12, 13, 17, 19, 26 and 30. From Lyman.
Price: Shellholder set **$19.95**
Price: Shellholder box only **$2.50**

LYMAN Weight Check Set

Consists of ten weights, totalling 210.5 grains, to check reloading scale accuracy. Weights provided are: one .5 gr., one 1 gr., two 2 gr., one 5 gr., one 10 gr., two 20 gr., one 50 gr., and one 100 gr.—enough to check a scale at several points through the weighing range. Made in accordance with national Bureau of Standards (NSF) Class F tolerances. Comes in a plastic box with forceps for handling the weights and instructions. From Lyman Products. **$24.50**

LYMAN Turbo Case Cleaner

A mild, non-etching solution for use with extremely fouled or corroded cases. Also removes resizing lube. Can be used with Lyman Turbo Tumblers. From Lyman Products. Per 16-oz. bottle. **$3.95**

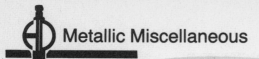

Lyman Turbo 3200

Lyman Accessory Bowl

Lyman Turbo Charger

Lyman Turbo 600 & 1200

LYMAN Loading Block

Accepts pistol cases through 45-caliber and rifle cases up to 458 Win. Mag. Made of durable plastic. From Lyman Products...**$3.95**

LYMAN Turbo Charger

After prolonged use the cleaning media supplied with Lyman's Turbo Tumblers becomes dark from absorbed lubricant and fouling and loses its effectiveness. By adding 1 ounce of Turbo Charger per 2 pounds of media, the polishing capability is restored. This 4-oz. bottle is enough for about four reactivations of the 1200 Tumbler. From Lyman Products.

Price: 4 oz. **$2.95**
Price: 16 oz. **$9.95**

LYMAN 3200 Turbo Tumbler

Similar to the 1200 Turbo except cleans and polishes up to 1,000 38 Spec. cases. Has an on-off switch and a replaceable integral fuse to protect against power overloads. Easily removeable lid. Operates on 120 VAC power (20 VAC unit also available). From Lyman Products.

3200 Turbo Tumbler. 120 VAC **$209.95**
3200 Turbo tumbler, 220 VAC.................**$210.00**

LYMAN Turbo Accessory Bowl

This orange pumpkin-shaped bowl converts the Turbo 600 Tumbler to a 1200 by increasing the capacity. Also serves as an alternate bowl when different media is used. Grid top serves as a sifter. From Lyman Products. **$34.95**

LYMAN Case Neck Dipper

A three brush set in the Dipper cleans cartridge cases from 17 to 45-caliber. The cases are dipped in the dry tube to reduce friction encountered when pulling the expander button back through the sized case neck. From Lyman Products.

Price: Case Neck Dipper with mica **$6.95**
Price: Replacement Mica Refill..................**$1.95**

LYMAN Turbo-Tumblers

This new system allows the media to swirl around totally immersed cases in a high speed agitated motion that cleans and polishes all interior and exterior surfaces. Two styles are offered. The Turbo 1200 with a 12-lb. capacity will process the equivalent of over 300 38 Specials or 100 30-06 cases. The Turbo 600 cleans half the 1200 capacity. A liquid 600 accessory bowl is also available for use of either dry or wet media. Quiet operation with easily removeable lid in place. Both operate on either 110V or 220V power, have a convenient on/off switch incorporated into the electrical cord, and come charged with a supply of Turbo media. From Lyman Products.

Turbo-Tumbler 600 110 V....................**$114.95**
　　　　　　　　　　220 V....................**$115.95**
Turbo-Tumbler 1200 110V **$144.95**
　　　　　　　　　　220V **$145.95**
Media, 1-lb. can **$3.95**
Media, 2-lb. box **$6.95**
Media, 1-lb. box **$19.95**

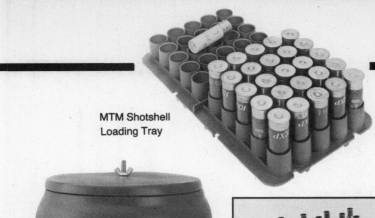

MTM Shotshell
Loading Tray

MTM Primer Flipper

MTM LT-50 Loading Tray

Olsens VT-30

Olsens VT-10

M&D Polishing Media

Corncob polishing media is excellent for use in rotary or vibrator tumblers. Available in 10-pound ($3.60), 25-pound ($8.00) or 50-pound ($14.00) quantities. From M&D Munitions, Ltd.

MRC Neck Reaming/Bullet Seating Kits

For precision reloading MRC offers three kits for neck reaming, bullet seating or a combination kit for both functions. The Bullet Seating kit comes complete with sizing die with built-in micrometer, knockout rod, bullet seater and depriming chamber. The Neck Reaming kit includes sizing die with built-in micrometer, neck reamer and knockout rod. The combination kit contains all the tools needed to perform both neck reaming and bullet seating. From Mequon Reloading Corporation.

Price: Bullet Seating Kit **$29.98**
Price: Neck Reaming Kit **$29.98**
Price: Combination Kit **$38.98**

MTM CASE-GARD 150 Loading Tray

Holds all cartridges for reloading. Front side has large and small openings (50 each) for cartridges from 17 cal. to 458 Win. Reverse side has holes for 45 and 9mm pistol cases. Made of durable polypropylene. From MTM **$3.71**

MTM Primer-Flipper

An indispensable time saver for the busy reloader. Especially useful if automatic feed priming tool is used. From MTM. **$1.88**

MTM Case-Gard Shotshell Loading Tray

Each tray holds 50 rounds and is precision moulded to hold shells rock-steady during reloading. Designed to fit MTM's Shotshell 100 carrier, they are ideal for storing reloads. From MTM. **$3.40**

MTM LT-50 Universal Loading Tray

A more compact version of the LT-150, this tray will accommodate almost all calibers sold in the U.S. Has two usable sides with more than 150 cavities for different calibers. From MTM. **$3.65**

OLSENS VT-10 and VT-30 Tumblers

These vibratory tumblers will clean and polish the reloader's cartridge cases. The VT-10 is a 3-quart capacity machine, with 10-inch diameter bowl; the VT-30 has a capacity of 12 quarts with a 15-inch diameter bowl. Both feature an adjustable amplitude which allows the finishing action to be set from aggressive to fine polishing; a thermally protected heavy-duty ball-bearing motor; a wear resistant bowl with cover made of one-piece, high-density polymer moulding; a heavy gauge Parkerized base; and an optional drain for flow-through operation. Both operate on 120 VAC. From Westfield Engineering.

Price: VT-10. . . . . **$129.95**
Price: VT-30 . . . . **$375.00**

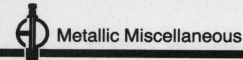
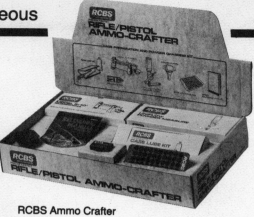

RCBS Ammo Crafter

Osage Arbor Press

RCBS Case Remover

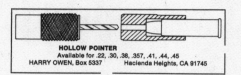

HOLLOW POINTER
Available for .22, .30, .38, .357, .41, .44, .45
HARRY OWEN, Box 5337   Hacienda Heights, CA 91745

Owen Hollow Pointer

OLSENS Polishing Media

Formula I and Formula II polishing media were designed for use in Olsens VT-10 and VT-30 tumblers but work well in all types of vibratory polishers. Formula I is a fine walnut shell media bonded with rouge — a fast dry media for cleaning brass. Formula II, a fine corncob media bonded with chromium oxide, brings a high luster polish to brass and will remove sizing lube and grease. Neither contain toxic solvents or grease and will not clog flash holes or damage primer pockets. From Westfield Engineering.

Price: Formula I (5 lbs.) **$9.95**
Price: Formula II (2½ lbs.)...................... **$6.95**

OSAGE Arbor Press

This press is all steel with a base measuring 4"x5"x½" with the top surface milled smooth. Clearance is 6 inches and is adjustable from 0 to 6 inches, with a ⅝-inch stroke on the spring return. Weight is about 5 lbs. and it can be disassembled to fit into the shooting box. From Vernon C. Seeley. Price does not include shipping charges. **$47.50**

OWEN Hollow Pointer

The Hollow Pointer is used to hollow point loaded cartridges. It can be used without any other tools. Adjustable drill holder acts as a positive stop to ensure depth consistency from cartridge to cartridge. May be used with an electric drill or drill press for large reloading jobs. Available for 22, 243, 25, 270, 7mm, 30, 8mm, 35, 357, 38, 9mm, 41, 44 and 45 calibers. From Harry Owen........................ **$13.95**

RCBS Rifle-Pistol Ammo Crafter Kit

Contains everything needed to prepare cases for reloading and handling powder charges in one easy purchase. Kit includes Speer #10 Manual, case loading block, deburring tool, powder funnel, case lube kit, 5-10 powder and bullet scale, Uni-flow powder measure combo. From RCBS. **$173.50**

RCBS Primer Tray

Designed to position primers anvil side up for fast, easy handling and insertion into the primer arm sleeve. Also can be used to load the automatic primer feed tubes by positioning primers with anvil side down. Tray holds 100 primers. Sturdy plastic. From RCBS............................ **$2.40**

RCBS Accessory Base Plate

A heavy aluminum casting measuring 9⅞" × 5½" × .820" thick with holes drilled and tapped for mounting reloading tools quickly and easily. The plate is mounted to the bench top with either four wood screws or two C-clamps. The following RCBS tools can be quickly attached and dismounted: Rotary Case Trimmer, and -2, Powder Measure Stand, Lube-A-Matic, and -2, Reloader Special-2 Press, Automatic and Standard Priming Tools. From RCBS............. **$17.90**

RCBS Sidewinder Case Tumbler

Designed specifically for handloaders, the Sidewinder Case Tumbler can clean and polish up to 300 38 Special cases, or 150 30-06 cases. Tilted, easy-access drum with a perforated cap that doubles as a screen to separate either liquid or dry polishing media from cleaned cases. Quiet motor; built-in timer adjusts for automatic shut-off of from 5 minutes to 12 hours. From RCBS.

129 VAC Sidewinder **$177.90**
240 VAC Sidewinder **$187.90**

RCBS Case Kicker

For RCBS JR., Reloader Special and Rock Chucker presses. This ejector spring assembly mounts on the right side of the press and pushes the case out of the shellholder into a box mounted to the left side of the press. A special Primer Deflector is included to catch decapped primers and direct them into a container on the floor. From RCBS......... **$18.40**

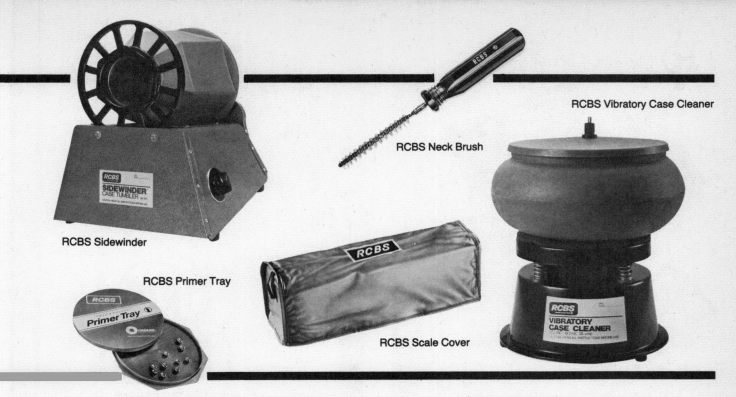

RCBS Sidewinder

RCBS Neck Brush

RCBS Vibratory Case Cleaner

RCBS Primer Tray

RCBS Scale Cover

RCBS Vibratory Case Cleaner

Designed specifically for cleaning and polishing larger quantities of cartridge cases using dry media. 3½-quart bowl cleans up to 550 38 Special cases or 190 30-06 cases at one time. Thermally protected ball-bearing motor cleans quickly and quietly. Operates on 120 VAC. A 2-pound package of dry media included. Limited lifetime warranty. From RCBS **$155.00**

RCBS Universal Scale Cover

Made of durable vinyl, this cover was designed for the RCBS 5-0-5 scale, but it may be used with other popular models. Protects the scale from dirt and foreign matter. From RCBS **$4.80**

RCBS Primer Seating Depth Gauge

A precise way to check primer seating depth without a micrometer. One end of the gauge is designed to "rock" on a case head which has a primer seated too low. The opposite end will rest flat on a case head which has a primer seated too deep. Made from hardened and ground steel. From RCBS **$5.00**

RCBS Case Cleaning Media

The RCBS liquid concentrate for use in the RCBS Sidewinder case tumbler is specially formulated to clean badly stained or soiled brass cases. Comes in 8-oz. bottle and makes approximately 4 gallons of cleaning agent.

The RCBS dry case cleaner works in either the Sidewinder or Vibratory units. Made of reusable black walnut shells ground to 12/20 sieve size, coated with two-special cleaning oxides. Available in 2-pound box. From RCBS.

Price: Liquid Case Cleaner **$2.90**
Price: Dry Case Cleaner **$7.40**

RCBS Pistol Ammo Crafter

The kit has everything needed to prepare handgun cases for the reloading process. Included are: Speer #10 Manual, case loading block, resizing lubricant, case lube pad, 5-0-5 powder and bullet scale, powder funnel, Little Dandy Pistol Powder Measure and two rotors. From RCBS.
Complete kit **$128.00**

RCBS Case Neck Brush

For lubricating inside of case neck before sizing. Nylon bristles withstand years of service. 22, 6mm, 270, 30, 35 and 45 calibers. From RCBS. Handle **$3.00**
Brushes **$1.80**

RCBS Reloading Accessory Kit

Kit contains the following accessories that simplify and speed-up reloading: powder measure stand, powder trickler, accessory base plate, primer tray, primer pocket brush combo, case loading block, and setscrew wrench combo. A handy package, especially for the beginner. From RCBS.
Kit, complete **$63.00**

RCBS Stuck Case Remover

This Williams-type device removes stuck cases from sizing dies quickly and efficiently. Case head is drilled and tapped, stuck case remover is placed over die and hex head screw is turned with wrench until case pulls free. Comes complete with drill, tap and wrench. From RCBS. **$11.20**
Stuck case remover kit **$8.00**

RCBS Primer Catcher

Attaches quickly without screws. Will fit RCBS Jr. and Pacific Super Presses. From RCBS. **$5.40**

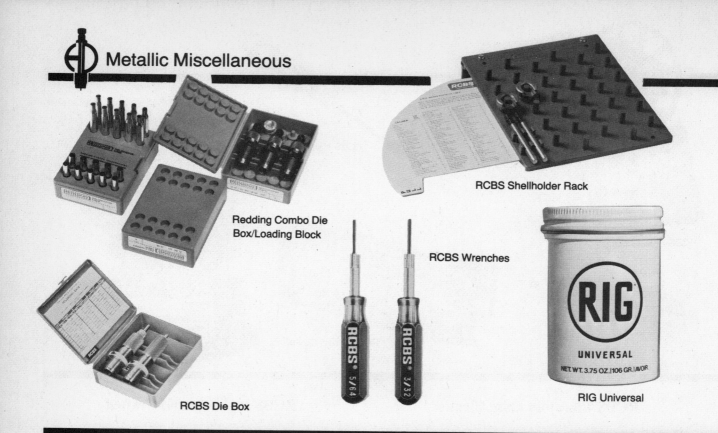

Redding Combo Die Box/Loading Block

RCBS Shellholder Rack

RCBS Wrenches

RCBS Die Box

RIG UNIVERSAL NET. WT. 3.75 OZ. (106 GR.) AVOIR.

RIG Universal

RCBS Shellholder Rack

This ABS plastic unit provides a method for keeping shell-holders and priming rod assemblies in one place. It measures 5¾" x 6⅝" and has pegs numbered through 32 for each size RCBS shellholder, plus an unmarked extra. A reference table listing the proper shellholder number for 114 common calibers pivots from the back of the unit. Can be mounted on bench or wall. From RCBS........................ **$9.90**

RCBS Die Box

Made of durable, green impact plastic this box will store any 2- or 3-die set and protect it from dust and dirt. Label on end of box for identification, another inside the lid to list pet loads for the dies. From RCBS **$3.20**

RCBS Loading Block

Made of unbreakable moulded plastic, this block fits all metallic cartridge cases. Flip over design allows for a full range of hole variations. 80 cavities on one side, 40 on the other, of 3 different depths and diameters are used to accommodate all cases. From RCBS............................. **$4.00**

RCBS Setscrew Wrenches

A handy item for every reloading bench. The convenient hexagonal plastic handle will not roll off the bench and is easy on the hands. Wrench size is stamped in large easy-to-read numbers for quick identification. Available in two sizes to fit all popular RCBS products. From RCBS.
Combination.................................. **$5.90**

REDDING No. 22 Stuck Case Removal Kit

This kit provides an easy and effective way to remove a stuck case from a resizing die. Case head is drilled, tapped, and the remover placed over the die; the hex-head screw is then turned to pull the case out. From Redding..... **$11.95**

REDDING Die Spacer Kit

For use with combination die sets and all ⅞-14 reloading dies to quickly compensate for case length or make a no-crimp adjustment, without moving the lock rings. Includes three spacers: .062—no-crimp or partial resizing; .125—44 Special/44 Magnum spacer; .135—38 Special/357 Magnum. From Redding.. **$5.00**

REDDING Combination Die Box/Loading Block

Unbreakable polypropylene box provides a convenient storage for dies when not in use and, also, has a provision for the storage of shellholders. Will accept any brand of dies regardless of lock ring diameter. Doubles as a loading block—top has provision for 20 cartridges with base size up to 30-06. Bottom has provision for 20 cartridges of Magnum base size up to 458 Win. or for large pistol cartridges. Included with all Redding Dies and available separately. From Redding. **$4.50**

REDDING Primer Catcher

Designed for the Redding Standard No. 7 "C" press. Eliminates the dropping of spent primers to the floor. From Redding.. **$6.50**

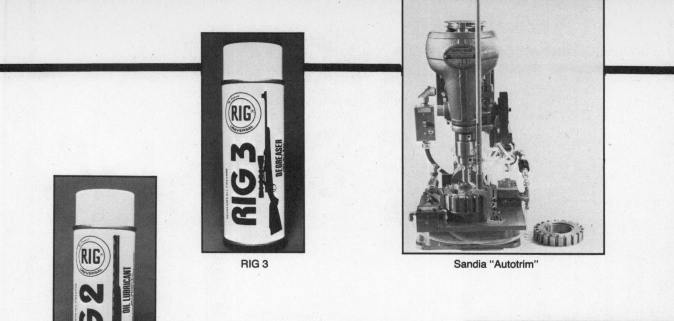

RIG 3

Sandia "Autotrim"

RIG 2

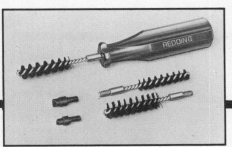

Redding #18 Kit

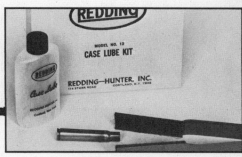

Redding Case Lube Kit

REDDING Model #18 Case Preparation Kit

Contains all the necessary tools you need for removing the dirt and powder residue from the inside of case neck and primer pockets. This all-in-one kit comes complete with accessory handle, both large and small primer pocket cleaners and three nylon case neck brushes which handle all cartridges from 22 thru 45 caliber. From Redding............ **$12.95**

RIG 2 and RIG 3

RIG 3 degreaser is an excellent die and brass cleaner for the handloader. One bath of RIG 3 removes both sizing and bullet lube from your favorite rifle or pistol dies. Once they have been thoroughly cleaned, spraying the dies with RIG 2 aerosol lubricant prior to storing them is an effective rust and corrosion preventative. This is a simple 2-step operation that extends die life and eliminates replacing ruined dies.

Another use for RIG 3 is in the area of brass cleaning. Once you've sized and/or polished the brass, spray them clean with RIG 3—it removes sizing lube and polishing rouge, instantly. Price per 8-ounce can of either RIG 2 or RIG 3, from RIG Products. About.................................... **NA**

RIG Universal Grease

RIG is an excellent preservative for long-term storage of reloading dies and firearms. A thin film of RIG, inside and out, keeps your dies like new until they're used again. Three sizes of RIG are available: 1-oz. (NA), 3¾-oz. (NA), and 15-oz. (NA). From RIG Products.

ROOSTER Brass Cartridge Polish

Removes tarnish and stain and provides a protective finish. Add it to any corncob or walnut shell media. Available in small or commercial quantities. From Rooster Laboratories.

Price: 4-oz.	**$3.50**
Price: 8-oz.	**$6.50**
Price: 16-oz.	**$12.00**
Price: 1-gallon...............................	**$50.00**
Price: 5-gallon	**$200.00**
Price: 55 gallons	**$1,500.00**

SANDIA "Autotrim"

This air operated automatic cartridge case trimmer processes 3500-plus cases per hour. Available for 223, 30 Carbine, 308 and 30-06. Tube or hand fed. Has micrometer-type head adjustment for raising or lowering the head. Adjustable speed control. Also available to ream primer pockets. From Sandia Die and Cartridge Co.

Complete for one caliber	**$4,860.00**
Additional caliber plates	**$216.00**

SANDIA Cartridge Cut-Off Machine

This tool attaches to a drill press and enables the operator to cut to length (not including final trim) about 700 cases per hour. Especially useful for cutting down military brass and such cases as 38 Special to 38 S&W or 308 Win. cases to 44 Auto Mag. From Sandia Die and Cartridge Co..... **$125.00**

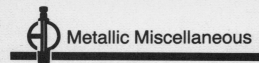
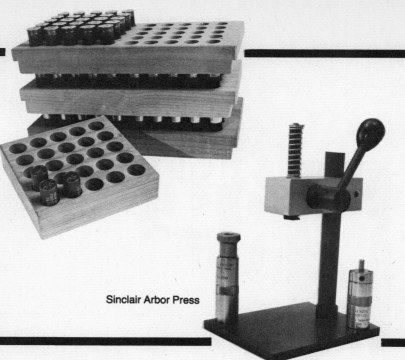

Stalwart Loading Blocks

Sinclair Arbor Press

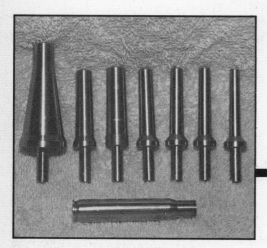

Sportsman Supply Case Spinners

SANDIA Processed Corn Cob Cleaner

Ground corn cob is used by large ammunition makers to clean and polish cartridge cases. This product is suitable for use in all vibratory and barrel tumbling machines. Useful for cleaning and polishing tools and parts as well. Packaged in 5-lb. box. From Sandia Die and Cartridge Co. **$6.95**

SCHARCH MANUFACTURING Range Master™ Case Inspector

Available for 38/357 brass, this four-stage automatic case inspector processes 5100 cases per hour. The first stage shuts off for bent or loaded rounds. The second stage checks for cracks. The third stage deprimes and the fourth stage checks the primer pocket. The second, third and fourth stages register all bad cases on the memory board and rejects them automatically without machine stoppage. If running 357 brass, the Rangemaster will automatically reject all 38 cases and vise versa. Has 12-inch diameter auto-case feeder and is set up to reject military crimped cases. Operates on 120-volt AC and weighs 340 pounds. From Scharch Mfg. Inc. **$5,495**

SINCLAIR Arbor Press

When used for bullet seating with straight line dies, the arbor press results in better uniformity of seating depth. Can also be used for neck resizing and depriming when the sizing die is fitted when an adequate base. This press is made of steel and anodized aluminum, has a 5″ × 5″ base and weighs 5 pounds. Adjustable head height of 6 inches under clearance. With spring return. From Sinclair Int., Inc. **$58.00**

SPORTSMAN SUPPLY Show Me Case Spinners

Show Me Case Spinners fit into any hand drill and provide a simple and inexpensive method of cleaning cartridge cases. Each spinner is individually machined from solid steel and they're available from 17-cal. to 45 ACP. Spinner No. 1 fits 22-6.5mm; No. 2—25-7mm; No. 3—270-8mm; No. 4—30- 35-cal.; No. 5—35-40-cal.; No. 6—41-47-cal.; No. 7—AU 45 pistol, 20-ga. and up shotshell through 45 ACP. From Sportsman Supply Company.

Price: Nos. 1-6, each **$6.00**
Price: 17-cal., each **$6.00**
Price: No. 7, each **$8.25**
Price: Nos. 1-7 (set) **$35.00**

STALWART Wooden Loading Blocks

For loading and sorting rifle and handgun cartridges from 25 ACP through 577 Nitro and shotshells in 10, 12, and 20 gauge. (The 20-ga. size also fits 12-ga. shells crimp down.) Made of solid hardwood, they are non-static and will not promote corrosion on brass during storage. Light and compact, they can be held beneath the powder measure for charging. The shotshell blocks, once loaded, are stackable for compact storage. From Stalwart Corp.

Price: 50-hole rifle and pistol block (50-70 and 577 sizes have 32 holes) **$3.49**
Price: 25-hole shotshell **$6.49**
Price: 50-hole shotshell **$12.49**

TRU-SQUARE Brass Polish Media

Treated crushed corn cob media for use in vibratory tumblers. This media removes only tarnish and oxidation without scratching. When cleaning action slows replace 25 percent of media with new. Also works well in rotary tumblers. From Tru-Square Metal Products. Comes in 3-pound packages. **$9.08**

Tru-Square Rotary AR-6

Tru-Square Ultra Vibe 18

Tru-Square Brass Polish

TSI 301 Lube

TRU-SQUARE Brass Separator

Sturdy 12-inch diameter plastic sifter that quickly separates cases from the polishing media. From Tru-Square Metal Products... **$6.95**

TRU-SQUARE UltraVibe Case Tumblers

Three models of vibratory tumblers are available from Tru-Square. Each features heavy steel construction, a wide stable base and an overload protected motor. The UltraVibe 45 is a 4¾-gal. capacity tumbler powered by a 115-volt, ¹⁄₂₀ hp motor. The 18, a 1½-gal. capacity unit with a 115-volt, ¹⁄₃₀ hp motor, and the UltraVibe 10 holds 3¾-gal. or 125-400 cartridge cases. All feature a heavy polyethylene bowl with lid. From Tru-Square Metal Products.

Price: UltraVibe 45 .... **$389.96**
Price: UltraVibe 18 .... **$142.98**
Price: UltraVibe 10 .... **$122.21**

TRU-SQUARE Rotary Tumblers

These high-speed tumblers clean and polish brass as quickly as a vibratory tumbler. Three models are available to handle large or small quantities of cases. The Model B features a steel barrel with rubber liner, 1¼-gal. capacity to hold 200-600 cases, a heavy steel base and a 115-volt, ¹⁄₅₀ hp motor. The AR-12's hexagonal steel barrel can clean 150-500 cartridge cases and is powered by a 115-volt, ¹⁄₇₅ hp motor. This same motor powers the smaller capacity AR-6 (100-400 cases). The AR-6 features a smooth exterior barrel with a 16-sided interior. From Tru-Square Metal Products.

Price: Model B **$125.94**
Price: AR-12................................. **$102.32**
Price: AR-6.................................. **$90.25**

TRU-SQUARE Brass Polish

Treated crushed black walnut shell media attacks oxidation without scratching. This media is reusable when used in conjunction with Tru-Square's reactivating cream. The cream will renew the media strength when cleaning action slows. From Tru-Square Metal Products. Price for 15 oz. **$3.73**
Reactivating cream per pound **$2.19**

TSI 400 Ammo Brass Cleaner

A safe non-polluting, non-flammable ammo cleaner that is instant-acting. No rubbing or wire-brushing necessary. A drip process that leaves brass shining and reduces the need for future cleaning. Comes in pint, quart and gallon containers.
Pint **$4.21**
Per gallon **$30.62**

TSI 301 Synthetic Lubricant

TSI 301 is a synthetic lubricant/degreaser that will clean, protect, and lube reloading presses, dies—anything metal. Removes both sizing and bullet lube. Once cleaned, spraying dies with TSI 301 prior to storage protects them against rust and corrosion. From American Gas and Chemical.

Price: 3 oz. aerosol spray **$3.53**
Price: 6 oz. aerosol spray **$3.94**
Price: 11 oz. aerosol spray **$5.49**
Price: 21 oz. pump **$6.87**
Price: 1-gal. drum **$23.80**
Price: 5-gal. drum **$98.70**

Vibra-Tek Polisher

Vibra-Tek Vibra Bright

The Loading Doc Case Annealer

Vibra-Tek Media

Wilcox Scoop

THE LOADING DOC Automatic Case Annealer

This unit anneals 1,000 cases per hour automatically. Fired brass is dropped into the shell wheel, the machine anneals and drops finished brass into a catch pan. Two propane torches supply the annealing heat while an electric motor turns the shell wheel. The machine comes equipped with one standard shell wheel of the reloader's choice. Shell-wheels are available in: 30-06, 223, 30-30, 44, 357, 41, 375 H&H, 284 Win., 224 Weath., 45-70, 45 LC, 240 Weath., 378 Weath. From The Loading Doc.................................. **$279.95**
Price: Extra Shell Wheels **$34.95**

VIBRA-TEK Brass Polisher

This polisher holds up to 300 pistol cases. It works at a very high vibrating speed and cleans and polishes the exterior, interior and primer pockets. Has an adjustable vibrating action to suit different needs. Works fast, no mess, and is relatively quiet. Can also be used with a cleaning solvent to clean gun parts. Comes with a full supply of polishing compound. From Vibra-Tek Co... **$69.95**
Magnum models holds 5 lbs. of polishing media and can process 2500 rounds of 30-06 brass per day. **$135.00**
Vibra-Bright media re-charging liquid, 2 oz. bottle. **$2.00**

VIBRA-TEK Polishing Media

This shell media is designed to be used in the Vibra-Tek brass polisher. It is made of finely ground black walnut shells impregnated with iron oxide. Small enough so it won't lodge in the brass. Can also be used in case tumblers. Comes in 1- to 2-lb. plastic bags and shipped in ½-gallon plastic tubs. From Vibra-Tek Co.
1-lb. bag **$2.50**
2-lb. bag **$4.50**
5-lb. box **$11.00**

WILCOX All-Pro Sifting Scoop

A fast, simple way for handloaders to separate polishing media from polished brass. Just pour it all into the scoop and the polishing media sifts through the 55 $\frac{5}{16}$"-diameter holes in the scoop back. From Wilcox..................... **$5.49**

> **The product prices mentioned in these catalog pages were correct at presstime, but may be higher when you read this.**

TOOLS AND
ACCESSORIES FOR

SHOTSHELLS

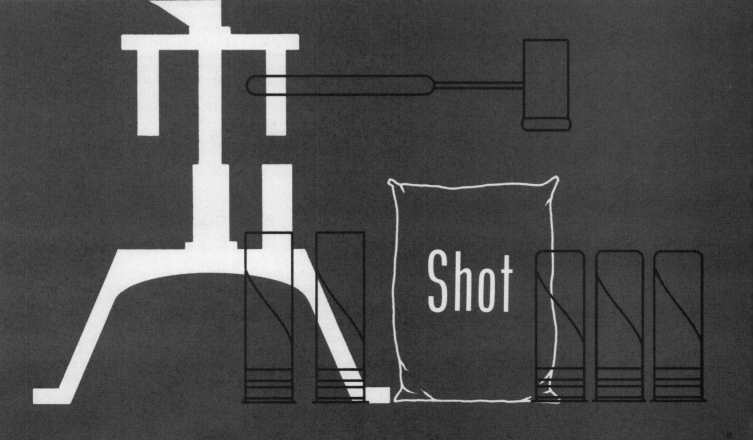

Shot

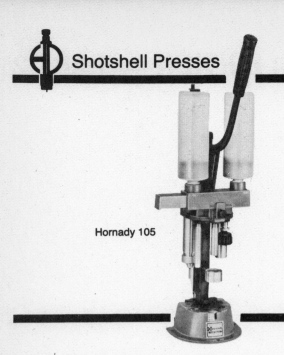

Hornady 105

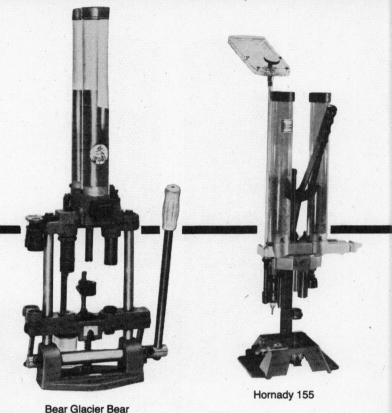

Bear Glacier Bear

Hornady 155

Notes on Shotshell Presses . . .

In the selection of a shotshell press the handloader may choose a tool that will produce handloads at rates from 10-20 per hour to 500 or more per hour, that range in price from just over $10 to $500 and more. He can make adequate match grade target loads or whatever suits his fancy.

Simpler types of shotshell tools offer the occasional shotgun shooter the opportunity to reload his cases with little outlay of cash. It takes a bit more time and effort with these tools as compared to the Skeet or trap shooter using the latest progressive tool, and the finished shells may not have the fine look of a commercially loaded shell, but his loads will do the job that he wants done.

The careful operator of a modern progressive tool can be assured of reloads second to none. His shells will be consistent performers at the traps or in the field and will have the clean crimp and smooth body of commercial loads; best of all, he'll have made them with little more than the up and down stroke of the operating handle of his tool.

There are the multi-station tools that range in efficiency—as well as price—from those using dippers for shot and powder measuring to the near-progressive types which charge the cases from shot and powder hoppers with a flick of the charge bar.

Select a press in the price bracket you can afford that has features that you want. Don't expect a lower price press to do things beyond its capabilities, and don't buy a $300 automatic loader unless you want to reload hundreds of shells. In the majority of the presses, the quality of the finished shell is inherent in the press, and is only varied by the competence of the operator.

BEAR Polar Bear 600

Available for 12, 16, 20, or 28 gauge, the Polar Bear features semi-automatic operation, six-station loading sequence, swing out wad guide, automatic primer feed and easy shot and powder shut off. Reloads at the rate of 24 boxes an hour. For the serious trap and Skeet shooter. Comes assembled ready to use. From Bear Co.

Price: **$150.00**
Price: Conversion kit for 12, 16, 20 or 28 gauge **$42.00**

BEAR Honey Bear

A progressive reloader available in 10M, 12M, 12, 20M, 20, 16, 28, 410M and 410. Features unique powder/shot shut-off that enables the reloader to stop flow any time during the cycle—also removable for fast changeover. Crimp die has adjustable taper lock and crimp depth. Can be ordered with automatic primer feed. From Bear Company.

Price: 12M, 12, 20M, 20, 16, 28, 410M, 410 w/Auto Primer installed **$75.00**
Price: 12M, 12, 10M, 20, 16, 18, 410M, 410 without Auto Primer **$65.00**
Price: Auto Primer Feed kit **$15.00**
Price: Conversion kit for 12M, 12, 20M, 20, 16, 28, 410M, 410 . . . . **$36.00**
Price: Conversion crimp die to convert standard gauges to 3″ Mag. **$9.50**

BEAR Glacier Bear

Reloads up to 250 rounds per hour. Three-station loading sequence eliminates extra handling. Hinged charging assembly makes changing shot or powder and respective bushings fast and simple. Easily converted to other gauges. Available for 12 Magnum, 12, 20 Magnum, 20, 16, 28, 410 Magnum and 410 gauge. From Bear Co.

Price: **$80.00**
Price: Conversion kit for 12M, 12, 20M, 20, 16, 28, 410M, 410 . . . . **$38.00**
Price: Conversion crimp die. (Converts standard gauges to 3″ Mag.) **$8.00**

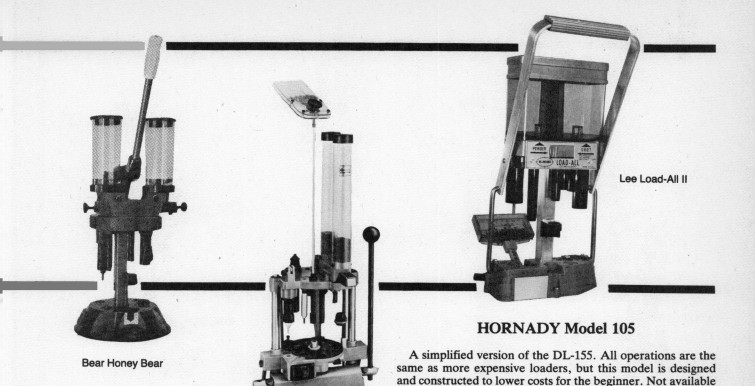

Bear Honey Bear

Hornady 366

Lee Load-All II

BEAR Bear Cat II

This loader full length resizes every case including head and rim. "Plastic Glas" crimp stations provide a crimped, locked and tapered shell that will function properly in the tightest automatic, pump gun, double or single barrel. The floating crimp starter self-aligns with the original crimp. 3" Magnum shells can be loaded with simple adjustment and changing of the final crimp die. Available for 12M, 12, 10M, 20, 16, 18, H10M or 410. From Bear Company.

Price: 12M, 12, 10M, 20, 16, 18, 410M or 410...... **$62.00**
Price: Conversion kit 12M, 12, 20M, 20, 16, 28, 410M, 410.......................................**$32.00**
Price: Conversion crimp die. Converts std. gauges to 3" Mag..................................**$9.50**

HORNADY 366 Auto Loader

A progressive tool that has an automatic turntable and swingout wad guide in addition to the regular features of the DL-366. Eight shells move around the turntable and eight different operations are performed automatically with each stroke of the operating lever. After loading, the finished shell is ejected. Operator simply sets an empty hull on the shell plate and inserts a wad in the machine. The new tool also has a shot and powder shutoff. Available in 12, 20, 28 or .410 gauge. The older standard 366 can be updated to automatic operation by returning the tool to the Hornady factory. From Hornady.

Model 366 Auto, 12, 20, 28....................**$485.00**
In 410...**$545.00**
Die set, 12, 20, 28..............................**$88.85**

HORNADY Model 105

A simplified version of the DL-155. All operations are the same as more expensive loaders, but this model is designed and constructed to lower costs for the beginner. Not available with auto primer fed. Comes in 12, 16 or 20 gauge only (specify). From Hornady.............................**$116.55**
Extra die set....................................**$37.00**
105 Magnum Conversion Set (Converts 2¾" dies to load 3" shells of same gauge).............................**$12.50**

HORNADY 155/155APF Loader

This loader sizes head and rim of cases before loading and the rest of the case after. Loads over 200 shells per hour and turns out a shell that functions in all types of actions. Model 155APF comes with automatic primer feed, 12 or 20. From Hornady...**$205.60**
M155APF, 16, 28 or 410.......................**$209.95**
Die set (12 or 20 gauge).......................**$56.70**
Die set (16, 28, 410)...........................**$56.70**
Charge bar bushings............................**$2.00**
10 gauge loader (no APF).....................**$194.45**
M155, 12, 20....................................**$180.15**
M155, 16, 28, or 410...........................**$185.15**
155/155 APF Magnum Conversion Set (Converts 2¾" dies to load 3" shells of same gauge.)....................**$24.40**
APF Conversion Unit **$33.00**
Extra Crimp Starters **$3.00**

LEE Load-All II

Has all the same basic features as the Lee Load-All but comes with a redesigned base which allows the addition of the optional primer feed for only $9.98. The new base has a built-in primer catcher with a door in front for emptying. The Load-All II converts to another gauge by replacing the die carrier, shellholder, wad guide and sizing die (all included in conversion kit). Available for 12, 16 and 20 gauge. From Lee Precision, Inc.

Price: Load-All II with 24 shot and powder bushings **$44.98**
Price: Primer Feed **$9.98**
Price: Conversion kit **$16.98**
Price: To convert Load-All to Load-All II **$19.98**

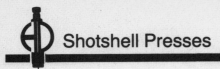

MEC Grabber

MEC Hustler

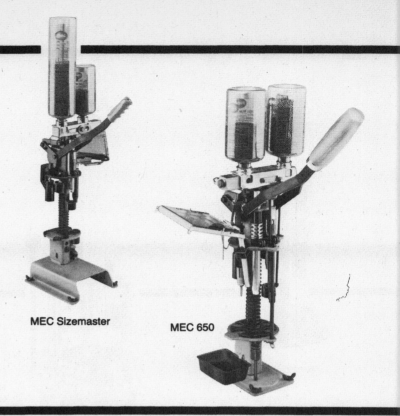

MEC Sizemaster

MEC 650

MEC Sizemaster

A single-stage reloader. The resizing station handles brass or steel heads and both high and low brass. Accurate "Power Ring" collet resizer returns base to factory specs. Standard equipment includes "E-Z Prime" automatic primer feed and "Pro-Check" to remind you of the proper loading sequence. The press is adjustable for 3″ shells and is available in 10, 12, 16, 20, 28 gauge and .410 bore. No automatic primer feed on .410 bore. Die sets are available. From Mayville Engineering Co.

Price: **$201.93**
Price: Die sets (12 or 20 ga.) **$4.95**

MEC 650

A progressive tool that works on six shells at once, producing a reloaded shell with each stroke. Standard features include Automatic Primer and Auto-Cycle charging to insure no powder is dropped until the shell is in the proper position. Three crimping stations close and taper the shell, important for proper feeding in pump or automatic shotguns. The 650 does not resize except as a separate operation. This reloader is ideal for the person who wishes to resize and inspect his shells as a separate operation. Available in 12, 16, 20, 28 gauge and .410 bore. No die sets available. From Mayville Engineering Co. **$263.97**

MEC Hustler

The "Hustler" utilizes all of the features of the Grabber and adds the benefits of hydraulic power. It features a toe-touch control that allows continuous action or stops anywhere in the cycle, as desired by the operator. The hydraulic 110 volt unit attaches with a single hose. From Mayville Engineering Co. **$972.88**

MEC 600 JR. Mark 5

Redesigned to include such popular features as the Spindex Crimp Starter for perfect alignment and a perfect crimp every time, and "Pro-Check" to keep the charge bar properly positioned and avoid spills. A single-stage tool, the MEC 600 Jr. loads eight to 10 boxes per hour or more with accessories. The press is adjustable for 3″ shells and is available in 10, 12, 16, 20, 28 gauge and .410 bore. Die sets are available in all gauges. From Mayville Engineering Co. **$133.52**
Price: Die sets (12, 16, 20, 28, 410) **$32.95**
Price: 10-gauge kit............................. **$37.95**

MEC Grabber

MEC's top-of-the-line progressive reloader. Fully automatic primer feed, Auto-Cycle charging and exclusive three-station crimp produce a finished shell with every stroke of the handle. The "Power Ring" collet resizer returns each shell base to its original size. Available in 12, 16, 20, 28 gauge and .410 bore (12 gauge for low brass only). No die sets available. From Mayville Engineering Co. **$361.06**

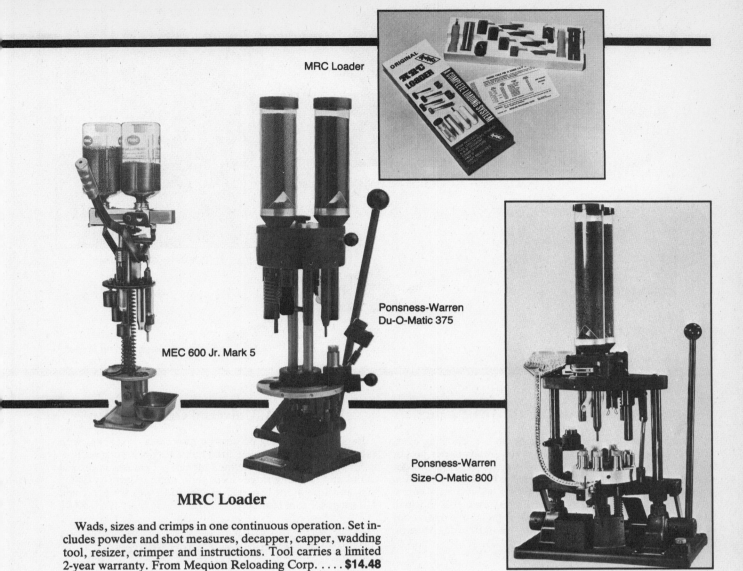

MRC Loader

Ponsness-Warren
Du-O-Matic 375

MEC 600 Jr. Mark 5

Ponsness-Warren
Size-O-Matic 800

MRC Loader

Wads, sizes and crimps in one continuous operation. Set includes powder and shot measures, decapper, capper, wadding tool, resizer, crimper and instructions. Tool carries a limited 2-year warranty. From Mequon Reloading Corp. **$14.48**

PONSNESS-WARREN Size-O-Matic 800 Convertible

The P-W 800 Convertible, available in 12, 20, 28 ga. and .410, is a progressive reloading tool which produces a reloaded shell with every pull of the handle—500 to 1000 rounds per hour. Handles both paper and plastic shells, "new or fired." Both high and low brass are fully resized to factory specifications in the patented full-length resizing dies. Shells remain in these dies through the entire reloading operation, producing a tapered crimped shell virtually undistinguishable from factory ammunition. Eight such dies are located in the die cylinder which indexes automatically to position shells for each operation. A cam-operated carrier receives and positions wads for seating. Baffled shot and powder reservoirs assure precise load-to-load consistency and can be shut off or drained at any time with the reservoir control switch. Primers are always in full view of the operator and are automatically fed. Changing tooling from gauge to gauge is quick and easy. From Ponsness-Warren.

Price: Complete (12, 20, 28, .410 ga.) **$499.00**
Price: Additional Tooling **$169.00**

PONSNESS-WARREN Du-O-Matic 375 10 Gauge

This press is exclusively for 10 gauge 3½" shells. An extra-large shot drop tube allows up to #2 shot to be loaded easily while a special bushing access plug allows direct shot drop for even larger sizes. Shells are held in a sizing die throughout the five station loading process. Press, complete with 6-point crimp starter. From Ponsness-Warren. **$199.00**

PONSNESS-WARREN Du-O-Matic 375

A single stage tool requiring only 4 moves to produce a loaded shell. Change gauges in 5 minutes. No crimp starter needed for paper cases. From Ponsness-Warren. Price complete for one gauge (12, 16, 20, 28, .410) **$179.00**
Additional tooling (12, 16, 20, 28, 410 gauge) **$79.00**
Crimp starter assembly (6, 8 point or cone) **$12.95**
10-gauge tooling (includes tool head) **$99.00**
Additional bushings **$2.50**
Conversion unit to change to 3½" 10 gauge. **$99.00**
Conversion unit for 3" 12, 20 410 . . . . **$29.95**

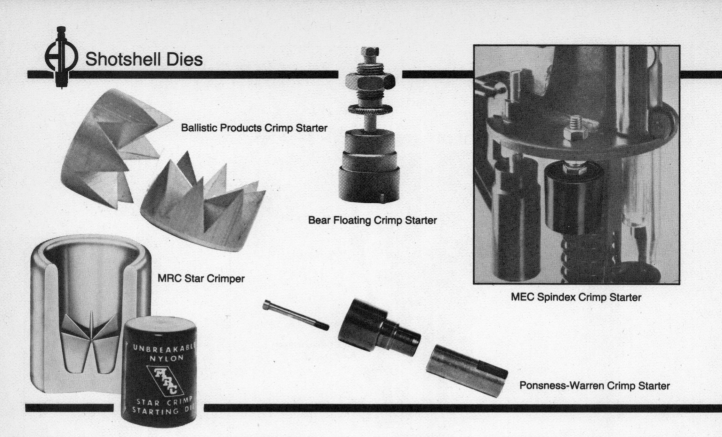

Ballistic Products Crimp Starter

Bear Floating Crimp Starter

MEC Spindex Crimp Starter

MRC Star Crimper

UNBREAKABLE NYLON MRC STAR CRIMP STARTING DIE

Ponsness-Warren Crimp Starter

Notes on Shotshell Loading Dies . . .

Shotshell dies are designed to perform the following operations: decapping and recapping; seating wads under proper pressure; sizing and crimping. Provisions for inserting powder and shot charges must also be made, but this is not a function of the die set. Sequence of the operations may vary somewhat, depending upon the dies and press used. All shotshell presses as such in this volume perform the above operations with dies designed specifically for the individual presses. Their dies will not usually interchange.

BALLISTIC PRODUCTS Super Crowncrimp Starter

Fits into the older MEC 600 Jr. and Sizemaster metal crimp starter Spindex housing. The crimp starter is interchangeable for 10-gauge and 12-gauge. 6 or 8-point crimp. From Ballistic Products Inc. **$10.95**

BEAR Floating Crimp Starter

Works in unity with a regular Bear crimping die and on Bear Loaders. Automatically aligns with original crimp. Available in six or eight segments in 12, 16 and 20 gauges; six segments in 28 and 410 gauges. From Bear Company.
Price: Floating Crimp Starter.....................**$9.50**
Price: Floating Head only.......................**$6.00**
Price: Solid Crimp Starter **$6.00**

HORNADY Universal Crimp Starter

Begins the crimping process on new cases or realigns with existing folds on previously fired hulls. Engineered specifically for cases with poorly-defined memory. Features improved radius and indexing ridges for a good, tight crimp. Available in 6- and 8-point for 12 and 20 gauges and 6 only for 10, 28 and 410 gauges. From Hornady. **$3.00**

MEC Spindex Crimp Starter

The Spindex Crimp Starter rotates automatically and realigns with the original crimp of the shell. Precision built, one-piece unit is made of rugged Celcon and is quickly changed from 6-point to 8-point. A standard component on the MEC reloaders. From Mayville Engineering Co...........**$4.14**

MRC Star Crimper

This starting die is made of unbreakable nylon, and can be used on all plastic or unfired paper shells. Available for 8-point crimping of 10, 12, 16, or 20 gauge; 6-point, 10, 12, 16, 20, 28, or 410 gauge shells, specify. From Mequon Reloading Corp...**$1.98**

MRC Shotshell Sizer

A simple hand tool comprised of the support tube and sizing ring that is slipped over the fired case to resize it. From Mequon Reloading Corp.
Support Tube....................................**$3.98**
Sizing Ring (10, 12, 16, 20, 28, 410, standard and magnums) **$3.98**

Ponsness-Warren Guide Fingers

MRC Deluxe Wad Guide

Ponsness-Warren Crimp Kit

MRC Shell Sizer

MRC Wad Guide Fingers

These replacement wad guide fingers are designed for all presses using the MEC type guides. Available in 10, 12, 16, 28 and 410 gauge. The fingers come packed two per package. From Mequon Reloading Corp. **$1.48**

MRC Wad Guide

Moulded of a new polycarbonate material that makes wad starting easy in all types of shells. Guaranteed for 2 years. In 12, 16 and 20 gauge. Mequon Reloading Corp.
Price: **$2.98**

MRC Deluxe Wad Guides

New aluminum full length wad guide with replaceable MRC Wad Fingers. A convenient and easy to use wad starting tool. Available in 10, 10 Magnum, 12, 12 Magnum, 16, 20, 20 Magnum, 28 and 410 (2½″ and 3″). Complete with an extra set of wad fingers. From Mequon Reloading Corp. **$3.98**

PONSNESS-WARREN Taper Crimp Kit

The P/W Taper Crimp Kit converts all models of P/W loaders to the "new, out-of-the-box" taper crimp. The Taper Crimp Kit enables you to round the crimp of all shotshell cases while retaining the full-length sizing. From Ponsness-Warren.
Prices:
   For 800B—8 new sizing dies + tooling **$145.00**
   For 600B—10 new sizing dies + tooling **$169.00**
   For 375—new sizing die + tooling **$50.00**
   The Taper Crimp kit is available in 12, 20, 28 and 410.

PONSNESS-WARREN Paper Crimp Assembly

This conversion kit is intended for shooters who reload paper shells predominately. The standard crimp assembly on Ponsness-Warren tools is primarily for plastic shells. This assembly can be installed in a matter of minutes. Specify gauge. From Ponsness-Warren. **$27.95**

PONSNESS-WARREN Wad Guide Fingers

Replacement wad guide fingers adaptable to most reloading tools and available in 10, 12, 16, 20, 28, and 410 gauge. These fingers accommodate all wads and assure exact wad seating. Specify gauge. From Ponsness-Warren. **$1.00**

PONSNESS-WARREN Crimp Starters

Six and eight point crimp starters have an automatic pick-up to assure perfect crimp alignment. From Ponsness-Warren.
   Crimp starter complete (6, 8 point or cone) specify **$12.95**
   Crimp Starter Head (6, 8 point or cone) specify **$3.95**

RCBS Shotshell Die Kit

RCBS shotshell dies allow loading 12-gauge shotshells on the Rock Chucker or Reloader Special 3 presses. Now both shotshell and metallic cartridges can be reloaded on the same press. Each die set also includes shot measure, case holder and case crimper. From RCBS. **$40.00**

Ballistic Products 12-ga. Roll Crimper

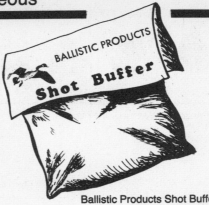

Ballistic Products Shot Buffer

Ballistic Products Loading Block

Miscellany for Handloaders . . .

Gadgets to lure the reloader are numerous indeed! Just about as many, if not more, have appeared and then disappeared. Some of the accessories available are worthwhile, even—to those ammo makers who load in quantity or who are concerned with ultra-precision shells—a real necessity. At the other extreme, of course, are items you can well do without, maybe, but you will have to decide that for yourself. In between there are small tools of real utility, products which can be helpful to you or not, as your personal needs—or fancied needs—demand.

By analyzing your needs carefully, these helpful items can speed up the loading process.

BALLISTIC PRODUCTS Hull Marks

Mark reloads with self-adhesive Hull Marks. Hull Marks come in yellow, orange, tan, light blue and light green to color code loads or mark with pen. The Hull Mark can be placed on the side of the shell or on the base. From Ballistic Products Inc. Price per 500 . . . . **$3.95**

BALLISTIC PRODUCTS Crow River Wad Cutter

Made from aluminum stock, this wad cutter is designed to three-petal or four-petal the Ballistic Products BPD or BP12 wad. A line on the cutter allows a ¾ or full length cut. The wad is pushed into the cutter tube base first, aligning the edge of the wad with the edge of the tube. Simply run an X-Acto knife along the slits in the cutter. Comes in either 10-gauge or 12-gauge. From Ballistic Products Inc.

Price: Crow River Cutter **$19.95**
Price: X-Acto Knife **$2.95**
Price: X-Acto extra blades (15) **$3.95**

BALLISTIC PRODUCTS Teflon Wraps

A slick, very thin plastic-tube material that makes shot wrappers for certain types of loads. The wraps are cut into small sheets for use in 20, 12 and 10 gauge. Can also be used to encase slugs as well as large buckshot. From Ballistic Products Inc. Price per 50 . . . . **$7.95**

BALLISTIC PRODUCTS Adjustable Shot Dipper

Made of tough plastic, this shot dipper dispenses 1 oz. or 1⅞ ounces of shot. The bottom of the cup screw slips down for the larger shot wad. From Ballistic Products Inc. **$2.00**

BALLISTIC PRODUCTS Powder Baffle

Fits all MEC reloading presses. Allows powder to flow evenly into the bushing. The baffle is of one-piece, high impact plastic construction. From Ballistic Products Inc. . **$3.95**

BALLISTIC PRODUCTS 12-Gauge Roll Crimper

This unit fits into a ¼-inch drill chuck and spins the roll crimp down. From Ballistics Products Inc. **$14.95**

BALLISTIC PRODUCTS 12-Gauge Loading Tray

Precision moulded plastic tray holds 50 12-gauge shotgun shells base up. Shell slips over plastic core for firm hold and is ready for reloading. Trays will stack for easy storage. From Ballistic Products Inc. **$3.95**

BALLISTIC PRODUCTS Hull Shape-Up Tool

The hull shaping tool fits easily in the hand and will quickly expand the mouth of hulls to accept a wad. From Ballistic Products Inc. **$5.95**

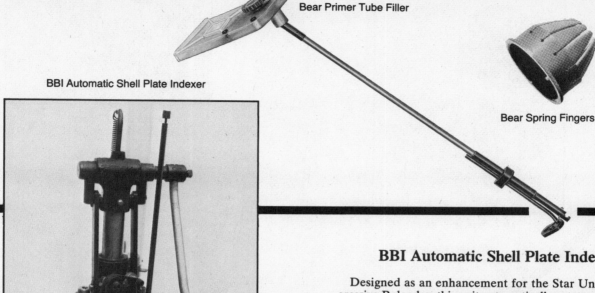

Bear Primer Tube Filler

Bear Spring Fingers

BBI Automatic Shell Plate Indexer

BALLISTIC PRODUCTS Super Slick

A liquid silicone treatment applied to hulls and wads that fills in the pores of the plastic with a slippery surface. One 8-oz. bottle is enough for hundreds of shells. From Ballistic Products Inc. **$12.95**

BALLISTIC PRODUCTS Reloading Block

This custom wood reloading block will hold 25 shotshells in the upright position. The holes are large enough to handle .410 bore to 10-gauge. From Ballistic Products **$4.95**

BALLISTIC PRODUCTS Original Shot Buffer and Special Shot Buffer Mix #47

Fine ground polyethylene shot buffer—original mix or special mix. Both come in plastic bags with enough buffering agent to load 150 shells. From Ballistic Products Inc.
Price: SB01 Original Buffer **$2.50**
Price: SB01 Case of 24 . . . . **$42.00**
Price: Mix #47 . . . . **$2.95**
Price: Mix #47 Case of 24 . . . . **$48.00**
Price: Buffer Dipper . . . . **$.25**

BBI Powder Magazine

A brass and Lexan powder magazine designed to be mounted on the Star Universal Progressive Reloader. It has a positive powder shut-off and capacity of 1 pound of powder. From Beal's Bullets, Inc. **$98.50**

BBI Automatic Shell Plate Indexer

Designed as an enhancement for the Star Universal Progressive Reloader, this unit automatically rotates the turret to the next station. Speeds reloading as no time is needed to manually index turret. Mounted on the Star reloader base. From Beal's Bullets, Inc. **$198.50**

BBI Manual Shell Plate Indexer

An enhancement for the Star Universal Progressive Reloader. The BBI Manual Shell-Plate Indexer mounts on the Star base. From Beal's Bullets, Inc. **$49.50**

BEAR Spring Fingers

A nylon insert for Bear loaders that replaces the old style metal fingers and prevents the points of the crimp of plastic shells from coming between the fingers. From Bear Company. . . . . **$.75**

BEAR Primer Tube Filler

A fast and simple method to load the primer tube on a shot-shell press. Turning the dial places a primer into the primer feed tube. For any Bear loading press, though it may be altered for use on other makes. From Bear Company . . **$12.50**

CRW Automatic Ejector

Spring activated shell ejector designed to fit MEC progressive presses. Attaches in seconds and increases reloading speed. For 12 and 20 gauge. Available through Magma Engineering. . . . . **NA**

HOLLYWOOD Shot Measure

Identical to the Hollywood powder measure except for having a patented tapered lead on the drum cavity's cutting edge. The wedging action of this lead displaces pellets, does not cut or deform them. Throws accurate charges of all shot sizes up to BB; maximum is 2⅛ oz. #9 shot. Furnished with flat bar and lock nut for attachment to bench or tool head, base is threaded ⅞-14 for use in most popular presses. From Hollywood Loading Tools. **$115.00**

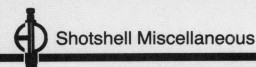

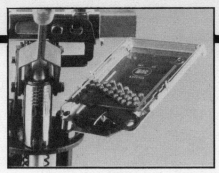

MEC E-Z Prime

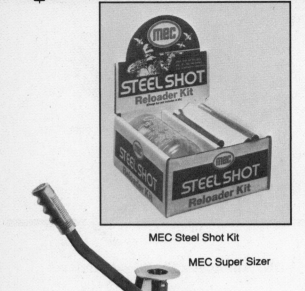

MEC Steel Shot Kit

MEC Super Sizer

MEC E-Z Pack

HOLLYWOOD Shell Processor

A complete die unit for reconditioning shotshell cases, including tightening the primer pocket. Available for 10, 12, 16, 20, 28, 410 gauges. From Hollywood Loading Tools . **$58.00**

HORNADY Steel Shot Bushings

Brass bushings adapt to Hornady's 155 and 266 shotshell reloaders for use with steel shot. They are marked "For Steel Shot Only" and should not be used with lead shot or in other reloaders. From Hornady........................**$3.00**

HORNADY Powder and Shot Baffles

These plastic baffles are standard with 366 Auto and 155 single-stage shotshell loaders. Available in a set of two. From Hornady. **$5.00**

HORNADY Primer Tube Filler

A fast and simple way to load primer tubes for shotshell presses—just turn the dial of this plastic device and the tube is filled. Will not drop primer with base inverted. From Hornady..**$13.80**

MEC Steel Shot Reloader Adapter Kit

Designed to be used with the 600 Jr. Mark 5 or Sizemaster to reload steel shot. MEC steel shot charge bars are available separately depending on powder and shot size desired. From Mayville Engineering Co. **$11.90**

MEC E-Z Pak

The easy way to pack shotshells. As each shell is reloaded, they're placed in this device as if they were being placed in the box. After each 25 shells, the original box is slipped over E-Z Pak which is then turned upside down and removed. Available in all gauges. From Mayville Engineering Co. **$6.21**

MEC Super-Sizer

The Super-Sizer accommodates 12-gauge and .410 bore shells. One pull forces eight steel fingers against the brass. Sizing pressure is spread out evenly over the entire surface of base metal. The metal is actually drawn back to factory specifications creating a resized shell that will work freely in any magazine tube and will chamber properly. Handles high or low brass. From Mayville Engineering Co.
Price:...**$75.71**

MEC E-Z Prime "S"

Standard feature on all MEC presses except the 600 Jr. Mark 5. Primers transfer directly from carton to reloader eliminating tubes and tube fillers. Adapts to all domestic and most foreign primers with adjustment of the cover. Not for .410-bore single stage reloaders. From Mayville Engineering Co. **$32.95**

MTM Shotshell Loading Tray

Precision moulded tray holds 50 shells during the reloading process. Trays fit the MTM Case-Gard 100 shotshell case. Perfect for storing reloads. Available for 12, 16 or 20 gauge shells. From MTM..................................**$3.02**

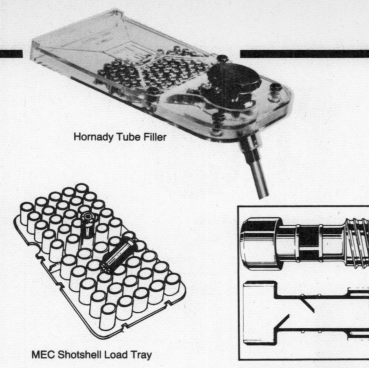

Hornady Tube Filler

MEC Shotshell Load Tray

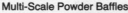

Multi-Scale Powder Baffles

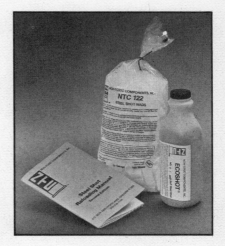

NTC Steel Shot Kit

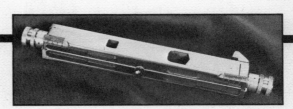

Multi-Scale Universal Bar

MULTI-SCALE CHARGE
Powder Baffles

Made of die-cast zinc, these baffles install between the powder bottle and charge bar of MEC loaders. They give even powder density for more consistent charges. From Multi-Scale Charge Ltd. Each **$5.75**

MULTI-SCALE CHARGE
Universal Charge Bars

This replacement charge bar is fully adjustable for shot and powder charges. Shot capacity (with #4 low antimony shot) is from ½ oz. to 2¼ oz.; power capacity from 12 to 55 grains. A powder and shot chart with 487 settings is included. All metal construction, with bottom guides for powder and shot valves, highly simplified method for reading and adjusting scales. Two models are available—Model D for the MEC 650 and Grabber, Model C for MEC 600 Jr., 700 Versamec, Sizemaster 77, MEC 600, 400, 250 and 250 Super, Texas LT, GT and FW models. Model C Steelshot comes with a rubber insert on the shot valve and must be used with components designed for the loading of steel shot. From Multi-Scale Charge, Ltd.

Price:...**$19.95**
Price: Model C Steelshot **$21.95**

NTC Wad Slitters

Used to slit four petals in NTC steel shot wads. This device attaches to single-stage MEC or Pacific presses. It is available for 2¾" or 3" presses. From Non-Toxic Components, Inc. **$6.95**

NTC Steel Shot Kits

NTC kits are available for 2¾" 12-ga. loading in 10, 20, 30 and 40-lb. units and for 3" 12-ga. loading in 20, 30 and 40-lb. units. Shot sizes available include: No. 6, 5, 4, 3, 2, 1 B, BB, BBB and T. Additional shotsizes offered for 10-ga. only are TT and F. Kits include shot, wads and reloading manual. From Non-Toxic Components, Inc.

NTC 122 Kits (for 1⅛ oz. 12-ga. 2¾" and select 12-ga. 3")
Price: 40-lb. Kit (40 lbs. shot, 640 wads, reloading manual) **$89.95**
Price: 30-lb. Kit (30 lbs. shot, 480 wads, reloading manual) **$75.95**
Price: 20-lb. Kit (20 lbs. shot, 320 wads, reloading manual) **$59.95**
Price: 10-lb. Sampler Kit (10 lbs. shot, 160 12-ga. wads, reloading manual) **$31.95**
NTC Kits (for 1¼-oz., 3", 12-ga.)
Price: 40-lb. Kit (40 lbs. shot, 520 wads, reloading manual) **$96.95**
Price: 30-lb. Kit (30 lbs. shot, 390 wads, reloading manual) **$81.95**
Price: 20-lb. Kit (20 lbs. shot, 260 wads, reloading manual) **$63.95**
NTC 105 Kits (for 1½-oz., 3½", 10-ga.)
Price: 40-lb. Kit (40 lbs. shot, 480 wads, reloading manual) **$109.95**
Price: 30-lb. Kit (30 lbs. shot, 360 wads, reloading manual) **$92.95**
Price: 20-lb. Kit (20 lbs. shot, 240 wads, reloading manual) **$69.95**

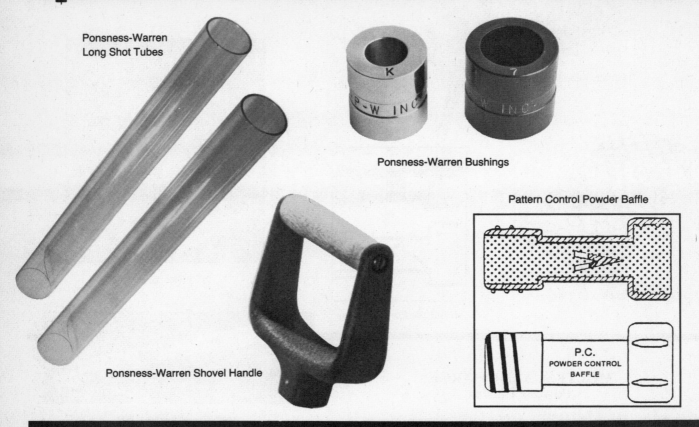

Ponsness-Warren Long Shot Tubes

Ponsness-Warren Bushings

Ponsness-Warren Shovel Handle

Pattern Control Powder Baffle

P.C. POWDER CONTROL BAFFLE

PATTERN CONTROL Shot Shell Box

Designed for shooters who want a sturdy box for reloads. The removeable lid allows the box to be inserted into leather shell holders—perfect for trap shooters. Holds 25 rounds. From Pattern Control.

Price: $1.95

PATTERN CONTROL Organizer Board

This 6½″ × 8″ plastic board has moulded-in posts and provides a handy place to hang powder and shot bushings and bars. Stick-on labels are included to identify the 17 available posts. Holes in the board allow it to be hung on the wall. From Pattern Control.

Price: $5.95

PATTERN CONTROL Powder Baffles

These baffles fit MEC and Pacific shotshell presses and improve loading accuracy to within two-tenths of a grain on every powder drop. Allows powder to flow evenly into the bushing. One-piece construction of durable high-impact plastic. From Pattern Control.

Price: For MEC presses $3.95
Price: As above with leak-proof seal $5.95
Price: For Pacific presses $2.95

PONSNESS-WARREN Shovel Handle

For the high-volume reloader, a shovel-type handle for the P-W Size-O-Matic. Some reloaders find this type of grip easier to use and more comfortable than the standard ball grip. Made of high-quality aluminum casting and finished with a matching baked-on wrinkle finish with smooth wood grip. From Ponsness-Warren. $19.95

PONSNESS-WARREN Shot Reservoir Tubes

Extra-long 2-foot shot reservoir tubes for high production loading. Used primarily in the P-W Size-O-Matic 800 and Mult-O-Matic 600 shotshell loaders which produce a high volume of shells. By using the extra large tubes, the operator needs to refill the reservoirs less often. Because P-W loaders utilize shot baffles, the extra length of the tubes does not affect the consistent flow of shot. From Ponsness-Warren. $14.95

PONSNESS-WARREN Shot, Powder Bushings

For use with the Ponsness-Warren presses, these bushings are made with extreme care to assure accuracy. Shot and powder bushings are of different diameters to eliminate any possibility of their being reversed. Powder bushings are of aluminum. From Ponsness-Warren. Each. $2.50

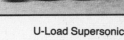
U-Load Supersonic
Steel Reloading Kit

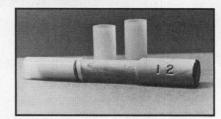

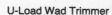
U-Load Wad Trimmer

U-Load 12-ga. Converter

Ponsness-Warren Dust Cover

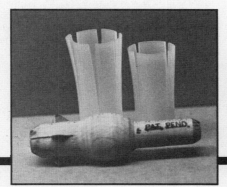

(Left and below) U-Load Wad Cutters

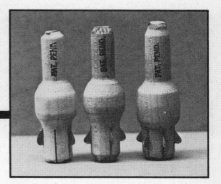

PONSNESS-WARREN Canvas Dust Cover

This rugged and handsome cover provides a practical way to keep dust and dirt off the press when not in use. From Ponsness-Warren.

Small..**$15.95**
Large **$19.95**

QUIVIRA Shotshell Reconditioner

An iron tool to assist the reloader in saving hulls and in reloading. The iron bar is heated to 300 degrees F., inserted into the mouth of the hull and used to "iron" the hull back into shape. Available in both 10 and 12 gauge. From Ballistic Products, Inc. **$17.95**

U-LOAD DFV Supersonic 12-Gauge Reloading Converter

Allows the reloader to load 12-gauge 2¾" shells on a 3" loader with no adjustment. Place the 2¾" hull on the converter and slide it around your press for loading. From U-Load Inc. **$9.95**

U-LOAD DFV Supersonic Wad Cutter

Three-, four- or six-blade wad cutter with case-hardened steel blades, inside a wooden body. The 3-blade is for extremely long range, 4-blade for long range and 6-blade for medium range. From U-Load Inc. $2 shipping/handling charge **$14.95**

U-LOAD Supersonic Steel Reloading Kits

U-Load offers four kits for the steel shotshell reloader. Each kit is available in either Basic or Deluxe form for reloading 10-gauge or 12-gauge shotshells. The Basic kits include 10 pounds of steel shot and 100/140 wads (depending on the kit). The Deluxe kits contain a higher grade of steel shot (10 pounds), 100/140 wads (depending on kit), 1 pound of Supersonic steel shot buffer, 30 grains of graphite and over and under shot wads. Shot sizes for kits: BB+, BBB, 4 Buck, 1 Buck—10 or 12 gauge kits #1 and #3; No. 1 steel shot—10 or 12-gauge, kits #2 and #4. Components also sold individually; contact manufacturer for prices. From U-Load Inc.

Price: Basic kit...............................**$31.95**
Price: Deluxe kit **$49.95**

Notes on Powder and Shot Measuring . . .

One of the most important phases of shotshell reloading is the complete understanding of shot and powder measurement. Shot loading is simple if the handloader will follow the recommended charges in the various manuals.

In the case of powder charges, there is some misunderstanding about the meaning of "drams equivalent" and "bulk" and "dense" powders.

Bulk powders were smokeless powders of a chemical composition which allowed them to be loaded "bulk for bulk"—that is, volumetrically equal—with black powder. This simplified reloading during the transition period between the black powder and smokeless powder eras.

Dense powders, simply, are those (smokeless powders) which, because of their chemical makeup, have a higher specific gravity and deliver a greater amount of energy than an equal weight of bulk or black powder. They *dare not* be loaded "bulk for bulk" with black powder as they create much higher pressures.

Drams equivalent. As explained by Du Pont, "a dram is a measure used for black powder and is normally used as a volume measure (although strictly speaking it is a weight measure equivalent to $1/16$ oz. or $1/256$ lb.) A certain dram charge of black powder imparts a certain velocity to a given weight of shot. For example, three drams of black powder with $1\frac{1}{8}$ oz. of shot in 12 gauge gives about 1200 fps muzzle velocity. When the change to smokeless powder was made, the dram equivalent designation was used as a measure of the approximate power of the load *regardless of the actual powder charge*. For example, in 12 gauge, a 3 dram equivalent load with $1\frac{1}{8}$ oz. shot gives a muzzle velocity of about 1200 fps. A method was devised to relate velocity and shot weight of commercial loads to the dram equivalent system, but modern loadings depart from the system in a number of instances."

"Some shooters mistakenly believe a low dram equivalent is synonymous with low pressure. This is not so, as all modern shotshells regardless of dram equivalent marking, gauge, brand, powder or shot charge are loaded to approximately the same pressure level.

Therefore, those who attach significance to the term 'dram equivalent' in respect to chamber pressure are in error."

Many people—particularly owners of damascus-barrel guns—think that Skeet and trap loads are low pressure shells because of their relatively light shot charges, but the reverse is true; these are among the highest pressure loads available and should not be used in guns of questionable strength.—Ed.

"The main problem is that people still confuse a 'dram equivalent' designation with a 'dram measure' of powder and this may be serious in the case of modern fast shotshell powders. Taking the density of black and smokeless powders into account, a volumetric 3-dram measure of such modern fast powders is approximately 40 grains (where a grain equals $1/7000$ lb.) *or about a double charge.*"

With this understood, any of the powder and shot measures, be they the simple dippers or mechanical measures, will do a good accurate job.

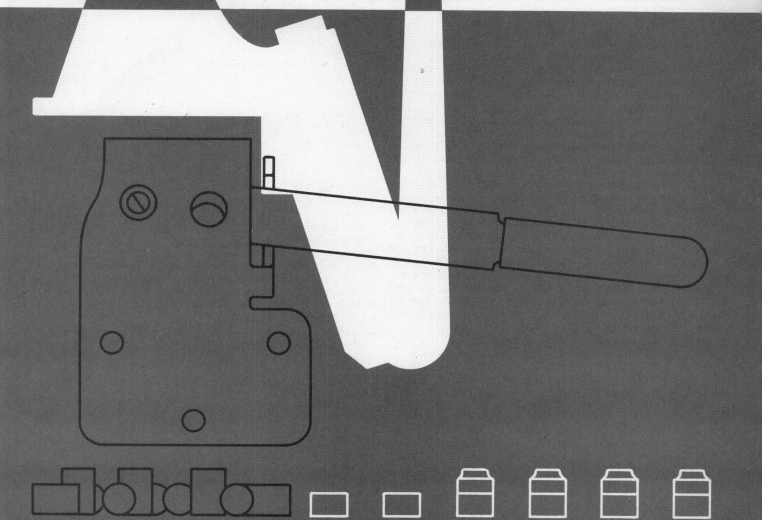

TOOLS AND
ACCESSORIES FOR
BULLET
SWAGING

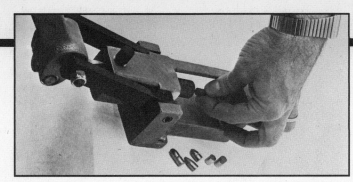

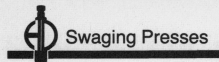

Corbin Mity Mite

Corbin Mity Mite

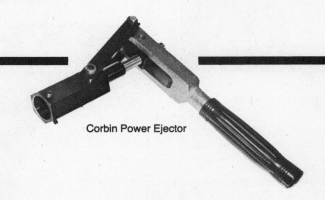

Corbin Power Ejector

Notes on Bullet Swaging Presses . . .

Swaging lead cores or slugs into bullets requires tremendous pressure, therefore presses for such use must be rigid, sturdy and have sufficient leverage to adequately cold form the lead.

Many of the more substantial presses available are adequate for swaging half-jacket pistol and rifle bullets, but only the more solid tools designed for heavy-duty work should be used for the swaging of *full jacket* rifle bullets because of the force required.

The handloader who now owns a press of sturdy construction may purchase bullet swaging dies for use in his press. Those who don't own a strong enough press, or who don't want to disturb their dies, should get a separate press for bullet swaging. The big advantage of the presses shown here, designed for bullet swaging only, is that they may be set up and used whenever the need arises without the bothersome task of removing the reloading dies, inserting the swaging dies, etc.

Obviously, because of the forces involved here, the need for a strong loading bench is of prime importance, too. Be sure to have your press properly anchored to a sturdy benchtop before doing any bullet swaging.

CORBIN Power Ejector

Powerful compound leverage unit slips over the top of Corbin bullet swage dies, gently pushes bullets from die cavity without hammering. Fits many standard ⅞″ diameter dies. Has adjustable ram so that maximum power can be obtained at the start of the stroke. Unit is a miniature press without the head, complete with ejector rod. From Corbin Mfg. and Supply Co. **$39.50**

CORBIN Model CSP-1 Mity Mite Swaging Press

Self-ejecting, horizontal ram bullet swaging press with floating alignment punch holder uses the special Mity Mite swage dies and punches made by Corbin. Extremely high precision for benchrest work, coupled with a wide range of special drawing dies and availability in any standard or custom caliber, style or weight of bullet. Built to custom order. Each order is a hand-built system for making a specific kind of bullet. Write for quote on the bullet swage system to suit individual purpose. Prices shown are typical examples only. From Corbin Mfg. and Supply Co.

Corbin Swaging Press **$198.50**
Press with typical rifle or handgun die set **$427.00**

CORBIN Mega-Mite

Universal swaging or reloading press. Accepts any kind of Corbin swage die (Mity Mite, Hydro-Press, or reloading press) and standard reloading dies. Machined steel construction, all moving interfaces run on bearings. A heavy-duty single-station press. From Corbin Mfg. and Supply Co. **$650.00**

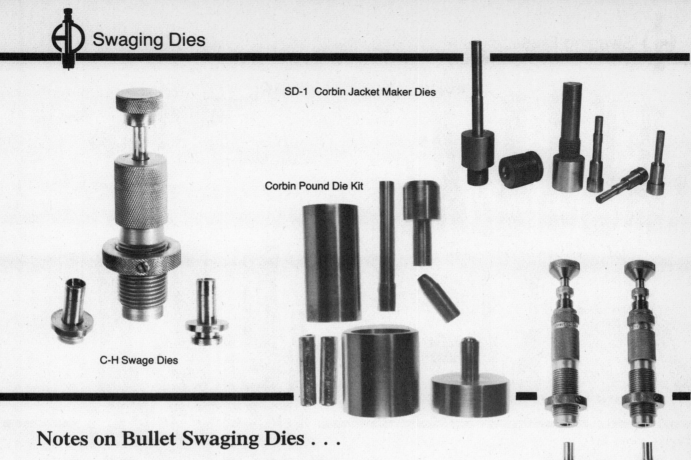

SD-1 Corbin Jacket Maker Dies

Corbin Pound Die Kit

C-H Swage Dies

C-H Swage Dies

Notes on Bullet Swaging Dies . . .

Bullet swaging dies are the keystone to the successful production of lead core, cold formed bullets. In selecting the correct dies the handloader should first decide what type of bullets he wants to make, and for what purpose. It would be foolish to buy expensive dies if the bullets were to be used only for plinking, but it would also be foolish for the perfectionist, the competitive target shooter or the person who wants to produce great quantities of bullets to expect lower priced dies to perform to his expectations.

All of the dies on the following pages will produce quite uniform half-jacket pistol or rifle bullets. The quality and degree of uniformity of the bullets made will depend on the workmanship, design and manufacturing tolerances of the press and dies in use. These qualities cannot be as high in mass-produced dies as in hand-honed and fitted ones; after all, they sell for a fraction of the cost of the others.

The operator is also important in the final quality of the finished bullet. A properly adjusted die that bleeds off just enough lead to assure you of a dense, completely filled bullet, but not enough to cause excessive pressure on the tool and dies, will produce a clean, uniform bullet, properly formed.

C-H Bullet Swaging Dies

These dies are for making ¾-jacket bullets for pistols. Available in: 38, 41, 44 and 45 calibers. Any bullet weight desired is possible. From C-H Tool and Die Corp.

Dies, complete	**$44.45**
Solid nose punches	**$3.65**
Hollow nose punches	**$4.20**

C-H Half Jacket Bullet Swaging Dies

An economical swaging die for the beginner. One die does the complete operation—forms and swages the bullet, automatically bleeds off excess lead. One tap on the ejector ejects the finished bullet, ready to load in the case. Available in .308″, .355″, .357″,. 429″ and .451″ diameters with either round nose or SWC nose punches. Can be used in any loading tool which accepts snap-in shellholder and ⅞ x 14 die threads. From C-H Tool and Die Corp.

Swaging die	**$21.75**
Nose punch	**$6.50**

CORBIN CTJM-1-H Jacket Maker for the Hydro-press

Manufacture any thickness of bullet jacket using the Corbin Hydro-press and this kit of tools. The set is tailor-made for each order, with experimental determination of the correct size and number of parts required to manufacture any bullet jacket, including partitioned styles, boattails, fully closed designs, steel, brass, or any copper alloy. Thicknesses of from .028- to over 0.125-inch. Standard sizes include calibers from 284 to 600 Nitro Express, standard wall thicknesses are 0.030-, 0.050-, and 0.065-inch. The set is not a specific number of parts but includes whatever is required to manufacture the jacket, including any necessary experimental work and development. Standard packages are available for immediate delivery as well. From Corbin Mfg. **$525.00**

Corbin Hyrdo-press Die and Punch Set

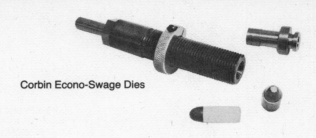

Corbin Econo-Swage Dies

Mity Mite Jacket
Maker Dies

Corbin Bullet Swage Dies

CORBIN FRBO-5-H Die and Punch Sets for Hydro-press

Use on Hydro-press to swage bullets of any caliber or weight, any jacket thickness or bullet style. 1, 2, 3, 4, 5 and 6-die sets are available to make semi-wadcutter, jacketed semi-wadcutter, full-jacketed, rebated boattail, flat base bullets. From Corbin Mfg.

Price: LSWC-1-H............................. **$149.00**
Price: JSWC-2-H............................. **$298.00**
Price: FJFB-3-H............................. **$486.00**
Price: LTFB-4-H............................. **$645.00**
Price: RBTO-4-H............................. **$743.00**
Price: RBTL-5-H............................. **$892.00**
Price: FRBO-5-H............................. **$892.00**
Price: FRBL-6-H............................. **$1041.00**

CORBIN Pound Die Swaging Kits

Corbin pound dies are replicas of the 1890-style bullet swages, operated with a brass mallet. They require no press and can be operated anywhere, but are limited to lead or paper-patched bullets (not jacketed bullets). Available in any caliber up to .520-inch. The kit includes: traditional brass mallet, lube, instructions and one 5-piece die set. From Corbin Mfg... **$250.00**

CORBIN .224/6mm Swaged Bullet Kit

Complete kit for manufacturing 224 or 6mm bullets using fired 22LR cases and scrap lead. The dies fit any standard ⅞-14 RCBS-type press. The kit includes a BSD-224R die set, RFJM-22R jacket maker, CM-4 core mould, CSL-2 lube and full instructions. From Corbin Mfg............... **$252.98**

CORBIN Bullet Econo-Swage Dies

Low-cost single dies for swaging rifle and handgun bullets, paper patched or dip-lubed in the following standard diameters:

.3570 (38/357 handgun)
.3580 (35 rifle)
.3920 (40 Sharps rifle paper patch)
.4100 (41 Mag. handgun)
.4290 (44 Mag. handgun/444 Marlin rifle)
.4480 (45 Sharps rifle paper patch)
.4520 (45 ACP, 454 Casull Mag. handgun)
.4980 (50 Sharps, 50 Lyman, 50 Contender ML paper patch)
.5020 (50 cal. dip-lube, cup-based rifle, no patch)

The dies will fit any standard ⅞-14 type press which takes an RCBS shellholder. Will *not* fit any progressive multi-station presses. Only round-nose bullet style available. Econo dies will make half-jacket (*not* full jacket), gas-checked or ¾ jacketed bullets. From Corbin Mfg............. **$59.50**

CORBIN Rimfire Jacket Maker

Turns fired 22 Long Rifle cases into either .224″ or 6mm rifle bullet jackets. Typical jacket length is 0.705″. Makes a 52 grain open tip or 65 grain lead tip 224-cal. bullet capable of varmint shooting accuracy at speeds up to 3,500 fps. Works in regular ⅞ x 14 reloading press, produces virtually free bullet jackets. From Corbin Mfg. and Supply Co.

224 jacket maker............................. **$49.50**
243 jacket maker............................. **$49.50**

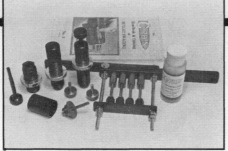

Corbin Swaged Bullet Kit

Corbin JSWC-2-M

Corbin RFJM-224R Jacket Maker Die and Punch Set

Corbin JRD-1-M Jacket Maker Set

Corbin Draw Dies

CORBIN CTJM-1-M Jacket Maker for the Mity Mite

Bullet jackets made from ordinary copper water tubing with a 0.030-inch wall thickness can be produced on the Corbin Mity Mite hand swage press using this kit. Practical alternatives to factory-made bullet jackets in calibers from 338 to 458, the tubing jackets are often used for 7mm and 308 simply because the shooter desires to control expansion or make a heavier bullet than existing jackets permit. Ends of tubing are rolled over, flattened, and the tubing is drawn to precise diameter. Standard tubing diameters used are ½-inch, ⁷⁄₁₆-inch, ⅜-inch, and ⁵⁄₁₆-inch O.D. From Corbin Mfg. **$298.00**

CORBIN Bullet Jacket Draw Dies

Die and punch sets for regular reloading presses to draw standard jackets to smaller calibers, to increase jacket lengths and thin walls, and to make oversized jackets smaller for proper fit in custom dies. Custom sizes made to order. All dies, write for details. All calibers available. From Corbin Mfg. and Supply Co.

Jacket Draw Die to reduce a jacket one caliber size **$59.50**
Die set to turn regular 38 cal. jackets into 30 Carbine jackets. **$59.50**
Die set to make 17 and 20 caliber jackets from 224 jackets (two steps including trim). **$119.00**

CORBIN Bullet Swaging Dies

Corbin Bullet Swaging Dies are made in all calibers from 17 to 458, in all styles from lead pistol wadcutters to copper tubing, multiple jacket African game bullets. Partitioned bullets, boattails, nylon tip bullets . . . even bullets made from fired 22 cases.

Shown are two of the basic kinds of Corbin dies . . . the reloading press (⅞-14) type which Corbin makes in all handgun calibers up to 357, in all styles including full jacket and partitioned designs, and in both the 224 and 243 rifle calibers; and the Corbin Swaging Press, a powerful horizontal stroke O-frame press brought out to replace the old Mity Mite C-frame. Every kind of bullet can be made on the Corbin press, using the Corbin self-alignment and automatic ejecting system. From Corbin Mfg. and Supply Co. Press and dies to make:

Semi-wadcutter bullets	**$337.50**
Flat base open tip bullets	**$427.00**
Rebated boattail bullets	**$536.50**
Flat or rebated, open or lead tip (all above)	**$496.50**
Corbin swaging press alone	**$198.50**
Corbin system die sets alone:	
1-die lead bullet pistol set.	**$69.50**
2-die lead bullet pistol set.	**$139.00**
3-die rifle or FMJ pistol set	**$228.50**
4-die RBT rifle set.	**$338.00**
5-die flat and RBT rifle set	**$408.00**

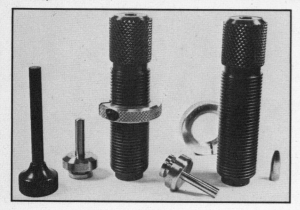

Corbin Rifle Swage Dies

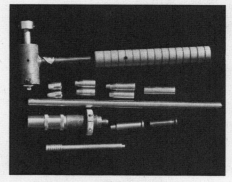

Hanned Precision Bullet Maker

Corbin Pistol Dies

Corbin Core-Band

CORBIN Core-Bond

This liquid permits the bonding of the lead core of a jacketed bullet to the jacket material as if the two were soldered together. Core-Bond is a flux that is applied either to the lead core or to the inside of the bullet jacket. From Corbin Mfg. and Supply Co. Price, 2-oz. **$2.98**
Price, pint................................... **$18.00**

CORBIN Power Cannelure Machine

This machine forms cannelures on lead or jacketed bullets at the rate of up to 100 bullets per minute. Designed to be incorporated into automatic production lines, or used as a stand-alone tool for handloaders. The ½-inch ground steel top provides a 6″ × 8″ work space. The steel cabinet is 10 inches high, machine weighs 27 lbs. and comes complete with one cannelure wheel (for all calibers) and one caliber of guide plate. Caliber plates available from 22 to 512 caliber. From Corbin Mfg. and Supply Co. Price, complete for one caliber. **$450.00**
Additional caliber guide plates **$75.00**

CORBIN Hand Cannelure Tool

This hand-operated tool duplicates the factory knurled grooves on commercial bullets. Does not require parts change to handle all calibers from 224 to 460. Depth and position are adjustable. Designed to be screwed to the bench, but a C-clamp will also hold it firmly. Works with lead or jacketed bullets. From Corbin Mfg. and Supply Co............. **$39.50**

HANNED PRECISION Hammerhead Bullet Making System

Makes super accurate, high-shock, high penetration 458-cal. jacketed rifle bullets from thick-walled (.040″), dead soft copper tubing. Die/mould set makes bullet weights from 200-gr. to 620-gr. "Cruise Missle" from same tubing. The tubing is cut to length, the jacket blank formed in the die, and then placed in the mould. The bullet is cast in place inside the jackets. The core is then compressed/expanded in the die. Includes tubing for 230 to 660 bullets. From Hanned Precision.
Price: Die, mould, punches, and tubing......... **$250.00**
Price: 10 extra 36″ length jacket tubing.......... **$50.00**

L.L.F. Die Shop

These dies fit nearly all presses suitable for bullet swaging. Adjustable for desired bullet weight, bullets are automatically ejected after forming. Dies are available in 17, 20, 22, 227, 228, 230, 234, 6mm, 25, 6.5mm, 270, 7mm, 7.35mm and 30 calibers. When ordering, give make and model of press, brand of jackets to be used and caliber. From L.L.F. Die Shop.
Complete set of rifle dies **$125.00**
Automatic pistol dies
Solid nose **$87.50**
Complete set Universal Dies
Solid nose **$67.50**

Corbin Power Cannelure

Sport Flite 22-cal.
Die Set

Corbin Power Cannelure

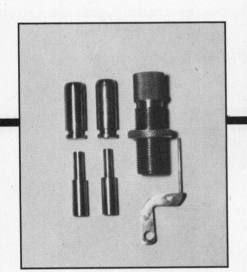

L.L.F. Swage Dies

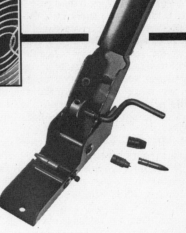

Corbin Hand Cannelure

SPORT FLITE 22-cal. 3-Die Set

A three-die set and ram for the Lyman or RCBS Rock-chucker reloading press featuring automatic ejection of the core, core/jacket or bullet. The three dies are for core forming, core seating in the jacket and bullet forming. Complete instructions accompany the die set. From Sport Flite Mfg. Co... **$99.95**

SPORT FLITE Swaging Dies

Dies are threaded ⅞-14 for standard presses and heat-treated to 52 Rockwell "C", then honed to a micro finish. Available in 30 cal. (.308-.309), 38/357, 9mm, 44, 45 caliber pistol solid nose punch styles, semi-wadcutter, round-nose and conical. Additional punches are available. Adjustable for a wide range of bullet weights. From Sport Flite. Complete **$20.95**
　　Nose punches **$6.95**
　　Extra base punch, zinc or jacketed **$4.95**

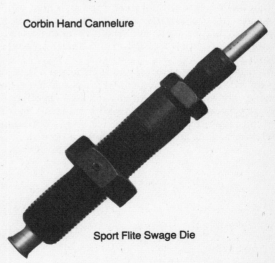

Sport Flite Swage Die

Corbin Jackets

Corbin Copper, Brass and Steel Bullet Jackets

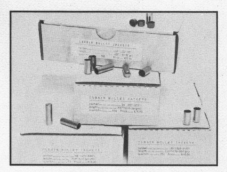

Corbin Bullet Jackets

Notes on Jackets and Gas Checks . . .

Ballistic performance with lead rifle bullets is limited. If an attempt is made to drive them fast, they often leave lead deposits in the bore—an inconvenience. Sometimes the base itself melts because of high powder combustion temperature. Both affect accuracy to a very noticeable extent.

To aviod these and other faults, a copper or alloy envelope called a jacket is added to part or most of the lead bullet. Being of harder, more durable material, this eliminates the barrel leading problem, as it prevents lead-to-bore contact. These jackets permit driving the bullet to the highest velocity practicable.

Jacketed rifle bullets have been factory manufactured for at least a century, but only since WWII have they been commonly made by handloaders using home-shop swaging tools. Several companies offer bullet-making dies for use in heavy-duty loading presses, while others sell jackets and lead wire for cores.

Commercial jacket material is usually gilding metal (a zinc-copper alloy), rather than pure copper, which sometimes causes fouling. Uniformity in length, weight, mouth concentricity, wall thickness, etc. are necessary for top results. Cores are normally of pure lead; occasionally a small amount of antimony is permitted.

A desire for high velocity and the success of the swaging dies for rifle bullets caused a similar interest in handgun bullet swaging. The addition of ½- and ¾-jackets—in effect, lengthened gas checks—gives them benefits similar to the rifle versions although the possibility of leading is not completely eliminated so long as any lead touches the bore.

CORBIN Bullet Jackets

Corbin supplies not only jackets but dies and tooling to make jackets from copper tubing, fired 22 cases, fired shotgun primers, and other scrap materials. From Corbin.

Caliber	Length	Quantity	Price
224	.600"	500	$22
224	.650"	500	22
224	.705"	500	22
243	.750"	500	24
243	.825"	500	28
257	.950"	250	14
284	1.00"	250	14
308	.375"	500	24
308	.925"	250	14
308	1.08"	250	14
308	1.05"	250	14
308	1.20"	250	14
38/9mm	.250"	500	22
38/9mm	.437"	500	24
38/9mm	.500"	500	24
38/9mm	.700"	250	14
44	.286"	500	24
44	.540"	250	14
44	.700"	250	14
45	.230"	250	24
45	.540"	250	14
45	.700"	250	14

Jackets other than those listed can be made from larger jackets with Corbin drawing dies, $59.50 each. Big bore jackets can be made from ordinary copper tubing (plumbing pipe) with Corbin Tubing Jacket Maker kits at $125 each.

CORBIN
Copper, Brass and Steel Bullet Jackets

Cut to length, deburred copper, brass and steel, ready to form into heavy-steel bullet jackets. Wall thickness of .030, .050, .065-inch. From Corbin Mfg.
Price: Per thousand . . . . **$16.00 to $30.00**

Lyman Gas Checks

Hanned Precision Gas Check Maker

HORNADY GAS CHECKS

Before sizing on bullets

After sizing on bullets

Caliber	#	Caliber	#	Caliber	#
22 cal.	#7010	7mm cal.	#7060	35 cal.	#7110
6mm cal.	#7020	30 cal.	#7070	375 cal.	#7120
25 cal.	#7030	32 cal. (8mm)	#7080	44 cal.	#7130
6.5mm cal.	#7040	338 cal.	#7090	45 cal.	#7140
270 cal.	#7050	348 cal.	#7100		

C-H TOOL & DIE Copper Jacket Cups

22 cal. (.705″) Copper Jackets	**$37.00/M**
6mm cal. (.825″) Copper Jackets	**43.88/M**
30 cal. 1/2 Jackets	**37.00/M**
38 cal. 1/2 Jackets	**38.38/M**
38 cal. 3/4 Jackets	**39.75/M**
38 cal. (extra long) 3/4 Jackets	**41.13/M**
41 cal. 3/4 Jackets	**43.88/M**
44 cal. 3/4 Jackets	**50.50/M**
45 cal. 3/4 Jackets	**50.50/M**

HANNED PRECISION
Freechec Gas Check Maker

Freechec dies make high-quality gas checks for plain based cast bullets out of aluminum pop can material. They swage on during lubri-sizing and won't come off in flight. For calibers other than 30 send a sample nose-damaged CB, a tool will be custom made. Fits on all standard reloading presses. All orders postpaid. From Hanned Precision.

Price: Each **$46.50**

HORNADY Crimp-On Gas Checks

Made with open edge thicker than the sidewall so that sizing die crimps them permanently to bullets. From Hornady. Price per 1000 in calibers 22, 25, 35, 6mm, 6.5 .... **$10.00**

In 270, 7mm, 30, 32, 338, 348, 375 .... **$11.55**

In 44, 45 .... **$14.40**

LYMAN Gas Checks

Protect bullet base from hot powder gases, permit higher velocities with cast bullets. Seated during sizing operation. From Lyman Products.

22 through 35, per M **$18.95**

375 through 45 .... **$19.95**

RCBS
Gas Checks

Caliber	Quantity	Price
22	1,000	$19.90
6mm	1,000	$19.90
25	1,000	$19.90
270	1,000	$19.90
7mm	1,000	$22.00
30	1,000	$22.00
32-8mm	1,000	$22.00
35	1,000	$22.00
375	1,000	$22.00
44	1,000	$22.00
45	1,000	$22.00

From RCBS

SPORT FLITE Copper Half Jackets

Caliber	Quantity	Price
30	1,000	$36.35
38	1,000	37.35
44	1,000	45.00
45	1,000	49.50

From Sport Flite Mfg. Co.

SPORT FLITE Zinc Bases

Zinc-based swaged bullets can be fired at the same velocity as half-copper-jacketed bullets. The price is about 1/7th of copper jackets. The zinc base remains with the bullet, even after impact. From Sport Flite Mfg. Co.

Caliber	Quantity	Price
30	1,000	$12.00
9mm/38/357	1,000	12.00
44	1,000	13.50
45	1,000	13.50

Corbin Core Cutter

Corbin Lead Wire

Corbin Extruder Kit

Notes on Lead Wire . . .

The lead wire used in bullet swaging should be, usually, of the highest quality pure soft lead. Alloys are generally too hard for the average swaging operation, but there are some that will swage satisfactorily in heavy-duty presses. For all practical purposes, pure soft lead is the best and easiest to use.

Pure lead will flow and yet stay in one piece, whereas harder lead alloys tend to shatter or disintegrate. Pure lead bullets have unsurpassed shocking power, and when combined with copper jackets to permit high velocities, make deadly missiles.

The companies in the boxed column offer lead wire in the following standard sizes for bullet swaging: ⅛″ for the 17 cal., ³/₁₆″, ¼″, .290″, .305″, ⁵/₁₆″, .365″ and .390″. This wire is generally available in 20, 25, 100 and 250-lb. spools, and in some instances in straight cut lengths.

C-H Core Cutter

A scissors-type cutter of all steel construction with a rubber handle to eliminate hand fatigue. Drilled for bench mounting and fully adjustable for weight of cores cut. From C-H Tool and Die Corp.

Complete **$29.95**

LESTER COATS Core Cutter

This lead wire cutter has six apertures drilled and reamed to accept wire sizes normally used in swaging bullets. All cutting surfaces are finely machined. Each aperture is fully adjustable for any desired bullet weight. Tension on the two cutting surfaces is adjustable.

Cutter, complete **$18.00**

CORBIN LED-1 Lead Wire Extruder Kit

An accessory kit for the Corbin CHP-1 Hydro-press which allows the extrusion of lead wire in any diameter from ⅛-inch to ½-inch. Special kits for hollow lead tubing are also available. Included in the kit is a package of four sample lead billets (approx. ¾-inch diameter by 4 inches long), a billet mould with extra tubes, the extruder body (a hardened steel die), a floating alignment punch, a retainer for the dies and a package of four heat-treated lead extruder dies in sizes for 22, 30, 38, 44/45 caliber wire. From Corbin Mfg. and Supply Co. **$450.00**

CORBIN Precision Core Cutter

A die-type cutter that uses two hardened tool steel dies in a steel frame with a fine thread stop screw to cut lead wire into precise lengths. Accuracy on the order of 0.1 grains in .224 is possible, with this handmade cutter. Four dies cover a full range of lead diameters. Comes with all dies. From Corbin Mfg. and Supply Co.

Corbin Core Cutter **$29.50**

CORBIN Lead Wire

Lead wire for bullet making is available in both 25-pound and 10-pound precision extruded spools. All calibers are available. From Corbin Mfg. and Supply Co.

Price: 25 lb **$39.50**
Price: 10 lb **$18.00**

CORBIN LED-2 Lead Wire Extruder Kit

Lead wire for tiny sub-caliber (14, 17 and 20) can be manufactured in short lengths using the Corbin Mity Mite press. The kit consists of a four-cavity adjustable weight mould that makes ⅜-inch diameter billets, a punch that fits into the Mity Mite ram, a die body that fits into the Mity Mite press head, a retainer bushing and a set of extruder dies. From Corbin Mfg. and Supply Co. **$169.00**

HOLLYWOOD Micrometer Lead Core Cutter

Accurately cuts lead cores from 22 to 45 caliber. Complete unit is ready to use on either the Hollywood Senior or Senior Turret tools. Micrometer thimble allows reference recording of lengths and weights. From Hollywood Loading Tools. **$57.50**

L.L.F. Lead Wire Cutter

A well-made tool for all sizes of lead wire. Adjustable stop to control length of cut core. From L.L.F. Die Co. . . **$24.00**

SPORT FLITE Lead Wire Cutter

A scissors-type cutter that cuts lead wire: .250″, .300″ and .365″ diameters. Length is regulated by an adjustable stop. Body and shear are of hardened steel. Adjustable for weights. A sturdy, economical tool. From Sport Flite Mfg. Co.

Price **$20.95**

**TOOLS AND
ACCESSORIES FOR**

BULLET
CASTING

Lee Production Pot IV

Ballisti-Cast Mark II   Ballisti-Cast Mark I

Notes on Furnaces & Pots . . .

Satisfactory bullet casting may be done with gas-heated lead pots, but electric furnaces will not only save time and labor, but also will improve the quality of the bullets cast.

It is important that the molten lead be stirred frequently, otherwise the tin and antimony (if any) will separate. If you are using a dipper, insert it into the bottom of the pot and bring it up from the bottom with the opening up. This not only keeps the mixture stirred, but gives you a ladle of clean metal without scum.

Lead and tin alloys require a temperature of about 600 degrees F., while an alloy containing antimony needs about 750 degrees F.

Beeswax or tallow is used to flux the alloy. A small ball (about the size of marble) of either should be added to the heated alloy, mixed in, and if it does not ignite by itself, it should be lit with a match. This will help mix the metals and cause any slag or impurities to rise to the surface where they can be skimmed off.

Some of the aids to bullet casting are available around the home. A blanket or soft pad should be used to catch the bullets dropped from the mould, and it is wise to use gloves when casting to prevent burns. Safety glasses or goggles should always be worn when working with molten metals.

BALLISTI-CAST INC. Mark I Hand Casting Machine

This hand-operated casting machine produces, cast bullets from #4 buckshot up to .54-caliber Maxi ball. Has a 2600-Watt heating element to bring the 100-lb. capacity furnace to operating temperatures. Furnace is thermostatically controlled. Uses most standard moulds which can be changed quickly. Each mold and sprue cutter is highly polished, hardened and specially treated to eliminate sticking. Operates on 220-volt, 20 amps. From Ballisti-Cast, Inc. Price with one mould of choice **$2,950**

BALLISTI-CAST INC. Mark II Casting Machine

The Mark II is fully automated producing 2400 cast bullets an hour from #4 buckshot to 54-caliber Maxi balls. The 2600-Watt heating element brings the 100-pound capacity furnace to operating temperatures and maintains proper heat control. The unit includes two heavy-duty air blowers, a dust-sealed control panel, indicator working lights, a thermostat, an electronic counter, a heavy-duty drive motor and an automatic lead control. Uses four 2-cavity Saeco, Ballisti-Cast or RCBS moulds, though most manufactured moulds can be adapted. Each mould and sprue cutter is highly polished, hardened and specially treated to eliminate sticking. Weighs 265 pounds with welded tubular frame. From Ballisti-Cast, Inc.
Price with one mould of choice **$4,195**

LEE Precision Melter

A high-speed melter with infinite heat control. Takes less than 15 minutes to melt 4 pounds of lead. Designed for continuous duty industrial soldering. Basically the same as the Bullet Caster model except has thermostat. 500 watts AC only. Guaranteed for 2 years. 220 volt 3-wire cord models for export are **$3.00** extra.
Price complete **$28.98**

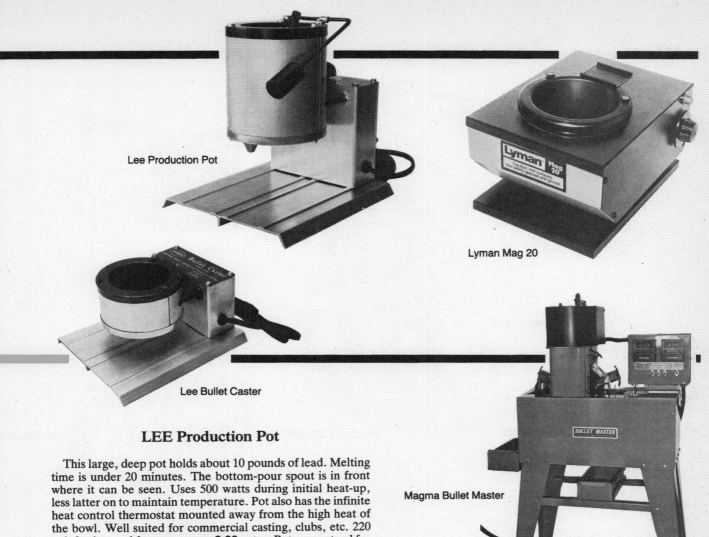

Lee Production Pot

Lyman Mag 20

Lee Bullet Caster

Magma Bullet Master

LEE Production Pot

This large, deep pot holds about 10 pounds of lead. Melting time is under 20 minutes. The bottom-pour spout is in front where it can be seen. Uses 500 watts during initial heat-up, less latter on to maintain temperature. Pot also has the infinite heat control thermostat mounted away from the high heat of the bowl. Well suited for commercial casting, clubs, etc. 220 volt 3-wire cord for export use ,3.00 extra. Pot guaranteed for 2 years. From Lee Precision Inc.

Price complete **$48.98**
Production Pot IV gives 4 inches of clearance under the spout instead of the standard 2 inches. This is high enough to accept all brands of bullet moulds and most sinker moulds. Same specs as standard Production Pot.

Price **$51.98**

LEE Bullet Caster

The perfect melter for the casual bullet caster. Holds over 4 pounds of lead. Drawn steel pot with an extruded aluminum jacket. Large stable base. Maintains adequate heat for all bullet alloys without thermostat. Has a 275-watt tubular heater. Two year guarantee. From Lee Precision Inc.

Price **$22.98**

LYMAN Mag 20 Electric Furnace

Low profile 20-lb. capacity furnace designed with both dip-casters and bottom pourers in mind. The Mag 20's 800-watt furnace melts cold metal in 20 minutes. Casting temperature thermostatically controlled. A fully adjustable mould guide is standard. Available in 110V and 220V. From Lyman Products.

Price: 110V **$199.95**
Price: 220V **$200.00**

LYMAN Magdipper Casting Furnace

Designed for the ladle-caster with 4⅜″ wide, 20-lb. capacity pot. Heat system controlled by the same industrial grade thermostat found on Mag 20. Available in both 110V and 220V. From Lyman Products.

Price: 110V **$149.95**
Price: 220V **$150.00**

MAGMA Bullet Master Mark V

This machine produces 2400 bullets per hour automatically. The heat controllers are solid state with LED readouts and control lead temperatures to ±7 degrees Fahrenheit. All springs and valve components are made of stainless steel. The pot is divided — a pre-melt side and pour side. A uniform lead level is maintained in the pouring side by using a float transfer mechanism to provide constant head pressure on the lead when pouring. Will cast as many as eight different bullets at one time. Mold sets can be changed in 10 minutes or less. Comes with 90-day parts and labor warranty. From Magma Engineering **$4,495.00**

Magma Cast Master

Magma Master Caster

Merit Pot

RCBS Pro-Melt

MAGMA Cast Master

The Cast Master is a hand-operated bottom pour type unit with a trip lever located on the right side (left side trip lever can be special ordered). Designed to cast large volumes of bullets using multiple cavity moulds. Pot can stand alone or be mounted on a bench. Valve components are of stainless steel with the orifice plate removeable to increase or decrease amount of flow. Holds 90 pounds of bullet alloy. Operates on 220 VAC. From Magma Engineering.............. **$350.00**

MAGMA Master Caster

A hand-operated automated caster. Machine includes the melting pot, two-cavity mold, sprue cutter and cutoff, mallet. Casting rate is 400-500 bullets per hour, depending on bullet size. Thermostatically controlled bottom pour melting pot, automatic sprue cutter and mould alignment. Moulds are opened automatically. From Magma Engineering. Price, with one mould..................................... **$495.00**
   Extra moulds (each) **$50.00**

RCBS PRO-Melt 10-Kilo Casting Pot

The Pro-Melt 10 Kilo (22-lb.) pot has temperature control of 450 to 850 degrees controlled by an industrial thermostat. The pot is made of steel and has a bottom pour valve. Pot liner is of stainless steel. A fully adjustable mould guide is standard, as is an "on-off" switch with indicator light. 800 watts, 120 volts AC. From RCBS...................... **$195.50**

MERIT Melting Pot

A 20-lb. capacity furnace with a controlled-flow downspout for slag-free mould filling. 2-piece design permits ready adjustment for bigger, multi-cavity moulds. Pot is used over a gas burner (not included). From Merit Gun Sight.
  Price: (F.O.B) **$72.50**
  Price: Replacement Valve and Pin **$8.75**

RCBS Pro-Melt

This heavy-duty furnace features an Incoloy sheathed heating element and a snap action, industrial quality thermostat. Thermostat is coupled to remote sensor on bottom surface of pot for added heating accuracy. Can be set up for either left- or right-hand operation. From RCBS.
  Price: 120 VAC Pro-Melt.................... **$217.00**
  Price: 240 Pro-Melt **$233.00**

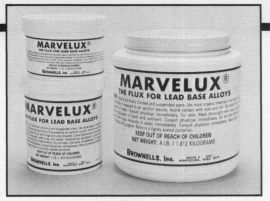

Brownells Marveleux

Lee Dipper

Lyman Mould Guide

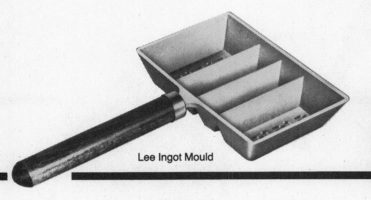

Lee Ingot Mould

Lee Pot

Lyman Pot

BROWNELLS Marvelux

This lead-alloy flux is non-corrosive to iron and steel and the manufacturer advises that its regular use will keep your lead pot free of rust. Marvelux reduces dross formation and increases fluidity of bullet alloys, thereby making it easier to obtain a well-filled bullet. Marvelux is nonsmoking, flameless and has no odor. From Brownells, Inc.

½-lb. **$3.56**
1 lb. **$5.85**
4 lbs. **$14.90**

LEE Lead Pot

This drawn steel pot holds 4 pounds of lead. The flat bottom makes it quite stable and provides good contact with the heat supply. From Lee Precision, Inc. **$2.78**

LEE Lead Ladle

A convenient size ladle for bullet casting. Works equally well for right or left handers. Handy for skimming and stirring the metal. From Lee Precision, Inc. **$2.78**

LEE Ingot Mould

A clever improvement on the standard 4-pig ingot mould, this new Lee unit is cast of an aluminum alloy and has a wooden handle that allows the mould to be flipped and emptied, and stays cool. There are four cavities—two for 1-lb. ingots, two for ½-lb. ingots. Perfect for alloying and storage. From Lee Precision, Inc................................. **$9.98**

LYMAN Mould Guide

Installs on bottom pouring electric casting furnaces. Makes precise positioning of mould beneath pouring spout easy. Usable with all moulds up to and including 4-cavity size. Guide is fully adjustable for easy positioning. From Lyman Products... **$19.95**

LYMAN Lead Pot

This Ideal unit is still the simplest and cheapest way of melting bullet metal. The pot can be used on almost any gas range or liquid fuel burner, or on an electric range if a high heat burner is available. From Lyman Products........... **$9.95**
Dipper...................................... **$8.95**

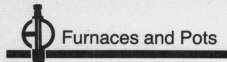

RCBS Dipper

RCBS Pot

RCBS Mallet

RCBS Mould

RCBS Lead Pot

This pot holds approximately 10 pounds of bullet alloy and is ideal for casting or blending metals. Flat, anti-tip bottom, pouring spout, bale handle lifter. From RCBS.
Price **$11.20**

RCBS Lead Dipper

This tool features an extra long handle and an ovaled spout contoured exactly to the sprue opening. The cup-shaped open top of the dipper allows for easy scooping and stirring of the bullet alloy. From RCBS. **$10.00**

RCBS Mould Mallet

This mallet is recommended for use when opening and closing the mould blocks and cutting sprues. The dense hardwood mallet is contoured for maximum efficiency and convenience. From RCBS **$8.40**

RCBS Ingot Mould

A heavy-duty iron mould which forms four easy-to-use ingots. Excellent for preparing alloys for future use and easy handling. From RCBS **$10.00**

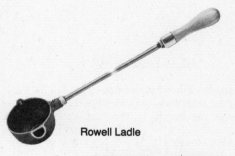

Rowell Ladle

ROWELL Bottom Pour Ladle

This bottom-pouring ladle delivers clean lead from the dipper via an internal spout that goes to the base of the bowl. Ten sizes are offered but only the numbers 1 and 2 are suitable for bullet casting. No. 2 ladle has a 2½-inch bowl and 14-inch handle. From Advance Car Mover Co.
No. 1, 1 lb. lead capacity **$11.50**
No. 2, 2 lb. lead capacity **$12.55**

Moulds

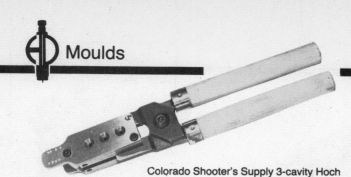
Colorado Shooter's Supply 3-cavity Hoch

Corbin 4-Cavity Mould

Colorado Shooter's Supply Hoch Custom Moulds

Notes on Moulds . . .

Cast bullets that do not perform accurately may have some internal defect that causes instability in flight. These defects may not be noticeable when weighing and sorting the bullets after casting, so every precaution should be taken to prevent them while casting.

The alignment of the two blocks is a critical factor in proper bullet casting. Extreme care should be taken that the mould is not dropped or hit with any force. The sprue cutter should be rapped only with a plastic or wood mallet—never steel! All moulds must be properly broken-in to do the best job of casting. After 100 or so bullets are cast, your mould will be putting out better bullets—or it should!

The first 10 to 12 bullets cast from a cold mould should be discarded—it takes at least that length of time for a mould to reach the proper temperature for accurate casting. If the bullet comes out of the mould with wrinkles or open spaces, the mould (or the lead) is too cold. Frosted bullets mean too hot a temperature, though the effect is harmless. Wait long enough for the bullet to harden before cutting off the sprue; cutting the sprue too soon results in a deformed base.

Lead should be poured into the mould slowly to permit the air in the mould cavity to escape, thus preventing air pockets or voids in the bullet.

The oil or grease on a new mould will not permit good bullets to be cast until the lube is burned away. Solvent or thinner can be helpful in removing this grease.

When you are through casting, leave a bullet in the cavity—this will help prevent rusting, thus eliminating the need to re-grease the cavity. For long term mould storage, however, the mould blocks should be coated with a rust preventative such as would be used on your guns.

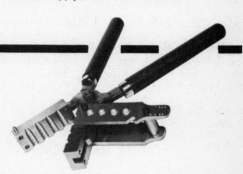
Colorado Shooter's Supply 4-Cavity Hoch

COLORADO SHOOTER'S SUPPLY
Hoch Custom Bullet Moulds

These 1-, 2-, 3-, 4-cavity moulds are made on a custom-basis only. All moulds are lathe-bored from fine-grain cast iron (meehanite) and are nose-pour only. Cylindrical (straight) or tapered. Pope and Hudson designs made to order. Machine tolerances: 0 to +.001″. From Colorado Shooter's Supply.

Single Cavity Moulds

Price: 22-51 caliber **$55.00**
Price: 52-75 caliber **$65.00**
Price: Hollow-based moulds...................... **$95.00**
Price: Adjustable moulds **$100.00**

Handles

Price: Hoch handles fitted to blocks **$15.00**
Price: 2-cavity with handles, 22-50 caliber **$100.00**
Price: 3-cavity with handles, 22-50 caliber **$150.00**
Price: 4-cavity with handles, 45-caliber only **$200.00**

CORBIN Core Moulds

Four-cavity style, these moulds mount to the bench, require no handles or mallets, and eject their fully-adjustable weight cores from precision honed cavities in tool steel dies. All calibers are available. Write for information on matching cores to jackets and caliber. From Corbin Mfg. and Supply Co.

Four Cavity Mould **$49.50**
Inserts to change calibers **$7.50**

LBT 4-Cavity Mould

LBT 6-Cavity Mould

LBT 1-Cavity Mould

Hensley & Gibbs

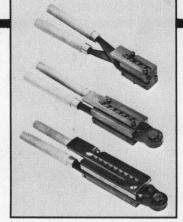

Lee Pistol Mould

HENSLEY & GIBBS Handgun Bullet Moulds

Made to give years of service. Many styles and weights available in 38, 44, and 45. Specify sized diameter of bullet and make of sizer when ordering. Moulds come complete with handles. Prices are approximate. From Hensley & Gibbs.

4-cavity	**$120.00**
6-cavity	**$170.00**
10-cavity (8 in 44 or 45)	**$275.00**

LBT Bullet Moulds

LBT makes 1-, 2-, 4-, and 6-cavity custom moulds in an unlimited selection of bullet designs from 22- to 45-caliber (50 to 75 caliber available in one cavity moulds only). Mould blocks are constructed of hard, stress-relieved aircraft grade aluminum alloy, sprue plates are of blued machine steel. All other critical parts are stainless steel. From Lead Bullets Technology. Contact LBT for prices.

LEE Pistol Bullet Moulds

These moulds have aluminum blocks that heat up faster and cool quicker. Moulds are substantially lighter than conventional steel types and can be preheated in molten lead without damage. Blocks are well vented reducing voids and, since lead won't stick to the aluminum, there is no "soldering" the blocks. Steel mould clamps with wood handles are light and the handles stay cool during casting operations. Available in 44 popular pistol sizes. Can be had with either single or double cavity blocks. Many hollowpoint styles are offered but only with single cavity mould. From Lee Precision, Inc.

Single cavity mould, complete with handles	**$17.98**
Single cavity mould, complete with handles and automatic core pin for hollowpoints	**$22.98**
Double cavity mould, complete with handles	**$22.98**

LEE Rifle Bullet Moulds

Same design and construction as the pistol bullet moulds except offered in 18 popular bullet styles in six calibers. Blocks are aluminum for rapid heating, come complete with handles. From Lee Precision, Inc.

Single cavity	**$17.98**
Hollowpoint	**$22.98**

LYMAN Mould Rebuild Kits

These kits provide replacement parts for worn moulds. Kits include sprue cutter, sprue cutter washer, screw and lock screw, and handle screws. From Lyman Products.

Single and double cavity kits	**$4.95**
Four cavity kit	**$6.95**

LYMAN Ingot Mould

Useful for melting down scrap lead or blending alloys. Each mould forms four, easy-to-use ingots that stack easily. From Lyman Products | **$8.95**

LYMAN Ideal Moulds

Made in single, double and 4-cavity types; available in over 100 bullet and ball styles. Precision machined and finished. Write to Lyman Products for their catalog for detailed descriptions.

Double cavity pistol, from	**$39.95**
Double cavity, rifle	**$39.95**
Four cavity	**$69.95**
Hollow base or hollowpoint	**$39.95**
Handles (not interchangeable), specify single or double cavity mould.	**$17.95**
Handles, four cavity	**$20.95**

LYMAN Shotgun Slug Mould

Casts unrifled, hollow base slugs in 12 or 20. Lyman recommends these be shot as cast, as extensive tests indicate slugs are not rotated by rifling grooves but travel head-on in the manner of a shuttle-cock because the greater mass is in the front of the projectile. From Lyman Products. Slug mould block only. | **$39.95**

Handles	**$14.95**

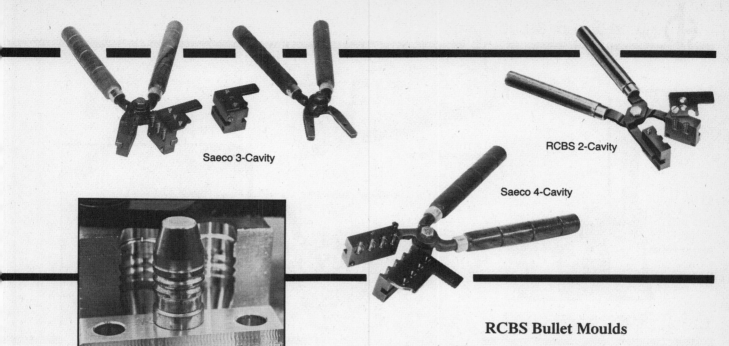

Saeco 3-Cavity

RCBS 2-Cavity

Saeco 4-Cavity

SSK Moulds

MAGMA Bullet Moulds

The following bevel-based bullet moulds are available from Magma Engineering. They are made to fit Magma's Bullet Master and Master Caster machines but can be altered for hand casting.

Caliber	Grains	Type	Caliber	Grains	Type
38	148	WC	41	215	SWC
38	148	WC DBB	44	215	SWC
38	158	RN	44	240	SWC
38	158	SWC	45	185	SWC
380	95	RN	45	200	SWC
9mm	122	FP	45	225	FP
9mm	125	CN	45	230	RN
9mm	125	RN	45	255	SWC

Price: Each **$50.00**

SAECO Match Precision Bullet Moulds

Designed with accuracy, consistency and speed in mind. Made from specially formulated steel to provide smooth bullets, rapid cavity filling and a high resistance to mould tining. Heavy mould blocks retain even temperatures. Long heavy-duty handles remain cool in use. One handle fits all moulds. Over 150 popular styles of bullets available: handgun, target, combat and silhouette, rifle, precision and target, roundballs and maxi balls and a wide selection of classic bullets for obsolete and turn of the century rifles. From Redding, Inc. Prices are approximate. Moulds without handles:

1 cavity	**$39.95**
2 cavity	**$46.00**
3 cavity	**$59.95**
4 cavity	**$79.95**
6 cavity	**$129.95**
8 cavity with handles	**$179.95**
Hardwood handles	**$24.00**

RCBS Bullet Moulds

Mould blocks are made of malleable iron allowing the sprue cutter to be hardened and sharpened. Tungsten carbide tooling is used to cut the cavity. Blocks are vented over the entire bullet surface to release trapped air. Alignment pins are hardened for durability. Most handgun and some rifle calibers available. Handles have extra long wood sheaths and are completely interchangeable between RCBS blocks. From RCBS.

Double cavity pistol bullet mould	**$43.00**
Double cavity rifle bullet moulds	**$44.50**
Silhouette bullet moulds, double cavity	**$44.50**
Single cavity mould, Minnie ball, less handles	**$50.00**
Double cavity, plain, gas check, or round ball, less handles	**$43.00**
Handles....................................	**$18.60**

SPORT FLITE Adjustable Core Mould

This is an economical means of casting slugs for swaged bullets. This mould is adjustable to give the length and weight desired. When the core is cast, cut the sprue and bump the spring-loaded ejector pin on the bench, popping the core out of the mould. Available in 30, 38 and 44/45 calibers. From Sport Flite Mfg. Co. Complete **$12.75**

SSK Bullet Moulds

Aluminum block bullet moulds available in 35-cal. (150-gr., 182-gr., 205-gr.), 41-cal. (225, 275, 310 grains), 44-cal. (220, 265, 320, 350 grains), 45-cal. (270, 340 grains) and 50-cal. (470 grains). From SSK Industries.

2 cavity mould	**$46.00**
4 cavity mould	**$69.00**

SSK 44-Caliber Bullet Mould

Aluminum block bullet moulds featuring two crimp grooves. Two crimp grooves allow the same bullet to be used utilizing the full cylinder length of both short and long cylindered guns. Available in weights of 285 and 320 grains. Add $3.00 for postage. From SSK Industries. **$46.00**

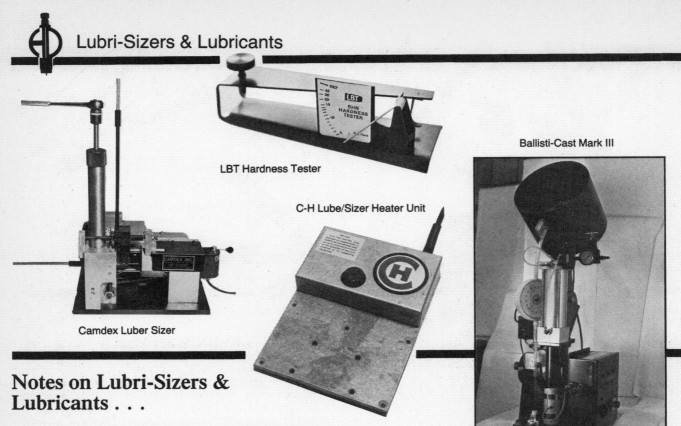

LBT Hardness Tester

C-H Lube/Sizer Heater Unit

Ballisti-Cast Mark III

Camdex Luber Sizer

Notes on Lubri-Sizers & Lubricants . . .

To be truly accurate, cast bullets are usually sized (forced through a die to bring diameter down to correct measurement), though some bullets shoot well "as cast." The combination tools shown on the following pages do this easily and quickly, and at the same time force a lubricant into the grooves of the bullet.

All lead alloy unjacketed bullets must be lubricated to prevent leading of the bore. Bullet lubricants should not only be able to lubricate properly at high temperatures, they should maintain this property in storage and must not melt in hot climates.

Operated properly, that is, maintaining the proper pressure on the lubricant and hesitating for a moment at the bottom of the downstroke to permit the lubricant to flow into all of the bullet grooves, these tools will help make your bullets more accurate, and they will also insure a minimum of bore leading.

Your sizing die-cast bullet combination should, ideally, be one in which a minimum amount of lead is displaced. In other words, let your lube-sizer swage only a thousandth or two from the bullet diameter. When you size away too much lead you decrease the lube capacity of the grooves, make the lead area in contact with bore greater, and you'll have to exert more effort, too, in doing the sizing-lubing. Regardless of the tool type used, care must be used in selecting dies. Bullet concentricity must be maintained. If all, or most of, the diameter reduction is on one side, the bullet's balance will be impaired, reducing its accuracy. Correctly designed dies contain a cylindrical cavity large enough to accept the as-cast bullet. A gradual, highly polished taper connects this portion to another cylinder of the diameter to which the bullet is to be sized. Both cylinders must be concentric. In this type of die the bullet is smoothly swaged to the correct diameter without loss of weight or concentricity.

Some older dies have a very short taper, or even an abrupt shoulder, connecting the two diameters. They simply shear excess metal off the bullet, usually more on one side than the other, producing a poorly balanced, inaccurate bullet. Casting is hot work — don't waste it by poor lubricating and sizing.

BALLISTI-CAST Mark III Lube Sizer

Lubes and sizes 4500 bullets per hour using Star sizing dies. A lube proportioning valve eliminates over-lubed bullets. The lube cylinder is air-pressure operated and needs no manual adjustments during operation. A lube preheater provides faster warm-up time on very hard lubes. The Watlow proportioner heat controller is 6 sec. thermocouple controlled. All moving parts of tool steel and case-hardened. From Ballisti-Cast, Inc.
Complete with collator. **$5,045.00**

CAMDEX Luber Sizer

A mass production unit that sizes and lubes cast or swaged bullets at 440 per hour. It feeds vertically and dispenses horizontally for bulk or tube packaging. Bullet lube is heated with a cartridge type element in an aluminum block. Lube pressure is held constant by a ratchet and spring assembly inside the reservoir. Powered by a ⅓-hp. electric motor. Comes with the cartridge heater, foot pedal and foward/reverse switch. From Camdex, Inc.
Price...................................... **$3,150.00**

C-H Lubricator/Sizer Heater Unit

Constant controlled heat is a necessity when lubing cast bullets with either the conventional or new hard lubes. Designed to work with Star, Lyman, RCBS or Saeco Lubricator/Sizers, the C-H heater unit will maintain heat up to plus or minus 10 degrees. Comes with bench attachment screws, long cord, and instructions. UL approved. From C-H Tool and Die Corp....................................... **$79.95**

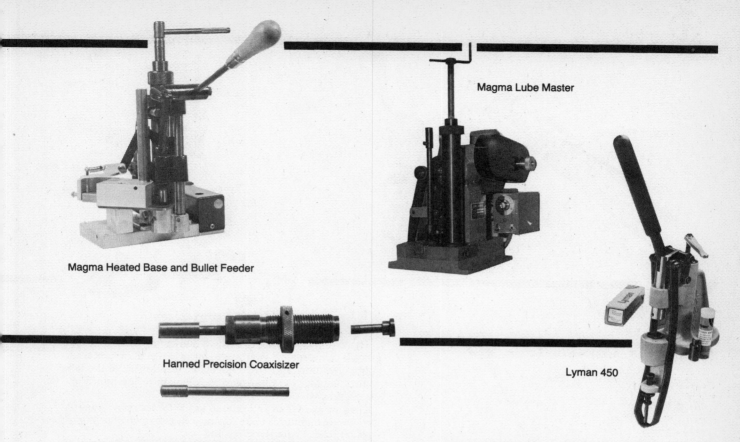

Magma Lube Master

Magma Heated Base and Bullet Feeder

Hanned Precision Coaxisizer

Lyman 450

HANNED PRECISION Coaxisizer

A set of coaxial sizer dies and punches that reshape the nose and base of 30-cal. or 22 centerfire (both rifle and pistol) so that they automatically align with the rifle bore during firing. Dies fatten-up or size down bullet nose and are available in .301, .302, .303, .304, .305, or .3135 (303 British). All 30-cal. dies produce a "drive band" diameter on the rear half of the CB of from .3085 to .310 and from .3125 to .3135 for 303 British. Die set includes choice one die size, a universal bottom punch, universal top punch and a L/SGB (Large and Small Game Bullet) top punch that changes a cast bullet into a semi-wadcutter. From Hanned Precision. **$60.00**
Price: Extra die **$30.00**
Price: Extra punches **$10.00**

LBT Hardness Tester

Test the hardness of any cast bullet ½ to 1⅜ inches long. Hardness scale runs from 5 bhn (pure lead) to 40 bhn (copper). Features direct scale readout, rugged all steel welded construction and guaranteed accuracy to ± 1 bhn. Comes with 1 year guarantee. From Lead Bullets Technology. . . . **$49.00**

LYMAN Lubricating & Sizing Die Sets

These current "G", "H" and "I" dies feature a precisely controlled entering taper, a smooth concentric bore, and dimensions held to minimum tolerances, and a grease-sealing O-ring that means clean bullet bases. Made in over 50 sizes from .224″ to .512″. "G" top punch. From Lyman Products. **$4.79**
"H" and "I" assembly (state bullet diameter) **$13.95**

LYMAN 450 Lubricator and Sizer

The short stroke, power link leverage of this tool sizes, lubes and seats gas checks with little effort. Large C-type iron-steel cast frame is line bored for best die alignment. Uses improved ram and leverage system. Comes with convenient Gas Check Seater and a stick of Lyman Alox lube. Adaptable to all bullets by changing sizing dies. From Lyman Products. Price less dies and top punch. **$104.95**

MAGMA Lube Master

This is a high-output machine that automatically sizes and lubricates cast lead bullets at the rate of 4300 per hour. Both bullet and lube feeds are vertical with bullet delivery coming through the bottom of the base plate. Powered by 110VAC ½-hp. electric motor. Comes complete with one size of die and one bullet feed tube. From Magma Engineering.
Price: **$2,795.00**
Conversion kit for caliber change.
Price. **$45.00**

MAGMA Heated Base and Bullet Feeder

Designed as accessories for the STAR Sizer. The heated base is an aluminum plate drilled and tapped to accept the mounting bolt pattern of the Star Sizer. A 150W-110V heating element connects to a snap action thermostat to control lube temperature.
The shuttle bar bullet feeder is shipped to feed one caliber. From Magma Engineering.
Price: Heated Base **$60.00**
Price: Bullet Feeder. **$75.00**

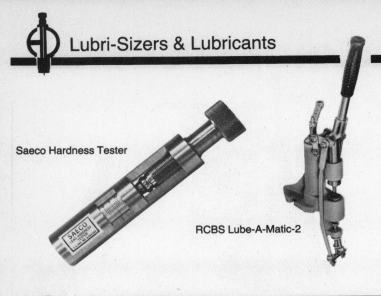

Saeco Hardness Tester

RCBS Lube-A-Matic-2

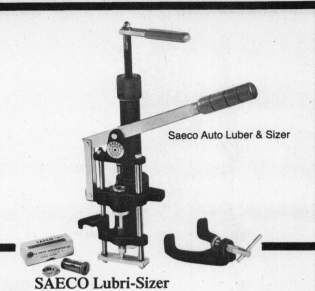

Saeco Auto Luber & Sizer

Pitzer

SAECO Lubri-Sizer

Heavy-duty cast bullet sizer and lubricating press with integral gas check seater. Features a spring loaded lubricant reservoir which lubricates 20-50 bullets between turns of the lube control handle. Parallel guide rods maximize top punch and die alignment.

Dies are hardened and ground to .0002″ accuracy. Tapered lead on die minimizes bullet distortion. Dies available in most popular sizes. From Redding, Inc.

SAECO Lubri-Sizer	$126.50
Lubri-Sizer dies	$17.50
Top Punches	$7.95

SAECO Lead Hardness Tester

A precision instrument to determine hardness of bullet casting alloy by measuring penetration of a hardened steel penetrator into a bullet. Hardness is read from a Vernier scale—reads in arbitrary units running from 0 (Brinell 5) for pure lead to 10 for linotype (Brinell 22). Wheel weights vary from 7 to 9 (Brinell 10-15). A hardness of at least 6 is required for medium handgun velocities, over 8 for magnum handgun and gas checked rifle bullets. Conversion to Brinell included. Use for quality control or sorting scrap to provide usable casting alloy. Should pay for itself many times over by allowing use of scrap lead. From Redding, Inc. About **$98.00**

PITZER Lubricator & Sizer

Pushing the operating handle completely foward sizes bullets and aligns the lube groove. Pulling the operating handle rearward forces the lube into the lube groove and the tool is ready to size and lubricate the next bullet. Features horizontal push-through design, "O" ring seals on die, a locknut that holds die firmly in place and a reservoir pressure screw that needs tightening down only every 10 to 20 bullets. Dies available for handgun bullets only—9mm to 45-cal. From Pitzer Tool Mfg. Co.

Price: Tool with one die and nose punch	$154.00
Price: Dies	$22.00
Price: Nose Punch	$8.25

RCBS Lube-A-Matic-2

This lubricator-sizer automatically controls lubricant pressure and feeds grease into the bullet grooves. Pressure is controlled with each stroke of the operating handle. Unit has finger tip adjustments for controlling depth of sizing for various bullets. Uses either Lube-A-Matic or Lyman dies. From RCBS. Price without dies. **$111.00**

Lube-A-Matic dies available in most popular sizes	$14.70
Top punches	$5.40

STAR Automatic Lubricator & Resizer

This lubricator, substantially and carefully built, is accurate and positive in its operations. A storage pressure system is used in the grease reservoir, which feeds the grease to a high pressure pump. This forces the lubricant into the grooves of the bullet. The bullet is then forced through the die by the entering of the next one. One setting of the pressure screw greases from 199 to 200 bullets. The bullets are forced through the die, and are processed about three times as fast as in the ordinary lubricator.

This item is equipped with hardened dies and is adaptable to any caliber.

Give bullet number (Lyman, SAECO or Hensley & Gibbs) and size of die wanted, or send sample bullet and state size of die wanted. From Star Machine Works. **$120.00**

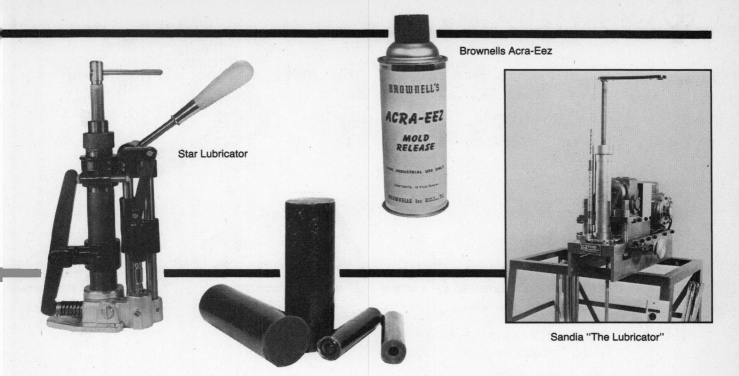

Star Lubricator

Brownells Acra-Eez

Sandia "The Lubricator"

C-H Ultra-Lube

SANDIA "The Lubricator"

A high-output lubricator/sizer for cast or swaged lead rifle and pistol bullets. Variable speed up through 15,000 pieces per hour through use of adjustable pulleys. A precise lube flow adjustment eliminates over or under lubrication. Cam-operated lube piston. Thermostatically controlled heater located under lube reservoir which holds enough lube for 6,000 to 8,000 38-cal. wadcutter bullets. Machine comes complete for one caliber, including counter, wrenches and tools necessary for maintenance, plus 10 bullet tubes holding 78 bullets each, and a ½-hp. 110 VAC motor. From Sandia Die and Cartridge.

Price....................................... **$3,700.00**
Caliber change (30, 9mm, 38/357, 41, 45) per caliber... **$350.00**
Steel machine stand (for two machines)........ **$212.00**
Extra bullet tubes, each **$3.50**

BALLISTI-CAST Wolverine Bullet Lube

Designed for two different applications — hot and cold. Wolverine Hot Lube is not sticky so it works well in automated loaders. After application, it does not get brittle but remains pliable, making for a better seal, eliminating blowby, lubricating the barrel and reducing leading. Since no oils are used, smoke is minimized. Wolverine Cold Lube has the same qualities except it is made softer for use with sizers with no heat plates. The 1"x4" sticks come in either hollow or solid configurations. 2"x6" sticks come in only solid form. From Ballisti-Cast, Inc.

Price: 1x4 (less than 100) each **$1.00**
Price: 1x4 (100 or more) each.................... **$.85**
Price: 2x6 (less than 25) each **$3.00**
Price: 2x6 (25 or more) each.................... **$2.75**

BROWNELL'S Acra-Eez

Lubricant and mould "separator" for casting bullets. Non-flammable, non-toxic, clean and quick drying, Acra-Eez is well suited for spraying bullet moulds, before and after casting. Prevents sticking when casting and offers rust and corrosion protection for storage. From Brownells, Inc.

Price: 16-oz. aerosol can **$8.15**
Price: Pint can................................. **$6.98**

C-H Ultra Lube

An extra hard cast bullet lube with a 340-degree melt-point and 450-degree flash. Shrinks for super hard bond. Prevents buildup in automatic loaders. From C-H.

Price: 1x5 hollow or solid stick (each)............. **$1.99**
Price: 2x6 solid stick (each) **$3.99**

CORBIN Dip Lube

Dip-type lubrication for cast or swaged lead bullets. Bullets are placed in a pan and lube is poured over them. Upon drying, a thin film of lubricant remains in the pores and on surface of the bullet. No lubricator-sizer machine required. Also makes pre-lubricated patches for muzzleloaders and paper patching bullets. From Corbin Mfg. and Supply Co.

2 oz. dispenser **$2.98**
Pint **$18.00**
Gallon **$75.00**

COOPER-WOODWARD Perfect Lube

Made in hollow or solid sticks, this lube works in any lubricating machine. Performs equally well in cold or hot weather because of its minimum contraction and high melting point. From Cooper/Woodward. **$1.75**

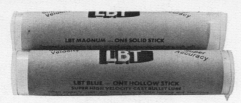

LBT Blue Lube

Lee Kit

Hodgdon Alox Lube

Lee Resizer

Lee Punch

Lee Alox Lube

HANNED PRECISION Quick-E-Wipe Bullet Lubricator

Dip-Lube your 30-cal. cast bullets then remove the extra lube with the Quick-E-Wipe tool: Just place the cast bullet atop the tool's post and slip the die down over it. The clean, ready to fire lubed bullet emerges from the top. Fast to operate, it takes tapered or Louvern-style bullets as well as the standard types. Use with either a press or freehand. From Hanned Precision **$36.50**

HODGDON Bullet Lube (Alox)

This high quality bullet lube gives increased accuracy and higher lead bullet velocity without leading. A mixture of pure beeswax and Alox 2138F. Available in hollow sticks only. From Hodgdon Powder Co. Price per 1¾-oz stick. **$2.76**

LBT Magnum Cast Bullet Lube

Somewhat softer than alox. Developed for soft, plain base handgun bullets to control leading. Available in solid or hollow 1x4 sticks. From Lead Bullets Technology.
Price: 1 to 4 sticks (each) **$4.00**
Price: 5 or more sticks (each) **$3.75**

LBT Blue Cast Bullet Lube

Developed for extremely heavy loads with hard gas-checked bullets in rifles. Comes in hollow or solid 1x4 sticks. From Lead Bullets Technology.
Price: 1 to 4 sticks (each) **$4.00**
Price: 5 or more sticks (each) **$3.75**
Price: 30 stick bulk pack **$63.00**

LEE Resizer and Punch

A quick and easy way of accurately resizing the bullets after lubricating. Generous taper leading to resize portion permits resizing without lead shaving. Order by bullet diameter. From Lee Precision, Inc.............................. **$7.98**

LEE Alox Bullet Lube

This famous NRA formula reduces leading, increases accuracy, and permits higher velocities. Contains 50% Alox 2138F and 50% commercial A-1 beeswax. Hollow sticks fit most lubricators. From Lee Precision, Inc. **$2.50**

LEE Lubricating & Resizing Kit

Everything needed for lubricating and resizing bullets. Kit includes 2 oz. Alox bullet lubricant, Lube Cutter, convenient sized lube pan, resizer die and punch and complete instructions. From Lee Precision, Inc.
Complete **$12.98**

LEE "Lube Cutter"

Aluminum cutter neatly wedges the lubricant away from the bullets, leaving holes in the lubricant for placement of the next batch of bullets and eliminating the need to re-melt the lubricant. From Lee Precision Inc................. **$4.98**

LYMAN Casting Thermometer

This all steel thermometer enables the caster to monitor the temperature of molten alloy. Calibrated from 200° to 1000° in 10° increments. The face is covered by heat resistant glass. Stainless steel stem is 6″ long and has a spring steel clip to hold the unit in place. From Lyman Products........... **$28.95**

LYMAN Safety Kit

Contains all of the required safety equipment needed by reloaders, bullet casters and "do-it-yourselfers." Kit contains sturdy leather gloves, safety glasses and strap, shop apron, ear plugs, reusable respirator, Lyman Guide to Bullet Casting. From Lyman Products........................... **$36.95**

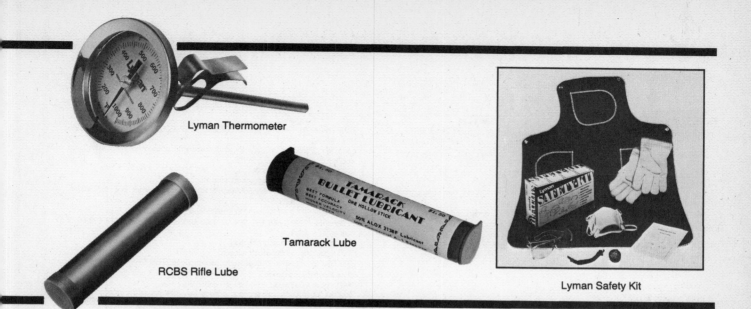

Lyman Thermometer

Tamarack Lube

RCBS Rifle Lube

Lyman Safety Kit

LYMAN Ideal Lubricant

The oldest such lubricant on the market and an excellent all-purpose formula. Available in solid or hollow sticks. From Lyman Products.................................. **$2.95**

LYMAN Alox Bullet Lubricant

This cast bullet lubricant increases accuracy and eliminates barrel leading. Sticks of this lube are moulded to fit the Lyman 450 sizer/lubricator. From Lyman Products...... **$2.95**

RCBS Rifle Bullet Lube

A special blend of Alox and beeswax formulated to NRA recommendations. Made primarily to withstand the higher velocity of rifle bullets, but works well for pistol bullets. Hollow stick. Comes in plastic storage tube. From RCBS..... **$2.70**

RCBS Bullet Lubricant

Designed to fit the RCBS Lube-A-Matic sizer-lubricator and others requiring a hollow stick lubricant. Alox free, heat and cold resistant. Long storage life. From RCBS. Per stick... **$2.70**

ROOSTER Liquid Bullet Film Lubricant

This emulsified liquid lube dries to a clear hard film and tightly bonds to cast or swaged bullets. Designed for lower velocity pistol loads. May be applied by dipping, tumbling or "flood-coating" in a container or funnel. Lubes 100,000 bullets per gallon. From Rooster Laboratories.

Price: 16 ounces................................ **$12.50**
Price: ½-gallon................................. **$40.00**
Price: 1-gallon................................. **$75.00**

ROOSTER Bullet Lubes

Rooster Laboratories produces a variety of bullet lubes in both solid and liquid form. Their C-3 and "Zambini" lubes come in 2″x6″ sticks or 1″x4″ solid or hollow sticks. SL-30 and SL-4 are available in 1″x4″ hollow sticks only. C-3 is primarily for commercial reloaders using automatic sizer-lubricators and is intended as a pistol lubricant. "Zambini" is similar to C-3 in both properties and use but has a lower melting point (220-degrees vs 250 degrees), is tougher and dries more quickly. For lubing rifle bullets Rooster has SL-30 and SL-4. SL-30 can be used for both pistol and rifle, is softer than C-3 but still forms a hard lube on the bullet. SL-4 is designed for the high velocity rifle bullet, is soft and sticky and needs no pre-heating. For further pricing break-down contact Rooster Laboratories.

Price: C-3 and "Zambini" 2″x6″ sticks (each) **$5.00**
Price: C-3 and "Zambini" 1″x4″ hollow or solid sticks (each) **$4.00**
Price: SL-30 and SL-4 hollow sticks only (each) **$3.00**

SAECO Gold Lube

SAECO Gold Lube lubricant is low in residue, will not separate under heat or pressure and keeps barrels bright and lead free. This lube also makes an excellent fluxing agent. From Redding Inc.

Hollow, 1.7 oz stick............................ **$3.00**
Solid, 1.9 oz stick............................. **$3.00**

TAMARACK Bullet Lubricant

This bullet lube is the same as that developed by the National Rifle Association. It consists of 50% Alox 2138-F and 50% commercial A-1 beeswax. Alox-based bullet lube raises the potential power limit of cast bullets and generally improves the performance of cast-bullet loads of all kinds. Sticks of Tamarack lube are available in either hollow or solid-core configuration. From Tamarack Products, Inc.

Price per stick................................. **$2.75**
100 2″x6″ sticks............................... **$198.00**
4-lb. bulk can **$20.25**
30-lb. bulk can................................ **$107.00**

OBSOLETE POWDERS

Make and name	Type	Remarks
DU PONT		
No. 1 Rifle Smokeless (1894-1926)	Irregular grains	Bulk type for low pressures (20,000-25,000 psi). For cartridges like .45-90.
Smokeless Rifle No. 2 (1894-1926)	"	Like No. 1 above, but for interchangeable rifle-revolver cartridges such as .44-40, etc.
Schuetzen (1908-1923)	"	Like Rifle Smokeless No. 1.
Schultz Shotgun (1900-1926)	"	Also light gallery charges in metallic cases.
Gallery Rifle No. 75 (1904-1928)	Irregular, smoothed	Previously called "Marksman," and widely used for reloading military rifle cartridges.
SR 80 (1913-1939)	Irregular grains	Bulk type for black powder cartridges.
MR 19 (1908-1909)	Tube	A double base type for full to medium loads in large to medium capacity cases.
MR 10 (1910-1915)	Tube	Designed for the .280 Ross.
MR 21 (1913-1926)	"	Full charges in medium cases.
IMR 15 (1914-1917)	"	For full loads with metal-jacketed bullets. The first IMR (progressive burning) powder.
IMR 13 (1917-1918)	"	IMR type. Made for special government use.
IMR 16 (1916-1927)	"	30,000-55,000-lb. pressures; a very flexible powder.
IMR 17 (1915-1925)	"	Military powder for .303 Lee-Enfield, .30-06, too.
IMR 18 (1915-1930)	"	Small to full rifle charges; a very flexible powder.
IMR 15½ (1919-1934)	"	For full loads in .30-06 size cartridges.
IMR 17½ (1923-1933)	"	Full and mid-range loads in large cartridges.
IMR 1147 (1923-1935)	Short tube	Full loads in military cases.
IMR 1204 (1925-1935)	Tube	For small capacity rifle cartridges.
Pyro Cal. .30, DG (1909-1927)	"	Military powder for the .30-06 not commercially offered. Also called MR 20 at one time.
IMR 1185 (1926-1938)	"	For 173-gr. Mark I bullet in .30-06. Never commercially available.
RSQ (Resque) (1909-1911)	Smooth, egg shaped	Pistol powder of bulk type.
Pistol No. 1 (1914-1915)	Disc	A nitroglycerine powder, never offered commercially, and like Bullseye.
Pistol No. 3 (1913-1921)	"	A dense gov't. pistol powder.
Pistol No. 5 (1920-1940)	Flake	Full and medium handgun charges.
Pistol No. 6 (1932-1953)	"	Reduced to medium handgun charges.
Ballistite (1909-1926)	"	A dense shotgun type, still a popular form in Europe.
MX Shotgun (1933-1953)	"	Designed for standard loads.
Oval Shotgun (1921-1942)	Disc	Maximum load shotshells.
HERCULES		
** E.C. Powder (1894-1931)	Irregular grains	Designed for shotguns, but useful also in light rifle loads.
308 (1915-1930)	Tube	Military powder for the .30-06 and like Pyro DG.
300 (1916-1932)	"	For full lodas with metal-jacketed bullets. A single base powder quite like Du Pont IMR 15.
Sharpshooter (No. 1 1897-1953; No. 2 1902-†)	Disc	Full or reduced loads in black powder cartridges. Fastest of the old double base powders.
W.A. .30 cal. (1898-1930)	"	Military powder for .30-40 Krag.
Lighting (No. 1 1899-1950; No. 2 1903-1917)	"	Full and reduced loads in medium to .30-06 size cartridges.
Pyro Pistol (1922-1928)	"	Dense .45 ACP (gov't.) powder.
HiVel No. 1 (1908-1915)	Tube	Military powder for .30-06.
HiVel No. 2 (1908-1964)	"	Full to medium loads in large to medium capacity cases.
HiVel No. 3 (1926-1940)	"	Full loads in medium capacity cases.
HiVel No. 5 (1929-1934)	"	Special for .30-06.
HiVel No. 6 (1933-1941)	"	High velocities with heavy bullets. Was not available to the public.
HiVel No. 6.5 (1937-1939)	"	High velocity .30-06.
1908 Bear (1908-†)	"	Not generally available to handloaders, this was intended for medium capacity cases.
1908 Stag (1908-1914)	"	Like 1908 Bear.
KINGS Semi-smokeless	Grain	Any and all black powder cartridges.

**Also manufactured by Du Pont previous to formation of Hercules.

†Still available to loading companies.

Most of the above powders were discontinued in the late 30's and early 40's. Kings Semi-smokeless powder, a bulk type, was manufactured and used from 1899 to about 1936. It was pouplar in small-bore match cartridges as it gave les smoke and fouling than black powder. Granulation range was similar to black powder, but there was also a size made called "Cg," for musket use, that was larger than Fg.

MR = Military Rifle   IMR = Improved Military Rifle

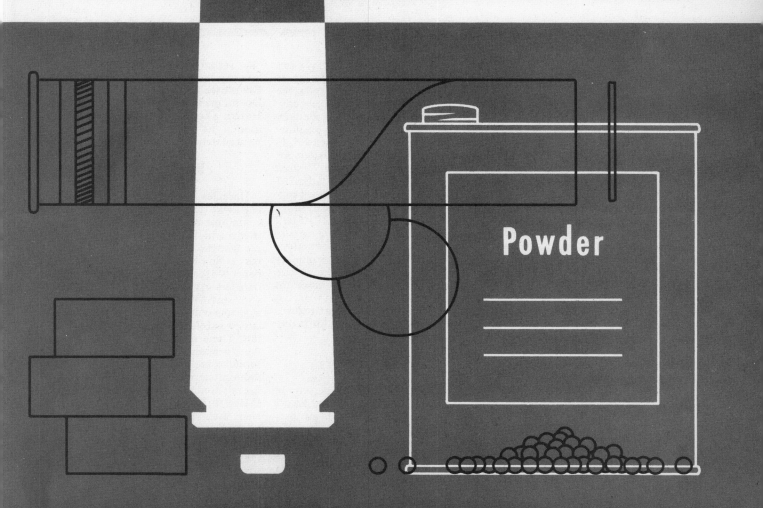

COMPONENTS

Powder

Notes on Powder . . .

Powders, generally, may be divided into three groups, depending on their use—pistol, rifle and shotgun. Some powders can be loaded for more than one use: Hercules 2400, basically a rifle powder, can be used for high velocity loads in some revolvers, or for 410 shotshells.

The manufacturers' suggested loads should be adhered to completely for accurate and safe loads (let the "max" loads go for awhile) and only those powders specified should be loaded. "Wildcatting" of shotshells, too, is unnecessary and dangerous!

Leave the experimenting to experienced reloaders.

Pistol Powders

Smokeless pistol powders are relatively fast burning. The short barrels of pistols demand this quality to achieve best results. Hercules' Bullseye, the oldest smokeless pistol powder made, has a nitroglycerin content and is finely granulated. This permits it to burn freely and ignite easily under all conditions. It is used successfully in large capacity cases made originally for blackpowder, in 38 Spl. and 45 ACP target loads, and is the powder most used for factory cartridges. Hercules' Unique for medium and heavy loads and 2400 for magnum loads have been consistently used, in their proper place, by handloaders for many years. The Winchester-Western Ball powder for standard loads, 231 (formerly 230P and 230), has been rapidly gaining in popularity since its introduction in 1960. W-W 295 HP, a ball powder for magnum loads, was discontinued shortly after its introduction. Hodgdon's H-4227 is a surplus military powder repacked into convenient size canisters. Norma powders have not been imported for a number of years but that may change in the near future. Hodgdon's Pyrodex CTG is for blackpowder cartridges.

Shotgun Powders

Shotgun powders are made only in dense form today, now that Du Pont's Bulk Shotgun Smokeless has been obsoleted. IMR's (Du Pont successor) dense powders are PB (porous base) for high velocity and magnum loads, and Hi-Skor for target loads. Hercules Unique is used primarily for medium loads, Red Dot is used for light target loads, Green Dot for medium loads and Blue Dot and Herco, a coarse-grained powder, are used in the heavier loads. 2400 should be used only in low velocity 410 shells.

Rifle Powders

Hercules offers Unique, RelodeR 7 and 2400. They are double base types, containing both nitrocellulose and nitroglycerine in percentages calculated to produce the desired performance. IMR makes an extensive line of rifle powders—IMR (Improved Military Rifle) numbers 4198, 4320, 4227, 3031, 4064, 4350 and 4831. Recently 4895, long available only as a surplus military powder, was released in standard canister lots. These powders are all single-base types containing no nitroglycerin. Their formulas are essentially the same; they differ primarily in granulation and coating required to vary their burning rates. IMR SR (Sporting Rifle) 4759 is especially useful in loading for obsolete cartridges at relatively low pressures. Hodgdon continues to offer many surplus powders, all excellent values.

Accurate Smokeless Powders

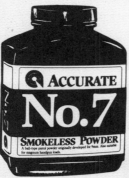

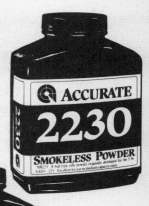

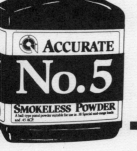

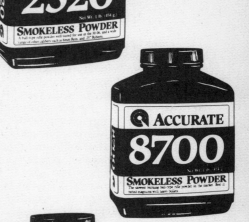

ACCURATE ARMS

No. 5 Relatively quick, flattened-ball-type pistol powder. Useful for target to moderate pressure loads in 32, 38, 9mm, 41, and 44. Great for 20-gauge field loads. 1 lb. **$10.95**

No. 7 Ball-type powder best suited for use in full-power 9mm and 10mm auto cartridges. Also good in moderate to magnum loads in revolvers. 1 lb. **$9.95**

No. 9 Very popular ball-type 44 Magnum powder. Applications include the other magnum handgun rounds and some small rifle cartridges. 1 lb. . **$9.95**

5744 Double-based extruded powder for large handgun or small rifle cartridges such as the 256 Winchester, 22 Hornet, and 7 T/CU. 1 lb. **$9.95**

2230 A perennial favorite for the 223 Remington. This ball-type powder is useful in other cartridges from the 6mms to the 458. 1 lb. **$9.95**

2460 Originally developed for the 308 Winchester, this ball-type propellant has won matches across the country in both silhouette and high-power competition. Serves well in cases from the 223 to the 30/06. 1 lb. **$9.95**

2520 A medium burning ball-type rifle powder that is replacing 4895 and 4064 at the ranges. Accuracy is outstanding in cartridges from the 22/250 up to the 30-06 size cases. 1 lb. **$9.95**

3100 An extruded single-based powder for cartridges from the 243 to the big magnums. Popular with varmint hunters using 6mms, 25/06, and 243s. 1 lb. **$9.95**

8700 The slowest ball-type powder available to the handloader today. Best suited for big cases such as the 264 and 7mm magnums, especially with the heavier bullets. 1 lb. **$5.25**

HERCULES SMOKELESS POWDERS FOR RELOADING.

Powder	Packaging				
	1-lb Canisters	4-lb Canisters	5-lb Canisters	8-lb Keg	15-lb Keg
Bullseye	X	X		X	X
Red Dot	X	X		X	X
Green Dot	X	X		X	X
Unique	X	X		X	X
Herco	X	X		X	X
Blue Dot	X		X		
Hercules 2400	X	X		X	X
Reloder 7	X				

Hercules

Hercules is offering seven double-base powders for the reloader. They discontinued their RelodeR powders, 7, 11 and 21 in 1971, although the RelodeR 7 has been reintroduced. Until recently Hercules was the only U.S. maker of double-base sporting powders (IMR's 700-X has a nitroglycerin component). Blue Dot is their latest addition to the line, intended for magnum shotshells.

2400 Powder A fine-grained powder intended for small-capacity rifle cartridges and for reduced loads, or light projectiles in larger capacity rifle cartridges, 410-gauge shotshells, and high-velocity loads in some revolvers.

RelodeR 7 Rifle Fastest burning of Hercules' rifle powders, it is adapted to the smaller size cases, from 222 Remington up through 30-30 for full charge loads. Performs well in some larger cases for reduced loads.

RelodeR 12 Rifle A versatile rifle powder for medium-caliber ammunition, such as 308 Win., 243 Win., 223 Rem.

Available in 1-lb. and 5-lb. canisters.

Bullseye Pistol A high-energy, quick-burning powder designed for pistol and revolver ammunition; available in 16-ounce canisters, 3-pound kegs, and 15-pound kegs.

Unique Powder An all-around powder, designed for large-caliber and for medium-gauge shotshells. It can also be used for gallery loads in rifle cartridges.

Red Dot Shotgun The powder preferred by many for light and standard shotshell loads.

Green Dot Shotgun Developed for light and medium 12-gauge shotshell loads. Uniform ignition and performance; minimum blast and residue, nonhygroscopic.

Blue Dot Shotgun The most recent addition to the Hercules line, Blue Dot is specifically designed for magnum waterfowl shotshells.

Herco Shotgun A coarse grained powder for use in heavy hunting loads.

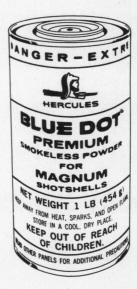

WINCHESTER®

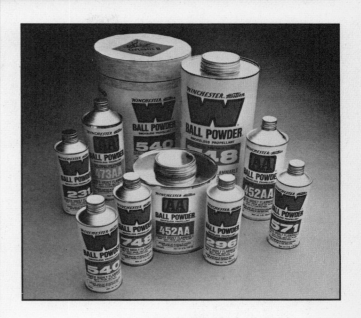

WINCHESTER-WESTERN® PROPELLANTS
Ball Powder

Ball powder, used for years by Winchester-Western in the loading of commercial and military ammunition, is offered to handloaders in five shotshell grades, two centerfire pistol types and four centerfire rifle types. It is highly suited to handloading because of its stability and clean burning. The smooth, round, graphited grains flow easily through powder measures, resulting in accurate charges.

452AA For 12 gauge trap, Skeet and field loads. Available in 1 lb. canisters, 3 lb. quarter kegs, and 10 lb. kegs.

473AA For 20 gauge Skeet and field, the same as used in factory 20 gauge AA but can also be used for 12 and 16 gauge. Same packaging as 452AA.

571 For 12 gauge 3″ magnum shotshells. Will also give superior performance in 20 and 28 gauge. Comes in 1 lb. canisters, 3 lb. quarter kegs, 8 lb. drums.

296 For 410 bore, magnum pistol and 30 Carbine. In magnum pistol cartridges, it requires heavy bullets and heavy crimps. Comes in 1 lb. canisters, 3 lb. quarter kegs and 8 lb. drums.

540 For heavy shot charges in 12 and 20 gauge. Excellent for 28 gauge. Higher density permits easier crimping of heavy loads. Comes in 1 lb. canisters, 3 lb. quarter kegs, 8 lb. drums.

231 Exceptionally fast, high energy, clean burning powder for target and standard velocity loads in handguns. Comes in 1-lb. cannisters, 3-lb. quarter kegs and 8-lb. drums.

748 For centerfire rifles. Excellent for a variety of cartridges including 222 Remington and 458 Win. Mag. Popular with bench rest shooters. 1 lb. canisters, 8 lb. drums.

760 For medium to large cartridges. Broad range of proven application in medium to large cases. 1 lb. canisters, 8 lb. drums.

IMR Powder Co.

IMR POWDER CO.

For many reloaders, Du Pont powders have long been considered the standard of excellence in quality and performance. Commercial loaders and the military services, as well, have confidence in Du Pont's consistently high quality.

Late in 1986 the Du Pont Co. sold its smokeless powder business to the IMR Powder Co., an affiliate of Expro Chemical Products of Canada. Expro has been the manufacturer of all Du Pont powders since 1978.

There will be no change in product offerings.

IMR-4227 Rifle Designed for relatively small capacity cartridges. It is too quick in burning to function to the best advantage in relatively large capacity cartridges, except in reduced loads.

IMR-4198 Rifle Developed especially for use in medium capacity cartridges and for reduced loads. An extremely popular powder for handloading.

IMR-4895 Rifle Used in billions of rounds of 30-cal. military ammunition and proved an excellent performer in cases from the 222 to the 458, now available in canister lots. Slightly faster than 4320.

IMR-4064 Rifle A powder for large capacity cartridges that has exceptional burning qualities. Consistent accuracy is easily achieved with this powder when it is loaded properly.

IMR-4320 Rifle Intended specifically for use in military cartridges, but is equally satisfactory in all ordinary high-velocity cartridges.

SR-4759 Single Base Powder. Ideally suited for cast bullet rifle loads. Long time favorite for single-shot rifles.

IMR-4350 Rifle An excellent powder designed especially for magnum cartridges. When properly loaded this powder will give very uniform results.

IMR-4831 Rifle Made for the first time by Du Pont as a canister-grade handloading powder. It is the slowest burning powder in the Du Pont line. Suitable for rifle calibers such as the 17 Rem. and 220 Swift up through the 375 H & H Mag. and 458 Win. Mag.

SR 7625 For use in 12-gauge high velocity shotshell loads; also suitable for a wide variety of centerfire handgun cartridges.

IMR-3031 Rifle Particularly recommended for medium capacity and midrange loads. One of the most satisfactory powders on the market.

PB Shotgun This powder replaces the old Du Pont MX. It is a dense powder for use in high base shells for high-velocity and magnum loads. Single base type.

SR 4756 Shotgun For magnum shotshells. Produces excellent 410-bore target ammunition when loaded per manufacturer's instructions. Useful in heavy centerfire handgun ammunition.

Hi-Skor 700X Shotgun Double Base. Developed for 12-gauge components, gives optimum ballistics at minimum charge weight. Wad pressures not critical.

H4227, H4198 Fastest burning of the IMR series. Well adapted to Hornet, light bullets in 222 and all bullets in 357 and 44 Mag. 1 lb. can.......... **$14.50**

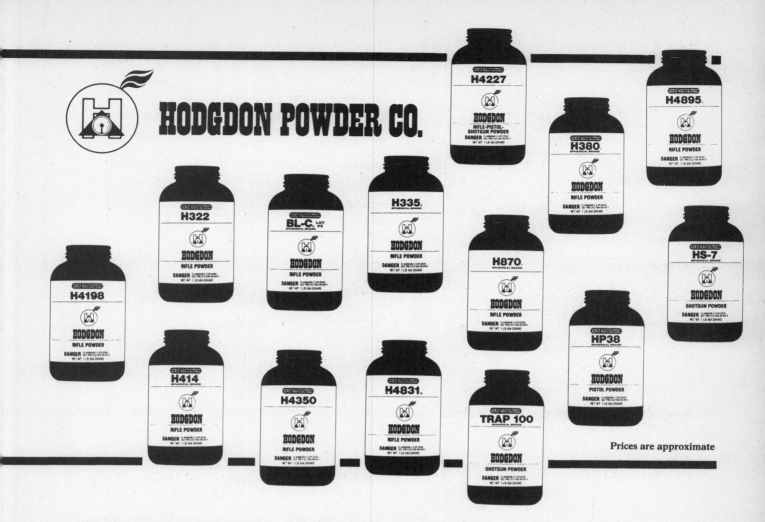

HODGDON POWDER CO.

HS-6 A spherical magnum shotshell powder. Leaves ample space for wad column. 1 lb. can. **$12.95**

H110 A spherical powder designed for the M1 carbine. Adaptable to heavy pistol and 410 shotshell. 1 lb. can. **$13.95**

Spherical BL-C2 A favorite of the benchrest shooters. Best performance is in the 222, and in other cases smaller than 30-06. 1 lb. can. **$11.50**

H4350 A favorite of many handloaders. Gives best performance and velocity in many large capacity metallic rifle cartridges. 1 lb. can. **$14.50**

H4895 May well be the most versatile of all rifle propellants. It gives desirable performance in almost all cases from the 222 to the 458. Reduced loads, as little as ⅗ of maximum, still give target accuracy. 1 lb. can. **$14.50**

Spherical H380 Excellent in the 22/250, 220 Swift, the 6mm's, 257 and 30-06; can be used in moderate charges in the 25-06 and bigger cases. 1 lb. can. **$14.50**

H4831 The most popular of all powders for the bigger magnums. Outstanding performance with medium and heavy bullets in the 6mm's, 25-06 and 270. Comes in 1 lb. can. **$14.50**

H450 A spherical powder with similar burning rate of H4831. Best results obtained in medium to large capacity cases. 1 lb. can. **$14.50**

Spherical H335 Best adapted to 222 and 308 Winchester. 1 lb. can. **$11.50**

H322 This extruded powder fills the gap between H4198 and BL-C (2), and performs best in small to medium capacity cases. Excellent in 22 and 308 benchrest guns. 1 lb. can. **$7.99**

H870 has a very slow burning rate adaptable to overbore capacity magnum cases such as 257, 264, 270 and 300 Mag. with heavy bullets. 1 lb. can. **$7.25**

Spherical H414 In many popular medium to medium-large calibers, pressure velocity relationship is better with this new spherical powder. 1 lb. can. **$7.99**

HP38 A fast pistol powder for most pistol loading, especially rcommended for 38 Special. 12 oz. can. **$13.25**

Trap 100 A spherical trap and light field load powder, also excellent for target loads in centerfire pistols. Mild recoil. Comes in 1 lb. can. **$11.95**

HS-7 For magnum field loads, HS-7 does not pack in the measure. Delivers uniform charges and is dense to allow sufficient wad column for best patterns. Comes in 1 lb. can. **$12.95**

Pyrodex P For blackpowder percussion single shot pistols and cap and ball revolvers. 1 lb. can. **$9.95**

Pyrodex RS Designed for use in all calibers of muzzleloading percussion rifles and shotguns. 1 lb. can. **$9.95**

Pyrodex CTG For blackpowder cartridges, CTG will duplicate blackpowder loads in rifle, pistol, and shotshell cartridges. 1 lb. can. **$7.95**

Prices are approximate

	Fiocchi	CCI	Federal	Rem.-Pet.	RWS	Win.-West.
Large Rifle	210	200	210	9½	5341	8½-120
			215	9½		
		250M	210M		5333M	
		BR2				
Small Rifle	100	400	200	6½	4033	6½-116
		450M	205	7½		
		BR4	205M			
Large Pistol	150; 100	300	150	2½	5337	7-111
		350M	155			7M-111F
Small Pistol	200	500	100	1½	4031	1½-108
		550M		5½	4047M	1½M-108
Shotshell Caps	209; 410	209B				
		PC57				
Shotshell[a]		209	209[c]			209
Shotshell[b]		209M		57		
		410		97[d]		
				97-4		
				209		
Percussion Caps		11		10 (.162")		
				11 (.167")		
				12 (.172")		

NOTE: Large rifle and large pistol primers measure .210"; small rifle and small pistol measure .175".

(a) For Winchester-Western, Monarch, J.C. Higgins, Revelation and Canuck cases.
(b) For Remington-Peters paper cases.
(c) Long battery cup type for Winchester-Western or Federal plastic shells.
(d) Battery cup; used in 12-ga. plastic trap and Skeet loads.

RWS Sinoxid Berdan Primers

Type	Per 250
Small Pistol	$5.15
Large Pistol	5.15
Small Rifle	5.15
Large Rifle	5.95

RWS #6507 Large Rifle replaces the now obsolete Eley #172 primer. All are non-mercuric, non-corrosive. From Old Western Scrounger, Inc.

Notes on Primers and Percussion Caps . . .

Small arms ammunition manufactured in the U.S. and Canada utilizes a single flash hole and Boxer primers. They consist of a brass cup into which is pressed a pellet of priming compound and a 2- or 3-legged anvil. Generally speaking, the rest of the world uses Berdan primers. They are similar except that the anvil is an integral part of the bottom of the primer pocket and two or more flash holes are used.

Boxer primers used in sporting and most military ammunition come in two basic sizes—.175" and .210" diameter—and two strengths. Those for handgun use contain less priming compound and have thinner and softer cups than primers for rifle use. Handgun cartridges contain less powder, thus require less flash for ignition, and pistols do not have the heavy firing pin blow necessary to properly indent the heavy rifle cups. Consequently, there are four basic primer types—large rifle, small rifle, large pistol and small pistol. In addition, Federal offers a special rifle primer for use in large capacity magnum-type cases with heavy powder charges. Also, CCI produces a "Magnum" primer in each of the four types for essentially the same reason. The magnum types reportedly produce a larger flash of longer duration, intended to give more uniform ignition of large charges than standard primers impart.

Remington introduced three new primers a few years back, the 9½M, 5½ and 7½. The 9½M is for magnum belted rifle cases, particularly those using very heavy charges. The 5½ and 7½, in general, supplement the older 6½ and replace it in several instances. For years the 6½ was used in such revolver cartridges as the 357 Magnum and in small rifle loads like the 222. However, on occasion it proved too hard and/or thick for the 357, yet at the same time too soft or thin for the 222. The 5½ is specifically designed for the 357 and the 7½ for small rifle cartridges from the 221 Fireball to the 222 Magnum.

Oil and grease kill primers. Do not handle them with greasy fingers or allow oil on any part of the reloading tool with which they come in contact. This applies especially to automatic primer feeds where only dry lubes can safely be used.

So far as can be determined all commercial primers available today are noncorrosive and nonmercuric. This means, simply, that their residues will neither cause the bore to rust nor the cases to be weakened—problems that existed in the past. Careful cleaning prevented the rusting, even then, but nothing could be done to salvage cases once they were contaminated by mercuric primers. They became brittle and unsafe. Now handloaders don't have that worry.

U.S.-made shotshells and some imports use battery cup primers. Reloading is normally done by replacing the complete primer; however, the battery cup and anvil can be re-used at a considerable saving if one cares to go to extra trouble. The battery cup is made of copper, open at one end and pierced by a flash hole at the other. First, a pointed anvil is pressed down into the cup, then a cap containing the priming compound is pressed into place. The cap looks much like a standard large pistol primer without its anvil.

Primers for Winchester-Western shotshells will not interchange with some of Remington-Peters make. Independent makers produce primers for both makes and those for W-W cases have the number 209 in their designation. When intended for use in R-P paper cases (or 28 gauge plastic), primers have 57 in the designation. In addition, R-P uses a special size battery cup in 28 and 410 gauge paper cases.

Remington-Peters No. 97 primer, introduced a number of years ago, has the same dimensions as other standard shotshell primers, and is interchangeable with them. Today most battery cup primers have the flash hole closed with a waterproof seal which also keeps powder granules from entering the cup.

"Gramps" Antique Cartridge Cases

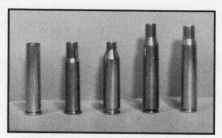
McConnellstown New and Fired Cases

A-Square Unprimed Brass

Cases, Metallic and Shotshell:

The average case can be reloaded many times, and it is not unusual to find handloaders who have reloaded a metallic case 20 or more times. Handgun cases, and those rifle cases that must be crimped every time they are reloaded, will have a somewhat shorter life span. Maximum loads shorten case life, too. Shotshell cases won't take as many reloadings, of course—particularly those of paper—for the mouth soon frays.

When a cartridge is fired, the case expands to the size of the chamber, then springs back slightly if the brass is correctly annealed. If such cases are to be fired again in the same rifle, only neck sizing is usually needed; full length sizing is generally required if cases will be used in a rifle other than the one they came out of. Standard ⅞-14 dies can do both jobs—for neck sizing only position the die ⅛″ or so away from contact with the shellholder. Full length sizing of paper and plastic shotshell cases is virtually a must, and all tools are made to do so.

Cases should be carefully examined before and during reloading, and any defective cases discarded. Watch for split necks and bodies; incipient head separations; swelling of head and primer pocket, torn or frayed mouths of paper cases.

You'll get better results from your handloads if you keep your cases segregated by make and lot. Mixed cases often will show considerable difference in weight (hence volumetric capacity), flash holes, temper or anneal, etc. Shotshells, because of the need for exact wad-column height, should be of the same make and type.

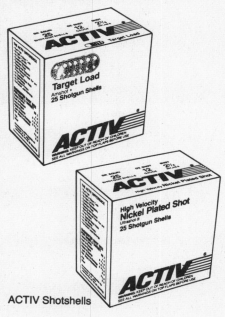
ACTIV Shotshells

ACTIV Empty Hulls

The ACTIV brass-free hull has a steel encasement in the plastic tube to reinforce the head, rim and primer pocket, eliminating the need for high or low brass. The steel primer pocket does not expand after repeated firing, and the hull does not need to be resized when reloading. ACTIV hulls have a greater internal capacity than most conventional types. Mouths are skived for a perfect 8-point crimp. Functions smoothly in all modern shotguns. Available in 12 and 20 gauge. From ACTIV Industries.
Price: 12 and 20 ga., unprimed, per 1000 . . . . **$135.30**

ACTIV Starter Kit

Designed for the first-time reloader or for those who would like to test the ACTIV brass-free hull, these kits come with a choice of 25 hulls in 12, 16 or 20 gauge, 25 wads, an ACTIV Reloading Booklet and an ACTIV patch. From ACTIV Industries.
Price: Per kit **$3.15**

Centerfire Primer/Cartridge Reference Chart

Large Rifle
219 Zipper
22 Savage Hi-Power
220 Swift
22-250
224 Weatherby
225 Winchester
240 Weatherby
243 Winchester
6mm Remington
25-35 Winchester
250 Savage
25-06 Remington
257 Roberts
257 Weatherby
6.5 Carcano
6.5 Japanese
6.5x54
6.5x55
6.5x57
6.5 Rem. Magnum
264 Win. Magnum

270 Winchester
284 Winchester
7mm Mauser
7x57R
280 Remington
7mm Exp. Rem.
7mm Rem. Magnum
7mm Weatherby
7x61 S&H
7x64
7.5x55 Swiss
30-30 Winchester
30 Remington
30-06 Springfield
30-40 Krag
300 Win. Magnum
300 H&H Magnum
300 Savage
308 Winchester
30 Herrett
300 Weatherby
308 Norma Mag.

7.62x39
7.62mm Russian
303 Savage
303 British
7.7 Japanese
32 Win. Special
32 Remington
32-40 Winchester
8mm Mauser
8x57J
8x57 JS
8mm Rem. Mag.
8mm/06
8mm/338
33 Winchester
338 Win. Magnum
340 Weatherby
348 Winchester
350 Rem. Magnum
35 Remington
357 Herrett
358 Winchester

358 Norma Mag.
9.3x57
9.3x62
375 Winchester
375 H&H Magnum
38-55 Winchester
444 Marlin
45-70 Gov't.
458 Win. Magnum
460 Weatherby
50-70 Gov't.

Small Rifle
17 Remington
218 Bee
22 Hornet
22 PPC
221 Rem. F'ball
222 Remington
222 Rem. Magnum
223 Remington
6mm PPC

6x47
25-20 Winchester
256 Win. Magnum
30 Carbine
32-20 Winchester

Large (Reg.) Pistol
357 Auto Mag.
38-40 Winchester
44 W&W Special
44 Auto Mag.
44-40 Winchester
45 Auto Rim
45 Colt
45 ACP

Small (Reg.) Pistol
22 Rem. Jet
25 ACP
30 Luger
30 Mauser
32 ACP

32 S&W
32 S&W Long
32 Short Colt
32 Long Colt
32 Colt New Police
9mm Luger
38 S&W
38 Special
38 Short Colt
38 Long Colt
38 Colt New Police
38 Super Auto
38 Automatic
380 ACP

Large (Mag.) Pistol
41 Rem. Magnum
44 Rem. Magnum

Small (Mag.) Pistol
357 Magnum

A-SQUARE™ Unprimed Brass

Caliber	Packaging	Retail
.338 A-SQUARE	WALLET	$18.49
.375 WEATHERBY	BOX	22.88
.375 A-SQUARE	WALLET	17.56
.378 WEATHERBY	WALLET	16.27
.416 HOFFMAN	BOX	18.89
.416 RIGBY	WALLET	21.82
.404 JEFFREY	WALLET	14.50
.450 NE (3¼")	WALLET	26.55
.450 #2	WALLET	38.80
.450 ACKLEY	BOX	18.89
.460 SH. A-SQ.	WALLET	18.49
.460 WEATHERBY	WALLET	18.22
.460 LONG A-SQ.	WALLET	19.29
.500/.465	WALLET	27.50
.470 RIGBY	WALLET	27.50
.475 #2	WALLET	39.75
.505 GIBBS	WALLET	32.00
.500 N.E. (3")	WALLET	32.60
.495 A-SQUARE	WALLET	19.29
.500 A-SQUARE	WALLET	18.62
.577 N.E.	WALLET	36.50

Note: Packaging labeled "BOX" denotes 20 rounds per re-usable, plastic, slip-top box. "WALLET" denotes 10 rounds per re-usable, plastic, ammo wallet.

Brass Extrusion Laboratories Ltd.

Case	May Be Formed To	Price/Per
600 Nitro	Formed	$89.95/10
577 N.E. Base 3"	577 2¾" & 3", 577/450 Martini Henry, 577 Snider, etc.	42.95/20
505 Gibbs Base		48.95/20
500 N.E. Base 3¼"	500 3" & 3¼", 476 N.E., 470 N.E., 500/465 N.E., 500/450 3¼", etc.	35.95/20
50 Sharps	50-140 3¼" Sharps, 50-90 Sharps, 50-70 Govt., etc.	35.95/20
475 #2 Base 3½"	475 #2 only.	69.95/20
470 N.E.	Formed.	39.95/20
465 N.E.	Formed.	39.95/20
450 #2 Base 3½"	450 #2 only.	69.95/20
450 Straight N.E. Base 3¼"	.040 std. & .060 Jeffrey rims. 333 Rimmed Jeffery, 360 #2, 369 Purdey, 11mm Murata, 11mm Gras, 7x66 Vom Hofe 9.5x73, 10.3x60R Swiss, and others.	35.95/20
45 RCBS Base 3¼"	45-100 Ballard, 40-75 Bullard, 40-60 Marlin, 44-70 Maynard, 40-50, 40-70 & 40-90 Sharps BN, and many others.	24.95/20
416 Rigby	Formed	39.95/20
11mm (.43) Mauser "A" Base	9.5 Turkish Mauser, 9.5x47R, 7.7x50R	24.95/20
43 Rem.-Spanish Base	44-60 & 44-77 Sharps/Rem., 44-90 & 44-100 Sharps, 11.7 Danish Rem., 11.15 Spanish Rem.	24.95/20
11mm Beaumont M/71/78	11mm Beaumont M/71/76, 11.3	39.95/20

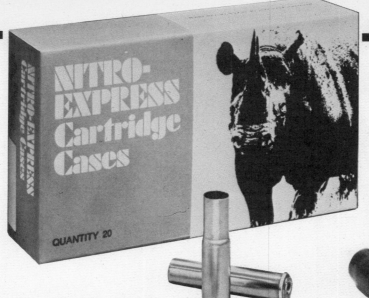

Brass Extrusion Laboratories

Hardin Unprimed Cases

Brass Extrusion Laboratories

Case	May Be Formed To	Price/Per
Base	Beaumont M/78, 11.43 Egyptian, 50-115 Bullard, 50-100 Maynard, 45-95 Peabody, 40-90 Peabody, and others	
425 Westly Richards Base	425 W.R. and 11.2x72 Schuler. Rebated rim.	39.95/20
405 Winchester Base 3¼"	38-72, 38-90, 40-72 Win., 40-50, 40-90 Sharps, 35 & 405 Win.	35.95/20
404 Jeffery	280 & 333 Jeffery, is base case for	35.95/20
Base	460 G&A Mag.	
401 Winchester	Formed.	49.95/50
375 H&H Mag. Flanged Base	275 Flanged Mag., Super 30 Flanged Mag.	35.95/20
280 Ross Base	280 Ross, 30 & 35 Newton, 280 Naiger Mag., 303 Mag., 8x68 Mag.	35.95/20
280 Flanged N.E. Base	280 Flanged only.	35.95/20
25-20 S.S.	2-R Lovell and others.	37.50/50
2-R Lovell	Formed	19.00/100
7.62x39		

Loaded Ammunition

600 N.E. Solids	900 gr.	174.95/10
600 N.E. Soft Point	900 gr.	174.95/10
470 N.E. Solids	500 gr.	79.95/10
500/465 N.E. Solids	500 gr.	79.95/10
416 Rigby Solids	410 gr.	65.95/10
416 Rigby Soft Point	410 gr.	65.95/10
7.62x39 FMC	123 gr.	7.95/20

Brass Extrusion Laboratories Ltd. (B.E.L.L.) New "Old" Brass

Brass Extrusion Laboratories Limited was started for the sole purpose of manufacturing obsolete "hard-to-get" brass cartridge cases. Shooting enthusiasts with classic or obsolete guns now have a source for many of those impossible or hard-to-get cases. In the near future B.E.L.L. will be offering the following cartridges; 416 Rigby, 280 Ross, 475 & 450 #2, 505 Gibbs, 500 Jeffrey and others as demand warrents. Those cases currently in production are listed in the chart at left.

HARDIN Unprimed Cases

These custom-made cases for 9mm Makarov, 7.62mm Tokarev and 30-cal. Mauser Broomhandle pistols are turned out from government surplus 223 brass. They are fully formed, sized and ready for loading. Cases are shipped, unprimed. Cost is about **$10.50** per hundred for the Tokarev and Mauser and **$9.50** per hundred for the 9mm Makarov. Load data is also available from the maker. 44 Auto Mag cases made from 308 brass are also available for about **$12.50** per hundred. Hardin Specialty Distributors.

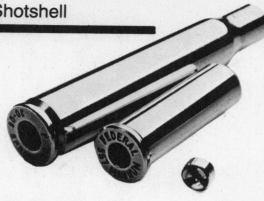

Federal Brass and Primers

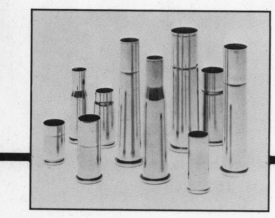

Winchester Cases

Ballistic Products Shotshell Hulls

Manufacturer	Gauge	Shell Length	Price	Comments
Federal	10	3½″	$24.50/50	New, primed
Federal Gold Medal	12	2¾″	$3.00/50	Class A
Federal	12	3″	$10.95/50	Class A, fiber based
Winchester	12	2¾″	$7.95/100	Class A
Cheddite	12	2¾″	$5.00/50	New, unprimed, plastic base
Cheddite	12	3″	$7.00/50	Unprimed, plastic base wad & high brass
Fiocchi	12	3″	$9.00/50	New, primed, ultra high brass, plastic base
Fiocchi	12	2¾″	$6.50/50	New, primed, plastic base
Fiocchi	16	2¾″	$8.95/50	New, primed, low brass
Fiocchi	20	3″	$6.95/50	New, primed
Fiocchi	20	2¾″	$6.95/50	New, primed
Remington	12	3″	$6.95/50	Type 5, Class A

New = Never fired; Class A = very clean, once fired
Available from Ballistic Products

FEDERAL Match Cases

In addition to their regular line of empty rifle and pistol cases, Federal is also offering unprimed, nickel-plated Match rifle cases in calibers 222 Remington and 308 Winchester. The cases are packed 20 per box. From Federal Cartridge Corp.

Price: 222 Rem. Match **$6.20**
Price: 308 Win. Match **$8.40**

"Gramps" Antique 222 Rimmed Brass

Imported from Australia, this empty, unprimed brass for the 222 Rimmed is fully formed and ready for reloading. Loading requires a 38 Special shell holder, 222 Remington sizing die. Cases come in boxes of 20. From "Gramps" Antique Cartridges.

Price: **$15.00**

"Gramps" Antique 577 English Brass

This Canadian firm imports from England two styles of the 577 case—the 577 Snyder and 577-450 Martini Henry. They are similar to the old Everlasting cases, are fully formed and take a Boxer primer. Loading dies for those two calibers (also from England) are available. From "Gramps" Antique Cartridges.

Price: 577 Snyder cases, each . **$3.25**
Price: 577 Martini Henry, each **$3.75**
Price: Dies for above and 43 Mauser, per set **$90.00**

McCONNELLSTOWN New and Fired Cases

Caliber	Price/20
Cases, New	
243 Winchester	$5.00
270 Winchester	6.20
30-30 Winchester	4.50
30-06 Springfield	6.20
Cases, Once-Fired	
243 Winchester	4.30
270 Winchester	4.30
30-06 Springfield	4.30
30-30 Winchester	3.00
375 Winchester	3.00

From McConnellstown Reloading

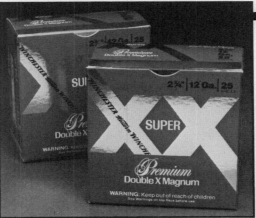

Winchester Premium Double X

O'Connor Steelhead Cases

B.E.L.L. Brass

O'CONNOR
Steelhead Cases

This company produces high-performance, formed or unformed cartridge cases with steel heads. The brass bodies utilize five-pitch pipe (tapered) threads to screw into the corrosion resistant, tempered steel heads. Since the bodies are of brass, they can be sized with ordinary dies. Include $2.50 (48 states)/$3.50 (Alaska & Hawaii) for shipping and handling. From O'Connor Rifle Products.

Caliber	Price/5
Formed Cases	
30-06 Springfield	$16.95
275 Win.	16.95
280 Rem.	16.95
300 Win. Mag.	18.95
8mm Rem. Mag.	18.95
338 Win. Mag.	18.95
375 H&H Mag.	18.95
458 Win. Mag.	18.95
Straight-Sided Cases	
.469″ rimless (30-06 type)	14.95
.530″ belted magnum	16.95
Replacement Brass	
Standard Calibers (30-06 type)	6.95
Magnum Calibers (375 H&H type)	8.95

PMC Unprimed
Rifle and Handgun Cases

Rifle (200-round pack)	Handgun (200-round pack)
222 Rem.	9mm
22-250 Rem.	357 Mag.
223 Rem.	38 Spcl.
243 Win.	38 Super Auto
270 Win.	41 Rem. Mag.
7.62x39	44 Rem. Mag.
30-30 Win.	44 S&W Special
30 Carbine	45 Auto
308 Win.	
30-06 Spring.	

Contact PMC Ammunition for prices.

Caliber	Per 20
22 Hornet	$13.25
222 Remington	13.25
5.6x50 Magnum	13.25
5.6x50R Magnum	13.25
5.6x52R (22 Sav. Hi-Power)	15.20
5.6x57	18.10
5.6x57R	18.10
243 Winchester	18.10
6.5x57 Mauser	12.50
6.5x57R Mauser	12.50
6.5x54 M.S.	15.15
6.5x68 Magnum	18.85
6.5x68R Magnum	18.85
270 Winchester	18.10
7x57 Mauser	13.30
7x57R	13.30
7x64	13.25
7x65R	13.25
7mm Remington Magnum	19.95

ROBERT POMEROY
Formed Cases

Custom forming of obsolete cases, all made from new 45-70 and 30-40 Krag cases. 45-90, 40-82, 40-70, 38-70, 35 WCF, 40-72 and 38-72 are just a few of the sizes available. Pomeroy also offers custom bullets: .365″, .375″, .318″, 9.3, .406″-.412″. Write about your needs. SASE please.

RWS Unprimed Brass

Caliber	Per 20
308 Winchester	13.50
30-06	13.50
300 Winchester Magnum	19.95
8x57JR (.318 dia.)	13.25
8x57JS (.323 dia.)	13.25
8x57JRS (.323 dia.)	13.25
8x60S (.323 dia.)	13.50
8x68S Magnum (.323 dia.)	19.95
8.15x46R	13.50
9.3x62	16.80
9.3x64	16.90
9.3x72R	15.25
9.3x74R	16.90
375 H&H Magnum	19.95
10.75x68 Mauser	18.10
10.75x73 (404 Jeffery)	19.90

All brass accepts standard .210″ Boxer primers. Available from Old Western Scrounger, Inc.

Cases, Metallic and Shotshell

NORMA
Cartridges Cases

Standard Rifle Cals.	Price, per 20
220 Swift	$ 8.74
222 Rem.	5.66
22-250 Rem.	7.90
243 Win.	7.90
270 Win.	8.25
280 Rem.	8.25
7mm Rem. Mag.	10.53
308 Win.	7.80
30-30 Win.	7.10
30-06	8.25
303 British	9.08

Handgun Cases	Price, per 50
32 S&W Long	$11.78
9mm Luger	11.45
38 Special	8.10
357 Mag.	9.09
10mm Auto	12.05
44 Mag.	12.05

Unique Cals.	Price, per 20
6.5 Jap.	$ 9.75
6.5 Carcano	9.75
6.5x55	9.75
308 Norma Mag.	13.00
7.5x55 Swiss	9.75
7.62 Russian	9.75
7.62 Argentine Mauser	9.75
7.7 Jap.	9.75

Prices are approximate.

WEATHERBY
Unprimed Cartridge Cases

Caliber	Per 20
224 Weatherby Mag	$14.25
240 Weatherby Mag.	14.25
257 Weatherby Mag.	14.25
270 Weatherby Mag.	14.25
7mm Weatherby Mag.	14.25
300 Weatherby Mag.	14.25
340 Weatherby Mag.	15.00
378 Weatherby Mag.	22.00
460 Weatherby Mag.	28.00

EMPTY CARTRIDGE CASES
Federal and Winchester Rifle and Handgun Cases

Federal and Winchester offer the most extensive lines of metallic cases available to handloaders in the U.S. Since they are for the most part identical, data are combined here to save space. Those cases available from only one source are marked thus: (W) Winchester; (F) Federal.

All rifle cases are packed 20 per box except those marked with an asterisk (*) which are 50 per box. All handgun cases are packed 50 per box except the 221 Rem., which is 20.

Handgun Cases

Caliber	Primer	Caliber	Primer
25 Auto (W)	S	380 Auto	S
256 Win. Mag. (W)	S	38 Auto (W)	S
32 S&W (W)	S	38 S&W (W)	S
32 S&W Long (W)	S	38 Special	S
32 Auto (W)	S	41 Mag.	L
357 Mag.	S	44 Rem. Mag.	L
357 Rem. Max.	S	44 Special (W)	L
9mm Win. Mag.	S	45 Colt	L
9mm Luger	S	45 ACP	L
		45 Win. Mag.	L

Rifle Cases

Caliber	Primer	Caliber	Primer
218 Bee* (W)	S	300 Savage (W)	L
22 Hornet* (W)	S	300 H&H Mag. (W)	L
220 Swift (W)	L	300 Win. Mag.	L
222 Rem.	S	303 Br. (W)	L
222 Rem. Match (F)	S	307 Win.	L
22-250	L	308 Win.	L
223 Rem.	S	308 Win. Match (F)	L
225 Win. (W)	L	8mm Mauser (W)	L
6mm Rem. (W)	L	32-20 Win.* (W)	L
243 Win.	L	32-40 Win. (W)	L
25-06 (W)	L	32 Win. Spl. (W)	L
25-20 Win.* (W)	S	338 Win. Mag. (W)	L
257 Roberts (W)	L	348 Win. (W)	L
250 Savage (W)	L	35 Rem. (W)	L
264 Win. Mag. (W)	L	356 Win.	L
270 Win.	L	358 Win. (W)	L
284 Win. (W)	L	375 Win. (W)	L
7mm Rem. Mag.	L	375 H&H Mag. (W)	L
7x57mm Mauser (W)	L	38-40 Win.* (W)	S
30-30 Win.	L	38-55 Win. (W)	L
30 Carbine* (W)	S	44-40 Win. (W)	S
30-40 Krag (W)	L	45-70	L
30-06	L	458 Win. Mag. (W)	L

Bullets

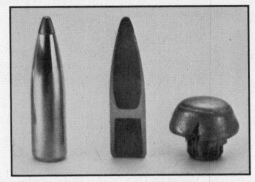

Federal 7mm Rem.
Mag. Nosler Part.

American Bullets

Notes on Handgun Bullets . . .

There are today three classes of handgun bullets. The cast lead bullet, relatively hard and lubricated, has been with us many years. It is excellent for target work and hunting at lower velocities.

The swaged lead, lubricated bullet is a relative newcomer. These bullets are just about as perfect as a lead bullet can be. They have no cavities, holes or off-balance hollows. They also make good target and low velocity game bullets.

The third class is the jacketed or half-jacketed handgun bullet. Some manufacturers use pure lead, others use lead alloys. The softer the lead the greater the shocking power on game. Jackets are swaged right onto the lead cores, permitting a high velocity bullet. For hunting it has no superior.

Some manufacturers not only swage the jacket right onto the lead core, they go further and crimp it on so that the jacket cannot come off in the barrel, in flight or on impact. This also reduces the bearing surface, thus increasing velocity with no increase in pressures. Unless the jacket completely covers all of the bearing surface, this type bullet leads the bore badly. Best are those in which the jacket is turned down at least to some extent over the ogive.

Notes on Rifle Bullets . . .

A basic rule for best rifle accuracy is to match the barrel twist to the bullet weight and length. As an example, a 30-06 barrel with a 1-in-10 twist will handle 150- to 220-grain bullets better than those of 90 to 150 grains, with some exceptions. If only lightweight, high velocity bullets are to be fired in a 30-06, then a twist of either 1-in-12 or 1-in-14 is generally preferable.

There are many types and classes of rifle bullets, each designed to do more or less specific jobs. Light, high-velocity varmint bullets should not be used on big game, nor ought long-range target bullets be used for varmint shooting. Try to choose the correct bullet for the job to be done.

It is just as imperative to select a load that will utilize the full potential of the bullet. A heavy hunting bullet must be driven at the velocity for which it was designed to obtain correct expansion, shocking power and penetration. For example, a 30-30 bullet, designed for the lower velocities, must not be driven too fast or it will tend to explode on contact and fail to give good performance.

Today virtually all bullet makers make good bullets. Choose one suitable for the job at hand, give it the right velocity and it will do that job—but only if you do your part!

One of the finest hunting bullets is the Nosler Partition bullet. It is designed to provide satisfactory expansion plus maximum penetration, while retaining approximately two-thirds of its original weight when recovered from game. It is also highly accurate.

Hornady, Speer, Sierra and others, also make a full line of fine hunting bullets.

Match bullets are another thing. Many of the best match bullets are handmade and hand-inspected. The fine Sierra 30 cal. 168-grain, soft-swaged bullets are superbly accurate. In this class it is usually a question of matching the barrel to the bullet, or vice versa. Several smaller makers (you'll find them listed in our Directory) offer excellent match bullets, particularly in the 22 to 6mm range.

AFSCO American, Foreign and Obsolete Loaded Ammunition

Afsco specializes in British hunting ammunition, from the 240 Apex to the 600 Nitro Express. Both softpoint and solid bullets for hunting dangerous game are offered. Hundreds of calibers available. Send for a free listing. From Afsco Ammunition.

AMERICAN BULLETS

American Bullets offers a line of hard lead and jacketed bullets for reloading in all popular pistol calibers. The hard lead bullets are designed for clean shooting at higher velocities. The jacketed bullets are designed for controlled expansion at high velocities and reliable expansion at lower velocities. The bullets are supplied, ready to use, and are packaged in either 100 packs or in bulk packs of 500. American Bullets are available through firearms retailers. From American Bullets.

Caliber	Weight	Style	Per 100	Per 500
Lead Bullets				
380	95	RN	$4.85	$18.40
9mm	125	RN	4.85	18.40
38/357	148	DEWC	4.85	18.40
	148	BBWC	4.85	18.40
	148	HBWC	4.85	18.40
	158	RN	5.05	19.75
	158	SWC	5.05	19.75
	158	SWC-HP	5.05	19.75
41	220	SWC	5.20	25.50
44	240	SWC	5.95	26.80
	290	SWC	4.75/50	31.90
45	185	SWC	5.90	24.35
	200	SWC	5.90	24.35
	230	RN	6.10	25.75
	230	FN	6.25	26.00
45 Colt	225	SWC	6.10	25.75
Jacketed Bullets				
38/357	125	JHP	8.95	23.50
	158	JHP	9.10	32.00

Bullets

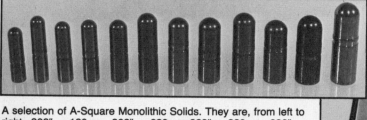

A selection of A-Square Monolithic Solids. They are, from left to right, .308″ — 180 gr., .308″ — 220 gr., 323″ — 220 gr., .338″ — 250 gr., 375″ — 300 gr., 416″ — 400 gr., 423″ — 400 gr., 458″ — 465 gr., 458″ — 500 gr., .475″ — 480 gr., .510″ — 600 gr., 510″ — 707 gr.

(Right) A-Square Dead Tough softpoints, Monolithic solids and Lion Load softpoints.

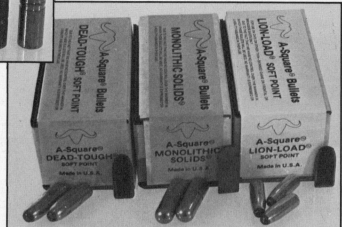

ACME Custom Bullets

Made in precision-machined Corbin dies, Acme bullets range in caliber from 224 to 458. Other calibers available on request. Bullets are formed in a four- to six-step process and inspected each step of the way. Price includes shipping and handling in contiguous 48 states. From Acme Custom Bullets.

BBI Bullets

Caliber	Type	Wt. (grs.)	Price/Per
40/10mm	Cast FP	165	$21.50/100
	SWC	185	23.50/100
	Bren Ten	200	26.00/100
38-40	JHP	170	22.50/100
	JHP	175	32.00/100
	JSP	180	30.00/100
	JHP	200	25.00/100
	FMJ-FP*	210	26.50/100
	JHP	210	26.50/100
	JSP	220	28.00/100
351 Win. SL	JSP	160	18.50/100
	FMJ	180	21.50/100
351 Win.	Cast		20.00/100
416	Cast RN	300	40.00/100
		350	45.00/100
416	JSRN	410	45.00/20
	SPBT	400	40.00/20
458	Cast	300 to 426	20.00/50
	JBT	460	50.00/20

BBI Brass

38-40		18.50/50
351 Win. SL		33.50/50

*Bren Ten
From Beal's Bullets.

ACME CUSTOM BULLETS

Caliber	Price/100	Caliber	Price/100
224-cal.		200 gr. HP	22.24
45 gr. HP	$14.12	225 gr. RNSP	22.98
50 gr. SP	14.26	225 gr. RNFMJ	22.98
53 gr. HP	14.36	235 gr. RNSP	23.42
55 gr. HP	14.42		
60 gr. SP	14.98	**32 Mag.-cal.**	
		100 gr. HJWC	16.92
228-cal.		115 gr. HJSWC	17.84
60 gr. SP	14.98		
70 gr. HP	16.06	**38/357-cal.**	
80 gr. HP	17.96	125 gr. HJHPSWC	17.28
		125 gr. HJWC	17.28
243/6mm-cal.		130 gr. JFP	18.24
70 gr. HP	16.06	160 gr. JFP	19.16
75 gr. SP	17.82	170 gr. JFP	20.98
85 gr. SP	18.10		
100 gr. SP	19.29	**358-cal. Rifle**	
		200 gr. SP	22.24
257-cal.		235 gr. SPHP	23.42
100 gr. SSP	19.49		
		375-cal.	
264/6.5mm-cal.		255 gr. RNSP	24.34
130 gr. SP	21.88		
		44-cal. (.429″)	
284/7mm-cal.		240 gr. HJSWC	23.92
130 gr. HP	19.88	240 gr. HJHPSWC	23.92
140 gr. SP	20.10	275 gr. RNSP	24.95
145 gr. SSP	20.26	360 gr. JSPSWC	27.90
150 gr. SSP	20.44		
150 gr. RNSP	20.44	**458-cal.**	
		335 gr. SSP	27.38
308-cal.		350 gr. SPFP	27.38
100 gr. HJRN	16.92		
130 gr. HP	19.88		
150 gr. SP	20.44		
165 gr. HP	20.86		
165 gr. SP	20.86		
190 gr. RNSP	21.66		

FMJ—Full Metal Jacket; FP—Flat Point; HJ—Half Jacket; HP—Hollowpoint; J—Jacketed; RN—Round Nose; S—Spitzer; SP—Softpoint; SWC—Semi-wadcutter; WC—Wadcutter.

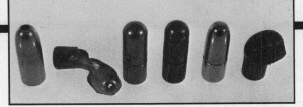

A selection of .458″ conventional and tubing FMJ's along with a Monolithic Solid. Note that the Monolithic Solid is absolutely undamaged.

Pairings of .458″ sectioned and unsectioned bullets. The pairs are, from left to right, a conventional FMJ, a tubing style FMJ, and an A-Square Monolithic Solid.

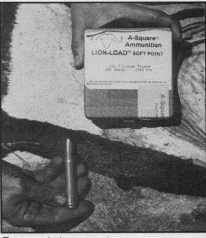

Entrance hole on a zebra struck with a .500 A-Square Lion Load. The animal was shot while struggling to get up, and death was instantaneous.

B.E.L.L.
Woodleigh Bullets

These large-caliber, dangerous-game bullets are offered in solid and soft nose form. Solids are drawn from solid copper-clad sheet steel; soft nose types are made from guilding metal. Bullet heel is folded to retain the core. They are said to be the best types since Kynoch stopped production. Imported from Australia. From B.E.L.L.

B.E.L.L. Woodleigh Bullets

Caliber	Wgt. (grs.)	Style	Dia. (in.)	Price/Per
600 Nitro	900	SN	.620	$45.00/25
600 Nitro	900	FMJ	.620	65.00/25
577 Nitro	750	SN	.585	45.00/25
577 Nitro	750	FMJ	.585	65.00/25
500 Nitro	570	SN	.510	65.00/50
500 Nitro	570	FMJ	.510	110.00/50
505 Gibbs	515	SN	.505	65.00/50
505 Gibbs	515	FMJ	.505	110.00/50
475 Nitro #2	480 & 500	SN	.483 & .488	65.00/50
475 Nitro #2	480 & 500	FMJ	.483 & .488	110.00/50
470 Nitro	500	SN	.475	65.00/50
470 Nitro	500	FMJ	.475	110.00/50
465 Nitro	480	SN	.468	65.00/50
465 Nitro	480	FMJ	.468	110.00/50
450 Nitro	480	SN	.458	65.00/50
450 Nitro	480	FMJ	.458	110.00/50
416 Rigby	410	SN	.416	65.00/50
416 Rigby	410	FMJ	.416	110.00/50
404 Jeffery	400	SN	.423	60.00/50
404 Jeffery	400	FMJ	.404	100.00/50
450/400 Nitro	400	SN	.411	60.00/50
450/400 Nitro	400	FMJ	.411	100.00/50

Styles: SN = Soft Nose; FMJ = Full Metal Jacket.

A-SQUARE Bullets

A-Square offers a triad of bullets to the handloader in either loaded or component form. Their Monolithic Solids™ are non-expanding bullets made from a single metal with no lead core. This solid construction ensures penetration on the heaviest of game. Dead Tough™ Soft Points are expanding bullets designed for close-range shots at heavy game. Lion Load™ Soft Points are designed for down-the-throat shots on a charging lion or leopard. They will penetrate a maximum of 18-24 inches and expand violently upon impact. From A-Square.

Diameter (Inches)	Weight (Grains)	Style	Price*
.284″	175	Monolithic Solid	$34.24
.308″	180	Monolithic Solid	34.24
.308″	220	Monolithic Solid	35.07
.323″	220	Monolithic Solid	41.75
.338″	250	Monolithic Solid	42.59
.375″	300	Monolithic Solid	41.75
.375″	300	Dead Tough S P	38.41
.375″	300	Lion Load S P	38.41
.416″	400	Monolithic Solid	25.46
.416″	400	Dead Tough S P	22.55
.416″	400	Lion Load S P	22.13
.423″	400	Monolithic Solid	27.97
.423″	400	Dead Tough S P	26.30
.423″	400	Lion Load S P	24.22
.458″	465	Monolithic Solid	26.72
.458″	500	Monolithic Solid	27.56
.458″	500	Dead Tough S P	24.63
.458″	500	Lion Load S P	19.62
.475″	480	Monolithic Solid	29.64
.510″	600	Monolithic Solid	29.64
.510″	600	Dead Tough S P	31.31
.510″	600	Lion Load S P	25.89
.510″	707	Monolithic Solid	30.06

*.375 and smaller packed 50 per box, .416 and larger packed 25 per box.

Action Ammo

ACTION AMMO

Importers of SAMSON and UZ1 ammunition manufactured by Israel Military Industries. Centerfire rifle offerings include 223 Rem., 30-06 Springfield and 308 Win. In pistol and carbine cartridge selections Action Ammo offers 357 Mag., 38 Spl., 38 Spl+P, 380 Auto, 44 Rem. Mag., 45 ACP, 45 HV Carbine, 9mm Luger, 9mm Carbine and 9mm Subsonic. Samson and UZ1 cases can be reloaded up to 20 times due to a special annealing process. From Action Ammo, Ltd.

C.W. Cartridge Sharps Bullets

Cast of pure lead, there are three different bullet styles available for 54-caliber Sharps percussion rifles, two each for 45 and 50-caliber guns. These bullets are designed to be used with the C.W. Cartridge Forming Kit to make combustible paper cartridges. From C. W. Cartridge Co.

Caliber	Wgt. (grs.)	Style	Price/20
54	380	HBBS	$5.40
54	415	HBCM	$5.40
54	425	SBS	$5.40
50	355	HBBS	$5.40
50	380	SBS	$5.40
45	280	HBBS	$5.40
45	300	SBS	$5.40

Styles: HBBS—Hollow Base Buffalo Slug; HBCM—Hollow Base Conical Minie; SBS—Solid Buffalo Slug.

Action Ammo

Caliber	Wgt. (grs.)	Style	Price/Per	Caliber	Wgt.(grs.)	Style	Price/Per
Rifle				380 Auto	90	JHP	10.90/50
223 Rem.	55	MCBT	$4.85/20		95	MC	10.90/50
	55	JHPBT	5.67/20	44 Rem. Mag.	180	JHP	14.95/50
	55	SPBT	5.67/20		240	JHP	14.95/50
	63	SFB	5.67/20		240	JHP	14.95/50
30-06 Spfld.	150	MCBT	7.60/20	45ACP	185	MCSWC	13.90/50
	150	SPBT	8.75/20	45 HV Carbine	185	MC-Mod. SWC	13.90/50
	165	SPBT	8.75/20	45 ACP	185	JHP	15.15/50
	180	SPBT	8.75/20		230	MC	13.00/50
308 Win.	150	MCBT	7.60/20	9mm Luger	115	MC	10.90/50
	150	SPBT	8.75/20	9mm Carbine	115	MC	11.75/50
	165	SPBT	8.75/20	9mm Luger	115	JHP	12.30/50
	180	SPBT	8.75/20	9mm Carbine	115	JHP	12.80/50
Pistol				9mm Subsonic	124	MC	10.90/50
357 Mag.	125	JHP	12.60/50	9mm Subsonic	158	MC	10.90/50
	125	JSP	12.60/50				
	158	JHP	12.60/50				
	158	JSP	12.60/50				
38 Spl.	148	HBWC	10.60/50				
	158	LSWC	10.60/50				
	158	LHPSWC	10.60/50				
38 Spl+P	110	JHP	12.30/50				
	125	JHP	12.30/50				
	158	JHP	12.30/50				
	158	JSP	12.30/50				
	158	LSWC	10.90/50				
	158	LHPSWC	10.90/50				

Styles: MCBT = Metal Case Boattail; JHPBT = Jacketed Hollow Point Boattail; SPBT = Soft Point Boattail; SFB = Spitzer Flat Base; JHP = Jacketed Hollow Point; JSP = Jacketed Soft Point; HBWC = Hollow Base Wadcutter; LSWC = Lead Semi-Wadcutter; LHPSWC = Lead Hollow Point Semi-Wadcutter; MCSWC = Metal Case Semi-Wadcutter; MC-MOD. SWC = Metal Case Modified Semi-Wadcutter; MC = Metal Case.

MANUFACTURED BY

ISRAEL MILITARY INDUSTRIES

IMPORTED EXCLUSIVELY BY

action ammo ltd.

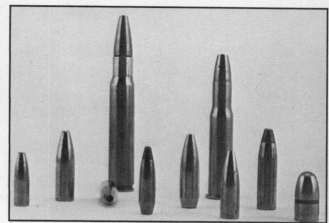

Black Mountain Arms bullets

BLACK MOUNTAIN Bullets

Custom bullets made to the reloader's specifications in 6mm, 7mm, 308 (7.62mm) or 9mm. Bullet options include: Fluid King construction*; FMJ with rounded points; soldered or bonded cores; heat-treated jackets; rebated and standard boattail designs; custom length cannelures; choice of 6 or 8-cal. ogives in 6 and 7mm; special preparation for match bullets; hand spun jackets; 7mm and 308 partition inserts; spire point, flat point or hollowpoint design; custom bullet weights, and determination of actual ballistic coefficient.

*Fluid King hollow tip bullets have a core with a large cavity swaged into the forward section filled with a non-toxic fluid which remains fluid and stable from well below 0-degrees Fahrenheit to over 300 degrees F. From Black Mountain Arms.

C. W. CARTRIDGE
Paper Cartridge Kit

Contains 200 precut, nitrated paper sheets, cartridge glue stock, and a 7" plastic forming dowel for making combustible cartridge tubers in the correct diameter to fit 45, 50 or 54-caliber Sharps bullets. For Sharps percussion rifles. From C. W. Cartridge Co.

Price: **$15.00**
Price: Special Refill Kit (500 nitrated sheets, two glue sticks) **$24.00**
Price: 100 nitrated sheets **$5.40**

Black Mountain

Caliber	Weight	Style	Per 20
6mm	60 gr.	FB/HP	$ 4.40
	80 gr.	Bonded/HP	6.00
	100 gr.	FB/HP	4.60
	115 gr.	FB/HP	4.40
7mm	100 gr.	FB/HP	4.60
	140 gr.	FB/HP	5.00
	155 gr.	Bonded/SP	5.80
		RBT/HP	6.20
	180 gr.	FB/SP	5.80
	200 gr.	FB/SP	6.00
30	100 gr.	FB/HP	4.60
	155 gr.	Bonded/SP	5.80
	168 gr.	Bonded/SP	5.80
		BT/HP (Match)	7.00
	190 gr.	BT/HP (Match)	7.80
		FB/SP	6.20
	200 gr.	Bonded/SP	7.60
		FB/SP	6.00
	220 gr.	Bonded/SP	7.60
		FB/SP	6.20
9mm*	158 gr.	Pistol/FMJ	5.60

Fluid King Bullets

6mm	80 gr.	Fluid King	7.00
7mm	130 gr.	Fluid King	6.80
	155 gr.	Fluid King	7.00
30	110 gr.	Fluid King	6.60
	125 gr.	Fluid King	6.60
	168 gr.	Fluid King (Match)	10.00
	190 gr.	Fluid King (Match)	11.00

Partition Bullets

6mm	80 gr.	FB/SP	8.40
7mm	140 gr.	FB/SP	8.80
	160 gr.	FB/SP	9.00
30	160 gr.	FB/SP	9.00
	190 gr.	FB/SP	9.40

FB—Flat Base; SP—Soft point; BT—Boattail; RBT—Rebated Boattail; Bonded—Soldered cores; Match—Bullets are made to rigid match standards. *This bullet is used for special subsonic loads in pistols. it is available in.354 or .355, FMJ or SP.

COR-BON
Custom Bullets

Custom jacketed rifle and handgun bullets made with a unique process that chemically bonds the bullet core to the jacket. This process eliminates jacket separation and reduces jacket brittleness. Cor-Bon also supplies custom bullets to customer specifications for order of 100 bullets or more. From Cor-Bon Custom Bullets.

Caliber	Type	Wt. grs.	Price/Per
30	OP	140	$24.95/40
30	OP	160	24.95/40
30	SSP	180	19.95/20
375	SSP	280	19.95/20
375	SSP	280	19.95/20
44	RNSP	260 & 280	19.95/20
44	FMJ	260 & 280	17.95/40
44	FMJ	305	24.95/40
(with cannelure)			
45/70	SP	300	19.95/20
454	SP	260 & 300	19.95/20
454	FMJ	300	24.95/40

OP—Open Point; SSP—Spitzer Softpoint; RNSP—Round Nose Softpoint; FMJ—Full Metal Jacket; SP—Softpoint

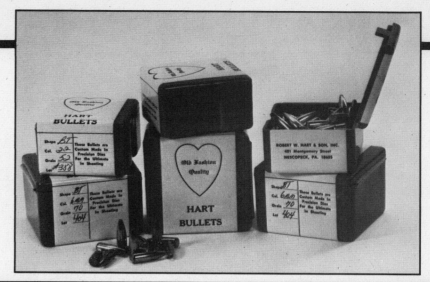

Hart Bullets

GREEN BAY Bullets

An excellent line of rifle and pistol bullets, produced under rigidly controlled conditions for high uniformity and accuracy. They also have a large line of blackpowder round balls, and bullets which are cast of very soft lead. They honor special requests for lead hardness, type of bullet lube, and custom sizing. Write for a current catalog, information sheet, and price list. From Green Bay Bullets.

HART Bullets

Caliber	Wgt. (grs.)	Type	Price/100
22	52	FB	$9.95
22	52	BT	9.95
243 (6mm)	62	BT	10.95
243 (6mm)	68	BT	10.95
243 (6mm)	68	FB	10.95
243 (6mm)	70	BT	10.95
243 (6mm)	65	BT	10.95
243 (6mm)	65	FB	10.95

FB (Flat Base), BT (BoatTail)
From Robert Hart & Son.

Green Bay Bullets

Caliber	Wgt. (grs.)	Style	Type	Caliber	Wgt. (grs.)	Style	Type	Caliber	Wgt. (grs.)	Style	Type
Rifle Bullets				30	165	RN	GC	348	250	FP	GC
22	45	RN	GC	30	120	FP		352	170	RN	GC
22	55	RN	GC	30	115	FP	GC	35	200	RN	GC
22	59	P	GC	30	125	P	GC	38/55	250	FP	GC
6mm	85	RN	GC	30	130	RN		38/40	175	FP	
25	90	RN	GC	30	155	RN	GC	40/65	245	FP	
25	90	FP	GC	30	170	RN	GC	44/40	210	FP	
25	115	RN	GC	30	180	FP	GC	405 Win.	290	RN	
6.5mm	125	RN	GC	303	190	P	GC	43 Span.	335	RN	
6.5mm	140	RN	GC	32/40	180	FP	GC	45/70	305	FP	
7mm	140	RN	GC	32/40	165	FP		45/70	345	FP	
7.35mm	145	RN	GC	8mm-32	170	RN	GC	45/70	395	RN	
32/20	75	RN		8mm-32	220	RN	GC	45/70	505	RN	
32/20	85	FP	GC	33	200	FP	GC	50/70	450	FP	
32/20	95	SWC		348	185	FP	GC	50/70	505	RN	
Pistol Bullets				38	148	WC		44	245	SWC	GC
25 Auto	65	FP	GC		BB			44	250	WC	
8mm Nambu	100	RN		38	148	WC		44	250	SWC	
380 Auto	90	RN		38	148	SWC		45 Auto	185	SWC	
9mm	95	FP		38	158	RN		45 Auto	185	SWC	
9mm	125	PFP		38	158	RN		45 Auto	200	SWC	
9mm	125	RN		38	160	SWC		45 Auto	220	SWC	
357	160	SWC		38	159	RN		45 Auto	225	RN	
357	160	SWC		38	200	SWC		45 Auto	240	RN	
357	160	SWC	GC	41 Long Colt	190	Heel		45 Auto	240	SWC	
38	90	RN		41	200	WC		45 Colt	255	SWC	
38	125	RN		41	210	SWC		45 Colt	260	SWC	
38	127	WC		41	210	SWC	GC				
38	140	WC		44	225	SWC	GC				
38	148	WC		44	245	RN					

RN—Round Nose; P—Pointed; FP—Flat Point; SWC—Semi-Wadcutter; WC—Wadcutter; BB—Bevel Base; GC—Gas Check

Excaliber Wax Bullets

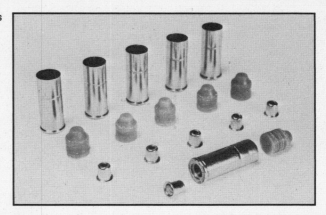

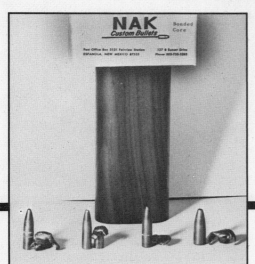

NAK Custom Bullets

EXCALIBER
Wax Bullets

Excaliber Wax Bullets are designed to be used as a training tool and are made of a special blend of waxes and oils. Powered by a CC1 209M shotshell primer, the small caliber bullets can reach a velocity of 750 fps, the larger calibers 650 fps. Bullets and primers are loaded into special Excaliber reusable brass cases with finger pressure only. Will feed from magazines in automatics but slide must be operated manually. Available in 38/357, 45 ACP or 45 Colt, 44, 41, 9mm or 380. Primers not included. From Excaliber Wax, Inc.

Price: 100 count bag with 6 brass cases **$5.99**

Price: 300 count bag with 6 brass cases **$12.99**

NAK
Custom Bullets

NAK makes bullets not usually offered by the large makers, in standard and custom weights. Jackets are made of guilding metal or copper tubing and are heat treated to improve performance. Tubing jackets for soldered or bonded core bullets are closed at the base by high heat and pressure. Jackets are thinned at the mouth to assure expansion over a wide range of velocities. From NAK Custom Bullets.

NAK Custom Bullets

Cal.	Wgt. (grs.)/Style	Jacket Thickness (in.)	Price/50
Guilding Metal Jackets			
22 (.224″)	53 OTS	.015	$ 9.00
	56 OTS	.015	9.50
	70 OTS	.023	12.00
6mm (.244″)	70 OTS	.023	12.00
	95 OTS	.023	12.50
7mm (.284″)	123 CTS	.024	13.00
	140 CTS	.024	13.50
	160 OTSBT	.024	15.00
	180 OTSBT	.024	16.00
	160 RN	.024	15.00
	180 RN	.024	16.00
30 (.308″)	130 OTSBT	.020	14.50
	150 OTSBT	.020	15.00
	172 OTSBT	.028	16.00
	150 RN	.020	15.00
	172 RN	.028	16.00
8mm (.323″)	195 OTS	.023	17.00
Copper Tubing Jackets			
7mm (.284″)	140 CTS	.035	26.00
	160 CTS	.035	27.50
	160 RN	.035	27.50
	180 CTS	.035	27.80
	180 RN	.035	27.80
30 (.308″)	150 OTS	.035	27.50
	165 OTS	.035	27.70
	180 OTS	.035	27.80
	200 CTS	.035	28.50
	180 RN	.035	27.80
8mm (.323″)	200 CTS	.035	29.00
35 (.358″)	220 CTS	.030	30.00
	250 CTS	.030	30.00
	250 CTS	.049	30.00
	250 RN	.049	30.00
	300 RN	.049	32.00
	300 RNFMJ	.049	19.00
44 (.429″)	265 FP	.032	30.00
	290 FP	.032	30.00
375 (.375″)	275 CTS	.049	30.00
	275 RN	.049	30.00
	300 RNFMJ	.049	19.00

Styles: OTS = Open Tip Spitzer; CTS = Compact Tip Spitzer; OTSBT = Open Tip Spitzer Boat Tail; RN = Round Nose; RNFMJ = Round Nose Full Metal Jacket; FP = Flat Point.

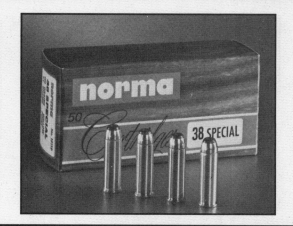

NORMA
Bullets

Norma bullets, at one time regularly offered, are only available from this supplier. The bullets have an excellent reputation on game, and there are two unique designs that have proven themselves in the field. Available from Huntington.

McCONNELLSTOWN
Cast Bullets

This firm offers hand-cast linotype rifle and pistol bullets and jacketed handgun bullets. They also have once-fired rifle cases (polished, trimmed and boxed) and new pistol cases. From McConnellstown Reloading.

McConnellstown Bullets

Cal.	Wgt. (grs.)/Style	Per 100
Pistol		
38	110 JHP	$ 6.25
38	125 JHP	6.00
38	150 SWC	5.00
38	158 JHP	7.00
9mm	115 FMJ	5.75
44	240 SWC	8.50
45 ACP	185 SWC	7.00
45 ACP	200 SWC	7.00
45*	220 Conical	4.00
Rifle		
30	170 FN	7.00
30	185 PT	7.50
30	220 RN	8.00
375	265 FN	10.00

*Ruger blackpowder bullet
Styles: SWC = Semi-Wadcutter; FMJ = Full Metal Jacket; JHP = Jacketed Hollow Point; FN = Flat Nose; RN = Round Nose; PT = Pointed.

M & D
Pistol Bullets

These swaged lead bullets are double dry lubed for less leading and are available only in 38/357 and 45 ACP. M&D is also an ammunition loader using either their own brass or the customer's brass. They load 38 Spec., 357 Mag., 9mm and 380 ACP. Contact M&D Munitions, Ltd. for quantity discount prices.

Norma Rifle Bullets

Diameter (In/mm)	Weight/Style		Price/100	Diameter (In/mm)	Weight/Style		Price/100
.224/5.56	45 gr.	HP	$20.00	.264/6.5	144 gr.	FMJBT Match	26.70
.224/5.56	50 gr.	SP	20.00	.308/7.62	180 gr.	SPBT	26.75
.224/5.56	50 gr.	FMJ	20.00	.308/7.62	180 gr.	SP-DC	36.40
.224/5.56	53 gr.	SP Match	26.40	.308/7.62	180 gr.	SP-RN	27.30
.228/5.6	71 gr.	SP	23.20	.308/7.62	180 gr.	SP-PPC	27.30
.228/5.6	71 gr.	FMJ	27.20	.308/7.62	200 gr.	SP-PPC	33.65
.243/6	100 gr.	FMJ	29.10	.308/7.62	150 gr.	SP-FN	27.20
.243/6	100 gr.	SP	29.10	.311/7.62	130 gr.	SP	26.40
.264/6.5	80 gr.	FMJ	25.40	.311/7.62	150 gr.	SP	26.40
.264/6.5	139 gr.	FMJBT Match	22.00	.311/7.62	180 gr.	SP	26.40
.264/6.5	139 gr.	HPBT Match	22.00	.323/8	165 gr.	SP-PPC	33.30
.264/6.5	144 gr.	FMJBT	22.00	.323/8	196 gr.	SP	30.95
.264/6.5	139 gr.	SPBT	26.40	.365/9.3	232 gr.	SP-PPC	39.50
.264/6.5	139 gr.	PPC	26.40	.365/9.3	286 gr.	SP-RN	22.35
.264/6.5	156 gr.	SP	26.40	.365/9.3	232 gr.	FMJ	30.10
.277	130 gr.	SP	26.40				
.277	150 gr.	SP	26.40				
.284/7	150 gr.	SP	26.40				
.284/7	150 gr.	FMJ	29.10				
.284/7	170 gr.	SP	30.10				
.308/7.62	130 gr.	SP	26.70				
.308/7.62	146 gr.	FMJBT Match	25.40				

Styles: HP = Hollow Point; SP = Soft Point; FMJ = Full Metal Jacket; FMJBT = Full Metal Jacket Boattail; SPBT = Soft Point Boattail; SP-DC = Soft Point Dual Core; SP-RN = Soft Point Round Nose; SP-FN = Soft Point Flat Nose; PPC = Protected Power Cavity.

Norma Pistol Bullets

Diameter (In/mm)	Weight/Style	Price/100	Diameter (In/mm)	Weight/Style	Price/100
.308/7.62	77 gr. FMJ	$18.20	.357	158 gr. JSP	21.90
.355/9	96 gr. FMJ	25.50	.401/10	200 gr. FMJ	30.50
.355/9	115 gr. JHP	25.50	.401/10	165 gr. JHP	30.50
.355/9	116 gr. FMJ	25.50	.430	240 gr. JSP	29.90
.355/9	116 gr. JSP	25.50			
.357	110 gr. JHP	23.70			
.357	158 gr. JHP	21.90			
.357	158 gr. FMJ	26.40			

Styles: FMJ = Full Metal Jacket; JHP = Jacketed Hollow Point; JSP = Jacketed Soft Point.

Cal.	Wgt. (grs.)/Style	Per M
38/357	148 HBWC	$19.50
	158 SWC	20.50
	158 SWCHP	20.50
45 ACP	200 SWC	27.50
	230 RNL	32.50

Styles: HBWC = Hollow Base Wadcutter; SWC = Semi-Wadcutter; SWCHP = Semi-Wadcutter Hollow Point; RNL = Round Nose Lead.

McConnellstown Bullets

KODIAK
Bonded Core Bullets

These bullets are designed to give deep penetration with positive expansion and maximum weight retention. They are made with pure lead cores bonded to heavy-walled copper jackets that guarantee them blow-up proof against heavy game at close ranges, even at magnum velocities. British caliber bullets have the exact weight and shape of the original Kynoch bullets. From Alaska Bullet Works.

Kodiak Bullets

Cal.	Wgt. (grs.)/ Style	Jacket Thickness (in.)	Per 50
284 (7mm)	160 PSP	.049	$34.00
	175 PP	.049	36.50
308	180 PSP,PP	.049	40.00
	220 PP	.035	40.00
	220 PP	.049	43.50
338	200 PSP, PP	.049	38.00
	250 PP	.049	43.50
	300 PP	.049	47.50
358	200 PSP	.049	38.00
	250 PP	.049	43.50
	275 PP	.049	45.50
375	270 PP, PSP	.049	43.50
	285 PP	.049	45.50
	300 PP, PSP	.049	47.50
458	400 FP	.035	46.50
	400 FP, RNSP	.049	50.00
	500 RNSP	.049	58.25
	600 RNSP	.049	63.25
British calibers*			
423 (404 Jeffery)	400 RNSP	.049	$50.00
411 (450/400)	400 RNSP	.049	50.00
416 (416 Rigby)	410 RNSP	.049	50.00
468 (465 H&H)	480 RNSP	.049	58.25
475 (470 Nitro)	500 RNSP	.049	58.25
483 (475 Nitro)	480 RNSP	.049	58.25
488 (475 #2 Jeffery)	500 RNSP	.049	58.25

*Available late 1987.
Styles: PSP = Pointed Soft Point; PP = Protected Point; FP = Flat Point; RNSP = Round Nose Soft Point.

MILLER TRADING CO.
Cast Bullets

This firm offers cast bullets for rifles and handguns in over 40 types and calibers, and seven diameters of round balls. These may be had as cast or sized and lubed. All bullets shipped postpaid and insured in wooden boxes. Write to them for their latest list.

PMC Bullets

Caliber	Wgt. (grs.)	Bullet Type	Bullet Dia. (ins.)
Handgun Bullets			
25	50	FMJ	.251
32	71	FMJ	.312
9mm	90	JHP	.355
9mm	90	FMJ	.355
9mm	115	JHP	.355
9mm	115	FMJ	.355
9mm	124	FMJ	.355
9mm	130	FMJ	.355
38	110	JHP	.357
38	125	JSP	.357
38	125	JHP	.357
38	132	FMJ	.357
38	150	JHP	.357
38	158	JSP	.357
44	180	JHP	.4295
44	240	JHP	.4295
45	230	FMJ	.451
Rifle Bullets			
22	55	FMJBT	.224
7mm	175	SP	.284
30	150	RNSP	.308
30	170	RNSP	.308
30	110	FMJ	.308
30	150	FMJBT	.308
30	180	SP	.308
30	123	FMJ	.311
30	125	SP	.311

FMJ—Full Metal Jacket; JHP—Jacketed Hollow Point; JSP—Jacketed Soft Point; FMJBT—Full Metal Jacket Boattail; SP—Spire Point; RNSP—Round Nose Soft Point.

From PMC Ammunition. Contact dealer or manufacturer for prices.

PRECISION MADE CARTRIDGES

Precision Components Cast Bullets

Magnus Bullets

Precision Components Bullets

Caliber	Wgt. (grs.)	Type	Price 100	Price 1000
380	95	RNBB	$12.25	$22.00
9mm	115	SWCBB	13.25	23.00
9mm	122	RNBB	13.25	23.00
38	148	WCDEBB	13.50	24.00
38	158	RNBB	13.50	24.00
38	158	SWCBB	13.50	24.00
41	210	TCBB	17.50	30.00
44	240	SWCBB	19.50	33.50
45	200	SWCBB	17.50	30.00
45	225	RNBB	19.00	32.50
45	225	FNBB	19.00	32.50

RN—Round Nose; SWC—Semi-Wad Cutter; WC—Wad Cutter; DE—Double Ended; TC—Truncated Cone; FN—Flat Nose; BB—Beveled Base

PRECISION COMPONENTS Cast Bullets

Precision produces a line of popular handgun cast bullets. Made from #2 alloy with a Saeco hardness factor of 9-10, these bullets are cast in Saeco and Hensley & Gibbs moulds. Three lube alternatives available on order: dry lube—molydenum disulphide epoxy; wax lube—precision beeswax/paraffin formula; or double lube—both a dry and waxed lube are applied. From Precision Components, Inc.

CBH BULLETS

Precision designed CBH bullets are cast of specially prepared alloys to assure uniformity of hardness and weight. They are sized and lubricated on automatic machines and are lubricated with a specially formulated bullet lubricant guaranteed not to crack or separate under heat or extreme pressure, giving a minimum of lead fouling. Cast pistol bullets are sized as follows: 9mm—.355", 38—.358", 44—.429", and 45—.452" and .454". Wholesale dealers write Sandia Die & Cartridge for pricing.

Caliber	Grs.	Type
9mm	125	RN
38	148	WC
38	150	SWC
38	158	RN
41	210	SERVICE
44	255	SWCGC
44	250	SWC
45	185	WC
45	200	WC
45	230	RN
45(.454")	250	SERVICE

WC—WADCUTTER
GC—GAS CHECK*
SWC—SEMI-WADCUTTER
RN—ROUND NOSE

MAGNUS BULLET CO.
INCORPORATED
PRICE LIST

No.		100	500*	1000 *
301	380-95-RN	3.50	14.00	25.00
401	09-122-FP	3.50	14.00	25.00
402	09-125-RN	3.50	14.00	25.00
501	38-148-DEWC	3.50	14.00	25.00
502	38-148-WC	3.50	14.00	25.00
503	38-158-SWC	4.00	15.00	28.00
504	38-158-RN	4.00	15.00	28.00
601	41-215-SWC	4.50	18.00	35.00
701	44-240-SWC *	5.00	16.00	31.00
801	45-185-SWC	4.25	16.00	30.00
802	45-200-SWC	4.50	17.00	33.00
803	45-225-FP	4.50	19.00	37.00
804	45-230-RN	5.00	19.00	37.00
901	45-255-SWC *	5.00	17.00	32.00

*NOTE: Bullets weighing 240 grains or more packed 400 per box. The prices shown on this list are per 100, 400 and 800 for these bullets.

MAGNUS BULLETS		MAGNUS BULLETS	
BULLET	DESCRIPTION	BULLET	DESCRIPTION
No. 301	380 Caliber RNBB 355 Dia. - 95 Grain Good 380 Bullet	No. 601	41 Caliber SWCBB 410 Dia. - 215 Grain Popular 41 Caliber
No. 401	9 MM Caliber FPBB 355 Dia. - 122 Grain Good Ballistics	No. 701	44 Caliber SWCBB 430 Dia. - 240 Grain Popular Heavy Wt. 44
No. 402	9 MM Caliber RNBB 355 Dia. - 125 Grain Good Feeding 9 MM	No. 801	45 Caliber ACP SWCBB 452 Dia. - 185 Grain Popular Light Target
No. 501	38/357 Caliber DEWC 358 Dia. - 148 Grain Excellent Target Bullet	No. 802	45 Caliber ACP SWCBB 452 Dia. - 200 Grain Popular Combat Bullet
No. 502	38/357 Caliber WCBB 357 Dia. - 148 Grain Excellent Target Bullet	No. 803	45 Caliber ACP FPBB 452 Dia. - 225 Grain Hornady Style
No. 503	38/357 Caliber SWCBB 357 Dia. - 158 Grain Popular 38/357	No. 804	45 Caliber ACP RNBB 452 Dia. - 230 Grain Best Feeding 45 ACP
No. 504	38/357 Caliber RNBB 357 Dia. - 158 Grain Good In 38 Super Also	No. 901	45 Caliber SWCBB 452 Dia. - 255 Grain For 45 Colt

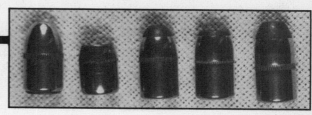
Precision Swaged 44-Cal. Bullets

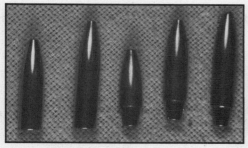
Precision Swaged 7mm Jacketed Bullets

Precision Swaged Paper Patch Bullets

PRECISION
Swaged Bullets

This firm offers a good line of useful swaged bullets for hunting and target shooting. To find which of their Paper Patch bullets shoot best, they offer the "Accurizor Kit" which includes four different weights per caliber (25 of each). Paper Patch bullets are not sold already patched. From Precision Swaged Bullets.

Precision Swaged Bullets

Copper Tubing Jacketed Bullets 360 N.E. No. 2, 400/360 W.R.N.E. (2¼)

Wgt. (grs.)	Jacket	Dia.	Price*
300	.032	.367	$25.00
320	.032	.367	25.00

Copper Tubing Jacketed Bullets: 9.3mm

Wgt. (grs.)	Jacket	Dia.	Price*
293	.032	.366	$26.00
300	.032	.366	26.00
320	.032	.366	26.00

*Price per 25.

Jacketed 44 Cal. Pistol Bullets

Wgt. (grs.)	Style	Price*
.429″		
265	CBRN	$22.86
275	CBRN	24.20
300	FBRN	25.40
260	FMJFB	24.00
162	CBHP	17.95
265	CBFN	23.86
275	CBFN	25.20
300	FBFN	26.40

*Price per 100. Styles: CBRN = Cup Base Round Nose; CBFN = Cup Base Flat Nose; FBRN = Flat Base Round ose; FMJFB = Full Metal Jacket Flat Base (heat-hardened core); CBHP = Cup Base Hollow Point. The .429″ 300-gr. also with Flat Nose; .429″ 265, 275-gr. also with FNFB.

Jacketed 7mm (.284″) Bullets

Wgt. (grs.)	Price/100
Rebated Boattail (Spitzer)	
138	$17.18
160	20.00
168	20.80
175	23.80
185	26.80
Flat Base (Spitzer)	
110	$13.80
125	15.00
138	16.40
160	18.40
168	19.20
175	22.20
185	25.20

Special "Coyote Killer" FMJ with alloy core in 120, 152-gr. also available; 120-gr.—$20.00/100, 152-gr.—$22.00/100.

Paper Patch Bullets

Dia.	Style	Price per 100 (according to weight)	
.395″*	RNFB	300-400 grs.	$14.50
.449″*	SSCB	401-500 grs.	15.00
.505″	RNCB	501-600 grs.	15.50
		601-700 grs.	16.00
		701-800 grs.	16.50

*Specify Cup or Flat Base. Bullets are of variable length and weight. Custom alloys or pure lead available.
Styles: RNFB = Round Nose Flat Base; SSCB = Semi-Spitzer Cup Base; RNCB = Round Nose Cup Base.

Patriot Custom Bullets

Bullet	Wgt. (grs.)	Type	Dia. (in.)	Price/50	Core Bonded Price/50
405 win.	300	JSP	.412	$18.25	$28.00
38-40 Win.	180	FNSPFB	.401	16.95	
38-40 Win.	180	HP	.401	16.95	
38-40 Win.	180	FNSPHB	.401	16.95	
45	275	JSPTC	.452	9.75	11.75
45	300	JSPTC	.452	10.50	12.50
338	200-250	Match Grade	.338	10.50	

JSP—Jacketed Soft Point; FNSPFB—Flat-Nosed Soft Point, Flat Base; HP—Hollow Point; FNSPHP—Flat-Nose Soft Point Hollow Point; JSPTC—Jacketed Soft Point Truncated Core.

PATRIOT
Custom Bullets

These bullets have been designed primarily with the hunter in mind and some duplicate original designs of the older cartridges like the 38-40 Win. and 405 Win. Contact the maker for further data. From Patriot Mfg. and Sales.

SWIFT
Core Bonded Safari Bullets

Designed for use on African game, Swift produces custom bullets with core bonded .055″ thick copper jackets in an "H" frame construction. The H-frame construction controls the threat of over-expansion on heavy game and prevents jacket/core separation. From Swift Bullet Co.

Caliber	Wgt. Grs.	Price/50
308	180	$65.00
358	250	65.00
375	300	65.00
416	400	95.00
458	500	95.00

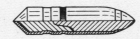

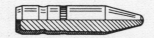

RWS Bullets

Caliber	Dia. (in.)	Wgt. Grs.	Type	Per 25
22	.223	46	SP	$44.00*
	.224	50	SP	44.00*
	.224	74	CP	24.90
	.224	74	FMC	21.25
	.228	71	PSP	18.90
	.228	71	FMC	20.60
6mm (.243)	.243	96	CP	14.00
6.5mm (.264)	.263	93	SP	14.25
	.264	127	CP	14.15
	.264	154	HMCHP	16.50
	.264	159	SPRN	15.00
270	.277	130	HMOHP	13.00
7mm	.284	116	CP	13.30
	.284	123	CP	13.30
	.284	139	SPRN	11.00
	.284	162	CP	14.50
	.284	162	TIG	14.50
	.284	173	HMCHP	18.00
	.284	177	TIG	14.50
308	.308	150	CP	14.50
	.308	181	HMCHP	18.00
	.308	181	TUG	14.50
	.308	190	FMCBT	16.75
8mm	.318	196	SPRN	11.25
	.323	181	CP	14.50
	.323	187	HMCHP	19.50
	.323	198	TIG	14.50
	.323	224	CP	15.50
8.15mm	.324	151	FNSP	14.50
9.3mm	.364	193	FNSP	15.50
	.366	247	CP	15.50
	.366	258	HMCHP	19.50
	.366	285	SPRN	13.00
	.366	285	FMS	15.00
	.366	293	TUG	15.50
375	.375	299	CP	17.00
	.375	299	FMS	17.00
10.75mm	.423	347	FMS	12.50
	.423	401	FMS	14.00**

*Price per 100. **Price per 20.
SP—Soft Point; CP—Cone Point; FMC—Full Metal Case; PSP—Pointed Soft Point; HMOHP—H-Mantel Open Hollow Point; SPRN—Soft Point Round Nose; HMCHP—H-Mantel Copper Hollow Point; TIG—Brenneke Torpedo Ideal; TUG—Brenneke Torpedo Universal; FMCBT—Special Match; FNSP—Flat Nose Soft Point; FMS—Full Metal Solid.
Available from Old Western Scrounger, Inc.

STAR "Tough-Bond" Bullets

These bullets are intended for African dangerous and plains game and offer a selection of options for the reloader/hunter for his hunting situations. The bonded core and jacket hold together where others are said to fail. Solid brass or pure copper jackets give a choice of performance. Wall thicknesses are offered in .032", .049", .065". Bullet styles of Solid RN, Spitzer RBT, Semi-Soft-Nose RN—all to match the game. All bullets are swaged and inspected by hand to insure precision. Bases are closed so the core can't be knocked out. Some bullets are reproductions of original English double rifle weights. Only a partial listing of bullets offered is shown. **Contact Professional Hunter Supplies for full data.**

Caliber	Wgt./grs.	Per 25
7mm (.284")	139	$22.50
	160	22.50
	175	22.50
30 (.308")	180	22.50
	200	22.50
	220	22.50
	250	22.50
8mm (.318" or .323")	185	22.50
	200	22.50
	225	22.50
	250	22.50
338	200	25.50
	250	25.50
	275	25.50
	300	25.50
35 (.358")	180	25.50
	250	25.50
	275	25.50
	300	25.50
9.3mm (.366")	250	25.50
	300	25.50
	320	25.50
375	270	28.00
	300	28.00
	350	28.00
400 (.407")	270	29.50
	300	29.50
	325	29.50
	400	29.50
416 (.416")	300	29.50
	410	29.50
404 Jeffery (.423")	300	32.50

Caliber	Wgt./grs.	Per 25
	410	$32.50
425 Westley Richards (.435")	410	32.50
11.2mm (.440")	401	32.50
458 (.458")	365	32.50
	400	32.50
	480	32.50
	500	32.50
	600	32.50
465 N.E. (.468")	365	32.50
	480	32.50
	500	32.50
470 N.E. (.475")	480	32.50
	500	36.50
	600	38.50
475 Jeffery (.483", .488")	480	38.50
	500	38.50
	520	38.50
500 (.505", .510")	400	36.50
	500	36.50
	535	38.50
	600	38.50
50 B.M.G. (.510")	750	40.00
577 (.585")	650	40.00
	750	40.00
600 N.E. (.622")	900	40.00
12 Bore Slugs (.720")	438	24.00
	550	26.50
	875	30.00
	1095	32.50

Prices are approximate.

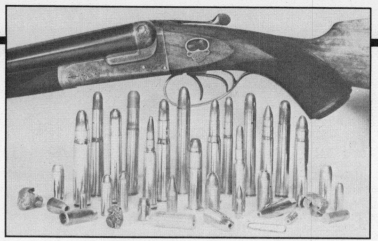

Professional Hunter's Supply Star "Tough Bond" Bullets

3-D Swaged Bullets

SUPREME Rubber Bullets

These primer-powered practice bullets are available in 38/357, 44 and 45 caliber. They are made of neoprene-like rubber in a wadcutter design with a bore-sealing skirt. By using magnum pistol primers, velocities of 400 to 500 fps can be achieved with excellent accuracy. Primer flash holes should be enlarged for best performance. Bullets are reusable up to 500 times. Bullets come 50 per bag with full instructions. From Supreme Products Co.

Price: 38/357, 44, 45 cals.,
per bag **$6.95**

3-D Brand Swagged Bullets

3-D offers swaged (not cast) hard alloy sized and lubricated (not dip lubed) bullets in 38 Spec., 357 Mag., 9mm, 45 ACP, 44 Mag. and 44 Spec. Eight bullet styles available—SWC lead, SWC copper PLT, RN lead, RN copper PLT, HBW lead, HBW copper PLT, DEW lead, DEW copper PLT. Available also are remanufactured or new 38 Spec. & 357 Mag. cases. Contact 3-D for prices.

TROPHY BONDED Big Game Bullets

Bear Claw Bullets: Semi-spitzer, protected softpoint, selectively annealed, precision machined, belted base, pure copper jackets. 100 percent fusion bonded to pure lead cores, 90 percent plus average retained weight, sharp cutting claw expansion. From Trophy Bonded Bullets, Inc.

Trophy Bonded Bullets

Caliber	Wgt. (grs.)	Price/25	Caliber	Wgt (Grs.)	Price/25
7mm (.284")	160	$42.00		400	47.50
	175	42.75		500	55.00
30 (.308")	165	42.00	465 (.468")	500	58.50
	180	42.75	470 (.475")	500	58.00
	200	42.75			
8mm (.323")	210	42.75			
	250	43.75			
338	210	42.75			
	250	43.75			
358	240	43.75			
	270	45.00			
9.3 (.366")	240	43.75			
	270	45.00			
	300	47.50	9.3 (.366")	300	$48.75
375	240	43.75	375	300	48.75
	270	45.00	404 (.423")	400	48.75
	300	47.50	411	400	48.75
404 (.423")	400	47.50	416	400	48.75
411	400	47.50	458	500	53.75
416	400	47.50	465 (.468")	500	57.25
45 (.458")	350	44.75	470 (.475")	500	56.75

Sledgehammer Solids: The hammerhead design provides straighter penetration and delivers greater shock power than any other type of solid. Precision machined massive naval bronze jacket with locked-in hard lead cores. Field tested on elephant, rhino, buffalo and hippo.

Trophy Bonded 375 Bearclaw (left) and 416 Bearclaw (below).

ZERO BULLETS

Zero is offering a fine line of swaged bullets in 38, 9mm, and 45 in different styles and weights for all applications. These bullets are high quality due to the quality control measures taken by the makers. They are available in 500 round lots up to 25,000 round lots and are priced accordingly. Write to Zero for the latest price sheet giving styles and weights. Zero is also offering loaded 38 Special, 357 Magnum and 45 ACP ammunition in a number of styles. Minimum 15,000 round order for best prices.

BULLETS MADE THE WAY THEY OUGHT'A BE SINCE 1939™

17 CALIBER - .172" Diameter
25 Gr. Spitzer Soft Point
.030" .121 .173

22 CALIBER - .224" Diameter
60 Gr. Spitzer Soft Point
.030" .171 .244

60 Gr. Spitzer F.M.J.
.030" .171 .215

70 Gr. Semi-Spitzer Soft Point
.030" .199 .284

(.228 Diameter also available)

6 mm CALIBER - .243" Diameter
90 Gr. Spitzer Soft Point
.030" .218 .370

105 Gr. Spitzer Soft Point
.030" .266 .428

NEW 115 Gr. Round Nose Soft Point
.030" .290 .322

25 CALIBER - .257" Diameter
90 Gr. Spitzer Soft Point
.032" .195 .309

90 Gr. Spitzer F.M.J.
.032" .195 .269

NEW 115 Gr. Spitzer Soft Point
.032" .249 .371

125 Gr. Spitzer Soft Point
.032" .270 .422

6.5 mm CALIBER - .264" Diameter
130 Gr. Spitzer Soft Point
.032" .266 .380

150 Gr. Spitzer Soft Point
.032" .307 .439

165 Gr. Spitzer Soft Point
.032" .338 .483

270 CALIBER - .277" Diameter
130 Gr. Spitzer Soft Point
.032" .242 .414

130 Gr. Spitzer F.M.J.
.032" .242 .387

150 Gr. Spitzer Soft Point
.032" .279 .468

160 Gr. Spitzer Soft Point
.032" .298 .481

180 Gr. Round Nose Soft Point
.032" .335 .372

7 mm CALIBER - .284" Diameter
125 Gr. Spitzer Soft Point
.032" .221 .378

140 Gr. Spitzer Soft Point
.032" .248 .436

160 Gr. Spitzer Soft Point
.032" .283 .491

175 Gr. Spitzer Soft Point
.032" .310 .520

195 Gr. Semi-Spitzer Soft Point
.032" .345 .570

(.228 Diameter also available)

30 CALIBER - .308" Diameter
150 Gr. Spitzer Soft Point
.032" .226 .377

165 Gr. Spitzer Soft Point
.032" .247 .436

180 Gr. Spitzer Soft Point
.032" .271 .468

200 Gr. Spitzer Soft Point
.032" .301 .544

225 Gr. Spitzer Soft Point
.032" .339 .595

250 Gr. Round Nose Soft Point
.032" .376 .417

250 Gr. Round Nose F.M.J.
.035" .376 .385

8 mm CALIBER - .323" and .318" Diameter
150 Gr. Spitzer Soft Point
.032" .205 .293

180 Gr. Spitzer Soft Point
.032" .246 .351

200 Gr. Spitzer Soft Point
.032" .274 .391

225 Gr. Spitzer Soft Point
.049" .308 .440

250 Gr. Semi-Spitzer Soft Point
.049" .342 .512

338 CALIBER - .338" Diameter
210 Gr. Spitzer Soft Point
.049" .263 .455

250 Gr. Spitzer Soft Point
.049" .313 .528

NEW 250 Gr. Round Nose "Super Solid"

300 Gr. Round Nose Soft Point
.049" .375 .416

300 Gr. Round Nose F.M.J.
.049" .375 .362

(.333 diameter also available)

348 WINCHESTER - .348" Diameter
250 Gr. Flat Nose Soft Point Cannelured
.032" .295 .327

35 CALIBER - .358" Diameter
200 Gr. Spitzer Soft Point
.032" .223 .319

250 Gr. Spitzer Soft Point
.032" .285 .407

275 Gr. Spitzer Soft Point
.049" .307 .470

300 Gr. Round Nose Soft Point
.032" .334 .371

300 Gr. Round Nose Soft Point
.049" .334 .371

300 Gr. Round Nose F.M.J.
.049" .334 .303

9.3 CALIBER - .366" Diameter
250 Gr. Spitzer Soft Point
.032" .267 .381

300 Gr. Spitzer Soft Point
.032" .320 .457

375 WINCHESTER - .375" Diameter
220 Gr. Flat Nose Soft Point Cannelured
.032" .223 .246

255 Gr. Flat Nose Soft Point Cannelured
.032" .259 .290

38/55 .375" and .377" Diameter
255 Gr. Flat Nose Soft Point Cannelured
.032" .259 .290

375 CALIBER - .375" Diameter
270 Gr. Spitzer Soft Point
.049" .275 .468

300 Gr. Spitzer Soft Point
.049" .305 .546

NEW 300 Gr. Round Nose "Super Solid"

350 Gr. Round Nose Soft Point
.049" .356 .370

350 Gr. Round Nose F.M.J.
.049" .356 .381

401 WINCHESTER - .406" Diameter
250 Gr. Round Nose Soft Point
.032" .217 .241

411 CALIBER - .411" Diameter
300 Gr. Semi-Spitzer Soft Point
.032" .254 .385

300 Gr. Semi-Spitzer Soft Point
.049" .254 .385

400 Gr. Round Nose Soft Point
.032" .338 .391

400 Gr. Round Nose Soft Point
.049" .338 .391

400 Gr. Round Nose F.M.J.
.049" .338 .399

(.408 Diameter also available)

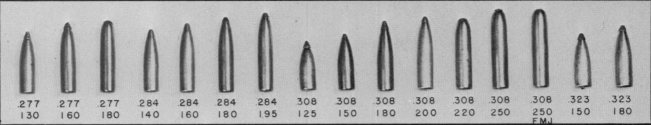

| .277 130 | .277 160 | .277 180 | .284 140 | .284 160 | .284 180 | .284 195 | .308 125 | .308 150 | .308 180 | .308 200 | .308 220 | .308 250 | .308 250 F.M.J. | .323 150 | .323 180 |

416 CALIBER - .416" Diameter

300 Gr. Semi-Spitzer Soft Point
.032" .284 .363

300 Gr. Semi-Spitzer Soft Point
.049" .284 .363

400 Gr. Round Nose Soft Point
.032" .330 .366

400 Gr. Round Nose Soft Point
.049 .330 .366

400 Gr. Round Nose F.M.J.
.049" .330 .376

NEW 400 Gr. Round Nose "Super Solid"

404 JEFFERY - .423" Diameter

400 Gr. Round Nose Soft Point
.032" .319 .354

400 Gr. Round Nose Soft Point
.049" .319 .354

400 Gr. Round Nose F.M.J.
.049" .319 .361

444 MARLIN / 44 MAGNUM - .430" Diameter

250 Gr. Flat Nose Soft Point Cannelured
.032" .193 .214

NEW 275 Gr. Flat Nose Soft Point Cannelured
.032" .212 .239

300 Gr. Flat Nose Soft Point Cannelured
.032" .232 .258

425 WESTLEY RICHARDS - .435" Diameter

410 Gr. Round Nose Soft Point
.049" .310 .344

410 Gr. Round Nose F.M.J.
.049" .310 .352

45/70 CALIBER - .458" Diameter

300 Gr. Semi-Spitzer Soft Point
.032" .204 .291

300 Gr. Flat Nose Soft Point Cannelured
.032" .204 .227

400 Gr. Semi-Spitzer Soft Point
.032" .272 .389

400 Gr. Flat Nose Soft Point Cannelured
.032" .272 .302

458 MAGNUM - .458" Diameter

400 Gr. Semi-Spitzer Soft Point
.049" .272 .389

400 Gr. Round Nose Soft Point
.049" .272 .302

500 Gr. Semi-Spitzer Soft Point
.049" .341 .487

500 Gr. Round Nose Soft Point
.049" .341 .379

NEW 500 Gr. Round Nose Soft Point
.070" .341 .379

500 Gr. Round Nose F.M.J.
.049" .341 .388

NEW 500 Gr. Round Nose "Super Solid"

600 Gr. Round Nose Soft Point
.049" .409 .454

600 Gr. Round Nose F.M.J.
.049" .409 .461

(.455 Diameter also available)

465 NITRO - .468" Diameter

500 Gr. Round Nose Soft Point
.049" .326 .362

500 Gr. Round Nose F.M.J.
.049" .326 .362

470 NITRO - .475"   A&M - .475" Diameter

500 Gr. Round Nose Soft Point
.049" .317 .352

500 Gr. Round Nose F.M.J.
.049" .317 .352

600 Gr. Round Nose Soft Point
.049" .380 .422

600 Gr. Round Nose F.M.J.
.049" .380 .422

475 No. 2 JEFFERY - .488" Diameter

500 Gr. Round Nose Soft Point
.049" .300 .333

500 Gr. Round Nose F.M.J.
.049" .300 .333

(.483 Diameter also available)

50 / 110 WINCHESTER - .510" Diameter

300 Gr. Flat Nose Soft Point Cannelured
.032" .165 .183

450 Gr. Flat Nose Soft Point Cannelured
.032" .247 .274

505 GIBBS - .505" Diameter

600 Gr. Round Nose Soft Point
.049" .336 .373

NEW 600 Gr. Round Nose Soft Point
.080" .336 .373

600 Gr. Round Nose F.M.J.
.049" .336 .373

700 Gr. Round Nose Soft Point
.049" .392 .436

700 Gr. Round Nose F.M.J.
.049" .392 .436

(.510 Diameter also available)

577 NITRO - .585" Diameter

*750 Gr. Round Nose Soft Point
.049" .313 .348

*750 Gr. Round Nose F.M.J.
.049" .313 .348

600 NITRO - .620" Diameter

*900 Gr. Round Nose Soft Point
.049" .334 .371

*900 Gr. Round Nose F.M.J.
.049" .334 .371

ALL BULLETS BOXED PER 50 EXCEPT *PER 20

FEDERAL SHOTSHELLS

HI-POWER® POWER MAGNUM LOADS — 25 rounds per box, 10 boxes per case.

LOAD NO.	GAUGE	SHELL LENGTH (INCHES)	POWDER DRAMS EQUIV.	OUNCES SHOT	SHOT SIZES	APPROX. CASE WT. (LBS.)	Retail Price Box
F103	10	3½	4¼	2	BB, 2,4	44	23.30
F131	12	3	4	1⅞	BB, 2,4	39	14.60
F129	12	3	4	1⅝	2,4, 6	36	13.50
F130	12	2¾	3¾	1½	BB, 2,4,5,6	33	12.20
F165	16	2¾	3¼	1¼	2,4, 6	28	12.00
F207	20	3	3	1¼	2,4, 6, 7½	27	11.30
F205	20	2¾	2¾	1⅛	4, 6, 7½	25	10.00

LIGHT MAGNUM LOADS — 25 rounds per box, 20 boxes per case. 500 rounds per case.

LOAD NO.	GAUGE	SHELL LENGTH	POWDER DRAMS EQUIV.	OUNCES SHOT	SHOT SIZES	APPROX. CASE WT.	Retail Price Box
F138	12	2¾	4	1⅜	4, 6, 7½	61	11.40

HI-POWER® LOADS — 25 rounds per box, 20 boxes per case. 500 rounds per case.

LOAD NO.	GAUGE	SHELL LENGTH	POWDER DRAMS EQUIV.	OUNCES SHOT	SHOT SIZES	APPROX. CASE WT.	Retail Price Box
F127	12	2¾	3¾	1¼	BB, 2,4,5,6, 7½,8, 9	57	9.90
F164	16	2¾	3¼	1⅛	4, 6, 7½	52	9.50
F203	20	2¾	2¾	1	4,5,6, 7½,8	45	8.70
F283	28	2¾	2¼	¾	6, 7½	37	8.75
F413	410	3	Max.	11⁄16	4,5,6, 7½,8	30	8.14
F412	410	2½	Max.	½	6, 7½	24	6.90

STEEL SHOT HI-POWER MAGNUM LOADS — 25 rounds per box, 10 boxes per case.

LOAD NO.	GAUGE	SHELL LENGTH	POWDER DRAMS EQUIV.	OUNCES SHOT	SHOT SIZES	APPROX. CASE WT.	Retail Price Box
W104	10	3½	Max.	1⅝	F,T,BB, 2	38	20.75
W149	12	3	Max.	1⅜	F,T,BB,1,2, 4	31	14.70
W140	12	3	Max.	1¼	BB,1,2, 4	32	13.50
W148	12	2¾	Max.	1¼	BB,1,2,3,4	28	13.50
W209	20	3	3¼	1	2, 4, 6	22	11.85

STEEL SHOT HI-POWER® LOADS — 25 rounds per box, 20 boxes per case. 500 rounds per case.

LOAD NO.	GAUGE	SHELL LENGTH	POWDER DRAMS EQUIV.	OUNCES SHOT	SHOT SIZES	APPROX. CASE WT.	Retail Price Box
W147	12	2¾	3¾	1⅛	BB, 2, 4, 6	54	12.40
W208	20	2¾	3	¾	4, 6	39	11.20

FIELD LOADS — 25 rounds per box, 20 boxes per case. 500 rounds per case.

LOAD NO.	GAUGE	SHELL LENGTH	POWDER DRAMS EQUIV.	OUNCES SHOT	SHOT SIZES	APPROX. CASE WT.	Retail Price Box
*F125	12	2¾	3¼	1¼	7½,8	56	10.15
F124	12	2¾	3¼	1¼	7½,8, 9	52	8.35
F123	12	2¾	3¼	1⅛	4, 6, 7½,8, 9	51	7.60
F162	16	2¾	2¾	1⅛	6, 7½,8	51	7.60
F202	20	2¾	2½	1	6, 7½,8	45	7.15

*Flyer Load

HI-SHOK® RIFLED SLUGS — 5 rounds per box, 50 boxes per case, 250 rounds per case.

LOAD NO.	GAUGE	SHELL LENGTH	POWDER DRAMS EQUIV.	OUNCES SHOT	SHOT SIZES	APPROX. CASE WT.	Retail Price Box
F103	10	3½	Mag.	1¾	Rifled Slug	40	5.65
New F131	12	3	Mag.	1¼	Rifled Slug	31	4.55
F130	12	2¾	Mag.	1¼	Rifled Slug	30	4.00
F127	12	2¾	Max.	1	Rifled Slug	26	3.25
F164	16	2¾	Max.	⅘	Rifled Slug	22	3.25
F203	20	2¾	Max.	¾	Rifled Slug	19	3.00
F412	410	2½	Max.	⅕	Rifled Slug	9	2.85

No split case orders accepted for shotshells

TRAP LOADS — 25 rounds per box, 20 boxes per case. 500 rounds per case.

LOAD NO.	GAUGE	SHELL LENGTH	POWDER DRAMS EQUIV.	OUNCES SHOT	SHOT SIZES	APPROX. CASE WT.	Retail Price Box
F114	12	2¾	**E.L.	1⅛	7½,8,8½	52	8.20
F115	12	2¾	2¾	1⅛	7½,8	52	8.20
F116	12	2¾	3	1⅛	7½,8	52	8.20
C117	12	2¾	2¾	1⅛	7½,8	54	8.20
C118	12	2¾	3	1⅛	7½,8	54	8.20
F113	12	2¾	2¾	1	8½	48	8.00

SKEET LOADS — 25 rounds per box, 20 boxes per case. 500 rounds per case.

LOAD NO.	GAUGE	SHELL LENGTH	POWDER DRAMS EQUIV.	OUNCES SHOT	SHOT SIZES	APPROX. CASE WT.	Retail Price Box
F114	12	2¾	**E.L.	1⅛	9	52	8.20
F115	12	2¾	2¾	1⅛	9	52	8.20
F116	12	2¾	3	1⅛	9	52	8.20
C117	12	2¾	2¾	1⅛	9	54	8.20
C118	12	2¾	3	1⅛	9	54	8.20
F206	20	2¾	2½	⅞	8, 9	41	7.65
F280	28	2¾	2	¾	9	37	9.05
F412	410	2½	Max.	½	9	24	7.45

SPECIAL SKEET LOAD — 25 rounds per box, 20 boxes per case. 500 rounds per case

LOAD NO.	GAUGE	SHELL LENGTH	POWDER DRAMS EQUIV.	OUNCES SHOT	SHOT SIZES	APPROX. CASE WT.	Retail Price Box
T122	12	2¾	3	1⅛	9	54	8.90

C117, C118 and T122 have paper tubes, all others are plastic
No split case orders accepted for shotshells.
**EXTRA-LITE ®

PREMIUM SHOTSHELLS

MAGNUM LOADS — 25 rounds per box, 10 boxes per case. 250 rounds per case.

LOAD NO.	GAUGE	SHELL LENGTH (INCHES)	POWDER DRAMS EQUIV.	OUNCES SHOT	SHOT SIZES	APPROX. CASE WT. (LBS.)	Retail Price Box
P109	10	3½	4½	2¼	BB, 2,4, 6	49	24.90
P159	12	3	4	2	BB, 2,4, 6	41	17.75
P158	12	3	4	1⅞	BB, 2,4, 6	39	16.60
P157	12	3	4	1⅝	2,4, 6	36	15.40
P156	12	2¾	4	1½	BB, 2,4, 6	33	14.50
P258	20	3	3	1¼	2,4, 6	27	12.85
P256	20	2¾	2¾	1⅛	4, 6	25	11.40

HI-POWER LOADS — 25 rounds per box, 20 boxes per case. 500 rounds per case.

LOAD NO.	GAUGE	SHELL LENGTH	POWDER DRAMS EQUIV.	OUNCES SHOT	SHOT SIZES	APPROX. CASE WT.	Retail Price Box
P154	12	2¾	3¾	1¼	4, 6, 7½	57	10.80
P254	20	2¾	2¾	1	6	45	9.40

FIELD LOADS — 25 rounds per box, 20 boxes per case. 500 rounds per case.

LOAD NO.	GAUGE	SHELL LENGTH	POWDER DRAMS EQUIV.	OUNCES SHOT	SHOT SIZES	APPROX. CASE WT.	Retail Price Box
P153	12	2¾	3¼	1¼	7½,8	56	9.45
P152	12	2¾	3¼	1⅛	7½	56	9.10
P252	20	2¾	2½	1	7½,8	45	8.30

BUCKSHOT — 10 rounds per box, 25 boxes per case. 250 rounds per case.

LOAD NO.	GAUGE	SHELL LENGTH	POWDER DRAMS EQUIV.	OUNCES SHOT	SHOT SIZES		APPROX. CASE WT.	Retail Price Box
New P158	12	3	Magnum	000 Buck,	10 Pellets	38	9.15
P158	12	3	Magnum	00 Buck,	15 Pellets	39	9.15
P158	12	3	Magnum	No. 4 Buck,	41 Pellets	40	9.15
New P158	12	3	Magnum	1 Buck,	24 Pellets	44	9.15
P156	12	2¾	Magnum	00 Buck,	12 Pellets	33	8.00
P156	12	2¾	Magnum	No. 4 Buck,	34 Pellets	34	8.00
P154	12	2¾	Max	00 Buck,	9 Pellets	28	6.85

HI-POWER MAGNUM BUCKSHOT — 5 rounds per box, 50 boxes per case. 250 rounds per case.

LOAD NO.	GAUGE	SHELL LENGTH	POWDER DRAMS EQUIV.	OUNCES SHOT	SHOT SIZES		APPROX. CASE WT.	Retail Price Box
G108	10	3½	Mag.	00 Buck	18 Pellets	52	5.35
G108	10	3½	Mag.	No. 4 Buck	54 Pellets	54	5.35
F131	12	3	Mag.	000 Buck	10 Pellets	38	4.00
F131	12	3	Mag.	00 Buck	15 Pellets	39	4.00
F131	12	3	Mag.	No. 1 Buck	24 Pellets	44	4.00
F131	12	3	Mag.	No. 4 Buck	41 Pellets	40	4.00
*A131	12	3	Mag.	No. 4 Buck	41 Pellets	40	20.00
F130	12	2¾	Mag.	00 Buck	12 Pellets	33	3.55
F130	12	2¾	Mag.	No. 1 Buck	20 Pellets	38	3.55
F130	12	2¾	Mag.	No. 4 Buck	34 Pellets	35	3.55
*A130	12	2¾	Mag.	No. 4 Buck	34 Pellets	35	17.60
F207	20	3	Mag.	No. 2 Buck	18 Pellets	30	3.55

*A131 and A130 are packed 25 rounds per box — 250 rounds per case.

HI-POWER BUCKSHOT — 5 rounds per box, 50 boxes per case. 250 rounds per case.

LOAD NO.	GAUGE	SHELL LENGTH	POWDER DRAMS EQUIV.	OUNCES SHOT	SHOT SIZES		APPROX. CASE WT.	Retail Price Box
F127	12	2¾	Max.	000 Buck	8 Pellets	30	2.80
F127	12	2¾	Max.	00 Buck	9 Pellets	27	2.80
F127	12	2¾	Max.	0 Buck	12 Pellets	32	2.80
F127	12	2¾	Max.	No. 1 Buck	16 Pellets	33	2.80
F127	12	2¾	Max.	No. 4 Buck	27 Pellets	30	2.80
F164	16	2¾	Max.	No. 1 Buck	12 Pellets	26	2.80
F203	20	2¾	Max.	No. 3 Buck	20 Pellets	25	2.80

FEDERAL 22 RIMFIRE CARTRIDGES

LOAD NO.	CARTRIDGES	BULLET TYPE	BULLET WEIGHT GRAINS	APPROX. CASE WT. (LBS.)	Retail Price Box

HI-POWER® 22's — 50 rounds per box, 100 boxes per case. 5000 rounds per case.

LOAD NO.	CARTRIDGES	BULLET TYPE	BULLET WEIGHT GRAINS	APPROX. CASE WT.	Retail Price Box
701	22 Short	Copper Plated	29	30	1.80
703	22 Short	Copper Plated, Hollow Pt	29	30	1.90
706	22 Long	Copper Plated	29	32	1.90
710	22 Long Rifle	Copper Plated	40	40	1.72
712	22 Long Rifle	Copper Plated, Hollow Pt	38	40	1.99
716	22 Long Rifle	#12 Shot	#12shot	34	4.58

HI-POWER® 22's — 100 PACK — 50 boxes per case. 5000 rounds per case.

LOAD NO.	CARTRIDGES	BULLET TYPE	BULLET WEIGHT GRAINS	APPROX. CASE WT.	Retail Price Box
810	22 Long Rifle	Copper Plated	40	45	3.44
812	22 Long Rifle	Copper Plated, Hollow Pt	38	45	3.98

MAGNUM 22's — 50 rounds per box, 100 boxes per case. 5000 rounds per case.

LOAD NO.	CARTRIDGES	BULLET TYPE	BULLET WEIGHT GRAINS	APPROX. CASE WT.	Retail Price Box
737	22 Long Rifle	Full Metal Jacket	40	50	6.25
747	22 Long Rifle	Jacketed Hollow Pt	40	50	6.25
	— 50 rounds per box, 50 boxes per case. 2500 rounds per case.				
New 757	22 Long Rifle	Jacketed Hollow Pt	50	25	6.25

SPITFIRE HYPER-VELOCITY 22's — 50 rounds per Sport-Pak™, 20 packs per carton, 6000 rounds per case.

LOAD NO.	CARTRIDGES	BULLET TYPE	BULLET WEIGHT GRAINS	APPROX. CASE WT.	Retail Price Box
720	22 Long Rifle	Truncated Cone, Solid	36	48	1.75
722	22 Long Rifle	Truncated Cone, Hollow Pt	33	45	1.99

No split case orders accepted for shotshells or 22's.

FEDERAL® AMMUNITION

FEDERAL CENTERFIRE RIFLE CARTRIDGES
20 rounds per box. 25 boxes per case, 500 rounds per case.

LOAD NO.	CARTRIDGES	BULLET TYPE	BULLET WEIGHT GRAINS	APPROX. CASE WT. (LBS.)	Retail Price Box
222A	222 Remington	Soft Point	50	15	9.00
222B	222 Remington	Metal Case Boat Tail	55	15	9.00
22250A	22-250 Remington	Soft Point	55	22	10.20
22250C	22-250 Remington	BLITZ, Hollow Point	40	21	10.55
223A	223 Rem., (5 56 mm)	Soft Point	55	15	9.85
223B	223 Rem., (5 56 mm)	Metal Case Boat Tail	55	15	9.85
223C	223 Rem., (5 56 mm)	Hollow Point Boat Tail	55	15	10.55
223D	223 Rem., (5 56 mm)	BLITZ, Hollow Point	40	14	10.55
6A	6 mm Remington	Soft Point	80	27	12.30
6B	6 mm Remington	Hi-Shok Soft Point	100	28	12.30
243A	243 Winchester	Soft Point	80	25	12.30
243B	243 Winchester	Hi-Shok Soft Point	100	27	12.30
257A	257 Roberts (High Vel · P)	Hi-Shok Soft Point	117	30	13.75
2506A	25-06 Remington	Hollow Point	90	28	13.35
2506B	25-06 Remington	Hi-Shok Soft Point	117	30	13.35
270A	270 Winchester	Hi-Shok Soft Point	130	31	13.35
270B	270 Winchester	Hi-Shok Soft Point	150	33	13.35
7A	7 mm Mauser	Hi-Shok Soft Point	175	33	13.60
7B	7 mm Mauser	Hi-Shok Soft Point	140	31	13.60
7RA	7 mm Rem. Magnum	Hi-Shok Soft Point	150	37	16.50
7RB	7 mm Rem. Magnum	Hi-Shok Soft Point	175	39	16.50
30CA	30 Carbine	Soft Point	110	16	8.55
30CB	30 Carbine	Metal Case	110	16	8.55
730A	7-30 Waters	Boat Tail Soft Point	120	25	12.35
3030A	30-30 Winchester	Hi-Shok Soft Point	150	27	10.45
3030B	30-30 Winchester	Hi-Shok Soft Point	170	28	10.45
3030C	30-30 Winchester	Hollow Point	125	25	10.45

We accept orders for split cases of centerfire — 5 boxes per individual load in increments of 5 boxes.

LOAD NO.	CARTRIDGES	BULLET TYPE	BULLET WEIGHT GRAINS	APPROX. CASE WT. (LBS.)	Retail Price Box
3006A	30-06 Springfield	Hi-Shok Soft Point	150	33	13.35
3006B	30-06 Springfield	Hi-Shok Soft Point	180	35	13.35
3006C	30-06 Springfield	Soft Point	125	31	13.35
3006D	30-06 Springfield	Boat Tail Soft Point	165	34	13.90
3006H	30-06 Springfield	Hi-Shok Soft Point	220	37	13.35
New 3006J	30-06 Springfield	Round Nose	180	35	13.35
300A	300 Savage	Hi-Shok Soft Point	150	30	13.50
300B	300 Savage	Hi-Shok Soft Point	180	32	13.50
300WB	300 Win. Magnum	Hi-Shok Soft Point	180	40	17.50
308A	308 Winchester	Hi-Shok Soft Point	150	31	13.35
308B	308 Winchester	Hi-Shok Soft Point	180	32	13.35
8A	8 mm Mauser	Hi-Shok Soft Point	170	32	13.75
32A	32 Win. Special	Hi-Shok Soft Point	170	29	11.15
35A	35 Remington	Hi-Shok Soft Point	200	32	12.30
†44A	44 Remington Magnum	Hollow Soft Point	240	29	10.20
4570A	45-70 Government	Hollow Soft Point	300	42	15.95

†For Rifle or Pistol
We accept orders for split cases of centerfire — 5 boxes per individual load in increments of 5 boxes.

NYCLAD® PISTOL CARTRIDGES — 50 rounds per box, 20 boxes per case, 1000 rounds per case.

LOAD NO.	CARTRIDGES	BULLET TYPE	GRAINS	CASE WT.	Price
New N9BP	9mm Luger Auto Pistol	Hollow Point	124	28	18.45
N38A	38 Special	Wadcutter	148	34	16.00
N38B	38 Special	Round Nose	158	35	15.15
N38C	38 Special	Semi-Wadcutter	158	35	16.00
N38G	38 Special (High Vel · P)	SW Hollow Point	158	35	17.55
N38H	38 Special (High Vel · P)	Semi-Wadcutter	158	35	17.55
N38M	38 Special	Hollow Point	125	30	17.55
N38N	38 Special (High Vel · P)	Hollow Point	125	30	17.55
N357C	357 Magnum	Semi-Wadcutter	158	37	19.55
N357E	357 Magnum	SW Hollow Point	158	39	19.55

FEDERAL CENTERFIRE PISTOL CARTRIDGES
50 rounds per box. 20 boxes per case. 1000 rounds per case.

LOAD NO.	CARTRIDGES	BULLET TYPE	GRAINS	CASE WT.	Box
*25AP	25 Auto Pistol (6.35mm)	Metal Case	50	12	6.60
32AP	32 Auto Pistol (7.65mm)	Metal Case	71	18	14.90
32LA	32 S&W Long	Lead Wadcutter	98	20	14.25
32LB	32 S&W Long	Lead Round Nose	98	20	13.25
32HRA	32 H&R Magnum	Lead Semi-Wadcutter	95	25	13.60
32HRB	32 H&R Magnum	Jacketed Hollow Point	85	21	16.50
380AP	380 Auto Pistol	Metal Case	95	23	15.25
380BP	380 Auto Pistol	Jacketed Hollow Point	90	22	15.25
9AP	9 mm Luger Auto Pistol	Metal Case	123	29	18.50
9BP	9 mm Luger Auto Pistol	Jacketed Hollow Point	115	28	18.50
9CP	9 mm Luger Auto Pistol	Jacketed Soft Point	95	28	18.50
38A	38 Special (Match)	Lead Wadcutter	148	34	14.65
38B	38 Special	Lead Round Nose	158	35	14.05
38C	38 Special	Lead Semi-Wadcutter	158	35	15.10
38D	38 Special (High Vel · P)	Lead Round Nose	158	35	15.60
38E	38 Special (High Vel · P)	Jacketed Hollow Point	125	30	17.80
38F	38 Special (High Vel · P)	Jacketed Hollow Point	110	28	17.80
38G	38 Special (High Vel · P)	Lead SW Hollow Point	158	34	15.25
38H	38 Special (High Vel · P)	Lead Semi-Wadcutter	158	35	15.60
38J	38 Special (High Vel · P)	Jacketed Soft Point	125	30	17.80
357A	357 Magnum	Jacketed Soft Point	158	39	19.55
357B	357 Magnum	Jacketed Hollow Point	125	34	19.55
357C	357 Magnum	Lead Semi-Wadcutter	158	37	16.55
357D	357 Magnum	Jacketed Hollow Point	110	30	19.55
357E	357 Magnum	Jacketed Hollow Point	158	39	19.55
357G	357 Magnum	Jacketed Hollow Point	180	44	19.55
41A	41 Remington Magnum	Jacketed Hollow Point	210	54	25.75
†44A	44 Remington Magnum	Hollow Soft Point	240	29	10.20
44B	44 Remington Magnum	Jacketed Hollow Point	180	50	25.55
**A44B	44 Remington Magnum	Jacketed Hollow Point	180	50	10.55
†44C	44 Remington Magnum	Metal Case Profile	220	56	27.20
44SA	44 S & W Special	Lead SW Hollow Point	200	50	19.65
45LCA	45 Colt	Lead SW Hollow Point	225	50	19.95
45A	45 Automatic (Match)	Metal Case	230	49	20.30
45B	45 Automatic (Match)	Metal Case, S.W.C.	185	42	21.45
45C	45 Automatic	Jacketed Hollow Point	185	42	21.45

†For Rifle or Pistol
*25AP packed 25 rounds per box   **A44B packed 20 rounds per box, 1000 rounds per case
We accept orders for split cases of centerfire — 5 boxes per individual load in increments of 5 boxes

PREMIUM CENTERFIRE RIFLE CARTRIDGES

LOAD NO.	CARTRIDGES	BULLET TYPE	BULLET WEIGHT GRAINS	APPROX. CASE WT. (LBS.)	Retail Price Box

20 rounds per box. 25 boxes per case 500 rounds per case

LOAD NO.	CARTRIDGES	BULLET TYPE	GRAINS	CASE WT.	Box
P22250B	22-250 Remington	Boat Tail Hollow Point	55	22	11.35
New P2506C	25-06 Remington	Boat-Tail Soft Point	117	30	14.79
P243C	243 Winchester	Boat Tail Soft Point	100	26	13.65
P243D	243 Winchester	Boat Tail Hollow Point	85	25	13.65
New P257B	257 Roberts (High Vel · P)	Nosler Partition	120	32	16.59
P270C	270 Winchester	Boat Tail Soft Point	150	32	14.79
P270D	270 Winchester	Boat Tail Soft Point	130	31	14.79
P270E	270 Winchester	Nosler Partition	150	32	17.99
P7RD	7mm Rem. Magnum	Boat Tail Soft Point	150	37	17.99
P7RE	7mm Rem. Magnum	Boat Tail Soft Point	165	38	17.99
P7RF	7mm Rem. Magnum	Nosler Partition	160	38	21.75
New P7RG	7mm Rem. Magnum	Nosler Partition	140	38	21.75
P3030D	30-30 Winchester	Nosler Partition	170	28	15.25
P3006D	30-06 Springfield	Boat Tail Soft Point	165	34	14.79
P3006F	30-06 Springfield	Nosler Partition	180	35	17.99
P3006G	30-06 Springfield	Boat Tail Soft Point	150	33	14.79
P300WC	300 Win. Magnum	Boat Tail Soft Point	200	41	18.95
P300WD	300 Win. Magnum	Nosler Partition	180	40	21.05
P308C	308 Winchester	Boat Tail Soft Point	165	31	14.79
P338A	338 Win. Magnum	Nosler Partition	210	31	21.45
New P338B	338 Win. Magnum	Nosler Partition	250	31	21.45

Terms of sale for these items are the same as set forth in our Hi-Power distributor price list

Nosler® BULLETS

Caliber	Diameter		Bullet Weight and Style
.22	.224″		45 Gr. Hornet
	.224″		50 Gr. Expander
	.224″		50 Gr. Spitzer
	224″		50 Gr. Hollow Point
	.224″		52 Gr. Spitzer
	.224″		52 Gr. Hollow Point
	.224″		52 Gr. Hollow Point Match
	.224″		55 Gr. Spitzer
	.224″		60 Gr. Spitzer
6 mm	.243″		70 Gr. Hollow Point
	.243″		70 Gr. Hollow Point Match
	.243″		75 Gr. Spitzer
	.243″		85 Gr. Spitzer
	.243″		100 Gr. Spitzer
.25	.257″		100 Gr. Spitzer
	.257″		120 Gr. Spitzer
6.5 mm	.264″		120 Gr. Spitzer
.270	.277″		130 Gr. Spitzer
	.277″		150 Gr. Spitzer
7 mm	.284″		120 Gr. Spitzer
	.284″		120 Gr. Flat Point
	.284″		140 Gr. Spitzer
	.284″		150 Gr. Spitzer
	.284″		162 Gr. Spitzer
.30	.308″		150 Gr. Flat Point
	.308″		150 Gr. Spitzer
	.308″		150 Gr. Hollow Point Match
	.308″		165 Gr. Spitzer
	.308″		168 Gr. Hollow Point Match
	.308″		170 Gr. Flat Point
	.308″		180 Gr. Spitzer

Caliber	Diameter		Bullet Weight and Style
.270	.277″		130 Gr. Ballistic Tip (Yellow)
	.277″		150 Gr. Ballistic Tip (Yellow)
7 mm	.284″		140 Gr. Ballistic Tip (Red)
	.284″		150 Gr. Ballistic Tip (Red)
.30	.308″		150 Gr. Ballistic Tip (Green)
	.308″		165 Gr. Ballistic Tip (Green)
	.308″		180 Gr. Ballistic Tip (Green)

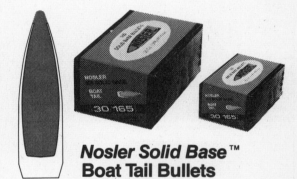

Nosler Solid Base™ Boat Tail Bullets

Competitively priced, Nosler Sold Base bullets offer both tighter groups and better game stopping power. The boat tail design improves the ballistic coefficient for better performance at long range.

Nosler Ballistic Tip™ Hunting Bullets

In this new series of Solid Base hunting bullets, Nosler has replaced the familiar lead point of the Spitzer with a tough polycarbonate tip. The purpose of this new Ballistic Tip is to resist deforming in the magazine and feed ramp of many rifles. The Solid Base design produces controlled expansion for excellent mushrooming and penetration.

Nosler® BULLETS

Caliber	Diameter		Bullet Weight and Style
6mm	.243"		95 Gr. Spitzer
	.243"		100 Gr. Spitzer
.25	.257"		100 Gr. Spitzer
	.257"		120 Gr. Spitzer
6.5 mm	.264"		125 Gr. Spitzer
	.264"		140 Gr. Spitzer
.270	.277"		130 Gr. Spitzer
	.277"		150 Gr. Spitzer
	.277"		160 Gr. Semi Spitzer
7 mm	.284"		140 Gr. Spitzer
	.284"		150 Gr. Spitzer
	.284"		160 Gr. Spitzer
	.284"		175 Gr. Semi Spitzer
.30	.308"		150 Gr. Spitzer
	.308"		165 Gr. Spitzer
	.308"		180 Gr. Spitzer
	.308"		180 Gr. Protected Point
	.308"		200 Gr. Spitzer
8 mm	.323"		200 Gr. Spitzer
.338	.338"		210 Gr. Spitzer
	.338"		250 Gr. Spitzer

Nosler Partition™ Bullets

The Nosler Partition bullet earned its reputation among professional guides and serious hunters for one reason: it doesn't fail. The patented Partition design offers a dual core that is unequalled in mushrooming weight retention and hydrostatic shock.

Nosler Handgun Bullets

Nearly four decades of bulletmaking experience have into producing Nosler jacketed handgun bullets. Manufactured by the industry's most advanced equipment, Nosler handgun bullets are made with the same care exercised in producing Partition, Solid Base and Ballistic Tip rifle bullets.

Caliber	Diameter		Bullet Weight and Style	Part Number
9mm	.355"		115 Gr. Full Metal Jacket	42059
.38	.357"		125 Gr. Hollow Point	42055
	.357"		150 Gr. Soft Point	42056
	.357"		158 Gr. Hollow Point	42057
	.357"		180 Gr. Non-Expanding Soft Point	42058
.44	.429"		200 Gr. Hollow Point	42060
	.429"		240 Gr. Hollow Point	42061
.45	.451"		185 Gr. Hollow Point	42062
	.451"		230 Gr. Full Metal Jacket	42064

Sierra Bullets

RIFLE

.22 Caliber Hornet (.223/5.66MM Diameter)

40 gr. Hornet Varminter #1100

45 gr. Hornet Varminter #1110

.22 Caliber Hornet (.224/5.69MM Diameter)

40 gr. Hornet Varminter #1200

45 gr. Hornet Varminter #1210

.22 Caliber (.224/5.69MM Diameter) High Velocity

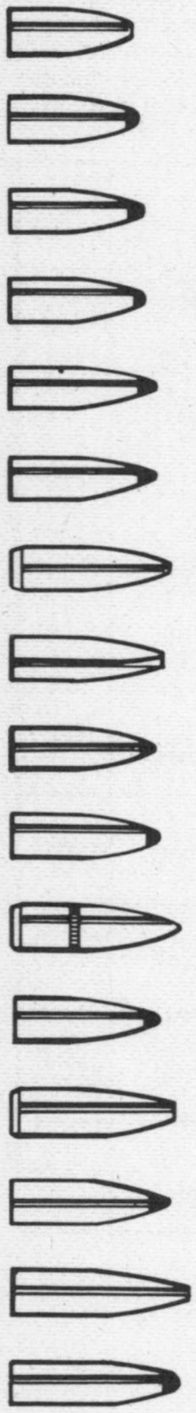

40 gr. HP Varminter #1385

45 gr. SMP Varminter #1300

45 gr. SPT Varminter #1310

50 gr. SMP Varminter #1320

50 gr. SPT Varminter #1330

50 gr. Blitz Varminter #1340

52 gr. HPBT MatchKing #1410

53 gr. HP MatchKing #1400

55 gr. Blitz Varminter #1345

55 gr. SMP Varminter #1350

55 gr. FMJBT GameKing #1355

55 gr. SPT Varminter #1360

55 gr. HPBT GameKing #1390

55 gr. SBT GameKing #1365

60 gr. HP Varminter #1375

63 gr. SMP Varminter #1370

69 gr. HPBT MatchKing #1380

6MM .243 Caliber (2.43/6.17MM Diameter)

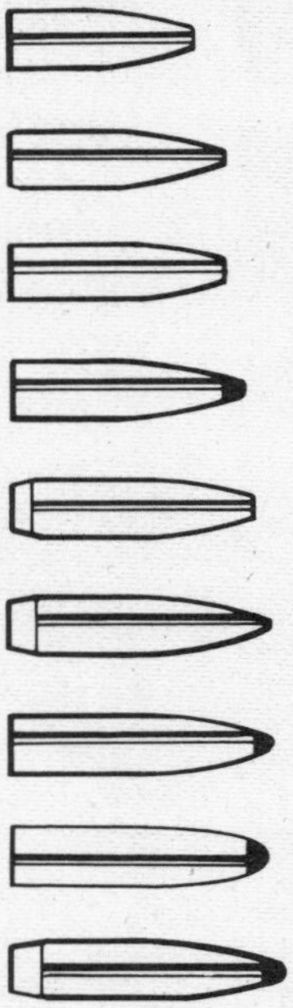

60 gr. HP Varminter #1500

70 gr. HPBT MatchKing #1505

75 gr. HP Varminter #1510

85 gr. SPT Varminter #1520

85 gr. HPBT GameKing #1530

90 gr. FMJBT GameKing #1535

100 gr. SPT Pro-Hunter #1540

100 gr. SMP Pro-Hunter #1550

100 gr. SBT GameKing #1560

.25 Caliber (.257/6.53MM Diameter)

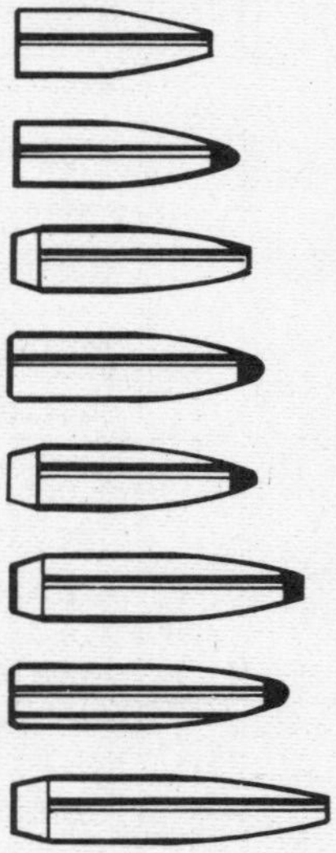

75 gr. HP Varminter #1600

87 gr. SPT Varminter #1610

90 gr. HPBT GameKing #1615

100 gr. SPT Pro-Hunter #1620

100 gr. SBT GameKing #1625

117 gr. SBT GameKing #1630

117 gr. SPT Pro-Hunter #1640

120 gr. HPBT GameKing #1650

6.5MM .264 Caliber (.264/6.71MM Diameter)

85 gr. HP Varminter #1700

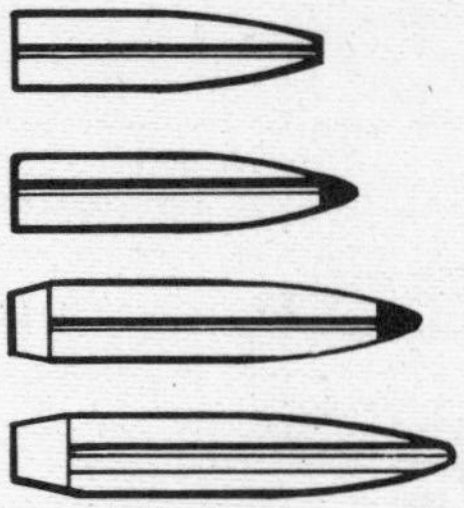

100 gr. HP Varminter #1710

120 gr. SPT Pro-Hunter #1720

140 gr. SBT GameKing #1730

140 gr. HPBT MatchKing #1740

7MM .284 Caliber (.284/7.21MM Diameter)

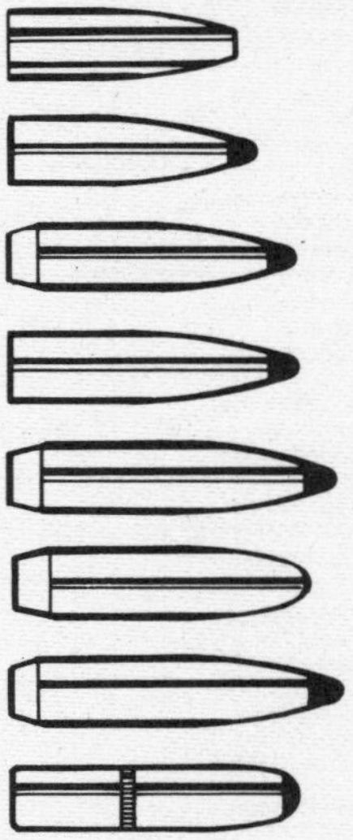

90 gr. HP Varminter #1800

110 gr. SPT Pro-Hunter #1810

130 gr. SBT GameKing #1820

130 gr. SPT Pro-Hunter #1830

140 gr. SBT GameKing #1845

140 gr. HPBT GameKing #1835

150 gr. SBT GameKing #1840

150 gr. RN Pro-Hunter #1850

.270 Caliber (.277/7.04MM Diameter)

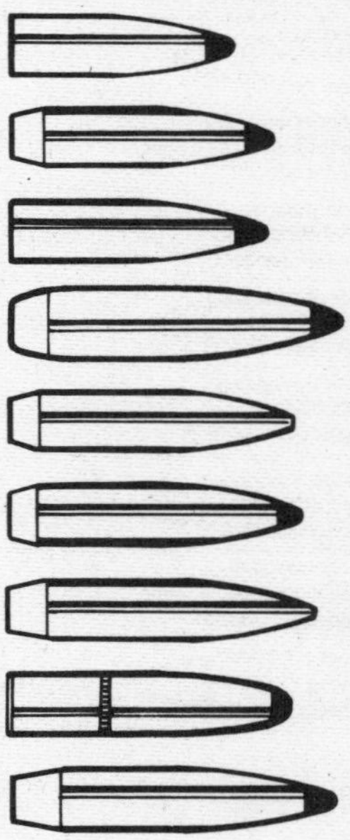

120 gr. SPT Pro-Hunter #1900

140 gr. SBT GameKing #1905

140 gr. SPT Pro-Hunter #1910

NEW 150 gr. SBT GameKing #1913

150 gr. HPBT MatchKing #1915

160 gr. SBT GameKing #1920

168 gr. HPBT MatchKing #1930

170 gr. RN Pro-Hunter #1950

175 gr. SBT GameKing #1940

.30 (30-30)Caliber
(.308/7.82MM Diameter)

125 gr. HP
Pro-Hunter #2020

150 gr. FN
Pro-Hunter #2000

170 gr. FN
Pro-Hunter #2010

.30 Caliber 7.62MM
(.308/7.82MM Diameter)

110 gr. RN
Pro-Hunter #2100

110 gr. FMJ
Pro-Hunter #2105

110 gr. HP
Varminter #2110

125 gr. SPT
Pro-Hunter #2120

150 gr. FMJBT
GameKing #2115

150 gr. SPT
Pro-Hunter #2130

150 gr. SBT
GameKing #2125

150 gr. HPBT
MatchKing #2190

150 gr. RN
Pro-Hunter #2135

165 gr. SBT
GameKing #2145

165 gr. HPBT
GameKing #2140

168 gr. HPBT
MatchKing #2200

180 gr. SPT
Pro-Hunter #2150

180 gr. SBT
GameKing #2160

*180 gr. HPBT
MatchKing #2220

*New & Improved. The angle of boat tail has been increased to allow more bearing surface, providing substantial improvement in bullet accuracy. Now one of the most accurate in the Sierra line.

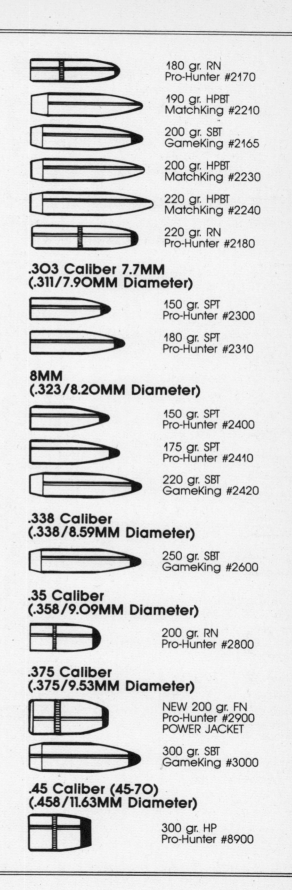

180 gr. RN
Pro-Hunter #2170

190 gr. HPBT
MatchKing #2210

200 gr. SBT
GameKing #2165

200 gr. HPBT
MatchKing #2230

220 gr. HPBT
MatchKing #2240

220 gr. RN
Pro-Hunter #2180

.303 Caliber 7.7MM
(.311/7.90MM Diameter)

150 gr. SPT
Pro-Hunter #2300

180 gr. SPT
Pro-Hunter #2310

8MM
(.323/8.20MM Diameter)

150 gr. SPT
Pro-Hunter #2400

175 gr. SPT
Pro-Hunter #2410

220 gr. SBT
GameKing #2420

.338 Caliber
(.338/8.59MM Diameter)

250 gr. SBT
GameKing #2600

.35 Caliber
(.358/9.09MM Diameter)

200 gr. RN
Pro-Hunter #2800

.375 Caliber
(.375/9.53MM Diameter)

NEW 200 gr. FN
Pro-Hunter #2900
POWER JACKET

300 gr. SBT
GameKing #3000

.45 Caliber (45-70)
(.458/11.63MM Diameter)

300 gr. HP
Pro-Hunter #8900

Sierra Bullets

HANDGUN

.25 Caliber
(.251/6.38MM Diameter)

50 gr. FMJ
SportsMaster #8000

.32 Caliber 7.65MM
(.312/7.92MM Diameter)

71 gr. FMJ
Tournament Master #8010

.32 Mag. .312/7.92MM Diameter

NEW 90 gr. JHC
Sports Master #8030
POWER JACKET

9MM .355 Caliber
(.355/9.02MM Diameter)

90 gr. JHP
Sports Master #8100
POWER JACKET

95 gr. FMJ
Tournament Master #8105

115 gr. JHP
Sports Master #8110
POWER JACKET

115 gr. FMJ
Tournament Master #8115

125 gr. FMJ
Tournament Master #8120

130 gr. FMJ
Tournament Master #8345

.38 Caliber
(.357/9.07MM Diameter)

110 gr. JHC Blitz
Sports Master #8300

125 gr. JSP
Sports Master #8310

125 gr. JHC
Sports Master #8320
POWER JACKET

140 gr. JHC
Sports Master #8325
POWER JACKET

158 gr. JHC
Sports Master #8360
POWER JACKET

158 gr. JSP
Sports Master #8340

170 gr. JHC
Sports Master #8365
POWER JACKET

170 gr. FMJ Match
Tournament Master #8350

180 gr. FJP Match
Tournament Master #8370

.41 Caliber
(.410/10.41MM Diameter)

170 gr. JHC
Sports Master #8500
POWER JACKET

210 gr. JHC
Sports Master #8520
POWER JACKET

220 gr. FPJ Match
Tournament Master
#8530

.44 Magnum
(.4295/10.91MM Diameter)

180 gr. JHC
Sports Master #8600
POWER JACKET

210 gr. JHC
Sports Master #8620
POWER JACKET

220 gr. FPJ Match
Tournament Master
#8605

240 gr. JHC
Sports Master #8610
POWER JACKET

250 gr. FPJ Match
Tournament Master
#8615

.45 Caliber
(.4515/11.47MM Diameter)

185 gr. JHP
Sports Master #8800
POWER JACKET

185 gr. FPJ Match
Tournament Master
#8810

200 gr. FPJ Match
Tournament Master
#8825

230 gr. FMJ Match
Tournament Master
#8815

240 gr. JHC
Sports Master #8820
POWER JACKET

NEW Single Shot
Pistol Bullets

NEW
7MM .284 Dia. 130 gr. SPT
Pro-Hunter #7250

NEW
7MM .243 Dia. 80 gr. SPT
Pro-Hunter #7150

NEW
30 Cal. .308 Dia. 135 gr. SPT
Pro-Hunter #7350

Abbreviations:

SBT—Spitzer Boat Tail
SPT—Spitzer
HP—Hollow Point

JHP—Jacketed
    Hollow Point
JHC—Jacketed
    Hollow Cavity

JSP—Jacketed
    Soft Point
FN—Flat Nose

RN—Round Nose
FMJ—Full Metal Jacket
HPBT—Hollow Point
    Boat Tail

SMP—Semi-Pointed
FPH—Full Profile Jacket
FMJBT—Full Metal Jacket
    Boat Tail

Hornady Bullets... A complete selection for every shooting purpose.

RIFLE BULLETS "I" denotes interlock bullets.

■ 17 CALIBER (.172)

25 gr. HP.............#1710

■ 22 CALIBER (.222)

40 gr. Jet.............#2210

■ 22 CALIBER (.223)

45 gr. Hornet.........#2220

■ 22 CALIBER (.224)

45 gr. Hornet.........#2230

50 gr. SPSX..........#2240

50 gr. SP.............#2245

■ 22 CALIBER MATCH

52 gr. BTHP..........#2249

■ 22 CALIBER MATCH

53 gr. HP.............#2250

55 gr. SPSX..........#2260

55 gr. SP.............#2265

55 gr. SP w/c .....#2266

55 gr. FMJ-BT w/c..#2267

60 gr. SP.............#2270

60 gr. HP.............#2275

■ 22 CALIBER MATCH

68 gr. BTHP .....#2278

■ 22 CALIBER (.227)

70 gr. SP.............#2280

■ 6MM CALIBER (.243)

70 gr. SP.............#2410

70 gr. SPSX ......#2415

75 gr. HP.............#2420

80 gr. FMJ..........#2430

87 gr. SP.............#2440

87 gr. BTHP..#2442

I 100 gr. SP .....#2450

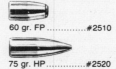

I 100 gr. BTSP ....#2453

I 100 gr. RN..........#2455

■ 25 CALIBER (.257)

60 gr. FP.............#2510

75 gr. HP.............#2520

87 gr. SP.............#2530

I 100 gr. SP.............#2540

I 117 gr. RN...........#2550

I 117 gr. BTSP ....#2552

I 120 gr. HP...........#2560

■ 6.5MM CALIBER (.264)

100 gr. SP.............#2610

I 129 gr. SP...........#2620

I 140 gr. SP...........#2630

■ 6.5 MM CALIBER MATCH

140 gr. BTHP......#2633

I 160 gr. RN...........#2640

■ 270 CALIBER (.277)

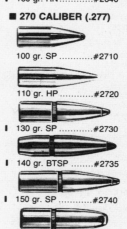

100 gr. SP ....#2710

110 gr. HP ....#2720

I 130 gr. SP ....#2730

140 gr. BTSP ....#2735

I 150 gr. SP ....#2740

I 150 gr. RN...........#2745

■ 7MM CALIBER (.284)

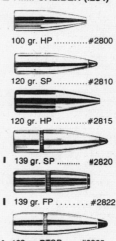

100 gr. HP ....#2800

120 gr. SP ....#2810

120 gr. HP ....#2815

I 139 gr. SP ....#2820

I 139 gr. FP ....#2822

I 139 gr. BTSP .....#2825

I 154 gr. SP ....#2830

I 154 gr. RN...........#2835

■ 7MM MATCH

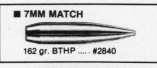

162 gr. BTHP .....#2840

I 162 gr. BTSP .....#2845

I 175 gr. SP ....#2850

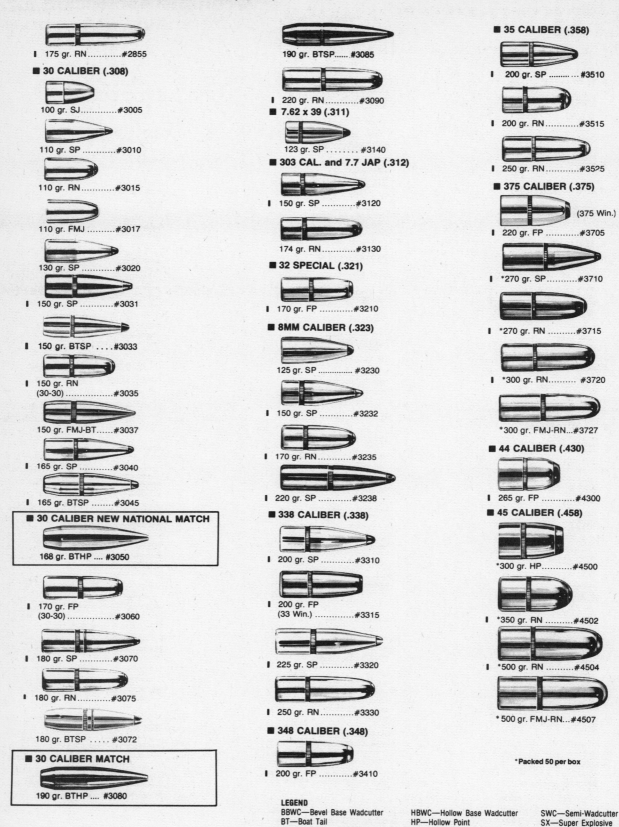

I 175 gr. RN ....#2855

■ **30 CALIBER (.308)**

100 gr. SJ ....#3005

110 gr. SP ....#3010

110 gr. RN ....#3015

110 gr. FMJ ....#3017

130 gr. SP ....#3020

I 150 gr. SP ....#3031

I 150 gr. BTSP .... #3033

I 150 gr. RN
(30-30) ....#3035

150 gr. FMJ-BT......#3037

I 165 gr. SP ....#3040

I 165 gr. BTSP ....#3045

■ **30 CALIBER NEW NATIONAL MATCH**

168 gr. BTHP .... #3050

I 170 gr. FP
(30-30) ....#3060

I 180 gr. SP ....#3070

I 180 gr. RN ....#3075

180 gr. BTSP ..... #3072

■ **30 CALIBER MATCH**

190 gr. BTHP .... #3080

190 gr. BTSP......#3085

I 220 gr. RN ....#3090

■ **7.62 x 39 (.311)**

123 gr. SP .... #3140

■ **303 CAL. and 7.7 JAP (.312)**

I 150 gr. SP ....#3120

174 gr. RN ....#3130

■ **32 SPECIAL (.321)**

I 170 gr. FP ....#3210

■ **8MM CALIBER (.323)**

125 gr. SP .... #3230

I 150 gr. SP ....#3232

I 170 gr. RN ....#3235

I 220 gr. SP ....#3238

■ **338 CALIBER (.338)**

I 200 gr. SP ....#3310

I 200 gr. FP
(33 Win.) ....#3315

I 225 gr. SP ....#3320

I 250 gr. RN ....#3330

■ **348 CALIBER (.348)**

I 200 gr. FP ....#3410

■ **35 CALIBER (.358)**

I 200 gr. SP .... #3510

I 200 gr. RN ....#3515

I 250 gr. RN ....#3525

■ **375 CALIBER (.375)**

(375 Win.)

I 220 gr. FP ....#3705

I *270 gr. SP...........#3710

I *270 gr. RN ....#3715

I *300 gr. RN......... #3720

*300 gr. FMJ-RN...#3727

■ **44 CALIBER (.430)**

I 265 gr. FP ....#4300

■ **45 CALIBER (.458)**

*300 gr. HP..........#4500

*350 gr. RN ....#4502

I *500 gr. RN ....#4504

* 500 gr. FMJ-RN...#4507

*Packed 50 per box

LEGEND

BBWC—Bevel Base Wadcutter	HBWC—Hollow Base Wadcutter	SWC—Semi-Wadcutter
BT—Boat Tail	HP—Hollow Point	SX—Super Explosive
DEWC—Double End Wadcutter	RN—Round Nose	JTC—Jacketed Truncated Cone
FMJ—Full Metal Jacket	SJ—Short Jacket	SIL—Silhouette
FP—Flat Point	SP—Spire Point	

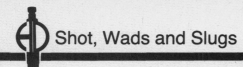

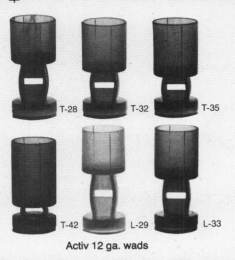

T-28 T-32 T-35
T-42 L-29 L-33

Activ 12 ga. wads

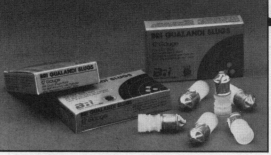

BRI Gualandi Slug

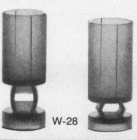

Activ 20-ga. wads

W-28 W-32

Notes on Shot, Wads and Slugs . . .

There are three basic wad types: over-powder, filler and overshot. The over-powder wads are available in card form (made of compressed paper), or as plastic wads. The over-powder wad separates the powder from the softer filler wads and effects a gas seal ahead of the powder. Filler wads are resilient to cushion the initial shock, and are available in a variety of thicknesses to give the proper wad column height for perfect crimps and correct pressure. Since the majority of shotshells loaded today are star crimped, they need no overshot wad. Only the older roll crimp shells require a wad which is held by the crimp to contain the shot.

Over-shot wads are made of compressed paper, similar to the over-powder type.

Lead shot is available from a number of makers in quite an array of sizes, ranging generally from #8 (.09″) to 000 buck (.36″) in the really useful sizes. Different grades of hardness are also offered, as well as plated shot for optimum performance.

Steel-shot reloading is now becoming reality as our technology increases, but this area of handloading is still somewhat clouded. The beginning reloader should leave this activity to the experts.

Hunting big game with shotgun slugs is popular and there are now a number of makers offering excellent new designs that give heretofore unheard of accuracy from smoothbores.

ACTIV Plastic Wads

These wads use a straight wall design for excellent tube resistance and are color coded to avoid reloading accidents and confusion. From ACTIV Industries.

Activ Plastic Wads

Model	Gauge	Color	Loads (oz.)	Per M
T-28	12	Green	1, 1⅛	$22.37
T-32	12	Yellow	1⅛, 1¼	22.37
T-35	12	Blue	1¼, 1⅜	22.37
T-42	12	Red	1½, 1⅝	22.37
L-29	12	White	1	22.37
L-33	12	Brown	1⅛	22.37
W-28	20	White	1	22.37
W-32	20	Yellow	1⅛	22.37

AMERICAN WAD

This black wad is moulded with a deep, tapered powder cup which gives an efficient gas seal. The design of the "X" mid-section provides even pressure on the shot column. The American Wad was designed for the trap shooter using a 1⅛-oz. shot load, but also works well with 1-oz. or 1¼-oz. loads. It will fit any standard shell such as Winchester, Remington and Federal. Load data available from American Products Inc. Price per M **$14.80**

BRI Gualandi Slug

This unibody full-bore slug has an integral base wad for stability and a conical nose for efficient air flow to deliver exceptional accuracy. Parallel driving bands insure an effective seal. Preset fractures break the slug into two parts upon impact, enlarging the wound cavity. Available in 12, 16, 20, 410 and police 12-ga. alloy models, loaded and in handloader sets. Contact Ballistic Research Industries for full data. Price **NA**

BRI Shotgun Slug

Designed for shotgun of big game, the BRI slug is a 50 cal. sabot bullet weighing 440 grains. The two-piece sabot falls away after leaving the muzzle. Made in 12 gauge only, it is available as loaded rounds or in handloading sets. Available from Ballistic Research Industries. Price . . . . **NA**

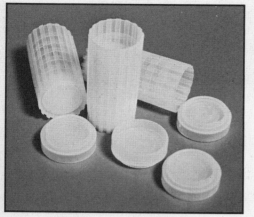

Ballistic Products BP-12 and gas seal

Ballistic Products
12-ga. Gas Seal

Ballistic Products
10-ga. Pattern Driver

Ballistic Products BPD 10-ga. Shotcups

BALLISTIC PRODUCTS
A-Q Round Ball Slugs

A 12-gauge 2¾" only slug with two-piece construction. Weighs a total of 1 ounce. The slug has a 12-bore tight fitting diameter that assures alignment during firing. The body is plastic with 10 spiral fins for spin. Load data comes with the slugs. From Ballistic Products Inc.
Price: Per 25 . . . . **$9.95**

BALLISTIC PRODUCTS
Slugmaster Shotgun Slugs

Hollowpoint slugs with fracture lines moulded into the body. This design allows the slug to burst apart into three parts upon contact. Available in 20 (275-gr., ⅝-oz.), 16 (339-gr., ¾-oz.) and 12 (410-gr., ⅞-oz.) gauges. They come in packs of 25. From Ballistic Products Inc. **$4.95**

BALLISTIC PRODUCTS
10-Gauge Tuff BPD and BP-12 12-Gauge Wads

A wad for both lead and steel loads. The "vented" design allows bleed-off when peak pressures are reached and provides good speeds with magnum loads. Special loading data and information included. From Ballistic Products, Inc.
Price: 100 10-gauge wads **$8.95**
Price: 100 12-gauge wads **$8.95**

Ballistic Products
12-ga. Magnum Shotcup

BALLISTIC PRODUCTS
Shot

BPI offers Super Buck Shot (3% antimony), Nickel-Plated Lead Shot (imported from Italy and extra penetrating), Magnum Lead Shot (extra hard), Copper-Plated Lead Shot, and Steel Shot. From Ballistic Products Inc.

BALLISTIC PRODUCTS
Overshot Wads

These wads are designed to be used with buffered shot loads and are offered in three sizes: .100" Nitro Cards; .030" Overshot Cards; ½" Fiber. Available in the following gauges; 8, 9, 10, 11, 12, 13, 14, 16, 20, 28 and 410. From Ballistic Products.
Price: .100" Nitro Cards, per 1000 . . . . **$5.95**
Price: .030" Overshot Cards, per 1000 . . . . **$5.95**
Price: ½" Fiber wads, per 500 . **$5.95**

Shot Size		Price/11 lbs. Nickel Lead	Price/10 lbs. Copper Lead	Price/lbs. Magnum Lead	Price/5 lbs. Steel Shot
000 Buck	.36"			$12.95/10	
00 Buck	.34"			12.95/10	
0 Buck	.32"			12.95/10	
1 Buck	.30"			12.95/10	
2 Buck	.27"			12.95/10	
3 Buck	.25"			12.95/10	
4 Buck	.24"			12.95/10	
F	.22"			12.95/10	
T	.20"			12.95/10	
BB	.18"	$18.95	$12.95		
1	.16"	18.95			
2	.15"	18.95	12.95	15.95/25	
3	.14"	18.95			
4	.13"	18.95	12.95	15.95/25	
5	.12"	18.95	12.95	15.95/25	
6	.11"	18.95	12.95	15.95/25	
7	.10"	18.95			
7½	.095"	18.95	12.95	15.95/25	
8	.09"	18.95		15.95/25	
Steel Shot					
F	.218"				$10.95
T	.200"				10.95
BB	.1875"				10.95
2	.156"				10.95
3	.140"				10.95
4	.125"				10.95

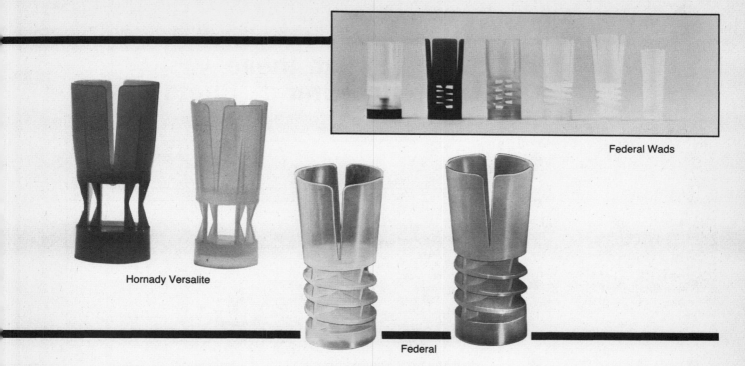

Hornady Versalite

Federal

Federal Wads

BALLISTIC PRODUCTS
Wool Felt Wads

Wool felt wads like the old-timers used. Made to fit the BPD 12-gauge shotcup (20-gauge wad), BPD 10-gauge shotcup (20-gauge wad) and BPD-Tuff 10-gauge cup (12-gauge wad). Comes in ⅛", ¼", ½" and ¾" thicknesses. From Ballistic Products, Inc.

20-Gauge Wads
Price: 250 ⅛" wads **$6.95**
Price: 250 ¼" wads **$6.95**
Price: 100 ½" wads **$5.95**
Price: 100 ¾" wads **$7.95**
12-Gauge Wads
Price: 250 ⅛" wads **$6.95**
Price: 250 ¼" wads **$7.95**

BALLISTIC PRODUCTS
Cardboard Spreader Wads

An "X" pattern of cardboard that goes down on the wad or inside the shotcup. Available for 20, 16, 12 and 10 gauge. The 250 pieces make 125 spreader loads. From Ballistic Products, Inc. **$3.95**

BALLISTIC PRODUCTS
12-Gauge Hard Cardboard Wads

These are ½" hard cardboard wads for buckshot and special Skeet loads for 12-gauge only. Wads are packaged 100 to a bag. From Ballistic Products, Inc. Per bag **$2.95**

BALLISTIC PRODUCTS
BPD 10-Gauge Pattern Driver Shotcups

Designed for extended range shooting. One-piece construction for 1½-oz. to 2½-oz. loads. can be used with shot, buck shot and slug loads. From Ballistic Products, Inc. Per bag of 100 . . . . **$6.95**

BALLISTIC PRODUCTS
BP12 Shotcup and Gas Seal

Designed to be used when reloading with slower burning powders. Loads 1¼-oz. to 1⅝-oz. in both 2¾" and 3" hulls. Ribbed body with tapered base. BP12 shotcups and BPGS Gas Seals come 250 to the bag. From Ballistic Products, Inc.
Price: BP12 Shotcups, per bag **$6.95**
Price: BPGS Gas Seals, per bag **$6.95**

BRENNEKE
Rifled Slugs

The Brenneke slug has a cylindrical head with a hemispherical tip of hard lead alloy. A felt wad between two discs is screwed to the rear. The 12 diagonal ribs around the slug are readily compressible and are pressed uniformly flat inside any choke bore. Can be fired from any smoothbore, regardless of choke. Available in 12, 16 and 20 gauge. From Old Western Scrounger, Inc.
Price: Per 25 . . . . **$10.00**

FEDERAL CARTRIDGE CO.
Shotshell Wads

Plastic Wad Columns

Type	Gauge	Number	Price/M
Champion	12	12C1	$31.10
Gold Medal	12	12SO	28.80
Gold Medal	12	12S3	28.80
Gold Medal	12	12S4	28.80
Gold Medal	20	20S1	28.80
Gold Medal	28	28S1	28.80
2½"	410	410SC	28.80

Packed 250 per bag, 20 bags per case of 5,000

HORNADY
Versalite Wads

A compressible center section in this wad will adjust to the correct wad column length. Available in 12 and 20 gauge, the Versalite provides an excellent gas seal and shot protection. Shot cup is slightly flared to slip easily over the wad seating punch. From Hornady Mfg. Co.
12 or 20 ga., per M **$23.00**

LAGE UNIWAD

This universal wad allows a change of powder charge for different cases and still stacks the proper height for a good crimp. Designed for 1⅛ oz. trap and Skeet loads, but it can be used for hunting loads too. Available in 12 and 20 gauge only. From Lage Uniwad Co.
Per M about . . . . **N.A.**

Check Lawrence Brand® Shot Sizes by these circles.

No. 12 .05	No. 11 .06	No. 10 .07
No. 9 .08	No. 8 .09	No. 7½ .095
No. 6 .11		No. 5 .12
No. 4 .13		No. 2 .15
BB .18	T .20	No. 4 .24
No. 3 Buck .25	No. 1 Buck .30	No. 0 Buck .32
No. 00 Buck .33	No. 000 Buck .36	

The circles printed here enable you to accurately check sizes of lead shot from No. 12 through 000 Buck. As you well know, the diameter increases by .01" for each number size from 2 through 12. Half sizes, like No. 7½, increase by .005" over the diameter of the full number (No. 7) preceding it.

The ounce counts shown apply to regular production packaging of Lawrence Brand® Magnum High Antimony Shot, counted pellet by pellet from a stock package. Although there is a "commercially acceptable" tolerance for "over" and "under" sizes, variations in Lawrence Brand® Shot sizes are held to a minimum. The shooter, target or hunter, can feel confident that his loads contain very close to the number of pellets indicated.

Choose from these Lawrence Brand® Shots

Chilled, Highly polished, uniformly round, accurately sized, and consistently dense. Graphite coated.

Type of Shot	Shot Name or Number	Diameter (in.)	Pellets/Ounce (approx.) Std. Chill Alloy	Weight/ Cu. Ft. (lb.)
Graphite-Coated	No. 12	.05	2335	435
LAWRENCE BRAND®	No. 11	.06	1350	435
CHILL SHOT	No. 10	.07	850	434
(American Standard)	No. 9	.08 (skeet)	570	426
Equivlent Hardness Factor:	No. 8½	.085 (trap)	475	426
Game Sizes	No. 8	.09 (trap)	400	436
BB, 2, 4, 5, 6-1% Antimonial Lead Alloy	No. 7½	.095 (game, trap)	340	
Target Sizes	No. 6	.11 (game)	220	435
7½, 8, 9-2% Antimonial	No. 5	.12 (game)	168	
Lead Alloy	No. 4	.13 (game)	132	439
	No. 2	.15 (game)	86	
	No. BB	.18 (game)	50	

High-Antimony Magnum Shot. Matches the performance of premier factory round ammunition, resulting in tight patterns, shorter strings, maximum density, and greater range. Graphite coated.

Type of Shot	Shot Name or Number	Diameter (in.)	Pellets/ Ounce (approx.)	Weight/ Cu. Ft. (lb.)
Graphite Coated	No. 9	.08	585	426
LAWRENCE BRAND®	No. 8½	.085	490	426
HIGH ANTIMONY MAGNUM SHOT	No. 8	.09	410	436
(American Standard)	No. 7½	.095	350	436
Equivlent Hardness Factor:	No. 6	.11	225	435
Game/Target Sizes	No. 5	.12	170	437
BB, 2-2% Antimonial Lead Alloy	No. 4	.13	135	439
4, 5-3% Antimonial Lead Alloy	No. 2	.15	87	440
6, 9-4% Antimonial Lead Alloy	No. BB	.18	50	442
7½, 8, 8½-6% Antimonial Lead Alloy				

Copper-Plated Magnum Shot. Retains more shot with less deformation, in shorter shot strings, at maximum velocity and penetration. Results: uniformly superior patterns required for long-range hunting. Wax coated.

Type of Shot	Shot Name or Number	Diameter (in.)	Pellets/ Ounce (approx.)	Weight/ Cu. Ft. (lb.)
Wax-Coated LAWRENCE BRAND® HIGH ANTIMONY COPPER-PLATED				
MAGNUM SHOT	No. 7½	.095	359	435
(American Standard)	No. 6	.11	226	435
Equivlent Hardness Factor:	No. 5	.12	172	437
Game/Target Sizes	No. 4	.13	135	439
BB, 2-2% Antimonial Lead Alloy	No. 2	.15	88	440
4, 5-3% Antimonial Lead Alloy	No. BB	.18	52	442
6, 9-4% Antimonial Lead Alloy				
7½, 8-6% Antimonial Lead Alloy				

Type of Shot	Shot Name or Number	Diameter (in.)	Balls/ Pound (approx.)	Weight/ Cu. Ft. (lb.)
Graphite-Coated	No. 4	.24	340	424
LAWRENCE BRAND®	No. 3	.25	299	426
BUCK SHOT	No. 2	.27	238	428
(American Standard)	No. 1	.30	152	437
	No. 0	.32	144	437
Composition: 100% Lead	No. 00	.33	130	437
	No. 000	.36	112	437
	No. T	.20	544	426

Ljutic Mono Wad

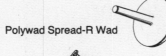

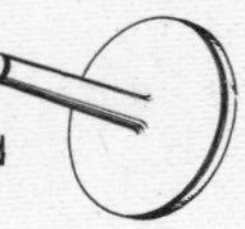

Polywad Spread-R Wad

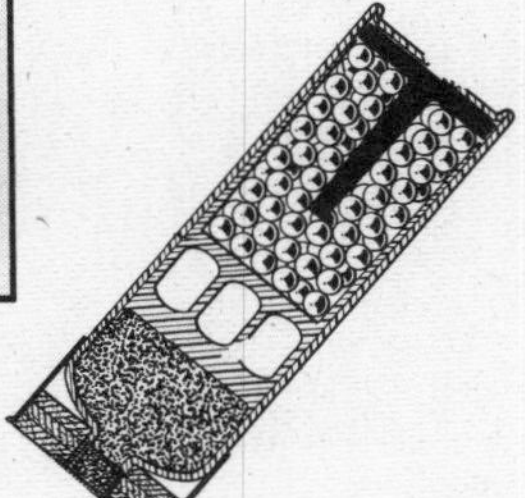

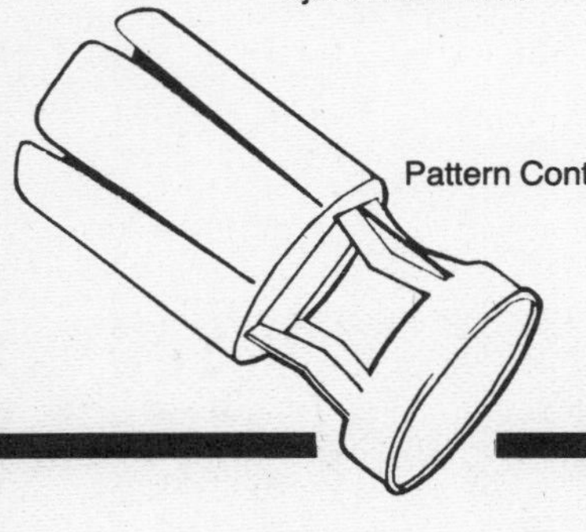

U-Load Shot Wads

Pattern Control Wads

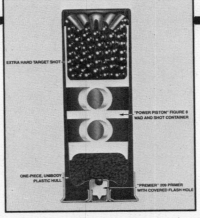

Remington "Premier" 12-ga. Load

LJUTIC
Plastic Mono Wad

Made in 12 gauge only, this wad features serrated runners the length of the wad to give less drag on the barrel. One piece design eliminates other wads and gives more consistent loads, greater speed with a reduction in powder charge. For use in Winchester AA plastic hulls and Federal plastic and paper shells. From Ljutic Inc.

Per M, FOB Yakima, WA . . . **$12.99**

NTC Card Wads

Card wads of .135″ thickness for occupying space in reduced-capacity 12 and 10 gauge loads. They may be split to fashion two .070″ wads. Wads come in .2-lb clear plastic sacks. From Non-Toxic Components, Inc. **$3.50**

PATTERN CONTROL
Plastic Wads

These wads are available in 12 ga. (1 oz., 1⅛ oz.), 20 ga. (⅞-oz.), and 28 ga. (¾-oz.) in six styles for hunting and competition. They give a complete seal and equalized pressure for controlled thrust. For full data contact Pattern Control.

Price: Per 1,000 (minimum 5,000). **$15.00**

POLYWAD
Spread-R Wad

New concept in pattern spreading inserts. An easy-to-load spreader device that can be used with any wad and any size shot. Opens patterns up from Full choke to Imp. Cyl. The Polywad is a small plastic disk (.05″ to .06″ thick) with a diameter of .707″ to .715″ which the reloader inserts ahead of the shot charge. A slender .680″ long center post is tapered to enter the shot column with ease. Install the Spread-R manually or use the wad guide and rammer tube of a loading tool. From Polywad, Inc.

Price: Per 150 . . . . **$5.00**

REMINGTON

Power Piston Wads
For Plastic Trap & Skeet Loads

Gauge	Wad No.	per M
12	RXP12	**$30.08**
12	PT12	30.08
20	RXP20	30.08
28	SP28	30.08
410	SPP410	30.08

RXP 20 wad replaces R20 wad.

Power Piston Wads
For Plastic Field Loads

Gauge	Wad No.	Per M
10 (1⅝ or 2 oz.)	SP10	**$37.00**
12 (1 oz. load)	R12L	30.08
12 (1⅛ oz. load)	R12H	30.08
1 (3¼x1¼ oz.)	RP12	30.08
12 (3¾x1¼ oz.)	SP12	30.08
16 (1⅛ oz. load)	SP16	30.08
20 (1 oz. load)	SP20	30.08

Prices are approximate.

U-LOAD
Supersonic Steel Shot Wads

One-piece, unslit wads constructed of tough polyethylene—uniform in both thickness and size. Available in two sizes—12-gauge 3″ which is easily trimmed to 2¾″ and the standard 10-gauge. From U-Load, Inc. . . . . **NA**

Hornady Versalite

Windjammer

Vitt/Boos Slug

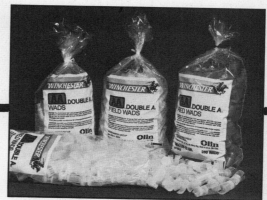

Winchester AA Wads

VITT/BOOS
Aerodynamic Shotgun Slug

Modified and improved from the old reliable Brenneke slug. The high, thin, helical ribs tightly fit the bore for accuracy, but because they are thin and soft they pass through the tightest choke with complete safety. Maker says the ribs induce rotation to improve accuracy. Weight 1.32 oz. (580 grs.)

For complete descriptive literature and prices, write to Raymond Boos.

Box of 25, 12 ga. only **$12.50**

SHOT			BUCKSHOT					
BB	T	F↓	No. 4	No. 3	No. 2	No. 1	No. 0	No. 00
.18	.20	.22	.24	.25	.27	.30	.32	.33

(Diameter in inches, actual size.)

WINCHESTER WADS

Type	Gauge	Per M
WAA12	12	N.A.
WAA12R	12	N.A.
WAA12F1	12	N.A.
WAA12F114	12	N.A.
WAA20	20	N.A.
WAA20F1	20	N.A.
WAA28	28	N.A.
WAA41	410	N.A.

The Double A is designed to give straight line compression—no tipped wad. The vented skirt at the base allows trapped air to escape when seating the wad during reloading. When fired, hinged posts progressively collapse to absorb recoil.

WINDJAMMER
Tournament Wads

The Windjammer wad features a flared eight-segment shot cup for enhanced patterns, compressible height to permit loading 1-, 1⅛- or 1¼-oz. shot charges with the same wad. Patented design produces less pressure resulting in less felt recoil. Fits all popular hulls. Available in 12 or 20 ga. From Windjammer Tournament Wads, Inc.

Price: Per thousand **$13.00**

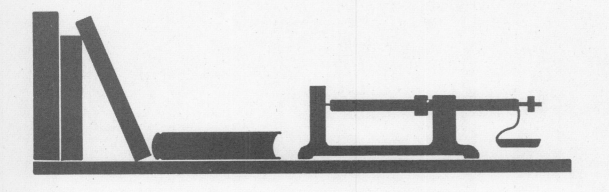

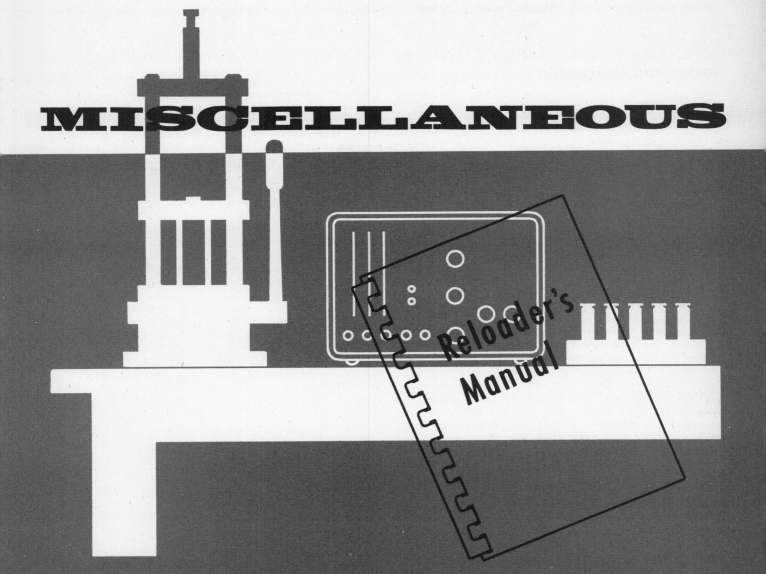

MISCELLANEOUS

Reloader's Manual

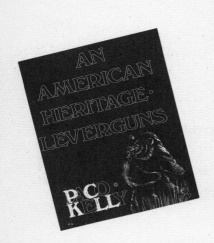

Notes on Books, Manuals, Videos and Computer Software

The reloading bench with a choice selection of books and/or manuals is by no means complete. No case should be charged or bullet seated until the reloader is sure that the load and bullet he is using are the correct ones to do the job he wants to have done. Whether you are new to reloading or a veteran of many years, a good selection of written material is a must if you are to produce safe, accurate ammunition each time you reload.

The man who wants to enjoy handloading will read as much material on the subject as he can, he'll go beyond the point of looking at the pictures, captions and bold face type and read and heed the cautions and warnings he'll find in all reloading literature. He'll use only the powder type recommended, approach maximum loads with extreme caution and double check the manuals along every step of his operation. He'll be safe, not sorry—slower, of course, but surer.

Best of all, he'll be able to take advantage of years of testing and experimentation by men who have devoted their lives to handloading. It is a sorry sight indeed to see a man buy a loading press, dies, components, etc., and walk out of the store without a manual of some sort.

Today's handloader is also keeping up with current technology with the use of computers. Many households now have personal computers and they can be put to good use as handloading tools with the proper programs. This software allows the reloader to compute most everything he'd want to know for any cartridge load—bullet design, trajectory, wind deflection, ballistic coefficients, paper patching, etc.

The beginning reloader may also want to take advantage of the videotape instruction now available. These tapes can be a good introduction to the handloading hobby, augmenting the many excellent books and manuals now on the market.

An American Heritage—Leverguns
by Paco Kelly

This book not only is a brief history of the truly American lever-action rifle but it's also an anecdoted trip through 40 years of using them. For handloaders, it has chapters on primers and pressure, cast bullets and their reloading into short and long-range loads, silent loads and hunting loads, most of which is directed toward the advanced reloader. Available from Paco-RD. **$12.95**
   Price: Collector Edition **$25.00**

ABC's of Reloading 3rd Edition
by Dean Grennell

A wealth of new information is included in this edition. Step-by-step instruction on reloading techniques, basic info on powders, cases, shot, etc. Everything about bullets from casting, sizing and lubrication to swaging, shotshell reloading, J.D. Jones Wildcats, homemade equipment. New ballistic information, testing reloads, mathematics and the reloader, shopping for components and equipment, building a reloading library—all facets of the hobby are covered. Complete with a directory of manufacturers of reloading equipment. From DBI Books. **$12.95**

Ackley's Pocket Manual
for Shooters and Reloaders
by P.O. Ackley

A durable handbook-size volume containing selected data from Ackley's bigger book. Many factory and wildcat cartridges are covered in detail. An excellent working reference for shooters and reloaders.
   Price **$4.95**

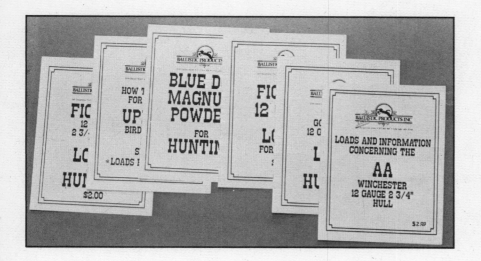
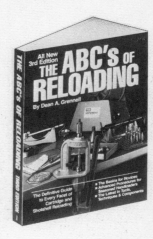

Ackley's Revised Handbook for Shooters and Reloaders by P.O. Ackley

The excellent reference work of this title described in the 4th Edition of HANDLOADER'S DIGEST has been expanded to two volumes totalling almost 1200 pages. Vol. 1 is a reprint of the original; Vol. 2 is a continuation of the first, with data on approximately 100 new wildcat cartridges, including a number based on the 284 Win. and 350 Rem. Magnum cases. All new factory cartridges are covered, new loading information on old designs is given, a shotgun load section has been added and, because of demand, Ackley's article on action blowups has been reprinted. The results of these tests should surprise a number of the newer guncranks who have accepted too much opinion and too little fact. Separately, **$9.94** each.

Both **$19.50**

BALLISTIC PRODUCTS
Shotgun Reloading Books and Manuals

Blue Dot Powder and the 12-Gauge
A discussion on the pressure and burning characteristics of Blue Dot powder under varying weather conditions. When to use Blue Dot and when not to. 8 pages. From Ballistic Products Inc. **$2.00**

Federal Gold Medal, 12-Gauge 2¾" Special Loads for Hunting
Over 23 hunting loads for Federal 12-gauge 2¾" hulls are detailed in this manual. Discussions of shell dimensions, reloading tips and more are in this pamphlet. From Ballistic Products Inc. **$2.00**

Federal 12-Gauge, 3" Hulls Plastic Base Loads for Hunting
Thirteen hunting loads tailored for the 12-gauge 3" Federal plastic-base hull. Loads for hunting geese, turkey and duck plus cold weather loads. From Ballistic Products Inc. . . **$2.00**

Fiocchi 12-Gauge 3" Loads for Hunting
Over 16 hunting loads for the Fiocchi 12-gauge 3" hull are detailed in this pamphlet with special loads for geese, ducks and loads for warm and cold weather. Eight pages. From Ballistic Products Inc. **$2.00**

Fiocchi 12-Gauge 2¾" Hulls Loads for Hunting
Specific loads for duck and cold weather shooting—17 loads in all. Also included are three slug loads for the Fiocchi 12-gauge 2¾". A discussion of Fiocchi 616 primers, the hull itself as well as an overview of reloading. 12 pages. From Ballistic Products, Inc. **$2.00**

Loads and Information Concerning the AA Winchester 12-Gauge 2¾" Hull
This 16-page pamphlet provides technical information on the AA Win. 12-gauge 2¾" hull plus 30 hunting loads for upland game, ducks, trap, cold and warm weather shooting. From Ballistic Products Inc. **$2.00**

Pagoda Loads for the 12-Gauge Hunter
Pagoda loads, as developed by the staff of BP, incorporate a second gas seal for better powder burning. Reloading tips and information plus reloading data (54 loads) for Activ (2¾", 3"), Federal (2¾", 3"), Fiocchi (2¾", 3"), Cheddite (3"), Remington (3"), Winchester Poly Formed (3") and Winchester Compression Formed (3") hulls. 20 pages. From Ballistic Products Inc. **$2.00**

Remington Type 5 SP12 12-Gauge 3" Hulls Loads for Hunting
Reloading tips plus 14 hunting loads for the 12-Gauge 3" #5 SP12 Federal hull. Loads are for turkey, duck, goose and swan plus special loads for warm and cold weather shooting. Eight pages. From Ballistic Products Inc. **$2.00**

Slug and Buckshot Manual Volume I
Thirty-three pages of slug reloading data with special sections on reloading tips, new slug reloading products, slug shot gun barrel performance, slug accuracy, shotguns, sights and

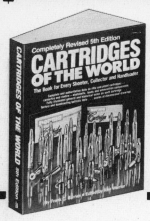

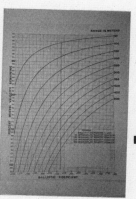

scopes for slug shooting, special crimping techniques and more. From Ballistic Products Inc. **$5.00**

How to Reload Better for Upland Bird Hunting

Loads for duck, pheasant, grouse, quail, sharptail, chukar, woodcock and specialty loads for doves—18 loads in all. Spreader loads, long and short range loads, 12-gauge to 20 gauge, warm weather to cold nasty weather loads are included in this 20-page manual. Subjects also covered are load strength, shooting stance, chokes, hunting dogs and reloading tips. From Ballistic Products Inc. **$2.00**

How to Reload Great Hunting Shotgun Shells Volume II by Dave Fackler

A basic shotgun reloading manual with 18 of its 56 pages devoted to specific reloading data. Other aspects of reloading and shotgun shooting covered are: pressure, forcing cones, powder, primers, hulls, crimps, shot and shot range, buffered loads, wads, reloading presses and slug and buckshot loads. From Ballistic Products Inc. **$5.00**

Load Log Book

Keep a record of loads and results. Pages are preprinted with outline of events to be logged. This book comes in loose leaf binder notebook. From Ballistic Products Inc. **$14.95**
Price: Log Replacement Pack **$5.95**

The Mighty 10-Gauge by Dave Fackler

A reloading manual with 20+ pages devoted to 10-gauge loading data. Components, reloading and shooting tips, 10-gauge shotguns, buckshot, slug and steel shot loads are also covered. 42 pages. Published by Ballistic Products Inc. **$5.00**

Status of Steel

Instructional guide to the reloading of steel loads in the 12-gauge and 10-gauge. 29 loads included. Reloading tips, components, primers, chokes, forcing cores, patterns and more discussed. From Ballistic Products Inc. **$3.00**

Buck Stix Ballistic Calculator

This easy-to-use chart tells the shooter the remaining velocity in terms of "percent" of muzzle velocity. It then becomes easy to figure remaining energy. Chart covers all ballistic coefficients from .100 up to .800 with ranges from 50 to 500 meters. From Buck Stix.
Price **$5.45**

Cartridges of the World 5th Edition
by Frank C. Barnes

This book is the standard general-purpose reference work on cartridges, for which scientists, technicians, collectors, and laymen alike reach first for answers to cartridge questions. It's a basic book, setting down the dimensions, performance parameters and physical characteristics for over 1,000 different cartridges. This is an encyclopedic reference work that covers rifle and pistol cartridges—rimfire and centerfire—shotshells, loads and components. Both general and historical notes are given for each cartridge, with factory and handloading data and dimensional drawings. From DBI Books, Inc. . . . **$16.95**

Corbin Bullet Swaging Books

Corbin publishes and sells all the bullet swaging books in print. These include the hardcover textbook, *Rediscover Swaging,* 283 pages, written by Dave Corbin. Price . . **$19.50**

The Corbin Handbook No. 7, is the guide to available swaging equipment, how to specify equipment and design bullets, and an introduction to bullet swaging technique. 200 pages. Price **$4.00**

The Corbin Technical Bulletins, Volume I, is a 66 page soft cover book full of questions and answers about swaging, problems and dealer questions, comparisons with casting, cost figures for making bullets, and other detailed information. Price **$6.50**

The Corbin Technical Bulletins, Volume II, is a 113 page metallic cover book with the history of swaging, future directions, chapters on each caliber range and how to make specific kinds of bullets for each group of calibers from the sub-cals to the nitro express. Full of photos and practical data. Price **$6.50**

The Bullet Swage Manual, T. Smith, is the old manuscript by famous pioneer die-maker Smith, published by Corbin in 1976, and is an interesting historical reference for students of bullet swaging. Price **$4.50**

The Corbin Technical Bulletins, Volume III (TB-3)

Bullet swaging for hunters, survivalists, experimental work and technical papers published in noted journals around the world are translated and republished here. 99 pages, illustrated. **$6.50**

Power Swaging (TB-4)

Complete course in commercial bullet manufacture on a small to medium scale, including charts, computer programs, math and a discussion on marketing, organizing, and running a custom bullet swaging business. Published in 1984, 180 pages, illustrated. **$10.00**

World Directory of Custom Bullet Makers

This 240-page 5½″ × 8½″ hardcover book lists custom bullet makers around the world, cross-referenced by location, calibers and company names. A wealth of information about special bullets, how they are made and what they are used for. Sources of lead wire, copper tubing, bullet jackets and specialty products made by bullet makers are also included. Filled with tables and unusual data relating to ballistic coefficients, minimum stable twist rates etc. From Corbin Mfg. **$24.95**

Complete Guide to Handloading
by Philip G. Sharpe

A comprehensive, authoritative coverage, but somewhat dated today. This revised 3rd edition (1953) of the "handloader's bible" gives much information on tools and techniques, old and semi-new, and on every phase of handloading. Containing over 8000 individual loads for rifle, revolver and pistol cartridges, it discusses practically every variety of shell and primer, bullet and bullet mould, for rifle and revolver. Funk & Wagnalls, New York. Fully illustrated, 734 pages. Although out of print and difficult to obtain, some copies are available from arms books dealers.

Du Pont Handloader's Guide

The Du Pont Company has published an updated edition of its "Handloader's Guide for Smokeless Powders." This 50-page guide lists more than 2,300 loads for shotgun, rifle and handgun ammunition using the 14 Du Pont smokeless powders. Many new loads using recently introduced components were developed for this edition, and several new rifle calibers are included. The new guide is available free at stores carrying Du Pont powders.

Elk Mountain Reloading Manual
for Advanced Handloaders
Vol. #1, 30-06

A new type of "reloading" manual claiming to contain more loading data than all other manuals. This is the first of a projected series of manuals—one for each cartridge to cover 243, 308, 270, 30-06 and 300 Win. Mag. Data presentation is graphical instead of tabular and both velocity and maximum peak pressure data are presented for all pressures from 20,000 psi to 60,000 psi, using an absolute pressure system with common crusher values noted. Bullet weights for the 30-06 range from 50 to 300 grains. Data for the 150-gr. bullet includes over 60 powders available from the six major distributors. Black powder loads are included but not lead bullets. From Elk Mountain Shooters Supply. **$11.95**

Elk Mountain Reloading Manual
Vol. #2, "The 243 & 6mm"

Similar coverage of the two subject cartridges as in Volume 1. Bullet weights from 60 to 155 grains and over 70 powders are covered. From Elk Mountain Shooters Supply. . . . **$11.95**

Handbook of Shotshell Reloading
by Kenneth W. Cougar

A very complete and detailed reference manual for shotshell reloaders based on MEC tools. Contains information for both beginner and expert reloaders with a fully illustrated "how-to" section, illustrated components section, 16 pages in color for shotshell hull identification, over 1,800 load recipes prepared by the four major powder makers, and a reference section of parts lists and drawings of MEC reloaders. From SKR Industries, Inc. **$17.95**

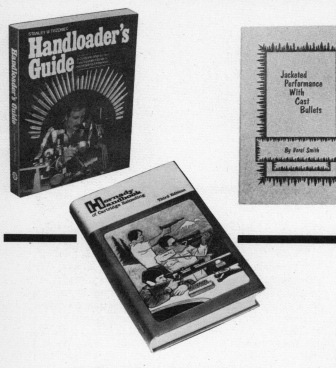

Handloader's Guide
by Stanley W. Trzoniec

This 256-page book is a step-by-step guide to handloading centerfire rifle and handgun ammunition and tailoring the handload to the individual firearm for maximum performace at the range or in the field. Well illustrated, the book covers many favorite calibers including the 357 Mag. Up-to-date information on equipment, loading techniques, powders, ballistics, and testing wads. 8″ × 10″, soft cover. From Stoeger Publishing. **$11.95**

Hodgdon Reloading Data Manual #25

544 pages of articles and data for every aspect of reloading. Includes data on Hodgdon, Hercules, Winchester and Du Pont rifle powders, popular military calibers not published before; rifle, lead bullet, pistol and silhouette data; plus a complete data and reloading section for blackpowder reloaders using Pyrodex. From Hodgdon Powder Co. Price **$14.95**

Hornady Handbook of Cartridge Reloading—Third Edition

First published in 1967 as a 360-page volume, the handbook has grown to 688 hardbound pages. Expansion of the new third edition provides a wealth of useful information. Details are provided on more than a hundred Hornady bullets for use in 117 different cartridges. This includes information on many popular European cartridges as well as a special section on wildcat and obsolete loads. There is also a special section covering both rifle and pistol calibers for silhouette shooting. Profusely illustrated and comprehensive in its scope. Include $2.00 for shipping. From Hornady. **$15.95**
Memorial Edition **$25.00**

Home Guide to Cartridge Conversions
by George C. Nonte, Jr.

The single reference book for handloaders who want to convert commercially available cartridge cases for use in shootable but obsolete arms. Tools and materials needed for case reforming are covered as well as step-by-step instructions on the procedures. Over 300 cartridge data sheets are included, giving complete information on adaptable cases, forming operations required and loading data. 404 pp. illustrated. From The Gun Room Press **$19.95**

Jacketed Performance with Cast Bullets
by Veral Smith

This 104-page monograph covers all facets of loading and shooting cast bullets with the emphasis on performance. Chapters include dope on "Bore Leading," "Gas Checks," "Bullet Fitting," "Alloying," "Cleaning Leaded Bores," "Hunting Bullets," and more. The author details many procedures for getting the most out of cast bullets in both rifles and handguns. An excellent guide for cast bullet users. Available from Lead Bullets Technology. **$9.00**

Lazy-X Handloaders Notebook

This is a big hardbound looseleaf notebook for recording data on handloads. It measures 10″ × 11½″ and has 8 plastic dividers to separate the data as to caliber, powders, etc. The book comes with 72 pages printed on heavy stock, each with spaces for load, powder, bullet, primer, case used and range data. Each page has room for 25 loads. The binder is covered with heavy duty vinyl and is easily cleaned of oil and dirt. From Lazy-X Notebook. Price, postpaid. **$8.95**

Lyman
Reloading & Cast Bullet Guide

This 64-page book provides all the basic how-to information on getting started in both reloading and bullet casting. It covers each step of the reloading process from start to finish, detailed assembly instructions and exploded view drawings on all major Lyman tools. From Lyman Products. **$1.95**

Lyman Reloading Handbook
46th Edition

A standard reloading reference for shooters the world over. Its easy-to-follow instructions will make the novice an expert in no time. The Handbook covers the entire field, including step-by-step instructions on the use of Lyman reloading equipment, complete information on reloading for rifles, pistols, shotguns, and muzzleloaders. Editorial sections include the history of Ideal/Lyman reloading products, accurate shooting, bullet design, chamber pressure and its measurement, bullet casting, step-by-step, introduction to muzzleloading. More than 8,000 loads are listed for more than 100 popular chamberings. Printed on 8½″ × 11″ pages and drilled for three-ring binder. It is a mine of valuable data, including up-to-date information on new loads, pet loads, bullets and techniques. From Lyman Products. **$17.95**

Lyman
Pistol and Revolver Handbook

This book features 2,065 fresh handgun loads as well as complete trajectory and wind-drift tables. There are 74 pages of data covering new bullets, powders, primers, and cases, plus a section on loading and shooting blackpowder revolvers. The 280-page book also describes Lyman's composite bullet system. 8½″ × 11″. From Lyman Products. Price **$13.95**

Lyman Shotshell Handbook
3rd Edition

This reloading handbook covers every aspect of shotshell reloading. It includes over 2,000 tested loads covering all gauges 10, 12, 16, 20, 28, and 410. Complete "How to Reload" section on choosing a load, factory velocities, assembling shotshells, etc. The large reference section covers up-to-date pressure information, full color case identification chapter, plus chapters on wads, patterns, powder and primers. Editorial sections include the history of Lyman Ideal shotshell reloading products, fresh guest editorial by some of shotshell reloading's best authors. Over 300 8½″ × 11″ pages. From Lyman Products. **$17.95**

Lyman
Cast Bullet Handbook 3rd Edition

Contains more than 5,000 tested loads for the cast bullet shooter, and over 100 pages of trajectory and wind-drift tables for cast, centerfire rifle bullets. It also includes a complete how-to section, special hunting section, a history of cast bullets and the Lyman/Ideal line, and advanced metallurgical information. Perfect-bound and three-hole drilled, this 419-page 8½″ × 11″ book is an important addition to the shooter's library. From Lyman Products. **$17.95**

MTM Handloaders Log

Designed to provide the handloader/shooter with a concise, written, easy-to-use scientific approach to load record keeping. The 3-ring looseleaf binder is vinyl covered and comes with 50 printed pages—enough for 1,000 entries. Log headings and spaces for: rifle model, serial number, date, yards, group size or score, number of shots, powder/grains, bullet weight, primer, case, conditions and notes. From MTM. **$10.94**
50 additional pages. **$5.53**

Metallic Cartridge Reloading
Ed. by Robert S.L. Anderson

A wealth of invaluable technical data by Ed Matunas, Ken Howell and other outstanding reloading experts. Covers components, propellants, pressure, safety, bullet casting, troubleshooting, benchrest loading, reloading for accuracy and a Q&A section on reloading problems. 256 easy-to-use load tables for over 70 rifle and pistol calibers. Included for each cartridge are its complete history, applications and an illustration showing all pertinent technical data. Emphasis is on modern rifle and handgun cartridges as well as selected obsolete ones. From DBI Books, Inc. . . . . **$13.95.**

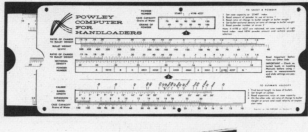

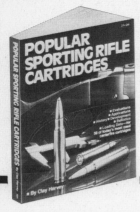

Popular Sporting Rifle Cartridges
by Clay Harvey

Provides the hunter/shooter with extensive information on most of the cartridges introduced during this century (with some carryovers from the 19th) that cannot be obtained from any other single source. Combines the hard data of a reloading manual with the author's interesting and informative analysis. Major sections are devoted to the .223 Remington, .243 Winchester, 6mm Remington, .270 Winchester, .308 Winchester, the .30-06, .375 H&H, 7mm Remington Magnum, many more. Covers history and development, application, general loading information on nearly 50 cartridges. Tabular ballistics data are included at the end of each chapter. From DBI Books, Inc. **$13.95**

Powley PSI Calculator

Used in conjunction with the Powley Computer and a counter chronograph, the 3″ × 8½″ slide chart supplies pounds-per-square inch chamber pressures. A very useful tool for handloaders. Available from Hutton Rifle Ranch **$6.00**

Combination price for Computer and Calculator, includes a special powder selection chart, available only from Hutton, postpaid **$12.50**; foreign orders **$14.50**

Powley Computer for Handloaders

This handy 4″ × 9″ slide chart computes quickly and accurately the following data for handloaders: Most efficient powder for guns using Military Rifle powders. Best powder for combination of bullet weight and case. Powder charge. Estimated velocity. Foreign orders add **$2.00**. From Marian Powley. **$7.00**

Combination price for Computer and Calculator. . . **$12.50**

Powley High Velocity Trajectory Chart

This 36″ × 24″ horizontal chart shows the bullet path to 500 yards for Ingalls' Ballistic Coefficients from 0.15 to .050 and 2600 to 5000 f/s muzzle velocities. Fast and easy to use. From Marian Powley. **$27.00**

Precision Handloading
by John Withers

An entirely new approach to handloading ammunition. The author tells the reader how to analyze his shooting needs, set objectives and how to meet those expectations by following a planned, logical sequence of steps based on the individual's particular requirements. Of course, all the procedures of modern reloading are covered and explained in full. Well illustrated, 8″ × 10″, soft cover. From Stoeger Publishing. **$11.95**

RCBS Cast Bullet Manual

A brand new book on an age old art. This comprehensive reference tool contains 178 pages of authoritative information, illustrations and specs. Includes step-by-step instructions on cast bullet prep/moulding and data for all current RCBS bullet moulds such as muzzle velocities and recommended powder charges for both rifles and handguns. From RCBS **$8.00**

RCBS Cartridge and Chamber Drawings

Scaled and completely dimensional engineering drawings printed on high-quality leatherette paper stock from original CAD ink tracings. The 11″ × 17″ size drawings are ideal for framing or technical reference. The same drawings are also available on 8½″ × 11″ heavy white stock, and are ring-binder punched for use at the reloading bench or in a reference library.

118 different drawings are available, encompassing all standard and wildcat calibers included in RCBS reloading die groups A-F. From RCBS, Inc.

Price: 11″ × 17″ each. **$7.00**
Price: 8½″ × 11″ for 5 . . . . **$7.00**

Reloader's Guide
3rd Edition
By R. A. Steindler

This practical book has been newly updated and revised to reflect the changes in this economical and rewarding adjunct to shooting and hunting. Contains the latest technical data, expanded loading tables, tips on solving handloading problems, bullet casting, swaging, and cartridge case conversions. Profusely illustrated with diagrams and photographs of the latest techniques and equipment. 244 pages, soft covers. Stoeger Publishing Co............................**$9.95**

Reloading For Shotgunners, 2nd Ed.
Ed. by Robert S. L. Anderson

Sound and savvy articles on "shorty" shells wildcatting, slug reloading, patterning, Skeet and trap loads. Shotshells for the small bores, the 10-gauge magnum and the 12-gauge. Tips and tricks to make reloading easier; how to recognize bad hulls and improperly loaded shotshells, how to avoid component spills and mixups, what wads for what hulls, proper storing of components. Complete listings for all available loading data from powder, press and shot manufacturers. Photos and descriptions of presses in operation and a separate catalog section on presses, components and prices. From DBI Books Inc. **$11.95**

Shoot Better
by Charles W. Matthews

Essentially a compilation of ballistics tables, the author lists the performance and characteristics of 457 commercial cartridges of 105 calibers made by five American and two European manufacturers. Most of the more popular centerfires are covered, from 17 Remington to the 458 Winchester. Velocity, energy, bullet drop, time of flight, wind deflection and amount of lead figures are given to 500 yards. From Bill Matthews, Inc. **$16.45**

Sierra Reloader's Manual

Recently expanded and up-dated, Sierra's Reloader's Manual 2nd Edition is a comprehensive ballistic reference guide. Published in two volumes—Rifle and Handgun—with 938 pages of reloading data and information. Includes loading data for 122 bullets and 90 calibers including the 7mms (7mm-08, 7mm BR and 7mm TCV); all rifle calibers from 22 Hornet-458 Win. Mag.; all pistol calibers from 25 ACP-45 Colt. Featured are articles by Art Blatt, Skip Gordon, Bob Milek, Larry Moore and Ross Seyfried.

For reloaders who already own the 2nd Edition two volume set Sierra offers the supplement package. It includes the handgun binder and 496 new and up-dated pages for both volumes. From Sierra Bullets.

Price: Reloader's Manual two volume set **$32.50**
Price: Supplement Package **$16.50**

Sinclair Data Log

This log book was designed for the serious handloader/shooter. The 8½" × 11" sheets have 18 columns of data and provide both a record of loads tested and a comparison of the results obtained with those loads. Sheets are printed on both sides. Each Log book contains 25 data sheets,—enough space to record the results of 1,350 loads. From Sinclair Int., Inc. **$4.50**

Speer Reloading Manual No. 11

This latest reloading manual shows the latest, most correct data on rifle and handgun loads, with very comprehensive sections on both. It includes many professional photographs and illustrations. All cartridge drawings have been revised to show both English and metric dimensions and new tables furnish detailed metric and English equivalents. All ballistic data has been retested, confirmed or updated and 200 yard holdover and energy is shown for all rifle loads. The glossary contains new definitions and is supplemented with detailed illustrations. Has 560 pages, 8,000 powder loads, bullet data, special techniques, etc. The book is hardbound and has plastic coated and soil proof covers to withstand constant use. From Speer Bullets.....................................**$13.60**

Books, Manuals, Videos and Computer Software

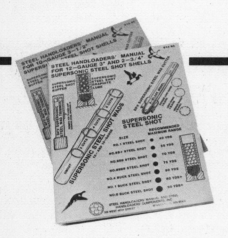

Speer Bullet Board

Speer has just released the latest in their series of bullet boards. Like earlier editions, this new board features another outstanding color painting by noted historical artist, Jack Woodson.

The theme of the board is "The Potlatch," a social event peculiar to several Indian tribes in the Pacific Northwest. The board measures 24″ × 14″ and contains one of all Speer bullets currently in production.

Price **$65.45**

U-Load Steel Handloaders' Manual

A fully illustrated manual for either the 12-gauge 2¾″ and 3″ or the 10-gauge to reload steel shot. Each manual is done in a step by step process with several loads (12-gauge 2¾″ and 3″—25 loads, 10-gauge—15 loads) that have been tested by H.P. White Laboratories, Inc. or Hodgdon Powder Company, Inc. All loads show approximate velocity and approximate chamber pressure (LUP's) and will eject from semi-automatic shotguns. From U-Load, Inc. **$14.95**

Winchester Ball Powder Propellant Loading Data

This 34-page booklet is a handy reference. It gives data on all of Winchesters powders and other components, tips on reloading and load data for rifle, handgun and shotshells. Available from Winchester Div., Olin Corp.

Software Programs for Reloaders

Corbin DC-1004 TPLOT Software Program

Terminal plot fires a bullet on screen and calculates the actual retardation due to skin effect, base drag, and nose drag at all speeds ever 0.01 seconds of flight, showing you the calculations and the graph of distance against vacuum distance, with retardation plotted on screen. Then it drops the bullet and calculates the energy as the bullet gathers speed, plotting distance versus energy: The lethality potential of the falling projectile can be seen on screen. From Corbin Mfg. **$25.00**

Corbin DC-1001 Bullet Design Software Program, Volume I

Enter data of bullet design—type in the weight, nose shape, caliber, manufacturing materials, specify the material it is to be fired into—and the program will give you the ballistic coefficient of that bullet. The minimum spin rate and all the physical parameters (volume of lead, amount of material in shank and ogive, weight of core and jacket, overall length of each part, etc.) of that bullet. Magnify it on screen from 10x to 1000x and then "fire" it on screen.

Compatible with any IBM-PC (or compatible running MS-DOS). For the graphics a CGS, EGA or Hercules-Graphics compatible monochrome video driver is needed. From Corbin Mfg.

Price: Monochrome DC-1001 . . . . **$25.00**
Price: Color DC 1001C **$29.50**

Corbin DC-1002 Corbin Handbook No. 7 Software

A two-disk set that acts as a guide to Corbin swaging equipment, how to specify equipment and design bullets. The program also introduces the techiques of bullet swaging. With the *SHOW* command, any word or phrase will be displayed in context. From Corbin Mfg. **$12.00**

```
        UPGRADE  YOUR  ABILITY
      TO  DESIGN  CUSTOM  BULLETS

     WEIGHT AND LENGTH FOR A GIVEN BARREL TWIST RATE...

     WHAT IS THE TWIST RATE of your barrel? 35.000 Default Value
DENSITY (LB/IN^3)  OVERALL LENGTH (IN)   SHANK LENGTH (IN)   WEIGHT (GR)
       0.40970        0.85797              0.40597            325.49
       0.40600        0.86187              0.40987            324.33
       0.39300        0.87601              0.42401            320.19
       0.38800        0.88164              0.42964            318.56
       0.37260        0.89967              0.44767            313.47
       0.36000        0.91528              0.46328            309.18
       0.35000        0.92827              0.47627            305.70
       0.26040        1.07618              0.62418            270.70
              Press any key to continue...

LEAD  TIN  ANTIMONY  DENSITY LB/IN^3    LEAD  TIN  ANTIMONY  DENSITY LB/IN^3
30%   0%   70%       .2604              37%   0%   63%       .2662
63%   0%   37%       .2974              90%   0%   10%       .3807
84%   16%  0%        .3726              92%   0%   8%        .3880
94%   0%   16%       .3930              96%   0%   1%        .3980
95%   5%   0%        .3970              80%   5%   15%       .3600
85%   5%   10%       .3000             100%   0%   0%        .4097
```

Corbin DC-1003 Bullet Design Programs, Volume II

Includes the PPATCH (paper patch design program), a four-section program that finds patch length, paper thickness, even bullet length for various alloys, bullet diameter for four different kinds of bullet to barrel fit, and more. Also includes the multi-density core program, which calculates charts of how much (length and volume) of each different material you need to make up a given weight of a certain caliber of bullet using from one to four different materials in the *same* bullet! Bullet jacket lengths for tubing (any alloy, including brass, steel, copper, etc.) are also calculated for any caliber or weight. From Corbin Mfg......................**$10.00**

Pro-Ware Ballistic Data Program

This easy to use software program provides a wealth of external ballistic information: Time of Flight, Distance, Energy, Elevation, Drop, Bullet Path, Uphill/Downhill Bullet Path, Wind Deflection, K-Factor, Recoil, Maximum Point Blank Range, Sight Resetting, Ballistic Coefficients, Mean and Standard Deviation. Handload data can be entered and listed on tables. English and metric systems supported. All data saved to disk file for storage. Comes with 20-page manual. For IBM AT, Tandy 2000, TI Pro, HP-150, C/MP80 (specify disk format), TRS80 w/MMCPM, Atari ST and Amiga. From Pro-Ware, Inc. **$49.95**

Pejsa Ballistic Computer Program

This program was designed for Apple, Atari, Commodore or IBM-PC computers and allows you to compute most everything you want to know for any cartridge load. Gives data on: bullet path, velocity, energy, time of flight, sight elevation, mid-range trajectory, point blank range, cross-wind deflection, ballistic tables, plots trajectory and wind curves. The serious shooter may even change the drag coefficient curve or compute ballistic coefficients. 5¼-in diskette. From Pejsa Ballistics.
Price:...**$29.95**

Sierra Exterior Ballistics Software

This software program can be used by the reloader to answer critical questions about a specific load's performance afield. It will give trajectories in meters or yards, compute the effect of a crosswind on a specific bullet and load, tell the shooter where his bullet will strike based upon a specific zero and much more. Compatible with the Apple II-C (5¼" floppy), Apple II-E (5¼" floppy), Commodore Pet (16K+) (5¼" floppy), Commodore 64 (5¼" floppy or tape) and the IBM PC. From Sierra **$199.00**

Video Cassettes for Reloaders

Basic Ammunition Reloading With Wally Berns
A comprehensive, basic coverage of the high points of reloading pistol, rifle and shotshell ammunition. Running time 1 hr. 8 min. VHS only. From All Sports Book & Video Distr. **$39.95**

Discover Reloading
This is a National Reloading Manufacturers Association production. Close-up footage of each reloading operation from case cleaning to bullet seating. Running time 30 min. VHS only. From All Sports Book & Video Distr.....**$29.95**

Handgun Reloading
This tape shows how to use a progressive loader and all the reloading equipment for handgun calibers. Includes an actual blow-up of a Smith & Wesson revolver due to an overload. Running time 90 min. VHS only. From All Sports Book & Video Distr......................................**$91.95**

Custom Chronograph 1000

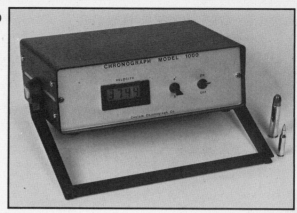

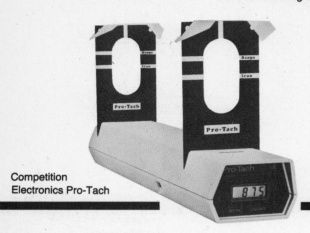

Competition
Electronics Pro-Tach

Notes on Chronographs . . .

The chronograph, at one time only for the advanced experimenter, is fast becoming a tool within the reach of more handloaders. Modern production methods and new, improved designs have aroused the interest in this instrument of more and more handloaders. Now many can purchase well-made, dependable instruments capable of accurate readings previously available only to the owners of expensive cumbersome machines. This, of course, is only the beginning. It is not difficult to foresee smaller, less expensive chronographs. Compact transistor types are already here that allow the shooter excellent mobility.

Though many chronographs cost less than many guns, clubs or groups of shooters can now easily afford one and operate it on a time-sharing basis. As advances in the electronics industry appear, the machines can only get better and less expensive.

COMPETITION ELECTRONICS, Pro-Tach

This self-contained chronograph, including electronics and skyscreens, can be mounted on any camera tripod, is easy to transport and simple to use. Powered by a 9-volt battery, the Pro-Tach gives direct readouts from 75-4500 fps on a large LCD display. It records the number of shots, velocity from shot to shot without resetting and the average velocity per shot string. For firing on bright days, diffuser hoods fit on the targets to aid the built-in skyscreens. For restricted range situations, an optional remote control allows resetting for number of shots and average velocity from up to 20 feet away. "Low Bat." indicator appears on the display if the battery is nearly dead. From Competition Electronics, Inc. Include $4.50 for shipping.

Price:	**$169.95**
Price: Optional Remote	**$30.00**
Price: Add'l targets (8) and diffuser hoods (2)	**$5.00**

CUSTOM CHRONOGRAPH
Model 500

A low-cost yet accurate chronograph, this unit is battery powered and compact. Size is 3½"×6"×2" and it takes a 6 volt battery giving a minimum life of 150 hours. Standard screen spacing is 2 feet, although it can be ordered with 4 foot spacing for a slight gain in accuracy. Screens are printed breaking-type that must be replaced after each shot. Velocity range is 490 to 5200 fps. Readout is via rotary switch scan and tables for velocity. Time base for the Model 500 is 500 Kc crystal controlled oscillator (250 Kc in 4-foot units). Comes with 50 printed screens, holders, cables and tables. From Custom Chronograph Co. **$69.95**
Extra screens, per hundred **$11.95**

CUSTOM CHRONOGRAPH
Model 600
Ambient Light Screens

This accessory directly replaces the printed screen holders supplied with every Custom Chronograph. Automatic gain control in the detectors assures optimum bullet detection whether sky is bright or overcast. Screens are powered by a 9 volt transistor battery with 50-hour life. Sensitive area is oval-shaped 8"x6".
Price, per pair **$79.95**

CUSTOM CHRONOGRAPH
Model 1000

This medium-priced system uses a direct readout in feet per second on a large four digit liquid crystal display, readable even in bright sunlight. Velocity range is from 244 to 5200 fps. Bullet detection is via printed screens (standard) or light screens (optional accessory) with a screen spacing of 2 or 4 feet. Time base is 500 Kc quartz crystal, with crystal accuracy of ±0.01%. Power is four internal C cell batteries with a life of over 200 hours of continuous use. The carrying handle also serves as an adjustable tilt stand. Comes with 50 printed screens, screen holders, cables, and instructions. . . . **$169.95**
Extra printed screens, per 100 . . . . **$11.95**
Model 600 light screens, per pair **$79.95**

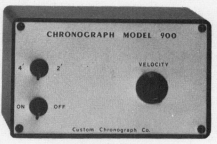

Custom Chronograph 900

Custom Chronograph 500

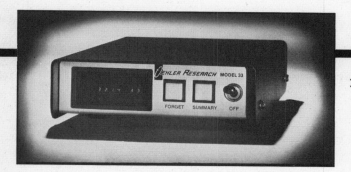

Oehler Model 33

Custom Chronograph Speed Tach

CUSTOM CHRONOGRAPH
Model 900

The Model 900 Ballistic Chronograph reads out velocity directly in feet per second. A single bright number displays the four velocity digits in sequence. For example, the velocity 3192 fps appears as 3, 1, 9, then 2 . . repeating the sequence until reset. The Model 900 Chronograph also features an instant choice of 2' or 4' screen spacing, and an extended velocity range of 245 to 5200 fps. This allows the instrument to measure the velocity of pellets and arrows, as well as rifles, handguns, and shotguns. Accuracy assured by a stable ±0.01% quartz crystal. Display reads out screen condition before shooting. Battery powered and very compact. Runs on 6 volt lantern battery. Can be used with printed (standard) or light screens (optional). Price includes 50 screens, screen holders, cables, and complete instructions......... **$109.95**
Extra printed screens, per 100................. **$11.95**

CUSTOM CHRONOGRAPH Speed Tach

A compact downrange housing that mounts on any camera tripod. The light screens, velocity computer and display are all combined into one neat package that is easy to transport, use and store. Operation is fully automatic—just shoot and read velocity. Each reading is held until the next shot.

The Speed Tach's light screen detectors are built into the chronograph and use skylight to determine the projectile's passage. A single 9-volt transistor battery powers the unit for over 30 hours of continuous use. Velocity is read out in feet per second on a liquid crystal display that also indicates when the battery needs replacing. All metal construction. From Custom Chronograph Co. **$189.95**
Price: Shooting window accessory with built-in diffusers **$10.00**

OEHLER Model 33 Chronotach

This new system provides many features not expected in a portable chronograph. Automatic display of both velocity and round number, automatic reset, and an automatic statistical summary of velocity test results are standard features. The statistical summary of up to 255 rounds includes minimum, maximum, extreme variation, average, and standard deviation. Computes velocity for any screen spacing from 1 to 99 feet, or will display time in micro-seconds. It will operate for near 60 hours on the set of flashlight batteries included in the 2"x6"x10" aluminum case. Price includes a pair of Skyscreen II detectors, batteries, instructions, and a 3-year warranty **$299.95**

OEHLER Model 34 Chronotach

The Model 34 differs from the Model 33 only in the respect that it is designed for operation with laboratory type screens or other sensors with a +12 volt pulse output signal and that it operates from 120 VAC power instead of batteries.
Price **$400.00**

OEHLER Model 55
Ballistic Screens

These screens provide a large shooting aperture of 28"x16" with a rectangular sensitive area of approximately 24"x14". Each screen is 36" high, 18¼" wide and approximately 3½" deep. The units are built of steel and can be joined to provide even larger apertures. The output (via BNC connector) is a 12 volt pulse with duration adjustable from 2 to 8 milliseconds. A sensitivity adjustment is provided. Price, per pair .. **$850.00**

PACT Mark II Championship Timer

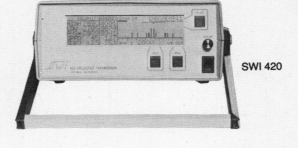

SWI 420

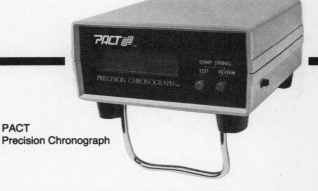

PACT
Precision Chronograph

PACT Precision Chronograph

Each time a round is fired over the PACT's skyscreens, the PACT PC displays the shot number and velocity to a tenth of a foot per second on the top line of the screen and the current average velocity on the bottom line. Up to 200 consecutive shots can be fired and then reviewed both in summary form and shot-by-shot. Displays the high and low velocity, extreme spread and average deviation. Features a retractable tilt stand for easy viewing and a self-contained rechargeable gel-cell battery with external charger. Economical PACT skyscreens can be adjusted from 6 inches to 5 feet. From Practical Applied Computer Technology, Inc.

Price: PACT Chronograph......................**$199.00**
Price: PACT Skyscreens (pair) **$25.00**
Price: Skyscreen bracket.......................**$24.00**

PACT MKII Championship Timer

Designed for the competitive shooter, PACT allows the practice of timed stages of fire in different ways. A sound activated timer, this unit is microprocessor controlled and can be programmed for any time interval up to 999.99 seconds. When the shooter presses "Go," a variable initial delay is followed by a clearly audible horn signal. As the shooter fires, shot number, time interval between shots and total elapsed time are recorded. The horn signals the end of the pre-programmed time period. Compatible with Oehler or PACT skyscreens and the unit can be programmed for any desired screen spacing. Using the factory installed Chrono-Mod (option), each shot is displayed on screen with the shot number, individual and running average. If the bullet weight is entered, the power factor will be calculated and displayed along with the round's velocity. At the end of a shot string, the high and low velocity, extreme spread, average for a series, and mean average deviation can be viewed. Powered by a rechargeable gel-cell battery; 110V charger included with the unit. From Practical Applied Computer Technology, Inc.

Price: Mark II Timer.........................**$329.00**
Price: Chrono-Mod **$49.00**
Price: PACT Skyscreens (pair) **$25.00**
Price: Screen Mounting Bracket **$25.00**

SWI 420 Projectile Chronograph

This portable chronograph provides features for complete ballistics measurement yet is simple to use. Information is displayed on a 1.7x5.9-inch 16384 pixel LCD graphics screen. Simultaneously displays: velocity, energy, shot number, min., max., extreme spread, standard deviation and graphs the results. Measure velocities to 9999 fps, energies to 9999 ft.-lbs., trap times to 640,000 microseconds and handles bullet weights to 999 grains. Constant memory stores up to 1000 shots in up to 99 groups even with the power off. Triangular 25-inch x 21-inch area photoscreens have built-in amplifiers and speed up circuits for improved sensitivity and accuracy. Any screen spacing from 1 to 160 ft. with 0.01-inch resolution may be used. User adjustable sensitivity. Chronographs automatic weapons. 500+ hr. battery life. Adjustable tilt stand/handle. Options include: Parallel printer interface. Third detector input for time-of-flight measurements allowing ballistic coefficient calculations. Serial computer interface for data transfer to a host computer for further processing or storage. Includes pair of photo-detectors, instructions, 1 year warranty. From Southwest Instruments. **$498.00**

TEPECO Time-Meter II

The Time Meter II gives time-of-flight readouts in millionths of a second on a four-digit liquid crystal display. The display is in decimal numbers (0-9) so velocity can be determined by using a calculator or by using the velocity tables that come with the unit (for distance intervals of 2, 5 and 10 feet). Fully automatic, the meter does not need to be reset or adjusted after each shot. Power is provided by six AA batteries. Comes complete with two Type 3 photo detectors, batteries, velocity tables and instructions. From Tepeco......**$119.95**

TEPECO Speed Meter IV

TEPECO Speed Master

TEPECO Timer-Meter II

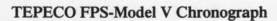

TEPECO Speed Master Chronograph

Direct velocity readout is shown on four-digit LCD display. The computer-type keypad provides individual access to readings of shot number, average velocity, high-low-extreme spread, standard deviation, kinetic energy, momemtum, bad shot rejection, spacing and bullet weight. Range is 76-5000 fps with allowable screen spacing of 1 to 15 feet. Bullet detection is via two Type 3 photo detector screens which come with the unit. Operates on 10-hour rechargeable sealed battery with 120 VAC charger. Battery condition is announced at 50 percent and 100 percent of allowable discharge. Price includes photo detectors, charger and operating instructions. From Tepeco. **$279.95**

TEPECO Model V

TEPECO FPS-Model V Chronograph

This unit gives direct velocity readouts on its large 4-digit LCD display. Range is from 76-5000 fps. The FPS-Model also features a choice of 1-foot to 10-foot photo detector spacing which allows measuring the velocity of pellets and arrows as well as rifles, handguns and shotguns. The Model V comes complete with Type 3 photo detector screens, rechargeable sealed battery and instructions. Battery condition is announced at 50% and 100% allowable discharge. From Tepeco. **$174.95**

TEPECO Photo Detector

TEPECO Speed Meter IV

A large four-digit LCD displays direct velocity readouts from 76-5000 fps. The Speed Meter IV keys select rejection of bad shots, average of up to a 20-shot series and display of extreme spread and detector separation. Operation is fully automatic with no adjustments or resetting between shots. Computes velocity for any screen spacing of 1-10 feet. Velocity range is 76-5000 fps. Comes with two Type 3 photo detectors, battery charger and instructions. From Tepeco **$199.95**

Midway Rifle

Ballistic Products Shell Box Labels

Ballistic Products Plastic Shell Box

Corbin Bullet Packaging

Cartridge Boxes and Labels

Cartridge boxes, be they plastic or cardboard, are a great convenience to the handloader, as they provide dust-free storage and a means to keep loads separated. The bottoms of the large-caliber plastic pistol boxes make excellent loading blocks for rifle cartridges.

Labels and record sheets, especially made for handloaders, provide a concise, uniform means of permanently recording all pertinent load data.

BALLISTIC PRODUCTS Factory-Style Shell Boxes

These factory-style cardboard shell boxes help organize shotshells. Available in 20-gauge 2¾" and 3", 12-gauge 2¾" and 3" and 10-gauge 3½". Shipped in packs of 10. From Ballistic Products, Inc. **$3.50**

BALLISTIC PRODUCTS Shell Box Labels

Self-sticking, heavy enameled and water-proofed labels. Note on label with pen Shot, Hull, Powder, Primer, Gauge, Wad and Date. From Ballistic Products, Inc.
Price: Pack of 20............................. **$1.95**

BALLISTIC PRODUCTS Plastic Shell Box

Strong, plastic, snaplid box for storing loaded shells. Holds 25 shells, 28 gauge through 12 gauge and all 3" hulls. From Ballistic Products, Inc. **$3.50**

CORBIN Bullet Packaging

Sturdy DOT-approved cardboard boxes for shipping bullets. The triple-fold tuck-top boxes can be used for direct shipment with no other packaging for protection. Special gray die-cut foam blocks sit inside the boxes to hold and protect bullets. Each block holds 25 to 50 bullets depending on size (from 22-50-cal.) A 4"x4" foam pad covers the bullet tips. Box, foam blocks, protector pad, cylinder comes as complete package. From Corbin Mfg.
Price: Carton of 25 complete packages........... **$29.50**

JASCO Reloader's Labels

Gummed shotshell box labels are printed in red. Space for 14 items of information. Per 40, postpaid **$1.50**
Pressure sensitive metallic ammo-box labels adhere firmly—even on plastic. Space for 14 items of information. Printed in red, per 27, postpaid.......................... **$1.50**

MIDWAY Bullet Boxes

Plain white stiff cardboard boxes in three sizes: BB-51 holds 100 bullets up to 130-gr.; BB-52 holds 100 bullets up to 160-gr.; BB-53 takes 100 bullets up to 250-gr. (also holds 50 rounds of 38, 357 or 45 ACP ammo, bulk packed). Corrugated "500 Count" cast bullet boxes available in two sizes: MAB-16 holds 500 9mm and 38 bullets; MAB-17 takes 500 41, 44, 45 bullets. From Midway Arms, Inc.
Price: BB-51, 52, 53, 100-400, per 100 .... **$17.50**
Price: As above, 500-900, per 100 .... **$15.00**
Price: As above, 1000 or more, per 100 .... **$12.50**
Price: MAB-16, per 100 .... **$28.25**
Price: MAB-17, per 100 .... **$30.75**

MIDWAY Plastic Boxes

An inexpensive, hinged-top, see-through plastic box with an orange tint. Each box holds 50 rounds. Sizes for 38/357 or 44/45 calibers. From Midway Arms, Inc.
Price: Per 50 boxes, 38/357, 50-450 .... **$34.75**
Price: As above 44/45, 50-450 .... **$39.95**

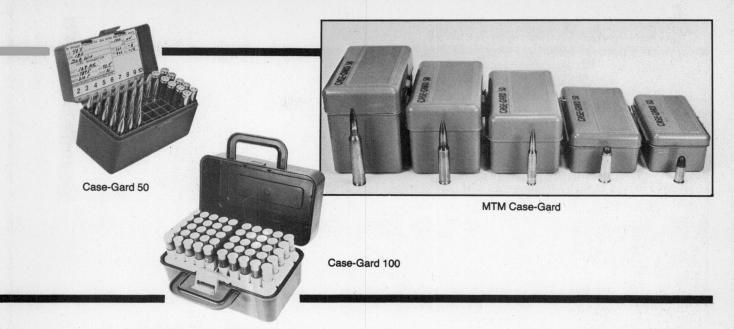

Case-Gard 50

Case-Gard 100

MTM Case-Gard

MIDWAY Ammo Boxes

Each box contains a styrofoam tray and a plain white outside carton. Box CB-01 holds 9mm and 38 Spec. WC (50 rounds); CB-02 holds 38 Spec. SWC (50 rounds); CB-03 takes 357 Mag., 38 Spec. RN, JHP, JSP (50 rounds); CB-05 holds 223 Rem. (50 rounds); CB-06 holds 41/44 Mag., 45 Colt (20 rounds); CB-07 holds 41/44 Mag., 45 Colt (50 rounds); CB-08 takes 45 ACP (50 rounds); CB-09 holds 308, 243, etc. (20 rounds); CB-10 holds 30-06, 7mm Mag., 300 Win. Mag., etc. (20 rounds). From Midway Arms.

    Price: 100 to 400 boxes, per 100 . . . . **$28.75**
    Price: 500 to 900 boxes, per 100 . . . . **$24.75**
    Price: 1000 or more, per 100 . . . . **$22.75**

MTM Case-Gard BUF-10 Ammo Box

Holds 10 rounds of the large African cartridges in secure, rattle-proof recesses, but rounds can be quickly removed when needed. Hinged top with Snap-lok latch. Suitable for 378, 460 Wby., 416 Rigby, 404, 500 Nitro, 470 Kynoch, etc. From MTM. **$4.86**

MTM

MTM CASE-GARD 20 This 20-round rifle ammo case rides on the belt or slips into the pocket and has a flip-open top for easy access. Comes in 3 sizes for small, medium or large case lengths. Has partitioned wells and the cover keeps out rain and dust. **$2.48**

MTM CASE-GARD Unique ammo boxes made of Polypropylene hold 50 rounds. Hinge is guaranteed for 1 million openings. Positive latch locks top. Load and sight data label inside top. Eight sizes available, three for pistol cases and five for rifles. Pistol sizes $1.86, rifle-sized boxes are. **$3.89**
    Same, 60 round capacity. **$4.20**

MTM CASE-Gard 100 This 100-round shotshell case features two loading trays holding 50 rounds each in 12, 16, or 20 gauge. "Tacklebox" latch and stainless steel hinge pin. Mea-

sures 7"x9"x11". Can also be used to hold factory load boxes, empties, etc. **$13.92**
    For 410-ga. **$6.96**

MTM CASE-GARD MAG 100 Each box holds 100 rounds of handgun ammo. Snap-lok latch, integral hinge. For 38 Spec., 357 Mag., 45 ACP, 41 Mag., 44 Mag. Available in MTM Green or Light Brown. **$3.96**

MTM CASE-GARD SILHOUETTE 100 Holds 100 rifle rounds securely. Originally designed for silhouette shooters, it is also excellent for serious ballistic experimenters, varmint hunters (especially prairie dog shooters), big bore competitors, etc. For any caliber from 22-250 to 375 H & H Magnum. Same tough polypropylene as the other MTM boxes. Snap-lok latch, handy folding carrying handle which lies flat for easy storage. Available in MTM Green or Grey. **$6.96**
    For smaller cartridges, 17-223 . . . . **$5.30**

MTM CASE-GARD H50 Similar to the Silhouette 100 box except holds 50 rifle rounds. Four sizes available for most calibers from 17 Rem. to 470 Kynoch. There is no #50 case for 378 Wea. Mag., 500 Nitro or 600 Nitro. Available in MTM Green or Light Brown. **$5.24**

MTM CASE-GARD 9 RIFLE AMMO WALLET Similar to the handgun ammo wallet except these hold 3, 6, or 9 rounds of rifle ammunition. For 22-250 to 8mm Mauser. Available in Dark Brown only.
    Three round wallet **$2.83**
    Six round wallet **$2.83**
    Nine round wallet **$3.60**
    Nine round wallet, for 22-250 to 375 H & H **$6.76**

MTM CASE-GARD AMMO-WALLET Slips into hip or coat pocket and flips open for 6, 12 or 18 back-up rounds. Rounds snap into individual compartments and are pressed downward to release. Weighs 2 ozs. empty. Five sizes are available for all pistol ammo.
    Six round. **$2.83**
    Twelve round **$3.05**
    Eighteen round **$3.60**

MTM Ammo Wallets

RCBS

Peterson Silhouette Targets

MTM CASE-GARD SHOTSHELL CARRIERS Made to carry 5, 10, or 25 shotshells, Snap-lok latch, integral hinge. Red color only. For 12 gauge 2¾" and 3" Mag.

Five-round	**$2.43**
10-round	**$2.76**
25-round, 12 ga.	**$3.07**
25-round, 20 ga.	**$2.83**
100-round, 12, 16 or 20-ga.	**$12.71**

MTM Slip-Top Boxes

Standard-type storage boxes made of tough plastic. Each holds 20 rounds of rifle ammo. Red or yellow color.

22-250 to 308 Win.	**$1.72**
270 to 375 Mag.	**$1.72**

Same type of box for handgun calibers is available with either round or square compartments. Red or yellow, 38/357 or 45 Auto sizes.

Square cavity	**$1.81**
Round cavity	**$2.03**

PETERSON Targ-Dots

Targ-Dots come in ½", 1", 1½", 2", 3", and 6" diameters. These fluorescent red, self-sticking aiming points help eliminate fuzzy cross-hairs and blurred iron sights. Size and number of dots per roll follow: ½"/110, 1"/100, 1½"/70, 2"/45, 3"/25, 6"/15—all sell for **$2.80** per package.

Peterson also has self-sticking target pasters in black or white, 200 per box **$2.80**

Slow fire, and timed and rapid fire target centers for 50-foot shooting are available, 3" diameter, 80 targets **$2.80**

Self-sticking 100 and 200-yd. benchrest squares on 75 and 60 rolls (respectively) are great for making your own targets. Per roll **$2.80**

All items shipped post paid; minimum order 4 rolls.

Scaled-down silhouette pistol targets for use on 50-foot indoor ranges. These are exact reductions from IHMSA outdoor targets. Self-stick, 40 targets per package **$2.80**

PETERSON Handload Labels

Pressure sensitive labels that allow you to record pertinent reloading data. Self-sticking to plastic, cardboard and metal cartridge boxes. They come rolled to feed through a typewriter.

2"x2½" (Size C), per 100 . . . . **$5.60**

1"x2" (Size B), to fit the end of a cartridge box, 250 per roll **$5.60**

RCBS Cartridge Boxes

Five one-piece, unbreakable boxes molded from light green transparent plastic with a flush latch and integral "living" hinge. Stacking legs are provided top and bottom. Rifle boxes have a raised collar for bullet tip protection in the bottom of each compartment. A compartment for a load description label is provided in the inside front of the box and is easily seen due to the clarity of the plastic. Available in Small, Medium and Large Rifle, each **$3.60**

Medium and Large Pistol sizes, each **$2.00**

SANDIA

Two-piece non-partitioned fiberboard boxes for most popular bullets and ammunition. Available for centerfire rifle (20 rounds, 30 Carbine 50 rounds) and handgun (50 round capacity). Bullet boxes hold 100 bullets. One-piece units available for 30 Carbine and 45 ACP also. Shotshell boxes for 12, 16, 20 and 410. Two-piece, unprinted boxes **$15.00** per 100 (**$85.00** per 1000), one-piece **$12.20** per 100 (**$56.00** per 1000). Quantity discounts are available.

HANDLOADER'S TRADE DIRECTORY

A

A-Square Co., Inc., Rt 4 Simmons Rd., Madison, IN 47250
Accurate Arms, P.O. Box 167, McEwen, TX 37101
P.O. Ackley Co., 2376 S. Redwood Rd., Salt Lake City, UT 84119
Acme Custom Bullets, 5708 Evers Road, San Antonio, TX 78238
Action Arms, P.O. Box 19630, Philadelphia, PA, 19124
Activ Industries Inc., 1000 Zigor Rd., P.O. Box F, Kearneyville, WV 25430
*Advanced Precision Products Co., 5183 Flintrock Dr., Westerville, OH 43081
Advance Car Mover Company, 112 N. Outagamie St., Appleton, WI 54911
AFSCO Ammunition, P.O. Box ''L'', Owen, WI 54460
Ainsworth (Denver Instrument Co.), 6542 Fig Street, Arvada, CO 80004
*The Alberts Corp., 519 E. 19th St., Paterson, NJ 07514
*All American Lead Shot Corp., P.O. Box 224566, Dallas, TX 75062
*Allred Bullets Co., 932 Evergreen Drive, Logan, UT 84321
American Bullets, P.O. Box 15313, Atlanta, GA 30333
American Gas & Chemical Co., 220 Pagasus Ave., Northvale, NJ 07647
American Products Inc., 14729 Spring Valley Road, Morrison, IL 61270
Ammo Load Inc., 1560 East Edinger, Suite G, Santa Ana, CA 92705
Ammo-Mart Ltd., P.O. Box 125, Hawkesburg, Ont., CANADA K6A 2R8
*Anderson Mfg. Company, RR1, Royal, IA 51357
Arcadia Machine & Tool, Inc., 536 North Vincent Avenue, Covina, CA 91722

B

B.E.L.L., 800 W. Maple Lane, Bensenville, IL 60106
BRI, 2825 S. Rodeo Gulch Rd. #8, Soquel, CA 95073
B-Square Company, 2708 St. Louis Ave., Ft. Worth, TX 76109
*Bill Ballard, 830 Miles Rd., Billings, MT 59101
Ballisti-Cast, Inc., Box 383, Parshall, ND 58770
Ballistic Products, P.O. Box 488, 2105 Shaughnessy Circle, Long Lake, MN 55356
Barnes Bullets, P.O. Box 215, American Fork, UT 84003
Beal's Bullets, 170 W. Marshall Rd., Lansdowne, PA 19050
Bear Machine Company, 2110 1st Nat'l. Tower, Akron, OH 44308
Belding & Mull, 110 N. 4th St., Phillipsburg, PA 16866
*Berdon Machine Company, Box 483, Hobart, WA 98025
*Bergman & Williams, 2450 Losee Rd., Las Vegas, NV 89030
Birchwood-Casey, 7900 Fuller Rd., Eden Prairie, MN 55344
Bitterroot Bullet Company, Box 412, Lewiston, ID 83501
Black Mountain Bullets, Rt. 3, Box 297, Warrenton, VA 22186
*Gene Boutin, Rt. 1, Box 890, Snyder, TX 79549
Brownells, Inc., RR 2 Box 1, Montezuma, IA 50171
*Brown Precision, Inc., 7786 Molinos Ave., W. Los Molinos, CA 96055
*Mr. A.V. Bryant, 72 Whiting Road, E. Hartford, CT 06118
Mr. Milton Brynin, 214 E. Third St., Mt. Vernon, NY 10710
Buck Stix, Box 3, Neenah, WI 54956

C

CRW Products Inc., Box 2123, Des Moines, IA 50310
*CBH, Rt. 5, Box 5400, Albuquerque, NM 87123
C-H Tool & Die, 106 N. Harding St., Owen, WI 54461
Camdex, Inc., 2330 Alger, Troy, MI 48083
*Mr. Russell L. Campbell, 219 Leisure Dr., San Antonio, TX 78201
*Carbide Die & Mfg. Co. Inc., P.O. Box 226, Covina, CA 91723
*Carter Gun Works, 2211 Jefferson Pk. Ave., Charlottesville, VA 22903
*Cascade Shooters, 60916 McMullin Dr., Bend, OR 97702
*Catco-Ambush, Inc., P.O. Box 300, Corte Madera, CA 94926
*Central Prods. For Shooters, 435 Rt. 18, East Brunswick, NJ 08816
Chevron Case Master, RR 1, Ottawa, IL 61350
*Mr. Kenneth E. Clark, 18738 Highway 99, Madera, CA 93637
*Clenzoil, Box 1226, Sta. C, Canton, OH 44708
*Cletes Custom Bullets, RR 6, Box 1348, Warsaw, IN 46580
Mr. Lester Coats, 416 Simpson Ave., North Bend, OR 97459
*Continental Kite & Key Co., (CONKKO), P.O. Box 40, Broomall, PA 19008
Cor-Bon Custom Bullets, P.O. Box 10126, Detroit, MI 48210
Colorado Shooter's Supply, P.O. Box 132, Fruita, CO 81521
Competition Bullets Inc., P.O. Box 5574 Station L, Edmonton Alberta, CANADA T6C 4E9
Competition Electronics, Inc., 753 Candy Lane, Rockford, IL 61111
*Container Dev. Corp., 426 Montgomery St., Watertown, WI 53094

Cooper-Woodward, Box 972, Riverside, CA 92502
Corbin Mfg. & Supply Co, Inc., P.O. Box 2658, White City, OR 97503
*Cumberland Arms, Rt. 1, Shafer Rd., Blatons Chapel, Manchester, TN 37355
*Custom Bullets by Hoffman, 2604 Peconic Ave., Seaford, NY 11783
Custom Chronograph Co., 5305 Reese Hill Rd., Sumas, WA 98295
*Custom Products, RD #1, Box 483A, Saegertown, PA 16443
Cutsinger Bench Rest Bullets, RR 8, Box 161-A, Shelbyville, IN 46176
C.W. Cartridge Co., 71 Hackensack St., Wood-Ridge, NJ 07075

D

*Dan Arms, P.O. Box 5040, Fort Washington, PA 19034
*Denver Instrument Co., 6542 Fig St., Arvada, CO 80004
J. Dewey Mfg. Co., 186 Skyview Dr., Southbury, CT 06488
Dillon Precision Products, Inc., 7442 E. Butherus Dr., Scottsdale, AZ 85260
*Division Lead Co., 7742 W. 61st Pl., Summit, IL 60502
*Dixie Shooter Supply, Hwy. 62 East, Blakely, GA 31723
Dynamit Nobel of America, 105 Stonehurst Ct., Northvale, NJ 07647

E

*EMCO-LUX, 2050 Fairwood Ave., Columbus, OH 43207
*Eagle Bullet Works, P.O. Box 2104, White City, OR 97503
*Eagle Products Co., 1520 Adelia Ave., S. El Monte, CA 91733
*Edmisten Co., P.O. Box 1293, Boone, NC 28607
*Efemes Ent., P.O. Box 122M, Bay Shore, NY 11706
Eldora Plastics, Inc., P.O. Box 127, Eldora, IA 50627
*Elk Mountain Shooters Supply, 1719 Marie, Pasco, WA 99301
*E. W. Ellis Sport Shop, RFD 1, Box 315, Corinth, NY 12822
*Estate Ctg. Inc., P.O. Box 3702, Conroe, TX 77305
*The Ensign-Bickford Co., 660 Hopmeadow St., Simsburg, CT 06070
Excalibur Wax, Inc., P.O. Box 432, Kenton, OH 43326

F

Federal Ctg. Corp., 900 Ehlen Dr., Anoka, MN 55303
Fiocchi of America, Inc., 1308 W. Chase, Springfield, MO 65803
*Fitz, 653 N. Hager St., San Fernando, CA 91340
Flambeau Prods. Inc., 15981 Valplast Rd., Middlefield, OH 44062
Forster Products, 82 E. Lanark Ave., Lanark, IL 61046
*Forty Five Ranch Enterprises, 119 S. Main, Miami, OK 74354
Francis Tool Co., P.O. Box 7861, Eugene, OR 97401
Fremont Tool Works, 1214 Prairie, Ford, KS 67842
*Mr. George M. Fulmer, 2499 Mavis St., Oakland, CA 94601

G

*GTM Co., 15915B E. Main St., La Puente, CA 91744
*Genes Gun Shop, Rt. 1, Box 890, Snyder, TX 79549
''Gramps'', Ellwood Epps Antique Ctgs., Box 341, Washago, Ont., CANADA LOK 2B0
Green Bay Bullets, P.O. Box 10446, 1486 Servais St., Green Bay, WI 54304
*Grills-Hanna Bulletsmith Co., Box 655, Black Diamond, Alb., CANADA T0L 0H0
Grizzly Bullets, 2137 Hwy. 200, Trout Creek, MT 59874

H

Hanned Precision, P.O. Box 2888, Sacramento, CA 95812
*Hansen Custom Bullets, 3221 Shelly St., Mohegan, NY 10547
Hardin Specialty Dist., P.O. Box 338, Radcliff, KY 40160
*Harrison Bullet Works, 6437 E. Hobart Street, Mesa, AZ 85205
Robert Hart & Son, 401 Montgomery St., Nescopeck, PA 18635
*J. Henry Customs, P.O. Box 3281, Texas City, TX 77592
Hensley & Gibbs, Box 10, Murphy, OR 97533
*Heppler's Gun Shop, 6000B Soquel Ave., Santa Cruz, CA 95062
Hercules Inc., Hercules Plaza, Wilmington, DE 19894
*Mr. R. Hock (The Gun Shop), 62778 Spring Creek Rd., Montrose, CO 81401
Hodgdon Powder Co., P.O. Box 2932, Shawnee Mission, KS 66201
Hollywood Loading Tools, Inc., 7117 South 400 West #5, Midvale, UT 84121
*Homak Mfg. Co., Inc., 4433 S. Springfield, Chicago, IL 60632
*Hondo Ind., 510 S. 52nd St., #104, Tempe, AZ 85281
Hornady, P.O. Box 1848, Grand Island, NE 68802
*Hulme Firearms Svc., Box 83, Millbrae, CA 94030
Huntington Die Specialties, P.O. Box 991, Oroville, CA 95965
*Hutton Rifle Ranch, P.O. Box 31868, Tucson, AZ 85751

*Unconfirmed address. Listed as a service to the reader.

I-J-K

IMR Powder Co., 122 Lakeside Dr., Glassboro, NJ 08028
I.S.W., 106 E. Cairo Dr., Tempe, AZ 85282
*Illinois Custom Bullet Mfg., RR 1, Dunlap, IL 61525
*Illinois Lead Shot, 7742 W. 61st Place, Summit, IL 60501
Imperial (LeClear Ind.), 1126 Donald, Royal Oak, MI 48073
Independent Machine & Gun Shop, 1416 N. Hoyes, Pocatello, ID 83201
*JASCO, Box 49751, Los Angeles, CA 90049
J.G.S. Precision Tool Mfg., 1141 South Sumner Rd., Coos Bay, OR 97420
*J&J Custom Bullets, 1210 El Rey Ave., El Cajon, CA 92021
*J-4, Inc., 1700 Via Burton, Anaheim, CA 92806
Jack First Dist., 44633 Sierra Hwy., Lancaster, CA 93534
*Jaro Mfg., P.O. Box 6125, 206 E. Shaw, Pasadena, TX 77506
*Javelina Products, P.O. Box 337, San Bernardino, CA 92402
*Jet-Aer Corp., 100 Sixth Ave., Paterson, NJ 07524
Mr. Neil Jones, RD 1, Box 483A, Saegertown, PA 16433
*Ka Pa Kapili, P.O. Box 745, Honokaa, HI 96272
*Kendall International Arms, 501 East North Street, Carlisle, KY 40311
*Kexplore, Box 22084, Houston, TX 77027
*King & Co., Box 1242, Bloomington, IL 61701
Kodiak Custom Bullets, P.O. Box 54, Douglas, AK 99824

L

LBT, P.O. Box 357, Cornville, AZ 86325
L.L.F. Die Shop, 1281 Hwy. 99N, Eugene, OR 97402
*LAC-CUM Bullet Puller, Star Rt., Box 242, Apollo, PA 15613
Lage Uniwad, P.O. Box 127, Eldora, IA 50627
Lazy-X-Notebook, P.O. Box 007, La Cresenta, CA 91214
*Leding Loader, RR 1, Box 645, Ozark, AR 72949
Lee Precision, 4275 Hwy. U, Hartford, WI 53027
*Lenz Products Company, Box 1226, Sta. C, Canton, OH 44708
*Mr. Dean Lincoln, Box 1886, Farmington, NM 87401
*Lindsley Arms Ctg., Co., P.O. Box 5738, Lake Worth, FL 33466
Ljutic Ind., P.O. Box 2117, Yakima, WA 98907
The Loading Doc, 1760 B-7 Monrovia, Costa Mesa, CA 92627
*Lock's Philadelphia Gun Exchange, 6700 Rowland Ave., Philadelphia, PA 19149
*Lomont Precision Bullets, 4236 W. 700 South, Poneto, IN 46781
Lortone, Inc., 2856 NW Market St., Seattle, WA 98107
Lyman Products, Rt. 147, Middlefield, CT 06455

M

M&D Munitions Ltd., 127 Verdi St., Farmingdale, NY 11735
MEC, Inc., 715 South St., Mayville, WI 53050
MMP, Rt. 6, Box 383-WP, Harrison, AR 72601
*M&N Bullet Lube, P.O. Box 495, 151 NE Jefferson St., Madras, OR 97741
*MSS Industries, P.O. Box 6, River Grove, IL 60171
MTM (Boars Head), N-73 Stedwick Village Dr., Budd Lake, NJ 07828
MRC, P.O. Box 253, Mequon, WI 53092
*Macks Sport Shop, Box 1155, Kodiak, AK 99615
Magnus Bullet, P.O. Box 2225, Birmingham, AL 35201
Magma Engineering, Box 881, Chandler, AZ 85224
*Marshall Ent., 792 Canyon Rd., Redwood City, CA 94062
Marquart Precision, Box 1740, Prescott, AZ 86302
*Bill Mathews, Inc., P.O. Box 26727, Lakewood, CO 80226
*Mathews & Boucher Inc., 1950 Brighton-Henrietta, Townline Rd., Rochester, NY 14623
*Mr. Paul McLean, 2670 Lakeshore Blvd. W., Toronto, Ont., CANADA M8V 1G8
McConnellstown Reloading, RD 3, Box 40, Huntingdon, PA 16652
McKillen & Heyer, Inc., 37603, Arlington Dr., Box 627, Willoughby, OH 44094
Merit Gun Sight, P.O. Box 995, Sequim, WA 98382
Michaels Antiques, Box 233, Copiague, LI, NY 11726
Midway Arms, Inc., 7450 Old Hwy. 40 West, Columbia, MO 65201
*Micro Shooter's Supply, P.O. Box 117, Mesilla Park, NM 88047
Miller Trading Company, 20 S. Front St., Wilmington, NC 28401
*Mirror-Lube, 1305 Simpson Way #K, Escondido, CA 92025
Morrison Custom Bullet Corp., P.O. Box 5574, Sta. L. Edmonton, Alberta, CANADA T6C 4E9

*Multi-Scale Charge Ltd., 3269 Niagara Falls Blvd., N. Tonawanda, NY 14102

N-O

NAK Custom Bullets, 127 Sunset Dr., Box 3131, Fairview Sta., Espanola, NM 87533
*National Lead Co., Box 831, Perth Amboy, NJ 08861
*Nevins Ammunition, 7614 Lemhi Suite 1, Boise, ID 83709
Non-Toxic Components, 1302 NW Kearney, P.O. Box 4202, Portland, OR 97208
Northeast Industrial, Inc., P.O. Box 249, 405 N. Canyon Blvd., Canyon City, OR 97820
Nosler Bullets Inc., 107 SW Columbia, Bend, OR 97702
*Nova Munitions Inc., 924 Logan St., Denver, CO 80203
O'Connor Rifle Products, 2008 Maybank Hwy., Charleston, SC 29412
Oehler Research, P.O. Box 9135, Austin, TX 78766
*Old West Bullet Moulds, 9900 Palmer Ct. NW, Albuquerque, NM 87114
Old Western Scrounger, Inc., 12924 Hwy. A-12, Montague, CA 96064
Omark Ind., Box 856, Lewiston, ID 83501
Oro-Tech Ind., 3909 S. Maryland Pkwy., Suite 300, Las Vegas, NV 89119
Osage Press, Box 6, Osage, WY 82723
*The Oster Group, 50 Sims Ave., Providence, RI 02909
Harry Owen, P.O. Box 5337, Hacienda Heights, CA 91745

P

PACO, Box 17211, Tucson, AZ 85731
PACT, P.O. Box 531525, Grand Prairie, TX 75053
*P&C Shooting Specialties, P.O. Box 10808, Pittsburgh, PA 15236
*PEM's Mfg. Co., 5063 Waterloo Rd., Atwater, OH 44201
PMC Ammunition, 4890 South Alameda, Suite 1400, Vernon, CA 90058
*PPC Corp., 627 E. 24th St., Paterson, NJ 07514
Patriot Manufacturing & Sales, Dept. GWK, Banyan Plaza, Suite 334, Box 900, Sebring, FL 33870
*Pearl Armory, Revenden Springs, AR 72460
Pejsa Ballistics, 2120 Kenwood Pkwy., Minneapolis, MN 55405
*Pennsylvania Arms, P.O. Box 128-H, Duryea, PA 18642
*Perazzi USA, 206 S. George St., Rome, NY 13440
Peterson Instant Targets, Inc., P.O. Box 186, Redding Ridge, CT 06876
Pitzer Tool Mfg. Co., RR 3, Box 50, Winterset, IA 50273
Plum City Ballistics Range, Rt 1, Box 29A, Plum City, WI 54761
*Polak Winters Co., Div. of Mallegg Inc., 580 Broadway, P.O. Box 1048, Laguna Beach, CA 92651
PolyWad, P.O. Box 7916, Macon, GA 31209
Mr. Robert Pomeroy, Morrison Ave., East Corinth, ME 04227
Ponsness-Warren, P.O. Box 8, Rathdrum, ID 83858
*Power Plus Ent., 6939 Macon Rd., #15, Columbus, GA 31907
Marion Powley, Petra Ln., RR 1, Eldridge, IA 52748
*Precision Components Inc., New Route 55, Box 337, Pawling, NY 12564
*Precision Ammo Co., P.O. Box 63, Garnerville, NY 10923
*Precision Prods. of Washington, N. 311 Walnut Rd., Spokane, WA 99206
Precision Swaged Bullets, 101 Mud Creek Lane, Ronan, MT 59864
Professional Hunters Supplies, P.O. Box 608, Ferndale, CA 95536
*Prospect Bullet Co., 1620 Holmes Ave., Prospect Park, PA 19076
ProWare Inc.1023 S.E. 36th Ave., Portland, OR 97214

Q

*Quartz-Lok, 5602 E. 20th St., Tuscon, AZ 85711
*Quickie Automation, P.O. Box 1116, Seabrook, TX 77586
Quinetics Corp., Box 29007, San Antonio, TX 78229

R

R.D.P. Tool Co., Inc., 49162 McCoy Ave., East Liverpool, OH 43920
*RIG Prods. Co., P.O. Box 1990, Sparks, NV 89432-1990
*RSR Corp., 1111 West Mocking Bird Lane, Dallas, TX 75247
*Radix Research & Mktg., Box 247, Woodland Park, CO 80863
*Reardon Products, 103 W. Market St., Morrison, IL 61270
*Redwood Bullet Works, 3559 Bay Rd., Redwood City, CA 94063
*Red Diamond Dist. Co., 1304 Snowdon Dr., Knoxville, TN 37912
Redding Inc. and Saeco Prod., 1089 Starr Rd., Cortland, NY 13045
*Reloaders Equipment Co., 4680 High St., Ecorse, MI 48229
*Reloaders Paper Supply, 2111 E. Santa Fe, Suite 323, P.O. Box 4000, Olathe, KS 66062

*Unconfirmed address. Listed as a service to the reader.

Remington-Peters, Dupont MCD, 2524—3 Nemours Bldg., Wilmington, DE 19898
Roberts Products, 25238 S.E. 32nd, Issaquah, WA 98027
*Rochester Lead Works, 76 Anderson Ave., Rochester, NY 14607
Rooster Labs, P.O. Box 19514, Kansas City, MO 64141
*Rorschach Precision Products, Box 1613, Irving, TX 75060

S

SSK Industries, Rt. 1 Della Dr., Bloomingdale, OH 43910
*S&S Precision Bullets, 22965 La Cadena, Laguna Hills, CA 92653
*SKR Industries, POB 1382, San Angelo, TX 76902
Anthony F. Sailer Ammunition, 707 W. 3rd St., P.O. Box L, Owen, WI 54460
Sandia Die & Ctg. Co., Rt 5, Box 5400, Albuquerque, NM 87123
*Bob Sanders Custom Gun Svc., 2358 Tyler Lane, Louisville, KY 40205
Scharch Mfg., 645 E. Hwy. 50, Salida, CA 81201
*Shannon Associates, P.O. Box 32737, Oklahoma City, OK 73123
Shooter's Edge Inc., P.O. Box 769, Trinidad, CO 81082
Sierra Bullets, 10532 South Painter Ave., Sante Fe Springs, CA 90670
* Jerry Simmons, 715 Middleburg St., Goshen, IN 46526
Sinclair Int. Inc., 1200 Asbury Dr., New Haven, IN 46774
Southwest Instruments, Box 91140, Santa Barbara, CA 93190-1140
*George W. Spence, 115 Locust St., Steele, MO 63877
Sport Flite Mfg. Co., 2520 Industrial Row, Troy, MI 48084
Sportsman Supply Co., 714 East Eastwood, P.O. Box 650, Marshall, MO 65340
Stalwart Corp., P.O. Box 357, Pocatello, ID 83204
Star Machine Works, 418 10th Ave., San Diego, CA 92101
Stoeger Publishing, 55 Ruta Court, South Hackensack, NJ 07676
*Super Vel, Hamilton Rd., Rt. 2, Fond du Lac, WI 54935
Supreme Products Company, 1830 S. California Ave., Monrovia, CA 91016
Swift Bullet Company, Route 1, Quinter KS 67752

T-U-V

3-D Inv., Inc., Main St., Box J, Doniphan, NE 68832

*Tallon Bullets, 1194 Tidewood Dr., Bethel Pk, PA 15102
Tamarack Prods. Inc., Box 224, Barrington, IL 60010
Taracorp Ind., Inc., Lawrence Brand Shot Div., 16th & Cleveland Blvd., Granite City, IL 62040
*Telepacific Electronics Co., Inc., POB 1329, San Marcos, CA 92069
Tepeco, P.O. Box 342, Friendswood, TX 77546
*Testing Systems Inc., 220 Pegasus Ave., Northvale, NJ 07647
*Traft Gunshop, P.O. Box 1078, Buena Vista, CO 81211
*Trico Plastics, 590 S. Vincent Ave., Azusa, CA 91702
Trophy Bonded Bullets, P.O. Box 262348, Houston, TX 77087.
Tru-Square Metal Prods. Inc., P.O. Box 585, Auburn, WA 98071
U-Load, Inc., P.O. Box 443-177, Eden Prairie, MN 55344
Vibra-Tek, P.O. Box 6969, Colorado Springs, CO 80903
Aerodynamic Slug, 2178 Nichols Ave., Stratford, CT 06497

W-X-Y-Z

*Walker Mfg., Inc., 8296 S. Channel, Harsen's Island, MI 48028
Weatherby, Inc., 2781 Firestone Blvd., South Gate, CA 90280
*Weaver Arms Corp., 115 N. Market St., Escondido, CA 92025
*Webster Scale Co., Box 188, Sebring, FL 33870
Westfield Engineering, 2401 East 27th St., Los Angeles, CA 90058
*H.P. White Labs, 3114 Scarboro Rd., Street, MD 21154
*Whitetail Design & Coloring, 9421 E. Mannsiding Rd., Clare, MI 48617
*Whits Shooting Stuff, Box 1340, Cody, WY 82414
Wilcox All-Pro Tools & Supply, RR 1, Montezuma, IA 50171
L. E. Wilson Company, Box 324, Cashmere, WA 98815
Winchester Group, Olin, Old Powder Mill Rd., East Alton, IL 62024
Windjammer Tournament Wads, P.O. Box 890, Conifer, CO 80443
*Worthy Prods, Inc., Box 88 Main St., Chippewa Bay, NY 13623
*Zenith Enterprises, 361 Flager Rd., Nordland, WA 98358
*Zero Bullet Company, P.O. Box 1188, Cullman, AL 35055

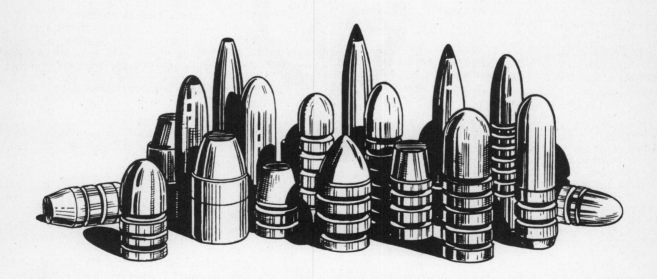

*Unconfirmed address. Listed as a service to the reader.

INDEX